Theories of Developmental Psychology

Theories of Developmental Psychology

FOURTH EDITION

Patricia H. Miller

University of Florida

WORTH PUBLISHERS

Theories of Developmental Psychology,
Fourth Edition

Printed in the United States of America
ISBN: 0-7167-2846-X

Sponsoring Editor: Marjorie Byers
Senior Marketing Manager: Renee Altier
Associate Managing Editor: Tracey Kuehn
Production Manager: Sarah Segal
Art Director: Barbara Reingold
Cover and Text Designer: Lissi Sigillo
Photo Research Manager: Patricia Marx
Cover and Chapter Opener Photo: Jen Fong/Photonica
Illustration Coordinator: Cecilia Varas
Illustrations (not otherwise credited): Alan Reingold and
Progressive Information Technologies
Composition: Progressive Information Technologies
Printing and Binding: R. R. Donnelley and Sons

Library of Congress Cataloging in Publication Data Available Upon Request
Third Printing, 2003

Worth Publishers
41 Madison Avenue
New York, NY 10010
www.worthpublishers.com

CONTENTS

Preface

"What is your theory of psychological development?" As an undergraduate I faced that very essay question on my final exam in an introductory child psychology class. Drawing on all the theories I had ever heard of, I modestly generated a 6 (age) × 20 (developmental tasks) matrix that covered all of development. My interest in theories was launched. Perhaps if I had been given a multiple-choice test this book would address a different topic.

In all four editions of this book I have tried to show the "big picture" of psychological development. Sometimes students are frustrated by fact-laden textbooks that do not provide frameworks in which to fit the facts. It is often not clear, for example, why a Swiss philosopher would be interested in children's numerical judgments after a row of objects is spread out or why it is noteworthy that infants cry when their mothers leave the room. This book provides frameworks for understanding and perceiving the significance of the research findings in developmental psychology.

Theories of Developmental Psychology can be used as a primary or supplementary text in undergraduate or graduate courses or as a resource book for instructors. In addition, it can provide perspectives on children's behavior for those who interact with children in any capacity. I hope that both developmental psychologists and readers from other disciplines will find something of interest in these pages.

I have used a parallel structure in the various chapters in order to help the reader compare the theories. To provide continuity, four central issues of development are addressed in each chapter. In addition, I have tried to convey what is exciting about each of the theories. The theories included are those that in my view are of most interest to developmental psychologists and professionals in related disciplines. Many important theories were necessarily excluded because of length restrictions. And some of the "theories" included are not formal theories, but they function as theories by identifying what to study, what questions to ask, and how to answer these questions.

The fourth edition updates the third. I have tried to show how each theory has changed in its emphasis, its data base, and its influence on developmental psychology since the last edition. In particular, I have expanded the sections on contemporary research in each theory. I added a number of new perspectives that recently have become influential in developmental psychology, such as connectionism, evolutionary psychology, Siegler's overlapping waves model, dynamic systems, the theory theory, modularity nativism, developmental neuroscience, and developing-person-in-context. Some of these are described in a new chapter labeled "Contemporary Minitheories and Emerging Approaches." In order to ground the theories in real-life settings, I added a section on applications to each chapter. Finally, the recent publication of a book by Eleanor Gibson and Anne Pick facilitated a substantial updating of the chapter on Gibson's theory, and I thank them for making a prepublication copy available to me.

I am grateful to a number of people who read and offered comments for one or more editions: Patricia Ashton, Fran Blumberg, William Charlesworth, Michael Cole, Jeffrey Farrar, David Forbes, Bridget Franks, Eleanor Gibson, Harry Grater, Richard Griggs, Gardner Lindzey, Richard Luftig, Thomas Mandeville, John McClure, Jack Meacham, Scott Miller, Stuart Miller, Joy Osofsky, Anne Pick, Sue Rosser, Robert Siegler, Debra Valencia-Laver, Robert Watson, and Rob Weisskirch. A number of undergraduate and graduate students made helpful suggestions as well. I am also grateful to John Flavell, who guided my meanderings into theories when I was a graduate student and has continued to be a source of inspiration. Finally, I want to thank Marjorie Byers at Worth Publishers, who expertly guided the fourth edition.

Patricia H. Miller

Introduction

Never trust an experimental result until it has been confirmed by theory.

—SIR ARTHUR EDDINGTON

Give us theories, theories, always theories.

—JAMES MARK BALDWIN

We have theories of development because observers of human behavior have been intrigued by what they saw children and adults do. A 3-year-old predicts that a crayon box holds crayons; then, after it is opened to reveal candles, he asserts that he always believed that it held candles. A 5-year-old claims that spreading out a row of buttons increases the number of buttons. A school-age child uses a good strategy to successfully solve an addition problem but shortly later she uses a less reliable strategy on the same problem. An adolescent selects an identity without seriously exploring other possible identities. An adult reports a dream that seems to be a thinly disguised attempt to deal with childhood anxieties.

Developmental theorists try to make sense out of observations such as these and, by doing so, construct a story of the human journey from infancy through childhood or adulthood. Some of the theories we will explore are grand, encompassing theories, often associated with a particular person, for example, Piaget's, Freud's, Erikson's, and Vygotsky's theories. Other theories actually are families of approaches under a general "theory" or framework, such as social learning theory, information processing, dynamic systems, and ethology and other evolutionary theories, and are not necessarily identified with a single person. Still other theories might be called "minitheories," for they limit themselves to a particular territory within development. An example is the "theory theory," which examines children's concepts about a domain, for example, the mind.

Some developmental theories are actually theories from areas outside of development that have been applied to developmental psychology, such as evolutionary theory, information processing, dynamic systems theory, and cultural psychology. Typically, a few key developmentalists see the potential of the theory for posing new questions about development or providing a new explanation of development and then translate the theory into a developmental framework. Thus, theory building in developmental psychology is a very rich, dynamic, and exciting enterprise that has come from many directions. The theories' stories are varied, but all give us insights into human behavior and change the way we look at the world.

This book attempts to convey not only the content of the theories but also the excitement and passion that developmentalists have felt as they constructed their theories or adopted those of others. In some cases certain observations, such as those described above, have captured the imagination of researchers and created a sense of excitement and progress in the field. They saw these intriguing behaviors as mysteries to be solved. In other cases certain ideas have expanded our vision of the nature of development. For example, Piaget's idea that the mental operations of adults have their origins in the sensory-motor behaviors of infancy opened up a whole host of new ways to think about cognitive development. Each theory tells us something important about the fundamental nature of human development.

To understand the contribution of these developmental theories, we must first look at the general nature of theories. In this Introduction, we ask the following questions about theories:

1. What is a theory?
2. What is a developmental theory?
3. Of what value is a developmental theory?
4. What main issues of developmental psychology do theories address?

WHAT IS A THEORY?

This is a deceptively simple question. In fact, a philosopher of science might "answer" our question by asking two more:

1. Are we asking what theories should be or what they typically are?
2. Are we asking about theories as they are stated formally or as they actually operate in a scientific community?

The philosopher's first question concerns the distinction between ideal and real theories and expresses the sad fact of scientific life that our theories fall short of their goal. Theories usually do not reach a complete, formal state. An ideal, complete, formal *scientific theory* is a set of interconnected statements—definitions, axioms, postulates, hypothetical constructs, intervening variables, laws, hypotheses, and so on. Some of these statements, which are usually expressed in verbal or mathematical form, are deduced logically from certain other statements. The function of this set of interconnected statements is to describe unobservable structures, mechanisms, or processes and to relate them to each other and to observable events. Perhaps the best way to contrast these types of statements is to show that they occupy different levels within a theory. That is, they vary in their distance from observable behavior. The "farther" a statement is from observable behavior, the less likely it is to be supported or refuted by empirical data.

At a point farthest from observable behavior are certain *assumptions* (axioms, postulates) that are accepted without being tested. (For example, in Piaget's theory, an assumption is that thinking is organized.) These assumptions may be so self-evident to the theorists that they are not even aware of them. As we move to a less general level, we find *hypothetical constructs*—concepts that posit relations among events, objects, properties, or variables. These constructs (such as "mental scheme" and "mental reversibility" in Piaget's theory) are unobservable themselves but refer to behavior that can be observed. Theorists translate hypothetical constructs into testable *hypotheses,* which are tentative statements about the relations among events, objects, properties, or variables. (One Piagetian hypothesis is that the infant tends to repeat interesting actions, such as shaking a rattle.) A hypothesis becomes a *fact* when it is sufficiently supported by research. As facts accumulate, they are tied together by a *law:* a relatively well established general statement concerning the relationship among a set of facts.

We build theories by going back and forth between *data* (repeatable empirical observations) and theory. New facts change the theory, and changes in the theory generate new experiments and thus new facts. The new facts again change the theory, and so the cyclical process continues. Empirical observations can provide strong support for a theory but can never completely prove that a theory is true because future observations could provide disconfirming evidence. In some theories, the theory does little more than summarize the facts (data). Particularly in Skinnerian learning theory, one finds statements such as "If a response is followed by a reinforcer for several trials, the frequency of that response increases." Such theories that stay close to the data are easier to test because they are easier to disconfirm. At the other extreme, Freud's "unconscious" or Piaget's "equilibration" process bears at best an uncertain and distant relationship to observable behavior. Because a large distance between theoretical notions and data makes it more difficult to test the theory, several such theories may be equally good at explaining the same set of data and thus may be retained for years, regardless of their accuracy.

Traditionally, psychologists have judged theories by certain criteria. A theory should be logically sound, that is, internally consistent, with no statements that contradict each other. A theory should also be empirically sound, that is, not contradicted by scientific observations. Furthermore, it should be clear, testable, and parsimonious, relying on as few constructs, propositions, and the like as possible. Finally, a theory should cover a reasonably large area of a science and should integrate previous research.

Psychology has had few formal theories in its history, and probably no current theory of development falls into this category. However, the above requirements give us a context for judging whether each theory or model of development is headed in the right direction. We can ask whether each theory could eventually reach the status of a formal, testable theory. In their present form, developmental "theories" serve as frames of reference for examining changes in behavior over time. For example, Piaget's theory directs our attention to the organization of thought rather than to specific pieces of knowledge, to stagelike changes during development rather than to a gradual accumulation of knowledge, and to children's active construction of knowledge rather than to their passive processing of information.

Today, theorists often use the term *model*—an informal theory of more limited scope. Models sometimes are presented visually, for example, in a drawing of boxes and arrows to indicate the flow of information. Models also can be like analogies, as when the mind is likened to a computer.

The philosopher's second question distinguishes between theories as they are stated (in books such as this one) and how they actually operate in a scientific community. A theory, in its tidy and polished form in a textbook, bears only a faint resemblance to the way the theory guides the behavior of real people doing real research. This section on theory building has presented the conventional view of theory building—an orderly, objective, logical process. This is a picture of scientists in their "dress clothes." Although science sometimes does proceed in this way, more often it proceeds in a much messier, irrational fashion to produce a polished final product.

More specifically, the conventional view of theory building implies that empirical observations are objective bits of information that we can use to make more general statements or to test statements derived from a theory. In reality, facts do not simply present themselves to eager scientists. When a person develops or adopts a particular theory, she takes on a whole set of beliefs concerning what questions about development are worth asking, what methods for studying these questions are legitimate, and what the nature of development is. A Freudian is not likely to study how rats learn to press bars in tightly controlled experiments, and a learning theorist is not likely to ask people to describe their dreams or memories of childhood. There are unwritten rules of the game that are very much a part of the theory as it is practiced.

Scientists' assumptions lead them to see certain facts more easily than others; in fact, it can be difficult to see what we are *not* looking for. As an illustration, radio signals from Jupiter had been heard, but ignored, for many years before two young American astronomers "discovered" these signals in 1955 and recognized their significance.

Scientists make decisions about how to divide up the "stream of behavior" and how to describe it. A 1-minute episode of a baby playing could be described in thousands of ways. There are different levels of behavior, from heart rate to exploration of the room, and different temporal units, from a fraction of a second to a behavioral unit spanning perhaps the entire minute. Which facts or observations the psychologist chooses from the thousands of candidates tells us as much about the psychologist or her theory as about the episode of behavior itself. These constraints on what is observed are necessary, of course, because it is not feasible to record everything.

Some philosophers and psychologists are "social constructionists," who propose that science and its theories are one particular view of reality and are always filtered through social-cultural beliefs, values, language, and categories. Social constructionism is not embraced by most practicing researchers, but social constructionists' critiques have alerted investigators to their own assumptions and biases, which can affect both their theory building and their research.

A scientist's social and political beliefs can be especially biasing in a field such as psychology, in which people are studying people. The psychologist holds a mirror rather than a telescope. If theorists assume that humans are basically rational, they are more likely to study thought than emotions, more likely to become a Piaget than a Freud. Developmental psychologists do not escape their culture's views. As Scarr observed, "We pose questions to fit our place and time; we get answers to fit our theoretical niches" (1985, p. 204). She argued that we change our scientific lenses as the culture changes. Scarr noted that in the 1950s and 1960s social scientists expected, and thus looked for, evidence that boys in "broken homes" were affected negatively by the lack of a father. The finding that these boys, when young, were low in aggression was taken as evidence for poor sex-role development. Since the women's movement and the emergence of nontraditional families, it is no longer automatically assumed that nontraditional family situations have a negative effect on children. Moreover, with today's less rigid view of desirable masculine and feminine traits or behaviors, low aggression in a boy may not be seen as a deficit.

Individual psychologists' personality and motivations also influence the particular direction their research takes, a point demonstrated by learning theorist E. C. Tolman:

> I started out . . . with considerable uneasiness. I felt that my so-called system was outdated and that it was a waste of time to try to rehash it and that it would be pretentious now to seek to make it fit any accepted set of prescriptions laid down by the philosophy of science. I have to confess, however, that as I have gone along I have become again more and more involved in it, though I still realize its many weak points. The system may well not stand up to any final canons of scientific procedure. But I do not much care. I have liked to think about psychology in ways that have proved congenial to me. Since all the sciences, and especially psychology, are still immersed in such tremendous realms of the uncertain and the unknown, the best that any individual scientist, especially any psychologist, can do seems to be to follow his own gleam and his own bent, however inadequate they may be. In fact I suppose that actually this is what we all do. In the end, the only sure criterion is to have fun. And I have had fun.
>
> (1959, p. 152)

Still another example of the informal side of theories is that some theorists draw heavily on imagery, such as diagrams or metaphors, to communicate their theories. Models of information processing may consist of diagrams of boxes and arrows to show the flow of information as it is processed. Examples of metaphors are the early image of the nervous system as a telephone switchboard or the eye as a camera and the later notion of an instinct as a hydraulic system. More recently, theorists have likened cognitive development to an equilibration system (Piaget), a computer (information processing), a neural network (connectionism), a staircase (Robbie Case, a neo-Piagetian), and a series of overlapping waves (Robert Siegler).

WHAT IS A DEVELOPMENTAL THEORY?

The above crash course in the philosophy of science suggests that developmental theories are somewhat informal frameworks at present and, like all theories, have a dynamic, nonpublic role as well as a static, public one. Our next question is, What makes these theories developmental? Simply studying children does not make a theorist a developmental theorist. For example, studying learning in 6-year-olds, or even children of several ages, does not necessarily lead to conclusions about development. What is critical about a developmental theory is that it focuses on *change over time.* Although developmental theories have nondevelopmental theoretical concepts such as ego, mental representations, and neural networks, they diverge from nondevelopmental theories by emphasizing changes over time in these concepts.

This concern with change presents developmental theories with three tasks. These tasks are (1) to *describe* changes *within* one or several areas of behavior, (2) to *describe* changes in the relations *among* several areas of behavior, and (3) to *explain* the course of development that has been described. Let us look more closely at each of these three tasks.

1 *A developmental theory describes changes over time in one or several areas of behavior or psychological activity, such as thought, language, social behavior, or perception.* For example, a theory might describe changes in the rules of grammar underlying language in the first few years of life. Although developmental theories tend to stress changes over months or years, an adequate theory must ultimately describe changes over seconds, minutes, and days. For example, the concept of object permanence, the notion that objects exist even when we do not see them, may develop over many months during infancy, but a full description would include many "minidevelopments" that occur during the child's moment-to-moment encounters with objects.

As we noted earlier, even direct observation is guided to some extent by theoretical notions that distort the flow of behavior in some way. Observers record certain behaviors and ignore others. They divide the stream of behavior into units. They encode the behavior into words that add connotations. They allow inference to creep into their observations. The following descriptions of the same behavior demonstrate that several degrees of inference are possible:

a. The baby's hand came closer and closer to the spinning top.
b. The baby reached for the spinning top.
c. The baby wanted to pick up the spinning top.
d. The baby applied her grasping scheme to the spinning top. (A scheme, according to Piaget, is an organized sequence of behavior that reflects an infant's knowledge in a particular area, such as grasping.)

Much of the early work in developmental psychology was focused on description. In the 1930s, Arnold Gesell's maturational theory of development established norms of physical, cognitive, and motor development through description. Although description is not sufficient for an adequate theory of development, it certainly is necessary. Without a database, we have an "edifice without a foundation," in White's (1969) words.

2 *A second task for a theory of development is to describe changes over time in the relations among behaviors or aspects of psychological activity within one area of development and, ideally, among several areas of development.* A developmental theory tries to deal with the simultaneous changes in thought, personality, and perception that we observe. Developmental theorists are "specialized generalists" in that they are knowledgeable about many areas of psychology but specialize in the developmental approach to studying these content areas and their relations.

In the case of the object concept described above, a theory might describe how the concept relates to children's developing memory system and their social relationship with one particular object, their mother. A theory would outline the temporal relations among these areas of development. For example, a theory might claim that a certain degree of memory capacity is developed before the object concept emerges, that the mother is the first permanent object, and that subsequent developments within the object concept are correlated with changes in the memory system and children's attachment to their mother. Another example concerns the relationship between thought and language. One position, that of the Russian psychologist Lev Vygotsky, is that thought and language are relatively independent until they merge to produce symbolic thought and children can think in words. Both examples describe the organization within children at various points in time. The descriptions refer to certain sequences (first *A*, then *B*) and concurrences (*A* and *B* at the same time) that occur during development.

Of course, any attempt to divide behavior into parts is somewhat arbitrary because there is an interrelated system, or the famous "whole child." Also, theories need to include the sociocultural context in any description, because behaviors occur in certain sociocultural settings. Nevertheless, not everything about the child and the environment can be studied at once. Developmentalists try to study the parts in the context of the whole child and the social and physical environment.

3 *Even if a theory provides a full description of development, it has not accounted for the transitions from point to point during development. Thus, a third task for a developmental theory is to explain the course of development that the other two tasks describe.* In fact, the sequences and concur-

rences identified in the first two tasks often suggest particular explanations. If skill *A* always appears shortly before the development of skill *B*, a psychologist may hypothesize that *A* causes *B*.

With respect to the third task, a developmental theory offers a set of general principles or rules for change. These principles specify necessary and sufficient antecedents for each change and identify variables that modify or modulate the rate or nature of each change. For example, Freud proposed that the biologically based drives "move" from the oral area to the anal and that the degree of the child's accompanying anxiety depends somewhat on the parents' child-rearing practices. In addition, principles of change hypothesize a set of processes for producing the change. These processes have been as diverse as dynamic equilibration in Piaget's theory, physical maturation in Freudian and ethological theory, and the strengthening of a response by reinforcement in learning theory.

One way to interpret developmental change is to hypothesize a continuity underlying the apparent change. For example, a theory might claim that dependency is expressed in different ways at different ages but that the underlying trait is the same. Or a theory might emphasize the underlying continuity in cognitive development by pointing to the gradual change in the understanding of number and by hypothesizing that what can be learned is limited by what number concepts the child already has. In more general terms, a theory may claim that concept, trait, skill, or behavior *A* is transformed into *B*, is replaced by *B*, combines with *B* to form *C*, and so forth. Most of the developmental theories we examine in this book posit an underlying continuity to the superficial changes during development.

When a theory explains why development proceeds in a certain way, it at the same time explains why certain other possible courses of development did not occur. Why did *A* lead to *B* rather than *X*? The significance of nonoccurrences is expressed by Sherlock Holmes:

> ". . . the curious incident of the dog in the nighttime."
> "The dog did nothing in the nighttime."
> "That was the curious incident," remarked Sherlock Holmes.
>
> —Sir Arthur Conan Doyle

These three tasks are not necessarily approached in the above order. A theory of development usually weaves back and forth among the three tasks. Progress on one of the tasks stimulates progress on another, which in turn feeds back to the first task or the third. A related point is that description and explanation are not as separate and independent as the list might imply. A theory's explanatory concepts influence the choice of what is described and how it is described, and the type of explanation that theorists offer is somewhat constrained by how they have described behavior. Finally, developmental theories are not equally concerned with these three tasks. For example, Piaget was much more successful at describing the development of thought than explaining this development.

These three monumental tasks, even if incompletely met in the near future, provide us with goals by which to measure the success of current theories of development. A more realistic expectation for the near future is that we can have theories that succeed in a more limited way. Theories may successfully describe and explain one particular area of development, such as language development, but not all areas. Or they may cover several areas but only achieve one or two of the three tasks. For example, a theory might competently describe changes in several areas but unsuccessfully explain these changes.

OF WHAT VALUE IS A DEVELOPMENTAL THEORY?

What does a developmental theory actually do for us when it describes and explains development? A theory makes two contributions: (1) it organizes and gives meaning to facts; (2) it guides further research. We examine each of these contributions in turn.

Organizing Information

The explosion of research on children in recent decades makes it especially important to look at current theories or develop new theories to make sense of our information about children. A theory gives meaning to facts, provides a framework for facts, assigns more importance to some facts than others, and integrates existing facts. Facts do not speak for themselves. As Jules Henri Poincaré (1952) said, "Science is built up of facts, as a house is built of stones; but an accumulation of facts is no more a science than a heap of stones is a house." Just as stones need an architect or a blueprint to become a house, so do facts need a theorist to give those facts structure and show their relation to the overall design. One by-product is that by summarizing and organizing information, we are saved from "information overload." It is easier (but perhaps more dangerous) for us to refer to "defense mechanisms" than to state all the separate behaviors to which they refer.

Just as the same stones can be used to make different houses, so can a set of facts be given different meanings by different theories—by organizing them differently, emphasizing different behaviors, and inferring different hypothetical constructs. Consider the following example (McCain & Segal, 1969): At one time, two theories explained the tendency of a falling rock to increase its speed as it approaches the earth. According to a popular Greek theory, rocks and earth like to be with each other because they are made of the same elements. As the rock gets closer to the earth, it travels faster because it becomes increasingly excited. The same fact can also be explained by Newton's theory of universal gravitation. All particles attract each other with a force directly proportional to the product of their masses and inversely proportional to the square of their distances. These two theories are based on the same set of observations, but they assign different meanings to these facts.

When we view development through the lenses of first one theory and then another, we experience a gestaltlike shift. We see the child as seething with sexual energy or reflecting on the origins of the universe. We see the child as a bundle of conditioned responses or a highly organized system. At times, we may wonder if we are looking at the same child in these different perspectives. These theoretical shifts have been likened to shifts in the perception of ambiguous figures (Averill, 1976), such as the sudden perceptual shift of young woman to old woman in Figure I.1. The information has not changed, but our organization of it has.

Guiding Research

In addition to organizing and giving meaning to facts, a theory serves a second function. It is a heuristic device, a tool to guide observation and to generate new information. A theory's abstract statements predict that certain empirical statements should be true. These empirical statements then must be tested. Theories sometimes stimulate new observations. For example, ethology, an approach borrowed from biology, stimulated developmental psychologists to search for innate social behaviors contributing to the adaptation of the species to the environment. A new theory may also cause us to reexamine familiar behavior. Piaget certainly was not the first person to watch babies play, but he

Figure I.1

Similar to the shift in perspective from one theory to another, the lines in this drawing can be perceptually organized to form an old woman or a young woman.

suggested a new way of looking at this behavior: the actions themselves are creating thought, according to Piaget.

Theory's dual role as a stimulator of and interpreter of data is nicely illustrated in a 22-year longitudinal study of aggression (Eron, 1987). Traditional learning theory, with its emphasis on drive reduction, guided the selection of the original variables in 1960. In later years, as new learning theories emerged, investigators interpreted the data first in terms of Skinnerian operant learning (early 1970s), then social learning (mid-1970s), and finally cognitive theory (mid-1980s). Thus, in these four phases of learning-theory development, investigators sought the causes of aggression in frustration (drive reduction), reinforcement of aggression (Skinner), aggressive models (social learning), and finally the child's attitudes toward and interpretation of potential instigators of aggression (cognition).

WHAT MAIN ISSUES OF DEVELOPMENTAL PSYCHOLOGY DO THEORIES ADDRESS?

Although the theories to be covered differ in their content, methods of investigation, and formal nature, all explicitly or implicitly take a position on certain core issues of development. Developmental change, by its very nature, leads to at least four critical issues:

1. What is the basic nature of humans?
2. Is development qualitative or quantitative?
3. How do nature and nurture contribute to development?
4. What is it that develops?

These issues, which serve as a way of summarizing and contrasting the theories, reappear at the end of each chapter. First, however, some discussion of each issue is in order.

What Is the Basic Nature of Humans?

Theorists' views of development are closely tied to their views of human nature. Their views of human nature, in turn, are closely tied to their world views, or their notions about how the universe works. Philosophers of science have identified several world views in the history of the Western world (Pepper, 1942). Three of these can be found in theories of developmental psychology (Overton, 1984; Reese, 1991): the mechanistic, the organismic, and the contextual. We examine each of these.

In the *mechanistic* view, the world is like a machine composed of parts that operate in time and space. For example, the world could be likened to a watch. Forces are applied to the parts and cause a chain reaction that moves the machine from state to state. In principle, then, complete prediction is possible because complete knowledge of the state and forces at one point in time allows us to infer the next state. The mechanistic view has its roots in Newtonian physics. It is also related to the empiricist philosophy of Locke (1632–1704) and Hume (1711–1776), which pictures the human as inherently at rest—a passive robot, motivated by environmental or bodily sources. Development, consequently, is caused by antecedent (prior) forces and events acting on a passive, machinelike mind composed of interlocking parts. One can almost see the wheels turning in the child's head!

In contrast, the *organismic* world view is modeled on living systems, such as plants or animals, rather than machines. This image derives from Leibniz (1646–1716), who believed that substance is in "a continuous transition from one state to another as it produces these states out of itself in unceasing succession" (Cassirer, 1951, p. 29). Leibniz pictured the world as composed of organized "wholes" that are inherently and spontaneously active and self-regulating. This organization and self-directed activity is necessary, or natural, given the nature of the organism. This view emphasizes the whole rather than its parts, the relations among the parts, and how the whole gives meaning to its parts. In the realm of psychology, for example, one can understand a child's behavior only by viewing it within a larger dynamic system that includes the context as well as the child.

Rather than look for antecedent causes, as the mechanistic world view has done, the organismic view considers inherent properties and goals. The human, by nature, is an active, organized whole and is constantly changing, not randomly but in a particular direction. Development, then, is inherent in humans. Self-initiated behavior and thought lead to changes in both the structure and the content of behavior and thought. White describes an active organism:

> Let us define an active organism as one that gives form to its experience, a passive organism as one that receives form from its experience. Active organisms have purposes and they attend, reason, and selectively perceive. All this enables the active organism to select, modify, or reject environmental influences pressing upon it.
>
> (1976, p. 100)

The organismic view is that children "construct" their knowledge by actively formulating and testing hypotheses about categories of objects and the causes of events. In contrast, the mechanistic view is that children passively acquire ("soak up" like a sponge) a copy of reality. Organismic, unlike mechanistic, theories often posit qualitative rather than gradual change, and sometimes they are stage theories.

In the third world view, *contextualism,* the main metaphor is not a machine or a living system but a historical act or a tapestry. A behavior has meaning (and can be “explained”) only in terms of its social–historical context. The pragmatist philosophers such as William James and George Herbert Mead provide the philosophical inspiration. As Pepper describes contextualism, it

> takes for its root metaphor the textured event, with its richly qualitied strands fading into a past that dies and guiding the changing pattern of a present duration into a future that dawns. The event through its texture extends sidewise in its present duration into neighboring contexts which are themselves textures extending into still other contexts. And the texture of each event is internally analyzable into strands, which have individual tensions and references into other textures.
>
> (1934, p. 183)

This tapestry extends from the distant past to the distant future and from the proximal to the distal. The horizontal temporal and vertical spatial threads intermesh into a pattern of a human life.

We study this tapestry of development by looking at ongoing action-event units consisting of meaningful goal-directed activities. As Reese explains it, “Writing is not an act; but writing something with something on something in some situation at some time is an act” (1991, pp. 191–192). Reese lists other components of the contextual metaphor: the meaning of a behavior varies from context to context; a math problem may involve feelings of competence in the school environment but survival for a homeless child who is a street vendor. Moreover, behavior has a purpose that reaches into the past (some proximal “cause”) and into the future (some goal). Finally, like the organismic view, the contextualist view is wholistic. Not only is a unit greater than the sum of its parts, but a unit-in-context is greater than the sum of a unit *and* its context. To continue the above example, writing a sentence “is an act but is also a part of the larger act that includes writing about the act of writing the sentence, which in turn is part of the larger act that includes writing an entire paper, which in turn is part of the larger act that is the writer’s lifetime, which in turn is part of the larger act that includes others’ lifetimes, etc.” (Reese, 1991, p. 194).

Thus, the contextualist belief that children’s patterns of development can differ from one culture, subculture, or historical time to another contrasts with the mechanistic and organismic focus on universal laws of behavior and development. The main mechanistic approach, learning theory (Chapter 3), posits laws of learning, such as the influence of reinforcement on behavior, that apply across time and place. A main organismic theory, Piagetian theory (Chapter 1), proposes universal stages and mechanisms of development. As will become clear in subsequent chapters, these world views ask different questions about development and use different methods to answer those questions.

In addition to these three metaphysical views of humans, the world, and causality are more specific and limited views based on particular economic and political ideologies. For example, Riegel (1972) relates views of childhood and of development to the capitalistic and mercantilistic politicoeconomic systems in the seventeenth to nineteenth centuries.

The capitalistic system, largely Anglo-American, saw humans as competitive, as struggling for success. Thomas Hobbes's (1588–1679) pronouncement of humans as selfish and competitive and of life as "nasty, brutish, and short" expressed this notion. The roots continue through Charles Darwin, who stressed the survival of the fittest. In the economic arena, the emphasis was on free trade, competition, and entrepreneurship. The standard of success (as a result of struggle and competition) was the white, middle-class adult male engaged in manufacturing or business. By this standard, children, the elderly, mental defectives, and women were considered inferior. Childhood, considered a state of incomplete adulthood, was a "disability." Normative descriptions of each age were developed to detect "abnormal" development and chart children's progress toward the adult standard of success. Society saw children as passive beings who must be molded ("socialized") into appropriate adult roles.

The mercantilistic ideology, in contrast, existed primarily in continental Europe in the seventeenth through the nineteenth centuries. The economy was based on land ownership and state-controlled trading more than on manufacturing and free trade. Distinct social classes enjoyed specified duties and privileges, and little competition between classes occurred. Society emphasized cooperation more than competition; differences between groups were tolerated. The main philosophical spokesman, Jean Jacques Rousseau (1712–1778), saw the child as a "noble savage," basically good but ruined by the adult world. Children were not to be judged by adult standards; children and adults were seen as qualitatively different. From this point of view, the goal of education was self-realization. Consequently, a child-oriented education was developed by Maria Montessori, Eduard Spranger, and others.

From even this brief account of changing history, it is easy to see how each theory of developmental psychology always has a view of the human being that reflects philosophical, economic, and political beliefs. This view is often implicit, and sometimes theorists themselves are not even aware of these assumptions. The view influences not only theory construction but also decisions about which research problems are meaningful, what method should be used, and how data should be interpreted. Even the meanings of the terms "explanation" and "fact" are different in theories with different world views. For these reasons, it is sometimes claimed that it is impossible to integrate or reconcile theories or make crucial tests that support one or the other if they have different world views.

Is Development Qualitative or Quantitative?

Closely related to these views of humans is the issue of the basis of developmental change: Is it qualitative or quantitative? The mechanistic and capitalistic views emphasize quantitative change, the organismic and mercantilistic approaches emphasize qualitative change, and contextualism permits both. *Qualitative changes* are changes in kind or type. An example from nature is the following sequence: egg → caterpillar → cocoon → butterfly (Spiker, 1966). New phenomena or characteristics emerge that cannot be reduced to previous elements. Qualitative changes typically involve changes in structure or organization. In contrast, *quantitative changes* are changes in amount, frequency, or degree. In some cases, the behavior becomes more efficient or consistent. The change is gradual and occurs in small increments. Bits and pieces of knowledge, habits, or skills are acquired during development.

An example of the contrast between quantitative change and qualitative change can be found in the development of memory. If a 4-year-old can recall three objects and a 7-year-old can recall seven objects from a set of objects seen several minutes earlier, we might infer a quantitative difference in their mental functioning. The older child can remember more. However, if the 7-year-old uses strategies such as sorting the objects into categories of food, furniture, and toys, and rehearsing them, whereas the 4-year-old does not, we would infer a qualitative difference in their mental functioning: they process the information in a different way.

At a more general level, the issue of qualitative versus quantitative change becomes an issue of stage versus nonstage development. When there are similarities in a number of new abilities or behaviors during a period of time, a theorist often infers that the child is in a particular "stage." For example, Piaget posited stagelike qualitative changes in the structure of thought from birth to adolescence. Stage theorists disagree about the possibility of being in more than one stage at the same time or of regressing to an earlier stage, and they argue about what causes children to differ in how quickly they pass through the stages.

Stagelike qualitative changes have been identified by scholars other than developmental psychologists. Historians identify periods in history, such as the "industrial age" or the "age of reason." Shakespeare saw seven ages of man from the "mewling and puking" infant to the old person "sans teeth, sans eyes, sans taste, sans everything."

Despite their arguments about which developmental changes are qualitative and which quantitative, most developmentalists agree that both types of changes occur. Some behaviors involve both qualitative and quantitative changes. In some cases the periods of quantitative and qualitative change appear to alternate. Using the memory example presented earlier, one might find that an increase in mental capacity (quantitative change) may facilitate the development of a sorting strategy (qualitative change). Subsequent increases in the speed and accuracy of this sorting would involve quantitative change.

How Do Nature and Nurture Contribute to Development?

Regardless of the extent to which development is qualitative or quantitative, a theorist must refer to the underlying causes of development. The basic issue is how knowledge and behavior arise from one's genetic endowment and physical maturation and from experience in the world. The nature–nurture issue is known by several other labels, such as "heredity versus environment," "nativism versus empiricism," "biology versus culture," "maturation versus learning," and "innate versus acquired abilities."

This controversy has raged not only within psychology but also within philosophy. The controversy began in classical Greek times when philosophers asked whether ideas are innate or acquired through the experience of the senses. Later, Descartes (1596–1650) believed that certain ideas are innate, while the British empiricist Locke (1632–1704) argued that the newborn's mind is a blank slate *(tabula rasa)* on which experience writes.

Anastasi (1958) pointed out that initially psychologists did not ask the right question. We should not have asked *which* (heredity or environment) causes a behavior or *how much* of each is needed for a given behavior. Instead, we should ask *how* (in what manner) nature and nurture interact to produce development. This is an interesting illustration of how progress in a field sometimes simply means learning how to ask the right question.

Today nearly everyone agrees that a complex interaction of innate and environmental factors accounts for both the development of a trait or behavior in an individual and the variations in a trait or behavior among individuals. Nature and nurture are inextricably intertwined. Both nature and nurture are fully involved in the development of any behavior. Hebb (1980) remarked that behavior is determined 100 percent by heredity and 100 percent by environment. Genes are never expressed directly in behavior. There is a long chain of events involving genes, physiological processes, and the prenatal and postnatal environment. The way that heredity is expressed depends on the specific environment in which this expression occurs. In other words, a given hereditary influence can have different behavioral effects in different environments. And, conversely, a given environment can have different effects on people with different genetic makeups. A jack-in-the-box might delight a placid baby but disturb a nervous, reactive infant who is upset by sudden change. Moreover, intense stressful events that cause disturbances in most children have little effect on so-called resilient children (Garmezy & Tellegen, 1984). To complicate matters even further, environmental influences actually can have a genetic basis. For example, an innately active, exuberant child and a passive, quiet, reflective child will select different types of play settings and playmates. Thus, they are exposed to different types of experiences. Finally, genes and the environment can be correlated, as when shy parents both pass on a tendency toward shyness genetically and provide an environment that encourages shyness.

The theories presented in this book differ in whether they emphasize the nature or the nurture part of the interaction. In addition, they disagree about the process by which either environmental or innate factors have their influence. For example, the environment can "stamp in" associations, provide models to be imitated, supply information to be assimilated, strengthen neural networks, or provide a supportive social system (a helpful parent). Finally, theories differ in how much importance they place on the timing of a particular experience. Are there "critical periods" in which the child is especially sensitive to a particular experience? Is early experience more influential than later experience?

What Is It That Develops?

Each theorist makes a claim concerning the "essence" of development, or at least the proper unit of analysis. Throughout this book, we encounter various phenomena, such as cognitive structures, psychic structures (id, ego, superego), strategies of information processing, neural networks, fixed action patterns, perceptual exploration, mental modules, and cultural tools. What theorists see as the essence of development depends on where their theoretical assumptions and methods of study place them along several dimensions:

1. Their level of analysis (from cells to societies)
2. Whether they focus on structure (organization of behavior, thought, and personality) or process (dynamic, functioning aspects of the system)
3. What content they emphasize (for example, personality or cognition)
4. Whether they emphasize overt behavior or covert thought and personality
5. What methodology they use to study development

These five dimensions have a chicken-and-egg relationship: Which came first, ethologists' decision to study complex, behavior acquired by species in their struggle to adapt to the environment or their choice of a methodology, namely, observations in natural settings? This interrelationship among the dimensions will become more obvious as we examine each theory.

SUMMARY

The traditional view of an "ideal" scientific theory is that it should be a hypothetico-deductive system and include a set of logically interconnected statements. It formally describes psychological structures and processes and relates them to each other and to observable events. Most psychological "theories," however, have failed to achieve the status of a theory in the strict definition of the term. A theory has not only a public, formal, static nature but also a private, informal, dynamic nature. Moreover, a theory guides the behavior of psychologists doing research. It helps them formulate questions, choose what to study, and decide how to study a problem.

We need developmental theories. They help us describe and explain developmental changes by organizing and giving meaning to facts and by guiding further research. Developmental theories have taken a stand on four issues that are of special importance to the study of development:

1. What is the basic nature of humans?
2. Is development qualitative or quantitative?
3. How do nature and nurture contribute to development?
4. What is it that develops?

We now have a framework for viewing each of the theories in turn.

ORGANIZATION OF THIS BOOK

The following nine chapters describe the major theories of development plus several minitheories. Piaget's theory is presented first because many of the current issues in developmental psychology were raised by his theory and several theories arose in reaction to his theory. Next come the other two big theories in the history of developmental psychology: psychoanalytic theory and social learning theory. The next three theories are directed toward more limited areas of development. The information-processing approach examines thinking, ethology focuses on early social behavior, and Gibson's theory analyzes perceptual development. Vygotskian and other sociocultural theories are presented next because they have had a more recent impact. Chapter 8 describes several emerging, influential approaches, and the final chapter looks both backward and forward regarding developmental theories. Each chapter follows roughly the same organization, in order to make comparisons among the theories easier. At the end of each chapter, theories are evaluated in terms of their strengths and weaknesses according to the current state of developmental psychology. That is, we ask what each theory can contribute to today's developmental researchers, professionals who work with children, and parents.

SUGGESTED READINGS

Lerner, R. M. (Ed.). (1998). Theoretical models of human development. Vol. 1 in W. Damon (Series Ed.), *Handbook of child psychology* (5th ed.). New York: Wiley. Several chapters examine the philosophical foundations of developmental theories, the notion of development, the intellectual history of the field, and issues of development.

The following books provide overviews of theories of development:

Goldhaber, D. (2000). *Theories of human development: Integrative perspectives*. Mountain View, CA: Mayfield.

Thomas, R. M. (1999). *Comparing theories of child development* (4th ed.). Belmont, CA: Wadsworth.

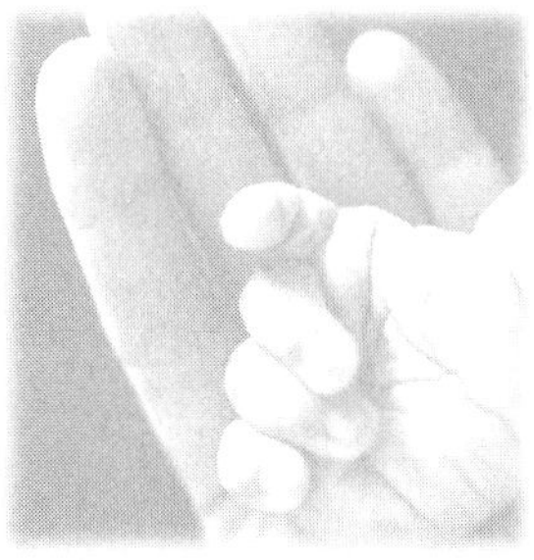

CHAPTER 1

Piaget's Cognitive-Stage Theory and the Neo-Piagetians

[At 7 months, 28 days] Jacqueline tries to grasp a celluloid duck on top of her quilt. She almost catches it, shakes herself, and the duck slides down beside her. It falls very close to her hand but behind a fold in the sheet. Jacqueline's eyes have followed the movement, she has even followed it with her outstretched hand. But as soon as the duck has disappeared — nothing more! It does not occur to her to search behind the fold of the sheet, which would be very easy to do (she twists it mechanically without searching at all).

— *Piaget, 1937 (1954, p. 36)*

Hub (age $6\frac{1}{2}$): Is the moon always round? — *No.* — What's it like? — *Sometimes a crescent, it is very worn out.* — Why? — *Because it has done a lot of lighting.* — How does it come round again? — *Because it is made again.* — How? — *In the sky.*

— *Piaget, 1926 (1929, p. 281)*

Intriguing glimpses of children's behavior and thought, such as those above, fired Piaget's imagination. In these unremarkable daily events, Piaget saw a remarkable process of cognitive development. In Piaget's view, moment-to-moment specific encounters with objects or people lead to general ways of understanding the world. This understanding changes during development as thinking progresses through various stages from birth to maturity. Moreover, children themselves actively construct this knowledge.

Piaget has been the most important figure in developmental psychology. His influence spread not only throughout the disciplines of psychology but also into areas such as education and philosophy. Moreover, his theory raised issues of development that the other theories must address. It is appropriate, then, to begin our look at theories with the cognitive-structural theory of Jean Piaget.

This chapter can only hint at the complexity of Piaget's theory. We first delve into Piaget's life in some detail in order to understand his theory better and to illustrate the close relationship between the personal history of a theorist and the nature of his theory. After this biography comes a general orientation to the theory, then a description of the stages and other developmental changes, followed by a discussion of the mechanisms of development. The next sections relate cognitive-structural theory to the critical issues of development and address applications of the theory. Near the end of the chapter, Piaget's theory is evaluated in a contemporary context. The chapter ends with a description of Piaget's modifications of his theory late in life and an overview of the work of neo-Piagetians.

BIOGRAPHICAL SKETCH

Most of the material in this biographical sketch comes from Piaget's (1952) autobiography. Jean Piaget was born in 1896 in Neuchâtel, Switzerland. Piaget described his father, a historian devoted to medieval literature, as "a man of a painstaking and critical mind, who dislikes hastily improvised generalizations, and is not afraid of starting a fight when he finds historic truth twisted to fit respectable traditions" (Piaget, 1952, p. 237). Piaget remembered his mother as intelligent, energetic, and kind, but with a neurotic temperament that drove him to both imitate his father and escape to what Piaget called a "private and nonfictitious world," a world of serious work. Piaget acknowledges that the turbulent family situation aroused his interest in psychoanalytic theory.

It would be easier to list what did not interest the boy Piaget than what did. A sampling of his interests includes mechanics, seashells, birds, and fossils. One of his early writings was a pamphlet (written in pencil because he was not yet allowed to write in ink) describing an "autovap," an intriguing union of a wagon and a locomotive. Piaget's first publication was a one-page article about a partly albino sparrow he had observed in a park. This achievement came at age 10—long before he had heard of "publish or perish"! Piaget's interest in the exhibits in the local natural history museum led to an invitation to assist the director with his mollusk (shellfish) collections. In this way, Piaget entered the field of malacology, the study of mollusks, which captivated him for years to come. Piaget's publications on mollusks attracted notice among natural historians. He was offered, sight unseen, the curatorship of mollusks at a natural history museum in Geneva. He had to decline the offer, however, because he had not yet finished secondary school!

Piaget did not escape the typical social and philosophical crises of adolescence. Conflicts between his religious and scientific teachings stimulated him to read hungrily through Bergson, Kant, Spencer, Comte, Durkheim, and William James, among others. This philosophical turmoil is expressed in his philosophical novel published in 1917. That this novel did not become a best-seller can be surmised from passages such as these: "Now there can be no awareness of these qualities, hence these qualities cannot exist, if there are no relationships among them, if they are not, consequently, blended into a total quality which contains them while keeping them distinct," and "positive theory of quality taking into account only relationships of equilibrium and disequilibrium among our qualities" (1952, p. 243). Piaget observed that "no one spoke of it except one or two indignant philosophers" (1952, p. 243).

Piaget continued to write on a variety of philosophical issues. He notes: "I wrote even if it was only for myself, for I could not think without writing—but it had to be in a systematic fashion as if it were to be an article for publication" (1952, p. 241). In these writings, one finds themes that are central in Piaget's later writings, for example, the logical organization of actions and the relationship between the parts and the whole.

Piaget continued his formal studies in the natural sciences and took his doctoral degree with a thesis on mollusks at the University of Neuchâtel in 1918 at age 21. Although he had published 20 papers by this time, he was not eager to devote his life to malacology. After visiting psychological laboratories in Zurich and exploring psychoanalytic theory briefly, Piaget spent 2 years at the Sorbonne. There he studied psychology and philosophy. By luck (for the field of developmental psychology), Piaget met Theodore Simon, a pioneer in the development of intelligence tests. Simon, who had at his disposal Alfred Binet's laboratory at a grade school in Paris, suggested that Piaget standardize Binet's reasoning tests on Parisian children. Piaget began the work with little enthusiasm. However, his interest was aroused when he began asking children to explain both their correct and incorrect answers. He became fascinated with the thought processes that appeared to lead to the answers, especially the incorrect ones. In these "conversations," Piaget used psychiatric interviewing techniques he had acquired at the Sorbonne while working with mental patients. Without Simon's knowledge, Piaget continued this research for 2 years. Piaget sums up this experience:

> At last I had found my field of research. . . . My aim of discovering a sort of embryology of intelligence fit in with my biological training; from the start of my theoretical thinking I was certain that the problem of the relation between the organism and environment extended also into the realm of knowledge, appearing here as the problem of the relation between the acting or thinking subject and the objects of his experience. Now I had the chance of studying this problem in terms of psychogenetic development.
>
> (1952, p. 245)

The subsequent publication of three articles based on this research in Binet's laboratory led to an offer in 1921 to become director of studies at the Institut J. J. Rousseau in Geneva. Piaget planned to spend only 5 years studying child psychology (a plan that, happily, went awry). The freedom and research facilities of this position nurtured Piaget's productive tendencies and led to the publication of five books: *The Language and Thought of the Child* (1923), *Judgment and Reasoning in the Child* (1924), *The Child's Conception of the World* (1926), *The Child's Conception of Physical Causality* (1927), and *The Moral Judgment of the Child* (1932). To his surprise, the books were read and discussed widely. He became known as a child psychologist, even though he had no university degree in psychology. He was much sought after as a speaker, and his fame grew rapidly in Europe.

In the following few years, Piaget continued his research at the institute, taught philosophy at the University of Neuchâtel, learned about

Gestalt psychology, observed his own babies, and even performed some research on mollusks in his free time! From 1929 to 1945, he occupied several academic and administrative positions at the University of Geneva, as well as international posts, such as president of the Swiss Commission of UNESCO. There were productive collaborations with Alina Szeminska, Bärbel Inhelder, and Marcel Lambercier on the manipulation of objects, the development of perception, and the notions of number, physical quantity, and space. Hearing of Piaget's work, Albert Einstein encouraged him to study the concepts of time, velocity, and movement. Two provocative books emerged from this suggestion: *The Child's Conception of Time* (1946a) and *The Child's Conception of Movement and Speed* (1946b).

The 1940s and 1950s were marked by research on an amazing range of topics: various aspects of mental development, education, the history of thought, logic, and his old passion, epistemology, or theory of knowledge. His titles included professor of psychology at the University of Geneva and the Sorbonne, director of the Institut des Sciences de l'Education, and director of the Bureau International de l'Education. In addition, he founded the Centre d'Epistémologie Génétique, a meeting ground for philosophers and psychologists.

In 1969, the American Psychological Association gave Piaget the Distinguished Scientific Contribution Award "for his revolutionary perspective on the nature of human knowledge and biological intelligence" (Evans, 1973, p. 143). He was the first European to receive this award.

Piaget pursued the riddle of children's thinking until his death in 1980, at the age of 84. Even in his final years, books and articles continued to emerge from behind the piles of papers and books in seeming disarray in his office. His flowing white hair, pipe, beret, and bicycle were a familiar sight in Geneva. We have the following description of Piaget at age 70: "He moves deliberately, but his blue eyes sparkle with youth, good humor and zest. Benevolent enough, but not heavy enough, to look like Santa Claus, he reminds one faintly of the pictures of Franz Liszt that have come down to us" (Tuddenham, 1966, p. 208).

One cannot help but be struck by Piaget's amazing productivity. A conservative estimate of his writing is over 40 books and more than 100 articles or chapters on child psychology alone. Adding publications on philosophy and education swells these numbers even more. In fact, he averaged about one and a quarter books per year from his first volume until his death (Brainerd, 1996). Piaget attributed his productivity, in part, to his helpful colleagues but also gave us the following interesting glimpse into his personality:

> And then, too, I owe it to a particular bent of my character. Fundamentally I am a worrier whom only work can relieve. It is true I am sociable and like to teach or to take part in meetings of all kinds, but I feel a compelling need for solitude and contact with nature. After mornings spent with others, I begin each afternoon with a walk during which I quietly collect my thoughts and coordinate them, after which I return to the desk at my home in the country. . . . It is this dissociation between myself as a social being and as a "man of nature" (in whom Dionysian excitement ends in intellectual activity) which has enabled me to surmount a permanent fund of anxiety and transform it into a need for working.
>
> (1952, p. 255)

GENERAL ORIENTATION TO THE THEORY

Like a short guided tour in an unfamiliar city, the following attempts to provide an overview of Piaget's theory before exploring the nooks and crannies—and perhaps becoming lost. We examine five salient characteristics of the theory: genetic epistemology, the biological approach, structuralism, the stage approach, and Piaget's methodology. These characteristics relate to Piaget's interests and goals, described earlier.

It should be noted that Piaget acknowledged the contributions of his coworkers. Although this is a chapter on Piaget's theory, much of the work it describes was done in collaboration with a number of people, especially Bärbel Inhelder.

■ *Genetic Epistemology*

Perhaps the most incomprehensible thing about the world is that it is comprehensible.

—ALBERT EINSTEIN

Piaget might well have agreed with Einstein, for he had a lifelong fascination with how humans comprehend the world. The branch of philosophy concerned with the study of knowledge is called *epistemology*. As Piaget viewed it, epistemology is "the problem of the relation between the acting or thinking subject and the objects of his experience" (1952, p. 245). Piaget tackled the same questions that have engaged philosophers for centuries: How do we come to know something? Is objective knowledge, unbiased by the nature of the knower, even possible? Are there certain innate ideas, or must all knowledge be acquired? All of Piaget's writings can be seen as attempts to answer these questions in different content areas, for example, mathematics, moral reasoning, and language. As we saw in our biographical sketch of Piaget, his philosophical quest led him through various schools of philosophy, biology, history, mathematics, and psychology. His search finally stopped at developmental psychology, which was not even an organized field of study at the time.

Piaget's journey to developmental psychology brings us to the "genetic" part of the term *genetic epistemology*. In this context, the word "genetic" refers not to what is innate, the more common meaning of the term today, but to "development" or "emergence." By studying developmental changes in the process of knowing and in the organization of knowledge, Piaget felt that he could find answers to the traditional questions of epistemology. His concern with the classical issues in epistemology explains his concern with what philosophers have considered the basic categories of thought: time, space, causality, and quantity. These categories of thought are obvious to an adult but, in Piaget's way of thinking, may not be obvious to children. Piaget wondered how and when children understand that no two objects can occupy the same place, that objects exist even when out of sight, and that two contiguous events can have a causal relationship. It may be as difficult for young children to understand these concepts as it is for most adults to understand "black holes" in space or the theory of relativity.

Piaget can be called an experimental epistemologist. Unlike most epistemologists, who use logical arguments to support their views, Piaget rejected the armchair approach and formulated empirical hypotheses that could be tested. For example, he examined the question of how humans acquire concepts of time, space, and causality by tracing the development of these concepts. One of Piaget's main contributions was his brand of epistemology—a marriage of philosophy and the scientific method, of logic and fact.

Piaget's simple but revolutionary solution to the problem of epistemology is that knowledge is a process rather than a state. It is an event or a relationship between the active knower and the known. A child knows or understands a ball or a rattle by acting on it—physically or mentally. In a sense, people "construct" knowledge. They have an active part in the process of knowing and even contribute to the form that knowledge takes. Cognitive humans actively select and interpret information in the environment. They do not passively soak up information to build a storehouse of knowledge.

Children's knowledge of the world changes as their cognitive system develops. As the knower changes, so does the known. A concrete example is the knowledge of relationships in space. Infants construct a practical knowledge of near and far, up and down. Older children construct a more abstract "cognitive map" of the relations among objects in their environment. Infants "know" space by crawling in it and reaching for objects, whereas older children know space by manipulating mental symbols in particular ways. Note that in both cases there is a constant interaction between the knower and the external world.

One implication of Piaget's theory of knowledge is that knowledge is biased, until perhaps the end of the final stage in certain domains. Experience is always filtered through the child's current ways of understanding. A child's mind is not a camera that takes faithful pictures of reality. However, as the mind develops, it becomes more in tune with reality.

■ *Biological Approach*

Beginning with the early boyhood interest in shells and birds, Piaget's thinking was firmly rooted in biology. Piaget's distinction is that he saw more in mollusks than did most biologists. In the humble mollusk he saw general principles of how living organisms adapt to the world. Mollusks both adjust themselves to the environment and actively assimilate it in ways allowed by their biological structure. Piaget felt that these principles also apply to human thought. His most general definition of intelligence is that it is adaptation to the environment. Just as human and nonhuman organisms adapt physically to the environment, so does thought adapt to the environment at a psychological level. Piaget hypothesized that the modes of psychological functioning involved in this adaptation are universal, that is, used by all humans.

Borrowing another concept from biology, Piaget proposed that cognitive growth is much like embryological growth: an organized structure becomes more and more differentiated over time. In fact, Piaget (1970) sometimes referred to cognitive development as "mental embryology."

Adaptation, organization, and structure, as well as such other biological concepts as equilibration, assimilation, and accommodation, are discussed later in the chapter, when we turn our attention to processes of development. At this point, however, it should be emphasized that these biological concepts serve as analogies for the way intelligence works. Biology did not lead Piaget to a neuroscience of intelligence.

Structuralism

Along with such other luminaries as anthropologist Claude Lévi-Strauss and linguist Ferdinand de Saussure, Piaget belonged to an approach called *structuralism*. Structuralists look at the organizational properties of whatever they are studying. Piaget proposed that a small set of mental operations (mental actions) underlies a wide variety of thinking episodes. Thus, there is an underlying structure to the apparent diversity of the content. Structuralists look at how parts are organized into a whole, and they abstract patterns of change. In particular, they are concerned with relationships—between parts and the whole and between an earlier and a later state. For example, the thinking of younger children and that of older children have similar elements, but these elements are combined in different ways to form the organized whole of thought.

According to Piaget the structuralist, the nature of mental structures changes as they develop. An infant's cognitive structures are labeled "schemes" (sometimes translated "schemas" or "schemata"). A *scheme* is an organized pattern of behavior; it reflects a particular way of interacting with the environment. For Piaget, a scheme is whatever is repeatable and generalizable in an action. The sucking scheme, then, describes the way children put various objects into their mouths and suck them. As the scheme becomes more differentiated, children classify objects into "suckables" and "nonsuckables," with various subcategories such as hard suckables, soft suckables, good-tasting suckables, and hairy suckables (daddy's leg).

In contrast, the cognitive structures of the older child, from roughly age 7 on, are described in terms of organized abstract mental operations similar to logicomathematical systems. The structuralist framework can be seen in the way these schemes and operations organize themselves into an organized whole and can be applied to various content. For example, addition, subtraction, multiplication, and division are operations that are coordinated in a concept of number that underlies (mediates) much mathematical behavior. (We return to the notion of cognitive structures later.)

Two points should be emphasized. First, children *actively* construct these structures. Second, Piaget emphasized the feeling of necessity that accompanies the acquisition of a cognitive structure. For example, he quotes a child who said, "Once one knows, one knows forever and ever" (1971, p. 5).

Stage Approach

Milestones, phases, and ages
render general gauges
While periods, levels, and stages
require pages and pages.

—*Leland van den Daele**

Perhaps the boldest and most controversial of Piaget's claims is that cognitive development proceeds through a series of stages. For Piaget, a *stage* is a period of time in which the child's thinking and behavior in a variety of situations tend to reflect a particular type of underlying mental structure. Piaget's emphasis on stages is not surprising, considering his years of careful observing and classifying, and studying evolution, while a student of zoology. The stages can be thought of as sequential levels of adapting. Just as various species have different ways of adapting to the environment, so do various cognitive levels provide different ways of adapting to the environment. Because stage theories abound in developmental psychology, it will be helpful to characterize Piaget's particular brand of stage theory. There are five salient characteristics.

1 *A stage is a structured whole in a state of equilibrium.* Piaget the structuralist sees a stage as an integrated whole that organizes the parts. The schemes or operations of each stage are interconnected to form an organized whole. Each stage has a different structure, which allows a different type of interaction between the child and the environment, and consequently provides fundamentally different views of the world. The essence of Piaget's stage approach is that movement through the stages involves structural changes that are qualitative (changes in type or kind) rather than quantitative (change in degree, amount, speed, or efficiency). For example, there is a qualitative change when the child moves from structures based on actions in infancy to structures based on mental representation in the preschool years. At the *end* of each major period of development, the cognitive structures are in a state of

*From "Qualitative Models in Developmental Analysis" by Leland van den Daele, *Developmental Psychology, 1,* 303–310 (quote is on p. 303). Copyright © 1969 by the American Psychological Association.

balance, or equilibrium. (More on the equilibration process appears later in this chapter.)

2 *Each stage derives from the previous stage, incorporates and transforms that stage, and prepares for the next stage*. The previous stage paves the way for the new stage. In the process of achieving this new stage, the previous stage is reworked. Thus, once children achieve a new stage, they no longer have the previous stage available. Although previous skills remain, their position or role in the organization changes. For example, elementary school children can still roll or hit a ball (a skill acquired during infancy), but they now embed this skill in a number of other skills. Furthermore, a more advanced level of thought controls the old skills of rolling and hitting. Rolling and hitting are now combined with other actions to win the game. One implication of this characteristic is that regression to an earlier stage should be impossible because the previous stage is no longer present. This notion is in contrast to Freud's theory of stages, in which a person overwhelmed with anxiety may regress to an earlier stage.

3 *The stages follow an invariant sequence*. The stages must proceed in a particular order. No stage can be skipped. In other words, since the first stage does not have all the building materials needed for the third stage, the second stage is required. This claim that stages follow an invariant sequence is implied by the second claim, that each stage is derived from the preceding stage.

4 *Stages are universal*. Because Piaget was interested in how humans as a species adapt psychologically to their environment, he focused on the structures and concepts acquired by humans everywhere. Of course, people with a low IQ may not progress through all the stages or may progress through them more slowly. And people in general vary on how fast they proceed through the stages. However, the crucial claim is that the same stages in the same order are found universally in children of the African jungle, the American suburb, or the Swiss mountainside.

5 *Each stage includes a coming-into-being and a being*. There is an initial period of preparation and a final period of achievement in each stage. Unstable, loosely organized structures mark the initial period of transition from the previous stage. Change both within a stage and between stages is somewhat gradual. The description of each stage later in this chapter refers to the final, stable, generalized, tightly organized structure of each stage.

In summary, stages are structured wholes that emerge from and transform a previous stage, follow an invariant and universal sequence, and proceed from an unstable period of transition to a final stable period.

Methodology

One message from the Introduction is that the scientist, the theory, and the methods for gathering data both facilitate and constrain one another. The three develop together in particular directions. Piaget the sparrow watcher and mollusk collector used his observation and classification skills when watching infants master the objects around them and when observing toddlers struggle to express their thoughts in spontaneous speech. Piaget as the Sorbonne student interviewing mental patients soon became known as the man who asked children questions about dreams, the origin of the universe, and quantity. Piaget's early work with preschool and school children typically involved the *clinical method*, which involves a chainlike verbal interaction between the experimenter and the child. Experimenters begin by posing a problem or asking a question, but subsequent questions are guided by the answer the child gave to the previous question. Through this interchange, experimenters try to understand the line of reasoning underlying the child's answers. A talented interviewer avoids biasing the child's answers by refraining from too much suggestion.

The following exchange between Piaget and a 5-year-old illustrates the clinical method:

> Where does the dream come from? — *I think you sleep so well that you dream.* — Does it come from us or from outside? — *From outside.* — What do we dream with? — *I don't know.* — With the hands? . . . With nothing? — *Yes, with nothing.* — When you are in bed and you dream, where is the dream? — *In my bed, under the blanket. I don't really know. If it was in my stomach(!) the bones would be in the way and I shouldn't see it.* — Is the dream there when you sleep? — *Yes, it is in my bed beside me* . . . . Is the dream in your head? — *It is I that am in the dream: it isn't in my head(!). When you dream, you don't know you are in the bed. You know you are walking. You are in the dream. You are in bed, but you don't know you are.* . . . Where do dreams come from? — *I don't know. They happen.* — Where? — *In the room and then afterward they come up to the children. They come by themselves.* — You see the dream when you are in the room, but if I were in the room, too, should I see it? — *No, grownups (les*

> *Messieurs) don't ever dream. . . .* When the dream is in the room, is it near you? — *Yes, there!* (pointing to 30 cms. in front of his eyes).
> [1926 (1929, pp. 97–98)]

In Piaget's later work, such interviews were often combined with the manipulation of objects by the experimenter or child. This was especially likely when Piaget studied numerical and physical concepts or perceptual development. For example, Piaget might spread out a row of objects and ask whether the number had changed.

Infants, of course, cannot fruitfully be questioned about their thoughts. Piaget and his psychologist wife, Valentine, kept a baby diary of observations of their own infants as the infants went about their normal activities. At times, Piaget became a participant-observer by inventing little experiments on the spot, such as hiding a toy and observing whether the infant searched for it.

Because these verbal protocols and behavioral observations were seen through the eyes of Piaget the philosopher and theoretical biologist, their description became more and more abstract. Piaget saw general structures of thought in the varied, concrete behaviors. Thus, his writings often had a high proportion of theoretical interpretation to actual observation.

One of the challenges to someone encountering Piaget's theory for the first time is to relate the many elusive, abstract features of the theory to the abundant specific behaviors found in each stage. Perhaps the best way to grasp the relationship between the abstract and the concrete is to swing back and forth between the two. Following this strategy, we now swing from the preceding abstract orientation to a description of specific stagelike changes and then swing back to abstract features found in mechanisms of change.

DESCRIPTION OF THE STAGES

In the Introduction to this book, it was proposed that a developmental theory should both describe and explain development. The present section describes the prototypic Piagetian child making her way through the stages of cognitive development. The subsequent section tackles the questions of how and why this particular course of development occurs.

To understand each stage, we need to know not only where it came from but also where it is going. Each stage holds both the fruits of the past and the seeds of the future. Here, then, is an overview of the stages, followed by a more detailed account. The ages listed with each stage are approximate because children vary somewhat in the ages at which they proceed through the stages.

1. *Sensorimotor period* (roughly birth to 2 years). Infants understand the world in terms of their overt, physical actions on that world. They move from simple reflexes through several steps to an organized set of schemes (organized sensorimotor behaviors).
2. *Preoperational period* (roughly 2 to 7 years). No longer do children simply make perceptual and motor adjustments to objects and events. They can now use symbols (mental images, words, gestures) to represent these objects and events. They use these symbols in an increasingly organized and logical fashion.
3. *Concrete operational period* (roughly 7 to 11 years). Children acquire certain logical structures that allow them to perform various mental operations, which are internalized actions that can be reversed.
4. *Formal operational period* (roughly 11 to 15 years). Mental operations are no longer limited to concrete objects; they can be applied to purely verbal or logical statements, to the possible as well as the real, to the future as well as the present.

The following description of the stages of development should be prefaced by a word about Piaget's terminology. Although Piaget refers to "stages" of development, each of the four major stages is designated as a "period," for example, the "sensorimotor period." When Piaget identifies substages within one of the four major periods, they are designated as "stages."

■ *Sensorimotor Period (Roughly Birth to 2 Years)*

In Piaget's view, a human starts life with a set of reflexes, a particular physical makeup unique to the human species, and inherited ways of interacting with the environment. These inherited ways of interacting reflect the tendency of thought to be organized and adapted to the environment. The thinking of even an Einstein has these humble beginnings. Although newborns know almost nothing about the world, they have the potential to know almost everything. Indeed, one of Piaget's books on infancy is aptly titled *The Origins of Intelligence in Children* (1936). We now trace the infant's active construction of a model of the world by means of the sensory (perceptual) and motor (physical movement) systems. The infant progresses through six stages in the construction of a sensorimotor system of thought.

Stage 1: Modification of Reflexes (Roughly Birth to 1 Month) ▪ A newborn is a bundle of reflexes, or "wired-in" responses that are triggered by particular stimuli. Touch a newborn's lips and she sucks, prick her foot and her knee flexes, place a finger in her hand and she grasps it. As these reflexes are activated a number of times, they very gradually are modified. The infant adjusts them slightly to meet the requirements of slightly different circumstances. For example, the infant's mouth must search out the nipple from different angles on different occasions. In addition, the way the mouth and tongue fit around a hard, plastic rattle differs from the way they fit around a finger.

As an expanding number and type of objects serve as "grist" for the sucking reflex, the category of "suckables" grows to include objects ranging from nipples to blankets to bars of the crib. However, at the same time that infants are generalizing their sucking behavior to many objects, they are also increasing their discrimination between objects. Hungry infants never confuse a finger with a nipple. In a sense, they "recognize" objects.

Behaviors such as sucking, grasping, and looking do not remain reflexes; babies can produce them spontaneously. In fact, the baby sometimes sucks when there is nothing to suck. Piaget claims that there is an innate tendency for humans to exercise their skills. Babies suck because they *can* suck. Sucking strengthens the sucking skill and leads to further sucking.

In short, in stage 1, the baby strengthens, generalizes, and differentiates behaviors that began as reflexes. At this point, Piaget begins to use the term "scheme," which was introduced in the earlier section on structuralism. These schemes—organized patterns of behavior—continue to strengthen, generalize, and differentiate throughout the rest of the sensorimotor period. The infant is constructing a world of things to suck, grasp, look at, hit, feel, listen to, and so on. The primitive schemes of the first stage are a small, but significant, step in this construction.

Stage 2: Primary Circular Reactions (Roughly 1 to 4 Months) ▪ The behaviors in stage 1 can be called schemes only in a very limited sense because there is so little modification of the reflex. In stage 2, there is widespread and rapid development of schemes because *primary circular reactions* can now occur. A circular reaction is a behavior that is repeated over and over again and thus becomes circular. By chance, the baby discovers an interesting result from some behavior and then attempts to recapture this result. As the behavior and its results are successfully repeated, it can be said that a "habit" is formed. These circular reactions are called "primary" because they involve response consequences that are centered on or around the infant's body rather than other objects.

Piaget observed many cases of primary circular reactions in his own infants. Consider the following example (the three numbers refer to the child's age in years, months, and days):

> From 0;2(3) Laurent evidences a circular reaction which will become more definite and will constitute the beginning of systematic grasping; he scratches and tries to grasp, lets go, scratches and grasps again, etc. On 0;2(3) and 0;2(6) this can only be observed during the feeding. Laurent gently scratches his mother's bare shoulder. But beginning 0;2(7) the behavior becomes marked in the cradle itself. Laurent scratches the sheet which is folded over the blankets, then grasps it and holds it a moment, then lets it go, scratches it again and recommences without interruption. At 0;2(11) this play lasts a quarter of an hour at a time, several times during the day. At 0;2(12) he scratches and grasps my fist which I placed against the back of his right hand. He even succeeds in discriminating my bent finger and grasping it separately, holding it a few moments. At 0;2(14) and 0;2(16) I note how definitely the spontaneous grasping of the sheet reveals the characteristics of circular reaction—groping at first, then regular rhythmical activity (scratching, grasping, holding and letting go), and finally progressive loss of interest.
>
> [Piaget, 1936 (1952, pp. 91–92)]

One primary circular reaction that is probably universal is thumb sucking. Although thumb sucking has occurred since (or before) birth, it now has developed into a systematic, coordinated behavior. The infant efficiently brings the thumb to the mouth and keeps it there. Other examples of primary circular reactions include active visual exploration of objects and listening to one's own vocalizations.

The performance of the circular reactions seems to be accompanied by feelings of pleasure. Piaget describes a baby who "played with his voice, not only through interest in the sound, but for 'functional pleasure,' laughing at his own power" [1945 (1951, p. 91)].

Stage 3: Secondary Circular Reactions (Roughly 4 to 8 Months) ▪ Infants are never content with the status quo; they continue to push themselves and expand their world. This expansion is especially striking in the movement from primary to *secondary circular reactions*. Whereas primary circular reactions are centered around the infant's body, secondary circular reactions are oriented to the external world. By chance, the infant does something that leads to an interesting effect in the environment: he shakes a rattle, which produces a noise; he slaps a ball, which causes it to roll. In the previous stage, the shaking or slapping itself was of interest; now the environmental consequences are.

When the secondary circular reactions generalize, Piaget calls them "procedures for making interesting sights last." If kicking their legs vigorously leads to a jiggling mobile a number of times, infants may make this kicking procedure a part of their repertoire. On future occasions when an interesting movement occurs, they may make kicking movements in an attempt to sustain or re-create this movement. Sometimes these procedures produce the desired result; sometimes they do not. On one occasion, after watching, in fascination, his father drum on a tin box, 7-month-old Laurent first stares at it, then shakes his arm, raises himself, strikes his covers, and shakes his head in an attempt to capture the box—all to no avail!

One of Piaget's novel observations is the "motor recognition" that emerges during this stage:

> What happens, in effect, is that the child, confronted by objects or sights which habitually set in motion his secondary circular reactions, limits himself to outlining the customary movements instead of actually performing them. Everything takes place as though the child were satisfied to recognize these objects or sights and to make a note of this recognition, but could not recognize them except by working, rather than thinking, the schema helpful to recognition.
>
> [1936 (1952, pp. 185–186)]

For example, when Piaget's infant daughter, Lucienne, sees a doll that she has often swung in the past, she simply opens and closes her hands or shakes her legs; this is a reduced, effortless version of the original behavior.

During stages 2 and 3, the infant achieves some simple coordinations of his schemes. The integration of vision and grasping is especially useful for developing circular reactions. Now the infant can see an object, reach for it, and run through his repertoire of "things to do to objects." This coordination of the schemes of looking, grasping, sucking, hearing, and so forth continues throughout the sensorimotor period. In this way, the cognitive structures are becoming increasingly integrated and organized.

Stage 4: Coordination of Secondary Schemes (Roughly 8 to 12 Months) ▪ In this stage, infants can combine their schemes in complex ways. In particular, planning and intentionality emerge. This new behavior sequence is made up of an instrumental (or means) behavior (scheme) and a goal behavior (another scheme). Infants know what they want and can put together schemes to achieve that goal. They have differentiated between means and end. In contrast, in stage 3, infants' discovery of interesting results was fortuitous; only *afterward* did they try to achieve the outcome again. A special feature of the means–end behavior found in stage 4 is that it is applied to *new* situations. The schemes are now mobile; they are freed from their original contexts and can be used at will to achieve a variety of goals.

Piaget relates various occasions on which he placed his hand in front of a desirable matchbox. Whereas in stage 3 Laurent simply applied (unsuccessfully) his familiar grasping scheme toward the matchbox, in stage 4 he hit his father's hand (means) and grasped the box (end). Laurent had removed a barrier in order to achieve a goal.

In addition to coordinating schemes to remove barriers, the infant can now use objects as instruments to obtain a goal. A modern example is the infant who places his mother's hand on the television knob in order to see the dark screen come alive.

Another outcome of the differentiation between means and ends is the anticipation of events:

> At 0;9(16) . . . she likes the grape juice in a glass, but not the soup in a bowl. She watches her mother's activity. When the spoon comes out of the glass she opens her mouth wide, whereas when the spoon comes from the bowl, her mouth remains closed. Her mother tries to lead her to make a mistake by taking a spoon from the bowl and passing it by the glass before offering it to Jacqueline. But she is not fooled.
>
> [Piaget, 1936 (1952, p. 249)]

Stage 5: Tertiary Circular Reactions (Roughly 12 to 18 Months) ▪ In this stage, we see infant scientists at work. The environment is their laboratory. They perform miniature experiments in which they deliberately vary an action in order to see how this variation affects the outcome. They exploit each object's potential. They seem to be asking, "Is there anything new about this object?" As in earlier circular reactions, there is repetition with variation.

Again Laurent thoughtfully provides us with a nice example:

> At 0;10(11) Laurent is lying on his back but nevertheless resumes his experiments of the day before. He grasps in succession a celluloid swan,

> a box, etc., stretches out his arm and lets them fall. He distinctly varies the positions of the fall. Sometimes he stretches out his arm vertically, sometimes he holds it obliquely, in front of or behind his eyes, etc. When the object falls in a new position (for example on his pillow), he lets it fall two or three times more on the same place, as though to study the spatial relation; then he modifies the situation. At a certain moment the swan falls near his mouth: now, he does not suck it (even though this object habitually serves this purpose), but drops it three times more while merely making the gesture of opening his mouth.
>
> [Piaget, 1936 (1952, p. 269)]

Through deliberate trial-and-error exploration, infants extend the means–end behavior of the previous stage to develop new means. They no longer simply coordinate old schemes. In fact, Piaget often characterizes stage 5 as "the discovery of new means through active experimentation." Examples of new means might include pulling a blanket to obtain an object resting on the blanket or positioning a long, thin object in such a way that it can be slipped through the bars of a crib.

Stage 6: Invention of New Means Through Mental Combinations (Roughly 18 to 24 Months) ■ Stage 6 both closes the curtain on the sensorimotor period and raises it on the preoperational period. The achievements of one period always make it possible for the child to begin the next period. In stage 6, thought begins to go underground. Up to this time, children have displayed their thinking to the world; now the overt is becoming covert. External physical exploration gives way to internal mental exploration. All of this is possible because children now can use mental symbols to *represent* objects and events.

Let us see how this mental representation leads to a new way of solving problems:

> At 1;6(23) for the first time Lucienne plays with a doll carriage whose handle comes to the height of her face. She rolls it over the carpet by pushing it. When she comes against a wall, she pulls, walking backward. But as this position is not convenient for her, she pauses and without hesitation, goes to the other side to push the carriage again. She therefore found the procedure in one attempt, apparently through analogy to other situations but without training, apprenticeship, or chance.
>
> [Piaget, 1936 (1952, p. 338)]

Earlier, Lucienne would have had to solve the problem through trial and error. Now she can solve the problem by "thinking" in symbols.

The emergence of a mental symbol can be seen in one of the most stunning of Piaget's observations. Piaget has been playing a game with Lucienne at age 1 year, 4 months, in which he hides from her a watch chain inside an empty matchbox. Lucienne has attained the chain by applying old schemes—turning the box upside down so that the contents spill out through the opening or, with a smaller opening, sliding her fingers into the slot to grasp the chain. (It should be noted that Lucienne has not observed her father sliding the box to change the size of the opening.) Then Piaget slips the chain through an even smaller opening, which, as Lucienne discovers, is too small to permit her fingers to reach the chain. Now we see the behavior of interest:

> She looks at the slit with great attention; then, several times in succession, she opens and shuts her mouth, at first slightly, then wider and wider! Apparently Lucienne understands the existence of a cavity subjacent to the slit and wishes to enlarge that cavity. The attempt at representation which she thus furnishes is expressed plastically, that is to say, due to inability to think out the situation in words or clear visual images she uses a simple motor indication as "signifier" or symbol.
>
> [Piaget, 1936 (1952, p. 338)]

When faced with a problem that past methods do not solve, Lucienne thinks through the problem, partly by means of movements of the mouth and partly by thinking. She is in transition to a true use of mental symbols. The movements of the mouth represent the idea of widening the opening of the matchbox.

One achievement of this stage is that an event that has been represented can be evoked at a later time. This absent event is reproduced in part, as seen in the following observation:

> At 1;4(3) J. had a visit from a little boy of 1;6, whom she used to see from time to time, and who, in the course of the afternoon got into a terrible temper. He screamed as he tried to get out of a play-pen and pushed it backwards, stamping his feet. J. stood watching him in amazement, never having witnessed such a scene before. The next day, she herself screamed in her play-pen and tried to move it, stamping her foot lightly several times in succession. The imitation of the whole scene was most striking. Had it been immediate, it would naturally not have involved representation, but coming as it did after an interval of more than twelve hours, it must have involved some representative or pre-representative element.
>
> [Piaget, 1945 (1951, p. 63)]

Overview of the Sensorimotor Period ■ The sensorimotor period has been presented in some detail because it provides a concrete illustration of the following general characteristics of all four periods:

1. *A child actively learns about properties of objects and relations among them.* In the sensorimotor period, the child achieves this knowledge through overt actions, thus, a "logic of action."

2. *Cognitive structures become more tightly organized.* The child coordinates schemes and applies them as solutions to new situations.

3. *Behavior gradually becomes more intentional.* The child differentiates between means and ends, invents new means, and applies them to new ends in new situations.

4. *The self is gradually differentiated from the environment.* Children discover the boundaries of their own body and see themselves as one object in a world of objects.

Concept of Object Permanence ■ Perhaps the most important concept acquired during the sensorimotor period is the notion of *object permanence*: an object continues to exist even when one cannot see, hear, or feel it. This knowledge is necessary for a notion of a stable, predictable world. According to Piaget, the concept develops as follows: During the first few months of life, if an object disappears, infants do not search for it (stages 1 and 2). Their behavior follows the rule "out of sight, out of mind." Later, they search if the object is only partially hidden or if they were doing something with the object when it disappeared (stage 3). However, they give up easily if the object does not reappear quickly. They still think of the object as an extension of their actions on it. Still later, as schemes are coordinated, children have the skills needed to look for hidden objects (stage 4). However, they persist in searching in the place where they searched previously. Thus, when Piaget hides a toy parrot twice under a mattress to his daughter's left and then hides it to her right (as she watches), she immediately searches to the left—in the original hiding place. Piaget's interpretation of this so-called A-not-B error is that she defines an object partly in terms of its position—a "parrot-under-the-mattress." This interesting error has been the subject of much recent research (e.g., Matthews, Ellis, & Nelson, 1996).

The next advance is that children can appropriately search for an object even if there are several displacements, but only if they are visible (stage 5). There is a problem with invisible displacements, as when Piaget puts a coin in his hand and moves it under a cushion, then under a coverlet, and then out again. However, in the final stage, Jacqueline continues to search for the coin because she now knows that it has to be somewhere (stage 6). She can represent the object mentally, so is not dependent on seeing, or otherwise acting on, the object. At last she understands that objects, including herself, are things that exist in and of themselves.

In variations on a (sensorimotor) theme by Piaget, his *Construction of Reality in the Child* (1937) traces babies' development of concepts of time, space, and causality. This should come as no surprise, given Piaget's interest in these classical philosophical problems of epistemology. The concepts of time, space, and causality are closely linked to the object concept because objects exist, move, and affect other objects in a spatiotemporal field.

■ *Preoperational Period (Roughly 2 to 7 Years)*

Ending the first period and beginning the next can be likened to climbing a mountain only to discover that it is merely a foothill to Mt. Everest. The achievements of the sensorimotor period, although monumental, are also preparation for what is to come. In a sense, children start all over again. What they have achieved in the realm of actions on the world is redeveloped, now in the realm of mental representations. They reconstruct notions about objects, relations, causality, space, and time in a new medium (mental representation) and a more highly organized structure. The sensorimotor actions become representational, in preparation for the move from overt physical actions to mental actions, which characterizes the first decade of life.

Semiotic Function ■ As we noted earlier, the emergence of mental representations in stage 6 of the sensorimotor period provides a bridge to the preoperational period. These mental representations are made possible by a more general developmental milestone: the *semiotic function*, or ability to use one object or event to stand for another. Stated more formally, a *signifier* evokes a *significate*. Words, gestures, objects, and mental images can serve as signifiers. A 4-year-old may use the word "airplane," a swooping hand, a mental picture of an airplane, or a toy airplane to stand for a real airplane.

There are precursors to the true use of signifiers. One precursor, which was mentioned in the description of stage 6, is imitation.

Lucienne's opening of her mouth to solve the problem of the watch chain in the matchbox illustrates the transition between overt behavior and a mental symbol. These reduced imitations become internal symbols during the course of development.

There are two types of signifiers: *symbols* and *signs*. Symbols bear some similarity to the objects or events they stand for. They have lingering traces of their origins in imitation. Symbols often appear in *symbolic play*, as when Jacqueline pretends that a cloth is a pillow and feigns sleep, laughing hard all the while.

In contrast to symbols, signs are arbitrarily related to certain events or objects. There is no relationship between the word "table" and the four-legged thing at which we sit, except that our language has assigned a relationship between them. This notion that words or other signs are arbitrarily assigned to objects is not easy for a child to grasp. Young children think that an object's name is as intrinsic to the object as are its color and form. When asked why spaghetti is called spaghetti, a young child may say that it looks like spaghetti and feels like spaghetti and tastes like spaghetti, so we call it spaghetti!

Representational thought has some obvious advantages over sensorimotor thought. It is faster and more mobile. It can deal with the past, present, and future in one grand sweep and can recombine its parts to create ideas that refer to nothing in reality (for example, monsters that go bump in the night). In contrast, Piaget describes sensorimotor intelligence as a motion picture in which the action is slowed down so that "all the pictures are seen in succession but without fusion, and so without the continuous vision necessary for understanding the whole" [1947 (1950, p. 121)].

It should be noted that Piaget does not hold the common view that the source of representational thought is the ability to use words. He believes that the opposite is true. The development of representational thought makes it possible to use words as well as other signifiers. Thus, thought is both prior to language and broader than language. Language is primarily a mode for expressing thought. Throughout development, thought is prior to language. For example, teaching a child to use the words "more," "taller," and "same" does not teach him the quantitative concepts underlying these utterances.

Although thinking is not dependent on language, language can aid cognitive development. Language can direct children's attention to new objects or relationships in the environment, introduce conflicting points of view, and impart abstract information that is not easily acquired directly. Language is one of many tools in our cognitive "toolkit" (Wertsch, 1991).

Characteristics of the Period ▪ Although thinking through symbols and signs is a tremendous advance over sensorimotor thought, such thinking is limited in a number of ways. As the term *preoperational* suggests, children in this period have not yet acquired reversible mental operations, which characterize the thinking of the next period, called concrete operations.

In many ways, this period is a time of preparation for the next stage, and Piaget himself typically described preoperational children in terms of what they cannot do, rather than what they can do. However, he also identified a number of positive acquisitions such as the structures of identities, functions, correspondences, and regulations, all described later. The main characteristics of preoperational thought are egocentrism, rigidity of thought, semilogical reasoning, and limited social cognition.

1 *Egocentrism*. The word "egocentrism" does not refer to selfishness or arrogance, and Piaget does not use it in a derogatory way. Rather, the term refers to (a) the incomplete differentiation of the self and the world, including other people, and (b) the tendency to perceive, understand, and interpret the world in terms of the self. One implication is that the child cannot take another person's perceptual or conceptual perspective and in fact has no sense of a "point of view." For example, preoperational children do not realize that a person viewing a display from a position different from their own sees the display from a different perspective. A child holding a book upright points to a picture and asks, "What is this?" He is unaware that his mother, who is facing him, can see only the back of the book. Egocentrism makes it difficult to take the role of another person. This can be seen in a card game when a 5-year-old giggles when she draws a good card. She does not perceive the need for a "poker face" as a card-playing strategy.

Because children cannot easily take another person's role, they make little effort to tailor their speech to meet the needs of the listener. In fact, Piaget notes that the child "feels no desire to influence his hearer nor to tell him anything; not unlike a certain type of drawing-room conversation where everyone talks about himself and no one listens" [1923 (1926, p. 9)]. He may tell his mother that at a birthday party "he hit her with it," without bothering to explain to what "he," "her," and "it" refer. He may omit essential events, so his mother cannot understand how "he cried" and "he blew out the candles" are related.

Egocentric speech is rampant in children's play groups. Children who apparently are talking together while playing in a group may not actually be talking together. Each child's remarks are unrelated to anyone else's. There is a collective monologue, of sorts, rather than a conversation. For example, one child's statement, "I think I saw Superman in a phone booth yesterday," might be followed by "This sweater makes me itch" from another child.

Although preoperational children are considered egocentric, they are less egocentric than they were in the sensorimotor period. Early sensorimotor functioning reflects a lack of differentiation between one's own actions and properties of objects. After the preoperational period, egocentrism continues to decline, but it never disappears completely, even in adulthood.

Recent work on children's "theory of mind" (see Chapter 8) suggests that by age 4 or 5 children know more about another person's perspective than Piaget thought (for a review, see Flavell & Miller, 1998). They know, for example, that a child would think that a crayon box holds crayons rather than candles, even though they themselves know it holds candles.

2 *Rigidity of thought*. Piaget characterizes preoperational thought as frozen. One example is *centration*, the tendency to attend to or think about one salient feature of an object or event and ignore other features. If two identical containers have equal amounts of water and the contents of one container are poured into a taller, thinner container, children center on the heights of the liquids, while ignoring their widths. Consequently, they erroneously conclude that there is now more liquid because the water level is higher. Centration and egocentrism are similar in that they both reflect an inability to deal with several aspects of a situation at the same time and that they both cause a biased view of the world.

We also find a rigidity, or lack of flexibility, of thought in the tendency to *focus on states* rather than on the transformations linking the states. When faced with the task concerning quantity of liquid in the containers, the child thinks about the "before" and "after" states but ignores the process of changing from A to B as the liquid is poured. Relatedly, children *focus on appearance* rather than reality. If a stick looks like it bends when it is plunged into a body of water, young children assume this perception is true.

Perhaps the clearest example of the rigidity of thought is its *lack of reversibility*. Preoperational children cannot mentally reverse a series of events, transformations, or steps of reasoning. For example, they are unable to return the poured liquid to its original container mentally. Their ability to internalize action is not yet complete because it is not bidirectional.

Toward the end of the preoperational period, we begin to see "the great thaw," as the child partially corrects the tendency of thought to be centrated, focused on states, and irreversible. We now see three positive achievements of the preoperational period: function, regulation, and identity. These cognitive skills serve as transitions to the mental reversibility of the concrete operational period.

A *function* is the notion that there is a relation between factors, as expressed in the equation $y = f(x)$. For example, the more one pulls a curtain, the farther a curtain opens. Or when the rope on a pulley is pulled, there is an increase in the length of one section of rope as the other section decreases in length. However, children cannot yet work out the precise and quantitative nature of the relationship.

A *regulation* is a mental act that is partially decentered. Again using the test of conservation of liquid quantity, we find that children switch back and forth between using liquid height and width to make their judgments about quantity. They think that a glass may contain more than another glass because it has a higher water level or that it may contain less because it is thinner.

The third achievement, *identity*, is the notion that an object can change its appearance without changing its basic nature, or identity. Water may look different after it is poured from one container to another, but it is the same water. Putting on a Halloween mask does not change a person into a witch, contrary to the belief of younger children. Thinking has become less rigid because a concept can be maintained despite superficial physical changes.

3 *Semilogical reasoning*. As a young psychologist, Piaget questioned children about their beliefs concerning the world. The interviews revealed various fascinating characteristics of preoperational reasoning. The conversations provide many examples of egocentrism and rigidity of thought, described above. They also demonstrate some surprising properties of semilogical reasoning. The following protocol illustrates several facets of semilogical reasoning in a 6-year-old child:

> How did the sun begin? — *It was when life began.* — Has there always been a sun? — *No.* — How did it begin? — *Because it knew that life had begun.* — What is it made of? — *Of fire.* — But how? — *Because there*

> *was fire up there.* — Where did the fire come from? — *From the sky.* — How was the fire made in the sky? — *It was lighted with a match.* — Where did it come from, this match? — *God threw it away.* . . . How did the moon begin? — *Because we began to be alive.* — What did that do? — *It made the moon get bigger.* — Is the moon alive? — *No . . . Yes.* — Why? — *Because we are alive.*
>
> [Piaget, 1926 (1929, pp. 258–259)]

The child tries to explain the mysterious natural events of everyday life. One solution is to explain natural events in terms of human behavior. The sun and moon, like people, are alive, are created by a human-like action (a god lighting a match), and are tied to human activities (the moon began because people began to exist). Similarly, a preoperational child may assert that snow is made for children to play in and clouds move because they are pulled when people walk.

Thoughts are often linked together in a loose way rather than in a logical relationship. For example, one afternoon when Lucienne had no nap, she reasoned that it could not be afternoon because she had not had her nap. Or a child might say that his friend fell down because he got hurt. The child reasons from the particular to the particular.

4 *Limited social cognition.* Piaget believed that his theory applies to social objects and events as well as physical ones. We saw this parallel between the physical and the social realms in deficits in role taking and communication resulting from egocentrism, confusions between natural events and human events, and notions about the identity of persons when physical appearances are changed. In addition, Piaget specifically examined social thought in his work on moral judgments. A preoperational child judges the wrongness of an act according to external variables, such as how much damage was done and whether the act was punished. He ignores internal variables, such as the person's intentions. Thus, a boy who breaks fifteen cups while trying to help his mother set the table is considered guiltier than a boy who breaks only one cup while trying to steal cookies from the cabinet.

In one study of children's social understanding, Piaget [1965 (1995)] asked 200 children about their notions of national identity and foreignness. Five-year-old Evelyne, a Swiss, said, "I like Italy. It's more beautiful than Switzerland . . . I was there this time during the holidays. They have very good cakes, not like in Switzerland where there are things inside that make you cry" (p. 254). And 7-year-old Herbert, when asked whether people differ from one country to another, said, "Yes, well,

Americans are stupid. If I ask them where the rue du Mont-Blanc is, well, they can't tell me" (p. 258). Their social conceptions are limited because they often are based on one or two concrete personal experiences

■ *Concrete Operational Period (Roughly 7 to 11 Years)*

Piaget sometimes combined ages 2 to 11 and labeled this period as "preparation for and achievement of concrete operations." Despite the considerable accomplishments in the preoperational period, in many ways the period is simply preparation for the pinnacle of cognitive development: the operation. Regulations, functions, and identities turn into operations as they become more complete, differentiated, quantitative, and stable. Let us now turn to these operations.

An *operation* is an internalized mental action that is part of an organized structure. With the ability to use operations, the child's representations are no longer isolated, rigid, or simply juxtaposed, as in the preoperational period. They are brought to life.

We can most easily see operations at work in Piaget's famous *conservation* task, which we described earlier with respect to liquid quantity. Let us consider this task in more detail. The child sees two identical containers equally filled with water and judges them to contain the same amount of water. As the child watches, one container is poured into a container with different dimensions or into several small containers. A "nonconserver" claims that the amount has changed, usually because the water level has changed. Typically, since the water rises higher in a taller, thinner container, the child concludes that the amount has increased. In contrast, a "conserver" believes that the amount has not changed. She realizes that quantity remains the same despite changes in appearance. Piaget usually requires that the child give a logical explanation for this judgment before he considers the child to be a true conserver, for example, "You didn't add any water or take any away."

Both nonconservers and conservers have a basis for their answers. Both think their conclusions are quite reasonable. In fact, if a tester happens to test the same child twice—once when the child is a nonconserver and later when he is a conserver—she may face the child's scorn on both occasions. The child on both occasions is likely to think that the tester is dumb to ask a question when the "correct" answer is so obvious!

Conservation is an important concept because it gives a certain stability to the physical world. In addition, Piaget assigns a great deal of importance to the conservation task because it reveals the presence or absence of mental operations. It is a diagnostic tool that probes the cognitive structures. Piaget asserts that children cannot conserve unless they have certain mental operations, especially *reversibility*. The negation aspect of reversibility is expressed by children who say, "If you pour it back where it was, they will have the same amount." The compensation aspect of reversibility is seen in the explanation, "This one's taller but this one's fatter." The preoperational child who lacks these operations centers on states, especially the water level.

Operations also can be seen at work in the common mathematical operations of multiplying, dividing, ordering (greater than, less than), and substituting (one thing equals another thing). Each operation is related to and obtains its meaning from the entire structure of which it is a part. Thus, addition is coordinated with subtraction, multiplication, and division to form a system of mental actions.

Piaget's interest in logic and mathematics appears in his attempt to describe these systems of concrete operations in terms of logicomathematical structures. Logic and algebra form purely formal, nonpsychological logicomathematical systems. However, Piaget felt that cognitive structures approximate these abstract logicomathematical structures and that it would be fruitful to look for various types of thinking suggested by the model. Furthermore, logical models are often clearer and more specific than verbal statements.

For example, in the concrete operational period there are nine groupings—logical structures that describe certain logical operations and relationships among these operations. Let us look at the psychological concept of class inclusion, which corresponds to what Piaget calls grouping I. This grouping describes the primary addition of classes and is the simplest grouping. For example, modes of transportation form a classification hierarchy, in which modes of transportation (C) at the top of the hierarchy have two subheadings: ground vehicles (B) and other classes of vehicles (B'). B, in turn, contains cars (A) and other ground vehicles (A'). The system's elements (A, A', B, B', C) can be manipulated according to certain rules. In the case of grouping I, the rules refer to the following properties of the grouping: composition ($A + A' + B$), association $[(A + B) + C = C]$, general identity ($A + 0 = A$), negation ($A - A = 0$), and special identities ($A + A = A$ or $A + B = B$). These properties, stated in formal, nonpsychological terms, serve as a model for the properties of thought that underlie the concept of class inclusion. They are logical representations that Piaget hoped would describe the essence of thought.

The grouping probably should be considered an idealized version of what cognitive structures the child must have in order to solve class-inclusion problems. The actual process of thinking may differ in various ways from that expressed by the grouping, because several different cognitive structures could produce the same answer. In other words, grouping I is a logically possible cognitive structure, but it is not necessarily the child's actual cognitive structure. But this is the nature of models. They are heuristic devices. They tell us what to look for, and they provide a framework for interpreting behavior. However, they may or may not reflect reality.

One useful aspect of Piaget's logicomathematical model is that it is possible to deduce new predictions from it. Because the model consists of sets of logically interrelated formal propositions, if certain logical operations are found in the child's thought, then one can predict (deduce) that the child should possess certain other logical operations. For example, Piaget's model would predict a particular type of logical relationship between the operation of classifying objects and the operation of ordering them along some dimension.

Piaget applied his logicomathematical model of concrete operations to a wide variety of physical and social situations, of which only a few can be described here. For example, various properties are conserved in addition to liquid quantity, described earlier. The number of objects in a collection remains the same when they are spread out; the total length of a stick remains the same if the stick is pushed ahead of another stick; and the weight of clay remains the same if the clay is broken into pieces.

Operations are evident in another basic acquisition: *class inclusion*. The experimenter shows the child 20 wooden beads, 17 of them brown and 3 white. He asks whether the child could make a longer necklace with the brown beads or the wooden beads. The preoperational child claims that there are more brown beads than wooden beads. She can deal only with the parts (brown or white beads) or the whole (wooden beads), but not with both of them simultaneously. She does not understand that the parts and the whole are reversible. In contrast, the concrete operational child has the underlying operations necessary to derive the correct answer.

Operations apply not only to classes but also to *relations*. If a concrete operational child knows that John is taller than Bill and that Bill is taller than Henry, she can infer that John has to be taller than Henry. In addition, she can order a row of dolls according to height and give the dolls sticks ordered according to length.

Figure 1.1

A typical error on the water-level problem during the preoperational period.

Operations are also applied to *temporal–spatial representations.* For example, preoperational children draw liquid in a container in such a way that it remains parallel to the base or a side (as in Figure 1.1). Their perceptions are influenced by the immediate surroundings. In contrast, concrete operational children keep the liquid parallel to the larger context, the surface of the earth.

Turning to the social realm, we see that children are overcoming many of the limitations in their reasoning about the social world. They are less egocentric but sometimes still have difficulties with role taking and communication. They are beginning to take intentions into account in their moral judgments. They also are increasingly aware of the subtle social relationships in the family, peer group, and larger society. In addition, children are beginning to sort out their various social identities. Piaget found that young children tended to draw two circles side by side to represent Geneva and Switzerland. Nine-year-old Pierre correctly drew the former as a smaller circle inside the latter but still was struggling to apply his class-inclusion concept to social understanding:

> What is your nationality? — *I am Swiss.* — How come? — *Because I live in Switzerland.* — Are you also Genevan? — *No, that's not possible. . . . I'm already Swiss, I can't also be Genevan.*

Two other 8-year-olds also do not quite have it right:

> Do you know any foreigners? — *Yes . . . those who live far away.* — For example, if you travel to France, could you also become a foreigner in

certain situations? — *No, I'm Swiss.* — A Frenchman, could he be a foreigner? — *Oh! Yes, a Frenchman is a foreigner.* — And in France is a Frenchman a foreigner? — *Oh yes.*

What is a Frenchman in Switzerland? — *French, but also a little Swiss if he's here.*

[Piaget, 1965 (1995, pp. 252, 263, 265)]

This list of acquisitions could continue to the end of this book, but the examples we have considered are representative. Two points about concrete operational acquisitions should be kept in mind. First, they do not develop at the same time. In fact, some concepts, such as conservation of weight, often do not appear until near the end of the period. Second, each cognitive acquisition develops over a period of time. At first, it is transitional in nature and is demonstrated only part of the time. It gradually strengthens, stabilizes, and generalizes to a variety of situations.

In summary of Piaget's stages to this point, children move from an understanding of the world based on action schemes, to one based on representations, to one based on internalized, organized operations. Thought now is decentered rather than centered, dynamic rather than static, and reversible rather than irreversible. For the first time, the lawful nature of the world seems to be reflected in a logical system of thought. Thought is in tune, in equilibrium, with the environment. However, the concrete operations are still "concrete." They can be applied only to concrete objects—present or mentally represented. They deal with what "is" rather than what "could be." The final step is to apply the operations to purely verbal or logical statements and to the possible as well as the actual. This story unfolds as we turn to formal operations.

Formal Operational Period (Roughly 11 to 15 Years)

Piaget and Inhelder studied the change from concrete to formal operations. During the concrete operational period, mental operations are applied to objects and events. Children classify them, order them, and reverse them. During formal operations, adolescents carry concrete operations one step further. They can take the results of these concrete operations and generate hypotheses (propositions, statements) about their logical relations. Thus, we now have operations on operations; thought has become truly logical, abstract, and hypothetical.

Formal operational thought resembles the kind of thinking we often call the *scientific method.* Children formulate a hypothesis about a present or potential event and test this hypothesis against reality. If necessary, they can generate all possible outcomes or all possible combinations at the beginning. Piaget typically presents a problem from physics or chemistry and observes how the adolescent goes about solving it. The problem-solving process, rather than the correct answer itself, is what is of interest.

A prototypic task is the pendulum problem. An adolescent observes an object hanging from a string and attempts to discover what determines how fast the object swings. He is shown how to vary the length of the string, the height from which the pendulum is released, the force of the push on the pendulum, and the weight of the object. One or several of these variables could control the speed of the swing. A concrete operational child experiments with the variables and may even arrive at the correct answer, but his approach is haphazard; he has no overall plan. He does not vary one factor while holding the other factors constant. For example, he may compare a long, light pendulum with a short, heavy one and conclude that both factors are important. In fact, the length of the string is the main determinant of the rate of oscillation.

In contrast to concrete operational children, formal operational adolescents imagine all possible determinants of the rate of oscillation before they begin, systematically vary the factors one by one, observe the results correctly, keep track of the results, and draw the appropriate conclusions (identify which factor controls the rate of oscillation). They systematically isolate the critical factor and deal all the while with propositions, not objects. By testing predictions from each hypothesis, they demonstrate hypothetico-deductive thought. More generally, as Flavell expresses it, "Reality is thus conceived as a special subset within the totality of things which the data would admit as hypotheses; it is seen as the 'is' portion of a 'might be' totality, the portion it is the subject's job to discover" (1963, pp. 204–205).

Piaget posed several other problems:

1. Determine which mixture of five colorless liquids produces a yellow color.
2. Discover which variables (for example, weight, length, types of material) cause a rod suspended over water to bend down far enough to touch the water.
3. Discover and state the law governing the relationship between the angle at which a billiard ball hits the table wall and the angle of its rebound.

4. Solve a geometric proof.
5. Discover proportional relationships (for example, 16 is to 4 as 4 is to 1).
6. Evaluate syllogisms, such as "All children hate spinach; girls are children; therefore, girls hate spinach."

It should be noted that direct instruction in scientific thought is not necessary for the development of formal operations. Years of common, unremarkable experiences contribute to this achievement. As Einstein remarked: "The whole of science is nothing more than a refinement of everyday thinking."

As in the concrete operational period, Piaget applied logicomathematical models to the child's thought. He identified 16 underlying mental operations that he believed are necessary for solving the various problems he presented to adolescents. This *system of 16 binary operations* forms a tightly knit organization of logical relations. Although his complex model is beyond the scope of this chapter, we look at two examples: conjunction and disjunction. *Conjunction* is an operation that refers to the co-occurrence of *x* and *y*. Another operation is *disjunction*, which refers to three possible outcomes: *x* and *y*, *x* and *not y*, and *y* and *not x*. In the problem of discovering what causes rods to bend, we consider two of many possible outcomes: (1) great length, great bending (conjunction) and (2) great length, great bending; short length, great bending; great length, little bending (disjunction).

In addition to the binary operations, a system of rules for manipulating the logical relations identified by the binary operations is included in Piaget's logical model. For example, in a weight-balance problem, an imbalance can be negated by subtracting the extra weight from the heavier side or adding more weight to the lighter side.

The ability to consider abstract ideas, the future, and various possibilities is evident in adolescents' social world. They dream about their future and imagine themselves in various occupational and social roles. They may experiment with some of these roles just as they experiment with hypotheses about physical events. They are concerned with the world of ideas. In sessions with friends, they debate various moral and political issues, such as whether wars can ever be moral, whether abortions should be legal, whether there are basic inalienable human rights, and what an ideal community would be like. They can consider these issues from a number of different perspectives and see how the issues are related to a larger set of social relationships. However, there is still a lingering egocentrism. Adolescents are impressed with the power of thought and naively underestimate the practical problems involved in achieving an ideal future for themselves or for society. They feel that the sheer force of their logic will move mountains. Piaget notes that this starry-eyed egocentrism is squelched when adolescents undertake their first real job!

One further difference between concrete operational thought and formal operational thought has implications for both social and physical development. Adolescents can reflect on their own thinking (and that of others). For example, they can think about propositions, which are thoughts. Or, in the social realm, we find the following line of thought: "He's thinking that I'm thinking that he's thinking about her."

By achieving formal operations, adolescents complete their cognitive structures. The various concrete operational logical systems have been combined to create a single, tightly organized system of thought—a unified whole. Thought is logical, abstract, and flexible. Thinking continues to develop throughout adulthood as formal operations are applied to more and more content areas and situations. Egocentrism continues to decline as people broaden their experiences in the world of work and social relationships. However, these changes after age 15 entail a change not in the structure of thought but only in its content and stability.

■ *An Overview*

Now that we have reached the height of Piaget's theory, it would be good to look back over our climb. Perhaps the best way to highlight the differences between periods is to see how a typical child in each period would understand several aspects of reality. First, what is an "object" for a child in each stage? During the sensorimotor period, an object that at first is simply a stimulus for feeding a reflex becomes something on which one can act. Then an object becomes an independently existing entity that is separate from one's actions and can be mentally represented. For a preoperational child, an object can represent other objects, can undergo physical changes while maintaining its identity (if not its amount), and can be joined with other objects to form a class of objects. During the period of concrete operations, various operations manipulate the representation of an object; for example, any changes in the object can be reversed, and the object can be fit into a series of objects ordered according to some dimension. Finally, during the period of formal operations, higher-order operations allow further mental manipulations of the representation of the object. All the object's possibilities can be examined scientifically.

Another way of slicing the periods vertically is to consider how a child in each period would attack a specific problem. Consider what would happen if we gave children in each stage a tub of water and various small objects of various densities, sizes, weights, shapes, and colors. Infants would immediately splash, throw the objects, push the objects to the bottom of the tub, and probably attempt to eat the objects. Toward the end of the sensorimotor period, children might drop the objects from various heights and note that the bigger, heavier objects make bigger splashes than do the smaller, lighter objects. They might also notice that some objects sink while others do not. Preoperational children might imagine that the objects are boats or fish. They would notice that some objects float while others sink, but they would be content to change their reasons from case to case. They might claim that one object floats because it is little, another because it is dry, another because it is a boat, and so on. Concrete operational children are bothered by inconsistencies that did not bother them in the previous stage, such as the fact that some small objects sink while other small objects float. They make comparisons between objects, but they are neither systematic nor exhaustive. For example, they do not hold their amounts constant while varying their weights. However, they do develop several categories of "sinkability," for example, always floats (light weight), always sinks (heavy), and sinks or floats depending on the circumstances (small objects, lids). Formal operational adolescents have both a plan and the necessary operations to solve the problem. They systematically vary the factors to determine their influence and use the results to test their hypotheses. They know that density is the proportion of weight to volume and that the relative density of the object to the water is the critical factor. Adolescents are able to form a proportion made up of two other proportions: the density for the objects and for the water. These are operations on operations. This general law allows them to predict whether any particular object will sink or float.

MEMORY

Some of Piaget's most dramatic claims stem from his work on memory. Consider the following typical experiment by Piaget and Inhelder (1969): They showed children an array of 10 sticks of various sizes that were ordered according to size. A week later they asked the children to draw from memory the array of sticks they had seen. Developmental differences emerged. In general, 3- and 4-year-olds lined up a few sticks having the same length. The 5- and 6-year-olds tended to draw some tall and some short sticks. By 7 years of age, most children could draw the original array correctly. Piaget and Inhelder concluded that the children had processed and interpreted the original array in terms of their present understanding of ordered relations. Only when this understanding is fully achieved can the child accurately remember the array. Thus, memory reflects and depends on the entire cognitive structure. Memory is active understanding rather than a static, passive state.

Although this is an interesting set of results, it is less surprising than that found 6 months later when the children returned. Although the children were not shown the sticks again, this time 75 percent of the children drew arrays that were more advanced cognitively than those they had produced 6 months earlier. For example, a child who originally lined up three tall sticks of the same height and three short sticks of the same height later made a row of three tall sticks, three medium-size sticks, and three short sticks. Piaget's interpretation was that such improvements are reasonable if one assumes that the children have developed cognitively during those 6 months. If the child's cognitive structures are expressed in his memory, then changes in these structures should produce changes in memory. Note that improvement in memory over time is the *opposite* of what one would expect from most theories of memory or from common sense. The typical view is that a memory trace fades over time and its recall is blocked by newer memories.

It should be mentioned that there are many methodological problems involved in this type of study. Furthermore, other researchers have not always replicated Piaget's results (see Liben, 1977, for a review).

Piaget's claim that memory is not always reliable is seen in the following intriguing account of a memory from his second year of life:

> I was sitting in my pram, which my nurse was pushing in the Champs Elysées, when a man tried to kidnap me. I was held in by the strap fastened around me while my nurse bravely tried to stand between me and the thief. She received various scratches, and I can still see vaguely those on her face.
>
> [1945 (1951, p. 188)]

When Piaget was 15, his parents received a letter from the nurse shortly after she had joined a religious order. She said she wanted to return the watch that had been given to her as a reward for protecting little Jean from the kidnapper. The truth was that she had made up the story and had even faked the scratches that Piaget so vividly "remembered"! Piaget believed that what he remembered was a visual memory that he created from the story his parents had told him as a child.

In addition to studying memory performance, Piaget examined children's concepts of memory. This topic was rediscovered by American and English psychologists 50 years later and labeled "metamemory," which is described in Chapter 4. A sample of Piaget's work is the following interview with an 8-year-old innatist:

> *Memory is something in the head which makes us think.* —What do you think this memory is like? — *It is a little square of skin, rather oval, and inside there are stories (les histories).* —What are they like? — *They are written on the flesh.* —What with? — *Pencil.* —Who wrote them? — *God, before I was born, he put them there.*
>
> [1926 (1929, p. 52)]

MECHANISMS OF DEVELOPMENT

Piaget recognized that it was important not only to describe cognitive stages but also to explain how and why children develop through those stages. In other words, by what processes does the child's thinking progress? How do new forms of thinking emerge? What facilitates or constrains the transition from step to step? Emphasizing the grand stages, which span several years each, can make us forget that thought actually develops in the moment-to-moment, everyday encounters between children and their physical and social environments. Stagelike changes ultimately are due to millions of these minidevelopments. An adequate theory of cognitive development must explain these small, but significant, steps.

In Piaget's theory, these small steps are spurred by certain functional invariants. The *functional invariants* are intellectual functions that operate throughout development. The two basic functional invariants are organization and adaptation. In yet another tie to biology, these invariants are also found in physiological activities. In both physiological and intellectual functioning there are certain abstract properties (functional invariants) that define the relationship between the organism and the environment. These functional invariants are part of the general heredity of living organisms. We are born with tendencies to organize our thinking into structures and to adapt to our environment. With apologies to Descartes, it could be said that "I am, therefore I think."

Cognitive Organization

Cognitive organization, described in the earlier section on structuralism, is the tendency for thought to consist of systems whose parts are integrated to form a whole. These systems, in turn, are coordinated; there are interrelationships among cognitive activities. The mind is not a grab bag of facts. Rather, it is a coherent view of the world. This view becomes more and more coherent and interrelated as the child develops. For example, the young infant has separate structures for sucking objects and for grasping them. Only later are these two structures organized into a higher-order structure that allows coordinated reaching for an object and bringing it to the mouth to suck.

Again, Piaget sees parallels between psychological and physiological activity. The human body is composed of systems, such as the digestive system, circulatory system, and nervous system. Each is organized within itself and interacts with other systems. A change in one system has repercussions for other systems. For example, digesting a meal changes not only the temporary state of the digestive system but also the flow of blood and body temperature.

Development through the stages involves changes in the nature of cognitive organization as the structures of thought change from stage to stage. As development proceeds, thought may be organized into schemes, regulations (partial reversibility), functions, concrete operations, or formal operations. Thus, an infant's sucking on a toy and Einstein's insights into relativity both reflect cognitive organization. In principle, one could trace a line of development from the former to the latter.

Cognitive Adaptation

The other basic functional invariant, *cognitive adaptation*, pertains to interaction between the organism and the environment. Piaget claims that all organisms have an innate tendency to adapt to the environment. Intelligent behavior is behavior that is appropriate to the demands of the environment. The following passage by Piaget expresses the close relationship between adaptation and organization:

> Organization is inseparable from adaptation: They are two complementary processes of a single mechanism, the first being the internal aspect

> of the cycle of which adaptation constitutes the external aspect. . . . The "accord of thought with things" and the "accord of thought with itself" express this dual functional invariant of adaptation and organization. These two aspects of thought are indissociable: It is by adapting to things that thought organizes itself and it is by organizing itself that it structures things.
>
> [1936 (1952, pp. 7–8)]

Adaptation involves two complementary processes: assimilation and accommodation. *Assimilation* is the process of fitting reality into one's current cognitive organization. In every cognitive encounter with objects or events, there is a degree of "bending" or distorting of experience as people attempt to incorporate, understand, or interpret this experience. In other words, people apply what they know in order to understand properties of objects and events as well as relationships between properties and events. To quote Anais Nin, "We don't see things as they are, we see them as we are."

Accommodation is the other side of the coin. This term refers to adjustments in cognitive organization that result from the demands of reality. Every object or event has special characteristics that must be taken into account sooner or later. In a sense, accommodation occurs because the current structures have failed to interpret a particular object or event satisfactorily. The resulting reorganization of thought leads to a different and more satisfactory assimilation of the experience. A particular stimulus is never again experienced in quite the same way. As Oliver Wendell Holmes tells us, "Man's mind stretched to a new idea never goes back to its original dimensions."

Assimilation and accommodation are closely intertwined in every cognitive activity from birth to death. Attempts to assimilate reality necessarily involve slight changes in the cognitive structures as these adjust to the new elements. Assimilation and accommodation are so related, in fact, that Piaget sometimes defines adaptation as an equilibrium between assimilation and accommodation. In a state of equilibrium, neither assimilation nor accommodation dominates.

In true Piagetian style, both a biological example and a psychological example are needed. In the biological realm, food is assimilated into the body as it is changed into a form the body can use. As Piaget expresses it, "A rabbit that eats a cabbage doesn't become a cabbage; it's a cabbage that becomes rabbit—that's assimilation" (quoted in Bringuier, 1980, p. 42). The digestive system accommodates to food by adjusting the mouth opening, chewing, secreting digestive juices, contracting the muscles of the stomach, and so on. Thus, the digestive system both changes and is changed by an environmental event, the presentation of food.

In the psychological realm, consider an infant who has happened onto a sheet of newspaper for the first time. In an attempt to make sense of this new experience, she runs through her repertoire of actions on objects. She applies her current structures (habitual patterns of behavior). She grasps the paper, hits it, sucks it, turns it over, shakes it, puts it over her head, and so on, in her attempts to fit this new object into something she already knows. However, a newspaper has certain characteristics foreign to her existing schemes. She is forced to stretch or reorganize (accommodate) these schemes in small ways. Her ideas about the way things sound when they are shaken must be altered to include the rustle of a newspaper. Similarly, the light weight and the new feel and sight make further demands on her comprehension of the world.

Most of the characteristics to be assimilated and accommodated to in our example are at least related to previous experiences, but some characteristics (for example, ripping the paper) may be quite foreign and startling. The varying degrees of discrepancy between current schemes and the experience at hand raise the issue of what the limitations are to accommodation. Piaget's answer is that only moderately discrepant events or characteristics can be accommodated to; great leaps are not possible. If reality is too different from the person's current level of understanding, she cannot bridge the gap. There can never be radical departures from the old. Thus, development necessarily proceeds in small steps.

To illustrate this gradual, continual development, consider what would happen if children of various ages were given a metal magnet for the first time. Six-month-olds might accommodate to the unfamiliar metallic taste, the peculiar (horseshoe) shape, and the sound of the magnet being dropped. However, they cannot accommodate to such features as magnetic properties. Three-year-olds, if given an assortment of objects, might accommodate to the fact that some of the objects cling to the magnet and might entertain explanations such as "stickiness" and "wanting to stay together." Nine-year-old children might hypothesize that only objects with certain characteristics are attracted to the magnet and might test out the conditions in which magnetism occurs—through glass, water, and certain distances. Only in adolescence could children accommodate by formulating an abstract theory of magnetism and simultaneously consider all of the variables involved, such as the size and shape of the magnet and the distance from the object. Thus, accommodation always occurs in small steps and is relative to the present cognitive level.

In summary, the functional invariants of assimilation and accommodation are simultaneously present in every act and stimulate cognitive development. Attempts to apply one's current intellectual structures typically are only partially successful because most encounters with the environment are new in some way. As a result of this failure to "understand" the object or event, minor cognitive adjustments or accommodations are made. These push children to a slightly more advanced cognitive level. They are one step closer to reality. However, this new level of understanding makes them aware of other discrepancies in experience, and again assimilation presents new elements and again accommodation occurs. Each accommodation makes new accommodations possible in the future. This spiral continues in our moment-to-moment encounters with the environment throughout development.

Cognitive Equilibration

The two basic functional invariants, organization and adaptation, imply a third functional invariant: equilibration. Piaget's equilibration model comes from the fields of physics (thermodynamics and mechanics) and biology. For example, a thermostat and a mollusk are self-regulating equilibration systems. In Piaget's view, every organism strives toward *equilibrium* with the environment and equilibrium within itself (among cognitive elements). When assimilation and accommodation are in balanced coordination so neither one is dominant, equilibrium is achieved. This balance is achieved through the development of organized structures that provide ways of interacting with the world. A change in either the organism or the environment leads to a state of disequilibrium, which must be corrected. It should be clear from other parts of Piagetian theory that equilibrium is dynamic rather than static. There is constant activity, but there is a balance, a pattern, to this activity.

For example, in the liquid-conservation task children are in disequilibrium if they switch back and forth between answers on the basis of liquid height or breadth. That is, they waver between saying that the tall thin one has more or the short fat one has more. Acquiring the mental operation, compensation, allows them to integrate information about the two dimensions. Seeing that one dimension compensates for the other eliminates the contradiction and reestablishes equilibrium.

Equilibration, while one of the most important concepts in the theory, is probably also the most difficult and evasive. Part of the difficulty may lie in the fact that equilibration can refer to several spans of time, ranging from a fraction of a second to a number of years. In each case, there is a period of equilibrium, followed by a state of disequilibrium, followed by equilibration, which leads again to equilibrium.

Piaget seems to have at least three spans of time in mind when he applies the notion of equilibrium:

1. A moment-to-moment equilibration process occurs as assimilation and accommodation operate in children's daily activities, even the most mundane. Temporary disequilibrium occurs when children encounter new properties of objects that do not fit into their present cognitive structures. Once the assimilation–accommodation process occurs and discrepancies are resolved, equilibrium is again achieved. Assimilation and accommodation are brought into balance once again.
2. Equilibration refers to moving toward the final level of achievement within each period or stage. A child enters a new period in a state of relative disequilibrium because the new cognitive organization is in the process of formation and therefore is incomplete and unstable. By the end of this new period, the child has achieved equilibrium with respect to the structures of the period. For example, at the end of the sensorimotor period, a child is in equilibrium with the environment in terms of action schemes but not in terms of operations. Each period achieves a different kind of equilibrium state. Equilibrium is reachieved in each period at a higher and higher level of abstraction.
3. The entire course of cognitive development can be seen as a process of equilibration as the child proceeds through increasingly "better" forms of equilibrium. The most complete equilibrium is achieved when formal operations bring fully reversible and abstract thought. The earlier states of equilibrium, because they are incomplete, inevitably break down at some point. In a sense, each period or stage eventually self-destructs.

For Piaget, equilibration is the grand process that puts together all of the elements of development. Equilibration integrates and regulates the other three main factors of development: physical maturation, experience with the physical environment, and the influence of the social environment. All of these factors together propel the child through the stages.

■ *Section Overview*

Perhaps the best way to summarize this section on mechanisms of development is to relate it to the earlier sections of this chapter. Knowledge of the world develops through a series of discrete states of equilibrium (stages) between the organism and the environment. This is the essence of Piaget's genetic epistemology. Mental structures, in equilibrium, are acquired as the organism interacts with physical and social objects in an organized way. Here we see Piaget's structuralism. In the innate tendencies toward organization and adaptation (assimilation and accommodation), we see Piaget the biologist. Finally, the particular stages are an inevitable outcome, given the nature of the human organism (its physical structures and cognitive functions) and the nature of the environment.

POSITION ON DEVELOPMENTAL ISSUES

The book's Introduction identified four basic developmental issues on which each theorist takes a stand. Using these issues, we can view Piaget's theory from a new perspective. The issues also provide a means for cutting across the diverse theories covered in this volume.

■ *Human Nature*

Piaget's world view clearly fits into the organismic rather than the mechanistic or contextual views. He posits an inherently active organism. Children tirelessly explore, hypothesize, test, and evaluate; they do this either overtly (particularly in the sensorimotor period) or covertly (as in the manipulation of symbols, concrete operations, and formal operations).

No external motivation is necessary. Children are intrinsically motivated; schemes are used simply because they exist. Once activated, they tend to be repeated. In other words, "To be is to do." The Piagetian child is a self-regulating, organized whole as he strives to maintain equilibrium both within himself and with the environment. He corrects any cognitive imbalance to the extent he is capable. The tendencies toward inherent activity and self-regulation produce an organism that is constantly changing.

Finally, the organismic world view can be seen in the fact that the parts can be understood only in terms of the whole. Any one behavior, scheme, or operation is influenced by and derives its meaning from the whole structure. The same behavior (for example, a child swinging a pendulum) obviously has a different meaning for a 2-year-old and a 12-year-old.

Qualitative Versus Quantitative Development

Although Piaget sees both qualitative and quantitative changes, he emphasizes the qualitative changes in structures from stage to stage. Just as the colored plastic fragments rearrange themselves when a kaleidoscope is turned, so does the organization of thought change to form new patterns as the child develops.

Quantitative changes occur as schemes, operations, or other cognitive skills become stronger, more easily activated, more efficient, and more consistent. One quantitative development is the increased number of schemes or habits in the child's repertoire or the number of "facts" available. The child who can name the capitals of all the states has more information at hand than the child who can name only five capitals. Of course, it should be kept in mind that this information is always assimilated into structures that undergo qualitative changes.

Qualitative and quantitative changes build on each other during development. A qualitative change in structure makes possible certain quantitative changes. For example, once class inclusion is understood, the child can quickly learn about the classifications and relationships in many different content areas, such as animals, people, trees, shapes, and colors. Quantitative increases in amount of information, in turn, may pave the way for further qualitative change as new information challenges the present structures. For example, talking with peers and adults rapidly expands children's knowledge and challenges their present understanding. This new information can stimulate subsequent qualitative change as the system attempts to resolve the contradictions in children's knowledge.

Whether we see quantitative or qualitative change in Piaget's theory depends, in part, on the unit of time we select. If we look at changes over minutes, days, and weeks, we are struck by the gradual nature of development. If we look at changes over months and years, we are struck by the qualitative changes from stage to stage or period to period. For example, from age 4 to $4\frac{1}{2}$, children may become more consistent in their grouping of objects according to shape; this is a quantitative change. However, the change from then to age 7, when they can sort objects into hierarchies of classes—for example, animals, mammals, brown mammals, and so forth—is qualitative.

Nature Versus Nurture

Piaget was an interactionist through and through. All knowledge, from the most specific and concrete sensorimotor behavior to the most general and abstract formal thought, is a by-product of the intertwined influences of innate and experiential factors. Innate factors include physical structures (for example, the structure and positioning of the particular species' eyes), reflexes, physical maturation, and the invariant functions (organization and adaptation). Given these innate factors and the nature of the physical and social world, development inevitably proceeds in the way it does. It could not be otherwise.

Piaget has proposed the following four-factor "formula" for development:

> Development = Physical maturation + Experience with the physical environment + Social experience + Equilibration

1 The first factor, physical maturation—of the nervous system, the muscular system, and the like—creates new possibilities for the cognitive system and requires certain adjustments of that system. For example, when physical maturation permits walking, new vistas open up for toddlers. As children actively exploit this new skill, they are forced to assimilate and, whenever possible, accommodate to new experiences. Also, recent neuropsychological research (see Chapter 8) has identified changes in the brain during development that appear to be linked to Piagetian qualitative changes in cognition.

2 Regarding experience with the physical environment, Piaget emphasizes *logicomathematical experience*. This term refers to reflecting on one's own actions on objects rather than on the objects themselves. To illustrate, Piaget refers to a friend's recollection from childhood:

> He was seated on the ground in his garden and he was counting pebbles. Now to count these pebbles he put them in a row and he counted them one, two, three up to 10. Then he finished counting them and started to count them in the other direction. He began by the end and once again found he had 10. He found this marvelous. . . . So he put them in a circle and counted them that way and found 10 once again.
>
> (1964, p. 12)

The child considered the results of repeatedly counting and arranging the pebbles and concluded that number is constant despite physical rearrangements. He discovered something (number) that is not intrinsic to the objects themselves. He went beyond simply noting the color, shape, size, and weight of the pebbles.

3 The third factor, social experience, refers to the effect of the cultural or educational environment. For example, other people transmit knowledge, either directly or through books, television, and so on. In this way, a child can benefit from the experience of others. Discussion also can spur progress: "Proof is born through discussion" (Piaget, 1932, p. 404). Of course, as always, the child must be cognitively advanced enough to assimilate the information if it is to be of value. Social experience can also be negative, as when social forces lead to conformity, as well as rigid and distorted thinking. Also, not all adult products provide good models to learn from, as seen recently in a sign that defies class-inclusion logic: "Please do not feed birds or animals."

These three factors, taken together, can address the question of what is universal about cognitive development. Given the similarities among cultures in the course of physical maturation, the nature of the physical world, and, to a lesser extent, the nature of the social environment, it is not surprising that the four major periods proceed in the same order in all cultures studied. However, it is not clear whether the  development of steps *within* the major periods occurs in an invariant sequence in all cultures. Even if some or all of the sequences identified by Piaget prove to be universal, we would still expect some variation in the *rate* of progress through the cognitive stages. This variation can arise from differences in physical maturation, physical experience, or social experience. We would expect some variation within a culture and some overall differences between cultures. For example, experience with clay may promote the development of conservation of substance (in which clay is the medium). Mexican children aged 6 to 9 who grow up in pottery-making families are more likely to be conservers of substance than are Mexican children who grow up in families engaged in other activities (Price-Williams, Gordon, & Ramirez, 1969). In addition, Piaget recalled that his daughter Jacqueline, who was born in the winter, was often bundled up in a carriage, so did not have as much opportunity as children born in warmer weather to develop eye–hand coordination.

4 The fourth factor, equilibration, ties together and controls the interaction of the innate and experiential factors. Maturation, experience with the physical environment, and the influence of the social environment constantly cause momentary disequilibrium. In this way, they force the cognitive system to change, to adjust. Through reestablishing equilibrium, the cognitive system reaches a higher level. Thus, it is in the interplay of forces within the equilibration process that experiential and innate forces together finally have their effect on cognition.

From this account, it is obvious that experience does not write upon a passive, blank slate. Intelligence is always active and self-regulating, from the first modification of a reflex to the formal operations of adolescent thought. Children construct, rather than receive, a model of reality.

What Develops

Piaget tells us that the essence of cognitive development is structural change—change in the schemes, regulations, functions, and various logicomathematical structures of the concrete and formal operational periods. Structural change gives meaning to and influences change in the content of thought. Thus, Piaget emphasizes change on a molar level, which leads to change at various more molecular levels.

The question of what develops is tied to Piaget's methodology. He relies on observations, interviews (the clinical method), and assessment situations in which the experimenter participates. In this way, he keeps the organization of the thought processes as intact as possible; too much experimental interference or control would distort the child's normal line of reasoning.

APPLICATIONS

Educators have applied Piaget's theory to instruction. One example is his notion of "readiness"—that a child can profit from instruction only if she is cognitively ready to assimilate it to her present cognitive structures or accommodate her structures to the experience. Instruction in calculus would not be successful with most 5-year-olds. Another important notion is that learning is most likely to occur when the child actively participates and, for children who have not yet reached formal operations, when teachers present problems in a concrete rather than abstract way. Moreover, the theory suggests that teachers should teach concepts in a particular sequence of developmental steps. In addition, for true understanding, children must learn the concepts underlying mathematical and scientific knowledge, rather than just memorize facts. Relatedly, Piaget criticized typical educational assessments for focusing on correct answers rather than on children's thought processes for reaching the answers. In short, a teacher mainly provides guidance and resources so that children can teach themselves.

The neo-Piagetians, to be described later in this chapter, would add a focus on the amount of support that teachers provide for the child's fragile new concepts, for example, their encouragement, hints, or collaboration. They also would encourage teachers to attend to whether the problems are presented in a way that does not overload the child's cognitive capacity. Finally, they expect differences among children, not only in how advanced they are in a particular domain, such as math versus science, but perhaps also in the route they take to acquire a new concept.

EVALUATION OF THE THEORY

When Piaget's first writings on children appeared, he was appalled that people evaluated them as though they were final statements on certain cognitive problems rather than the tentative solutions he intended them to be. In fact, he continued to modify his theory even into his eighties. After this section on strengths and weaknesses, we will look at some of the modifications that attempt to address some of the weaknesses.

■ *Strengths*

We focus on four strengths of Piaget's theory: its recognition of the central role of cognition in development, its discovery of surprising features of young children's thinking, its wide scope, and its ecological validity.

Recognition of the Central Role of Cognition ■ Cognition now is such a central part of the study of development that it is hard to imagine that this was not always the case. If a developmental psychologist were somehow plucked out of the 1950s and set down today, he would be bewildered by the talk around him. He would hear psychologists discussing children's "theories," strategies, cognitive structures, plans, and representations, instead of stimulus generalization, mean length of utterance, mental age, conditioning, and discrimination learning. To a great extent, Piaget is responsible for this change. He altered the course of psychology by asking new questions that made developmentalists wonder why they had ever asked the old questions in the first place. Once psychologists looked at development through Piaget's eyes, they never again saw children in quite the same way.

Both the state of academic psychology and the history of developmental psychology in the United States created a state of readiness for the assimilation of Piaget. Academic psychology had pushed behaviorism in general and learning theory in particular to their limits and found them wanting. Even when learning theory was modified by such notions as verbal mediation, social reinforcement, modeling, intrinsic reinforcement, and attention, it did not completely satisfy psychologists. There was dissatisfaction with the explanation of language development in terms of imitation, practice, and reinforcement. At the same time, alternative cognitive approaches were emerging, such as Noam Chomsky's transformational grammar and computer scientists' work on information processing.

Within child psychology, until the 1950s researchers could be found less often in departments of psychology than in "child institutes" or departments of home economics, pediatrics, public health, education, clinical psychology, and nursing. Developmental psychologists were concerned with poor nutrition, physical and mental retardation, learning disabilities, and emotional disturbances. Because of this physical and ideological separation from psychology departments, many developmental psychologists did not become immersed in the behaviorist–experimental zeitgeist of academic psychology of the times and kept one foot in the laboratory and one foot in real-life settings. In addition, developmental psychologists at that time were primarily interested in collecting normative data—descriptions of the behaviors that could be expected at each age. For all these reasons, there was room for Piaget's naturalistic, descriptive approach. The field of developmental psychology was ready for Piaget.

A newcomer to developmental psychology might wonder why Piaget had produced almost a lifetime of work before American academics became interested in him. Certainly the state of academic psychology at that time provides part of the answer. A further reason is the language barrier. Until the 1960s, much of Piaget's work had not been translated into English. An additional language problem is that Piaget's writings are difficult to understand in any language! Fortunately, John Flavell, David Elkind, Hans Furth, and Joachim Wohlwill, among others, served as psychological translators of Piaget's work in the late 1950s and early 1960s. In particular, Flavell's timely book, *The Developmental Psychology of Jean Piaget* (1963), made Piaget understandable to English-speaking psychologists.

The rest, as they say, is history. Psychology witnessed both a flurry of Piagetian replication studies and an attempt to fit Piaget into the existing field of developmental psychology. For example, Berlyne (1965) attempted to integrate learning theory and Piagetian theory. Next came efforts to train children to acquire various Piagetian concepts, especially conservation. At the same time, there emerged American-style laboratory studies of variables such as the nature of task materials and instructions, the scoring criteria, and the socioeconomic level of the children. Piagetian-influenced research peaked in the late 1970s through the early 1980s when approximately one-third of the articles in major developmental journals cited Piaget (Iaccino & Hogan, 1994). Piaget's theory spread into areas such as social development, clinical psychology, and education. This was the "Piagetian stage" of developmental psychology.

The purpose of this historical side trip has been to show the impact of a theory that recognized the central role of cognition in development. Piaget searched for the modes of thinking underlying the overt behavior studied by behaviorists and by child psychologists constructing norms of development. This focus on cognition provided a new perspective and inspiration for a generation of developmental psychologists. As Lourenco and Machado observe, "Paraphrasing Einstein on Euclid, if Piaget failed to kindle your youthful enthusiasm then you were not born to be a developmental psychologist" (1996, p. 157)

Discovery of Surprising Features of Children's Thinking ▪ Piaget's main legacy may be his rich description of what it is we develop. The thousands of observations by Piaget himself, combined with the thousands of studies inspired by him, constitute a remarkable body of information. Regardless of the final judgment on his theoretical claims and the exact ages at which each concept is acquired, his detailed, sensitive, and astute observations remain with us.

Piaget revealed new developmental phenomena, many of which strike people as surprising, or counter to common sense. Especially notable are the following: Young infants often act as though they do not think that objects are permanent. Preschoolers believe that rearranging objects can change their number and assert that the wrongness of an act depends on how much damage resulted. More generally, most concepts not only take longer to develop than we might think but also go through a number of interesting steps along the way. A further surprise is that children think about such a wide variety of things. Children's thinking ranges from pondering the origin of the universe to solving the problem of how to open doors without dropping what they are holding, from penetrating the nature of society's moral system to determining the speed of the swing of a pendulum. In a discipline that has few real "discoveries" to rival the discovery of a new planet or the structure of DNA, Piaget's surprises about cognitive development are refreshing and his observations remarkable, especially considering that they came from seemingly mundane, everyday behavior.

Wide Scope ▪ Piaget's theory is ambitious, drawing its net over behavior ranging from playing with pebbles to causal reasoning, from the sucking reflex to formal operational structures. The theory attempts to describe and explain both cognitive states and transitions between those states. Piaget not only tackled cognitive development but also followed up on its implications for other areas of development, such as social and emotional development and learning. In addition, he addressed other disciplines, such as epistemology, philosophy of science, and education. In Piaget we catch a glimpse of how a complete theory of development might look.

The theory's wide scope obviously increases its attractiveness. At the same time, it increases its vulnerability. The theory may try to do too much.

Ecological Validity ▪ Every psychologist has an intuitive list of what a good theory should do. Many lists would include the requirement that the theory tell us about the real world of children. Although even the most basic research in laboratories has some relevance for day-to-day behavior, some approaches have a closer relationship than others to common, everyday behavior. Piaget's theory seems to rate well in this respect. The focus is on children's adaptation to the world they encounter every day. Infants try to grasp a rattle just out of reach, replace a pacifier, and figure out where a ball has rolled. Preschoolers divide their cookies with friends, try to express their ideas to others, and chastise those who break the rules of games. School children struggle with math problems, try to make sense of social rules, and find their way around their neighborhood or city.

The ecological validity of the theory is more striking for infancy than for the later stages of development. When studying children beyond infancy, Piaget tended to interrupt the flow of behavior with questions or even pose problems from the beginning. The reason is that infants' thinking is expressed in their overt actions, whereas older children's thinking is more covert and must be prodded.

Weaknesses

Although Piaget's theory broke much new ground, it has been heavily criticized in recent years. The theory provides an easy target because of its methodology, wide scope, and ties to biology and philosophy. We examine the following weaknesses: inadequate support for the stage notion, inadequate account of mechanisms of development, need for a theory of performance, slighting of social and emotional aspects of development, underestimation of abilities, and methodological and stylistic barriers. We review some of the recent research, particularly in North America, stimulated by the recognition of these weaknesses. Lourenco and Machado (1996) can be consulted for a defense on behalf of Piaget against some of the criticisms described below as well as additional criticisms.

Inadequate Support for the Stage Notion ■ The strongest attacks on Piaget's theory concern his notion of stages, the heart of the theory. Are there, in fact, broad stretches during development that have characteristics that apply to all the psychological events during that period? Or does the notion of stages simply confuse and mislead by oversimplifying development and claiming more coherence among concepts than there actually is? A basic issue here is how stages are related to the child's actual intellectual functioning. Developmentalists disagree as to whether Piaget thought that the logical structure of each stage should lead to similarity in thought over a variety of content areas (Chapman, 1988; Lourenco & Machado, 1996). The structural model may be an idealized model of thought that differs somewhat from the psychological functioning of the child. Perhaps the problem of interpreting what Piaget meant is that "Piaget used too much logic for psychologists and too much psychology for logicians" (Lourenco & Machado, 1996, p. 156).

The evidence certainly does not support a strong structural version of stages, in the sense of concurrent changes across all content areas. In fact, Piaget himself acknowledged that a structure may apply only to a particular content area and may have to be constructed anew in various domains during a stage. He referred to *horizontal décalages* that occur when a general concept emerges earlier on some tasks than others. For example, in the case of conservation, the conservation of substance typically develops a year or two before conservation of weight. He also would probably not have been bothered by child prodigies whose cognitive achievements in one particular area, such as math, are much more advanced than they are in other areas of thinking. Thus, a weaker structural version of stages may be still viable; some unevenness across domains would even be expected. However, inconsistency over trials in applying even a single concept, such as number conservation, poses a problem even for this weaker version. For instance, Siegler (1995) found that slightly over half of his 5-year-olds classified as nonconservers had generated a correct answer and satisfactory explanation on at least one pretest problem. Thus, variability is as common as consistency, which contrasts with Piaget's emphasis on variability mainly during transitional periods. Moreover, as described later, a concept is demonstrated with simpler task demands earlier than with more complex ones. In addition, "formal operational" adults who can test hypotheses like a scientist in some situations often are poor at testing hypotheses regarding matters about which they have intuitive, often erroneous, theories (Kuhn, 1989). They even ignore or distort data that contradict their beliefs. Given this inconsistency, is the mind less a coherent cognitive system than a "collection of different and unrelated mindlets" (Flavell, 1992) devoted to different contents?

Even if one accepts a weaker stage notion, the problem remains that Piaget did not provide a satisfactory account of what determines whether a structure will be applied to a particular content area. When should we expect generalization, and when should we not? Piaget did not work out in detail his claim that décalages are caused by differences in how various stimuli "resist" the application of the cognitive structures.

It is difficult to decide whether the notion of stages is wrong or simply incomplete. Are the logicomathematical structures a philosopher's dream, or, as described at present, are they simply too vague, general, and distant from behavior? Looft and Svoboda voice some of these doubts:

> While reading Piaget's most recent writings one sometimes acquires an eerie, cold feeling that something very strange is going on in this man's work. In his early writings we read about delightful children playing on the banks of Lake Geneva, expressing their surprise and exhilaration as they make new discoveries about their little worlds. Today we are

> presented with some sort of cybernetic automata, regulating themselves and pushing themselves to ever higher levels of differentiation and complexity. In short, it would seem that as Piaget's theory has evolved over the past five decades to higher and higher levels of abstraction, people have somehow dropped out and have been replaced by sterile logicomathematical structures.
>
> (1971, p. 15)

Analyses of the stage notion by Flavell (1971b, 1982) demonstrate both its incompleteness and the potential for revision within the theory. Flavell suggests several modifications of Piaget's conception of stages:

1. Stagelike, qualitative changes appear to be causally linked to more gradual, quantitative sorts of developmental changes, such as an increasing attentional capacity or an increasing stability and generality of concepts.

2. The development of a cognitive skill is an extended process. In fact, children may not achieve the "full functional maturity" of a stage until after that stage has officially ended.

3. Concepts or structures that characterize a stage are often only roughly synchronous in their development. For example, two concepts might begin their development at the same time but complete it at different times. Or they might begin and end their development at different times but have a considerable temporal overlap. There are other possible temporal relationships as well. The temporal relationships among various developments are especially important for an adequate account of the logicomathematical structures. In what sense are they a simultaneously developing, tightly knit system of structures?

4. The cognitive items of a particular stage may *eventually* become tightly organized and interrelated into a true stage, even if there is not synchrony throughout the stage.

5. In cognitive performance, there are several different types of homogeneity and heterogeneity, and these vary in their implications for Piaget's theory. For example, there may be more cognitive homogeneity in spontaneous, everyday thinking than in testing situations and more in some cognitive domains than in others.

Even though the stages may be less coherent units than Piaget would have us believe, they still are useful ways to organize a large number of diverse behaviors. They are convenient points of reference for accounting for the orderliness of thought. As Flavell and Wohlwill conclude, "To paraphrase Voltaire's dictum concerning the deity: if there were no such structures in the mind of the child, we should have to invent them, to account for the degree of consistency and orderliness that we do find in his cognitive development" (1969, p. 94).

As suggested earlier, the most reasonable way to use Piaget's notion of stages may be to look for stagelike changes limited to a particular content area. Each domain may develop somewhat independently of the others, and thus we would have domain-specific knowledge. This possibility was explored by the neo-Piagetians and by information-processing knowledge-based approaches (see Chapter 4). In the latter view, a child shifts from novice to expert status after experience in a particular domain such as chess, soccer, or dinosaurs. Domain-specific knowledge also is posited by modularity approaches (Chapter 8), certain evolutionary approaches (Chapter 5), and the "theory theory" (of mind, biology, physics) approaches (Chapter 8).

Inadequate Account of Mechanisms of Development ▪ We need clarification not only of the criteria for stages but also of the transitional mechanisms both within a stage and from stage to stage. Although Piaget considered explanations of change quite important, he more successfully described than explained the course of development. The functional invariants, such as assimilation and accommodation, provide at best a general framework with which to examine cognitive change. There are no specific, precise statements as to how sensorimotor thought becomes preoperational thought or how preoperational thought becomes operational thought. Furthermore, although the equilibration process is an intuitively appealing idea, it is not clear how children's awareness of a contradiction would lead them to the solution that resolves the contradiction (Bryant, 1986). Simply knowing that something is wrong does not identify the cause of the problem. Moreover, young children do not seem to be very good at detecting logical inconsistencies that might cause cognitive conflict. Not until age 6 do children see a problem with the claim that a man is both tall and very short (Ruffman, 1999).

One way to study mechanisms of change is to supply certain experiences and see whether they cause cognitive change. Piaget was dubious about the value of trying to intensively teach concepts to children and cautioned that "each time one prematurely teaches a child something he could have discovered for himself, that child is kept from inventing it and consequently from understanding it completely" (1983, p. 113). However, even Piagetians, especially Inhelder, have attempted to provide empirical support for the mechanisms of change by studying how training studies stimulate learning (Inhelder, Sinclair, & Bovet, 1974). In addition, hundreds of training studies have been conducted by American and British psychologists, though they have tended to try to disprove Piaget by showing that a concept can be acquired earlier than Piaget believed. Many of these studies have successfully taught a new concept by creating cognitive conflict, teaching underlying operations such as reversibility or compensation, verbalizing the rule for the child, or providing a model who illustrates the new concept. Other approaches have focused on removing barriers to the child's performance by redirecting attention to the relevant feature, such as number, or by ensuring memory of relevant information.

Unfortunately, training studies have only minimally illuminated mechanisms of development. First of all, even if we find that training based on one of Piaget's mechanisms of development (for example, cognitive conflict) causes the child to acquire the concept, there is no guarantee that children progress by this mechanism in real life. Spontaneous, natural development may proceed in other ways. Second, when a training study does succeed, that success may be based on mechanisms other than those the investigators thought they were providing. Gelman's (1969) training procedure was intended to redirect the child's attention from irrelevant dimensions (for example, length of a row of objects) to the relevant dimension (number). However, as Beilin (1971) points out, this procedure's success could have stemmed from cognitive conflict created when the child's initial answer did not consistently lead to reinforcement. Third, there is not a specific account of why a particular training experience stimulates change in some children but not others. In general, the older children are, the more likely they are to acquire the concept as a result of training, presumably because they are closer to acquiring the concept naturally. However, more refined predictions are more difficult because it is not clear how to assess degree of readiness in children. Finally, since even successful training often does not generalize (transfer) to other materials, procedures, or related tasks, the mechanisms permitting a new concept to generalize remain a mystery.

Need for a Theory of Performance ■ Piaget created an elaborate system of cognitive structures that represent children's knowledge about the world. He also provided a rich description of behavior. There is, however, a missing link: a detailed account of exactly *how* the structures are translated into specific problem-solving strategies "on line" in a particular context. Such a theory of performance would explain how a child's knowledge is expressed in her behavior at any particular time, with particular materials in a particular context. Critical cognitive processes include memory, attention, social influences, mental capacity, and self-regulation. Variables that influence these processes might include, for example, the salience of each attribute (shape, color) in the materials, familiarity of the materials, the amount of information to remember, and the complexity of instructions about the task. A number of researchers (see Miller, 1978), including the neo-Piagetians (e.g., Fischer, Case) described later in this chapter, have examined performance factors. These factors may account, in part, for the extended, gradual, uneven development of concepts. For example, it may be that the early, fragile form of a concept can be used only if there are not large demands on the child's memory, attentional capacity, and verbal ability.

The conservation-of-number task can supply us with a concrete example of how a theory of performance would analyze the way children use their cognitive structures. A test of conservation of number requires that the child proceed through a number of steps as the stimuli (objects and instructions) make contact with the mental operations relevant to conservation. A partial list of steps is as follows: (1) understanding that the task concerns the number of the objects rather than some other feature and (2) attending to the relevant attribute (number) while ignoring irrelevant attributes (color, length, and orientation). Other steps might include (3) counting the objects, (4) encoding information about the number of objects, (5) observing the experimenter move the objects, and (6) remembering the initial equality and the lack of addition or subtraction during the transformation. In addition, the child may (7) recall previous experiences with counting or moving objects, (8) search for an appropriate rule or mental operation, and (9) carry out the appropriate operation, for example, mentally reversing the transformation. Final steps involve (10) inferring the correct answer and (11) translating this answer into words, including a logical explanation. It should be noted that some of these steps may occur at the same time rather than in sequence.

Piaget recognized the importance of these cognitive activities, and in his later years he and his colleagues began to give more attention to a performance model. They studied "procedural knowledge," such as strategies for gathering relevant information or processing it further during problem solving [Inhelder & Piaget, 1980; Piaget, 1981 (1987)]. Piaget thought that it was more important to describe development and to identify general cognitive structures first. In contrast, certain other theoretical approaches discussed later, particularly information processing, Gibson's perceptual learning, and learning theory, focus on the nature of performance. Such theories may eventually provide the missing link between structures and behavior in Piaget's theory.

Slighting of Social and Emotional Aspects of Development ▪ Piaget thought that social and emotional influences on cognitive development were very important. For example, in his *Sociological Studies* he says, "Human knowledge is essentially collective and social life constitutes an essential factor in the creation and growth of knowledge" [1965 (1995, p. 30)]. Recall that social experience was one of the variables in his developmental equation, described earlier. Interacting with other people provides new information to be assimilated. And a concept may be expressed earlier in a social context, as when Piaget's daughter Jacqueline showed a more advanced object concept when she played peekaboo skillfully with her mother at $8\frac{1}{2}$ months than when tested on nonhuman objects [Piaget, 1937 (1954)]. Regarding affect, Piaget thought that it was very intertwined with intelligence: "Feelings express the interest and value given to actions of which intelligence provides the structure" [1945 (1951, pp. 205–206)]. In a sense, emotions provide the energy behind cognition. For example, feelings influence the content to which structures are applied. A child with a passion for airplanes is likely to learn a great deal about them.

For Piaget, the social realm was important not only as an influence on cognition but also as the content of cognition, for example, the concepts of morality and of national identity described earlier. More generally, he thought that cognitive structures are applied to social, as well as nonsocial, content.

Despite this importance that Piaget assigned to the social and emotional realms, he paid relatively little attention to them in his theoretical or research activities. Moreover, he underestimated the role of sociohistorical influences. It has been said that Piaget's epistemic subject has no social class, sex, nationality, culture, or personality—and also has no fun (Murray, 1983, p. 231).

Fortunately, other researchers have filled in the gaps or corrected Piaget's account of social cognition. Kohlberg (1969) adopted Piaget's stage approach to moral judgments and expanded and modified the model considerably. Social cognitive researchers have addressed children's concepts of self, other people, minds, and social interaction (e.g., Flavell & Miller, 1998). Finally, the cultural and person-in-context approaches discussed later in this volume greatly expand our knowledge of sociocultural influences on cognitive development. One contemporary example is work on peer interactions, thought by Piaget to be important for creating cognitive conflict that could cause cognitive progress. For example, interactions between nonconservers and conservers prior to deciding on a mutually agreed-upon answer tend to be tilted toward the conserver. These interactions often are very brief—in one study (Russell, 1982) an average of 40 seconds, consisting of little more than the conserver saying, "Same size, OK? . . . Ready!"

Underestimation of Abilities ▪ Piaget's requiring infants to search for a hidden object before being credited with the concept of object permanence may have caused underestimations of their competence. Baillargeon (1987) found that 4-month-old infants, who should not yet possess the concept of object permanence, were surprised when a screen falling away from them seemed to pass through a now out-of-view box they had seen there earlier. Other studies find infant precocities in areas such as understanding physical concepts, causality, time, problem solving, number, and categorization (see Haith & Benson, 1998, and Spelke & Newport, 1998, for reviews). A main controversy in infant research today concerns how early infants acquire representation (Mandler, 1998).

With children older than infancy, the verbal nature of much of Piaget's testing raises the possibility of underestimating children's knowledge if they do not understand the language used during testing, for example, the meaning of "same number" and "amount." Or children may not be able to express in words their ideas about quantity, the origin of the universe, the nature of dreams, and so forth. Moreover, children may have the concept of conservation but not be able to give an adequate reason for their answer—one of Piaget's criteria for conservation. Or the standard Piagetian procedures may actually be tapping into children's understanding of conversation. An adult asking children about quantity twice (before and after the transformation) may cause children to think that they should change their answer (Siegal, 1991). Specifically, children may think that when an authority figure asks a question a second time, this usually means that the first answer was not satisfactory. In short, children's knowledge may be underestimated.

This concern with the considerable verbal requirements of tasks has led to a number of interesting attempts to devise nonverbal, or at least less verbal, procedures. Psychologists have cleverly devised ways of using expressions of surprise (Gelman, 1972), heart rate (Bower, 1974), predictions (Siegler, 1978), and choice of candy (S. A. Miller, 1976) to test for the presence or absence of certain concepts. For example, Gelman (1972) found that 3-year-olds notice, and are surprised, when the number of toy mice changes (because the experimenter has surreptitiously removed one). Some of the studies employing nonverbal assessment found better performance than did Piaget, but others did not.

Underestimation also can come from complex procedures. One way to simplify the task is to use simpler materials. For example, young children demonstrate more knowledge about counting when there are only a few objects than when there are many (Gelman & Gallistel, 1978).

What should we conclude from these many demonstrations that Piagetian concepts appear to emerge earlier than Piaget thought if motor, verbal, and information-processing demands are addressed? One possible conclusion is that Piaget did in fact underestimate children's competencies. Some psychologists see this as evidence against Piaget's theory that should lead us to seek alternative accounts. For example, unearthing the early competencies in infancy has led some developmentalists to argue for powerful biological constraints that permit the rapid acquisition of certain knowledge about language, mental states, and objects and their behaviors (Gelman & Williams, 1998; Spelke & Newport, 1998). Others have sought explanations of infant behavior in terms of social contextual support (Fischer, later in this chapter) or in terms of connectionist (see Chapter 4) neural networks that, for example, integrate information about the object (Mareschal, Plunkett, & Harris, 1999). However, recall that Piaget's main claims concerned the sequence in which behaviors are acquired rather than the particular ages, which he thought would vary. Thus, showing that an ability emerged earlier than Piaget claimed is not necessarily damaging to his theory.

A more intriguing conclusion from these demonstrations of earlier competencies is that they may show less advanced versions of, or precursors of, the later, more advanced concepts identified by Piaget. For example, the apparent understanding of object permanence in young infants may reflect a competency that is more perceptual than conceptual (e.g., Meltzoff & Moore, 1998). And preschoolers' apparently successful performance on modifications of concrete operational tasks may actually reflect only preoperational concepts, such as functions, rather than concrete operational concepts (Chapman, 1988; Lourenco & Machado, 1996). That is, the simplified task provides so much perceptual support that the conditions theoretically necessary for operational reasoning are not present.

The differences in the methodology of Genevan Piagetians, on the one hand, and North American and British psychologists, on the other, reflect different goals of assessment. Piaget especially wanted to avoid "false positive errors," namely, concluding that children have the concept when in fact they do not. Thus, he sometimes even considered it desirable to have complex materials, a misleading visual array, and heavy verbal demands so that only children who see the concept as logically necessary will prevail. In contrast, the other camp is more concerned about "false negative errors," concluding that children do not have the concept when in fact they do.

In any case, research on early competencies has been quite fruitful, for it has revealed positive acquisitions during the infancy and preschool years that complement Piaget's emphasis on the deficiencies of young children. For example, it turns out that preschoolers know a great deal about number. Gelman and Gallistel (1978) found a sequence of simple principles of counting, such as the principle that numerals must always be used in the same order. That is, children who say "1, 2, 6, 9" follow this counting principle correctly if they always use these numerals in this order for counting. These early principles supplement Piaget's account of the full-blown concept of number acquired several years later. Techniques that simplify the Piagetian tests are more sensitive to earlier forms of concepts than are Piaget's procedures.

It is interesting, however, that in addition to finding Piagetian underestimations, researchers also have found overestimations. One example is formal operations. As discussed earlier, adolescents and even adults appear to use these concepts rather infrequently. In fact, Piaget (1972) later concluded that the stage continued until age 20 or later.

Methodological and Stylistic Barriers ▪ Piaget's critics attack his methodology not only with respect to issues of underestimation and overestimation but also because much of it does not meet the conventions of developmental science. With respect to his infancy research, Piaget observed his own three children. Unfortunately, he did not have 40 or 50 children of his own to give us a more respectable sample size! The small number of subjects, the possible biases in interpreting the behavior of one's own children, the absence of measures of reliability from two independent observers, and the lack of control over the children's immediate environment, possible only in a laboratory, did not endear Piaget to American experimental psychologists. However, subsequent studies, with more subjects and better-controlled testing situations, generally have replicated the sequence of development within infancy, though not always the exact ages at which the changes occur.

In his work with older children, Piaget often tested large samples of children [for example, 2159 for *Early Growth of Logic in the Child* (1964)!]. He usually employed the clinical method. Although this method has certain advantages, such as flexibility in tailoring questions to the particular answers given by each child, it also has a number of disadvantages. Two main disadvantages are the danger that examiners may be too leading in their questions or not leading enough and that different children often are asked slightly different questions. Uniform instructions, materials, and measures of response are the backbone of testing in experimental psychology. We are asked to make the leap of faith that Piaget was in fact a sensitive and accurate observer. Piaget himself seemed aware of these problems:

> It is so hard not to talk too much when questioning a child, especially for a pedagogue! It is so hard not to be suggestive! And above all, it is so hard to find the middle course between systematization due to preconceived ideas and incoherence due to the absence of any directing hypothesis!
>
> [1926 (1929, p. 9)]

Piaget's reporting of his experiments is frustrating to contemporary psychologists. His reports do not allow the reader to evaluate the research. He typically does not report the number of children, their race or socioeconomic level, and details of the testing procedure. Sometimes it is even difficult to tell whether Piaget is referring to hypothetical children or children he has actually tested! He was not impressed with tightly controlled laboratory experiments and statistical analysis. In his words, "Psychologists over-generalized their methods and arrived at delightful trivialities, particularly when an army of scientists translated their results into mathematical terms" (1918, p. 63). Furthermore, "acute observation, especially when made by [a good observer] . . . , surpasses all statistics" [1936 (1952, p. 72)]. Instead of presenting statistical summaries of the findings, Piaget provides sample protocols, which he interpreted at great length. The reader has no idea whether these protocols are representative of all children tested.

What are we to make of these characteristics of Piaget's methodology and writing? Flavell (1963) concluded that Piaget was primarily interested in satisfying his own curiosity, not the requirements of the scientific community. Consequently, he played by his own rules when doing research and wrote almost as though he were talking to himself.

Although Piaget's methodology and reporting are annoying to anyone trying to understand and evaluate his theory, they may be somewhat responsible for Piaget's success. His qualitative methods captured the richness of children's thinking, which sometimes is lost when quantitative methods are used. If Piaget had used standardized procedures from the beginning, he might have missed some fascinating facets of cognitive development. In fact, as Ginsburg and Opper suggest, "If Piaget had attempted to establish every point with the maximum of certainty, then he probably would not have advanced beyond the study of children's verbal communication (one of his first research topics)" (1979, pp. 94–95).

PIAGET'S OWN MODIFICATIONS OF HIS THEORY

Piaget considered himself one of the primary revisionists of "Piaget's theory." As his later works are translated, the "classic Piaget" is being modified (see Beilin, 1992; Beilin & Fireman, 2000; Lourenco & Machado, 1996; Montangero & Maurice-Naville, 1997). Although some of this more recent work was presented throughout this chapter, several theoretical changes should be highlighted, particularly regarding developmental change, equilibration, and the logicomathematical model.

In his later years, Piaget [1975 (1985)] put less emphasis on stages. In fact, Vuyk concluded that Piaget "now considers development a spiral and though one may call a stage 'a detour of the spiral,' this indicates that periods of equilibrium are relatively unimportant" (1981, p. 192). Piaget began to view development as less steplike, with longer transition periods between stages. He increased his attention to mechanisms of cognitive change, especially the equilibration process. He further worked out the equilibration subprocesses of assimilation, accommodation, feedback from actions, and reflective abstraction. In *reflective abstraction,* children construct new knowledge by taking their knowledge from a lower level to a higher one and reorganizing it at this higher level. Piaget gave the example that a young child can know how to get from home to school in a practical way, using cues to guide him from one point to another. In reflective abstraction, this knowledge is projected onto a representational level—an overall cognitive map of the spatial relations between home and school (Montangero & Maurice-Naville, 1997, p. 58).

Piaget also worked out a new way of describing developmental change, both within a stage and over all the stages: *intra-*, *inter-*, and *trans* changes. Knowledge about properties of objects (intra) leads to knowledge about relations between object properties or actions (inter) and then to a structure that organizes these relations (trans). For example, a child moves from "A car can be ridden in" to "Cars and buses can be ridden in," and thus go together, to "Cars and buses and other vehicles are modes of transportation within a hierarchical logical system."

Piaget expanded on the role of "possibilities" (the way things might be) and "procedures" (strategies) in the process of development. This contrasts with his earlier emphasis on logical necessity. A new cognitive structure generates new possibilities, which cause the child to try out new procedures on objects. Through accommodation to these new experiences, the child can establish equilibrium again. In this process possibility and necessity are intertwined because new possibilities may lead to a new necessity, which in turn may lead to new possibilities, and so on, back and forth.

As an example of the increasing awareness of possibilities during development, Piaget (1981) showed children a box with only one side visible under a cloth. At age 5 or 6, children would accept only a single possibility for the color of the hidden side of the box—the same color as the visible side. Thus, a sense of necessity occurs in young children because they can imagine only a single possibility. By age 7 to 10, children recognized multiple, though limited, possibilities: the hidden side might be "green, violet, blue, white, yellow . . . that's all" (Piaget, 1981, p. 44). At age 11 to 12, children realize that the number of possibilities is essentially unlimited. One reason that this development is interesting is that the concept of unlimited possibilities cannot be observed in the environment. It must be constructed internally.

An important aspect of equilibration is contradiction. An example of Piaget's later [1974 (1980)] research in this area involved a row of seven disks, each of which was slightly, but imperceptibly, larger than the one before it. Because the last and largest disk was unattached, it could be moved to, and compared with, each of the six disks attached to the board. Thus, the contradiction facing the child was that any two adjacent disks appeared to be equal in size but the disk at the end of the series was obviously larger than the first disk. Three stages of understanding contradiction emerged. In the first stage, young children were unaware of the contradiction. Next, children had some awareness of the contradiction, but their attempted solutions were not satisfactory. For example, a child might categorize the disks as small ones and large ones, thereby accounting for some of the perceived equivalences between adjacent disks (both are "small") and also explaining the difference in size of the first ("small") and last ("large") disk. Finally, by age 11 or 12 children resolved the contradiction and reestablished equilibrium by creating a new structure—quantified seriation of size.

Piaget's most radical changes concern his logicomathematical model of thinking. Piaget had intended to "restructure the entire logical architecture of the theory" (Beilin & Fireman, 2000, p. 239), but his death prevented completion of the project. He tried to incorporate a *logic of meanings* and *category theory*, a branch of mathematics developed since the 1960s. A logic of meanings is described in a posthumous publication (Piaget & Garcia, 1991). Briefly, Piaget emphasized that logic comes from the meanings of objects, developed from infants' actions. Specifically, infants learn that one action on an object is related to other actions; the meaning of actions comes from "what they lead to." That is, one action can be inferred from another, in a sort of "logic of meaning in actions," a "psycho-logic" on objects. For example, an infant who pushes an object away from herself may infer that the object can be pulled toward herself. Another example is that grasping a rattle implies relations between grasping and seeing, as well as the reasoning that "if I release the car down the ramp it will crash into the house at the bottom." This action-based logic later leads to a logic of operations, such as when the pushing–pulling relation leads to the reversal or negation of a mental action. The meaning of an object comes not only from what can be done with the object but also from children's description of the attributes of an object and their classification of it. Remarkably, Piaget perceived in infants' coordinations of their actions a sensorimotor counterpart to the 16 binary combinations of formal operations thought.

In category theory, Piaget's previous emphasis on action in the form of mental transformations is supplemented with "correspondences" between two static states (Piaget, 1979). Comparisons of static states are central, as when a preoperational child sees the similarity between a currently perceived object and a previously encountered one, and thereby assimilates the current one. The current object or event is recognized, categorized, or characterized; it therefore "corresponds" (is seen as similar) to other objects or events. Or a child may perceive that each of five dolls of increasing size maps onto five dresses of increasing size (Davidson, 1988). Detecting correspondences can, of course, lead the child to notice a transformation. For example, when a picture corresponds to the same picture hung upside down, a mental rotation links the two states and underlies their correspondence.

Piaget's final contributions raise enough important questions to occupy cognitive theorists and researchers for years to come. Only after this critical examination will we be able to judge the ultimate value of these new ideas.

THE NEO-PIAGETIANS

Many of the problems and limitations raised concerning Piaget's theory have been addressed by a group of developmental psychologists labeled "neo-Piagetians." They are Piagetian in their belief in the active construction of some sort of stages, sequences, and structural change. In particular, they believe that lower-level concepts are integrated to form higher-level concepts. However, they are "neo" in their inclusion of information-processing (see Chapter 4) constructs such as skills, limited memory capacity, and domain-specific concepts, and the social-contextual (see Chapter 7) idea of social supports for emerging cognitive skills. Domain-specific concepts or stages are those that pertain only to a particular area or areas, such as role taking or number. Thus, a careful analysis of particular tasks is necessary. In contrast, Piaget tended to emphasize the domain-general application of cognitive structures. We examine the theories of Robbie Case (e.g., Case, 1998; Case & Okamoto, 1996) and Kurt Fischer (e.g., Fischer & Bidell, 1998), the two most influential neo-Piagetians.

Robbie Case

Case, like Piaget, addressed cognitive changes from one level to the next. Case, however, attributed much of such change to increased capacity in working memory or, in his words, *executive processing space:* "the maximum number of independent schemes a child can activate at any one time" (1985, p. 289). An increase in the efficiency of using one's capacity, rather than the equilibration process, is a major mechanism for development. Capacity can increase in two ways. First, practice with a skill, such as counting, makes it faster and more automatic. Consequently, counting becomes less effortful and more efficient, thus freeing previously needed capacity. A given amount of capacity goes a lot further if many elements can be processed, rather than a few. This increase in available capacity can be used for new or additional cognitive activities, for example, both counting and remembering. The faster a child can count objects, the better she is at remembering the number of objects in sets in a counting span test (Case, 1985). Second, brain maturation increases the amount of information children can handle on many different tasks. Increased myelinization (insulation of neurons) and perhaps increased physical connections between the frontal and posterior lobes may increase the efficiency and integration of cognitive functioning. Neurological spurts are correlated with cognitive spurts (Case, 1985).

Case differed from Piaget in his view of how children's mental structures should be modeled. Case remarked that "it seemed that Piaget's theory was better equipped for representing the structure in the mind of logicians than the structure in the minds of young children" (1992, p. 6). Rather than draw on symbolic logic, Case used constructs from the information-processing framework, particularly (a) children's rich networks of concepts and their relation and (b) *executive control structures*, which are devices for dealing with specific problem situations. He viewed children as problem solvers, with these control structures as their tools. These structures use processes such as setting goals, activating procedures (sequences of schemes) in novel ways for reaching these goals, and evaluating the results of these procedures. Other processes include restructuring successful procedures so that they later can be produced intentionally and practicing and integrating successful procedures until they are consolidated. For example, with respect to counting, children set a goal (determining the number of objects), generate counting procedures for attaining it, evaluate their success, "mark" the successful sequence, and integrate the successful counting procedures.

When children experiment during attempts to solve problems, they explore objects, observe and imitate other people, and interact with others as together they solve a problem. For example, children might learn about counting by using their own verbal labels as they touch each object during problem solving, counting different types of objects during exploring, observing others count, and trying to count a large set with the help of an adult. If children have the necessary processing capacity, they can take advantage of these experiences to construct more advanced executive control structures (for example, procedures for determining quantity).

Case addressed the debate about general versus task-specific cognitive structures by proposing a small set of *central conceptual structures* at an intermediate level of generality. They are less general than Piaget's structures but more general than a single task. Each central conceptual structure is a representational system of a domain of knowledge such as number, space, or social interaction that should permit a child to apply that knowledge to all tasks in that domain. These structures interpret specific tasks in the domain and assemble problem-solving procedures for these tasks (the executive control structures mentioned earlier), a process which can cause cognitive change at this specific level. The specific-level changes, along with increases in capacity, in turn can contribute to changes in the central conceptual structure *for that domain*. In this way they bootstrap each other during development.

Children can show both consistency and inconsistency across situations. A child might show the same level of thinking across tasks because the tasks fall within the same central conceptual structure. When children learn about number on one sort of task, they may generalize their new understanding to new tasks in that domain. Evenness also occurs when capacity sets the same upper limit on all tasks. Tasks may fall within different central conceptual structures, such as number, space, and social thought, but involve the same amount of capacity. In addition, changes in the central conceptual structures can be similar across domains. For example, in the early elementary school years, due to capacity, changes and schooling, children merge two schemes into a superordinate unit with a linear chainlike structure that can be expressed across areas that on the surface appear quite different. In number, children begin to mentally count "1, 2, 3 . . . " In space, a drawing of a dog corresponds grid by grid to a real dog. In social thought, one state or action enables or causes the next state or action in the story line. In this example, a stagelike change across domains has occurred.

Piaget and Case offer different mechanisms for change. Specifically, Case gives more attention to capacity limits and cultural experiences. The two theorists also propose different models for mental structures, as described above. However, they both view development as structural change resulting in a series of stages (see Case, 1985, for a description of his earlier theory, which gave more attention to stages). In both theories, lower-order concepts are differentiated and coordinated into higher-order concepts.

Case thought that, on a given task, children develop in a qualitative stagelike way: "on a wide variety of scientific, cultural, social, and mathematical tasks, children appear to move from a predimensional, to a unidimensional, to a bidimensional, to an integrated bidimensional form of response" (Case & Okamoto, 1996, p. 55). For example, when children are told to tell a story about a little child and an old horse, predimensional (preintentional) children relate a social situation with no mention of motives, whereas slightly older, unidimensional (uni-intentional) children create a story around the intentions of the central character. Later, bidimensional (bi-intentional) children create a chain of two or more event sequences in which the first sequence does not lead to goal satisfaction while the second sequence does. Finally, at the integrated bidimensional (integrated bi-intentional) level, children integrate multiple attempts at satisfaction into an overall, complex, organized plot. As another example, the representations of spatial relations in Chinese children's drawings show a similar sequence (see Figure 1.2): (a) no real concern with spatial relations, (b) placement of objects into a single spatial dimension, (c) depiction of both foreground and background, and (c) creation of a coherent, unified picture.

As a final example of qualitative change, consider the concept of "juiciness" (Noelting, 1980).There are two sets of small glasses. In each set some glasses contain orange juice and some contain water. Children must predict which pitcher would taste more strongly of orange juice if the liquid were poured from one set of glasses into one pitcher and from the other set into a second pitcher. Thus, children must determine which pitcher would have the higher proportion of orange juice. Preschoolers judge solely on a perceptual basis, on whether one set looks as if it has a lot of juice and the other set does not. Then, 5- to 7-year-olds judge on a single quantitative basis and believe that whichever set has more glasses of juice would taste more strongly of juice. Thus, they are correct when there is an equal total number of glasses in the two sets but are incorrect when, for example, set A contains four glasses of juice and four of water and set B contains three glasses of juice and two of water. That is, the children choose set A. Next, 7- to 9-year-olds attend to the numbers of both types of glasses and say, for example, "the same, since there's more juice here but more water here." Finally, 9- to 11-year-olds note the difference in the number of water glasses in the two sets and the difference in the number of juice glasses

Figure 1.2

Typical pictures drawn by children aged 4(*a*), 6(*b*), 8(*c*), and 10(*d*) in Nanjing, China, when told to "draw a picture of a mother and a father holding hands in a park. A baby is in front of them and a tree is very far away behind them."

SOURCE: Reproduced with permission from "The role of central conceptual structures in the development of children's thought," by Robbie Case and Yukari Okamoto, in *Monographs of the Society for Research in Child Development*, 1996, *61*(1-2), Serial No. 246, p. 139. Copyright 1996 by the Society for Research in Child Development.

in each set. If the juice difference is greater, they pick the set with more juice as "juicier," and if the water difference is larger, they pick the set with more water as less juicy.

With these tasks, as well as others used by Case, what changes during development is that (1) children consider more elements (because processing capacity has increased) and (2) these elements become more organized into a structure. These changes are made possible mainly by an increase in mental capacity.

Case's theory is an exciting attempt to integrate a structural model and a processing model of development. He shows how limits in processing capacity and social experience limit logical reasoning and constrain what the child can learn at any developmental level. By the same token, an increase in capacity creates a new opportunity for the further development of logical thinking. He studies children of various ages, social classes, and countries. He examines a variety of skills, such as spatial representation, social cognition, eating with utensils in infancy, using vocalizations for social purposes, manipulating other people's feelings, storytelling, understanding emotions, and judging intelligence in others.

Kurt Fischer

Kurt Fischer (e.g., Fischer & Bidell, 1998) agrees with Case in many ways but focuses on cognitive variability and children's activities in social-cultural context. Unlike Piaget, Fischer downplays consistency across behaviors. In Fischer's view, "Variations in developmental level are routine and pervasive and they need to be explained, not ignored" (1996, p. 209). His *dynamic skill theory* addresses why and how that variability occurs. The context, especially the supportive social context, is key. Children gradually construct their thinking and learning skills as they use them in activities in various contexts. Skills include abilities such as storytelling, counting, forming relationships with others, and reading. A child is most likely to be advanced in her concept of number, and use it, if she is raised in an environment with support for developing and using this skill. She may be less advanced with respect to skills generally considered to be in the same stage if she has had little support or training. Thus, she is not "in" one stage or another. Rather, she will show various levels of cognitive functioning across various domains, depending on the opportunities for developing a particular skill in her social context.

Similarly, variable testing conditions with different levels of support produce various levels of performance. Each child has a *developmental range*. At one end, with contextual supports such as prompts, models, or coparticipation with someone more advanced, the child operates at her maximal, *optimal level* (see also Vygotsky, Chapter 7). At the other end, in a setting devoid of meaning, value, or support, or under conditions of fatigue, emotional stress, or distraction, she is unlikely to express her skill. Her highest skill level when functioning independently, under low support, is her *functional level*. In short, the child's level of cognitive functioning has to do with the fit between a child and her environment, not the child alone.

Children also show variability in their skill levels because they are constantly having to adjust their skills to changing conditions and people and even to reorganize their skills. They use "not only their brains but also their bodies, the objects and people around them, and the roles, norms, and values of their culture" (Fischer & Bidell, 1998, p. 545). Moreover, "People's activities are embodied, contextualized, and socially situated—understood in terms of their ecology . . . as well as their structure" (Fischer & Bidell, 1998, p. 468). Through studying children's actions in context, Fischer tries to map the "dynamic structures" of human behavior. He tries to capture the orderly patterns of development within variability.

Still another aspect of variability in Fischer's model is that a child may follow several different developmental routes for different skills. He contrasts his view with traditional metaphors of development, such as a ladder, in which a child begins at one point and moves from one formal structure to the next to a final point. He offers an alternative metaphor—a "constructive web," illustrated in Figure 1.3: "Unlike the steps in a ladder, the strands in a web are not fixed in a determined order but are the *joint product* of the web builder's constructive activity and the

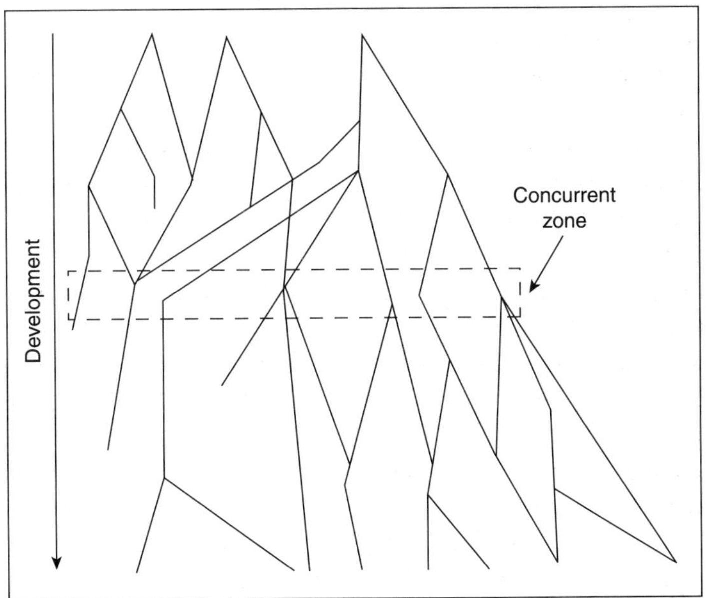

Figure 1.3

In Fischer's developmental web, the branching, joining of strands, and changes in direction indicate discontinuities in development. Discontinuities often cluster across strands in a stagelike period called a concurrent zone, an example of which is shown by the box.

SOURCE: Reproduced with permission from "Infants' construction of actions in context: Piaget's contribution to research on early development," by Kurt Fischer and Rebecca Hencke in *Psychological Science,* 1996, *7,* p. 206. Copyright 1996 by the American Psychological Society.

supportive context in which it is built (like branches, leaves, or the corner of a wall, for a spider web") (Fischer & Bidell, 1998, p. 473). The various strands represent the various pathways along which a person develops in different domains, such as object permanence and pretend play. At some points along this web there may be simultaneous change across several strands—a *concurrent zone*—as several new abilities emerge at approximately the same time across domains. That is, the strands may come together to cause a developmental spurt, which is a qualitative change that looks like a stage. At other times, disparities across domains are more obvious because two strands change at different times. Thus, Case and Fischer agree that development can sometimes appear stagelike and sometimes not, sometimes domain-general and sometimes domain-specific.

Because different children encounter different settings that call for different sorts of integrations of skills, they may follow different developmental pathways to the same skill. For example, children follow different sequences of skills in the process of learning to read, and subsets of poor readers follow different, less-integrated, routes than good readers rather than simply show delay along the path of the good readers (Knight & Fischer, 1992). And seemingly abnormal behavior sometimes reflects a nonnormative developmental pathway rather than psychopathology, as when abused children are not simply socially unskilled but have developed alternative cognitive and social pathways to cope with their abuse.

Like Piaget and Case, Fischer believes that over a larger developmental time scale skills develop in a sequence through four tiers, as depicted in Table 1.1 (see Fischer & Bidell, 1998, for a detailed description). For our purposes much of the detail in the table can be ignored. Three points about this table are important. First, within each tier, children go through the same four sorts of levels, beginning with a single unit formed by the final level of the previous tier. For example, a single sensorimotor action, such as reaching, is both the final achievement of the reflex tier and the first level of the sensorimotor tier. This single action is followed by a two-action connection or mapping, in which children differentiate and integrate two specific actions, as when they reach for a ball in order to look at it. Next come connections between two sensorimotor systems, such as moving a rattle in various ways in order to look at different parts of it. Finally, a single representation that reflects a coordination of two or more sensorimotor systems emerges, as when a toddler pretends that a doll is walking. This sequence then is repeated at the representational level and then at the abstract level. At the

Table 1.1 Fischer's levels of skill development

	TIER*				
Level	**Reflex**	**Sensorimotor**	**Representational**	**Abstract**	**Age†**
Rf1: Single reflexes	[A] or [B]				3–4 wk
Rf2: Reflex mappings	[A—B]				7–8
Rf3: Reflex systems	$[A^E_F \leftrightarrow B^E_F]$				10–11
Rf4/S1: Systems of reflex systems, which are single sensorimotor actions	$\begin{bmatrix} A^E_F \leftrightarrow B^E_F \\ \Updownarrow \\ C^G_H \leftrightarrow D^G_H \end{bmatrix}$	≡ [I]			15–17
S2: Sensorimotor mappings		[I—J]			7–8 mth
S3: Sensorimotor systems		$[I^M_N \leftrightarrow J^M_N]$			11–13
S4/Rp1: Systems of sensorimotor systems, which are single representations		$\begin{bmatrix} I^M_N \leftrightarrow J^M_N \\ \Updownarrow \\ K^O_P \leftrightarrow L^O_P \end{bmatrix}$	≡ [Q]		18–24
Rp2: Representational mappings			[Q—R]		3.5–4.5 yr
Rp3: Representational systems			$[Q^U_V \leftrightarrow R^U_V]$		6–7
Rp4/Ab1: Systems of representational systems, which are single abstractions			$\begin{bmatrix} Q^U_V \leftrightarrow R^U_V \\ \Updownarrow \\ S^W_X \leftrightarrow T^W_X \end{bmatrix}$	≡ [Y]	10–12
Ab2: Abstract mappings				[Y—Z]	14–16
Ab3: Abstract systems				$[Y^C_D \leftrightarrow Z^C_D]$	19–20
Ab4: Systems of abstract systems, which are principles				$\begin{bmatrix} Y^C_D \leftrightarrow Z^C_D \\ \Updownarrow \\ A^C_D \leftrightarrow B^C_D \end{bmatrix}$	24–25

* Long straight lines and arrows designate a relation between components. Brackets enclose a single skill. The large letters stand for a main component of the skill and subscripts and superscripts indicate subsets of the main components. Note that structures from lower tiers continue at higher levels, as when reflexes become sensorimotor actions.

† Ages are approximate.

SOURCE: Reproduced with permission from "The development of representation as the coordination of component systems of action," by M. F. Mascolo and K. W. Fisher, in *Development of mental representation*, I. E. Sigel (Ed.). Copyright 1999 by Lawrence Erlbaum Associates.

representational level, for example, single representations of doctor and patient become mapped into each other in the doctor–patient roles; during play, the doctor doll gives medicine to the patient doll after she complains of a stomachache. Later, children coordinate two mappings and thus show a person in two roles simultaneously, such as a father who goes to the doctor. Finally, the various roles of two or more people are integrated into a system of representations and a single abstraction.

The second point is that brain growth and activity sometimes occur in spurts, such as a new type of neural network, that correspond to movement from one level to the next or one tier to the next (Fischer & Bidell, 1998). Third, the tiers become increasingly abstract and bear a marked similarity to Piaget's. Fischer has studied this integration of earlier skills into later ones in diverse content areas such as gender-role development, reading, emotional development, adolescents' relationships, and planning.

Fischer cautions about focusing on stages, however:

> When multiple levels of skill are analyzed in each person, the debate about the existence of stages disappears. Under optimal, highly supported conditions, people show jumps in performance that act much like stages; but under ordinary, low-support conditions, the same people show no systematic stages, often progressing in smooth, monotonic growth.
>
> (Fischer & Bidell, 1998, p. 545)

Neo-Piagetian Themes

Neo-Piagetians other than Case and Fischer have gone in various directions. Some have continued themes already discussed in this section. For example, one of the first neo-Piagetians, Pascual-Leone (1970), also emphasizes the role of capacity in cognitive development (e.g., Pascual-Leone & Johnson, 1999). Halford (1993, 1999) similarly emphasizes capacity, particularly regarding its influence on the development of the ability to perceive analogical relationships, such as mapping from tall and short people to long and short walking sticks. Other neo-Piagetians have emphasized other themes, such as stages that develop after adolescence (e.g., Commons, 1994). Demetriou and colleagues (Demetriou, Efklides, & Platsidou, 1993; Demetriou & Raftopoulos, 1999) have developed a comprehensive theory that is a synthesis of Piagetian, information-processing, psychometric (e.g., IQ), and theory-of-mind approaches. They see the architecture of the mind as a three-level universe consisting of a processing system, a set of specialized systems for various knowledge domains, and a "hypercognitive system" that monitors and controls the activities of the other systems. The specialized knowledge systems are visual creativity (drawing, spatial imagination), analytical inferential thought (quantitative, causal), and interpersonal thought (social, verbal). Thus, neo-Piagetian theorizing is alive and well.

For the most part, neo-Piagetians enrich and specify Piaget's theory, rather than contradict it. Their two main contributions are (1) to propose a promising set of processes to account for developmental change and intrachild and interchild variability and (2) to clarify and refine the notion of stages, for example, by attempting to differentiate domain-general and domain-specific achievements. As Flavell has observed, "Cognitive development might appear to be more general-stagelike than many of us believed, if only we knew how and where to look" (1982, p. 1).

In a broad sense, many cognitive developmentalists today are neo-Piagetian. Although many psychologists claim that the influence of Piagetian theory is waning, this decline may be more apparent than real. Even though there are fewer studies with such Piagetian tasks as conservation and class inclusion, many Piagetian concepts are still studied, for example, object permanence, number, space, scientific reasoning, causality, moral judgments, and understanding of mental states and activities. Moreover, so many of Piaget's assumptions about the nature of cognitive development are assimilated into the thinking of researchers that Piaget's ongoing influence often is not recognized. As Flavell notes, "I think we are in more danger of underappreciating Piaget than of overappreciating him, for much the same reason that fish are said to underappreciate the virtues of water" (1996, p. 202). Examples of this pervasive but invisible influence are the following: Researchers search for a general concept underlying several different behaviors, for example, the "theory theory" (see Chapter 8), and for the process by which a new concept arises from a previous one. The "wrong" or "cute" notions that preschool children have about the world are a symptom of a complex, probing intellectual system trying to understand reality. Children actively construct knowledge; to a great extent they teach themselves. The list could, of course, go on.

SUMMARY

Piaget's theory posits invariant stages in how children acquire knowledge about the world (genetic epistemology). In the first 2 years of life, children construct sensorimotor schemes based on physical action upon the world. The schemes become more intentional and more intercoordinated during that time. During the preoperational period, approximately age 2 to 7, children exploit their newly acquired symbolic ability. Despite the limitations of egocentrism, rigid thought, and limited role-taking and communication abilities, children combine symbols into semilogical reasoning. During the concrete operational period, roughly age 7 to 11, children acquire logicomathematical structures. Now thought is operational and consequently more flexible and abstract. Actions are still the main source of knowledge, but the actions now are mental. Finally, during the formal operational period, age 11 to 15, these operations are no longer limited to concrete objects. Operations can be performed on operations, verbal propositions, and hypothetical conditions.

These stagelike changes involve changes in the structure of thought. Thought becomes increasingly organized, always building on the structure of the previous stage. Evidence for these structural changes comes from observations of infants and from interviews or problem-solving tasks with older children.

Movement through the stages is caused by four factors: physical maturation, experience with physical objects, social experience, and equilibration. Experience brings cognitive progress through assimilation and accommodation. These functional invariants help children adapt to the environment by strengthening and stretching their current understanding of the world.

Piaget viewed children as active and self-regulating organisms who change by means of interacting innate and environmental factors. He emphasized qualitative change, but he identified certain quantitative changes as well. The essence of cognitive development is structural change. Piaget drew on the equilibration model and the logicomathematical model to describe these changes. His theory has contributed many educational concepts, for example, "readiness to learn" and the "active learner."

The theory's main strengths are its recognition of the central role of cognition in development, discovery of surprising features of young children's thinking, wide scope, and ecological validity. The main weaknesses include its inadequate support for the stage notion, inadequate account of mechanisms of development, need for a theory of performance, slighting of social and emotional aspects of development, underestimation of abilities, and methodological and stylistic barriers. Some of these problems have been addressed by the neo-Piagetians, particularly Case and Fischer, who include the roles of capacity and cultural support in explanations of the variability and consistency of children's thinking. In addition, Piaget himself continued to modify his theory in his later years, particularly with respect to the nature of logic and the mechanisms of development.

What should be our final judgment on Piaget's theory? This flawed but amazingly productive theory gives us a framework for viewing the richness and complexity of cognitive development. Even when it has failed, for example, where an adequate explanation for conservation cannot be found despite hundreds of studies, the theory has led to interesting discoveries about development, such as rudimentary numerical skills that may lead to conservation. Furthermore, the theory has raised issues that all theories of development must address. All new theories for years to come will inevitably be compared to Piaget's theory. In short, we have not made a mistake by paying attention to this "giant in the nursery" (Elkind, 1968).

SUGGESTED READINGS

Numerous books and articles have been written about Piaget. Especially notable efforts are the following:

Flavell, J. H. (1963). *The developmental psychology of Jean Piaget*. Princeton, NJ: Van Nostrand. This classic is still the most comprehensive account of Piaget's theory.

Wadsworth, B. J. (1996). *Piaget's theory of cognitive and affective development* (5th ed.). White Plains, NY: Longman. This book presents a readable account of the theory.

Brainerd, C. J. (Ed.). (1996). *Psychological Science* celebrates the centennial of Jean Piaget. [Special section of journal]. *Psychological Science*, 7, 191–225.

Lourenco, O., & Machado, A. (1996). In defense of Piaget's theory: A reply to 10 common criticisms. *Psychological Review*, *103*, 143–164.

Montangero, J., & Maurice-Naville, D. (1997). *Piaget or the advance of knowledge*. Mahweh, NJ: Erlbaum. This book describes Piaget's work in various periods of his life and provides a useful glossary of important terms in the theory.

The following books by Piaget are two of his more readable and clearly written publications:

Piaget, J. (1967). *Six psychological studies*. New York: Random House.

Piaget, J., & Inhelder, B. (1969). *The psychology of the child*. New York: Basic Books.

Piaget's research has stimulated a number of thoughtful publications on issues raised by his theory. Three are listed here:

Case, R., & Okamoto, Y. (1996). The role of central conceptual structures in the development of children's thought. *Monographs of the Society for Research in Child Development, 61* (1–2, Serial No. 246). The authors describe their neo-Piagetian approach to various research areas.

Fischer, K., & Bidell, T. R. (1998). Dynamic development of psychological structures in action and thought. In W. Damon (Series Ed.) & R. M. Lerner (Vol. Ed.), *Handbook of child psychology: Vol. 1. Theoretical models of human development* (5th ed., pp. 467–562). New York: Wiley. The authors describe their neo-Piagetian approach.

Scholnick, E. S., Nelson, K., Gelman, S. A., & Miller, P. H. (Eds.). (1999). *Conceptual development: Piaget's legacy*. Mahwah, NJ: Erlbaum. Each chapter describes Piaget's influence on some aspect of contemporary research on cognitive development.

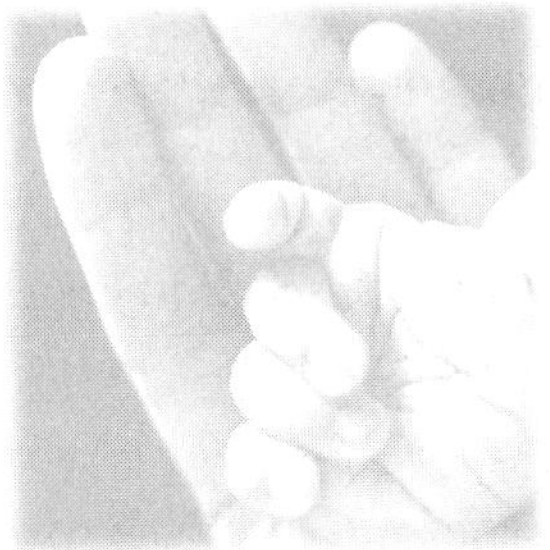

CHAPTER

Freud's and Erikson's Psychoanalytic Theories

I dreamt that it was night and that I was lying in my bed. . . . Suddenly the window opened of its own accord, and I was terrified to see that some white wolves were sitting on the big walnut tree in front of the window. There were six or seven of them. The wolves were quite white, and looked more like foxes or sheep-dogs, for they had big tails like foxes and they had their ears pricked like dogs when they pay attention to something. In great terror, evidently of being eaten up by the wolves, I screamed and woke up.

— "THE WOLF MAN" QUOTED IN FREUD, 1918 (1955, p. 29)

The most significant sex difference was the tendency of boys to erect structures, buildings, towers, or streets . . . the girls tended to use the play table as the interior of a house with simple, little, or no use of blocks. . . . Simple enclosures with low walls and without ornaments were the largest item among the configurations built by girls. However, these enclosures often had an elaborate gate. . . . A blocking of the entrance or a thickening of the walls could on further study be shown to reflect acute anxiety over the feminine role.

— ERIKSON, 1963, pp. 102–105

Psychoanalytic theory has great historical significance for developmental psychology. To meet the source of the theory, we move from Geneva to Vienna, where Freud spent most of his life. The development of the theory followed a tortuous course, full of dazzling insights, diverging ideas, and clashing personalities. Although many figures are responsible for the psychoanalytic movement, we must limit our attention to Sigmund Freud, who began the movement, and Erik Erikson, who subsequently constructed a life-span view of development. Both proposed that personality development proceeds through a series of stages. In each stage, the child copes with certain conflicts stimulated, to a great extent, by biological changes in development. Freud's theory, although developed prior to Piaget's theory, is presented here after the Piagetian chapter because Freud's stage theory can be more easily understood after the fuller discussion of issues about stages in the Piagetian and neo-Piagetian tradition. This chapter proceeds in the following order for both parts of this chapter: biography, general orientation, description of stages of development, contemporary developmental research, mechanisms of change, the theory's stand on critical issues, applications, and an evaluation.

Freud

BIOGRAPHICAL SKETCH

Much of the material in this section comes from Ernest Jones's three-volume biography (1953, 1955, 1957). Sigmund Freud was born in Freiberg, Moravia, in 1856. When he was 4, his family moved to Vienna, where he lived for nearly 80 years. He was the eldest of eight children born to a wool merchant and his wife. Freud believed that he was a favored child and that great things were expected of him. As he expressed it, "A man who has been the indisputable favorite of his mother keeps for life the feeling of a conqueror, that confidence of success that often induces real success" (quoted in Jones, 1961, p. 6). He had a voracious appetite for books on history and philosophy, as did Piaget. He and a friend taught themselves Spanish so that they could read

Don Quixote in the original. In secondary school, he read an essay by Goethe on nature that awakened an interest in science. He entered medical school with the expectation that he would devote his life to scientific research. In retrospect, it is interesting, given the eventual focus of his theory, that his first major research project was on the structure of the testes in eels.

The goal of becoming a research scientist had to be set aside when his poor economic situation and the barriers against advancement for a Jew in academia forced him to enter private practice. Freud's longstanding interest in neurology led him naturally into the treatment of nervous disorders. At the time, this branch of medicine was at a very primitive level, and its practitioners could give little help for the mentally ill. Patients typically received hydrotherapy (various types of baths) and electrotherapy (mild electric currents passed through the body).

Freud was fascinated with hysteria, a disorder characterized by such symptoms as paralysis, numbness, squinting, and tremors. His interest in a possible new treatment, hypnosis, was aroused by his contact with the French neurologist Jean Charcot and the Viennese physician Josef Breuer. The fact that Charcot could produce symptoms of hysteria in people by means of hypnotic suggestion was evidence that the malady had a psychological basis. As Freud began to use hypnosis with his patients, he was impressed that they could recall important incidents and feelings while under hypnosis that were otherwise inaccessible. Despite the general belief among neurologists that hypnotism was both fraudulent and dangerous, Freud enthusiastically experimented with this technique: "There was something positively seductive in working with hypnotism. For the first time there was a sense of having overcome one's helplessness; and it was highly flattering to enjoy the reputation of being a miracle-worker" [1925a (1959, p. 17)].

Freud was also influenced by Breuer's discovery that symptoms of hysteria could be alleviated simply by having his patients talk about (and "relive") their emotion-laden experiences from early life. It eventually became clear that hypnosis was often not even necessary in order to remove hysterical symptoms. With a sense of excitement, Freud experimented with what Breuer called the "talking cure." In a letter to his friend Wilhelm Fliess in 1895, he described how psychology possessed him: "A man like myself cannot live without a hobbyhorse, without a dominating passion: in fact, without a tyrant, to use Schiller's expression, and that is what it has become. For in its service I know no moderation. It is psychology . . ." (quoted in Jones, 1961, p. 226)

Freud's study of his patients' dreams and childhood memories led to his first major publication, *The Interpretation of Dreams*, in 1900. Although this book was ignored by medical and scientific circles, as well as the general public, Freud was not discouraged. A succession of fascinating books appeared in the following years. Although he worked almost completely in isolation for years, he eventually began to attract a small following.

Carl Jung and Alfred Adler, in particular, strengthened the new psychoanalytic movement even while the European medical establishment spurned it. A turning point came in 1909, when the eminent American psychologist G. Stanley Hall invited Freud to speak in the United States. As Freud described it, "In Europe I felt as though I were despised; but over there I found myself received by the foremost men as an equal" [1925a (1959, p. 52)]. Freud began to achieve international recognition, especially in the years following World War I. Psychoanalysis began to influence not only psychiatry and the social sciences but also fields such as literature, art, ethics, and education. "Subconscious" and "ego" became household words. It should be noted that much of the reaction was far from positive. Many people were shocked at the claim that children have a sexual nature. The attacks on psychoanalytic theory continued throughout Freud's lifetime.

Freud continued to develop his theory over the years. In fact, he made some basic changes in his views when he was in his seventies. By the end of his life, his psychoanalytic writings filled 23 volumes. In his last years, he worked while in considerable pain from cancer of the jaw. When the Nazis took over Austria in 1937, he was forced to flee to England. He died in 1939 in London.

Freud's notion that behavior and development are directed by powerful unconscious drives struck twentieth-century thought with force. Concepts such as infantile sexuality, the anal personality, and the teeming desires of the unconscious jarred a Victorian society that covered piano legs to hide their nakedness. Freud's view of the human potential for destructive behavior could not be so easily dismissed after two world wars and the political crimes of the times. It was a theory whose time had come.

Regardless of one's judgment about the scientific merit of the theory, it is, without doubt, the most widely influential psychological theory in history. Its impression on society may equal that of Marx and Darwin. The theory's influence reaches into nearly every area of twentieth-century thought. Freud described unconscious motivation in the areas of anthropology (*Totem and Taboo*, 1913), art ("The Moses of Michelangelo," 1914), religion (*The Future of an Illusion*, 1927), literature ("Dostoevsky and Parricide," 1928), sociology (*Civilization and Its Discontents*, 1930), and history (*Why War?* 1933b). The general public became familiar with many of his ideas. Slips of the tongue became more embarrassing than before, and millions of people began to take their dreams seriously. The belief that weaning and toilet training should not be sudden and harsh is often attributed to Freud's ideas.

Within psychology and psychiatry, the influence of Freud's work on emotional and nonrational aspects of personality has also been far-reaching. He left his mark on every area from social psychology to sensory processes, from adult therapy to child therapy. The diversity of viewpoints among psychoanalysts today can be traced to the various followers of Freud who further developed his theory and, in some cases, broke away from Freud. Some of the best-known neo-Freudians were Carl Jung, Otto Rank, Alfred Adler, Karen Horney, Harry Stack Sullivan, Erik Erikson, Melanie Klein, Anna Freud, Heinz Hartmann, and David Rapaport.

Since Freud's stage theory is thoroughly developmental, it is not surprising that it has deeply influenced developmental psychology. Salient psychoanalytic developmental work in the 1940s and 1950s included Erikson's stage theory of psychosocial development; direct observations of children by Anna Freud, Ernst Kris, Sybill Escalona, and Rent Spitz; John Whiting and Irvin Child's cross-cultural work; and John Bowlby's early studies on infant social attachment. Psychoanalytic theory also touched the early work of social learning theorists, especially Robert Sears, Neal Miller, and John Dollard, who began to incorporate psychoanalytic content. For instance, a concern with unconscious motivation is very clear in Sears's work on defense mechanisms, dependency, identification, and parent–child relations. Prominent contemporary psychoanalytic theorists include Otto Kernberg, Heinz Kohut, Stephen Mitchell, and Charles Brenner.

Freud's theory remains a vital force within child clinical psychology, child psychiatry, and counseling psychology. However, an anti-Freudian attitude has pervaded developmental experimental psychology for many years, in part because his theory is not based on empirical research. In the major journals of contemporary developmental research, one rarely finds "tests" of the theory or references to psychoanalytic work.

GENERAL ORIENTATION TO THE THEORY

Accounts of Freud's theory are somewhat contradictory, because various sources give differing accounts. The problem in part is that Freud revised his ideas over the years. Fortunately, despite changes in the details of the system, there is constancy in the general approach. Six general characteristics emerge: a dynamic approach, a structural approach, a topographic approach, a developmental stage approach, a normal–abnormal continuum, and the psychoanalytic methods. We look at each of these characteristics and, when useful for clarifying the theory, compare them with those of Piaget's theory.

Dynamic Approach

Freud described his theory as "a sort of economics of nervous energy" (quoted in Jones, 1953, p. 345). This nervous energy is variously termed *psychic energy, drive energy, libido*, and *tension*. In an analogy to energy in the field of physics, nervous energy builds up and can be distributed, tied to certain mental images, transformed, and discharged. Just as mechanical, electrical, or thermal energy performs physical work, so does psychic energy perform psychological work.

In the same way that physical energy is transformed but not destroyed, psychological energy is transformed into anxiety; displaced into a physical structure that causes a symptom, such as paralysis; transformed into a thought, such as an obsession; and so on. The *pleasure principle* states that whenever possible, energy is discharged without delay. The organism strives toward the immediate, direct reduction of tension, which reduces pain and produces pleasure. Hunger leads to eating; the need to suck leads to sucking one's thumb. In the *reality principle*, small amounts of energy are discharged, but only after a delay and only after following an indirect route. The mental apparatus scans reality and evaluates various possible courses of action before allowing energy to be discharged. For example, an angry child may tell his friend he is angry with him rather than hit him and risk punishment.

Where does this psychological energy come from? The human body has certain instincts (biological drives) that make demands on the mind. Freud posited two basic instincts—*Eros* (sex, self-preservation, love, life forces, striving toward unity) and the *destructive instinct* (aggression, undoing connections, the death instinct, hate). Freud assigned the term *libido* to the available energy of Eros. There is no analogous term for the energy of a destructive instinct. His interest in the destructive instinct came late in life and is attributed to his horror at the atrocities of World War I and the anti-Semitic feelings of his times. In Freud's words, "The aim of all life is death" [1920 (1955, p. 38)].

Instincts involve excitation in some region of the body, particularly the oral, anal, and genital areas for the sex drive. The change in the site of excitation underlies the movement from stage to stage, as we shall see later. This internal excitation stimulates the mind and creates a "need." Thus, psychic energy is derived from biological energy. Freud maintained that "mind" and "body" have a constant interplay: an instinct is "a concept on the frontier between the mental and the somatic" [1915 (1957, p. 121)].

The *aim* of the sex drive, or of any instinct, is to remove this bodily need, discharge tension, and experience pleasure. This ultimate goal is achieved through such subordinate goals as finding and investing energy in sexual objects, either a real person or object or a representation of a person or object. Libido becomes attached or, in Freud's terminology, "cathected" to an object. Infants cathect to their mother and other objects that satisfy their needs.

Diverse human behaviors can ultimately be traced to the two general instincts, with their various subinstincts. Freud would claim that writing a book, jogging, watching television, and making a bookcase have their origins deep in human needs. The route between the instinct and the behavior may be very indirect because of the mobility of the instincts. Psychic energy is a general energy source that can be likened to an electricity supply, which can be used to toast bread, shave, bake, and so forth (Hall, 1954, p. 84). Drives can be satisfied either fully or in a partial and roundabout way. Freud believed that da Vinci's interest in painting Madonnas was a way of partially satisfying his desire for his mother, from whom he had been separated early in life. One object can substitute for another object, as when an adult's oral needs are satisfied by playing a trumpet. In some cases, a culturally or morally "higher" goal object is substituted for the truly desired object. This is labeled *sublimation*. An angry person might sublimate his desire to attack other people by painting violent scenes. Another common type of object substitution is *compensation*, in which people make up for their failure in one area by applying themselves in another area. A 5-foot, 6-inch basketball player may eventually become a sports announcer.

Structural Approach

The previous section creates the image of a human hydraulic system with powerful forces surging through the body and the mind. We now look at the psychological structures through which these forces flow. These structures mediate between the drives and behavior; drives do not lead directly to behavior. There is, then, an architecture of the mind. Mental processes take place within the structures, between the structures, and by means of the structures. There are three major structures: the id, ego, and superego. Roughly speaking, the *id* is the seat of biologically based drives, the *ego* is the mechanism for adapting to reality, and the *superego* is analogous to the conscience. We examine each "province of the mind" [Freud, 1933a (1964, p. 72)] in turn and then portray their overall organization.

Id ▪ As the novelist Peter De Vries humorously expresses it in *Forever Panting*, "'Id' isn't just another big word." The id is the seat of innate desires and is the main source of psychic energy. It is the "dark, inaccessible part of our personality . . . a chaos, a cauldron full of seething excitations" [Freud, 1933a (1964, p. 73)]. The id wants immediate satisfaction, in accordance with the pleasure principle described earlier. The energy of the id is invested either in action on an object that would satisfy an instinct or in images of an object that would give partial satisfaction. For example, infants may satisfy their oral-hunger drive directly by sucking a nipple and receiving milk or partially and indirectly by imagining a bottle of milk. This hallucinatory wish fulfillment is called *primary-process thought*. The id's energy is so mobile that it is easily discharged or transferred from object to object or image to image.

In contrast to young infants, older infants, children, and adults have an ego and a superego in addition to an id. The id, however, continues to operate throughout life, especially in our nighttime dreams, daydreams, imagination, and impulsive, selfish, and pleasure-loving behavior. The id has been called the "spoiled child of the personality" (Hall, 1954, p. 27).

Much of Freud's knowledge about the id came from his study of dreams. The desires of the id appear in dreams in either an obvious or a disguised fashion. One does not need psychoanalytic training to interpret a hungry person's dream about a chocolate cake. However, some urges are so threatening that they must be rendered less obvious. According to Freud, clothes and uniforms sometimes represent nakedness; water can stand for birth; a journey can mean death.

Ego ▪ In the beginning, there is id. The id, armed with primary-process thought (hallucinatory wish fulfillment), makes its demands. However, babies soon discover that thinking something does not make it so. The image of the mother and milk and the memory of warmth do not quiet the pangs of hunger. They learn that there is a difference between images and reality, between the self and the outer world.

The id's inability to always produce the desired object leads to the development of the ego. (However, near the end of his life, Freud altered his theory and began referring to an early, undifferentiated ego–id.) The ego, the mind's avenue to the real world, is developed because it is needed for physical and psychological survival. It aids in survival because it possesses *secondary-process thought*. Secondary-process thought is rational and includes intellectual activities such as perception, logical thought, problem solving, and memory. It is more organized, integrated, and logical than primary-process thought, in which contradictions abound. Most of the intellectual abilities studied by Piaget would fall into Freud's ego domain. The ego is the director who must make the tough, high-level decisions. It evaluates the present situation, recalls relevant decisions and events in the past, weighs various factors in the present and future, and predicts the consequences of various actions. The ego's decisions are aided by feelings of anxiety, which signal that certain actions would be threatening. Above all, the ego's decision making involves the *delay* of energy discharge, the reality principle mentioned earlier. Freud described the thinking of the ego as "an experimental action carried out with small amounts of energy, in the same way as a general shifts small figures about on a map before setting his large bodies of troops in motion" [1933a (1964, p. 89)].

The small quantities of energy at the disposal of the ego come from the id. As the ego acquires more and more energy and gains experience using secondary-process thought during development, it becomes stronger and more differentiated. Of course, the ego, with its secondary-process thought, does not replace the primary-process thought of the id. Rather, it simply adds another level to thought. Gratification can be achieved either by finding appropriate real objects in the environment after a delay or by hallucinating and dreaming. Throughout life, we use a mixture of primary- and secondary-process thought. However, as development proceeds, the secondary-process aspects of thought become more dominant.

The ego serves "three tyrannical masters": id, superego, and external world [Freud, 1933a (1964, p. 77)]. Freud described the ego's position in an analogy:

> The ego's relation to the id might be compared with that of a rider to his horse. The horse supplies the locomotive energy, while the rider has the privilege of deciding on the goal and of guiding the powerful animal's movement. But only too often there arises between the ego and the id the not precisely ideal situation of the rider being obliged to guide the horse along the path by which it itself wants to go.
>
> [1933a (1964, p. 77)]

The ego mediates between the id and the external world: "Thus the ego is fighting on two fronts: it has to defend its existence against an external world which threatens it with annihilation as well as against an internal world that makes excessive demands" [Freud, 1940 (1964, p. 200)].

These constant threats and dangers from the id and the environment arouse anxiety. When possible, the ego tackles the problem in a realistic way, using its problem-solving skills. However, when the anxiety is so strong that it threatens to engulf the ego, *defense mechanisms* come into play. They control and thereby alleviate anxiety by distorting reality in some way. Although defense mechanisms allow only partial satisfaction of the drives, for the organism in a state of tension some satisfaction is better than none at all. Freud and his daughter, Anna Freud, identified five main defense mechanisms: repression (denying or forgetting the danger), reaction formation (acting the opposite from the way one feels), projection (attributing one's unacceptable impulses to others), regression (returning to an earlier form of behavior), and fixation (remaining at the present level).

1 In *repression*, a person prevents a threatening thought from emerging into awareness. The principle seems to be "What we don't know can't hurt us" (Hall, 1954, p. 85). If anxiety-arousing thoughts cannot surface, we do not experience anxiety. A thought may be anxiety-arousing because it threatens a breakdown in self-control or arouses frustration or guilt. To avoid anxiety, we forget to pay a bill that would put a severe strain on the budget and cause worry.

Often a whole constellation of memories must be repressed because recalling neutral memories would elicit associated painful memories.

According to Freud, there is massive repression of memories of childhood sexuality once children reach grade school age. Only with great difficulty could Freud help his adult patients recover these memories.

Freud's ideas about repression developed from his observations in therapy. When a patient reported her thoughts during "free association," she would often stop abruptly and claim that her mind had suddenly gone blank, just at the moment when important memories of the past seemed about to emerge. As Nietzsche remarked, "One's own self is well hidden from oneself: of all mines of treasure one's own is the last to be dug up."

If a person depends too heavily on this defense mechanism, she may develop a repressed personality: withdrawn, inaccessible, nonspontaneous, and rigid. Also, there can be some loss of contact with reality as the person makes serious and frequent mistakes in remembering, speaking, and perceiving or develops symptoms of hysteria. For example, hysterical deafness may prevent a person from hearing something she does not want to hear.

2 In *reaction formation*, the ego masks an unacceptable emotion by focusing on its opposite, often in an exaggerated way. A child's jealousy and hatred for a newborn sibling is experienced as love, extravagantly displayed.

3 *Projection* is the attribution of anxiety-arousing thoughts to people and objects in the external world, rather than to the self. "I want to kill him" is changed to "He wants to kill me."

4 In *regression*, a person reverts to an earlier level of development. If the anxiety of the present is too much to handle, one retreats to simpler times, when there were fewer controls. Thus, people act in childish ways. They fight, play practical jokes, eat too much ice cream, yell obscenities at the referee at a football game, and seek cuddling.

5 In *fixation*, one component of personality development comes to a halt. A portion of the libido remains tied to an earlier period of development and does not allow the child to proceed fully to the next stage. Fixation can occur when the present mode of satisfaction, for example, sucking a breast or bottle, is so gratifying that the child does not want to give it up, even under pressures to become weaned. Fixation can also occur when the next step appears to be too frightening or demanding or unsatisfying. The initiation of toilet training, if too

harsh, may cause the toddler to remain partially in the oral stage rather than progress through the anal stage. Fixation is tied to regression in that a person is more likely to regress in the face of a barrier if there has been fixation at an earlier point in development.

Other psychological processes discussed elsewhere in the chapter are sometimes considered defense mechanisms. These include sublimation of an unacceptable desire to a more socially accepted activity, identification with the aggressor (usually a boy's father), and displacement of drives.

Defense mechanisms are a necessary evil. We need them to deal with high anxiety, but at the cost of "wasting" our energy when it could be put to better use in ego development, for example, for creative thought or the development of problem-solving skills. Furthermore, if too much energy is tied up in the defense mechanisms, personality may not develop normally because the person distorts reality and deceives himself. This situation makes subsequent adjustments to reality even more difficult.

Superego ▪ The superego is the last to develop. It arises when children resolve their Oedipus complex and develop identification with their parents. That story is told in the section on stages.

The superego is composed of two parts: the conscience and the ego ideal. In general, the conscience is negative, and the ego ideal is positive. The *conscience* is composed of the parents' prohibitions, their "Thou shalt nots." Just as the parent has punished the child for his transgressions, so does the conscience punish the person with feelings of guilt, the "accidental" cutting of one's finger, or intentionally self-destructive behavior. Curiously, the superego often becomes even more severe than the parents were.

The term *ego ideal* refers to standards of conduct toward which the child strives. Just as the child has been rewarded for certain behavior by the parents, she is rewarded by the ego ideal with feelings of self-esteem and pride. These are echoes of early years when a parent said "Good girl!" to the young child.

The superego opposes both the id and the ego. It rewards, punishes, and makes demands. It tries to do away with both the pleasure principle and the reality principle. The superego watches over not only behavior but also the thoughts of the ego. Thinking is as bad as doing, from the superego's point of view. As in the case of the id, the superego does not distinguish between the subjective and the real.

The superego is society's way of achieving order. Unrestrained sexual and aggressive behavior would destroy the always tenuous social

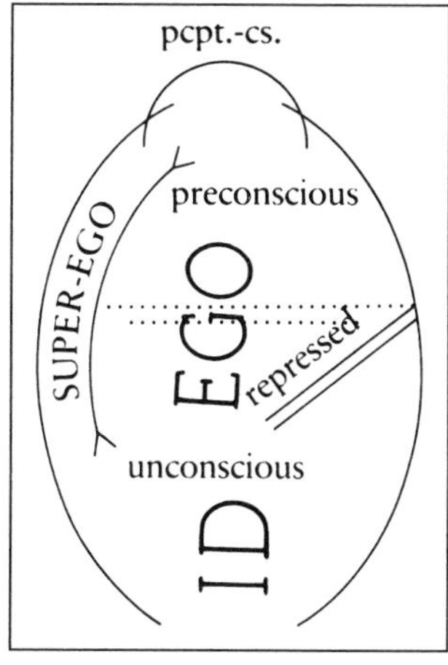

Figure 2.1

In Freud's sketch of the structure and topography of the mind, which also depicts the process of repression, the label "pcpt.-cs." refers to the perceptual-conscious, usually termed the conscious.

SOURCE: Reproduced from *New Introductory Lectures on Psycho-Analysis*, by Sigmund Freud, translated and edited by James Strachey, with the permission of Hogarth Press and W. W. Norton & Company, Inc. Copyright ©1965, 1964 by James Strachey.

structure. Freud noted that if the ego represents the "power of the present" and the id represents the "organic past," then the superego represents the "cultural past" [1940 (1964, p. 206)].

Structural Relationships ▪ We have dissected the personality into id, ego, and superego. However, personality is an organized whole—a unique constellation of forces and structures. Freud sketched out the relationship among the mental "areas," as seen in Figure 2.1. He cautioned that we should not regard the id, ego, and superego as sharply defined areas and certainly not as locations in the brain. Rather, they are "areas of color melting into one another as they are presented by modern artists" [Freud, 1933a (1964, p. 79)]. The superego, for example, blends into the id and, in fact, is intimately related to the id. This close relationship is most clearly seen in the Oedipus complex, discussed later, in which strong urges in the id necessitate the development of the superego and are subsequently controlled by the superego. Or in another instance, the id and superego may join forces in attacking supposedly "immoral" persons as in witch-burning or the cruelty of the Inquisition (Hall, 1954, p. 48).

These structures contain a closed energy system, in which a certain amount of energy is distributed to the three parts. A gain in energy in one part strengthens that part but at the same time weakens the other parts. Under ordinary circumstances, the three systems work together as a team in relative harmony rather than war against each other.

The ego is central in this structural relationship. It is brought into all conflicts between the id and the superego because each is trying to use the ego to meet its own needs. The ego must both obey and control the id, superego, and external reality. It survives by compromising. If the id says "yes" and the superego says "no," then the ego says "wait" (Hall, 1954, p. 47). Freud summed up this relationship as follows:

> Thus the ego, driven by the id, confined by the super-ego, repulsed by reality, struggles to master its economic task of bringing about harmony

> among the forces and influences working in and upon it; and we can understand how it is that so often we cannot suppress a cry: "Life is not easy!"
>
> [1933a (1964, p. 78)]

Yet Freud remained optimistic about human reason:

> The voice of the intellect is a soft one, but it does not rest till it has gained a hearing. Finally, after a countless succession of rebuffs, it succeeds. This is one of the few points on which one may be optimistic about the future of mankind, but it is in itself a point of no small importance.
>
> [1927 (1961, p. 53)]

Topographic Approach

Everyone is a moon and has a dark side which he never shows to anybody.

—MARK TWAIN

Freud's geography (or topography) of the mind also is depicted in Figure 2.1. The map of the mind displays three regions: the unconscious, preconscious, and conscious. The unconscious is largely unknown territory; the preconscious and, especially, the conscious have familiar terrains.

1 The *unconscious* consists primarily of thoughts and feelings that are repressed and therefore unknown. This material is incapable of breaking into consciousness without certain changes or interventions, such as an increase in the drive, a weakening of ego defenses, or the guidance of a therapist.

2 The *preconscious* is capable of becoming conscious because it is not actively barred from consciousness. It is a great deal closer to the conscious than is the unconscious. Preconscious thought becomes conscious by forming mental images or linking up with language.

3 The *conscious* (or perceptual conscious) is synonymous with what a person is aware of at the moment. It is a "highly fugitive state" [Freud, 1940 (1964, p. 159)] because thoughts can rapidly slip back and forth between the preconscious and the conscious. Since energy is required for a thought to enter into consciousness, only a few thoughts can be conscious at any one time.

Freud used a metaphor to describe the relationship between the unconscious and the preconscious and conscious:

> Let us therefore compare the system of the unconscious to a large entrance hall, in which the mental impulses jostle one another like separate individuals. Adjoining this entrance hall there is a second, narrower, room—a kind of drawing-room—in which consciousness, too, resides. But on the threshold between these two rooms a watchman performs his function: he examines the different mental impulses, acts as a censor, and will not admit them into the drawing-room if they displease him.
>
> [1917 (1963, p. 295)]

Returning to Freud's sketch, we see how the id, ego, and superego (structures) are related to the unconscious, preconscious, and conscious (topography). All the id resides in the unconscious. The unconscious id is a large area, and in fact Freud corrected his drawing by noting that the space taken up by the unconscious id should have been much greater than that of the ego or the preconscious. If the mind is like an iceberg, then the conscious is only the exposed tip of the iceberg; most of the iceberg (the unconscious) remains hidden. Both the ego and the superego span the three layers. For example, the ego is unaware of the action of its defense mechanisms.

Developmental changes also occur in the relative size of the unconscious, preconscious, and conscious. The infant's mind is almost completely unconscious. With increasing age, the preconscious and conscious occupy more and more of the mental territory. Even among adults, however, the unconscious is the largest area.

Although Freud described the unconscious, preconscious, and conscious as though they were separate entities, he constantly noted that no such separation exists. Rather, he was simply abstracting three aspects of mental functioning. Reading obituaries in the newspaper can be traced to both unconscious (fear of death) and conscious (keeping track of elderly friends) motivations.

Freud placed great importance on the role of the unconscious: "For the property of being conscious or not is in the last resort our one beacon-light in the darkness of depth-psychology" [1923 (1961, p. 18)]. The notion that there is a vast unconscious that controls behavior emerged from Freud's early psychoanalytic sessions with his patients. Patients had sexual fantasies or impulses of which they were unaware but which led to certain inexplicable behavior. For example, a patient with a healthy visual system was unable to see because seeing was too painful; seeing activated painful memories in the unconscious. Additional evidence for the existence of an unconscious came from posthypnotic suggestion, in which patients perform some action that was suggested to them while under hypnosis, or from slips of the tongue, accidents that were not really accidental, selective forgetting (as when someone forgets a dental appointment), and dreams.

Stage Approach

Freud made two bold claims about human development. One is that the first few years of life are the most important years for the formation of personality. The other claim is that this development involves psychosexual stages.

The notion that early experience is crucial seems obvious and noncontroversial to the modern student of development. This idea, however, had not really been taken seriously until Freud systematically developed it. According to Freud, a behavior can be understood only if one knows how it developed in the person's early history. Both normal behavior and abnormal behavior have their roots in the early years, when the basic structure of the personality is laid down. The early interactions between children's drives and their social environment set the pattern for later learning, social adjustment, and coping with anxiety.

It is interesting that a therapist who studied and treated adults would develop a theory of child development. Early in his work, Freud discovered that attempts to trace the cause of a disturbed personality usually led to traumatic, unresolved sexual experiences of childhood. The distant past was very much alive in his patients' current lives in dreams, anxiety from repressed childhood desires, and defense mechanisms acquired in childhood. From information revealed in sessions with patients, Freud was able to reconstruct the sequence of stages of childhood.

Freud, like Piaget, focused on stages. We look at their general nature here and leave a fuller description for later. Four distinct stages and a period of latency mark developmental time. Each stage is defined in terms of the part of the body around which drives are centered. The eye of the storm shifts from the oral to the anal to the phallic area during the first 5 years. Then a period of latency in middle childhood is followed by the genital stage of adolescence. Each stage presents new needs that must be handled by the mental structures. The way in which these needs are met (or not met) determines not only how sexual satisfaction is achieved but also how children relate to other people and how they feel about themselves. Children develop characteristic attitudes, defenses, and fantasies. Unresolved conflicts in any stage may haunt people throughout their lifetime.

Because the movement from stage to stage is biologically determined, it occurs whether or not there is unfinished business in the stage that is ending. This notion of stage development is very different from Piaget's, in which one stage must be essentially completed before the next stage may begin. The two theories, however, coincide in their claim that the stages follow an invariant order. For Freud, the invariant order comes almost entirely from physical maturation. For Piaget, it comes not only from physical maturation but also from physical and social experiences and innate ways of functioning mentally.

The two theories differ in the relationship between the stages. In Freud's theory, each stage is characterized by one dominant trait (for example, anal concerns) but does not form a tightly knit, structured whole, as does a stage in Piaget's theory. Freud's stages form layers, with each stage only loosely integrated into the next. The reorganization of previous knowledge that characterizes each of Piaget's stages is much less apparent in Freud's stages. Furthermore, one stage does not contain the germ of the next, as it does in Piaget's theory. The oral stage does not *become* the anal stage, in the way that concrete operations become (are transformed into) formal operations.

Although a stage builds upon and is dominant over the previous stage, it does not completely replace that stage, according to Freud. No stage is ever given up entirely. Freud offered a simile of an army that advances into new territory but leaves forces en route to send on supplies or provide a place to retreat if difficulties arise. In the same way, a child can escape unbearably tense experiences by regressing to earlier behavior, such as sucking the thumb or hallucinating the desired object.

We can see many remnants of earlier stages in later stages. Earlier modes of satisfaction may be retained, as when thumb sucking persists throughout the preschool years. Or these earlier modes of gratification may be integrated into later sexual gratification, as when kissing becomes a subordinate part of adult sexuality. Anal concerns may still be present, but they are suppressed, sublimated, and displaced until they bear little resemblance to their earlier form (for example, giving gifts in adulthood). There is a partial integration in the last stage, the genital, when the component instincts (oral, anal, and phallic) merge to form adult genital sexuality.

Normal–Abnormal Continuum

Psychologists often study the unusual or exotic in order to understand the usual or mundane. The unusual may include the mentally ill, the developmentally delayed, another culture, or impoverished environments. And Freud's profession, medicine, studies diseased or malfunctioning organisms in order to understand normal organisms.

Freud's first evidence about the normal functioning of the unconscious arose from his early study of hysteria. For example, certain patients suffered from delusions of being observed by unknown persons who distrusted them and expected them to transgress and be punished. This abnormal behavior revealed the workings of the conscience in normal people. The only difference was that the internal was projected to the external in abnormal cases. Freud explains the value of studying abnormal behavior:

> Pathology, by making things larger and coarser, can draw our attention to normal conditions which would otherwise have escaped us. Where it points to a breach or a rent, there may normally be an articulation present. If we throw a crystal to the floor, it breaks; but not into haphazard pieces. It comes apart along its lines of cleavage into fragments whose boundaries, though they were invisible, were predetermined by the crystal's structure. Mental patients are split and broken structures of this same kind. . . . They have turned away from external reality, but for that very reason they know more about internal, psychical reality and can reveal a number of things to us that would otherwise be inaccessible to us.
>
> [1933a (1964, pp. 58–59)]

So far, we have followed Freud's argument that his study of the abnormal heightens our understanding of the normal. Freud, however, makes a further claim. He sees no sharp cleavage between the abnormal and the normal. Abnormal and normal personalities obey the same principles and merely occupy different positions along a continuum ranging from the very disturbed to the very healthy. In an abnormal personality, psychological processes are exaggerated or distorted. A melancholic patient has an overly strong superego. A sadistic killer has a strong, uncontrolled aggressive drive. An amnesiac must repress all of a painful past. Yet every normal personality has traces of melancholia, sadism, and unaccountable forgetting, as described in the appropriately titled *The Psychopathology of Everyday Life* [Freud, 1901 (1960)]. When reality becomes too painful or impulses of the id intensify, the ego's frantic attempts to keep in touch with reality or fortify the barriers against the id or superego ultimately fail. Neurotic symptoms or even a psychosis results. In Freud's words, "The threatened ego throws itself into the arms of the unconscious instinctual forces in a desperate revolt" [1933a (1964, p. 16)].

Methodology

It might seem odd that Freud did not study children directly as he built a theory of development. His rationale was that our childhoods remain with us always, in that our adult personalities are residues of our childhoods. In addition, his patients happened to be adults rather than children. For these reasons, he devoted his efforts to developing methods for eliciting information about childhood from adults. Freud also conducted a self-analysis, beginning in 1897 and continuing throughout his life. He reserved the last half hour of each day for this purpose. This increased his confidence, if not that of the scientific community, in his theory of personality.

Freud's methods of free association, dream analysis, and transference at first shocked the psychiatric profession and the public but eventually won the acceptance of many therapists. The method of *free association* requires that patients verbally report their ongoing stream of thought. During the free-association sessions, the patient would relax, usually on the famous couch, in a quiet room. Freud sat near the patient's head but out of sight. He instructed his patients to report every thought, regardless of how trivial it seemed, omitting or censoring nothing. This relaxed, accepting state promoted the ego's relaxation of control over unconscious thoughts. Repressed thoughts might then emerge, though often in disguise. Occasionally, if the patient fell silent, Freud would ask a question or even "lay on hands"—put his hand on the patient's forehead—and tell him that new memories would come!

The theoretical rationale for the free-association technique is as follows: Freud believed that every psychological event has a meaning. That is, a thought or feeling is caused; it does not occur randomly. If one thought typically leads to another, there is a reason for it. If the patient talks about her deceased father and then abruptly changes the subject to a trip she is thinking about taking, Freud may infer that she is troubled by her father's death. (Freud found that a journey is often a symbol for death.) The patient may not be aware of the anxious feelings. In this way he abstracted common themes underlying seemingly unrelated thoughts or behaviors. More generally, he tried to describe the organization of the patient's mind. The central concepts of Freud's theory arose from the free-association sessions.

A second method is *dream analysis*. If all thoughts are causally related and significant, then psychologists cannot ignore dreams. In fact, Freud concluded that more unconscious material may emerge when one is asleep than when awake. During dreams, the usual psychological controls are "sleeping" and allow disturbing thoughts to be expressed and wishes to be fulfilled. These thoughts, however, are often disguised until they are unmasked during psychoanalysis. For example, kings and queens might represent parents, little animals or vermin might stand for siblings, and snakes and trunks might represent sex organs [Freud, 1916 (1963, pp. 153–157)].

The method of *transference* involves a particular type of relationship that develops between the patient and the analyst during therapy. In the analyst the patient sees some important figure from childhood, such as a parent. He consequently transfers to the analyst feelings and reactions that he felt toward this person. Transference helps the analyst discover the nature of patients' relationships with their parents in childhood. Certain patterns of social interaction are repeated throughout life in various settings, including the therapist's office.

In summary, Freud's methodology was to listen to troubled adults talk. He did not perform controlled experiments (though later researchers did) and, unlike Piaget, did not observe children's behavior in natural situations. Instead, he studied single individuals in depth, sometimes spending hundreds of hours with a single patient. As if putting together a jigsaw puzzle, he put together pieces of information from patients' free associations, dreams, expressions of emotion, use of defense mechanisms, slips of the tongue, and so on:

> He that has eyes to see and ears to hear may convince himself that no mortal can keep a secret. If his lips are silent, he chatters with his finger tips; betrayal oozes out of him at every pore. And thus the task of making conscious the most hidden recesses of the mind is one which it is quite possible to accomplish.
>
> [Freud, 1905a (1953, pp. 77–78)]

Freud organized this information into a coherent picture in his case studies. Several long case studies were published and became well known. For example, the "Rat Man" [1909b (1955)] had the obsession that his father and girlfriend would be punished with hungry rats fastened to their buttocks. The "Wolf Man" [1918 (1955)] reacted to viewing the "primal scene" (sexual intercourse between his parents) by dreaming about wolves (see the dream report at the beginning of this chapter, page 105).

DESCRIPTION OF THE STAGES

Oral Stage (Roughly Birth to 1 Year)

During infancy the mouth rules. Oral experiences introduce the baby to both the pleasure and the pain of the world. Pleasure flows from the satisfaction of the oral drives. Sucking, chewing, eating, and biting give sexual gratification by relieving uncomfortable sexual excitations. The oral activities cause pleasant sensual feelings in the lips, tongue, and membranes of the mouth. These pleasant feelings need not be linked with the satisfaction of hunger because the oral activities themselves are satisfying. The outcome of all of this, in Freudian terminology, is that libidinal energy is cathected (invested) in the oral erogenous zone. The salient social and nonsocial experiences in the oral stage center around oral concerns.

In addition to experiencing oral pleasure, the infant meets pain from frustration and anxiety. Sexual tensions are pleasant if they are satisfied but painful if they are not and continue to intensify. A preferred object, such as a nipple, may not be present at the moment the infant wants it. She must wait, a situation that she finds frustrating and anxiety-arousing. She may lapse into hallucinatory wish fulfillment as she imagines the desired nipple. Or she may suck her fingers, a blanket, or a soft toy. Still, satisfaction is not complete. Other frustrations come when parents demand that the nighttime feeding be given up, that certain objects not be chewed because they are unsanitary or unsafe, and, especially, that the breast or bottle be given up for the cup. The cultural demands of one's society are expressed through the parents. Parents teach the infant how to satisfy her drives in ways that are acceptable to the society. Conflict is inevitable. In small ways, the infant discovers that life has its frustrations as well as its pleasures, its "downs" as well as its "ups." She develops ways of coping with these frustrations that will form the basis for her later personality.

As babies seek gratification and valiantly struggle to overcome barriers to this satisfaction, there is an important psychological principle at work: infants are in trouble if they obtain either too little or too much oral gratification. The side effects of too little gratification are obvious: frequent anxiety, continual seeking of oral gratification in later years, and pessimism. The outcome of too much gratification is less obvious. If oral satisfaction is especially gratifying, children may find it difficult to shift their cathexes to new objects, as demanded by a new stage. In this case, fixation can occur. Furthermore, relatively minor anxiety in a later stage may cause regression to highly cathected objects of the oral stage. For example, the initiation of toilet training during the anal stage may cause a child to return quickly to thumb sucking. The goal, then, is to achieve an optimal level of oral gratification so that one need not carry unfulfilled needs into later stages or feel unwilling to move on to a new stage.

The oral stage shows humans' ambivalence toward other people and objects. Both positive and negative emotions arise, often in quick succession. Just as an infant both sucks and bites a nipple, a person may both love and hate another person.

Freud claimed that the way that infants develop during the oral stage forms the foundation for their personality as an adult. This claim is now elaborated. There are at least five oral "modes of functioning": (1) taking in, (2) holding on, (3) biting, (4) spitting out, and (5) closing (Hall, 1954, p. 104). Each of these modes forms a prototype (model, plan, or blueprint) for later personality characteristics. Infants learn certain oral reactions to situations they encounter. These five characteristic reactions lead to certain attitudes, behaviors, and life goals in adulthood:

1. The infant who found pleasure from taking in food becomes an adult who voraciously "takes in," or acquires, knowledge or power and who incorporates or identifies with significant other people.
2. Trying to hold on to the nipple when it is removed may lead to determination and stubbornness.
3. Biting is the prototype for destructiveness, "biting" sarcasm, cynicism, and dominance.
4. Spitting out becomes rejection.
5. Closing the mouth firmly leads to rejection, negativism, or introversion.

Note that these adult behaviors range from the literally oral, as in smoking, nail biting, and eating, to the metaphorically oral, as in being gullible (swallowing anything) and obstinate (holding on).

All these characteristics are found in every personality to some degree. However, some people have a personality structure that is dominated by one or several of these prototypes from the oral modes. In particular, certain traits may dominate because of extremely pleasant or unpleasant experiences in infancy. For example, an infant with an unaffectionate mother may become an adult who seeks to "take in" love symbolically by acquiring power or vast amounts of money.

Perhaps the most momentous event of the oral stage is the formation of attachment to the mother (though fathers' contributions are also addressed today, e.g., Lamb, 1997). Freud proclaimed that the mother's importance is "unique, without parallel, established unalterably for a whole lifetime as the first and strongest love-object and as the prototype of all later love-relations" [1940 (1964, p. 188)]. Because typically it is the mother who satisfies needs such as food, sucking, and warmth, she becomes the primary love object in the infant's life. The infant invests a great deal of libidinal energy in her. The notion of an emotional attachment to the mother is one of Freud's main legacies to the field of developmental psychology, and it inspired Spitz's (1945) work on disturbed mother–infant relationships. After observing that many infants left in foundling homes became depressed and that some even died, Spitz concluded that the lack of mothering contributes to psychological and health problems in infants. Subsequently, Bowlby's (1958) seminal work on attachment led to research by many other investigators in recent years.

Although it may seem counterintuitive, attachment seems to lead to the infant's healthy sense of separateness from his mother. Winnicott (1971) stressed that this gradual differentiation is necessary for a clear sense of self and for normal interpersonal relations later. Before this differentiation, an infant–mother matrix gives little sense of a separation of the self and the world. What Winnicott calls "good-enough mothering" involves a synchrony, or match, between the infant's needs and spontaneous behaviors and the caretaker's activities. Consequently, the infant feels omnipotent because he can magically obtain his every desire. Gradually, the baby's ego develops as he encounters delays in gratification, interacts with various "not-me" objects, and discovers his own resources for interacting with the world. The "holding environment" with the mother provides a secure base for this threatening process of individuation.

Mothers also design "play dialogues," which involve a mutual regulation of the interaction between themselves and their infants. The mother uses the infant's gaze and state of arousal as cues for the timing and intensity of her facial expressions and talking (Stern, 1974, 1985, 1995). Thus, the ideal mother tries to avoid both stimulus overload and boredom. The important outcome is that in the context of a social relationship, the child uses feedback regarding his effect on the mother to construct his self-concept. In other words, the baby expresses and defines his true self by being with his mother and seeing the effects of his spontaneous actions toward the mother.

The individuation process continues during development as children use "security blankets" or other cuddly, comforting objects to ease their separation from their mother. Winnicott (1953) described a series of steps in the differentiation of the self from the mother. The toddler has ambivalent feelings about this growing independence, and in severe cases child psychosis results from a faulty individuation process (Mahler, Pine, & Bergman, 1975). Object loss, particularly the real or perceived loss of the mother, is one of the most significant events that can occur in early life.

Attachment is a vital process for development because it serves as a building block for later social relationships. Furthermore, it facilitates the mother's attempts to socialize her child by using her attention to reward desirable behavior. However, in Freud's somewhat pessimistic theory, all silver linings are covered by clouds. Thus, attachment has its dangers. If the attachment is too strong, the infant may become overly dependent on the mother or anxious about her possible rejection of him. Then, later in life, he may depend on others to do things for him and even do his thinking for him. He may develop a generally passive personality.

Anal Stage (Roughly 1 to 3 Years)

By the end of the oral stage, infants have developed the rough outlines of a personality. This personality consists of attitudes toward themselves and other people, mechanisms for achieving gratification within the demands of reality, and interests in certain activities and objects. As maturation moves infants to the anal stage, the concerns move from the oral area to the anal area. The new needs of this stage set in motion new conflicts between children and the world. The way in which children resolve these new conflicts further differentiates and crystallizes the rudimentary personality structure. The expression of oral needs does not stop, of course. Children simply face a new set of needs and demands that require their immediate attention.

The physiological need to defecate creates tension, which is relieved by defecation. This anal stimulation and subsequent reduction of tension produces pleasure. As in the oral stage, the erogenous zone brings frustration and anxiety as well as pleasure. Society, as represented by the parents, demands toilet training, and thus self-control. The desire for immediate gratification is frustrated. In a small but momentous way, children enter into conflict with authoritarian adult society. Children all over the world face and resolve this conflict in some way. Obviously, many variables affect how much conflict the child feels and how she adapts to the demands placed on her. These variables include the age at which toilet training is begun, how strict or relaxed the training is, and the mother's attitude toward defecation, control, and cleanliness.

If toilet training is particularly harsh or premature or overemphasized by the parents, defecation can become a source of great anxiety for children. This anxiety can generalize to other situations in which an external authority makes demands or children must control their own impulses. Some children react to strict toilet training by defecating at inappropriate times or places, such as the supermarket. The child may become a messy, dirty, and irresponsible adult or, at the other extreme, a compulsively neat, orderly, and obstinate adult. These potential negative outcomes in the anal stage certainly are not comforting to the prospective parent!

As in the oral stage, the goal is to allow enough, but not too much, gratification and to develop enough, but not too much, self-control. If this goal is adequately achieved, the child will have developed a more mature ego because it has been sharpened by its confrontation with reality. The child who survives the anal period relatively unscathed is ready to tackle the third stage, the phallic stage, when it arrives.

Phallic Stage (Roughly 3 to 5 Years)

The child's solution to problems of the oral and anal stages sets a pattern for solving later problems of adjustment. This development is continued in the phallic stage, so named because the possession of the phallus in boys and its absence in girls is a major concern of children, according to Freud. In this stage, pleasures and problems center on the genital area. Stimulation in the genital area brings tensions and, if the tensions are relieved, pleasure. The problem of this stage is that the sexual urge is directed toward the parent of the other sex. In boys, this situation is the well-known *Oedipus complex*. (In Greek mythology, Oedipus killed his father and married his mother.)

Freud emphasized the development of boys more than girls in the phallic stage because he believed that the conflict is more intense for boys. A young boy has sexual desires for his mother and does not want to share her with his father. At the same time, the boy fears that the father, in retaliation, will castrate him. As a way out of this highly anxious situation, the boy represses both his desire for his mother and his hostility toward his father.

The most important outcome of the Oedipus complex is that the boy comes to identify with his father. That is, he develops a strong emotional bond with the father, strives to be like him, and "internalizes" him—his beliefs, values, interests, and attitudes. Identification serves as a basis for much of socialization. In particular, the development of the superego and behavior considered appropriate to one's sex are by-products of this identification. The superego increases the child's self-control and adherence to the parents' morality.

Identification is a reasonable solution to the demands of the ego and id in this stage. The ego is partially satisfied because anxiety is reduced. The id is partially satisfied because the child can "have" the mother vicariously through the father. Again, as the child tries to cope with both his drives and the prohibitions of society, he achieves a compromise solution that advances his psychological maturity.

Freud argued that, in comparison with boys, girls face a similar, but much less intense, conflict during the phallic stage. He proposed that a girl desires her father and experiences penis envy as she realizes that the father has a prized object that she does not have. In Freud's words, "She makes her judgment and her decision in a flash. She has seen it and knows that she is without it and wants to have it" [1925b (1961, p. 252)]. The girl begins to feel that she has been castrated and blames her mother for this loss because she "sent her into the world so insufficiently equipped" [1925b (1961, p. 254)].

As in the case of boys, society does not allow the full expression of the sexual desire for the parent. However, because castration is not possible, the girl feels less threat from the mother than the boy does from the father. Since there is less anxiety and consequently less repression, the girl supposedly has a weaker identification with the mother than does the boy with the father. Freud then concludes that girls have a weaker conscience than do boys, a claim that is not supported by research. Freud's views on the Oedipus complex and penis envy are perhaps the most controversial aspect of his theory and have been rejected by feminist scholars.

In actuality, there is always identification with both parents. Both sexes retain a strong cathexis for the mother because she is the most important object in the two previous psychosexual stages.

In psychoanalytic sessions, Freud found powerful and lasting influences from the phallic stage. For example, women often had disturbing sexual fantasies about their fathers that had never been resolved. More generally, lasting attitudes toward the opposite sex and toward people in authority could be traced to this stage.

With the achievement of identification and the waning of the phallic stage, children's basic personality is set, and conflicts are resolved in characteristic ways. Personality changes, but it does so primarily by further differentiation of the basic structure.

Period of Latency (Roughly 5 Years to the Beginning of Puberty)

After the *Sturm und Drang* of the first three stages, there is a period of relative calm, when sexual drives are repressed and no new area of bodily excitement emerges. Children conveniently "forget" the sexual urges and fantasies of their earlier years. They turn their thoughts to school activities and play primarily with children of the same sex. This is a time for acquiring cognitive skills and assimilating cultural values as children expand their world to include teachers, neighbors, peers, club leaders, and coaches. Sexual energy continues to flow, but it is channeled into social concerns and into defenses against sexuality. Thus, the ego and superego continue to develop.

Genital Stage (Adolescence)

The sexual impulses, which were repressed during the latency stage, reappear in full force as a result of the physiological changes of puberty. These sexual impulses are fused with the earlier ones but are now channeled into adult sexuality. Love becomes more altruistic, with less concern for self-pleasure than in earlier stages. The choice of a partner is influenced by attitudes and social patterns developed in the early years. For example, a woman may choose a "father figure."

Although some internal conflict is inevitable throughout life, a relatively stable state is achieved by most people by the end of the genital stage. Typically, an individual achieves a fairly strong ego structure that makes coping with the reality of the adult world possible. One important achievement is a balance between love and work.

Case Study of "Little Hans"

The above outline of the psychosexual stages cannot capture the vivid, powerful conflicts that operate in an individual child's life. Thus, we turn to one of Freud's most famous case studies, the "Analysis of a Phobia in a Five-Year-Old Boy" [1909a (1955)] or, as it is more commonly known, "Little Hans." This case study was unique because it was Freud's only analysis of a child and because Freud conducted the analysis by mail in a series of letters with the boy's physician-father, who made the observations. Nevertheless, the study was a central force in the formation of one of Freud's most important developmental concepts: identification.

When Hans was 5 years old, anxiety attacks, a phobia, and a fantasy appeared. His phobia, the fear that a horse would bite him or fall down, was so strong that he would not leave his house. He was especially afraid of horses that pulled heavy loads in carts or vans or were white with a black muzzle and wore blinders. In Hans's fantasy, during the night "there was a big giraffe in the room and a crumpled one; and the big one called out because I took the crumpled one away from it. Then it stopped calling out; and then I sat down on top of the crumpled one" [quoted in 1909a (1955, p. 37)].

After sifting through the evidence, Freud identified three themes: an Oedipus conflict, sibling rivalry, and fear of punishment for masturbation. Thus, in the phobia, the horse represented Hans's father, who had a mustache (a black muzzle around the horse's mouth) and eyeglasses (blinders) and was, as Hans remarked, "so white" (like the white horse). Hans feared that the horse would bite (castrate) him because of his sexual longing for his mother and his masturbating. Anxiety about masturbation may have been prompted by his mother's threat that if his masturbation continued, she would send him to the doctor to cut off his "widdler." The fear that a horse might fall down was interpreted as a fear that his father might die or go away, as he sometimes wished when he wanted his mother alone. Significantly, Hans had remarked, "Daddy, don't trot away from me" (p. 45). The giraffe fantasy might be interpreted as a wish for possessing the mother, as Hans imagines he sits on the smaller giraffe (mother), which he has taken from the larger giraffe (father). Note the phallic symbol in the giraffe's long neck.

Hans's feelings of loss of attention and love after the birth of his sister are expressed in the fear that a cart might be upset and spill its contents (his mother might give birth again). In the fantasy, Hans destroys his younger sister when he sits on her (the small giraffe).

Hans eventually identified with his father, thereby resolving his conflicts and recovering from his fear of horses. He continued to develop a healthy personality.

CONTEMPORARY RESEARCH ON RELATIONSHIPS

The most active current Freudian-inspired topic in developmental psychology is early relationships. Freud's emphasis on the early relationship between mother and child, later psychoanalysts' work on object relations, and, particularly, Bowlby's study of infant attachment (see Chapter 5) stimulated much research on infants' attachment to their parents. A "hot" topic in this area currently is *internal working models* (e.g., Bretherton & Munholland, 1999), both in infancy and across the life span. As an infant becomes attached to her caregivers (mothers usually are studied), she constructs a mental representation of each significant adult, of herself, and of their interactions. This representation includes certain assumptions and expectations about whether or not the parent will be responsive to her needs and the self is worthy of love. Such models later lead to expectations about other relationships, for example, with peers, and to the nature of behaviors toward others and to one's self concept. Internal working models serve as "interpretive filters through which new relationships and other experiences are construed, providing implicit decision rules for relating to others that may, for better or worse, help to confirm and perpetuate intuitive expectations about oneself and others" (Thompson, 1998, p. 36). Disturbing relationships can lead to disturbed working models and thus to psychopathology.

Even as adults, people still have these "states of mind" concerning self and others (Main & Goldwyn, 1998) that spill over into romantic relationships (Shaver & Hazan, 1993) and relationships with their children. Secure or insecure relationships are transmitted from one generation to another. Pregnant women's reports of the security or insecurity of their childhood attachment to their mother are related to the types of attachment relations they form with their own infants (Steele, Steele, & Fonagy, 1996). Some mothers respond more sensitively to their infants than do others. A mother's mode of communication then biases her child's development of working models (Bretherton & Munholland, 1999), and the cycle continues. Thus, the infant and preschool years are a critical time for the development of working models that influence social relationships throughout the lifetime. These working models are self-perpetuating because they encourage people to make decisions that are consistent with them. However, they change throughout life to a lesser or greater degree, depending on social experiences. We examine attachment further in Chapter 5.

An influential critique of Freud's analysis of girls' development has focused on gender differences in the development of relationships. Chodorow (1978) proposed that infant boys and girls become attached to their mother but later follow different developmental pathways. Boys are encouraged to separate themselves from their mother and establish autonomy, whereas girls are encouraged to develop further their close relationship with their mother. Consequently, the self-concept of girls, but not boys, is based on a sense of relatedness that directs the child toward interpersonal relationships.

MECHANISMS OF DEVELOPMENT

Both Freud and Piaget have a "trouble" theory of development. Development proceeds because of disturbances to the system (disequilibrium). Development is hard work. Children must continually try to reestablish a state of relative calm. For Freud, emotion-laden thoughts rather than objective information about the physical world cause the disequilibrium. He was more concerned with psychological pain than logical inconsistency, with energy in repose than mental actions in balance. Freud's equilibration system is less open (less responsive to external information) than Piaget's. Piaget spoke of continual assimilation and accommodation as new experiences are encountered. In Freud's system, there is more resistance to change. The system is also closed in that there is a certain amount of energy that can be changed in form but never in amount.

Freud identified several sources of conflict or psychological disruption: physical maturation, external frustrations, internal conflicts, personal inadequacies, and anxiety (Hall, 1954, p. 72):

1. *Maturation* involves changes in the nervous system, motor development, hormonal changes, drives, and so on. Each of these maturational changes brings new possibilities and new problems. As we saw earlier, the drives are particularly important. These maturational forces both propel children into activity as they try to satisfy the drives and move them from stage to stage as the bodily site of pleasure changes.

2. *External frustrations* come from people or events that do not allow the immediate expression of needs. They cause a painful buildup of tension and force children to delay and detour their discharge of energy.
3. *Internal conflicts* arise from the battle among the id, ego, and superego or, more specifically, between drives and forces of repression.
4. *Personal inadequacies* are certain skills, knowledge, expertise, or experience that the person needs but lacks. For example, a child may want to join a peer group but be too shy to enter the group or too clumsy at the game they are playing.
5. Finally, *anxiety* is an unpleasant feeling that occurs when the child anticipates physical or psychological pain. The fear of losing a valued love object is a common example.

All these elements cause an unpleasant state of tension, which the child attempts to rectify in accordance with the pleasure principle and the reality principle. These disturbances, however, merely initiate change. Other mechanisms actually accomplish change. The ego has the primary responsibility for guiding the course of change. Its perceptual and cognitive systems gather relevant information about the current situation, recall useful information from past experiences, and use whatever defense mechanisms are most appropriate. The ego develops methods for keeping distressing sexual thoughts from becoming conscious and placates the id and superego. The ego, then, mediates change from moment to moment. The accumulation of these small changes adds up to long-term change. Over time the ego gathers strength, and personality crystallizes and becomes further differentiated into complex attitudes, interests, and behaviors.

Several developmental "products" also serve as mechanisms of development. The most notable are attachment and identification. As mentioned earlier, both lead to other important acquisitions, such as sex typing and moral development in the case of identification.

POSITION ON DEVELOPMENTAL ISSUES

Human Nature

Hall and Lindzey summarize Freud's view of the person as

> a full-bodied individual living partly in a world of reality and partly in a world of make-believe, beset by conflicts and inner contradictions, yet

> capable of rational thought and action, moved by forces of which he has little knowledge and by aspirations which are beyond his reach, by turn confused and clearheaded, frustrated and satisfied, hopeful and despairing, selfish and altruistic; in short, a complex human being.
>
> (1957, p. 72)

This description of the conflicted, contradictory nature of humans stands in sharp contrast to Piaget's rational human, calmly searching for epistemological truth in a predictable world. Freud is concerned with emotions, particularly their role in forcing the development of personality and thought as children strive to cope with these emotions. By nature, people have strong passions that color their perceptions throughout life.

Although not all interpreters of Freudian theory would agree, Freud's world view seems to fit more comfortably into the organismic than the mechanistic camp. The classification, however, is less clear than for Piaget. For Freud, a psychological being is a loosely organized whole rather than the tightly knit, integrated, equilibrated whole described by Piaget. Freud's holistic approach is clearest in his claim that a given behavior is caused by a structured whole consisting of id, ego, and superego.

Although human beings are passive, in that drives force them into action, they are active, and therefore organismic, in their attempts to cope with these drives and maintain a state of equilibrium. The ego, in its executive role, is the most active agent of the personality. It organizes incoming information from the self (for example, anxiety about some impending event) and the social environment and directs the behavior chosen. Still, for Freud children act because drives force them to act, whereas for Piaget children act because they are inherently active and self-regulated.

■ *Qualitative Versus Quantitative Development*

As in Piaget's theory, the stagelike changes proposed by Freud imply that development involves qualitative change. There is a change in which aspect of the sexual drive is dominant: the oral, anal, phallic, or genital. There is also qualitative change in the psychological organization as new acquisitions, such as defense mechanisms and the superego, appear. Still, there is some quantitative change, as the developing child exhibits a gradual strengthening of the ego, superego, and various defense mechanisms.

Nature Versus Nurture

It is sometimes claimed that Freud has a biologically based theory of development. Although he emphasizes maturation and the biologically based drives, he is, in fact, an interactionist: "The constitutional factor must await experiences before it can make itself felt; the accidental factor must have a constitutional basis in order to come into operation" [Freud, 1905b (1953, p. 239)]. Although drives derive from a person's biological nature, their expression is always modified by the social milieu. The people or objects available and the behaviors allowed by parents or other authorities direct the satisfaction of the drives. The demands of civilization are as real as the demands of the body.

Within the category of nurture, not all experiences make an equal impact. The experiences of the first 5 years of life are especially important. These experiences need not be traumatic in order to be influential. In fact, many intense, violent events of childhood have only a fleeting effect. In Freud's words, "Harsh rulers have short reigns" [1905b (1953, p. 241)]. The recurrent, day-to-day enduring patterns of satisfying one's drives in a socially and psychologically acceptable way have the most influence on later life.

Variations in either the social environment or the physical constitution can cause personality differences among people. Examples of the latter are innate differences from person to person in the strength of the various components of the sex drive (oral, anal, phallic) and in the time at which each psychosexual stage emerges.

What Develops

The essence of development is the emergence of structures—the id, ego, and superego—that channel, repress, and transform sexual energy. These structures and their dynamic processes are both affective (emotional) and cognitive. Although Freud typically is not considered a cognitive psychologist, in many ways he was. Thought—whether unconscious, preconscious, or conscious and whether primary or secondary process in nature—always accompanies feeling.

APPLICATIONS

This chapter provides many examples of applications of Freud's theory to clinical practice, and these applications continue today. The Little

Hans case study shows how one might analyze a single child in depth. Freud's message for parents is to be sensitive to the conflicts between id, ego, and superego in their child and to try to provide neither too much nor too little satisfaction for the child's drives. A secure attachment between parent and child is particularly important, as is the later relationship during the child's identification with her parents.

Freud's claim that people can repress painful memories for years has arisen again in recent clinical and legal issues about adults' recall, after decades, of childhood sexual abuse. Freud at first believed that such events actually happened but later concluded that it was unlikely that there were so many Viennese parents who had sexually abused their children. He then viewed these memories as fantasies or perceptions distorted by sexual desire, but he still thought that, true or false, they were important because they affect the course of personality development. This issue about his patients has never been resolved, and psychologists disagree as to whether to accept the accuracy of current claims of remembered early abuse that has been repressed.

EVALUATION OF THE THEORY

Although rejection of certain aspects of Freud's theory is reasonable, experimental psychologists' overall rejection of the theory may have deprived the field of a valuable perspective on development. Despite the paucity of research today that is explicitly Freudian, this approach can provide some insights into current issues in developmental psychology. Thus, the following section on strengths focuses on two that are of potential contemporary relevance, namely, the theory's discovery of central developmental phenomena and its focus on nonlogical thought.

■ *Strengths*

Discovery of Central Developmental Phenomena ■ Although Freud's influence is rarely acknowledged explicitly in current developmental research, many core concepts are his: developmental stages, psychological structures, unconscious motivation, and the importance of early experience. In addition, the theory stimulated research in the areas of moral development, sex typing, identification, parent–child relations, attachment, aggression, and self-regulation. These remain active areas of research even today. Although a number of Freud's specific claims may be inaccurate, he told us what is important in development. Researchers have found something of value in the theory, even if they have not accepted it in its entirety.

Focus on Nonlogical Thought ▪ Psychoanalytic theory could enrich contemporary research on cognitive development. In the last 30 years, cognitive developmentalists have focused on rational problem solving: how thought becomes increasingly organized, efficient, abstract, and objective. This type of thought characterizes that of an adult scientist. It is assumed that this is the goal of cognitive development. This viewpoint emerges clearly in Piaget's emphasis on logical operations and on concepts of the physical world. The information-processing approach, described in a later chapter, also pictures a developing child as an organism that relentlessly searches for truth in an increasingly efficient and rational way. Although this view characterizes part of cognitive development, it does not tell the whole story. Humans probably are not as rational as these theories propose. As Wason and Johnson-Laird express it, "At best, we can all think like logicians; at worst, logicians all think like us" (1972, p. 245).

Irrational thought processes are as important as the more frequently studied rational ones; in fact, the former may occur more frequently than the latter. Thus, Freud's theory poses two challenges for developmentalists. One challenge is to study how emotions affect thinking in children. Do children reason differently when angry or frustrated than when calm? A second challenge is to examine whether the mental processes underlying primary- and secondary-process thought and the defense mechanisms (such as projection, reaction formation, repression, and sublimation) differ from the mental processes described by Piaget and the information-processing psychologists. For example, how is Piaget's notion of mental reversibility related to Freud's notion of reaction formation, in which a negative attitude toward a person or an object is transformed into a positive attitude? Are conflicting feelings and logically contradictory ideas resolved in the same way? What are the mental processes underlying self-deception? What cognitive acquisitions are necessary for understanding displaced aggression (taking one's anger out on an innocent person)?

Psychoanalytic theory also suggests that the *content* of children's thought is more wide-ranging than recent research would indicate. Freud would point out that children do not think only about quantity, spatial relationships, justice, objects, and causality. They also try to understand, and mentally adjust to, the violence on television or in their home, hunger, their parents' physical and emotional relationship, their own sexual or aggressive feelings, the tendency of adults to say one thing and do the opposite, rejection by their peers or parents, failure in social interactions, and so on. Adding this content to the logical, rational, linear thinking studied by Piagetian and information-processing (see Chapter 4) theorists would give a more balanced view of children's thinking.

This suggested new direction for research on cognitive development is particularly promising because it is compatible with current interest in *social cognition*, especially *theory of mind*. Research on social cognition, thinking about people and their behavior, seldom addresses the problematic or troublesome content of thought just described. As described in the previous chapter, theory of mind refers to a person's understanding of the nature of mental states, particularly representations. A child's theory of mind would influence his understanding of the psychological defenses used by others as well as himself, desires, the nature of dreams, and the distinction between fantasy and reality.

■ *Weaknesses*

Freud made it difficult for anyone to criticize his theory: "No one has a right to join in a discussion of psycho-analysis who has not had particular experiences which can only be obtained by being analyzed oneself" [1933a (1964, p. 69)]. Nevertheless, we now critically look at two weaknesses of the theory: uncertain testability of central claims concerning development and overemphasis on childhood sexuality.

Uncertain Testability of Central Claims Concerning Development ■ The scientific community requires that theories be based on empirical observations that can be replicated by other scientists. Freud's methodology makes this type of data gathering nearly impossible. His primary methods—free association, dream analysis, and transference—pose three major difficulties:

1. According to Freud, these methods require that the experimenter be trained in psychoanalysis. Because such training is a long, expensive process, few people would be qualified to test the theory. Furthermore, those who are psychoanalytically trained tend to be "believers." An involved, possibly biased participant-observer, who

records only a portion of the patient's responses, is a dubious source of objective data for testing the theory.

2. Freud's methods lend themselves to experimenter error. Freud made notes about the psychoanalytic sessions after they occurred, often hours later. It is ironic that someone who demonstrated the distortions of memory in his patients should be so oblivious to that possibility in himself. There is a danger that he selectively remembered only that which fit into his theory. Another source of experimenter error is the possibility that the patient's line of thought is influenced by the nature of the therapist's questions or even the timing of his grunts and silences.

3. Adults' recollections of childhood and recent dreams are unlikely to be completely accurate. Introspection has a poor reputation in psychology. It is not easy to report objectively even one's current mental state or recent dream states; mental states from 50 years earlier pose even more difficulties. Freud himself knew that these verbal reports are not reliable, but he felt that the patient's experience of the earlier events, whether accurate or distorted, is what is most relevant to therapy. Still, the fact that therapists usually do not have the means to discern when the reports are real and when they are not limits their assessment of the patient's perception of reality.

The problem of definition also poses a challenge to the experimental psychologist. There are many vague, imprecise, poorly defined terms. Because Freud relies heavily on analogies to communicate the meaning of the terms, the meaning conveyed is intuitive. Freud's reply to this criticism was that terms are imprecise in the early years of any science. For example, when physics was a young science, the notions of force and mass were elusive.

One facet of the problem of definition is that many of Freud's notions have an uncertain relationship to observable behavior, in part because of the considerable distance between the two. The therapist takes verbal reports and, to a lesser extent, nonverbal behavior (for example, facial expressions, crying, and physical accidents) and interprets them in terms of distant theoretical concepts, such as defense mechanisms, drives, and unconscious motivation. In particular, the evidence for the unconscious from dreams, forgetting, and puns sometimes seems rather far-fetched. For example, Freud made a large jump from a report of a dream about an oven to the interpretation that this image represents the uterus.

One way to state the problem with Freud's methods is that in Freud's system a psychological attribute can refer to several different behaviors or, conversely, a particular behavior can stem from several different psychological attributes. As an example of the former, an "anal personality" can be expressed in either a compulsively neat or an overly messy person. Or a patient's problem can be diagnosed as an Oedipus complex if he either talks constantly about his mother or never mentions her (due to repression). As an example of the case in which a behavior can have several possible causes, the inability to eat can stem from hysteria (perhaps caused by a fear of seeming to be pregnant) or paranoia (perhaps a fear of being poisoned). It is unclear how one would "test" these notions. The theory must be stated more systematically before it is clearly testable. Rapaport (1960) has taken a significant step in that direction.

There have been numerous attempts to test Freud's theory either clinically, often with hypnosis or projective tests in which the subject must interpret inkblots or pictures, or experimentally (see Fisher & Greenberg, 1996). The latter approach, however, has been criticized for not adequately testing the theory. For example, exposing a boy briefly to an aggressive, hostile male adult and subsequently observing how much the boy imitates the male's behavior is not a fair test of the notion that the Oedipus complex leads to identification with the aggressor. The long-term, emotionally powerful experiences of real life cannot be translated easily into brief, simplistic, experimental episodes. In short, psychologists are in a bind: they cannot adequately test the most crucial theoretical notions outside the psychoanalytic session, but the psychoanalytic session does not lend itself to experimental procedures.

If the theory itself cannot be tested scientifically, perhaps the best use of the theory is as a springboard for more limited, testable hypotheses. For example, in the 1950s, learning theorists took Freudian notions such as sex typing, dependency, identification, and defense mechanisms and studied their development within a learning framework (see Chapter 3). Also, hypnosis has been used to test hypotheses concerning the unconscious (Hilgard, 1965). Reyher (1967) provides an example. Hypnotized college students were told a story designed to arouse unconscious Oedipal feelings. They were told they would not remember anything about the story after awakening but would have strong sexual feelings when certain words were mentioned after they awakened. As predicted, the critical words, but not neutral words, aroused sweating, trembling, and guilt. Thus, it is possible to test hypotheses about unconscious conflicts. Finally, there have even been attempts to formulate computer models based on information-processing constructs (see Chapter 4) of Freud's notions concerning the repression of painful memories (Wegman, 1985).

Freud's notion of the scientific approach differed from that of the scientific community. He looked for converging evidence for a particular interpretation. If dream reports, memories from childhood, physical symptoms, slips of the tongue, and accidents all suggested that the patient had not resolved her feelings of sibling rivalry in childhood, then Freud believed he had proved his case. He integrated facts from several sources to form a consistent picture. He felt that his interpretations were further bolstered if several patients illustrated the same relationship between variables. For example, patients with paralysis of a limb (hysteria) often reported unresolved sexual conflicts from childhood. We are not, however, told how many patients exhibited these two behaviors. Furthermore, we cannot know whether the co-occurrence of the variables would be statistically significant or was simply coincidental. However, this lack of experimental rigor was not of great concern to Freud. His goal, after all, was to provide clinical insights that would help him formulate a theory that would improve therapy.

Overemphasis on Childhood Sexuality ▪ Freud's emphasis on sexuality brings to mind the greeting card that begins, "SEX—Now that I have your attention." Not surprisingly, claims about childhood sexuality both captured the attention of psychologists and the public and alienated many. Freud's answer to those who saw little evidence that sexuality pervades childhood was that his critics were repressing their own strong sexual memories from childhood!

For most developmental psychologists, claims about infantile sexuality in normal children strain the theory's credibility. The bulk of the developmental research of the last 20 years portrays infants and children as curious, self-motivated, social creatures who seek stimulation and relationships, rather than driven, anxiety-ridden beings who seek the reduction of tension. Recent research on attention and thinking in infants demonstrates that even a young infant is much more than id. Of course, the Freudian and cognitive views are not necessarily incompatible. Decarie's (1965) study of parallels in the development of Freud's object relations and Piaget's object permanence, neo-Freudian advances in ego psychology (e.g., Hartmann, 1958), and Furth's (1987) integration of Freudian and Piagetian theory are particularly notable attempts to bridge the two areas.

Freud's theory demonstrates the mutual constraints among culture, method, data, and theory mentioned in the Introduction. His data on the sexual fantasies of neurotic middle- and upper-class adults during the sexually repressive Victorian era may have little generality to children developing today. Furthermore, recent feminist critiques point out that the specific claims about sexuality may reflect the biases of a male-oriented society. Even years ago, Horney (1967) suggested that one could find as much evidence for womb envy in boys, due to their inability to have children, as for penis envy in girls. Still, it is possible to reject Freud's focus on sexual content without rejecting the entire theory.

Erikson

Powerful theories spawn "neo's": neo-Piagetians, neo-Freudians, neobehaviorists, and so on. Freud's theory, despite its limitations, inspired a diverse group of brilliant and creative theoreticians, researchers, and therapists. They stretched, patched, and rearranged Freud's vision in two main ways that had consequences for developmental psychology.

First, several neo-Freudians, especially Hartmann (1958), stressed the development of conflict-free ego functions, such as perception, memory, and logical thought. Whereas Freud's ego defends and inhibits, the neo-Freudian's ego integrates and organizes personality. Hartmann described an ego that is partly independent of the id and its drives. The emphasis on the ego's cognitive processes as a way of adapting to reality can be found in works by Rapaport (1960), Gill (1959), and Klein (1970). Furthermore, White (1963) identifies such ego satisfactions as exploration and competence at performing tasks well. These satisfactions are independent of satisfactions of the id. It is clear that psychoanalytic theory can address normal, as much as abnormal, behavior. (See Gedo, 1999, for an account of recent psychoanalytic approaches.)

Second, many neo-Freudians moved away from Freud's biological approach and considered the vast influence of society on development. The trends toward ego and social concerns came to developmental psychology largely through the work of Erik Erikson, who now commands our attention.

BIOGRAPHICAL SKETCH

Erik Erikson was born in 1902 near Frankfurt, Germany, and grew up in Karlsruhe. His wanderlust and desire to be an artist drew him away from formal schooling. After several years of drifting, studying art, and painting children's portraits, Erikson was hired to teach art and other subjects to children of Americans who had come to Vienna for Freudian training. This accidental entry into the vigorous Freudian circle resulted in his admittance into the Vienna Psychoanalytic Institute. His own psychoanalysis, part of the usual training program, was conducted by Anna Freud. Erikson also learned from Freud himself, Heinz Hartmann, Ernst Kris, Helene Deutsch, and other gifted analysts.

The threat of fascism brought Erikson to the United States in 1933. Despite his lack of any college degree, he became Boston's first child analyst and obtained a position at the Harvard Medical School. Later he held positions at several eminent institutions, including Yale, Berkeley, and the Menninger Foundation. During the McCarthy era, Erikson's (1951) concern that California's loyalty oath was a danger to personal and academic freedom precipitated his move back to the East Coast and to the Austen Riggs Center at Stockbridge, Massachusetts to Harvard and to several other eastern universities. He died in 1994 at age 91.

These diverse settings, from clinician's chair to professor's podium, fueled an energy that spread Erikson's interests over a remarkable area. He studied combat crises in troubled American soldiers in World War II, child-rearing practices among the Sioux in South Dakota and the Yurok along the Pacific Coast, the play of disturbed and normal children, the conversations of troubled adolescents suffering identity crises, and social behavior in India. These observations molded his ideas, which he expressed in many publications, including the well-known *Childhood and Society* (1950a) and *Identity: Youth and Crisis* (1968). He was constantly concerned with the rapid social changes in America and wrote about issues such as the generation gap, racial tensions, juvenile delinquency, changing sexual roles, and the dangers of nuclear war. He was a gifted author whose writings have been described as "Freud in sonnet form" (Hopkins, 1995, p. 796). It is clear that psychoanalysis had moved far from a doctor's couch in Vienna.

GENERAL ORIENTATION TO THE THEORY

Erikson accepts the basic notions of Freudian theory: psychological structures, the unconscious and conscious, drives, psychosexual stages, the normal–abnormal continuum, and psychoanalytic methodology. However, he expanded Freud's theory by developing a set of eight psychosocial stages covering the life span, by studying the development of identity, and by developing methods that reach beyond the structured psychoanalytic setting used with adults. A look at these three contributions serves as an orientation to the theory. He has been described as "a moralist, artist, and intellectual trying to deal with a culture that has begun to lose its power as an instrument for fulfilling the potential and the aspirations of those who live within it" (Bruner, 1987, p. 8).

Psychosocial Stages

Erikson's work in various cultures convinced him of the need to add a life-span psychosocial dimension to Freud's theory of psychosexual development. In Table 2.1, columns A to D describe several aspects of Erikson's theory, and column E names the Freudian psychosexual stage corresponding to each of Erikson's psychosocial stages. To illustrate the psychosexual and psychosocial components, Erikson (1959, p. 115) contrasts a toddler's oral pleasure when making speech sounds (psychosexual component) with the role of speech communication in shaping his relationship with his parents and significant others (psychosocial component). In the psychosocial view, physical maturation has personal and social repercussions. Maturation brings a new skill that opens up new possibilities for the child but also increases society's demands on him, in this case, pressure to talk instead of cry when he wants something. There is a "fit" between the child and his culture. Societies have evolved agreed-upon ways of meeting the child's new needs in each step of his maturation. These include parental care, schools, social organizations, occupations, a set of values, and so on. Erikson speaks of a "cogwheeling" of life cycles, as when adults' needs to become caretakers coincide with children's needs for caretaking. In other words, each child is a life cycle in a "community of life cycles" (Erikson, 1959, p. 121). The child is surrounded by others who are also passing through various stages. While the culture, over many generations, has adapted itself to the child, the child in turn adapts himself to the culture, as when a new kindergartner adjusts to a bewildering new set of experiences called "school."

Table 2.1 Erikson's "worksheet" summarizing the eight stages of development

Stage	A **Psychological crises**	B **Radius of significant relations**	C **Related elements of social order**	D **Psychosocial modalities**	E **Psychosexual stages**
1	Trust vs. mistrust	Maternal person	Cosmic order	To get To give in return	Oral-respiratory, sensory-kinesthetic (incorporative modes)
2	Autonomy vs. shame, doubt	Parental persons	"Law and order"	To hold (on) To let (go)	Anal-urethral, muscular (retentive-eliminative)
3	Initiative vs. guilt	Basic family	Ideal prototypes	To make (= going after) To "make like" (= playing)	Infantile-genital, locomotor (intrusive, inclusive)
4	Industry vs. inferiority	"Neighborhood," school	Technological elements	To make things (= completing) To make things together	"Latency"
5	Identity and repudiation vs. identity diffusion	Peer groups and outgroups; models of leadership	Ideological perspectives	To be oneself (or not to be) To share being oneself	Puberty
6	Intimacy and solidarity vs. isolation	Partners in friendship, sex, competition, cooperation	Patterns of cooperation and competition	To lose and find oneself in another	Genitality
7	Generativity vs. self-absorption	Divided labor and shared household	Currents of education and tradition	To make be To take care of	
8	Integrity vs. despair	"Mankind" "My kind"	Wisdom	To be, through having been To face not being	

SOURCE: Reproduced from *Identity and the Life Cycle* by Erik H. Erikson, with the permission of W. W. Norton & Company, Inc. Copyright © 1980.

Psychosocial development is culturally relative in two ways. First, although children in all cultures go through the same sequence of stages, each culture has its own idiosyncratic way of directing and enhancing the child's behavior at each age. For example, Erikson observed that the Sioux allowed nursing for several years in the spirit of overall generosity that pervaded the Sioux value system. They also thumped the teething male babies on the head for biting the mother's nipples in the belief that their crying rage would turn them into good hunters, and they trained their girls to be bashful and afraid of men in preparation for serving their hunter-husbands. Second, there is cultural relativity within a culture as it changes over time. Institutions that meet the needs of one generation may prove inadequate for the next. Industrialization, urbanization, immigration, the Depression, and the civil rights movement brought changes in what children needed to be taught in order to develop a healthy personality at their time in history.

Psychosocial development proceeds according to the *epigenetic principle,* a term derived from *epi,* which means "upon," and *genesis,* which means "emergence." This principle is borrowed from fetal development:

> Somewhat generalized, this principle states that anything that grows has a ground plan, and that out of this ground plan the parts arise, each part having its time of special ascendancy, until all parts have arisen to form a functioning whole. At birth the baby leaves the chemical exchange of the womb for the social exchange system of his society, where his gradually increasing capacities meet the opportunities and limitations of his culture.
>
> (Erikson, 1968, p. 92)

Like the fetus, the personality becomes increasingly differentiated and hierarchically organized as it unfolds in, and is shaped by, a particular environment. As summarized in Table 2.1, this unfolding involves several dimensions. There is movement through a set of psychosocial "crises" or issues as the child matures, and there is an expansion of his radius of significant relations. Other dimensions include the translation into the child's terms of certain elements of social order or structure and the progression through a set of psychosocial modalities or ways of "being" and interacting in society. Put succinctly, the child has inborn laws of development "which create a succession of potentialities for significant interaction with those who tend him" (Erikson, 1968, p. 52).

We now look at the general nature of the eight stages and leave a specific description of each stage for a later section. Maturation and society's expectations together create eight crises, or issues, that the child must resolve. Each issue is most evident at a particular stage in the life cycle but appears in some form throughout development. For example, autonomy is the dominant concern of the second year of life, but it is prepared for in the first year and elaborated on in later stages.

Erikson describes each crisis in terms of a dimension with both positive and negative outcomes possible, for example, autonomy versus shame and doubt. Ideally, the child develops a favorable ratio, in which the positive aspect dominates the negative. For instance, a person needs to know when to trust and when to mistrust but generally should have a trusting attitude toward life.

If the childhood crises are not handled satisfactorily, the person continues to fight his early battles later in life. Many adults are still struggling to develop a sense of identity. Erikson optimistically claims that it is never too late to resolve any of the crises.

With respect to the integration of successive stages, Erikson's theory lies between that of Piaget, with his tight integration, and that of Freud, with his loose integration. Each stage builds on the previous stages and influences the form of later stages. As Erikson expresses it, "Each stage adds something specific to all later ones, and makes a new ensemble out of all the earlier ones" (quoted in Evans, 1967, p. 41).

■ *Emphasis on Identity*

In contrast to Freud's concern with how people defend themselves from unpleasant tensions—a somewhat negative approach—Erikson's concern is more positive. He holds that a main theme of life is the quest for *identity*. This term refers to "a conscious sense of individual identity . . . an unconscious striving for a continuity of personal character . . . a criterion for the silent doings of ego synthesis . . . a maintenance of an inner solidarity with a group's ideals and identity" (Erikson, 1959, p. 102). Stated differently, identity is the understanding and acceptance of both the self and one's society. Throughout life, we ask "Who am I?" and form a different answer in each stage. If all goes well, at the end of each stage the child's sense of identity is reconfirmed on a new level. Although the development of identity reaches a crisis during adolescence, Erikson notes that it begins when the baby "first recognizes his mother and first feels recognized by her, when her voice tells him he is somebody with a name and he's good" (quoted in Evans, 1967, p. 35).

Thus, identity is transformed from one stage to the next, and early forms of identity influence later forms. This process is similar to the reworking of a concept (such as causality) in each successive stage in Piaget's theory.

Erikson—the child with a mixed cultural heritage, the wandering youth, and the American immigrant—had felt marginalized in society. He lived with the need to establish an identity: "As an immigrant . . . I faced one of those very important redefinitions that a man has to make who has lost his landscape and his language, and with it all the 'references' on which his first sensory and sensual impressions, and thus also some of his conceptual images, were based" (quoted in Evans, 1967, p. 41). His conversations with Huey P. Newton (Erikson, 1973) demonstrate that he was particularly sensitive to the problems that minority groups have when trying to form an identity. He began using the term "identity crisis" to describe the loss of identity he observed in World War II soldiers. He saw a similar problem among troubled adolescents "who war on their society" (Erikson, 1968, p. 17). Eventually, Erikson realized that the problem of identity appears, though usually on a smaller scale, in all lives. Furthermore, he recognized that identity is a central problem of our times: "If the relation of father and son dominated the last century, then this one is concerned with the self-made man asking himself what he is making of himself" (quoted in Evans, 1967, p. 41).

Expansion of Psychoanalytic Methodology

Erikson contributed to three methods for studying development: direct observation of children, cross-cultural comparisons, and psychobiography. His early experiences with children and his contact with Anna Freud, who was developing child observations and play therapy, immersed him in the world of both normal and disturbed children from the beginning of his career. In moving from the couch to the playroom, he asserted that "we must study man in action and not just man reflecting on reality" (quoted in Evans, 1967, p. 91).

Erikson's writings are sprinkled with contrasts between cultures. He was fascinated with how the solutions to the universal stages vary from culture to culture. His forays into cultural anthropology pointed out the inherent limitations to basic Freudian theory, which was based almost completely on psychologically troubled patients in turn-of-the-century Vienna.

Some of Erikson's most interesting writing is found in his "psychobiographies." These are analyses of the psychosocial development of well-known people, which show how a single person can represent the central preoccupation of a society at a particular time. Erikson believed that Hitler's rise illustrates the meshing of an individual's particular needs for identity and a nation's need for a more positive identity (Erikson,

1950a). In *Young Man Luther* (1958), Erikson describes a troubled youth who defied his strict father, who wished him to study law; rebelled against the authority of the church; and followed a belief that gave him an honest sense of identity. Other historical "patients" include Maxim Gorky (1950a) and George Bernard Shaw (1968). His biography *Gandhi's Truth* (1969) won a Pulitzer Prize and the National Book Award in philosophy and religion.

DESCRIPTION OF THE STAGES

Erikson divides the entire life cycle into "the eight ages of man." These eight ages refer to eight critical periods, when various lifelong ego concerns reach a climax. (Table 2.1 provides an overview of each stage.)

Stage 1: Basic Trust Versus Basic Mistrust (Roughly Birth to 1 Year)

In Table 2.1, we see that the main task of infancy is to acquire a favorable ratio of trust to mistrust. If the balance is weighted toward trust, the child has a better chance of weathering the later crises than if it is weighted toward mistrust. Erikson defines *basic trust* as "an essential trustfulness of others as well as a fundamental sense of one's own trustworthiness" (1968, p. 96) and the sense that "there is some correspondence between your needs and your world" (quoted in Evans, 1967, p. 15).

Infants with an attitude of trust can predict that their mother will feed them when they are hungry and comfort them when they are frightened or in pain. They will tolerate having their mother out of sight because they are confident she will return. The mother, then, is all-important. Babies also develop trust in themselves from the feeling that others accept them and from increased familiarity with their bodily urges. This faith in themselves and their small world corresponds to religious faith in the "cosmic order" of the universe (column C). From the mother's side of the interaction, there must also be trust—trust in herself as a parent and in the meaningfulness of her caretaking role. Erikson (1950b) refers to a remark from Benjamin Spock: "To be a good parent you have to believe in the species—somehow."

Some mistrust is necessary at all ages in order to detect impending danger or discomfort and to discriminate between honest and dishonest persons.

However, if mistrust wins out over trust, the child, or later the adult, may be frustrated, withdrawn, suspicious, and lacking in self-confidence.

The specifically oral experiences—sucking, biting, teething, and weaning—are prototypes for the psychosocial modality of getting and giving (column D). The baby "takes in," or "incorporates," stimulation through all the senses, much as a Piagetian child "assimilates." By taking from the mother and the world, the baby is laying the foundation for her later role as a giver to others.

Stage 2: Autonomy Versus Shame and Doubt (Roughly 2 to 3 Years)

With further neurological and muscular development come walking, talking, and the potential for anal control. As the child becomes more independent physically and psychologically, there are new possibilities for personality development. At the same time, however, there are new vulnerabilities, namely, anxiety over separation from the parents, fear that anal control may not always be possible, and loss of self-esteem when failure does come.

A clash of wills is inevitable. Erikson refers to the "sinister forces which are leashed and unleashed, especially in the guerrilla warfare of unequal wills; for the child is often unequal to his own violent drives, and parent and child unequal to each other" (1959, p. 66). Ideally, parents create a supportive atmosphere in which the child can develop a sense of self-control without a loss of self-esteem.

While the positive component of this stage is autonomy, the negative components are shame and doubt: "Shame supposes that one is completely exposed and conscious of being looked at—in a word, self-conscious . . . 'with one's pants down.' Shame is early expressed in an impulse to bury one's face, or to sink, right then and there, into the ground" (Erikson, 1959, pp. 68–69). Doubt has to do with the unknown "behind" that the child cannot see yet must try to control. Shame and doubt about one's self-control and independence come if basic trust was insufficiently developed or was lost, if bowel training is too early or too harsh, or if the child's will is "broken" by an overcontrolling parent.

The culture, expressed through the parents, shapes and gives meaning to the toddler's new competencies. For example, cultures vary in how seriously they take training for anal control. Erikson points to the machine age's ideal of a "mechanically trained, faultlessly functioning, and always clean, punctual, and deodorized body" (1959, p. 67), in contrast to the lack of concern with such matters in the Sioux culture. By simply imitating older children, Sioux children achieve bowel control by the time they begin school.

The psychosocial modality is holding on versus letting go, the counterpart to retention and elimination. This ambivalence pervades the child's behavior and attitude. For example, toddlers often zealously hoard toys or other objects and anxiously guard them in their hiding place but then casually throw them out the window of a moving car or give them to a friend. One morning a mother is late to work because her 2-year-old adamantly has insisted on buttoning every single shirt button himself, while the next morning the young Dr. Jekyll–Mr. Hyde screams with rage because his mother has not helped him get dressed. Failure to coordinate the opposing tendencies to hold on and let go can lead to the "anal personality" described by Freud—overcontrolled, compulsive, messy, stingy, or rigid.

In this second stage, the child encounters such rules as when he can have bowel movements or which areas of the house he is allowed to explore. These rules are an early hint of the "law and order" society he will face (column C of Table 2.1). The issue here, according to Erikson, is "whether we remain the masters of the rules by which we want to make things more manageable (not more complicated) or whether the rules master the ruler" (1959, pp. 72–73). In a well-functioning society, the sense of autonomy encouraged in children is maintained throughout their lives by that society's economic and political structures.

■ *Stage 3: Initiative Versus Guilt (Roughly 4 to 5 Years)*

"Being firmly convinced that he *is* a person, the child must now find out *what kind* of a person he is going to be. And here he hitches his wagon to nothing less than a star: he wants to be like his parents, who to him appear very powerful and very beautiful, although quite unreasonably dangerous" (Erikson, 1959, p. 74). The theme of this stage is children's identification with their parents, who are perceived as big, powerful, and intrusive. Erikson accepted the basic outline of Freud's account of how children achieve identification through the Oedipus complex, but he emphasized the social components more than the sexual. As we saw in Freud's theory, identification brings with it a conscience and a set of interests, attitudes, and sex-typed behaviors.

The basic psychosocial modality is "making," namely, intrusion, taking the initiative, forming and carrying out goals, and competing. We might conclude, with T. S. Eliot, that the stage-3 child dares to disturb the universe. The child intrudes "into other bodies by physical attack . . . into other people's ears and minds by aggressive talking . . . into space by vigorous locomotion . . . into the unknown by consuming curiosity" (Erikson, 1959, p. 76). This initiative is supported by advances in mobility, physical dexterity, language, cognition, and creative imagination.

The child settles somewhere along a dimension ranging from successful initiative to overwhelming guilt due to an overly severe conscience that punishes sexual fantasies and immoral thoughts or behavior. In addition to guilt, another danger is that the child may forever feel that he must always be doing something, always competing, always "making," in order to have any worth as a person. For this stage the related elements of social order are "ideal prototypes" (column C). These are social roles, such as police officer, teacher, astronaut, president, and "hero."

■ *Stage 4: Industry Versus Inferiority (Roughly 6 Years to Puberty)*

The "industrial age" begins. Children now want to enter the larger world of knowledge and work. Their theme is "I am what I learn" (Erikson, 1959, p. 82). The great event is entry into school, where they are exposed to the technology of their society: books, multiplication tables, arts and crafts, maps, microscopes, films, and tape recorders. Learning, however, occurs not only in school but also on the street, in friends' houses, and at home.

Successful experiences give the child a sense of industry, a feeling of competence and mastery, while failure brings a sense of inadequacy and inferiority, a feeling that one is a good-for-nothing. Children strive to make things well and complete what they have begun. The years spent establishing basic trust, autonomy, and initiative were preparation for this energetic entry into our technological society. Erikson notes that this stage differs from the first three in that "it does not consist of a swing from a violent inner upheaval to a new mastery" (1959, p. 88). It is a calmer period, a time of psychosexual latency.

■ *Stage 5: Identity and Repudiation Versus Identity Diffusion (Adolescence)*

Erikson quotes a saying that hangs in a cowboys' bar in the West: "I ain't what I ought to be, I ain't what I'm going to be, but I ain't what I was" (1959, p. 93). In an earlier section, we saw that the quest for identity is the undercurrent running through all the stages:

> The process of identity formation emerges as an *evolving configuration*—a configuration which is gradually established by successive ego syntheses and resyntheses throughout childhood; it is a configuration gradually integrating *constitutional givens, idiosyncratic libidinal needs, favored capacities, significant identifications, effective defenses, successful sublimations, and consistent roles.*
>
> (Erikson, 1959, p. 116)

Trust, autonomy, initiative, and industry all contribute to the child's identity. In the fifth stage, however, this concern reaches a climax. Rapid physiological changes produce a "new" body with unfamiliar sexual urges. These changes, along with social pressure to make rational and educational decisions, force the youth to consider a variety of roles. The basic task for adolescents is to integrate the various identifications they bring from childhood into a more complete identity. Erikson emphasizes that this whole (the identity) is greater than the sum of its parts (previous identifications). This reassembled identity is appropriate for the new needs, skills, and goals of adolescence. If adolescents cannot integrate their identifications, roles, or selves, they face "identity diffusion." The personality is fragmented, lacking a core. Erikson quotes Biff in Arthur Miller's *Death of a Salesman*, "I just can't take hold, Mom, I can't take hold of some kind of a life" (1959, p. 91). The problem may be exacerbated by one's minority-group status, uncertainty about one's sexual orientation, an overly strong identification with a parent, or too many occupational roles from which to choose.

The psychosocial modality of this stage is to be oneself or not to be oneself. Hamlet's "to be or not to be" soliloquy voices this alienation and role confusion (Erikson, 1968). Youths seek their true selves through peer groups, clubs, religion, political movements, and so on. These groups provide opportunities to try out new roles much in the way someone might try on jackets in a store until finding one that fits. The ideology of society, this stage's counterpart in the social order, guides this role playing by conveying which roles are valued by society.

■ *Stage 6: Intimacy and Solidarity Versus Isolation (Young Adulthood)*

Only if a reasonably well integrated identity emerges from stage 5 can psychological intimacy with other people (or even oneself) be possible. If a youth fears that she may lose herself in someone else, she is unable to fuse her identity with someone else. Although young people usually form important relationships with the opposite sex during this time, their friendships with the same sex and even their access to their own intimate feelings and thoughts also mark this stage. These relationships, by enhancing one's own identity, further the growth of personality. One aspect of intimacy is the feeling of solidarity of "us" and the defense against "them," the threatening "forces and people whose essence seems dangerous to one's own" (Erikson, 1959, pp. 96–97). If a youth's attempts at intimacy fail, she retreats into isolation. In this case, social relationships are stereotyped, cold, and empty.

Stage 7: Generativity Versus Stagnation and Self-Absorption (Middle Adulthood)

Generativity refers to "the interest in establishing and guiding the next generation" (Erikson, 1959, p. 97) through child rearing or creative or productive endeavors. Simply bearing children does not, of course, ensure that the parent will develop a sense of generativity. Faith in the future, a belief in the species, and the ability to care about others seem to be prerequisites for development in this stage. Instead of having children, one may work to create a better world for the children of others. Stage 7, then, provides the mechanism for the continuity of society from generation to generation. A lack of generativity is expressed in stagnation, self-absorption (self-indulgence), boredom, and a lack of psychological growth.

Stage 8: Integrity Versus Despair (Late Adulthood)

In this final stage, people must live with what they have built over their lifetime. Ideally, they will have achieved integrity. *Integrity* involves the acceptance of the limitations of life, a sense of being a part of a larger history that includes previous generations, a sense of owning the wisdom of the ages, and a final integration of all the previous stages. The antithesis of integrity is despair—regret for what one has done or not done with one's life, fear of approaching death, and disgust with oneself.

CONTEMPORARY ERIKSONIAN RESEARCH

Unlike Piaget and Freud, Erikson emphasized development over the entire life span and thus stimulated later work on life-span development, a very strong area today. Some contemporary research continues to examine Eriksonian issues, such as generativity and adult development (McAdams & de St. Aubin, 1998). During aging, a person needs to continue to stimulate and challenge the environment, as the environment simultaneously has that effect on the person (Erikson, Erikson, & Kivnick, 1986).

A main active area of current research is ego development and the search for identity during adolescence and early adulthood (e.g., Grotevant, 1998; Loevinger, 1976; Noam, 1996). For example, Marcia (1967, 1999) has expanded two of Erikson's notions, crisis and commitment: "Crisis refers to times during adolescence when the individual seems to be actively involved in choosing among alternative occupations and beliefs. Commitment refers to the degree of personal investment the individual expresses in an occupation or belief" (1967, p. 119). The presence or absence of crisis or commitment defines four *identity statuses*. The *identity-diffused* person, because she has experienced neither an identity crisis nor a commitment, is easily influenced by others and changes her beliefs often. The *foreclosure* person has made commitments without experiencing an identity crisis. She unquestioningly accepts beliefs, attitudes, and an occupation based on the views of others. The *moratorium* person is in a severe state of identity crisis and is not yet able to make commitments. Finally, the *identity-achieved* person has successfully passed through an identity crisis and has made a set of personal commitments.

As feminist critiques point out, Erikson's sequences regarding identity may not be universal across cultures and for both men and women. Although identity may precede intimacy for men, Gilligan points out that "for women these tasks seem instead to be fused. Intimacy goes along with identity" (1982, p. 12). Recent research has examined whether adolescents and adults in the four identity statuses have different backgrounds and characteristics and whether the four statuses do in fact follow a developmental sequence (Marcia, 1999).

MECHANISMS OF DEVELOPMENT

The epigenetic principle describes the forces that underlie movement through the stages. Physical maturation writes the general timetable for development. Within these limits, one's culture pushes, slows down, nurtures, and destroys. In Erikson's view, society exerts its influence on the developing organism at many levels, ranging all the way from its abstract ideology to a parent's caress. Many of Freud's mechanisms of development can join Erikson's list of mechanisms of development: drives, frustrations from external and internal forces, attachment, and identification. However, Erikson makes little use of Freud's tension-reduction equilibration process. Instead, he seems to view development as the resolution of conflict from opposing forces. The child integrates holding on and letting go, initiative and guilt, the biological and psychological, and so on.

Erikson (1977) has elaborated on a more specific mechanism of development: play. Play is used in a broad sense to mean the use of imagination to try out ways of mastering and adapting to the world, to express emotions, to re-create past situations or imagine future situations, and to develop new models of existence. Problems that cannot be solved in reality can be solved through doll play, dramatics, sports, art, block play, "playing house," and so on. Play, however, is not limited to children. Play includes Einstein visualizing a model of time and space, an adolescent fantasizing about entering various occupations, or a man rehearsing what he will say to his boss the next day. Play is often ritualized and becomes a somewhat formal, enduring, culturally agreed-upon way of interacting with others. For example, an adolescent who is "messing around" with his friends is acquiring culturally approved patterns for interacting with other people. Another example is that the child-care rituals of infancy pass on "proper" ways of recognizing and greeting other people. Rituals are mechanisms of development because they bring humans in every stage into the cultural mainstream and provide ready-made solutions to the problems of everyday life.

POSITION ON DEVELOPMENTAL ISSUES

Erikson's position on the four issues is close to Freud's but differs in emphasis. Erikson, like Piaget, has a more optimistic view of human nature. Children and adults not only seek to avoid pain but also actively seek to develop a positive sense of identity. The existential human is in a process of "becoming" throughout life. This development is primarily qualitative because changes are stagelike, but it is also somewhat quantitative in that one's identity becomes stronger and one's convictions solidify.

Unlike Freud's theory, Erikson's has elements of the contextualist world view. He saw a changing child in a changing world and a system of culturally constructed contexts devoted to the socialization of children into that culture. The nature of these settings contributes to, and affects the resolution of, the crisis of each stage.

Like Freud, Erikson believed that nature determines the sequence of the stages and sets the limits within which nurture operates. If heredity ensures that certain crises arise, then the environment determines how they are resolved. Erikson, however, more than Freud, emphasized the role of culture in nurturing and shaping the developing child or adult. Not only the person's past and present but also society's past and present influence the developing person. In addition, Erikson did not accept Freud's claim that development is essentially complete after the first 5 years of life. Development is a lifelong process; sometimes childhood conflicts are not resolved satisfactorily until adulthood. Finally, for Erikson, the essence of development is the formation of an identity that gives coherence to one's personality.

APPLICATIONS

As mentioned earlier, Erikson applied his theory to problems such as adolescent identity crises, conflict between generations, postwar adjustment of soldiers, race relations, and child rearing. Today, counselors continue to draw on his work on adolescence in particular to help young people successfully make personal and occupational decisions. Adults can facilitate their children's development by helping them achieve a balance between each end of the continuum in each stage, such as both trust and healthy mistrust.

EVALUATION OF THE THEORY

Because Erikson's theory is an extension of psychoanalytic theory, the earlier evaluation of Freud's theory is relevant here. Instead of reiterating those comments, the present section focuses on the unique strengths and weaknesses of Erikson's theory.

■ *Strengths*

Expansion of Psychoanalytic Theory ■ By widening the empirical base of psychoanalytic theory, Erikson increased its credibility and application. He added the psychosocial to the psychosexual, the cultural to the biological, the ego identity to the ego defenses, the normal to the abnormal, the cross cultural to the culture specific, child observations to adults' reconstructions from childhood, and adult development to child development. He helped start the life-span developmental approach. The theory is remarkable in its power to integrate a wide variety of situations. Erikson's version of development seems well grounded in the everyday lives of the majority of people, as they struggle to find coherence and meaning in their lives. He "looks for the hopeful and active part of the person and for how human experience and human potential are organized in the communal environment, within a radius of significant social encounters" (Schlein, 1987, p. xxv). This broadened psychoanalytic framework has been a valuable heuristic for counseling and therapy, especially with adolescents. Erikson's emphasis on cultural factors and life-span development was especially important for developmental psychology. However, his work stimulated little research on the specific claims of his theory, such as the ordering of the stages or, at a more concrete level, sex differences in children's play.

Broad Perspective ▪ Erikson's relevance for contemporary views of development lies in the broad perspective he gives to a child's behavior. He has been described as "perhaps one of the last great synthesizers in the behavioral sciences" (Hopkins, 1995, p. 796). A specific behavior of a specific child is influenced by his past history, the present situation, and the past and present history of his own culture and even the world society. All levels of society, from international relations to the nation's political structure to the interaction within the family, influence behavior. Erikson's writings conjure up the image of a system of interlocking forces uniting the child and the universe, the distant past and the distant future. Although many developmentalists pay lip service to this position, with few exceptions (see Vygotskian and sociocultural theories in Chapter 7 and person-in-context theories in Chapter 8) they do not seriously examine these social and historical variables. Instead, the behavior of children is typically studied in isolation.

▪ *Weaknesses*

Lack of Systematicity ▪ Erikson's theory is a loose connection of observations, empirical generalizations, and abstract theoretical claims. Consequently, it is difficult to state his claims in a way that can be tested or relate his empirical findings to the more abstract levels of the theory. As with Freud, much of the problem lies in the methodological inadequacies, particularly the lack of controlled experimentation. In Erikson's case, the observations are laden with interpretations that are difficult to evaluate. For example, in Erikson's observation at the beginning of this chapter, do boys build towers because of their phallic, intrusive orientation, as Erikson claims, or simply because they like to knock tall things down? His psychobiographies are fascinating but are necessarily speculative. A related problem is that the terms he selects often mislead rather than elucidate. For example, "generativity" and "integrity" do not have their usual meanings. It is not surprising, then, that many of Erikson's concepts are often misunderstood.

Lack of Specific Mechanisms of Development ▪ It became clear in the earlier section on mechanisms of development that Erikson did not explain in any detail how a child moves from stage to stage or even how he resolves the crisis within a stage. He states *what* influences the movement (for example, physical maturation, parents, cultural beliefs, the extent to which earlier crises were resolved) but not specifically *how* the movement comes about. By what mechanisms does an infant learn when to trust and when to mistrust? Why does the resolution of the initiative–guilt polarity lead to the industry–inferiority conflict rather than to some other conflict? The validity of many of Erikson's notions, such as the conflict-resolution model, rests on the ability to describe in detail the mechanism of development.

SUMMARY

Two of Freud's ideas have formed the backbone of developmental psychology. First, he proposed that the first few years of life are critical because the basic personality is formed during that time. Second, he believed that personality is developed as the child copes with an invariant sequence of conflicts. Each conflict involves a different domain: oral, anal, phallic, and adult genital. The way that children satisfy the drives in each stage forms the basis of their personality. Although Freud's psychosexual focus is less influential today in academic psychology, the notion of stages has greatly influenced research and therapy with children. Also, his account of attachment has stimulated current research on internal working models and their long-term effects on development.

Using an energy model from physics, Freud described a system of psychological energy that is distributed, transformed, and discharged within a psychological structure. This structure consists of the id, ego, and superego in a delicate balance. The ego considers its available defenses, its perceptions of reality, the demands of the id for drive reduction, and the prohibitions of the superego before deciding on a course of action. Most of the "mind" is unconscious because knowledge of the thoughts and wishes hidden in the id, ego, and superego would cause unbearable anxiety.

Most of Freud's evidence came from his patients' free associations concerning their childhood, dreams, and present concerns. Freud believed that the workings of the abnormal mind clarify the nature of normal personality because there is a continuum of behaviors ranging from the abnormal to the normal.

Freud viewed humans as being driven by instincts but actively trying to cope with various internal and external conflicts. He stressed qualitative, stagelike changes in development but also included quantitative change. Although he emphasized biological influences, especially drives, he also recognized the role of experience, particularly in the first 5 years of life. The essence of development is the emergence of psychological structures that mediate all experience and behavior. Freud's theory introduced new psychological phenomena to Western culture and has the potential to broaden future research on cognitive development by including emotion-laden thoughts and defense mechanisms. However, the theory has methodological inadequacies, and its claims may not be testable. In addition, its focus on infantile sexuality has limited its acceptance in academic psychology.

What is Freud's heritage for developmental psychology? He began by asking why his patients suffered and ended by giving us a new perspective on human development. Hall and Lindzey note that whereas Freud may not have been the most rigorous scientist or theorist, "he was a patient, meticulous, penetrating observer and a tenacious, disciplined, courageous, original thinker" (1957, p. 72).

Erikson's psychosocial theory of development modified Freudian theory in two important ways. First, Erikson identified important social influences on development throughout the life span. His research in various cultures and various social settings within a culture suggests that every society tries to deal with the biologically based changes occurring during development. Ideally, there is a fit between the child's needs and the society's needs at each point in development. In each of eight stages, there is a psychosocial crisis in which there are two possible extreme outcomes: (1) trust versus mistrust, (2) autonomy versus shame and doubt, (3) initiative versus guilt, (4) industry versus inferiority, (5) identity and repudiation versus identity diffusion, (6) intimacy and solidarity versus isolation, (7) generativity versus stagnation and self-absorption, and (8) integrity versus despair. Eriksonian-inspired research on identity continues today.

Erikson's second major contribution to psychoanalytic theory is his notion that life is a quest for identity. Thus, he focused on ego processes. The work on both social and ego processes greatly expanded psychoanalytic theory and provided a broad perspective on development. However, the theory is rather unsystematic and lacks specific mechanisms of development.

Freud and Erikson produced unique yet complementary perspectives on development. A remark by Kierkegaard expresses an integration of the two views: "Life can only be understood backwards; but it must be lived forwards."

SUGGESTED READINGS

This paperback is a short, lucid introduction to Freud's theory:

Hall, C. S. (1954). *A primer of Freudian psychology*. New York: World.

This book includes applications of psychoanalytic theories to development:

Masling, J. M., & Bornstein, R. F. (1996). *Psychoanalytic perspectives on developmental psychology*. Washington, DC: American Psychological Association.

Because Freud is a talented and provocative writer, his ideas should be explored in his own writings:

Strachey, J. (Ed. and Trans.). (1953–1966). *The standard edition of the complete psychological works of Sigmund Freud* (24 vols). London: Hogarth Press. Particularly recommended are "An Outline of Psycho-Analysis" (Vol. 23, pp. 144–207), "New Introductory Lectures on Psycho-Analysis" (Vol. 22, pp. 5–182), and any of the case studies.

The following is a comprehensive introduction to Erikson's theory:

Gross, F. L. (1986). *Introducing Erik Erikson: An invitation to his thinking*. Lanham, MD: University Press of America.

Three of Erikson's books, including his last one, provide a comprehensive look at his ideas:

Erikson, E. H. (1950). *Childhood and society*. New York: Norton.

Erikson, E. H. (1968). *Identity: Youth and crisis*. New York: Norton.

Erikson, E. H. (1982). *The life cycle completed: A review*. New York: Norton.

Erikson's psychobiographies are a source of fascinating reading, especially this Pulitzer Prize–winning one:

Erikson, E. H. (1969). *Gandhi's truth*. New York: Norton.

This biography clarifies some of Erikson's ideas:

Coles, R. (1970). *Erik H. Erikson: The growth of his work*. Boston: Little, Brown.

CHAPTER 3

Social Learning Theory

Subjects were tested for the amount of imitative learning. . . . Three measures of imitation were obtained: Imitation of physical aggression: *This category included acts of striking the Bobo doll with the mallet, sitting on the doll and punching it in the nose, kicking the doll, and tossing it in the air.* Imitative verbal aggression: *Subject repeats the phrases, "Sock him," "Hit him down," "Throw him in the air," or "Pow."* Imitative nonaggressive verbal responses: *Subject repeats, "He keeps coming back for more," or "He sure is a tough fella."*

—*Bandura, Ross, & Ross, 1961, p. 33*

The experimenter introduced the training task as follows: "Now let's give this lady (model) a chance to play the game. Then you (child) can play the game. Here are some cards. Which ones are the same? Which ones go together?" The model grouped the stimuli according only to the size dimension. The experimenter queried the model, "Why are they the same?" and the model responded, "Because these two are pictures of big things (pointing) and these two are little things (pointing)." Then the same item was presented to the child in identical fashion (asking about only one dimension). "Now it's your turn to play the game. Play the game just like the lady did."

—*Zimmerman, 1974, p. 1035*

Mark Twain once remarked, "Training is everything. The peach was once a bitter almond; cauliflower is nothing but cabbage with a college education." This optimistic view of learning captures learning theorists' belief that development comes primarily from experience. Children acquire new behaviors and modify old behaviors as they encounter their social and physical world. As specific learning experiences accumulate, the child develops, but not in the stagelike way described by Freud and Piaget.

The previous two chapters presented theories flowing mainly from a single person. In contrast, learning theory came from many researchers working over a span of more than 60 years. More than any other theoretical approach, learning theory was responsible for bestowing scientific respectability on developmental psychology. The theory's rigorous, objective research methods made laboratory studies of children possible in the 1950s and early 1960s, developmental psychology's formative years.

Learning theory is the most truly American theory. Most of the theories in this volume arose in Europe and only later influenced North American psychology. Although early Russian work on reflexes and conditioning had already begun and Hermann Ebbinghaus's verbal-learning studies were already history, learning theory developed and had most of its influence on U.S. soil. To a great extent, the history of psychology in the United States and the history of learning theory were synonymous until the 1960s. Learning theory has become part of our culture and has entered our language as "behaviorism," "rat psychology," "behavior modification," "Skinner box," and "reinforcement."

This chapter focuses on social learning theory because it is the version of learning theory that most clearly influences current developmental thinking and research. Work by Albert Bandura (born 1925) will be highlighted. However, in order to understand the assumptions and goals of social learning theory, it is necessary to take an extended look at its heritage in "classical" learning theory. The next sections include a general orientation to social learning theory, examples of developmental research, and an overview of mechanisms of development. The final topics include the theory's position on developmental issues, its applications, its strengths and weaknesses, and its position within developmental psychology today.

HISTORY OF THE THEORY

Learning theory up to the time of social learning theory raised many of the issues to which social learning theory responded. This history, then, is critical to our understanding of social learning theory. As Henri

Bergson (1911) noted, "The present contains nothing more than the past, and what is found in the effect was already in the cause."

Behaviorism

Early in this century, psychologists' attempts to examine systematically the structure of the mind and the nature of consciousness relied on introspection—verbalizing one's own thoughts or feelings. This unsatisfactory state of affairs led to John Watson's "declaration of behaviorism" in 1913. In this strongly worded statement, he asserted that the goal of psychology should be to predict and control overt behavior, not to describe and explain conscious states. Thus, Watson redefined the field of psychology. In 1917, he was awarded the grand sum of $100 to study reflexes in infants. In his most famous study, he conditioned a fear response in "Little Albert" (a feat described later). Watson (1924) considered children "lumps of clay" to be shaped by their environment. He carried his ideas to parents in his manual *Psychological Care of Infant and Child:*

> There is a sensible way of treating children. Treat them as though they were young adults. Dress them, bathe them with care and circumspection. Let your behavior always be objective and kindly firm. Never hug and kiss them, never let them sit in your lap. If you must, kiss them once on the forehead when they say goodnight. Shake hands with them in the morning. Give them a pat on the head if they have made an extraordinary good job of a difficult task. Try it out. In a week's time you will find how easy it is to be perfectly objective with your child and at the same time kindly. You will be utterly ashamed of the mawkish, sentimental way you have been handling it.
>
> (1928, pp. 81–82):

It speaks well for the wisdom and common sense of parents that they did not adopt his philosophy wholeheartedly. By the 1920s Watson had left academia and become an advertising executive.

Learning theorists asked questions that could be answered and provided a fruitful methodology for examining those questions. Central questions included the following: Can learning occur if a stimulus and a response simply occur together, or is reinforcement always necessary? Why is a learned response more persistent if it has been reinforced only part of the time rather than all of the time? Is there "latent" learning—knowledge that is acquired simply by being in a particular environment without any immediate reinforcement? In Sheldon White's words, learning theories were so influential "because they found for Psychology a reasonable species of psychological reality, and because they then laid down a paradigm of cooperative research procedures which might search that reality with a hope of significant findings. . . . one could stop the hair-splitting and throat-clearing and one could move into intensive scientific development" (1970, p. 662). Thus, learning theory served a need at a particular point in history.

After several decades of great research activity, learning theory ran into trouble in the 1960s. Part of the discontent came from within; hundreds of studies of verbal learning had not led to a satisfactory account of memory or learning. In addition, new evidence suggested that biological predispositions limit or modify the laws of learning. For a given species, some kinds of learning are easier than others. For example, rats learn to associate nausea with a certain taste but not with a light or a sound (Garcia & Koelling, 1966). At the same time, learning theory faced external challenges. Noam Chomsky's (1959) attack on B. F. Skinner's account of language acquisition was a serious blow because it showed that learning approaches could not explain the acquisition of a skill as complex as language. In addition, alternative conceptions of learning were developing. Information processing (see Chapter 4), Chomsky's transformational grammar, and Piaget's cognitive theory provided attractive opposing explanations of behavior: they characterized learning as a change in knowledge rather than as a change in the probability of response. Attempts to patch up learning theory by positing verbal mediation (associations involving verbal labels), generalized rules, and complex hierarchies of mental associations did not halt the declining influence of the theory. With the entrance of cognitive psychology, psychology began what Hebb (1960) called its "second American revolution," the first being the elimination of any psychology based on introspection.

■ *Early Research on Children's Learning*

A parallel, but delayed, scenario unfolded within developmental psychology. The learning studies with children in the first few decades of the twentieth century were simply translations of paradigms used with animals and college students. The experiments differed from the earlier ones only in that the participants happened to be children. Children underwent operant and classical conditioning, solved simple discrimination-learning problems, and even wandered through mazes seeking prizes rather than cheese at the end (Hicks & Carr, 1912). It should come as no surprise that children learned faster than rats but more slowly than college sophomores. In 1954, a review of children's learning concluded that the laws of learning are the same in children and other populations (Munn, 1954).

However, children soon showed that they were unlike rats in many ways. As learning theorists used slightly more complex tasks in the 1950s and 1960s, they came to view children as "rats with language." Children could label attributes of objects, such as their color or size, and use the labels to guide their learning which attribute always led to reinforcement. Learning seemed to be under cognitive control in other ways as well. Attending to relevant information, forming hypotheses about the correct answer, and generating strategies for gathering information increased their speed of learning. In fact, learning per se—choosing the stimulus that always leads to reinforcement—is rather trivial and anticlimactic. As Flavell and Hill noted, the learned response, such as choosing the black stimulus, is "correct for today only in this specific situation. The 'organismic change' thus amounts to a temporary pairing of two items which are already in the cognitive repertoire rather than any genuine and substantive modification of the repertoire itself" (1969, p. 44). Such "learning" comes after all the developmentally interesting processes described above have occurred. Furthermore, researchers used abstract, meaningless stimuli, usually colored, geometric shapes. They used simple, meaningless tasks because they wanted to measure "pure" basic processes of learning, uncontaminated by previous learning. It is ironic, then, that the most interesting information from learning research has to do with children's use of their previously acquired cognitive, linguistic, and social abilities as they attempt to make sense of the simple, meaningless task put before them. The "contamination" was interesting indeed. By the late 1960s, the attitude of many developmentalists toward learning research was that it is probably more fruitful to study the development of these skills directly, rather than indirectly through learning tasks. Also, the active, strategic, hypothesis-forming child seen in learning tasks looked very much like a Piagetian child.

Another line of research on children's learning came from Skinner, one of the most well-known psychologists in the world. Skinner considered thoughts and feelings inappropriate for empirical study and therefore examined only observable behavior. His work concerned the way rats' and pigeons' behavior could be shaped and controlled by schedules of reinforcement. In operant conditioning, a particular behavior becomes more frequent if it is reinforced. This work led psychologists to wonder if children's behavior could be similarly influenced. In fact, in a novel, *Walden Two* (1948), Skinner proposed that children in his utopian society would be raised by behavioral engineers, specialists in operant conditioning. Such desirable behaviors as self-control and independence would be fostered by reinforcement, whereas such undesirable behaviors as jealousy and poor work habits would be extinguished because of lack of reinforcement from the environment. Skinner (1967) even kept a cumulative record of his writing output as a way of providing self-reinforcement.

In the 1960s, research showed that a wide variety of behaviors in infants and children could become more frequent if they were reinforced. There was particular interest in the fact that social reinforcers, such as attention, smiles, and praise from other people, were especially potent.

The hope that studies of children's learning would lead to an adequate account of developmental changes in learning was not fulfilled. Research produced a complex literature, and investigators sometimes became so involved in examining parameters of a small set of tasks that they lost sight of the developmental issues that caused them to choose these tasks in the first place. Finally, one limitation, not unique to learning theory, was that much of the research was conducted with bright, upper-middle-class children in university towns. (Some 4-year-olds greeted experimenters with "What reinforcement do I get this time?") Despite the problems, this phase in the history of developmental psychology, from the early 1960s to the mid-1970s, was an exciting and fruitful time. The discipline was becoming a laboratory science, and "facts" were accumulating rapidly. A number of astonishingly productive and enthusiastic researchers conducted programmatic research using cleverly designed experimental tasks. There was confidence that developmental psychology was progressing.

Social Learning

The above historical context helps us understand early social learning theory. Social learning theory was born in the 1930s at Yale University, perhaps when Clark Hull offered a graduate seminar on relating learning theory to psychoanalysis. Many of those who would become the pioneers in social learning theory—O. H. Mowrer, Neal Miller, John Dollard, Robert Sears, Leonard Doob, and John Whiting—attended this seminar. One of the seminar topics led to the group's first major publication, *Frustration and Aggression* (Dollard et al., 1939), which explored the causes of aggression.

The young group of scholars, trained in learning theory by Hull but also inspired by Freud, combined these two traditions. In fact, one of their publications, *Personality and Psychotherapy* (Dollard & Miller, 1950), was dedicated to both Freud and Pavlov. Social learning theorists took interesting and important content from Freudian theory, such as the concepts of dependency, aggression, identification, conscience formation, and defense mechanisms, but sought explanations for behavior in principles of *S–R* (stimulus–response) learning, which could be observed, rather than the unconscious, which could not. In Dollard and Miller's words, "The ultimate goal is to combine the vitality of psychoanalysis, the rigor of the natural-science laboratory, and the facts of culture" (1950, p. 3). The guiding belief of social learning theorists was that personality is learned. They brought the parts of Freudian theory that were testable into the laboratory and ignored the rest. Thus, social learning theorists extended learning theory and changed its focus. By extending learning principles to important real-life social behaviors, they increased the plausibility of the theory.

Social learning theorists explored much territory in the 1940s and 1950s: imitation, neuroses, cross-cultural influences on personality, identification, and parental attitudes toward child rearing. Dollard and Miller were interested in developing psychotherapy based on social learning theory:

> If neurotic behavior is learned, it should be unlearned by some combination of the same principles by which it is taught. . . . We view the therapist as a kind of teacher and the patient as a learner. In the same way and by the same principles that bad tennis habits can be corrected by a good coach, so bad mental and emotional habits can be corrected by a psychotherapist. There is this difference, however. Whereas only a few people want to play tennis, all the world wants a clear, free, efficient mind.
>
> (1950, pp. 7–8)

A major focus of social learning theory was socialization, the process by which society attempts to teach children to behave like the ideal adults of that society. As Dollard and Miller observed, "A system of child training built on the laws of learning might have the same powerful effect on the neurotic misery of our time as Pasteur's work had on infectious diseases" (1950, p. 8). Research examined correlations between characteristics of parents (for example, authoritarianism) or their child-rearing practices (early toilet training) and the child's personality at a later time. A prototypic study examined dependency, identification, guilt, and conscience formation (Sears, Rau, & Alpert, 1965). A child, placed in a roomful of attractive toys, was asked to watch a hamster, which was in a box with no lid. The experimenter left the room to finish making the lid for the box. When the temptation to take a closer look at the toys became too great and the child took her eyes off the hamster for a moment, the hamster silently disappeared through a false floor in the box. Measures of conscience, specifically guilt, in the study included the length of time before deviating, the child's emotional reaction to the deviation, whether the child confessed, and on what the child blamed the disappearance.

Social learning theorists proposed that there are important learned drives, such as aggression and dependency, derived from primary biological drives. Thus, the need for food leads to a dependency drive, a need to be near the mother and nurtured by her. The presence of the mother becomes reinforcing. Psychologists rarely use the drive notion today.

In a major theoretical change in social learning theory, Miller and Dollard (1941) set out to show that one of the most powerful socialization forces is imitation. They proposed that a general tendency to imitate is learned because various imitative behaviors are reinforced, a process of operant conditioning. This reinforcement of imitation may start very early, as illustrated in the following episode involving an 11-month-old:

> Shamini (11 months), noticing great-grandmother snoring with open mouth, makes a face with jaws open wide but mouth pulled down to form a small "o" as an imitation of what was an extreme facial gesture. This causes enormous though slightly embarrassed hilarity in [the] rest of [the] family. Shamini responds directly to the laughing others, looking at their faces, laughing, and repeats her "face" with great amusement several times.
>
> (Reddy, 1991, p. 145)

Social learning theory gives two of Freud's key concepts a new perspective. First, identification with the same-sex parent involves a great deal of observational learning. Freud's notion that children "incorporate" the parent and acquire a superego actually may involve children's observing or inferring, from observation, the parent's values, beliefs, and behaviors. Children also control their own behavior by repeating to themselves the parent's approving or disapproving statements. Adults may praise a boy for being "just like his father." Children tend to imitate models, such as parents or siblings, who have been rewarding in the past. Second, children acquire defense mechanisms, such as displaced aggression, projection, and regression, by observing others use these defenses, especially if these behaviors appear to ward off punishment or unhappiness.

Bandura and Walters (1963) then carried the concept of modeling one step further by demonstrating that relatively new behaviors can be acquired by simply watching a model. (This cannot have been a stunning discovery to any parent!) The observer need not make an overt response or be reinforced. The punishment or reinforcement of the model's behavior has the same effect on the observer as it does on the model. Children who see a hard-working classmate praised by the teacher learn to try that behavior. And, on the side of evil, children who get away with a naughty behavior are quickly imitated as well. Bandura and Walters called this process *vicarious reinforcement*. Thus, learning occurs without overt behavior—"no-trial learning," in Bandura's words.

Bandura and Walters's theory greatly influenced developmental psychology in the 1960s and early 1970s. It guided the majority of laboratory and observational studies of aggression, sex typing, and resistance to temptation. There was great interest in discovering which characteristics of models, such as warmth, power, and similarity to the observer, encouraged imitation. In addition, the list of social reinforcers was expanded to include peers.

In recent years, Bandura's theory has become more cognitive. He now calls his theory "social cognitive theory" and defines learning as "knowledge acquisition through cognitive processing of information" (Bandura, 1986, p. xii). He rejects what he calls the radical behaviorist "cognitive bypass operation" (Evans, 1989, p. 83). He is less concerned with the literal duplication of behavior (imitation) than with observational learning as a more general process of acquiring information from another person, verbally or visually. In 1980, the American Psychological Association recognized Bandura's contributions with a Distinguished Scientific Contribution award "for masterful modeling as researcher, teacher, and theoretician" (*American Psychologist*, 1981, p. 27). The rest of this chapter emphasizes his current account of social learning.

GENERAL ORIENTATION TO THE THEORY

Fashioning a general orientation is difficult because learning theory is actually many theories, including some approaches, particularly Skinner's, that claim not to be theories at all. It is outside the scope of this chapter to explore the differences among these theories. Fortunately, despite their differences, they share important assumptions or characteristics. This orientation focuses on social learning theory (designated as "SLT" in the headings below) but also traces its conceptual roots in traditional learning theory (TLT). Within each section, discussion centers first on traditional learning theory and then on modern social learning theory, especially Bandura's position. The topics are the emphasis on learning (TLT), especially observational learning (SLT); a causal model that includes the environment (TLT) or an environment–person–behavior system (SLT); the view that acquired behaviors can be simple (TLT) or complex (SLT); the focus on both observable behaviors (TLT and SLT) and underlying cognitive processing (SLT); self-efficacy (SLT); and the use of experimental methods (TLT and SLT).

Emphasis on Learning (TLT), Especially Observational Learning (SLT)

Traditional Learning Theory ▪ Learning theorists emphasize environmental, nonbiological influences on behavior, in contrast to Piaget and Freud, who address the interaction of innate and experiential influences. However, learning theorists acknowledge that biology sets limits on what each species can learn, when it can learn the behavior, and how quickly it can learn it. Species-specific behaviors sometimes intrude on learned behaviors, as demonstrated dramatically by two of Skinner's former students, Breland and Breland (1961), who trained animals commercially. While trying to train raccoons to drop tokens into a slot, the Brelands found that the animals stopped to "wash" the tokens, as if they were food, even though there was no water around.

Although there are many definitions of *learning*, a common one is "a more or less permanent change in behavior which occurs as a result of practice" (Kimble, 1961, p. 2). At its simplest, learning consists of some sort of association or connection between a stimulus and a response. At its most complex, learning involves acquiring abstract rules or a chain of reasoning.

Traditionally, learning has been divided into two types: *operant conditioning* (also called *instrumental conditioning*) and *classical conditioning*. Skinner thoroughly explored operant conditioning, which begins with a behavior that a child spontaneously produces. A child "operates" on the environment. This behavior becomes conditioned when it comes under the control of a particular stimulus. Some stimulus leads the child to produce a certain behavior in order to receive a reinforcement. Babies learn that when a parent appears, if they smile at the parent (the operant behavior), the parent will pick them up and play with them (the reinforcement). If this sequence occurs a number of times, smiling can be said to be operantly conditioned as it increases in frequency. Thousands of behaviors can be operantly conditioned in the same way, ranging from rats' pressing a bar to children's drooling (Johnston, Sloane, & Bijou, 1966) to pigeons' guiding missiles to their targets in Skinner's Project Pigeon during World War II.

Behavior modification is the application of principles of operant conditioning to naturally occurring undesirable behaviors, such as temper tantrums, avoidance of social interaction, and, with autism, the lack of spoken language. The approach assumes that a common set of learning principles underlies both normal and abnormal behavior. A psychologist changes the reinforcement contingencies so that desirable behavior is reinforced and thereby maintained while undesirable behavior is ignored and thereby weakened. That is, in behavior modification, you try to catch the child doing something right and reinforce it. Harris, Wolf, and Baer (1967) observed an extremely withdrawn child who spent 80 percent of the time at nursery school in solitary activities. Their observations revealed that the teachers had unintentionally reinforced this behavior by talking to him and comforting him when he was alone. The teachers ignored the child when he played with others. The program of behavior modification reversed the above contingencies. The teachers attended to the boy when he joined a group and ignored him when he withdrew. He soon spent 60 percent of his time playing with other children.

In contrast to operant conditioning, classical conditioning begins with a reflex—an innate connection between a stimulus and a response. Behaviors that can be classically conditioned include salivating when food is placed in the mouth, sucking when a nipple is placed in the infant's mouth, and constricting the pupil when a light is shone into the eye. The response is elicited, rather than spontaneously emitted, as was the case in operant conditioning. An unconditioned stimulus (nipple placed in the mouth) elicits the unconditioned response (sucking). A conditioned stimulus (sight of the bottle) occurs just before the bottle is given. After repeated pairing of the bottle and sucking, simply showing a bottle produces sucking. A new stimulus substitutes for an old one. Sucking has become a conditioned response. More exotic examples are asthmatic attacks triggered by stimuli such as elevators, children's choirs, bicycle races, political speeches, and the national anthem (Dekker & Groen, 1956).

The most famous case of classical conditioning in children is the "Little Albert" experiment. Watson and Rayner (1920) conditioned a fear response in 11-month-old Albert. They placed a white rat in front of the toddler. As he reached for it, they struck a steel bar behind him with a hammer, producing a noxious, painful sound. Albert started violently and cried. After several repetitions of this pairing of the rat and the sound, Albert cried and crawled away when the rat alone was presented. Albert's fear was a conditioned response to the conditioned stimulus, the white rat. The initial reflex was that the noxious sound (unconditioned stimulus) produced pain (unconditioned response). The conditioned response generalized to objects such as a rabbit, a fur coat, and a Santa Claus mask. Unfortunately for Albert, his mother removed him from the experiment before Watson had a chance to decondition him. Harris (1979), however, points out that although the Little Albert experiment is one of psychology's most famous, it apparently was not as successful at establishing a conditioned fear response as is commonly believed. Over the years, textbook writers have "improved" the results of this now-famous case. In addition, there were methodological problems that muddy any interpretation of the results.

At a later time, one of Watson's students, Mary Cover Jones (1924), found that a naturally acquired fear of animals in a 2-year-old child, Peter, could be eliminated by extinguishing this response, which presumably was a conditioned response. Peter was seated in a highchair and given a snack, which produced a positive response. As he ate, a white rabbit in a cage was brought closer and closer. The conditioned stimulus (the white rabbit) was not allowed to become powerful enough to evoke the response of fear by, for example, suddenly being brought too near. As the stimulus occurred without the related fear response, this association was weakened. At the same time, eating, the positive response, was replacing the negative fear response to the rabbit. The procedure was quite successful. By the end of the study, Peter was stroking the rabbit and letting it nibble his fingers. This treatment obviously requires a skillful experimenter who does not inadvertently teach the child to associate eating with fear!

There is an interesting footnote to this research. Peter had to enter a hospital for treatment of scarlet fever. As Peter was leaving the hospital, an unfortunate incident occurred. A large dog lunged at him, frightening him terribly. When Jones then retested Peter, he had reacquired his fear response to animals and had to be deconditioned again.

This deconditioning technique for overcoming fears contrasts with Freud's psychoanalytic study of Little Hans's fear of horses. Whereas Freud was concerned with the deep-seated, underlying anxieties, learning theorists try to change the behavior. If Hans would very gradually approach horses and at the same time establish some positive response to horses, his conditioned fear response should weaken. Freud's view would be that these procedures treat only the symptoms, not the underlying psychological cause of the problem. If one symptom is removed, another may appear in its place.

It is difficult to extinguish phobias without intervention because they are self-perpetuating. By avoiding the feared situation, people reduce the rising anxiety. Thus, the phobia is reinforced. In addition, they have no opportunity to extinguish the fear because they do not allow the feared stimulus to be present. There is an old joke about a man who is asked why he always holds a banana in his ear. His answer is that it keeps the lions away. When told there are no lions around, he replies, "See? It works!" Behaviors that are perceived to bring reinforcement are difficult to unlearn.

In summary, for learning theorists, development involves the accumulation of operantly and classically conditioned responses. In Bijou and Baer's words, "The developing child may be adequately regarded, in conceptual terms, as a cluster of interrelated responses interacting with stimuli" (1961, p. 15). Both operant and classical conditioning can be established within the first few days of birth, although with classical conditioning the learning is accomplished only after a large number of trials. Thus, learning changes behavior, and thereby causes development, from birth.

Modern Social Learning Theory ▪ Social learning theorists retained the focus on learning but broadened the notion of learning in two main ways. First, they were especially interested in social behavior and the social context of behavior. They argued that learning theories based on animal research are inadequate to account for human behavior, which occurs in a social milieu. Children act aggressively, share, play with peers, learn sex-typed behaviors, and develop independence. Much of the socialization of children involves the shaping of behaviors directed toward other people. Thus, social learning theorists broadened the *content* of learning theory by proposing that even social behaviors could be explained by principles of learning.

Even behaviors that are not social in nature are influenced by the social *context* in which they occur. A boy's attempts to learn to play the piano may be reinforced by his parents but actively discouraged by his baseball teammates. As children grow older, others' expectations of them become greater. A 4-year-old who cannot add is not a cause for alarm to adults, but a 7-year-old who cannot add faces a social environment in school directed toward learning this concept.

Second, social learning theorists broadened the *types* of learning to be explained. They saw the importance of observational learning: acquiring new skills or information or altering old behaviors simply by watching other children and adults or even reading a book. In fact, Bandura (1986) claims that most learning comes from observational learning and instruction rather than from overt, trial-and-error behavior. Children may not even show they have learned from observing until much later, and the model need not be reinforced in order for the observer to learn. Thus, observational learning is particularly important for explaining how novel, complex behaviors are acquired during development. Operant conditioning can gradually produce relatively new behaviors by shaping, but it cannot explain how complex new behaviors emerge suddenly after the child watches peers play a new game or watches the antics of superheroes on television. Observational learning is especially important for acquiring behaviors in areas where mistakes are costly or life-threatening. There cannot be much trial-and-error learning in studying brain surgery or learning to drive a car.

How observational learning occurs can be illustrated by a real-life example and a laboratory study. One skill acquired by many boys and girls today is playing soccer. This skill includes a complex set of conceptual- and perceptual-motor skills. It is doubtful that this skill could be taught simply by telling the child how to play the game (just try telling a child how to do a "header"—hitting the ball with one's head), though this type of instruction is important. Much of the learning comes from observing models playing—older children, parents, coaches, and professional soccer players on television. These models are particularly likely to be imitated because they are perceived as having high status, competence, and power—characteristics that encourage imitation (Bandura, 1986). Books on how to play soccer provide symbolic models. These various types of models demonstrate how to travel with the ball, pass, attempt goals, make corner kicks, and express elation appropriately after scoring a goal.

To a great extent, children learn the game through what Bandura calls *abstract modeling*—abstracting a general rule from observing specific behaviors. The child gradually extracts general concepts of group action in the game: team defensive strategy, the prediction of where one's teammates will be at a particular moment, strategies concerning how to play one's position, and so on.

During the course of observational learning, children try to reproduce the behaviors they have seen and receive feedback regarding how closely their behavior matched that of the model. A skillful pass meets with success when it reaches another player. Also, the coach may praise this behavior. An attempt to score that misses the goal gives immediate feedback, and players may adjust the angle of their kick next time or seek further verbal instruction or demonstration from others. This reinforcement or nonreinforcement serves primarily as a source of information to children concerning their behavior. This feedback also serves as an incentive, encouraging children to seek future self-satisfaction, achievement, competence, or attention from others by participating in soccer. Still, reinforcement or punishment to the model or the child is not *necessary* for observational learning to occur: "After the capacity for observational learning has fully developed, one cannot keep people from learning what they have seen" (Bandura, 1977, p. 38).

Of the numerous laboratory studies that illustrate observational learning, an early influential one by Bandura, Ross, and Ross (1961) is described at the beginning of this chapter. Preschool children saw an aggressive adult model punch a large, inflated Bobo doll and hit it on the head with a hammer, saying "Sock him in the nose" and "Pow." In a comparison group, the model played nonaggressively with Tinkertoys, and a control group had no model. Later, the children played in a room that contained a variety of aggressive toys (Bobo doll, dart guns, tetherball with a face painted on it) and nonaggressive toys (tea set, teddy bears, trucks), including the toys the adult model had used aggressively. The children who had observed the aggressive model were more aggressive than the children who had seen a nonaggressive model or no model. It is debatable, however, whether the children were expressing "aggression" or simply playing vigorously in a setting in which doing so seemed to be approved by adults.

It is clear that Bandura and Freud give us opposite predictions concerning the effects of watching aggression in other people. Freud would see such an activity as a way of reducing aggressive tensions, thus lessening subsequent aggression. In contrast, Bandura would predict that viewing aggression, especially if the aggression is not punished, is likely to cause imitation, thereby increasing aggression.

We can conclude that children may become more aggressive as a result of observing an aggressive model. But how, exactly, does the model cause aggression? A model can cause imitative behaviors in several ways:

1. *Teaching new behaviors.* Perhaps the children in the above study learned new forms of aggression, such as hitting a Bobo doll over the head with a hammer.

2. *Strengthening or weakening children's inhibitions.* Although parents presumably had taught the children not to be aggressive (and the comparison groups were not aggressive), the aggressive model may have disinhibited the children's aggression. Disinhibition was especially likely because the model was not punished. Evidence for a general disinhibition of aggression comes from the fact that some of the aggressive behaviors differed from those presented by the model, for example, firing imaginary shots at objects in the room and saying "Stupid ball" and "Knock over people."

3. *Drawing attention to particular objects* and thereby increasing their use in various ways.

4. *Increasing emotional arousal,* which typically increases responsiveness.

A further result in this study is noteworthy. Boys were physically more aggressive than girls. Thus, characteristics of the child influence imitation. However, other studies (e.g., Bandura, 1965) revealed that one must make a distinction between learning and performance. We know that girls *learn* as much aggression from the model as do boys, because they can produce the aggressive behaviors when asked to or rewarded for doing so. However, they typically do not *produce* as much physical aggression, perhaps because there are stricter inhibitions of this behavior in girls than boys. The finding that children learn and remember what they observe even if it is not reproduced immediately is of interest to people concerned with violent models on television shows watched by children. Even if children do not immediately reproduce the aggression, they may store it for future use.

Researchers have used the basic paradigm of Bandura's study to examine a variety of models (filmed, symbolic, real) and a variety of behaviors (prosocial behavior, styles of information processing, conservation of number). It is clear that observational learning is widespread during childhood. Much of the enculturation of children involves exhibiting desirable social behaviors and strategies of problem solving. Many of the behaviors pervasive within a culture reflect the fact that children in the culture are exposed to the same or similar models.

Observational learning also accounts in part for differences in personality among cultures. For example, cultures vary in how much effort they put into teaching aggression. The Dugum Dani, a warrior society in the New Guinea highlands, have a training program that brings boys closer and closer to real warfare (Gardner & Heider, 1969). War games include skewering the enemy (berry seeds) on a sharp stick, spearing a hoop tossed by the opposition, battling with grass "spears," and watching real battles from a distance. In contrast, the Polynesians of the Society Islands actively discourage aggression and rarely provide aggressive models (Levy, 1969). They teach their children that spirits punish aggression with illness and injury.

Observational learning not only is a process of normal socialization but also can be a therapy for problem behaviors. For example, observational learning can help children overcome fears. In another study by Bandura (1967), nursery school children who were afraid of dogs watched a child happily approach a dog gradually and play with it. After the therapy and even 1 month later, most of the previously fearful children would hand-feed a dog and even climb into a playpen with it. Showing the modeling sequence on film also proved effective in reducing fears.

■ *Causal Model Includes Environment (TLT) or Environment–Person–Behavior System(SLT)*

I imagine the mind of children as easily turned, this or that way as water itself.

—*John Locke*

Traditional Learning Theory ■ The belief that changes in behavior are largely brought about by experience is closely linked with the interest in environmental influences on behavior. Skinner claimed that "a person does not act upon the world, the world acts upon him" (1971, p. 211). The environment is viewed as a set of stimuli. Stimuli can play several roles. They can serve as signals for the onset of reinforcement if the proper response is emitted; become linked with unconditioned stimuli and eventually elicit conditioned responses; become associated with responses, as in the verbal learning of pairs of nonsense stimuli; or serve as punishment or reinforcement. Thus, stimuli control behavior by determining which behavior occurs, when and where it occurs, and how frequently it occurs. In this way, a child's development takes a particular course.

It is interesting that learning theory's emphasis on the role of the environment fits so well with American egalitarian ideals. If the environment offers equal opportunity for all, then all humans can achieve their potential. A strong version of this belief in the influence of the environment is expressed in a famous quote from Watson:

> Give me a dozen healthy infants, well-formed, and my own specified world to bring them up in and I'll guarantee to take any one at random and train him to become any type of specialist I might select—doctor, lawyer, artist, merchant, chief, and yes, even beggar-man and thief, regardless of his talents, penchants, tendencies, abilities, vocations, and race of his ancestors.
>
> (1924, p. 104)

It should be noted that Watson goes on to say: "I am going beyond my facts, and I admit it, but so have the advocates of the contrary and they have been doing it for many thousands of years."

The environment changes not only the frequency of behavior but also its form—through *shaping*. Pigeons do not naturally play table tennis. However, by beginning with the table-tennis-related behaviors they do have, it is possible to slowly modify these behaviors into a chain of movements appropriate to table tennis. The experimenter "ups the ante" (raises the requirement for obtaining reinforcement) as the behavior gradually comes to approximate the desired behavior. Early in training, moving toward the ball might be sufficient to receive reinforcement, but later on it may be necessary to make the ball drop onto the opponent's side in order to receive reinforcement.

Skinner has described his first attempt to use shaping on a human:

> I soon tried the procedure on a human subject—our 9-month-old daughter. I was holding her on my lap one evening when I turned on a table lamp beside the chair. She looked up and smiled, and I decided to see whether I could use the light as a reinforcer. I waited for a slight movement of her left hand and turned on the light for a moment. Almost immediately, she moved her hand again, and again I reinforced. I began to wait for bigger movements, and within a short time, she was lifting her arm in a wide arc— "to turn on the light."
>
> (1980, p. 196)

Modern Social Learning Theory ▪ Although social learning theorists agree that the environment exerts a great deal of influence on behavior, they consider it only one of many forces operating in any situation. The entire learning context includes biological and psychological characteristics of the person (*P*), the person's behavior (*B*), and the environment (*E*). These three factors are highly interdependent, and each factor influences, and is influenced by, each of the others. The factors interact via a process that Bandura calls *triadic reciprocal causation*. Consider a situation in which a child observes another child giving some of his pennies to help poor children. Several characteristics of the observing child influence whether she will imitate this behavior ($P \rightarrow B$). Is she cognitively and socially developed enough to understand what it means to be poor? What are her standards of fairness or social justice? Is she even attending to the model's behavior at all? Has she observed her parents contributing to charities in the past? The environmental factors might include the social attractiveness of the model, whether the model was praised after he gave, the salience of the model in that situation, and other social influences ($E \rightarrow P$, $E \rightarrow B$). If the girl feels pleased with herself after sharing, the behavioral act of sharing affects the observing child psychologically ($B \rightarrow P$). Cognition is important in this process; children symbolically represent the relationships among the situation, their behavior, and the outcome.

Bandura (1997) describes three types of environments: imposed, selected, and created. An *imposed environment* is thrust on people. They cannot control its presence, but they have some control over how they construe it and react to it. For example, children must attend school but vary in whether they feel positive or negative about it. A *selected environment* is the part of the potential environment that people actually experience. Only the parts of the environment that children select and activate can affect them. A high school student selects certain school courses but not others. A student may take advantage of extracurricular activities and engage in rewarding leadership experiences or become entangled in peer pressure to engage in risky behaviors such as heavy drinking. *Created environments* are those that children construct through their behavior ($B \rightarrow E$, $P \rightarrow E$). Children who watch television a great deal expose themselves to a different set of models from that of children who usually play with friends instead. Or children may perfect a skill, such as drawing or ballet dancing, that creates an environment of social reinforcement in the form of praise from others. In the sharing situation described above, the child who has habitually shared in the past and thereby elicited warmth and gratitude from others has created a positive, supportive milieu for herself. In contrast, an aggressive child may create a hostile world for herself wherever she goes, causing others to react negatively toward her. Thus, people are active agents who can create or change their environments.

Evidence that children's behavior can change their social environment comes from a study by Brunk and Henngeler (1984). Two 10-year-old child actors exhibited either anxious–withdrawn or aggressively noncompliant behavior in a setting in which mothers (not theirs) attempted to engage each boy in a game of checkers. The mothers used more helping and rewards with the anxious–withdrawn child and more ignoring, commands, and discipline with the aggressively noncompliant boy. Thus, the boys "created" two different social environments.

Acquired Behavior Can Be Simple (TLT) or Complex (SLT)

Traditional Learning Theory ■ Behavior is complex. People learn to play chess, write computer programs, organize governments, and create soufflés. Learning theorists' *reductionist* strategy for understanding complex behavior is to break it down into simple units, study the units, and then put the behavior back together again. The simplest units are *associations*—the atoms of psychology. The research strategy, then, is to study simple associations, then chains of *S–R* associations, and perhaps even hierarchies of chains. Metaphorically, many simple units of Tinkertoy sticks and joiners are combined to form a larger structure. During development, *S–R* associations can be strengthened, weakened, or chained with other associations.

The breakdown of complex concepts into simpler parts and the sequencing of units to be learned also characterize programmed instruction, a precursor of computerized instruction. In this technique, inspired by Skinner's analysis of operant learning, children read a short passage, answer a question, and then are told whether they are correct.

In contrast to learning psychologists, Freud and Piaget claimed that a simple behavior has meaning and can be understood only in its structural context. If complex behavior is reduced to simpler elements, the structure is destroyed and consequently the behavior is destroyed, in a sense. Thus, one can understand a child's smiling and crying only by knowing the overall structure of the parent–child relationship and the child's organized perception of this relationship

Modern Social Learning Theory ■ After children acquire new behaviors by observing various models, they can combine these behaviors to form more complex behaviors. A girl may become sex-typed by imitating behaviors of her mother, older sister, female teachers, and females on television. Learning to play basketball requires integrating a number of simpler subskills, such as dribbling, guarding, and shooting baskets. Children cognitively reorganize behaviors learned earlier. By mentally manipulating symbols, children can form unique combinations of these behaviors.

In addition to forming complex behaviors by drawing on various previously observed behaviors, it is possible to learn whole complex behaviors all at once. A young child may learn to play Monopoly after watching peers play one game. Acquiring large chunks of behavior by observation is a very efficient way to learn.

Focus on Observable Behavior (TLT and SLT) and Underlying Cognitive Processing (SLT)

What is Matter? — Never mind.
What is Mind? — No matter.

— Punch, 1855

Traditional Learning Theory ■ When the behaviorists revolted against the introspectionist psychologies of the early 1900s, they carved out what they believed to be the proper object of study: observable behavior rather than mental structures or conscious experience. Just as physical scientists could observe physical events, psychologists could now point to physical events (behaviors) as the content of their science. Rats press bars, children push buttons, and adults say words. Observable behavior is available to public inspection and can be objectively measured. Of course, there have always been some unobservable entities in learning theory. For example, no one has ever directly observed an "association" between a stimulus and a response. And over the years, the observable stimuli and responses went underground, and mental *S–R* chains, expectations, concepts, and rules entered the vocabulary of learning theory.

Modern Social Learning Theory ■ Bandura's social learning theory is a synthesis of earlier versions of social learning, which focused on overt, imitative behaviors, and cognitive theory, particularly information-processing theory (see Chapter 4). Figure 3.1 presents Bandura's (1986) outline of the cognitive processes underlying observational learning and, to provide a context, the other component processes involved in observational learning. Much like a computer program, the child selects and processes information, applies general rules or principles, weighs infor-

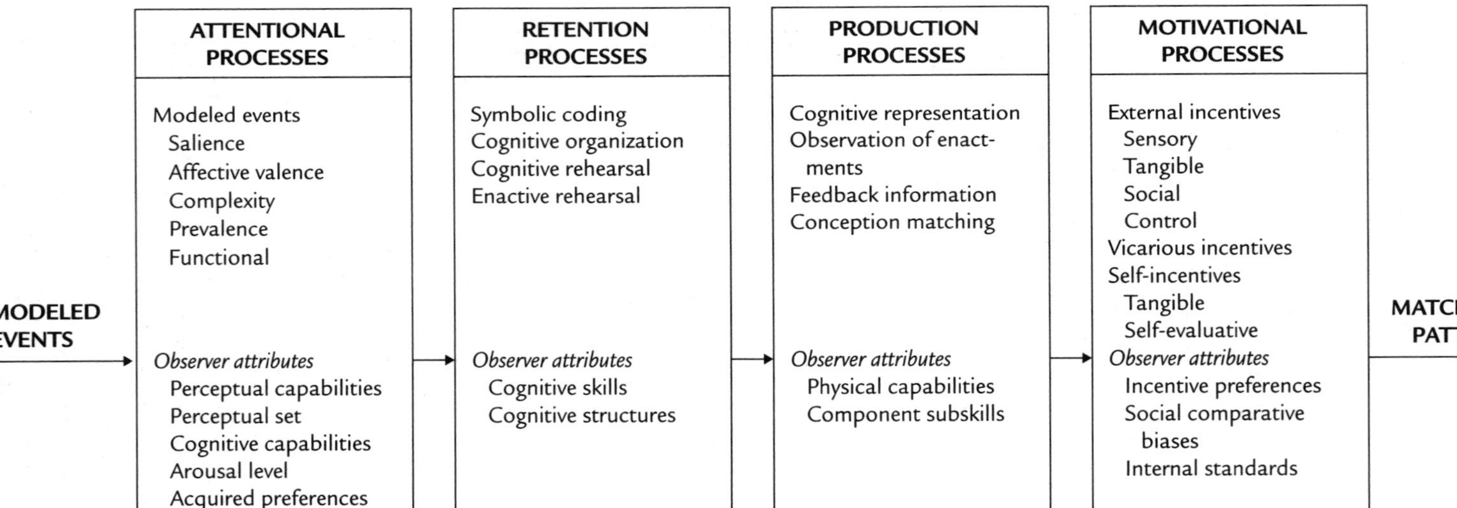

Figure 3.1

Subprocesses underlying observational learning, according to Bandura.

SOURCE: From Albert Bandura, *Social Foundations of Thought and Action,* ©1986, p. 52. Reprinted by permission of Prentice-Hall, Inc., Englewood Cliffs, NJ.

mation, and makes a decision. Cognitive factors influence what is observed, how that person or event is perceived, how this new information is organized for the future, whether the observational learning has a lasting effect, and what this effect is.

Information-processing theory stresses both attention and retention processes. Children must attend to a model before it can have an influence. They attend to the important features of the model's behavior and ignore unimportant features. Characteristics of both the model and the observer control attention. Certain models command attention because of their attractiveness, based on their high status or power. Certain behaviors of models, such as aggression, are more salient than others. Models appearing on television in adventure-filled programs are particularly effective at capturing attention. As summarized in Figure 3.1, attention to a model and its behavior is most likely if the model is salient and attractive, if the model's behavior is not too complex, if there are many opportunities to see the behavior (prevalence), and if the model's behavior has proved to be effective (functional value).

Children's ability to attend selectively and their past experiences influence which models they attend to and how effectively they attend. Mature perceptual capacities and an optimal level of arousal encourage attention to important aspects of the model's behavior. Children's perceptual set (what they expect to see), their cognitive ability to comprehend the event, and their preferences (interests) also influence which features they select for processing.

Even if children attend to the model's behavior, it has little influence unless they retain it for future use when the model no longer is present. Children must translate the event into symbols, integrate it into their cognitive organization, and rehearse it cognitively. *Cognitive rehearsal*, or visualizing oneself successfully carrying out the desired sequence of activities, is a skill that outstanding athletes develop to a high degree as they mentally prepare for competition. *Enactive rehearsal* involves activities such as actually practicing the modeled behavior or verbally rehearsing it. Symbols are either visual images or verbal codes, depending on the behavior modeled and the child's developmental level. Bandura emphasizes that the representation of the model need not be structurally similar to the model's behavior. It may be a conception, rule, or set of propositions that abstracts the underlying conceptual structure rather than the concrete event itself.

The two remaining component processes, production processes and motivational processes, pertain to the performance of behaviors once they are learned through observation. Although both components have been topics of interest for learning theory throughout its history, social learning theory gives them a cognitive interpretation. During production, children mentally select and organize responses to serve as a representational model with which to compare the performed behavior. As a result of receiving feedback while monitoring this performance, children may modify their initial response. Finally, through motivational processes, children tend to reproduce behavior they see resulting in desirable outcomes. In contrast to Piaget, who examined only the cognitive development underlying imitation, Bandura is interested also in why a child is motivated to imitate only certain actions of certain models at certain times and places.

Bandura's notion of abstract modeling, described earlier, is a radical departure from traditional learning theory. Bandura proposes that children can formulate an abstract rule by pulling out the relevant elements from a number of specific episodes of observational learning. Abstract modeling is the main mechanism for explaining language learning. As children observe that the past tense is usually formed by adding *-ed*, they abstract this as a general rule and correctly say "walked" and "talked" and incorrectly say "hitted" and "doed." They may even make very complex incorrect utterances such as "He was disingappeared."

Unlike the case in Piaget's theory of cognition, thinking stays near the surface in Bandura's theory. That is, children detect regularities in the environment and generalize them; for example, "I'm usually good at that sort of game." These external events are translated into a symbolic form and combined with other symbolically represented events or used as information to develop a more general rule; however, the theory does not specify a complex reworking of the information or the construction of broad cognitive structures of the type described by Piaget. Bandura's concepts are more like summary statements about the world.

■ *Self-Efficacy (SLT)*

"I think I can. I think I can. I think I can."

—*Piper*, The Little Engine That Could, *1989/1930.*
(quoted in Maddux, 1998)

In recent years, Bandura has emphasized *self-efficacy*—people's perception of their competence in dealing with their environment. A more formal definition is "beliefs in one's capabilities to organize and execute the courses of action required to produce given attainments" (Bandura,

1997, p. 31). These courses of action may include behavior, thoughts, and emotions. Self-efficacy affects all types of behavior—academic, social, or recreational. Children may have the necessary skills for mastering a task, but if they do not perceive themselves as capable of actually using their skills to master the task, they may fail or, unlike "the little engine that could," may not even attempt the task. For example, Collins (1982) gave difficult math problems to children with high or low math self-efficacy within each of two groups, differing in levels of math ability. Although math ability obviously influenced their performance, significant effects of self-efficacy emerged as well. Within each ability level, children who perceived themselves as efficacious solved more problems, more quickly rejected strategies that did not work, more willingly reworked failed problems, and displayed more positive attitudes toward mathematics. This positive reaction to failure among highly efficacious children reflects their attributions of their failure to insufficient effort. In contrast, low-efficacy children attribute their failure to low ability, an attribution that does not encourage them to try again.

The work on self-efficacy has two particularly important implications for development. First, in Bandura's view, the efficacy judgments most conducive to development are slight overestimations, because these motivate children to try moderately challenging tasks that could hone their present skills. The second implication concerns children's motivation to become self-directed learners. High self-efficacy is essential for persisting in the face of rejection. Bandura recounts the many rejections encountered by talented people who persisted:

> James Joyce's *The Dubliners* was rejected by 22 publishers. Gertrude Stein submitted poems to editors for about 20 years before one was finally accepted. Hollywood initially rejected the incomparable Fred Astaire as "a balding, skinny actor who can dance a little." Decca Records turned down a recording contract with the Beatles with the unprophetic evaluation, "We don't like their sound. Groups of guitars are on their way out." . . . Walt Disney's proposed theme park was rejected by the city of Anaheim on the grounds that it would only attract riffraff.
>
> (1997, p. 73)

During development, children gradually construct their self-knowledge about their efficacy in various situations from four main types of information. The most authentic and direct source of information is the success or failure of previous similar attempts. A second source is the vicarious experience of observing others fail or succeed on similar tasks. If children perceive themselves as similar to a model who succeeds, their self-efficacy is enhanced. In addition, children can acquire new coping strategies by observing successful others. A third source of information is verbal persuasion: Others talk children into believing they have the ability to achieve their goal. An example is a coach's locker-room halftime pep talk. Finally, information comes from one's physiological and affective states: arousal, anxiety, fatigue, and physical pain. Cognitive development contributes to children's learning to integrate these four sources of information.

For all four sources of information, developmental changes influence how accurately children can process the information. The acquisition of language, the broadening of social awareness, increased differentiation of internal states, and the development of self-appraisal skills all play a role. Beginning in infancy, humans gradually develop a sense of personal agency, a sense that they can cause effects in their environment, which is essential for self-efficacy. Differentiating oneself from others during infancy and accurately comparing oneself with others during childhood contribute as well. The family is the main contribution to the young child's self-efficacy. Parents' self-efficacy regarding their parenting skills mediates many of the correlates of parenting quality such as maternal depression, child temperament, social support, and poverty (Coleman & Karraker, 1997). The peer-group and school context become increasingly important during middle childhood. Children with low social self-efficacy "exhibit social withdrawal, perceive low acceptance by their peers, and have a low sense of self-worth" (Bandura, 1997, p. 173). Children with high self-efficacy for aggression are quick to use aggression with their peers to obtain goals. Schooling, of course, contributes greatly to children's sense of intellectual efficacy in various areas.

Throughout the life span there are changes in which aspects of self-efficacy are most important. For example, adolescence and young adulthood bring new challenges to self-efficacy regarding interpersonal relationships, physical appearance, and occupational competence. During middle age, people may reevaluate their lives, doubt their efficacy concerning physical performance, and seek to achieve efficacy in new areas. A divorce or retooling for a new occupation may be the outcome. The elderly may face damaged self-efficacy as a result of perceived memory loss, slowed reactions, and lessened self-esteem because they no longer hold a job. A self-fulfilling prophecy can occur: if the elderly are insecure about their efficacy and expect to fail, they may limit their range of activities and invest little effort in any activity, thus ensuring their failure. Bandura argues that true declines as a result of aging can be offset to a great extent by real-world knowledge and coping strategies acquired throughout one's lifetime.

Self-efficacy is related to the processing of information outlined in Figure 3.1. Interesting processing biases may be at work. People who tend to attend to and recall the negative features of their performance may underestimate their efficacy. Thus, parents and teachers can enhance children's self-efficacy by drawing attention to the positive aspects of their performance and thereby increasing the salience of those aspects.

Bandura recently has introduced the idea of *collective efficacy*—a group's shared belief in its ability, through collective action, to produce valued outcomes. For example, efficacious schools have characteristics such as strong academic leadership by administrators, high academic standards and the belief that students can meet them, and instruction that encourages students to exercise control over their performance. Bandura believes that collective political efficacy in local communities and nationally can bring about social change that addresses social problems such as poor schools, illiteracy, poor health practices, risky behaviors, unwanted pregnancies, and the threat of nuclear war. Collective efficacy can empower individuals, and individuals can increase collective efficacy.

Methodology (TLT and SLT)

Traditional Learning Theory ▪ Learning theory took the physical sciences as its model, an emphasis that has been called "physics envy." The preferred method of study, therefore, was the tightly controlled, small-scale laboratory experiment. This precision was an important step, historically. Researchers adopted William James's (1920) attitude: "I wished, by treating psychology like a natural science, to help her become one." Researchers described stimuli and responses in an objective and precise way so that the experiment could be replicated in other laboratories. They measured learning by the number of trials needed to solve the problem or to establish the conditioned response or by the number of responses per unit of time.

The investigator's need to define and control the environment led to the development of certain apparatuses and paradigms suited to this purpose. One such apparatus is the Skinner box, a cage-box containing a lever that the animal presses, thereby delivering a food pellet to the tray below. Skinner's concern with controlling the environment can be seen in another invention: a completely enclosed, temperature-controlled, soundproof "baby tender" constructed for one of his own infants. This device has been called a "baby box" and even an "heir conditioner" (Bradley, 1989). It was not, as many people believed, a Skinner box for conditioning babies.

Many studies include a number of participants in each experimental condition and compare conditions by looking at group characteristics, such as the average number of trials required to learn a problem. However, studies of operant conditioning sometimes examine changes over time in an individual. In behavior modification, a common design is the *A-B-A* design. After determining the child's usual frequency of hitting behavior (*A*), the experimenter causes a decline in hitting as that behavior is ignored and prosocial behaviors are rewarded (*B*). Then, to prove that the changed contingencies are responsible for the change in behavior, the experimenter discontinues these new contingencies (*A*) and hitting increases. Afterward, of course, the desirable behavior is reinstated by further behavior modification.

Modern Social Learning Theory ■ Social learning theory retains the methodological spirit of traditional learning theory—rigorous, well-controlled laboratory experiments, such as the ones at the start of this chapter, that determine which variables affect learning. Bandura's theory is a loosely organized set of modest, limited hypotheses that have been modified as a result of experimental evidence.

EXAMPLES OF DEVELOPMENTAL RESEARCH: MORAL JUDGMENTS AND GENDER ROLES

■ *Moral Judgments*

For Piaget, learning is a sort of "applied cognition" as one's cognitive structure is used to interpret new situations. What children can learn about morality depends on their cognitive level. Piaget posited changes in the organization of thought. The child moves from an objective perspective, in which the amount of damage and degree of punishment are considered, to a subjective perspective, in which intentions and extenuating circumstances (such as fatigue or life-or-death factors) are taken into account. Change occurs because of the equilibration process, which brings into harmony social experience, experience with physical objects, and physical maturation.

Social learning theorists (e.g., Rosenthal & Zimmerman, 1978) argue that because structuralists like Piaget are primarily concerned with underlying cognitive structures, they do not have a robust theory of performance. That is, structuralists do poorly at explaining how the child's knowledge is expressed in behavior and why a child might apply her moral knowledge in one situation but not another. Social learning theorists carefully consider how the particular situation, the child's previous history of observational learning, and the particular content area determine the child's moral judgments.

Social learning theorists attribute developmental changes in moral judgments to changes in a child's criteria for judgments, such as intentions, clumsiness, amount of damage, and long-range consequences. Also important are the child's personal standards, adults' prohibitions, the expected punishment or reward, and peer influence. The particular factors the child thinks are important vary from situation to situation, depending on variables such as which situational factors are operating, which causes are most salient, and what the child processes cognitively. Moral judgments involve a complex process of considering and weighing various criteria in a given social situation. Thus, moral judgments are expected to be much more variable from time to time and from situation to situation within a social learning framework than within a Piagetian framework. In some situations the child makes subjective judgments (based on intentions) and in other situations makes objective judgments (based on amount of damage). This is true from preschool age through adulthood. Rosenthal and Zimmerman argue that there are no dichotomous, mutually exclusive types of moral reasoning. Rather, the frequency of using various criteria changes from situation to situation and from age to age. Still, social learning theorists recognize that children must attain a certain level of cognition before they can comprehend certain types of moral reasoning.

The increase in making subjective judgments as a function of age reflects the increasing exposure to models making subjective judgments, adults' heightened expectations of older children, older children's ease of inferring internal states from situational cues, the lessening effect of the salience of consequences, and the more refined analysis of moral criteria by older children. For example, when disciplining a child, parents are more likely to explain their reasons for doing so if the child is 8 years old rather than 3 years old. The younger child is not impressed with arguments about fairness and equality and may respond better to physical controls. Similarly, parents' presentation of legal codes and societal punishment may be reserved for preadolescents and adolescents. An example of evidence for the role of parents is that young boys use moral-judgment rules that are similar in form and complexity to those of their mothers (Leon, 1984). Some mothers use a simple unidimensional rule based on damage alone, whereas others use a more complex integration that combines both intent and damage or even weighs damage differently, depending on the person's intent.

The main evidence bolstering the social learning account is that children's moral judgments can be altered by a brief social experience in the laboratory. In a prototypic study, Bandura and McDonald (1963) first assessed whether 5- to 11-year-olds had an objective or a subjective moral orientation, based on Piaget's stories depicting moral dilemmas. One actor had good intentions but produced great material damage, whereas the other actor had bad intentions but produced minimal material damage. First the model and then the child made judgments about stories. Then the researchers exposed the most extremely subjective or objective children to a model whose judgment was always opposite that of the child's from the first phase. A final phase tested for generalization. In another room, a different adult presented new stories that the child judged.

As predicted by social learning theory, the children adopted the model's moral standards. Note that no verbal praise was given to the child. This new moral perspective generalized to the new stories in the third phase. This generalization suggests that the children abstracted a general rule rather than imitated specific responses. Thus, even without being reinforced, children observed and accepted the moral judgments of others. A control group that had no model showed no change. In a later study (Dorr & Fey, 1974), children maintained these changes for at least 1 month.

One developmental acquisition central to social learning theory's account of moral development is setting standards of conduct concerning one's own behavior. These are rules, goals, and expectations for one's own conduct abstracted from experiences such as observing others' standards of self-reinforcement or punishment and observing which behaviors of others occur in each situation. For example, after seeing a model criticize his own behavior as undeserving of a reward, children are less likely to reward themselves for similar behavior (Bandura, 1971). If children's models are older, such as older siblings and parents, they may set impossibly high standards of conduct for themselves. It is noteworthy, however, that when models require little of themselves but much of others, their attractiveness and influence decrease (Ormiston, 1972). The hypocrisy is detected. There are clear implications for parents who do not practice what they preach.

Children's internal standards of conduct constitute what Freud would call the superego. However, social learning theorists stress that the parent of the same sex serves as only one of many models from whom the child learns. These internal standards, along with self-reward and self-punishment, are especially effective because children can apply them to many situations; an external authority need not be present.

■ *Gender-Role Development*

Social learning theory also suggests mechanisms of gender-role development (Bussey & Bandura, 1999). The various processes already described in this chapter can be applied here as well. However, children's learning in this area is particularly revealing in several ways. Because the transmission of gender roles pervades a culture, the theory "favors a multifaceted social transmission model rather than mainly a family transmission model" (Bussey & Bandura, 1999, p. 676). Moreover, childhood provides numerous opportunities to observe gendered behavior because children tend to seek out same-sex playmates and, even when both sexes are available, to imitate same-gender models more than other-gender models. As children become aware of the social significance attached to gender, they increasingly attend to and regulate their own gender-relevant behaviors, especially in mixed-sex groups. For example, girls learn that others disapprove of their physical aggression, and thus girls make greater use than boys of relational aggression (Crick & Grotpeter, 1995), for instance, by saying "You can't be my friend any more."

By age 3 or 4, or even earlier, children disapprove of boys feeding, diapering, and comforting dolls and girls playing with trucks. In fact, in one study (Bussey & Bandura, 1992), when children of this age were confined to a playroom with only toys gender-typed for the other gender, they ignored the toys. One boy even flung the doll across the room and turned his back on it. Some boys tried to transform the feminine toys into masculine ones, for example, by using an eggbeater as a gun or a drill. The boys tried to have the "feminine" toys removed. One boy pointedly told the departing experimenter, "No, I'm finished with those toys," even though he had not played with them at all.

Self-efficacy comes into play in many ways, for example, regarding probable success if one enters male-dominated versus female-dominated occupations. This has been particularly true for fields requiring math skills; females tend to underestimate their efficacy in this area. In addition, Bandura notes that a low sense of social efficacy contributes more heavily to depression in girls than in boys.

Bandura's account adds sociocultural and motivational components to cognitive theories of gender development. Cognitive factors alone, such as gender identity and knowledge of gender stereotypes, do not consistently predict gender-linked behavior. In Bandura's view, such behaviors can best be understood through "an integrated perspective in which social influences operate through psychological mechanisms to produce behavioral effects" (Bussey & Bandura, 1999, p. 694). As family structures become more diverse, the gender roles that children observe are changing. Bandura concludes that collective efficacy can bring about social change to ensure gender equity.

MECHANISMS OF DEVELOPMENT

There is controversy as to whether social learning theory or any current learning theory is truly a developmental theory. Is developmental change simply short-term change accumulating over a longer period of time? Are the central laws of learning the same, regardless of the child's cognitive level? If development is merely accumulated learning, then it should be possible to speed up development by providing appropriate experiences.

Social learning theorists focus on *processes* of change, in contrast to Piaget and Freud, who were also interested in *structural* change as the child goes through the stages. Social learning research has examined the situational variables that encourage or discourage observational learning more than it has studied how age and cognitive level affect observational learning. However, Bandura has identified a number of developmental variables. Development occurs because of three main factors: physical maturation, experience with the social world, and cognitive development. These three factors cause developmental changes in all of the processes in Bandura's model in Figure 3.1. The first factor, *physical maturation*, holds little interest for social learning theorists. Its main relevance is that young children may not have the physical maturity to reproduce certain motor patterns they observe. The other two factors are much more important.

Experience with the social world causes development in the following way: As children interact with other people, they acquire a repertoire of behaviors, learn the appropriate situations for these behaviors, and, because these behaviors are reinforced by others, become motivated to perform them. Thus, with increasing age, children have a larger and increasingly differentiated set of behaviors. Much of this increased exposure to social behaviors comes from the growing number and types of models children encounter from television, movies, books, school, and the neighborhood. Moreover, as children become older, their social environment changes simply because society, ranging from their parents to the legal system, changes its expectations of them. Older children, by observing a model, are expected to learn complex new skills quickly, with a minimum of verbal instruction. A teacher provides much more help with reading to a first-grader than to a third-grader. In short, children of different ages face different social environments.

Regarding the third factor, *cognitive development*, children's conceptions of the world and of themselves are formed by direct experience of the effects produced by their actions and vicarious experience of the effects produced by others' actions. Also important are judgments articulated by others and the inference of new knowledge from their preexisting knowledge.

Bandura's model in Figure 3.1 describes these cognitive changes more specifically. As described in the next chapter, on information processing, the child's attention, memory, and cognitive organization undergo dramatic changes during development. For example, older children have much better comprehension and recall of characters, behaviors, motivations, and outcomes of the behaviors in a television story (Newcomb & Collins, 1979). Young children often do not even make a connection between the model's behavior and the consequences of that behavior later on. Another relevant developmental change is that older children are more likely to rehearse verbally what they have observed than are younger children. Motor reproduction and motivational processes also become more complex, differentiated, and efficient as children become more able to integrate several pieces of information, accurately interpret feedback, develop standards for their own performance, and so forth.

Bandura points out one particularly critical developmental change in thinking: the growing ability to translate observations into symbols and to recombine these symbols. Very young children must rely heavily on visual images to represent past observations. Once children can use symbols, their observational learning is much more flexible and enduring. Symbols can be rehearsed and thereby stored in memory more efficiently than can visual images. Children can formulate hypotheses about physical or social events and test them. An increasingly sophisticated symbolic ability also makes it possible to model behavior by reading a description of it or listening to instruction rather than by having to see the behavior and trying to reproduce it. The modeling can be symbolic rather than behavioral. Even the effect of vicarious reinforcement is influenced by the observer's symbolic ability. A young child may be more likely to imitate when another child is rewarded with candy or toys, whereas an older child can infer more subtle consequences, such as the model's feelings of self-worth and achievement.

As an example of research on symbolic functioning, a group of 7-year-olds recalled more of the behavior they observed on film if they were told to verbally describe the model's actions rather than told simply to watch the film carefully (Bandura, Grusec, & Menlove, 1966). The children recalled even less if the experimenter told them to count while viewing the film—an activity that interfered with symbolization. Thus, verbal encoding facilitated observational learning. However, in interpreting this study, we should note that the adults' or children's verbalizations may have increased attention to the model as well as encouraged symbolic representation.

POSITION ON DEVELOPMENTAL ISSUES

Human Nature

For years, learning theory has served as textbook writers' favorite example of a theory with a mechanistic view of human behavior. The infant— "a lively squirming bit of flesh," in Watson's words—is material to be fashioned by parents and society. The theory views the learner as passive, nudged by the whim of the environment, influenced in a machinelike way by a chain of events. In this "mechanical mirror" model, "the child is born empty of content into a world of coherently organized content. Like a mirror, however, the child comes to reflect his environment" (Langer, 1969, p. 51).

The mechanistic model, however, does not accurately represent the views of modern social learning theory, in which "people are self-organizing, proactive, self-reflective, and self regulating" (Bussey & Bandura,

1999, p. 691). In triadic reciprocal causation, discussed earlier, people actively operate on the environment, just as the environment acts on them. People filter their experience through their current knowledge and expectations about the world, create their own environment as their own behavior influences the environment, and generate new behavior by reorganizing previously learned behaviors. People are also active in their self-regulation. They set their own standards, reinforce themselves when they act in accord with these standards, and use feedback to judge their success at observational learning and to construct their self-efficacy.

Bandura certainly considers people to be more actively involved in their own development and learning than does Freud. Piaget, however, posits an even stronger role for activity than does Bandura. Although both Bandura and Piaget describe symbolic activity, this mental activity has a greater role in Piaget's theory. According to Piaget, children do not simply learn more or less automatically by watching or listening to others. As they assimilate and accommodate to new information, there is distortion of the information and a slight reorganization of their present cognitive structure. Although Bandura occasionally refers to these processes, he does not stress them.

There is a more basic difference in the role of interaction in Piaget's and Bandura's theories. For Piaget, the interaction or exchange between the child and the environment forms a structure that later becomes an internalized cognitive structure. The actions of sucking, hitting, and manipulating become mental schemes that serve as concepts. In contrast, for Bandura the structure of the interchange between the child and the environment is less important than the new information acquired as a result of this interchange. The child observes a new behavior in the model or learns that certain behaviors in others lead to reinforcement.

Social learning theory has elements of the contextualist world view in that it emphasizes the influence of social contexts on children. However, it gives little attention to historical–cultural influences.

One point of comparison among social learning, Piagetian, and Freudian theories is the view of humans as rational or irrational. For Piaget, the essence of development is that children become more logical as their mental structures gradually come to reflect reality. Adults, having achieved formal operations, possess equilibrated, logical thinking. Although all three theorists consider logical thinking important, both Freud and Bandura see a larger role for illogical, irrational thought than does Piaget. This may be due to their focus on social and emotion-laden events. For Bandura, children may think logically or illogically, depending on the types of models in problem-solving situations they have encountered. They acquire styles of processing information from others.

■ *Qualitative Versus Quantitative Development*

Both traditional and modern learning theories view development primarily as a process of quantitative change, in which learning episodes gradually accumulate over time. Development simply involves a multitude of short-term changes. Observational learning may change somewhat from toddlerhood, when symbolic functioning is severely limited, to middle childhood, when thinking is more advanced. However, we do not find either rapid qualitative changes in movement from one stage to another or massive cognitive reorganization. Bandura considers the search for stages counterproductive because stages draw attention away from individual differences and differences in the way a given child functions in different environments. Furthermore, a failure to learn may be dismissed as a lack of cognitive readiness, when it actually reflects a poor learning environment. Bandura thinks that an analysis of which subskills are needed to produce a certain behavior or knowledge is much more promising.

If smaller, more limited qualitative changes are considered, there are several candidates within social learning theory. Acquiring a new rule or adopting a new strategy of gathering information is more than a change in amount or strength.

■ *Nature Versus Nurture*

A young branch takes on all the bends that one gives it.

— CHINESE PROVERB

The early militant environmentalism of traditional learning theory viewed the young mind in the way British empiricist John Locke viewed it: a blank slate on which experience writes. This extreme position has evolved into a more moderate position. Children are malleable, but within limits. Within the constraints of children's biological makeup, experience provides data for forming rules through models and instruction and helps them polish the component skills needed for observational learning. The types of behaviors children encounter in their models and the reactions of others to these behaviors influence the particular set of behaviors they develop.

Bandura's view of the roles of biology and experience is captured in his notion of triadic reciprocal causation. The environment, the person (including physical maturation), and the person's behavior are interdependent forces operating in any event. Freud and Piaget focused on the interaction of biological maturation and experience with the physical world (especially Piaget) and the social world (especially Freud). To this view, Bandura adds the idea that one's behavior can change one's environment.

Biology not only constrains learning but also makes learning possible. An organism's learning ability is innate. It has evolved as a way of surviving in a changing environment. The ability to learn from experience, especially the advanced capability for observational learning, allows an organism to adapt to whatever demands the environment makes. The ability to process and store information, manipulate symbols, abstract general rules, and translate this information into behavior is obviously adaptive for humans. A society's advances also can affect the course of evolution because they create new selection pressures for the evolution of specialized biological systems for functional consciousness, thought, language, and symbolic communication (Bussey & Bandura, 1999).

What Develops

Because what is learned depends greatly on what the environment has to offer, learning theorists propose few universal behaviors, those that we would be certain to find developing in every culture. Whereas Piaget, with certainty, would predict that all physically normal children in the world would develop concepts of object permanence, causality, and conservation, and whereas Freud would predict universal concern with sexuality and aggression, social learning theory appears to be almost content-free. Investigators have directed their energy toward process rather than content. One culture may encourage aggressive behavior, whereas another may discourage it. Superstitious behavior may be valued and nurtured in one culture, whereas scientific, analytic thinking may be fostered in another. In other words, there is no universal goal or endpoint to development. Piaget, in contrast, sees development moving toward a particular way of thinking: formal operations. And Freud sees mature sexuality and freedom from excessive anxiety as the goal of development.

What is universally developed is a skilled ability to learn by observing or listening to other people or by attending to symbolic characters—in television and in books in some societies. Although social learning theorists have researched many kinds of behavior, they have been especially interested in self-efficacy, aggression, altruism, sex roles, and the ability to regulate the self.

APPLICATIONS

Psychologists have used learning theory to change a variety of problem behaviors, for example, the behavior modification of maladaptive behaviors and the deconditioning of fears, as described earlier. In addition they have addressed children's learning of aggression observed on television and the roles of self-efficacy and collective efficacy in bringing about social change. Moreover, social learning theorists have tried to help families function better.

Families sometimes unknowingly develop coercive systems (Patterson & Bank, 1989; Patterson & Reid, 1984). During hostile interchanges, certain behaviors habitually lead to certain other behaviors through a system of reinforcement. For example, a mother asks her son to clean his room, the child whines, the mother intensifies her command, the child resists, and the conflict rapidly escalates. Patterson notes that "rapid escalation is thought to be an important component in the repertoire of the trained fighter and well practiced coercive children" (1980, p. 7). When the behavior of the child becomes unbearably aversive for the mother, as when the child throws a temper tantrum, the mother gives up and the child stops his aversive behavior. Each person has ended the aversive behavior of the other. The mother has increased the chances that the child will act aversively in the future to obtain negative reinforcement (removing an aversive stimulus). The child has negatively reinforced the mother (the temper tantrum stopped), which increases the likelihood that the mother will give in on future occasions. This pattern of reinforcement should also increase the likelihood that a rapid escalation of conflict will occur in their future interactions. More generally, parents in functional and problem families differ in their discipline skills. In functional families the parents set up specific consequences for the child's misbehavior and consistently apply them. In contrast, in coercive dysfunctional families the child learns that parents may react explosively to misbehavior and make vague punishment threats but will not follow through on these threats.

Another example of how families develop a complex set of contingencies occurs when a young sister's teasing of her older brother leads to his hitting her, which in turn leads to punishment from the parents, which finally may even escalate the boy's aggression. The family can become a coercive system, in which each family member learns to cope with aversive behavior from others, such as hitting, teasing, ignoring, verbal abuse, and requests to do work, by counterattacking, which often ends the aversive behavior. Thus, aggressive behavior works. Each family member is periodically reinforced for behaving aggressively and coercively when overpowering another family member through negative behaviors. After the psychologist makes the problem family aware of these correlated events, together they try to reduce the amount of aversive behavior with which the child must cope and try to lower the "payoff" for the child's coercive behaviors. If the child is old enough, the family may write a contract that includes the child, specifying what behaviors will be punished by withdrawal of rewards. Thus, they present expectations for behavior and the consequences of disobeying in a clear and consistent way that the aggressive child can easily grasp and represent symbolically.

Psychologists have also applied social learning theory to the problem of violent adolescent boys. An early study by Bandura and Walters (1959) examined the puzzling fact that these boys often came from "privileged," middle-class families in neighborhoods that supported law-abiding behavior. In fact, the parents of the boys discouraged their sons' aggression toward them. However, the parents encouraged the boys to use aggression to solve their problems with their peers and with adults outside the home. The following interchange between the interviewer (I) and a mother (M) illustrates this encouragement of aggression:

> I: Have you ever encouraged Earl to stand up for himself?
>
> M: Yes, I've taught young Earl, and his Dad has. I feel he should stand up for his rights, so you can get along in this world.
>
> I: How have you encouraged him?
>
> M: I've told him to look after himself and don't let anybody shove him around or anything like that, but not to look for trouble. I don't want him to be a sissy.
>
> I: Have you ever encouraged Earl to use his fists to defend himself?
>
> M: Oh yes. Oh yes. He knows how to fight.
>
> (Bandura & Walters, 1959, p. 115)

These lessons were learned well. One of the boys interviewed mentioned his pride in his prowess at "stomping"—fighting with his feet: "Like my Dad, he said, 'If you know how to fight with your feet, then it's in your hands, you've got it made,' or something like that. 'You never need to be afraid of anybody'" (Bandura & Walters, 1959, p. 122). This information is consistent with laboratory studies of reinforcement and modeling, but it provides insights into real-life aggression that could not emerge in a controlled laboratory setting.

EVALUATION OF THE THEORY

This evaluation focuses on modern social learning theory rather than traditional learning theory, for which there are several excellent critiques (Bowers, 1973; White, 1970). As in the previous chapter on psychoanalytic theory, the focus is on what the theory *could* contribute to present and future research and theory building in developmental psychology. Social learning theory has been eclipsed by the theories in the following chapters (plus neo-Piagetian theories). Social learning theory's strengths are its focus on the situational, social, and emotional influences on behavior and its testability. Two weaknesses are an inadequate account of cognitive development and an inadequate description of development in natural settings.

■ *Strengths*

Focus on Situational Influences on Behavior ■ One characteristic of structural, trait, and many other organismic theories is that they locate the causes of behavior primarily in the person and therefore predict that a person will act similarly in different situations. Thus, Freud would expect a child with a strong superego to be overly controlled in most situations. Similarly, Piaget was relatively uninterested in the fact that conservation is acquired for certain content areas (substance) before others (weight) or that a newly acquired piece of knowledge might be exhibited in one situation but not in another. In contrast, in social learning theory behavior typically varies from situation to situation, depending on which models and reinforcers are found in each situation and on what the person's previous experiences in these situations have been. The person, her behavior, and the situation all exert an influence, but much of Bandura's research has analyzed situational variables, such as the type of model present or the consequences to the model. More generally, social learning theorists today are part of a movement toward a person-in-context (see Chapter 8) account of cognitive functioning that emphasizes connections between the person and the environment.

This attention to situational variables is sorely needed in current work on children's thinking, remembering, and learning. It is now common to find that the child applies a given concept to some materials but not others or on one trial but not another, that a concept is acquired earlier in one culture than another, and that teaching the child a concept or strategy does not ensure that it will be transferred to another task. There is, however, no generally accepted explanation of these results, although, as described in Chapter 1, neo-Piagetians tried to address this problem. Social learning theory would help fill this gap. For example, Rosenthal and Zimmerman (1978) suggest that Piagetians have underestimated the role of observational learning in the acquisition of conservation. Some sorts of conservation are more frequently modeled and reinforced than are others. Children observe other people comparing quantities by counting in many settings from very early in life. Learning to count to 10 before kindergarten is a heavily valued and reinforced skill in Western middle-class societies. Moreover, children count pennies, keep track of the number of days until their birthday, and make sure that they are given the same number of cookies as their siblings receive. Comparing the weights of objects is considered a less critical skill. It is used less in a child's day-to-day living and thus is less salient. Moreover, it is much easier to keep track of the number of objects than the amount of a continuous substance, because counting can be used to verify the former. Thus, one would expect décalages.

Social learning theory also has the potential to show how children acquire a "theory of mind"—a belief system about others' mental states and how such states cause behavior. Observing others deceive, manipulate, and comfort people may contribute to this knowledge.

Not only proximal social influences, such as parental and peer pressures, affect development, but also the broader social institutions and belief systems. Bandura has applied his work to a wide range of social concerns. Examples are terrorist tactics, sexual and racial stereotypes, transcultural modeling through satellite telecasting, pornography, deterrents to crime, and encouragement of healthy behavior.

Unlike Piagetian and information-processing theories of cognition, Bandura's considers what has been called "hot" cognition (Zajonc, 1980), as opposed to "cold." Hot cognition consists of the emotional, motivational aspect of thinking; cold cognition includes the nature of thinking but not its emotional aspects. Examples of hot cognition are children's thinking about how to please their parents, experiencing sadness when they fail at a task, and feeling disappointed in themselves when they do not meet their own standards of conduct. Also, children are much more interested in some activities than others and thus apply their knowledge inconsistently. Motivation is a critical part of learning in real life, but it has been virtually ignored by Piagetian and information-processing theories.

Testability ■ Even those who have attacked learning theories admit that they are among the most testable theories in psychology. Learning researchers have defined terms clearly, stated hypotheses precisely, and kept unobservable, intervening variables to a minimum. Parsimony is highly valued. Bandura's theory has a greater proportion of difficult-to-test concepts than do earlier learning theories but fewer than does Piaget's or Freud's theory. For example, symbolic representation, abstract modeling, and expectations are not unambiguously related to observable behavior. Although even more emphasis on cognition would enhance the theory (as noted in the next section), it is desirable to have a theory that reminds us that we are interested in behavior as well as in thinking. Thus, social learning theorists can serve as watchdogs on cognitive psychologists, who sometimes seem to have forgotten about behavior. We must remember that representations, mental operations, and concepts of other people ultimately are related to behavior.

■ *Weaknesses*

Inadequate Account of Cognitive Development ■ Bandura's theory has loosely adopted information-processing theory's (Chapter 4) account of thinking. However, it includes only general features, such as symbolic representation, attention, storage, rule construction, and verification. A child integrates a sequence of events in the world with other events and abstracts more general concepts. Knowledge seems to consist of a storehouse of observed empirical regularities. Perry (1989) calls these representations "summary cognitions" because they are summaries of a history of social experiences. Cognition still remains quite close to behavior. Bandura has not yet developed a detailed account of exactly how these cognitive processes—especially abstraction and integration—work, how the cognitive system changes during development, and how changes in cognitive development change observational learning.

One such problem to be worked out is how children's thinking is organized and how that organization changes during development. Bandura clearly does not endorse complex cognitive organizations that characterize a particular stage and that change in a qualitative way as the child moves from one stage to another. However, he does not take the opposite view, from traditional learning theory, that children acquire specific associations, chains of associations, or specific facts piecemeal and join them together in very simple ways. He takes an in-between position: Children have domain-specific knowledge, plus skills that operate on this knowledge to make it more abstract and to organize it to some extent. They construct schemes, such as gender schemes, and through abstract modeling abstract common features from several related events. Through creative imitation they reorganize previous knowledge to produce a novel behavior. Thus, Bandura seems to allow for simple cognitive organization and restructuring, but he stops far short of Piaget's equilibrated, highly organized structures. The exact nature of these developmental changes, however, is not yet described.

This description of cognitive changes is important because the way the child's knowledge is organized surely influences how an observed behavior is interpreted at each point in development. For example, watching another child share a toy with a friend may be regarded as an isolated behavior by a 4-year-old but may imply a set of meanings concerning fairness and reciprocity for an 8-year-old. The two children differ in what they learn from this observation. Furthermore, children's cognitive level limits their observational learning. A 4-year-old does not learn the rules of division after watching a 10-year-old do division problems. Social learning theorists recognize that one's developmental level influences what is learned during observation, but they do not have a detailed account of this process.

A specific portrayal of developmental changes in cognitive reorganization is also necessary for evaluating the criticism that, for social learning theory, development is simply learning accumulated over a long period of time. If children organize their thoughts differently over the course of development, then the theory is more clearly a developmental theory.

An account of a developing cognitive organization would show how imitation and observational learning themselves change during development. The ability to imitate develops very early in life (Meltzoff & Moore, 1989). Bandura proposes that with further cognitive, perceptual, and motor development, this ability becomes more efficient and abstract. However, there is little experimental evidence concerning these changes. Which cognitive abilities must be developed before children can form a cognitive representation of what they have observed or read about? What differences underlie infants' ability to copy their mother when she sticks out her tongue and 10-year-olds' ability to operate a computer after reading the instruction manual?

Inadequate Description in Natural Settings ▪ From learning theory, we know much more about the variables that *can* affect the learning of social behaviors than about what variables *actually* operate in the lives of children or what behaviors actually occur at various ages. We know how variables operate to produce short-term changes in the laboratory but not how they operate in natural environments. We do not know the ecology of aggression, sex typing, or dependency. For example, laboratory studies stimulated by social learning theory have identified many processes, such as imitation, abstract modeling, reinforcement, and concept formation, that mold sex-typed behaviors. Which processes, in fact, are most important in particular natural settings at each age? We need a taxonomy of the various situations in which children typically find themselves in each developmental period. The theory's contribution would be much greater if investigators would examine the models and reinforcement contingencies usually found in the typical environments of each phase of development. Our culture presumably rewards different behaviors at different developmental levels. It appears, for instance, that the elderly, in order to obtain reinforcements, often must learn "old, sick, helpless" behaviors and unlearn independent behaviors (Baltes & Barton, 1979).

Moreover, observational learning and patterns of reinforcement need to be tied systematically to social-ecological variables, such as both parents working outside the home, diversity in what constitutes a family, urbanization, racial discrimination, and changing sex roles. A complete account of social learning must also consider demographic variables, such as socioeconomic level, race, sex, and geographic location. For instance, we need a description of developmental changes in aggression that takes into account the type of peer models in the neighborhood that are seen by children in various subgroups of the population, the type of day care the child has, and the father's role in child rearing.

SOCIAL LEARNING THEORY TODAY

Social learning theory peaked in its direct influence on developmental psychology in the 1960s and 1970s. Although today it still is included in most standard accounts of development, few studies appear to be directly stimulated by the theory. Even the recent work on self-efficacy has focused on adults, including elderly people, and has addressed child development only sporadically. Bandura's preferred label for his theory, "social cognitive theory," has never really caught on in developmental psychology, and developmentalists seem to be more familiar with the older, less cognitive aspects of the theory. Developmentalists usually reserve the term "social cognition" for children's thinking outside Bandura's framework, for example, in areas such as theory of mind (see Chapter 8), social attributions (children's perceptions of what causes their own behavior or that of others), self-concepts, and perceptions of other people. Although Bandura's recent accounts include the broad network of social influences in the larger social-cultural context of development, the person-in-context accounts in Chapter 8 are much more influential in developmentalists' thinking about how the social environment impacts children's behavior and thinking.

A similar story could be told about other learning theories. Although modern research within learning theories sometimes involves children, especially in the modification of severe problem behaviors, this work remains isolated from mainstream developmental psychology.

In a more general sense, however, social learning theory is indirectly responsible for much of the current research on children's social behavior, particularly in the areas of aggression, gender development, peer relationships, prosocial behavior, and influences of television and other media. Important social learning theory concepts such as observational learning, social motivation, and the importance of adults' and peers' reactions to a child's behavior are simply assumed. Moreover, learning paradigms such as operant conditioning have proved to be valuable procedures for assessing other behaviors of interest, such as infants' memory (Rovee-Collier, 1999).

The current slighting of learning theories, including social learning theory, is unfortunate because they offer a valuable perspective. No other approach provides such a testable account of social behavior, specifies clear mechanisms by which environments enter into the developmental formula, and addresses emotions and motivation. Developmentalists recently have shown a renewed interest in learning, in the sense of acquiring new knowledge or changing the relative probabilities of using a particular skill (Siegler, 2000). However, they conceptualize learning within frameworks other than the traditional learning or social learning one. Examples include connectionism (see Chapter 4), microgenetic changes (Chapter 4—information processing), training studies (Chapter 1—Piaget), acquisition of new behaviors through cultural learning (Chapter 7), and neural changes (Chapter 8). In fact, because learning is now viewed as the acquisition of new knowledge, it is virtually indistinguishable from cognitive change over short periods of time.

SUMMARY

Social learning theory retains the spirit of the behaviorist movement: the experimentally rigorous study of how basic learning occurs as a result of environmental forces. The spotlight, however, has switched from a hungry rat pressing a bar to a child interacting with other people. Children learn new behaviors by observing others. Moreover, the effect of environmental influences is cognitively mediated, as seen in children's use of language and strategies during problem solving.

Bandura contributed three key concepts:

1. *Observational learning can be much broader than mimicking another person's behavior*. The child can symbolically construct a new behavior by listening to another person or simply by reading. Complex new behaviors as well as simple modifications of previously acquired behaviors can be learned in this way. Furthermore, overt behavior is not even necessary in order for learning to occur. As Bandura summarizes the influences of models, they "can serve as instructors, motivators, inhibitors, disinhibitors, social facilitators, and emotion arousers" (1989, p. 17).

2. *Children are self-regulatory*. Although reinforcement is not necessary for learning, it is helpful for self-regulation. Children observe which behaviors occurring around them lead to reinforcement and punishment and use these observations as sources of information to help them abstract rules, evaluate their efficacy, develop standards of conduct, set goals, and decide in which situations to use the observed behavior.

3. *Triadic reciprocal causation provides a model of behavior change*. Three sources of influence—the person, his behavior, and the environment—interact. The environment does not always exert the greatest control. The most novel features of this three-pronged model are that children select certain environments and their behavior even helps shape their environment, which in turn acts on them.

Children develop five skills that are very important for social learning: symbolization, vicarious learning, self-regulation, self-efficacy, and the ability to see the future consequences of present behaviors (Perry, 1989). During development, children become more skilled at the four component processes of observational learning: attention, retention, production, and motivation. In particular, the growing ability to use visual and verbal symbols boosts the child's observational learning. Much of social development results from the accumulation and integration of episodes of observational learning. Social learning theory has examined a wide variety of developmentally important behaviors, such as aggression, concept formation, language, gender-related behaviors, and moral development.

Bandura's theory is testable. It also is integrative in that it brings together several areas that, by themselves, are somewhat limited. These areas include operant conditioning, information processing, reinforcement processes (direct and vicarious), and socialization processes. Social learning theory could correct several shortcomings of cognitive approaches, providing a way to conceptualize why the child's behavior or demonstrated knowledge might vary from situation to situation. There are two needed directions for further developing social learning theory. First, the interface between cognitive development and observational learning must be worked out in greater detail before the theory can be considered a truly developmental theory. Second, the theory could become much more powerful in predicting and exploring behavior if it acquired a broader ecological base. The theory has shown us that processes of social learning can guide development; the next step is to discover how these processes are tied to the environments typically found at various points in development, in various types of families, and in various socioeconomic and ethnic niches.

SUGGESTED READINGS

Bandura, A. (1997). *Self-efficacy: The exercise of control*. New York: Freeman.

Bijou, S. W. (1989). Behavior analysis. In R. Vasta (Ed.), *Annals of child development* (Vol. 6). Greenwich, CT: JAI Press. This chapter provides a contemporary account of children's learning, now called the "experimental analysis of behavior."

Bussey, K., & Bandura, A. (1999). Social cognitive theory of gender development and differentiation. *Psychological Review, 106,* 676–713.

Evans, R. I. (1989). *Albert Bandura: The man and his ideas—a dialogue*. New York: Praeger. This long interview with Bandura provides some interesting insights into his thinking.

Grusec, J. E. (1992). Social learning theory and developmental psychology: The legacies of Robert Sears and Albert Bandura. *Developmental Psychology, 28*, 776–786.

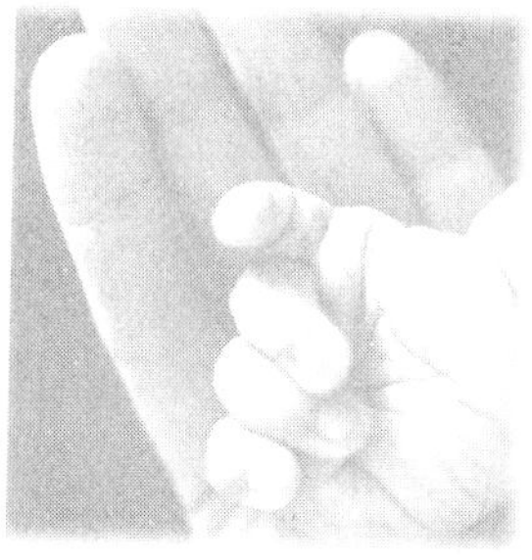

CHAPTER 4

Information-Processing Theory

*1PDV1 ((> * < GOAL GETREL BLUE RED) (HEARD (BIGGER)) (VALUE RED) (VALUE BLUE) (HEARD BLUE) (HEARD RED) NIL NIL NIL NIL NIL)*

*2P4 ((> * < GOAL COMPARE BLUE RED) > * < (GOAL GETREL BLUE RED)(HEARD (BIGGER)) (VALUE RED) (VALUE BLUE) (HEARD BLUE) (HEARD RED) NIL NIL NIL NIL)*

— *Performance on a Conservation Task, Klahr & Wallace, 1976, p. 137*

E: How much is 6 + 3?
L: (Long pause) Nine.
E: OK, how did you know that?
L: I think I said . . . I think I said . . . oops, um . . . I think he said . . . 8 was 1 and . . . um . . . I mean 7 was 1, 8 was 2, 9 was 3.
E: OK.
L: Six and three are nine.
E: How did you know to do that? Why didn't you count "1, 2, 3, 4, 5, 6, 7, 8, 9"? How come you did "6, 7, 8, 9"?
L: Cause then you have to count all those numbers.
E: OK, well how did you know you didn't have to count all of those numbers?
L: Why didn't . . . well I don't have to if I don't want to.

— *Siegler & Jenkins, 1989, p. 66.*

This is the information age. We use computers, cellular phones, and fax machines to transfer information from one form to another and to communicate with each other, often at great distances. It is not surprising, then, that at least one developmental theory would use a technology metaphor and focus on how humans deal with information.

In the last three decades, the information-processing approach, along with the cognitive revolution, has spread quietly through the field of cognitive development and currently is one of the most dominant approaches. It is said that the approach "was never born; it gradually coalesced" (Kendler, 1987, p. 364). Information processing arrived with little fanfare and, surprisingly, with only moderate clashes with Piagetian theory. The approach attracted psychologists seeking a more rigorous experimental approach than Piaget's and a more cognitive approach than learning theory.

Piagetian, Freudian, and learning theories are easily recognized as theories, and most psychologists who adhere to these theories are aware of their allegiance. In contrast, many developmental psychologists who study memory, representation, and problem solving—the focus of information processing—are not aware that they have accepted certain assumptions and methods of that approach. They feel they are simply performing empirical, atheoretical studies of various aspects of thinking. This chapter makes explicit this implicit agreement about what thinking involves, what aspects of thought change during development, what questions are worth asking, and how those questions should be studied. We begin with a brief description of the information-processing approach and then continue with a historical sketch, a general orientation, descriptions of major developmental approaches, and an account of mechanisms of development. Later sections address the theory's position on developmental issues, applications, and the theory's strengths and weaknesses.

Information processing is not a single theory but, rather, a framework characterizing a large number of research programs. Information-processing investigators study the flow of information through the cognitive system. This flow begins with some *input*, such as a written passage, a problem to be solved, or an event, into the human information-processing system. The flow ends with an *output*, which can be information stored in long-term memory, motor behavior, speech, or a decision. Mental operations occur between input and output during real time. For example, the information may be attended to, transformed into some type of mental representation, compared with information already in long-term memory, assigned meaning, and used to formulate a response. These mental processes are similar in some ways to computer programs that accept information, perform certain operations on it, and store it. More generally, both humans and computers manipulate symbols and transform input into output. Both computers and humans are limited in the amount of information that can be attended to simultaneously and in the speed with which this information can be processed. The correspondence is, of course, only partial. The circuitry of a computer is quite unlike the anatomy of the brain. However, as we shall see later, the computer metaphor served as a valuable heuristic for developing the field of information processing.

To illustrate this description of the information-processing approach, consider what happens when a young child first encounters the Dr. Dolittle story with the pushmi-pullyu, a horselike creature with a head at each end. The delighted child attends to the picture of the creature while ignoring other objects on the page and encodes it visually, as an image, or verbally, as a "pushmi-pullyu" or "two-headed horse." He processes this visual or verbal representation further as he compares it with previously stored information about horses or fantastic creatures such as unicorns. Furthermore, the child may derive certain implications about having two heads ("How does it know if it's coming or going?"), store the new information in a way that allows him to recognize pushmi-pullyus on future occasions, and finally laugh, ask his father to reread the page, or look ahead in the book for more pictures of the pushmi-pullyu.

Thus, the child transforms information over a period of time. Information-processing psychologists (who specialize in concepts of pushmi-pullyus?) might ask the following questions: Did the child process the input superficially, noting only its physical characteristics, or deeply, relating it to a system of meaning? How fast did he process the information? Did he process the pushmi-pullyu's features simultaneously or successively or in both ways? Were there limits to how much information he could analyze during the time he could see the picture? Did he "rehearse" the label "pushmi-pullyu," by repeating it several times aloud or to himself? How is the pushmi-pullyu as it is finally stored in long-term memory different from the input, the physical stimulus? If the child is shown another picture of a pushmi-pullyu, how does he retrieve the relevant information from memory and "recognize" the picture? If investigators can answer these questions, they can write a set of rules describing how the child processes information.

As this example illustrates, information-processing psychologists look at what mental processes children apply to the information and, as a result, how they transform, manipulate, and use that information. In other words, they are primarily interested in exactly how the processing system actually operates in real time in a particular situation—how the system changes external objects or events into a cognitively useful form according to certain rules. They examine both how changes in processing occur during development and the constraints on these changes. They try to explain "both how children of given ages have come as far as they have and why they have not gone further" (Siegler, 1998, p. 64).

Although the pushmi-pullyu example illustrates the "style" of information-processing psychologists, it masks the diversity of approaches within the field. The main division is that the approaches vary in the type of role that computer programs play in research and theorizing. At one extreme, we have *computer simulation*, in which cognitive scientists try to develop computer programs that model human thought. A sample of an influential early simulation appears at the beginning of this chapter.

At the other extreme, the computer serves as a loose metaphor to help researchers think about the processes a person uses to represent, store, and solve problems about words, pictures, objects, or events. This "soft-core" (Klahr, 1989) information-processing approach is much more common than the "hard-core" simulation model among developmental information-processing psychologists. The soft-core researchers adopt the informal, but not the formal, language of computer science. That is, they talk about "information," "capacity," and "rules" but do not translate cognitive processes into a formal computer language in a computer program. They accept many of the assumptions and concepts of computer science. However, they tend to study cognition using the experimental method, much as experimental psychologists have for years in the study of processes of learning (see Chapter 3). A simple example of soft-core information processing would be a study in which some children see a group of pictures and some children see a list of words for those pictures. Psychologists compare the children's memory in the picture-only and word-only conditions. By looking at the relationship between different inputs (visual–pictorial or visual–verbal) and their outputs (types of errors, order in which the objects were recalled), they try to infer what mental processes the children in the two groups

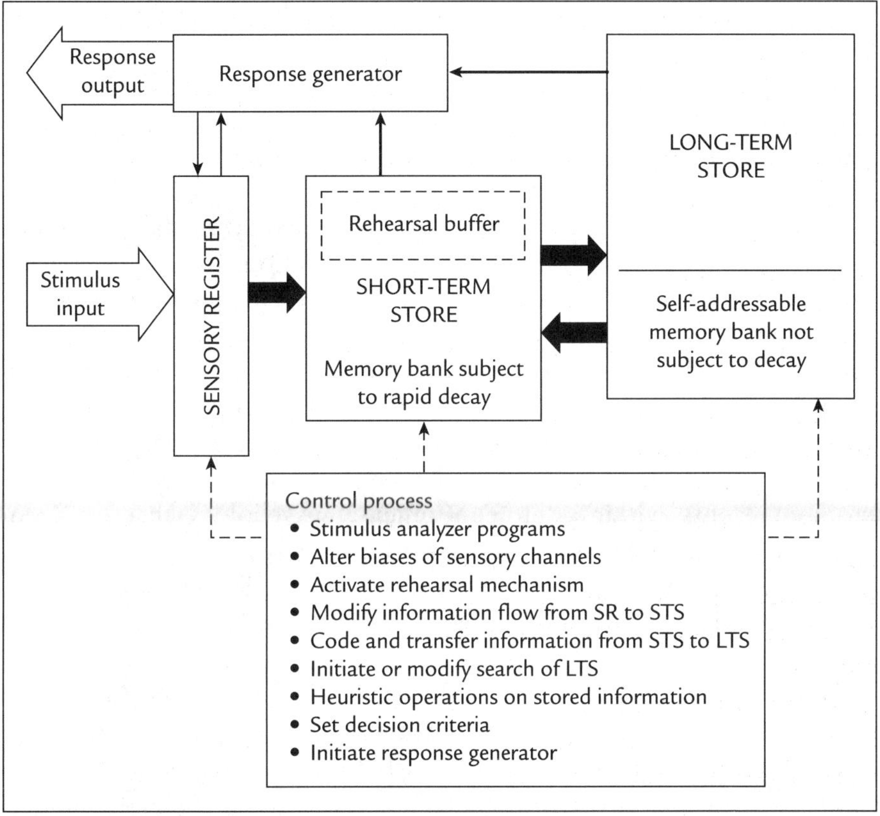

Figure 4.1

A flowchart of the memory system: SR = sensory register, STS = short-term store, and LTS = long-term store.

SOURCE: From "Storage and Retrieval Processes in Long-Term Memory," by Richard M. Shiffrin and Richard C. Atkinson, in *Psychological Review,* 1969, *76*, 179–193. Reproduced by permission of the authors.

applied over time to the input. These processes might include verbal rehearsal, organizing the objects into categories, or constructing visual representations.

In between computer-simulation "computational" approaches and approaches that use computer processing as a loose metaphor, we find other information-processing psychologists. Some investigators develop flowcharts (see Figure 4.1, which is described later)—diagrams that depict how information flows through the cognitive system. Such flowcharts can be used, at least in principle, to develop computer simulations of thought. (We look more carefully at such simulations later.)

HISTORY OF THE THEORY

Once developmentalists entered the domain of experimental psychology en masse in the early 1960s, they felt reverberations from every significant event in adult experimental psychology. Information processing was the first major theory of adult cognition to arise since developmental psychology had become an experimental science. This minirevolution within adult experimental psychology gradually changed the prevailing view of thinking in children. The attraction of information-processing theory for developmentalists can be understood only by tracing the chain of events within adult experimental psychology that led from neobehaviorism to the information-processing approach.

Two general developments in the 1940s and 1950s eventually transformed adult experimental psychology. First, a crisis occurred within neobehaviorism. Second, technological advances in society changed the thinking of psychologists forever; theories reflect their times. The crisis in neobehaviorism, described in Chapter 3, arose partly because many psychologists lost confidence that verbal-learning research, the hallmark of neobehaviorism, was actually advancing our understanding of adult learning (Lachman, Lachman, & Butterfield, 1979). This verbal-learning research examined how people remember material stripped of meaning and context, such as learning an arbitrary association between nonsense syllables, for example, "GAV-HIG." The research also systematically varied parameters in learning tasks, such as the length of the list to be remembered and the degree of prior association between words. All of this led to much information about learning in laboratory settings but not much understanding of human thought in day-to-day living outside the laboratory. The previous knowledge and strategies believed to contaminate any "pure" measure of memory or association would later be considered interesting in their own right.

At about the same time, the feeling of crisis was increased by a serious challenge to learning theory from outside psychology. A young linguist named Noam Chomsky attacked the learning account of language acquisition, particularly in his now-famous review (1959) of Skinner's book *Verbal Learning*. Chomsky argued that learning theory's account of language is wrong because it focuses on language output and a simple set of specific conditioned associations between words. Chomsky proposed that the essence of language is the set of underlying abstract rules that generate sentences. These rules are unobservable and must be inferred from the relations between language input and output.

The second influential development was the exposure of psychologists to conceptions of the human implicit in much of society's new technology (Lachman et al., 1979). World War II drew psychologists out of the laboratory because they were needed to improve the human operation of wartime equipment and weapons. Psychologists began to think of humans as information transmitters and decision makers when they examined how military personnel divided their attention between a plane's controls and instructions from a radio, detected blips on a radar screen, and interpreted a plane's instrument readings. A human and a machine (plane or weapon) operate together as a unit. It is desirable that this unit operate efficiently to avoid unfortunate errors, such as plunging into the ocean.

Another technological influence came from communication engineering and information theory. Engineers working on communication systems, such as the telephone, telegraph, radio, and television, developed the notion of "communication channels," which came to serve as a metaphor for human thought. Psychologists began to speak of "limited-capacity channels," "serial" (successive) and "parallel" (simultaneous) processing, "coding information" into large units, and "uncertainty" (ambiguous information). Thus, psychologists were not only willing to talk about the mind but also had a language for doing so. Later, computer scientists' work on digital computers, robots, and other symbol-manipulating systems suggested to psychologists that people might also be considered symbol-manipulating systems. Newell and Simon (1961), in particular, argued convincingly that the logical capabilities of people could be simulated by appropriate computer programs. The cognitive revolution had begun!

The field of *cognitive science* is an amalgamation of cognitive psychology, computer science, philosophy, neuroscience, and linguistics. Also, the field of *artificial intelligence* develops robots, computer programs, or other devices that can play chess or other games, translate texts, serve drinks, perform mathematical calculations, keep track of a store's inventory, and move documents from one office to another. The goal is to produce maximally efficient and intelligent systems. Such devices typically do not model human intelligence and in some cases they surpass average mental skills, as anyone who has been humiliated by a computer in a chess game can attest. For example, even an early computer chess whiz, "Deep Thought," beat nearly all of its human opponents (Lindsay, 1991), and more recently "Deep Blue" beat Kasparov.

Regarding developmental psychology, by the late 1960s researchers were beginning to recognize the potential of information processing for studying children's thinking. Many developmentalists had misgivings about the ultimate value of studies based on learning theory, along with uncertainty that Piagetian stage theory had a viable account of cognitive change. The information-processing approach was appealing because it permitted controlled experimental studies, as had learning theory, but it also supplied a fruitful new methodology, language, and metaphor for studying the development of thought. In addition, there already was interest in some of the topics studied by information-processing psychologists, particularly memory. Developmentalists had studied attention in discrimination learning and were becoming increasingly interested in language acquisition because of Chomsky's work. There was a sense of excitement and anticipation about the future of developmental psychology.

As a result of all of these factors, information processing became a major force in the field of developmental psychology. Numerous studies have examined children's memory, attention, representation, comprehension, and problem solving over the last 30 years. Recently, connectionist models, discussed later in the chapter, have caused another surge of interest in information processing. Most of the early information-processing studies were simply direct translations of the adult research, using children as subjects. For example, researchers gave children simpler versions of the memory and attention tasks they gave to adults. Eventually, as happened in learning theory years earlier, developmental research began to go beyond these simple translations and look at specifically developmental issues.

GENERAL ORIENTATION TO THE THEORY

How do we recognize an "information-processing cognitive developmental psychologist" when we see one? This species has distinctive markings that help "psychologist watchers" identify it. The following field guide describes several characteristics: viewing humans as information-processing systems, conceptualizing development as self-modification, conducting task analyses, and using information-processing methodology.

Humans as Information-Processing Systems

We find striking correspondences in how people and computers manipulate input according to certain rules and store the results of these operations. We can compare perceiving with "input," thinking with a "computer program," storage capacity with number of "K," forgetting with hitting the "delete" key, a decision with "output," and mental operations with "subroutines." An information-processing psychologist asks, "How are humans programmed to make sense out of the complex world around them?" and "What would an information-processing system require in order to exhibit the same behavior as a child?" (Klahr & Wallace, 1976, p. 5). Information-processing psychologists make a step-by-step analysis of what a person does to the information. How this new orientation breaks with the past is illustrated in its language. For example, "input–output" connotes a different sort of thinker than does "stimulus–response" or "assimilation–accommodation."

The input to the information-processing device is information, which can come in many forms. It might be a word, a paragraph, a mathematical or logical symbol, a blip on a radar screen, or a mental image. The device performs certain operations on this information, such as comparing it with previously stored information or transforming it into a representation *(encoding)*, for example, by transforming a written word into a mental image.

The adult mind can efficiently organize millions of pieces of information. How is such a remarkable device developed? Information-processing psychologists view children at various ages or cognitive levels as being in different knowledge states. Psychologists infer each knowledge state from the relationship between the input and the output. Thus, each developmental level is characterized by a particular input–output relationship, and developmental change involves going from one such relationship to another. As we will see later, developmental changes are apparent in nearly every phase of processing—from attention through encoding to recall and decision making.

Now that we have noted the general nature of the human information-processing device and its development, let us look more specifically at the flow of information through this device. Information processing has been called the "psychology of boxes and arrows," because psychologists construct flowcharts, sometimes called "models," such as the early classical one in Figure 4.1. These models communicate the theorist's claims about the structure, or "architecture" (blueprint), of the mind. Models also depict the temporal and functional relations among the stages of processing in the information-processing system. The information "goes" in and out of boxes or may be "lost" at any point. Typically, these stages are not intended to correspond to areas of the brain.

Some information-processing models of memory (see Figure 4.1 on page 217) posit sensory registers, a short-term store (short-term memory), and a long-term store (long-term memory). *Sensory registers* (sometimes called *sensory memory*) in each modality retain all information reaching the sense organs, but only for perhaps a fraction of a second or several seconds, depending on the sense organ. Children's sensory registers appear to have as great a capacity as those of adults. However, children form sensory representations more slowly than do adults.

Any information selected for further processing continues to a short-term store. The *short-term store* can maintain a limited amount of information (perhaps 5 to 9 units in an adult) for up to approximately 15 to 30 seconds, or longer if the person verbally rehearses (repeats) or otherwise acts upon this information. Material that is not attended to further in the short-term store and not transferred to the long-term store is quickly lost forever. Thus, we must either immediately dial the phone number we have looked up or keep repeating it. Information from the sensory register and information from the long-term store can be brought together to perform calculations or other activities in the short-term store. Thus, the short-term store is sometimes aptly called the "working memory." Older children can keep more information in working memory than can younger ones, mainly because they can say words faster (Hitch & Towse, 1995).

Finally, the *long-term store* includes our knowledge about the world. It has a large capacity and retains information indefinitely within a complex mental organization. During retrieval, information is summoned out of the long-term store and once again enters the short-term store.

A crucial set of processes called *control processes*, listed in Figure 4.1, consists of the "executives of the company." Like computer software, they direct the activities in each stage of processing, keep track of what is going on in all parts of the system, and make sure the entire system is working in harmony. Control processes help humans overcome structural limitations on how much information can be handled. Some of the most impressive developmental changes in information processing occur in these control processes.

With respect to development, both description and explanation (see the Introduction) questions could be raised about the stages of processing outlined in the flowchart. First, in what way, if any, do the stages of processing differ at various ages? Do they differ quantitatively or qualitatively? Second, what causes a child to progress from one state to the next? Are changes in how a child solves a problem due to an increase in the capacity of the short-term store, the more efficient retrieval of a relevant rule from the long-term store, or both?

Development as Self-Modification

Information-processing theories focus on mechanisms of change during development, which will be described later. Like Piaget, they see the child's activities as leading to changes in her thinking through a process of self-modification. For example, as children try out various strategies and see which they like best, they begin to use some increasingly often and others less often. They learn how to select the most promising routes to solving a problem. If children reject useless methods and retain helpful ones, they gradually become more efficient information processors.

An important breakthrough in the computer simulation of cognitive development was the development of self-correcting, self-modifying programs. Simon and Klahr (1995), for example, generated models of 3-year-olds and 4-year-olds solving number problems that could modify themselves, or "learn." Although both models could learn from extensive experience with number problems, only the model of 4-year-olds could learn from more limited experience (due to better memory and counting). Thus, the models captured age differences in the ability to learn. The models corresponded closely to the observed behavior of 3- and 4-year-olds.

Computer simulations can ruthlessly reject procedures that turn out not to be useful, reorganize units already available, and increase or decrease the number of situations in which a particular operation will be used. These self-modifications, then, propel the program from state to state, or from one developmental level to another. Examples of such models will appear later in the chapter.

Task Analysis

One hallmark of the information-processing approach is the careful, almost compulsive, analysis of the experimental or real-life task facing the child or adult. The investigator asks, "What cognitive skills and capacities does a child have to have in order to do this task well?" This concern with the specific features of a particular task follows naturally from the approach's focus on the information available in the task setting, the limits to the person's processing capacity, the goals of the task, and the person's processing skills. The unique demands of each particular task elicit a different set of processing activities. For example, children may verbally rehearse conceptually unrelated objects, but they may categorize related objects into "kitchen objects" and "living-room objects" and then only briefly rehearse them. By analyzing task demands, the investigator can distinguish between the behaviors that children produce because they are necessary for adapting to the particular task and those they produce because of their inadequate information-processing abilities (Siegler, 1998). The latter should appear on a variety of tasks.

This issue of task demands is of particular concern to developmentalists. Is there so much information that it exceeds the child's capacity and therefore cannot be comprehended, even though the child has the appropriate rule? If so, the child's knowledge may be underestimated. A child may be able to use a balance scale to order blocks according to weight if there are four blocks but not if there are seven. Is there salient, but irrelevant, information that draws a child's attention away from the important information? For example, a child may attend to differences in the sizes of the blocks, thereby ignoring their weights. Are there developmental changes in what behaviors a child has available to apply toward the goal of the particular task? Children may weigh the blocks, compare their weights, and place them in a line differently at various ages.

Piaget had little interest in task analysis, but the neo-Piagetians did. For example, they raised the issue of domain-specific versus domain-general knowledge. Information-processing investigators tend to propose that the child acquires a set of rules or strategies that is specific to a particular domain, that is, limited to a certain task or set of tasks. A careful analysis of various tasks clarifies why a child may apply a rule (for example, a counting rule) or set of rules to certain tasks (adding) but not other relevant ones (class inclusion).

There is a common spirit in the information-processing and learning approaches. Both often break down tasks or behavior into their simple components. In addition, both are very concerned with the nature of the task stimuli. The information-processing approach, however, allows for more complexity in how people operate upon stimulus information. They can, for example, relate it to an organized set of knowledge about objects, people, and events.

Methodology

Information-processing psychologists typically use rigorous experimental methods to conduct a fine-grained analysis of the course of problem solving. The experiments sometimes are microscopic, in that they often look at very brief events, such as detecting whether a particular design that is flashed briefly on a screen is a spatial rotation of a design seen earlier. The studies often examine such temporal variables as the amount of time, in milliseconds, the stimulus is exposed and take temporal measures, such as reaction time (how long it takes the person to decide whether the design was rotated). It is assumed that any mental activity takes a certain amount of time. There may be differences in speed of processing between different ages, between normal and low-IQ children, and between good and poor readers. Researchers' concern with time is not surprising, given their focus on the flow of information over time. Under certain conditions, it can be assumed that the longer the time between input and output, the greater the cognitive activity that is taking place. Consequently, it might be assumed that if two tasks are identical except that one additional cognitive operation is required for one of the tasks, the difference in the time required to perform the two tasks provides a measure of the time needed to perform the additional operation. Long reaction times can also indicate slower processing of information. For example, researchers interpret elderly people's slower reaction times as indicating a slowing of their cognitive processing (e.g., Kail & Salthouse, 1994).

Another powerful method is the *rule-assessment* approach based on error analysis. The pattern of correct and incorrect answers over various types of trials reveals the rule or rules the child is using to solve the problem. A classic example is Siegler's (1978) work with the balance-scale task, to be described later. Although Piaget also made considerable use of children's errors, he did not analyze them in the elegant, systematic way often found in information-processing work. Still another assessment is eye-movement analysis. What children look at, how long they look at stimuli, and the order in which they examine stimuli provide clues to their processes of attention and encoding.

Information-processing psychologists, particularly Robert Siegler, have also adopted the *microgenetic method* advocated by Vygotsky (see Chapter 7). In this method, children are given a large number of trials on the same general type of problem (Siegler & Crowley, 1991). There can be multiple sessions spread over weeks or months. This design reveals moment-to-moment changes in the child's cognitive performance during the session and across sessions, for example, changes in which strategies are used. The microgenetic method permits investigators to observe change directly, while it is happening. They can see moments of sudden change, or cognitive insight—"cognitive moments," as it were. For instance, children sometimes show "hemming and hawing" behaviors on the trial just before the one on which they use a new strategy (Siegler & Jenkins, 1989), as illustrated by the quote from a child at the start of this chapter. They may suddenly fall silent before giving the answer, sometimes as long as a minute or more! These odd behaviors may indicate increased cognitive activity associated with the discovery of a new strategy. The method also reveals whether children differ in the developmental route they take to the same end point or their speed of reaching that point. In short, the microgenetic method brings the magnifying glass in very close to the child's behavior.

In addition to using these experimental methods, information-processing psychologists have developed two tools: models and computer simulation. The use of *models* in the form of flowcharts, described earlier, is not, of course, unique to the information-processing approach. As we saw in an earlier chapter, even Freud occasionally tried to express his theoretical notions through diagrams. However, no other approach has relied so heavily on schematic models for theory building as has the information-processing approach.

The advent of the computer not only gave psychologists and other scientists an efficient way to analyze their data but also provided a way to test theories of human thought. *Computer simulation* is an attempt to write a program that is specific enough, accurate enough, and complete enough to generate an output similar to that of humans. Information-processing psychologists pose the question: What would an information-processing system have to be like in order to behave as a child does? Psychologists try to develop a computer program that, given the same input as a child, produces the same output. The computer program and the child should make the same errors and succeed on the same problems. The closer the correspondence, the better the simulation.

The development of a successful simulation can be a long and arduous task. Usually psychologists begin by gathering descriptions of how people solve a particular problem. For example, they might describe the sequence in which a child selects pairs of blocks to weigh on a balance scale when ordering a set of blocks or have her describe what she is thinking and doing as she solves the problem. These data make up the "protocol." Researchers may videotape the problem-solving session so that they can view it many times. They then try to write a set of rules or procedures that the child or a group of children used to order the weights. Next, they write a computer program that gives instructions based on this set of rules. The program must make specific statements about the capacity of the system, the representation of information, and the nature of the cognitive processes. If psychologists have left out some steps in the rules they wrote into the program, if their instructions are logically inconsistent, or if they have incorrectly inferred a rule from the child's behavior, the program will give an output that does not correspond to the child's. Psychologists then try to correct the program and run it again. Often, this cycle must be repeated many times. With each repetition, the number of unexplained behaviors of the child becomes smaller and smaller. Eventually a satisfactory correspondence between the outputs may be achieved. In other words, the program essentially reproduces the protocol from which it was generated.

At this point, researchers apply more stringent tests. Can the program predict what other children of the same age or a different age would do? Can it predict what the child would do if there were 15 blocks to order instead of 7 or if the blocks were a different set of sizes? Can it predict what the child would do on a task of ordering objects according to length? Further modification of the program may be necessary to achieve this generalization. For example, for arithmetic skills it may be necessary to add information about the level of difficulty of backup strategies—such as adding by counting one's fingers—the frequency of problem presentation, and the effects of related knowledge (Siegler & Jenkins, 1989). The final simulation and the children should find the same problems difficult and make the same strategy choices on these problems.

At some point, psychologists find that they have a satisfactory model of how humans behave in a particular type of task, such as seriating weight or playing chess. Ideally, they can develop a more general model that explains behavior on a wider set of tasks, for example, a model of memory during problem solving. Thus, as they make further changes in the program, it may become both more specific and more general. A good model will generalize to more behaviors than the small set of protocols on which it was based but be specific enough to be supported or refuted by empirical findings.

One unexpected bonus of computer simulation is that it can suggest new hypotheses to psychologists. There may be unexpected outcomes of the simulation that suggest a new variable that should be examined. For example, if researchers found that the program predicted the same level of recall with 5 and with 10 items, they might look for a "chunking" mechanism that operates when there is a large number of items.

The information-processing approach may illustrate that researchers' methods sometimes encourage certain metaphors. It has been argued, for example, that the use of the rat maze as an experimental apparatus by the early learning theorist Tolman led to his spatial view of cognition, particularly cognitive maps (Gigerenzer, 1991). Similarly, present-day cognitive researchers, who typically use computers heavily for data gathering and data analysis, may find computer-program metaphors particularly appealing. Their tool becomes their metaphor.

MAJOR DEVELOPMENTAL APPROACHES

The study of information processing in children is a diverse, multifaceted enterprise. Some information-processing psychologists use letters flashed briefly on a screen, while others make the materials available for half an hour. Some look at reaction time, while others look at children's own explanations of how they solved a problem. The common orientation presented earlier should not mask this diversity. The following smorgasbord offers a sampling of current information-processing research programs and influential earlier studies. We look at the development of memory, strategies, rules for problem solving, production and connectionist simulations of problem solving and learning, and intelligence. This division into five areas is strictly for convenience of presentation. In actuality, all five make up a child's indivisible cognitive system.

For a look at exciting findings on other topics, see Siegler (1998), Bjorklund (2000a), and Flavell, Miller, & Miller (2001). These areas of study include, for example, the neural basis of information processing; social information processing; infants' problem solving, mental representations, imitation after a delay, and precocious processing of sensory information and language; scientific reasoning; event knowledge; executive functioning (for example, inhibition, planning); and learning to read. Information-processing psychologists obviously study topics that are somewhat different from those studied by Piaget. Also, Piaget was less interested in the actual online functioning of a cognitive system than in its structures.

Memory

Memory is a net; one finds it full of fish when he takes it from the brook; but a dozen miles of water have run through it without sticking.

— Oliver Wendell Holmes

Children's memory is a fascinating phenomenon, in part because it is fraught with contradictions. On the one hand, it is widely believed that young children have poor memories. On memory subscales of IQ tests or on laboratory memory tasks they perform poorly compared with adults, and in more natural settings young children find it difficult to memorize their phone numbers and street addresses. Yet parents or teachers who read stories to preschoolers know that children often memorize a story word for word after only a few readings. In fact, children become quite indignant if the reader inadvertently (or because it is past bedtime) leaves out a word or two.

Children's memory probably has been the topic most often studied by information-processing psychologists and in fact has been one of the largest research areas in developmental psychology. This investment of psychologists' time and energy has paid off handsomely in knowledge not only about children's memory but also, as a bonus, about the development of language, attention, and complex cognitive structures such as the organization of knowledge.

Memory involves three main steps. First, children encode information, either verbatim or the gist of the event, either the exact words of a conversation or the essence of its meaning (Brainerd & Reyna, 1998). Next comes the storage of the information, and finally children retrieve the information. Developmental changes occur in each step, as the following research examples indicate. Still, even very young infants appear to be able to encode, store, and retrieve within limits. In one demonstration of this, a ribbon connected to a mobile is tied to an infant's ankle (Rovee-Collier & Gerhardstein, 1997). She quickly learns, to her delight, that kicking her feet makes the mobile move. A week later when she again is placed in the crib she sees the mobile and again kicks in anticipation of the dancing mobile, even though the ribbon is no longer attached to her ankle. She has "remembered" what she discovered at the first event. Two-month-olds remember for as long as 2 weeks, and older infants can remember for longer periods and, during the test of recall, require fewer cues from the original learning situation. This ability to recognize a situation and retrieve a very simple event is, of course, a very rudimentary sort of memory, and there is much still to develop.

What happens after infancy? Do children possess a single, underlying memory ability that applies to all content areas? Are individual differences in memory stable throughout development? The answer to both questions seems to be "not really." This is the conclusion from an important 10-year longitudinal study with a number of different sorts of memory tasks, the Munich Longitudinal Study (Schneider & Weinert, 1995, 1999). How well a child recalled, relative to other children, on a particular memory task bore little relation to how well he recalled on other memory tasks. Recall was significantly correlated only when the tasks were very similar, such as two memory-span tasks. Thus, memory skills seem to be somewhat specific to a particular task. Regarding the stability of memory skills over time, children who remembered well, compared to other children, at one age did not necessarily remember well on a similar task several years later, especially if doing so required a strategy.

We now examine four main factors that cause developmental changes in memory, illustrated with several studies that convey the flavor of the research. The factors are strategies, knowledge, metamemory, and capacity. Researchers have examined each of these factors and, more recently, their complex interactions, such as whether the effectiveness of a strategy depends on the child's knowledge about the task if the capacity demands are large.

Strategies ▪ Some memory activities are effortless and seemingly automatic: a baby recognizes her father's face, a boy relates to his friend the plot of his favorite television show seen the night before, an adult hums "White Christmas" while Christmas shopping. The person is not conscious of trying to remember and does not make an effort to remember. These acts of memory "just happen." There is little change in these types of memory during development. Simple recognition memory (indicating that an object or a picture has been seen before) is good even in infants. By the end of the preschool years, children recall coherent, comprehensible stories or past experiences that are of interest to them. This memory is a by-product of a meaningful activity or event.

When the material to be recalled is *not* part of a context that is meaningful to the child and memory itself must become the primary goal, then there *is* striking improvement in memory during development. Remembering phone numbers, a group of unrelated objects, and the order in which pictures of toys were presented all fall into this category. Much of the information-processing research on children's memory addresses these sorts of remembering.

Children of different ages do different things when they are trying to remember. Older children know that in order to store unrelated information, they must do something special to the material. This "something special" is a strategy. Defined more formally, *strategies* are "subject-controlled activities that are employed in the service of a memory goal" (Ornstein & Naus, 1985, p. 118). For example, if people want to remember what to buy at the store, they could say the items over and over again to themselves or put the items into categories such as "dairy products" and "vegetables." Or they could make up a silly story about the items ("The carrot swam through the sea of milk on the back of a tuna . . . "), mark the location of the items on their mental image of the supermarket, or, best of all, simply write a list. These strategies are tools that humans have devised in their constant struggle to overcome their processing limitations.

In an early influential study of children's strategies, Flavell, Beach, and Chinsky (1966) asked young children to remember the order in which the experimenter pointed to several pictures of objects. During the delay between the presentation and the recall tests, a visor on a space helmet was lowered over the child's eyes so that he could not see the pictures. A trained lip reader noted any overt verbal rehearsal. Few 5-year-olds, over half of the 7-year-olds, and most of the 10-year-olds rehearsed. In a later experiment, Keeney, Cannizzo, and Flavell (1967) found evidence for a direct link between rehearsal and memory. First, children who spontaneously rehearsed recalled more items than those who did not. Second, when the experimenter directed nonrehearsers to say the names of the objects during the delay between the presentation and the recall test, they successfully rehearsed. Consequently, they remembered the order of the objects. Thus, young children are capable of using rehearsal to aid memory if they are told to rehearse, but they are deficient at spontaneously producing the strategy. Flavell dubbed this a *production deficiency*. Young children have appropriate strategies but are deficient in knowing when, where, and how to use (produce) them effectively. Since the Flavell studies, researchers have documented a production deficiency with many other memory tasks and many other strategies, such as leaving clues that will help in retrieval or classifying the items into categories (animals, furniture, and food). This research shows that older children are more likely than younger children to use the higher-order relations among items, such as categories.

Children begin to develop simple strategies well before grade school age. For example, toddlers age 18 to 24 months watched the experimenter hide a Big Bird stuffed animal (DeLoache, Cassidy, & Brown, 1985). They were told to remember Big Bird's location so that they could find him later. Even though the experimenter then distracted them with attractive toys for several minutes, they frequently stopped playing to talk about Big Bird or his hiding place (the "Big Bird chair"), look at or point to the hiding place, hover near it, or try to get Big Bird. These strategylike behaviors were much less frequent in control conditions, such as when the experimenter rather than the child was to remember the locations.

Even after children develop and use more complex strategies, they continue to refine them. Ornstein, Naus, and Liberty (1975) found that verbal rehearsal becomes more systematic and organized during development. During the memory task, the children were to say the words aloud as they were presented. Third-graders tended to say each word alone as it was presented or perhaps with the previous word. In contrast, eighth-graders rehearsed cumulatively, including previously presented words as well as the new word.

By the preteen years, children typically can pick a strategy that fits the particular task and carry out the strategy spontaneously, quickly, and efficiently. Certain strategies, however, continue to develop during adolescence. An example is "elaboration," or constructing an image out of the materials to be remembered (Pressley, 1982).

A major developmental change during the grade school and adolescent years involves learning to make maximal use of one's limited capacity. For example, during the grade school years, children become more efficient in their use of study time. Older grade school children are more likely than young children to select relevant material and ignore irrelevant material (Miller, 1990). For example, older children focus more on the important elements of a text, as reflected in their underlining and note taking (Brown & Smiley, 1978). Children learn to control their strategies and other cognitive processes. As if conducting a great orchestra, children eventually bring the parts into perfect harmony and increase their control over the whole process (Brown, 1978).

Children's use of strategies for remembering has turned out to be quite complicated. First, children sometimes produce good strategies that, surprisingly, do not help their recall or provide less help for younger than for older children (Bjorklund, Miller, Coyle, & Slawinski, 1997; Miller & Seier, 1994). This is called a strategy *utilization deficiency*. It is puzzling why children would continue to use a strategy that provides little or no help. Second, children often use several strategies together when trying to remember something, rather than just one (Coyle & Bjorklund, 1997). Third, they tend to change their strategies from trial to trial, as we will see in the later section on Siegler's strategy research. Fourth, strategy development appears to benefit from the development of knowledge, metamemory, and capacity, to be described next.

Knowledge ▪ Memory is not a mental process separate from the rest of cognition. It is intermeshed in a broad system of thought. In fact, memory has been called "applied cognition" (Flavell, 1971a) because the cognitive system is simply directed to a particular set of problems, namely, storage and retrieval. There are two implications for development. First, children are more likely to remember material that they know about and understand, such as a child-oriented movie or familiar words. In fact, this factor may account for more of the difference in memory performance than any other factor on some tasks (Alexander & Schwanenflugel, 1994). When there is a match between what the child knows and what is to be remembered, there is what Brown (1975) called "headfitting." Moreover, children in fact often extract the "gist"—the essence of the material—and construct "fuzzy" memory representations rather than memorize the story or paragraph verbatim (Brainerd & Reyna, 1998). Second, as children become "worldwise" and acquire a growing store of knowledge about objects, events, and people in the world, their recall improves.

Numerous studies show that knowledge helps recall. Piaget's studies of memory, described in Chapter 1, showed that children's memory of seriated (size-ordered) sticks improved (became more seriated) after their understanding of seriation improved. Moreover, when children become experts in a particular domain, they demonstrate good memory in that domain. For example, children who are skilled chess players have better recall of the locations of chess pieces on a chessboard, positioned as if in the middle of a game, than do adults who know less about chess (Chi, 1978). Thus, children's greater knowledge in a particular domain can outweigh adults' other cognitive advantages. Knowing about chess permits children to "chunk" the chess pieces into significant units (for example, an attack), whereas novices must memorize individual pieces and locations. Expert knowledge also benefits children's recall in areas such as soccer (Schneider, Körkel, & Weinert, 1989) and baseball (Recht & Leslie, 1988). Young children could be considered "universal novices" (Brown & DeLoache, 1978) who only gradually acquire expertise across various domains.

A rich knowledge base may allow children to access automatically items to be recalled because these items have a rich network of associations with other items and with category labels (Bjorklund, 1987). Thus, thinking of either "tulip" or "flowers" can help a child remember that there was a "rose." Multiple associations increase the chances that a child can recall the item. Another example involves a 4-year-old who was obsessed with dinosaur lore (Chi & Koeske, 1983). He knew the names of 40 different dinosaurs, understood the differences between a pachycephalosaur and a rhamphorhyncus, and persuaded his patient mother to spend an average of 3 hours a week reading his dinosaur books to him. The boy could remember more of his better-known than his lesser-known dinosaurs. An analysis of what dinosaurs and traits were highly associated showed that the better-known dinosaurs had many links to other dinosaurs and were better organized according to their characteristics.

The importance of the structure of knowledge for recall also is suggested by a study that showed that simply increasing a child's factual knowledge in a domain does not ensure improved recall (DeMarie-Dreblow, 1991). Children were given approximately 1 hour of instruction about various species of birds over 1 week. They significantly increased their knowledge of birds, but memory did not improve. In addition, equating knowledge between younger and older children does not equate performance (Barnes, Dennis, & Haefele-Kalvaitis, 1996). Thus, the increase in knowledge (quantitative change) may have to lead to a shift in the organization of this knowledge (qualitative change) before recall improves.

In addition to increasing access to items to be recalled, a well-formed knowledge base helps children use an appropriate strategy, which in turn facilitates recall. Thus, a strategy may mediate the effect of the knowledge base. According to one version of this argument, the ability to quickly process the information by relating it to previous knowledge frees capacity that can be applied to deliberately using a strategy (Bjorklund, 1987). Thus, Siegler concludes that "familiar content may serve as a kind of practice field upon which children exercise emerging memory strategies" (1998, p. 206). Six-year-olds, who typically do not group similar items together during recall, can, when asked to remember the names of classmates, show a great deal of grouping according to seating arrangement, reading groups, and sex of the children (Bjorklund & Zeman, 1982). In addition to these two main explanations of why knowledge helps recall (access to items and freed capacity) is the suggestion that a rich knowledge base may facilitate recall by enhancing motivation or increasing children's understanding of the goal of the task.

As children increase their store of knowledge, they tend to make inferences that go beyond the information given. Hebb (1949) likens this feature of remembering to the way a paleontologist reconstructs a prehistoric creature. Just as a paleontologist generates a complete dinosaur from lone fragments and his general knowledge about the anatomy of dinosaurs, so does a person reconstruct an event by filling in among remembered fragments. For example, in one study (Paris & Carter, 1973), children were told "The bird is inside the cage" and "The cage is under the table." Later the children were presented with sentences, some new and some heard earlier. Children as young as 7 often recalled, erroneously, that the sentence "The bird is under the table" had been presented earlier. They had spontaneously made a reasonable inference from the information they had been given.

Children's social knowledge, such as social beliefs, attitudes, and expectations, also affects memory. For example, school-age children with the most stereotyped views of gender-appropriate behavior recalled more pictures of traditional (for example, female secretary) than nontraditional (for example, male secretary) activities (Signorella & Liben, 1984). In addition, they sometimes even reconstructed the pictures, for example, recalling that a secretary was female when in fact the person was a male. Racial stereotypes have a similar biasing effect on Euro-American children's recall of the personal characteristics of African-American and Euro-American children in stories (Bigler & Liben, 1993). Children had trouble accurately recalling the characteristics that ran counter to their racial stereotypes. A final example is that 7- and 10-year-olds "remembered" that a character known to them to be powerful, such as "The Six Million Dollar Man," had been strong in a story heard 3 weeks earlier. In fact, the character had been weak in the story (Ceci, Caves, & Howe, 1981). This distortion of memory did not occur with unfamiliar characters. Thus, memory does not simply copy the world. Children "construct" a memory from inferences based on their knowledge. In short, "creative memory" is a by-product of cognitive development.

One cognitive change in knowledge that affects memory is the development of *scripts* (e.g., Nelson, 1986, 1996). Scripts are generalized, coherent mental representations of a series of events that occur in a consistent temporal order in everyday life. These scripts describe "what's supposed to happen" in certain situations, and they lead children to expect that certain events will occur in a particular order. If this order is violated, children may become confused. For example, a 2-year-old who once was given a bath before dinner, rather than after, became very upset because she thought she would not be fed that evening (Hudson, 1990). Scripts also allow children to understand and interpret both old and new objects and events. As Nelson defines it, a *script* "(1) contains certain basic and obligatory events in sequence, (2) predicts open slots for options, objects and events and what they may contain, and (3) designates appropriate roles and actors" (1978, pp. 256–257). Nelson found that even young children develop scripts for familiar situations. To illustrate, a child might have a script for eating at a fast-food hamburger restaurant:

> I walk in there and I, I, I ask my daddy and then the daddy ask the lady and the lady gets it. One small coke, one cheeseburger. . . . They want to eat here so they don't need a tray. Then we go find a table. I eat it all up. All. And throw the . . . paper . . . the cheeseburgers in the garbage can. . . . Goodbye. Goodbye. Jump in the car. . . . Vroom! Vroom! Goodbye.
>
> (Nelson, 1978, p. 260)

Three features of scripts are noteworthy. First, scripts are about events and thus are less verbal and less static than representations in semantic networks, which emphasize information about the meanings of words and concepts. Even preverbal infants have memory for simple events, which may form the basis for the later script concepts. For example, they can later repeat a sequence of events such as putting a ball into a cup, inverting a smaller cup on top of the larger one, and shaking the cups (Bauer & Mandler, 1992). Second, scripts involve t. world of people and events. Scripts seem to correspond to the wa, dren represent complex events of their day-to-day lives. Third, scr. both help and hinder memory. They help a child "fill in" details when re calling an event. However, scripts also hinder the recall of one specific event because, for example, the various trips to the restaurant blend together into the script and the child recalls what happens at restaurants in general rather than what happened on one particular visit.

A final observation about the relationship between knowledge and recall is that since children's interests and knowledge differ from those of adults, their most salient memories may differ from those of adults. One 5-year-old, when asked if he remembered the place he had moved from 2 years earlier, answered: "I remember lots about Michigan. I remember you left a piece of cheese at the back of the refrigerator and it got green stuff all over it."

Metamemory ▪

"The horror of that moment," the King went on, "I shall never, never *forget!"*
"You will, though," the Queen said, "if you don't make a memorandum of it."

— LEWIS CARROLL

Taking notes while listening to a lecture, underlining key points in a textbook on developmental theories, writing a shopping list before leaving for the supermarket, leaving one's completed homework by the front door the night before school, and mentally walking through the previous day in order to recall where a jacket might have been left all reflect *metamemory*. Metamemory is knowledge about memory and is a special case of *metacognition*, which is knowledge about any aspect of human thought. During development, we acquire an understanding that sometimes it is necessary to make an extra effort or do something special in order to remember and that certain factors facilitate or hinder memory. These factors can include person, task, or strategy variables (Flavell & Wellman, 1977). Examples are knowing that there are limits to how much can be remembered (person variable), that recognition is easier than recall (task variable), and that verbal rehearsal aids recall (strategy variable). Thus, children become amateur psychologists.

Preschoolers have limited knowledge about memory. For instance, they claim superhuman memory abilities, such as when they predict that they can remember 10 items even though they can remember only

3 or 4 (Flavell, Friedrichs, & Hoyt, 1970). With simple testing procedures, however, they do reveal some competence at metamemory. For example, 4-year-olds who view two strategies on videotape can choose the more helpful one. They know that they can better help themselves remember where Cookie Monster is hidden by marking his hiding place with a colored chip rather than by looking away when the stimulus array is rotated (Justice, 1989).

The more sophisticated facets of metamemory develop later. Kreutzer, Leonard, and Flavell (1975) asked children whether it mattered if, after being told a phone number, they made the call immediately or got a drink of water first. Approximately 40 percent of the kindergartners but more than 75 percent of the fifth-graders thought it would be better to phone first. Presumably, children become increasingly aware that short-term memory fades rapidly. This study also provides an example of increasing knowledge about strategies. When given a retrieval problem in which a child is trying to remember at which Christmas he received his dog, nearly half of the kindergartners were unable to suggest a way to recall the correct Christmas but all of the fifth-graders could. The fifth-graders thought of aids such as taking a trip through the mind back to each Christmas and recalling the gifts received or trying to recall other things that happened when the dog was received in the hope that doing so would provide a cue.

Kreutzer et al. found that children's thinking about strategies can become rather complex, as the following exchange with a third-grader demonstrates:

> Say the number is 633-8854. Then what I'd do is—say that my number is 633, so I won't have to remember that, really. And then I would think, now I've got to remember 88. Now I'm 8 years old, so I can remember, say, my age two times. And then I say how old my brother is, and how old he was last year. And that's how I'd usually remember that phone number. (Is that how you would most often remember a phone number?) Well, usually I write it down.
>
> (1975, p. 11)

Children not only learn about the nature of memory and the variables that affect it but also learn to monitor their memory performance and the strategies they use to help it. Metacognition in this sense and strategies appear to form a feedback loop in which feedback about the success or failure of each strategy increases meta-awareness of the goal and of the power and limitations of each strategy with respect to meeting that goal (Kuhn, 1999; Kuhn & Pearsall, 1998). Thus, effective strategy training must be directed toward metacognition as well as strategic behavior (Pressley, Borkowski, & Schneider, 1987).

An important theoretical question concerns the relationship between knowledge about memory and memory behavior. Intuitively, it seems that there should be a close relationship. If children think that memory is automatic and do not realize that they need to do anything special to remember, they are not likely to bother to rehearse the material, look for similarities among the objects, and so on. Thus, young children might fail to produce a strategy simply because of their poor metamemory. In addition, even if children do produce strategies, they should draw on their ability to detect whether their chosen strategy is working when deciding whether to continue or drop that strategy. It appears, however, that the relationship between knowledge about memory and memory performance is not so simple. Knowledge does not necessarily lead to the use of that knowledge, though recent studies are more optimistic in this respect than were earlier studies (see Schneider & Bjorklund, 1998, and Schneider & Pressley, 1997, for reviews). For example, children are more likely to continue to use a strategy if they attribute their success on the task to using that strategy and understand why the strategy helps them (Fabricius & Hagen, 1984).

Capacity ■ A commonsense explanation of developmental improvement in memory would be that the memory span (the capacity of short-term memory) increases as the brain matures physically. For example, with increasing age children can repeat back, in order, a longer string of numbers (for example, 3281734). This view connotes a container metaphor in which children have small boxes in their heads and adults have larger boxes (Schneider & Weinert, 1989) or a weight-lifter metaphor in which older children have greater "raw mental muscle power" (Flavell et al., 2001). The full story is more complicated, however. As mentioned earlier, when cognitive skills are practiced, they become more automatic and thus less capacity-demanding. For example, as children become more skilled readers, they can recognize words more quickly; as a result, a given amount of capacity goes much further. Also, increasing knowledge probably helps children use what they have more efficiently. Consequently, some of the developmental increase in capacity reflects children's improved efficiency in using a constant amount of capacity rather than a neurological–structural increase in capacity. Thus, thanks to both maturation and experience, older children have a larger memory span than do younger ones.

This developmental increase in capacity appears to be somewhat domain-general. Studies of reaction time (latency between presentation of a stimulus and the child's response) have examined this. They show that across a number of tasks the ratio between the capacity of adults and that of children of a particular age is the same (Kail, 1997). In other words, the pattern of age differences in reaction time seems to be the same for a variety of tasks. Reaction time is important because speed of processing information, particularly identifying it, is thought to underlie children's capacity. The faster the child can process information, the more information he can deal with at any one time. This domain generality supports the argument of the neo-Piagetian Case that an increase in capacity during development can contribute to simultaneous changes across domains, as discussed in Chapter 1.

Regardless of whether increased capacity proves to involve mainly maturation-based, "hard-wired" structural changes or experience-based changes in efficiency, the effects on memory are clear. As described in earlier sections, older children use this greater capacity to keep more items alive in short-term memory and invest it in memory strategies and metamemory activities—a wise investment, as we have seen.

Finally, one challenge to young children's attempts to use their strategies efficiently is their limited capacity. They find strategy production more effortful than do older children (Guttentag, 1995). This may account for young children's utilization deficiencies, described earlier, in which children produce a good strategy but it does not help their recall or it helps recall less than it does for older children. After producing the strategy, the young child has less remaining capacity to devote to memorizing per se than does an older child for whom the strategy itself requires less capacity-draining effort.

Current Issues About the Development of Memory ■ In addition to exploring the traditionally studied areas of strategies, knowledge, metamemory, and capacity, researchers currently are examining many other exciting areas as well. Here is a tantalizing sampling: Can children accurately report what they have witnessed others do, particularly when it involves an emotion-laden event such as physical abuse to themselves? Can older children or adults remember very early events that occurred before they acquired language? Are young children particularly suggestible—easily swayed by false information given to them by adults? How early do infants possess what we would call "memory"? How important is implicit memory—memory without awareness of remembering—for cognitive development? What leads to the development of the ability to inhibit the intrusion of task-irrelevant stimuli and thoughts into working memory? How do parents and their young children co-construct autobiographical memories of earlier personally experienced events (see Chapter 7)? What does it mean that children sometimes recall information that appeared not to be remembered initially? For accounts of these and other issues, see Schneider and Bjorklund (1998) and Schneider and Pressley (1997). Many of these lines of research incorporate other theoretical frameworks quite different from information processing. Thus, memory research no longer can so easily be taken to represent only the information-processing approach.

Strategies: Acquisition, Variability, and Choice

Siegler's Microgenetic Research ▪ Children use strategies not only for remembering, as described above, but also for a variety of other sorts of cognitive work. Siegler's (e.g., 1996) microgenetic research on how children develop new strategies over several problems and sessions and select from their toolbox of current strategies is a major example of research in this area. In the slice of laboratory life at the start of this chapter, a young girl is trying to solve an addition problem. She worked on a large set of addition problems, and Siegler observed her pattern of errors and correct answers, recorded her use of strategies, and asked her about her strategies. Siegler found that at any age a child uses a variety of strategies to solve basic addition problems. To solve 4 + 3, a child might put up four fingers on one hand and three fingers on the other hand and then count all the fingers. Or she might put up her fingers and recognize their number without counting. Or she might start with the larger of the two numbers and count on from that point (4, 5, 6, 7).

In this experiment and others, children show the following interesting behaviors: At any age, a child typically uses several different strategies from one problem to the next on the same sorts of problems or even the same problem on different days. Children often use six strategies or more on addition problems (Siegler & Jenkins, 1989). Sometimes the variation is quite sensible: On easy problems with small numbers, a child uses the simple recognition strategy because she can easily detect the number of fingers or even just give a correct answer that she has memorized. On other problems that are easy because one number is small, such as 8 + 2, she can use the strategy of counting up from 8. On harder problems, she has to use the harder strategy of counting all of the fingers. This seems smart. She is using a fast, low-effort strategy on easy problems, where it is likely to be accurate, and slower, more effortful strategies on harder problems. Over time she increases her use of the most efficient strategies, decreases her use of the less efficient strategies, and discovers new strategies. However, children sometimes seem to act in irrational or surprising ways. They may construct a new strategy right after using an existing one successfully. They may successfully use a new, more efficient strategy but then abandon it for a while and go back to an earlier strategy. Still, these seemingly inefficient temporary rejections of successful strategies are useful, because they help the child keep old strategies available while discovering new ones.

Even toddlers are strategic, and their ways of acquiring this skill look very much like those of older children (Chen & Siegler, 2000). Consider the following dilemma presented to children 18 to 35 months old: A child sees a desirable toy turtle tantalizingly out of reach. Between him and the turtle are six objects, for example, a rake, a banana, a stick, a cane head, and other elongated objects. Only the rake could effectively pull the turtle to within reach. Few toddlers used the rake initially, but most eventually learned to do so with a prompt or with an adult as a model and even transferred the strategy to other tools and toys. As in the Siegler research with older children, the toddlers' strategy discovery and choice seemed to involve the use of multiple strategies, much switching of strategies both within a trial and between trials, an initial intuitive sense about the general sort of tool that would work, and strategy choice that becomes increasingly adaptive. Thus, the microgenetic method seems fruitful for illuminating strategies in toddlers as well as older children.

Although children sometimes are taught strategies or learn them by watching others, they at times invent a new strategy by themselves during the course of problem solving. Some children show a great deal of insight into their discovery. Others do not and, during questioning, even claim, for example, not to have counted at all, even though videotapes clearly showed that they had used a new counting strategy (Siegler & Jenkins, 1989). In fact, children's new strategies often seem to stay unconscious for a while. Siegler and Stern (1998) found that almost 90 percent of their second-graders discovered a new strategy but could not yet report it.

Siegler has successfully modeled strategy discovery, variability, choice, and change in his Strategy Choice and Discovery Simulation (SCADS) model (Shrager & Siegler, 1998). The model shows most of the above patterns observed in children. The model, like a child, tries various strategies and records their success or failure along with information about the speed and accuracy with which the problem was solved. This feedback affects the subsequent choice of a strategy. The model gradually learns which strategies work best for which types of problems. Also, with more and more experience with a particular problem the association between the problem and the answer becomes very strong and it becomes possible to simply give a low-effort, memorized answer.

Thus, the contemporary view of children's strategies emphasizes variability more than consistency. Strategy variability seems to be the rule rather than the exception during development. That is, Siegler (1996) sees all of development as a transition period; children are always thinking in multiple ways, rather than just one. This going back and forth among various strategies appears in areas as diverse as motor behaviors in infants (Adolph, 1997), conceptual understanding in school-age children (Karmiloff-Smith, 1992), and scientific reasoning in adolescents and adults (Schauble, 1996). Trying a variety of approaches seems to be part of being human. Psychologists' past tendency to consider variability a nuisance rather than a phenomenon of interest may have directed attention away from behaviors that could provide important clues to developmental change.

Strategies of Selective Information Gathering ▪ A second illustration of children's strategies comes from studies of children's strategies for selecting information. Because children's worlds are full of information, an important part of development is learning what *not* to attend to and ponder. In these studies (for example, Miller, 1990, and Welch-Ross & Miller, 2000), a child sits in front of a box with doors, as shown in Figure 4.2. On half of the doors is a drawing of a cage, which indicates a drawing of an animal concealed behind the door; on the other doors is a drawing of a house, indicating a household object behind the door. The researcher tells half of the children to remember where each animal is located (the other half of the children are told to remember household objects instead). During a 30-second study period the children can open whatever doors they wish. Typically, preschoolers jump right in and open each door, row by row. Although their door opening is not random, it also is not efficient, for they are wasting their precious working-memory space viewing irrelevant household objects as well as relevant animals. In contrast, older children open only the relevant

Figure 4.2

Apparatus for Miller's selective-memory door-opening task. (Photo supplied by Patricia Miller.)

(animal) doors. In an interesting transitional phase children are partially selective; some begin by using the selective strategy but then seem unable to sustain it and lapse back to opening all of the doors.

Sociocultural Context of Strategic Behavior ▪ Children do not acquire strategies in a social vacuum. Their culture encourages them to acquire some strategies more than other strategies and gives them an opportunity to practice these valued strategies. Cultures vary, for example, in their views of whether a child's asking an adult for help is an appropriate strategy and whether it is better to choose a strategy that ensures speed or accuracy. Although information-processing psychologists have given little attention to social factors in the past, this is beginning to change.

Some information-processing research has looked at strategic behavior in dyads (Ellis, Klahr, & Siegler, 1993). When child dyads worked together to solve decimal problems, some dyads were more successful than others. The most successful ones were those in which one child reacted with interest and enthusiasm to the other child's correct explanation. Thus, a child who generates a correct strategy may abandon it if peers do not respond positively. In addition, dyads who generated the correct solution together, rather than one child before the other or one child not at all, gave the clearest explanations. Thus, using strategies by oneself and with others, for example, at school, may differ in important ways.

Collaborative problem solving with a peer or adult presumably involves some "reading" of the mental states of the other person. Consider a child who gives a nonconservation answer on Piaget's conservation task and then hears a conservation answer from an adult (Siegler, 1995). The adult then says, "How do you think I knew that?" This question was more effective in promoting learning about conservation than was the situation in which children just heard the adult's conservation answer and had to explain their own reasoning. Having to think about another person's thinking, or "attempting to learn not from another but through another" (Tomasello, Kruger, & Ratner, 1993, p. 496), may turn out to be an important mechanism of development.

It is interesting, however, that when children first acquire conservation they may have trouble taking the perspective of a nonconserver. Ellis and Johns (1999) found that few conservers could predict and explain the behavior of a child on videotape who gave nonconservation answers, even though the conservers had been nonconservers themselves not so long ago and presumably followed the same line of reasoning as the nonconserver they were observing! Children who had been conservers longer were better able to understand the thinking of the nonconserver. Thus, a child's understanding of others' misconceptions during collaborative problem solving may be influenced by her knowledge about the task at hand. Children may find it difficult to think about other beliefs that conflict with what they know to be true, especially if their own grasp of this "truth" is rather fragile.

Rules for Problem Solving

Because computer programs often consist of a set of rules, it was natural for information-processing researchers to ask what rules children use to solve problems. Examples are in areas such as planning, causal inference, analogy, tool use, scientific reasoning, and logical deduction. For example, a dog-cat-mouse problem presented to preschoolers requires moving each animal to its favorite food (Klahr, 1985). Only certain types of moves are permissible. Children's series of moves to place the dog with the bone, the cat with the fish, and the mouse with the cheese reveal their approaches to problem solving.

Siegler's (1978) rule-assessment approach, mentioned in the section on methods, examines the rules children use to solve problems about many physical phenomena studied by Piaget. One task is a balance-scale (teeter-totter) problem, shown in Figure 4.3. On each arm of the scale are four equally spaced pegs on which weights can be placed. The child predicts which side, if either, is heavier and will go down. Two pieces of information are relevant: the number of weights (all of equal weight) on each side and their distance from the midpoint (fulcrum). Siegler identified a developmental sequence of four rules:

1. Children consider only the number of weights, so they predict that the side with more weights will go down.
2. Children consider only the number of weights, unless the numbers are equal on the two sides, in which case they also take the distance into account.
3. Children examine both number of weights and distance but do not know what to predict when one side has greater distance and the other side has more weights.
4. Children can assess the exact contribution of both number of weights and distance by multiplying the number of weights on each peg by that peg's ordinal distance from the fulcrum. (The ordinal position can be used because the pegs are an equal distance apart. The fourth peg from the midpoint is four times as far away as the first one.) By comparing the outcome of this computation for the two sides, children can predict which side will go down.

Siegler could determine which rule a child was using by systematically varying the number of weights and their distance in a series of problems. Each rule would lead to a characteristic pattern of correct and incorrect predictions over the series of problems. This study is an example of the error-analysis method mentioned earlier. Consider, for example, a "conflict-weight problem," in which there is more weight on one side but the weights are more distant on the other side. The config-

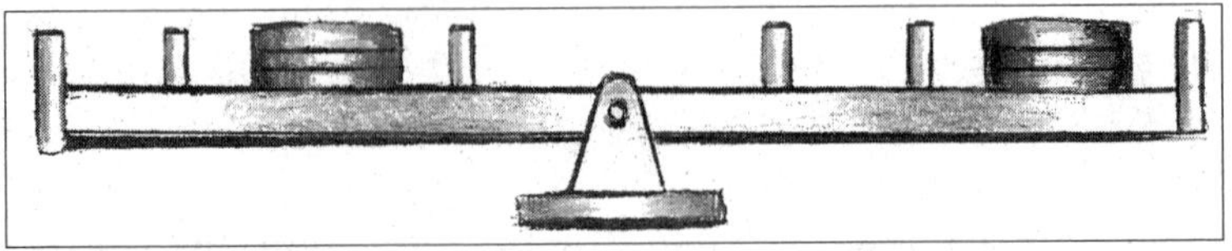

Figure 4.3

Examples of a trial on Siegler's balance-scale task. The arms of the scale are locked into place until after the child predicts which side, if either, will go down.

uration is such that the side with more weights goes down. Children using rule 1 or 2 always correctly predict that the side with more weights will go down because they consider only the number of weights. Children using rule 3, however, are correct only about one-third of the time because they simply guess. They know that both distance and number of weights are important but cannot determine the exact contribution of each. Children using rule 4 are correct. Notice that the children's errors are as informative as their correct answers. The results were that the four rule models accurately described the pattern of predictions over the various types of trials of 89 percent of the children ages 5, 9, 13, and 17. Furthermore, as expected, the older children used more sophisticated rules than did the younger children. Siegler has conducted similar analyses on many other tasks, including conservation, projection of shadows, probability, speed, and mathematical calculations.

Siegler and Chen (1998) recently used the microgenetic method to reexamine children's learning of these rules on the balance scale in order to track the moment-to-moment changes and to try to identify the causes of these changes. They found that what their 4- and 5-year-olds brought to the task—their age, initial rule, and initial encoding of the task—affected what they could learn during the task. For example, because 83 percent of the 4-year-olds failed to encode the distance of the weights from the fulcrum, they were unable to learn that this feature might be related to the problem. Although they saw 12 problems on which the weights were equal and the side with weights farther from the fulcrum went down, and each time they were asked "Why do you think that side went down?" they never seemed to notice the dimension of distance!

The way that information-processing psychologists study the balance-scale task contrasts with Piaget's approach to the same task. Although both were concerned with how children reached their answer, Piaget used the task to diagnose whether children have underlying mental operations. Siegler, in contrast, inferred what specific rules the child used for the task at each step en route to developing an understanding of balancing weights. He made a more detailed analysis of the child's actions and, because he had done a task analysis, could relate them to the stimulus characteristics of the task—the number of objects and their distance from the fulcrum. He also looked at children's learning, using a microgenetic design. Finally, he wrote a computer program based on the inferred rules to see if they could generate the child's sequence of actions.

The simple set of rules revealed by Siegler is an elegant and appealing model of development, yet this simplicity has been a focus of criticism. It has been suggested (Strauss & Levin, 1981) that these simple rules emerge because Siegler's methodology restricts children to these rules. Presenting the same task in an open-ended, rather than forced-choice, manner may reveal other, perhaps more complex, rules.

Production and Connectionist Simulations of Problem Solving and Learning

As described earlier, simulations are attempts to describe human thinking in terms of processes that can be modeled within computer programs. The two main types of computational models that have attempted to simulate cognitive development are production systems and connectionist systems. *Production systems* tend to include rules, expressed in symbols, and address complex cognitive processes such as problem solving. An example of a rule is "If *X* is present, then do *Y*." In contrast, *connectionist systems* tend to focus on the underlying microstructure of basic cognitive processes that is analogous to neural networks. Both production and connectionist systems can simulate change and thus serve as examples of the self-modifying systems described earlier, but this is especially true of connectionist systems (Klahr, 1999). Connectionist approaches have been particularly "hot" in recent years, perhaps because of the recent interest in cognitive neuroscience (see Chapter 8). Below is a description of each type of system, followed by an example.

Production Systems ■ Klahr, sometimes in collaboration with Wallace, Siegler, Simon, Newell, or other colleagues, has developed production-system computer programs to simulate problem solving in children. He has examined class inclusion, conservation, transitivity, counting, balancing weights, as well as other concepts. Klahr has sought the "programmable Piaget" (Quillian, Wortman, & Baylor, 1964). For our example, we will examine Klahr and Siegler's (1978) research in which Siegler's four rules for solving the balance-scale problem, described earlier, are translated into a computer program.

The first step is to translate the four rules into the flowchart in Figure 4.4. This diagram shows the steps involved in applying each rule.

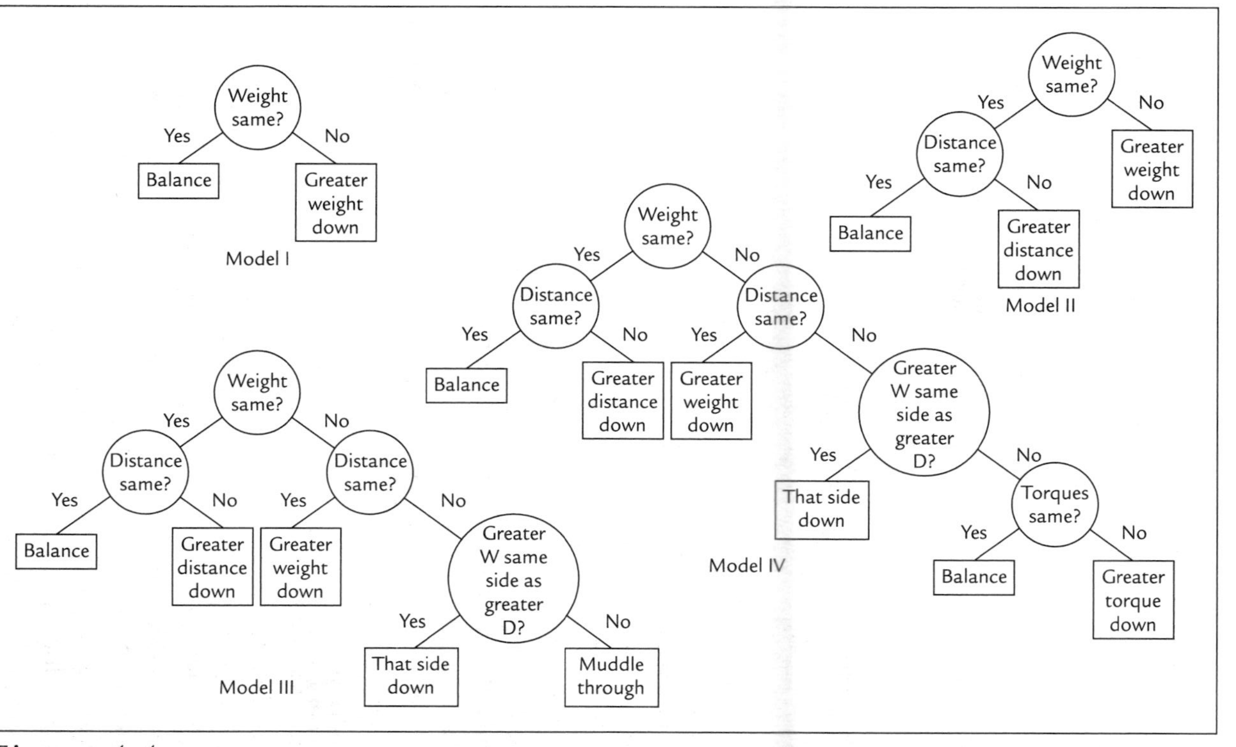

Figure 4.4

Decision-tree diagrams for models I–IV, which describe rules underlying judgments on the balance-scale task. Torque = downward force, D = distance, W = weight.

SOURCE: From "The Representation of Children's Knowledge," by David Klahr and Robert S. Siegler, in *Advances in Child Development and Behavior,* Vol. 12, edited by H. W. Reese and L. P. Lipsitt.

```
Model I
        P1: ((Same W) --> (Say "balance"))
        P2: ((Side X more W) --> (Say "X down"))

Model II
        P1: ((Same W) --> (Say "balance"))
        P2: ((Side X more W) --> (Say "X down"))
        P3: ((Same W) (Side X more D) --> (Say "X down"))

Model III
        P1: ((Same W) --> (Say "balance"))
        P2: ((Side X more W) --> (Say "X down"))
        P3: ((Same W) (Side X more D) --> (Say "X down"))
        P4: ((Side X more W) (Side X less D) --> muddle through)
        P5: ((Side X more W) (Side X more D) --> (Say "X down"))

Model IV
        P1: ((Same W) --> (Say "balance"))
        P2: ((Side X more W) --> (Say "X down"))
        P3: ((Same W) (Side X more D) --> (Say "X down"))
        P4: ((Side X more W) (Side X less D) --> (get Torques))
        P5: ((Side X more W) (Side X more D) --> (Say "X down"))
        P6: ((Same Torque) --> (Say "balance"))
        P7: ((Side X more Torque) --> (Say "X down"))
```

Transitional requirements

	Productions	Operators
I -> II	add P3	add distance encoding and comparison
II -> III	add P4, P5	
III -> IV	modify P4; add P6, P7	add torque computation and comparison

Figure 4.5

Production-system (P) representations for models I-IV, which describe rules underlying judgments on the balance-scale task. Written in a special language called PSG. Torque = downward force. D = distance. W = weight.

SOURCE: From "The Representation of Children's Knowledge," by David Klahr and Robert S. Siegler, in *Advances in Child Development and Behavior,* Vol. 12, edited by H. W. Reese and L. P. Lipsitt. Copyright © 1978. Reproduced by permission of Academic Press, Inc., and the authors.

"Yes" and "no" answers lead to different events. Constructing a flowchart is an intermediary step between rules stated in everyday language and rules stated in a production system in a language that can be fed into a computer. Figure 4.5 describes, in computer language, the production system for the four rules. Models I to IV correspond to the four rules described earlier.

A production system consists of two main structures—declarative ("working") memory and production memory. *Declarative memory* is knowledge that is relevant to the current problem-solving situation.

Production memory consists of a set of condition–action rules (productions) for changing the set of information currently activated in the cognitive system. Productions take the following form: "If *X* is present (condition), *Y* occurs (action)." That is, a particular situation leads to a particular action, decision, new goal, or piece of new information. For example, in production 1 (P1) in Figure 4.5, if the number of weights is the same (*X*), the child says that they balance (Y). Thus, there is recognition (*X* is present) and then action (*Y* occurs). Recognition occurs if the conditions are satisfied, that is, if there is a match. If the conditions are not satisfied, that production does not "fire."

A whole set of productions is tested simultaneously. If two or more productions are satisfied, then some conflict-resolution principle must decide which production should fire. For example, the satisfied production with the most recently added conditions or the most conditions might be favored. As condition–action rules are applied for several cycles, they transform the initial knowledge state regarding the task into its final state by adding, deleting, or changing the elements of the state. Thus, learning involves acquiring and changing productions. As the production system goes through these cycles, it leaves a record, or "trace," of what it knew and did at each step, as shown in the trace for one child in Figure 4.6.

Let us now look more closely at one of the models in Figure 4.5. Recall that in model II the distance is considered only if the weights are equal. Model II is a production system containing three productions (condition–action rules). The "condition" part of the condition–action rule refers to tests for the sameness or difference in weight or distance. The "action" part, after any arrow in Figure 4.5, refers to a behavioral response. Thus, in P1 if the number of weights is the same on both sides (condition), the child says they will balance (action). P2 says that if side *X* has more weights than side *W*, then side *X* will go down. Finally, in P3 if the number of weights on each side is the same but there is more distance on side *X* than on the other side, then the child predicts that *X* will go down. At the bottom of the figure is a list of what changes in the set of productions occur when the child moves from one model to the next during development.

The formal representation of production systems may make its greatest contribution by describing the behavior of individual children. Figure 4.6 shows how the production system runs for a 7-year-old child, Jan.

```
        (0003|0020)
Cycle 1
 WM: ((PREDICT) (CRITERION) WEIGHT))

 Fire P8: ((PREDICT) (<DIMENSION.1>) ABS --> ATTEND)
     Output from ATTEND (input to WM) ::> (weight more left)(distance more right)

Cycle 2
 WM: ((DISTANCE MORE RIGHT) (WEIGHT MORE LEFT) (PREDICT) (CRITERION WEIGHT))
    CONFLICT.SET: (P2 P4)
 Fire P4: ((PREDICT) (WEIGHT MORE) (DISTANCE MORE) --> FIND.BIG)
     Output from FIND.BIG (input to WM) ::> (distance big right)(weight big left)

Cycle 3
 WM: ((WEIGHT BIG LEFT) (DISTANCE BIG RIGHT) (PREDICT) (WEIGHT MORE LEFT)
       (DISTANCE MORE RIGHT) (CRITERION WEIGHT))
    CONFLICT.SET: (P2 P4 P5 P6 P7)
    CONFLICT.SET: (P4 P5) AFTER SPECIAL.CASE.ORDER
    CONFLICT.SET: (P5) AFTER WM.ORDER
 Fire P5: ((PREDICT) (CRITERION <DIMENSION.1>)(<DIMENSION.1 BIG <SIDE.1>)
        (<DIMENSION.2> BIG <SIDE.2.) --> (MADE **) (EXPECT <SIDE.1> DOWN) SAY.D)

********** LEFT down

Cycle 4
 WM: ((EXPECT LEFT DOWN) (MADE (PREDICT)) (CRITERION WEIGHT) (WEIGHT BIG LEFT)
       (DISTANCE BIG RIGHT) (WEIGHT MORE LEFT) (DISTANCE MORE RIGHT))
 Fire E1: ((EXPECT) --> LOOK)
     Output from LOOK (input to WM) ::> (see right down)

Cycle 5
 WM: ((SEE RIGHT DOWN) (EXPECT LEFT DOWN) (MADE (PREDICT)) (CRITERION WEIGHT)
      (WEIGHT BIG LEFT) (DISTANCE BIG RIGHT) (WEIGHT MORE LEFT) (DISTANCE MORE RIGHT))
    CONFLICT.SET: (E1,E3)
 Fire E3: ((EXPECT <SIDE.1> <DIRECTION>)
          (SEE <SIDE.1> <DIRECTION>) ABS (SEE) --> (DID **) (SEE ---> SAW)
(RESULT WRONG))

Cycle 6
 WM: ((RESULT WRONG) (DID (EXPECT LEFT DOWN)) (SAW RIGHT DOWN) (MADE (PREDICT))
       (CRITERION WEIGHT) (WEIGHT BIG LEFT) (DISTANCE BIG RIGHT) (WEIGHT MORE LEFT)
        (DISTANCE MORE RIGHT))
 Fire SW2: ((RESULT WRONG) (CRITERION WEIGHT) --> (OLD **) (WEIGHT ---> DISTANCE))

Cycle 7
 WM: ((OLD (RESULT WRONG)) (CRITERION DISTANCE) (DID (EXPECT LEFT DOWN))
      (SAW RIGHT DOWN) (MADE (PREDICT)) (WEIGHT BIG LEFT) (DISTANCE BIG RIGHT)
       (WEIGHT MORE LEFT) (DISTANCE MORE RIGHT))
```

Figure 4.6

Trace of 7-year-old Jan's production system (P) running on a conflict-distance problem in the balance-scale task. ABS = absent, WM = working memory, E = problem number.

SOURCE: From "The Representation of Children's Knowledge," by David Klahr and Robert S. Siegler, in *Advances in Child Development and Behavior,* Vol. 12, edited by H. W. Reese and L. P. Lipsitt. Copyright 1978. Reproduced by permission of Academic Press, Inc., and the authors.

For our purposes, we need not be concerned with most of the notations; the interested reader is referred to Klahr and Siegler (1978) for a detailed account. The important sections are the descriptions of the state of working memory (currently available information) after each cycle of applying the production system. For example, as cycle 2 begins, working memory (WM) has four elements: more distance on the right arm, more weights on the left arm, task is to predict, and criterion is weight. During recognition tests, P2 and P4 (productions 2 and 4 in the particular model Jan uses) match (recognize) these elements, and since P4 happens to be a special case of P2, P4 fires. The output directs the system to find what is big (FIND.BIG). After doing so, the production system moves on to cycle 3. The result of cycle 2 appears at the beginning of cycle 3, and the process continues. Notice that on some cycles the system recognizes conflict between two productions and attempts to resolve the conflict.

As this example shows, a formal model produces a detailed, explicit, moment-by-moment description of how the child solves the problem. The model becomes more complex as the child changes her strategies during the task as a result of training. Ideally, the simulation contains all relevant information about the child and the general problem-solving abilities and semantic knowledge that the child brings to the task at each developmental level. The simulation also includes the demands of the experimental situation, for example, the nature of the feedback and the way the scale is presented. Since both the cognitive state and the situation affect performance, especially in children, it is important that they both be specified in any theory of problem solving. The Klahr and Siegler work is an excellent example of the task-analysis approach described in the general-orientation section.

Connectionist Systems ▪ Unlike most other simulations, connectionist simulations (e.g., Elman et al., 1996) are loosely modeled on the structure and processing of the brain. Similar to the brain, a connectionist system consists of elementary nodes or neuronlike units, connected by pathways, each with some degree of activation. These are called *neural networks*. A connectionist model posits several layers or levels of processing, as illustrated in Figure 4.7 (p. 254). At the input level, simple processing units, analogous to neurons in the brain, encode the situation. These signals can come from other networks. At the next level, so-called hidden systems, or internal representations, use information from the input level to compute more complex relations. A final complex level consists of output such as decisions, words, or thoughts. The modeler tries to bring the network to a state in which it can take a given input and produce the same output as a child.

Not surprisingly, in connectionist models the connections are all-important. Each unit is connected to units in different layers and some-

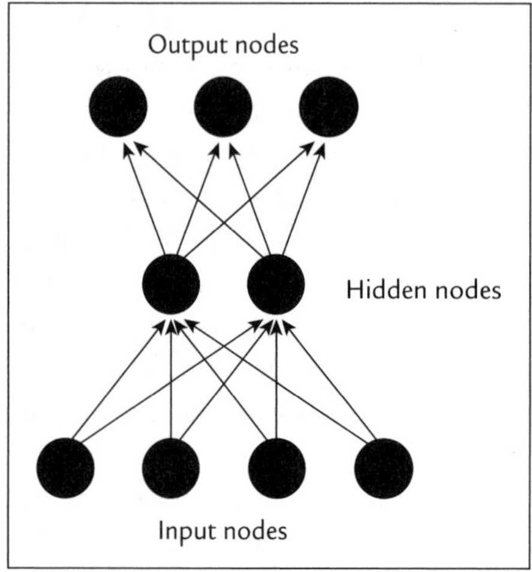

Figure 4.7
A simple connectionist model.

times in the same layer as well. These units can excite or inhibit other units. As in the brain, the strength of any given connection depends on the frequency of "firings" between the two elements of the connection. That is, with experience certain units are consistently fired and thus become highly associated (heavily weighted), while other units do not. A helpful analogy is a map with some routes between towns, such as interstate highways, thicker and more heavily traveled than other routes. In a connectionist model, as in the brain, a unit fires if the amount of activation it receives from all of the other units connected to it exceeds a certain threshold. Note that, as in the brain, the excitation of processing units is occurring at the same time, in parallel. Thus, these are *parallel-processing models*, rather than *sequential-processing models*, which usually characterized earlier information-processing models.

In this connectionist world, a piece of knowledge does not reside in a single place in the system. Rather, knowledge is a distributed pattern of activation over many connections. It is a pattern of connections with various weights. And any one unit may take part in representing many different pieces of knowledge if it is part of several patterns of activation. The goal is to show that different distributions of connections—patterns of connectivity—correspond to different knowledge levels in children of different ages. Thus, connectionists have replaced production systems' depiction of thinking as the manipulation of rules expressed in symbols with a view of thinking as a pattern of activation in neurallike networks. If Descartes had been a connectionist, he would have declared, "I have a pattern of activation in a neurallike network, therefore I am."

Learning occurs when the pattern of connections changes because of changes in the relative strength of the connections. The system learns by example, actually a large number of examples. Let us now consider one model (MacWhinney, Leinbach, Taraban, & McDonald, 1989), which describes how German children learn which of the six forms of the German definite article "the" goes with which nouns. The appropriate article is determined by the noun's gender (masculine, feminine, neuter), number (singular or plural), and role in the sentence (for example, subject, direct object). The input level consists of 35 units that analyze these features of nouns. Two levels of hidden units consist of units formed by combinations of the input-level features, such as the gender and number of the noun, and six output units represent the six possible German articles.

Repeated experience with a set of common German nouns and their correct article led to changes in the strengths of connections between particular articles and particular nouns in the model. Some pathways fired many times and became stronger; some never or rarely fired and remained weak. The model became more accurate as correlations between nodes began to approximate correlations between particular articles and nouns in the real world of German language. In this process the model compared its answer with the correct answer; a match strengthened the rule, whereas a mismatch did not. Once the model constructed a set of rules for which articles go with which sorts of nouns in which contexts, it was tested with unfamiliar nouns. The model was fairly successful at choosing the correct article. Other evidence that the model is a good simulation of language development is that when the model was learning, it made some of the same sorts of errors that young German children do, such as overusing the article that is used most often in German. And the same article–noun combinations that are most difficult for the children were also the most difficult for the model.

Connectionists have constructed developmental models in a number of areas, for example, second-language learning (MacWhinney, 1996), the concept of object permanence (Munakata, McClelland, Johnson, & Siegler, 1997), causal reasoning (Shultz, Schmidt, Buckingham, & Mareschal, 1995), number conservation (Shultz, 1997), and early reading acquisition (Plaut, McClelland, Seidenberg, & Patterson, 1995). Also, connectionist models of the balance-scale task described earlier have captured children's relative weighting of the cues of weight and distance from the fulcrum on that task (Shultz et al., 1995). These models have produced impressive matches with child behaviors, and they have the advantage of being very precise and thus testable. Moreover, as the models become more closely tied to the organization of the brain, they can describe how this organization constrains or facilitates development. For example, one model of infants' processing of visual information about objects suggests that successful performance on tasks that require the baby to integrate representations that are separated in the cortex comes later than it does on tasks that do not require this integration (Mareschal et al., 1999).

Intelligence

Robert Sternberg's (1985, 1999) theory is an attempt to combine the best aspects of several frameworks. His focus on cognitive processes, capacity, and the time course of thinking, along with his careful task analyses, is in the tradition of the information-processing approach. The concern with individual differences reflects the psychometric (IQ testing, for example) approach. His interest in cognitive development and logical operations shows the influence of Piaget. Finally, his concern with context is within the tradition of social-cultural approaches (Chapter 7).

Sternberg calls his theory a "triarchic theory of intelligence" because it includes three subtheories. The *componential* subtheory focuses on the components of intelligence, which are described below in some detail because they are most closely related to the information-processing approach. The *experiential* subtheory involves the ability to deal with novel demands and to automatize information processing. In an older child or an expert, the increasing automaticity of the components in a particular domain frees capacity for other tasks. Sternberg proposes that low-IQ children have poor automaticity. If they are not able to automatize subskills such as recognizing letters or words, the higher-order skills needed for smooth reading will be very slow to develop.

The *contextual* subtheory emphasizes social and practical behavior in its cultural context. That is, what is intelligent in one culture might not be intelligent in another. People are intelligent if they adapt to their everyday particular real-world environments, shape their environments to create a better fit for them, or select environments that draw on their strengths or help them to compensate for their weaknesses. Thus, a nonathletic boy in a high school that values athletic achievement might begin a weight-lifting program, organize a science club at school, or switch to a more academically oriented school. Examples of Sternberg's tests for everyday intelligence are asking people to identify real couples and fake couples in photographs or assessing their knowledge about managing their careers.

Regarding the componential part of the triarchy, Sternberg characterizes intelligence as a set of components—elementary processes that operate on internal representations of objects, events, or symbols. There are three types of component: knowledge-acquisition components, metacomponents, and performance components. When a child does not have the knowledge needed to solve the problem, *knowledge-acquisition components* obtain relevant information. The *metacomponents*, which are used in planning and decision making in task performance, then combine this new information with previous knowledge to construct an appropriate problem-solving strategy from among the performance components. The *performance components* then actually solve the problem. If the child already has the understanding required for solving the problem, then only the metacomponents and performance components come into play. We now look at each of these components in more detail.

The knowledge-acquisition components appear to provide a striking difference between average and intellectually gifted children. Gifted children are particularly adept at *selective encoding* (differentiating relevant and irrelevant information), *selective combination* (integrating information in a meaningful way), and *selective comparison* (relating newly encoded information to knowledge the child already has). Consider the follow problem:

> You have black socks and blue socks in a drawer, mixed in a ratio of 4 to 5. Because it is dark, you are unable to see the colors of the socks that you take out of the drawer. How many socks do you have to take out of the drawer to be assured of having a pair of socks of the same color?
>
> (Sternberg, 1986, p. 213)

Selective encoding is necessary for detecting that the ratio of the socks is irrelevant. Regardless of the ratio, taking out three socks would ensure that a *pair* of socks was obtained.

The other two knowledge-acquisition components can be illustrated by examples of insight among famous scientists. Selective combination was crucial to Darwin's ability to combine facts, known to him for years, into a coherent framework that became his theory of evolution. Insight based on selective comparison can be seen in the chemist Kekulé's dream about a snake curling back on itself and catching its tail. Upon awakening, he realized that this image was a metaphor for the structure of the benzene ring.

The metacomponents, much like the control processes and metacognitive processes described earlier, orchestrate the other two components into goal-directed behavior. Metacomponents perform duties such as deciding how to best allocate mental capacity to the other components during the limited time for problem solving, keeping track of what one has done, and deciding how to respond to feedback. Inadequate metacomponents can be seen when young children or low-IQ children choose the wrong performance and knowledge-acquisition components for their strategies or do not shift to an alternate strategy if the chosen one is not successful.

As an example of the performance components, consider the following analogy problem used by Sternberg (1979): N.J.:N.Y.::N.H.:(*a*.R.I., *b*.N.D.). The correct answer is R.I. The seven performance components for these types of problems include the following: The first involves *encoding,* identifying various attributes of the first two terms. For example, N.J. might be encoded as New Jersey and N.Y. as New York. Second, *inferring* specifies the relation between the first and second term; for example, both are abbreviations, are adjacent states, and begin with N. Third, in *mapping* the person compares the encoded attributes of the first and third terms; for example, both are states and begin with N. Fourth, *application* derives a relation between the third term and one of the possible answers that is analogous to the relation between the first and second terms. Fifth, *comparison* involves comparing and contrasting the possible answers. Sixth, *justification* entails comparing the chosen answer with one's notion of the ideal answer to decide whether the chosen option is good enough. And seventh is *responding.* Such a task analysis is typical of the information-processing approach.

Although school-age children and adults use the same performance components to solve analogy problems, they differ in their allocation of cognitive resources to the various performance components (Sternberg & Rifkin, 1979). For example, adults spend more time encoding the terms than they spend in the subsequent steps. Seven-year-olds do the opposite. High-IQ children are more like adults in this respect. This concern with how problem solvers allocate their cognitive resources is another hallmark of the information-processing approach.

Sternberg believes that people apply their intelligence to tasks involving analytical, creative, or practical thinking, or a combination of these. *Analytic* problems usually are familiar sorts of problems requiring abstract judgments, such as the analogy problem above. *Creativity* is best tapped by novel tasks. For example, Sternberg asked children to write a very short story for a title such as "The Octopus's Sneakers" or to draw a picture of "Earth from an Insect's Point of View" (Sternberg & Lubart, 1995). More than average individuals, gifted persons are able to deal with novel situations in insightful, original ways. *Practical* intelligence involves applying the components of intelligence so as to adapt to, shape, and select environments, as described above.

Recently, Sternberg has studied what he calls *mental self-government:*

> The mind carries out legislative, executive, and judicial functions, just as do governments. The legislative function of the mind is concerned with creating, formulating, imagining, and planning; the executive function of the mind is concerned with implementing and doing; and the judicial function of the mind is concerned with judging, evaluating, and comparing.
>
> (Ferrari & Sternberg, 1998, p. 927)

He goes on to develop other parallels with government, such as a conservative versus a liberal style of thinking.

Sternberg's theory of intelligence is broad and complex. And it becomes even more complex when he adds developmental changes as well as individual differences to his various aspects of intelligence. Thus, the theory has developed far from its start in Sternberg's childhood in his seventh-grade science project, in which he constructed an IQ test that has been referred to as the "less-than-widely-used Sternberg Test of Mental Abilities" (*American Psychologist,* 1982, p. 74)!

MECHANISMS OF DEVELOPMENT

Klahr and Wallace have voiced the research priorities of the field of information processing in children: "A theory of transition can be no better than the associated theory of what it is that is undergoing that transition" (1976, p. 14). Stated differently, "One never sees transitions, only by-products of transitions; so the empirical snapshots provide a major source of support for theories of transition" (Klahr, 1984, p. 106). Thus, the first task is to describe carefully each step in the acquisition of a concept, such as each of the four models in Figure 4.5. Only then is it possible to identify the sort of mechanisms that might cause the change.

Siegler (1998) has advanced our conceptualization of mechanisms of development by identifying three themes in children's behavior. First, changes in thinking are omnipresent during childhood. They do not occur only during brief transitions from one consistent way of thinking to another. Second, children show variability. Any child at any age approaches a task in several different ways. Consequently, and third, children constantly have to choose among alternative ways of thinking. In this conceptualization, opportunities for developmental change are always present.

Siegler expresses these ideas in his influential *overlapping-waves model*: "A wave, like children's thinking, never stands still" (Siegler, 1996, p. 239). As applied to strategy development, in Figure 4.8 each wave represents a strategy. The strategies, like waves, overlap in that a child continues to use an old strategy even after a new strategy begins to develop. Many strategies look like waves because they gradually gather strength, peak, and then crash as the child discontinues them. We saw in an earlier section that at any age a child has several strategies that she could use to solve a problem. In the figure, a child discovers new strategies (3, 4, and 5) and adds them to her repertoire. Some waves never become the most prominent one but still influence the other waves. The wave model contrasts with the staircase model that depicts development as a series of levels, with brief periods of transition between levels. During each level a child has a particular way of approaching problems, as in Piaget's concrete operational stage. Siegler, in contrast, sees change and variability throughout development.

Siegler makes an analogy to biological evolution. As in evolution (see Chapter 5), change comes about through variation, competition, and selection. Various strategies compete for dominance. Through experience a child learns that some strategies are more adaptive (useful, accurate, or efficient) than others and thus retains ("selects") these. Thus, a process of competition among skills or ideas, in this case, strategies, leads to "survival of the fittest." Moreover, it is adaptive to have multiple strategies because if one strategy fails to solve a problem, the child can go to "plan B." Variability in approaches to a problem also is adaptive because it seems to set the stage for children's ability to profit from new experiences or training (Graham & Perry, 1993). That is, children who show variability seem to be more ready to change. Siegler has used this evolutionary model of cognitive change to account for changes in a variety of areas, such as arithmetic, reading, problem solving, and spelling (e.g., Siegler, 1996).

Information-processing theorists have identified at least four specific mechanisms of development: automatization, encoding, generalization,

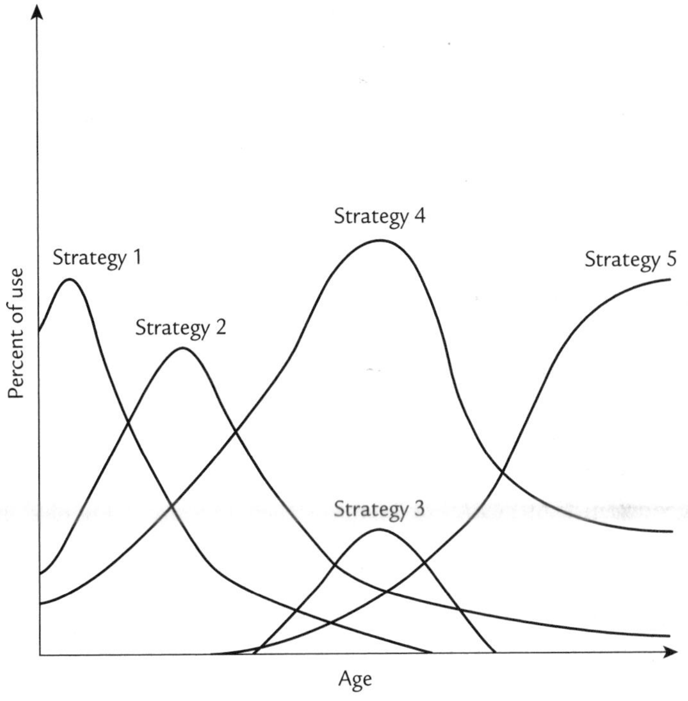

Figure 4.8

Siegler's overlapping-waves model of cognitive development.

SOURCE: From *Children's Thinking* (3rd ed.), by Robert Siegler. Copyright © 1998. Reproduced by permission of Prentice-Hall and the author.

and strategy construction. As seen in addition strategies (Siegler, 1998), *automatization* of identifying numbers occurs, for example, when a child has counted five fingers on one hand so many times when learning to count that what originally was highly effortful now is automatic. She now automatically says "five" when she holds up one hand with all fingers extended. Automatization can cause cognitive change during addition problems by freeing capacity for use for other cognitive activities, such as constructing a new strategy.

Changes in *encoding* features of the environment can encourage a child to notice, and thus use, different information, as when a child learns to check whether the problem has one large digit (5) and one small one (2), which leads to efficient use of the strategy of counting "5, 6, 7." When information contradicts a person's beliefs, children and even adults can have trouble "seeing," and encoding, what is in front of their very eyes. In one study (Kaiser, McCloskey, & Proffitt, 1986), participants watched a ball released by an electric toy train fall in a curve forward and down to the floor. Most school-age children and many adults encoded the event as the ball falling straight down. Even later, when confronted with the actual curved trajectory of the ball, many still had trouble accepting, and encoding, this information that violated their beliefs.

A third mechanism of change, *generalization*, operates when a child applies an adding strategy to new problems with a similar structure. Finally, *strategy construction* occurs when a child has an insight into the problem and tries a new approach. These mechanisms work together to bring about cognitive change. General cognitive developmental changes, such as increased knowledge and organization of this knowledge, can facilitate the work of these mechanisms.

Information-processing investigators have examined change through three main techniques: microgenetic methods, training studies, and self-modifying computer programs. As discussed earlier, microgenetic designs can provide a fine-grained description of change that suggests the cause of the change. Training studies that have brought about changes in processing suggest that changes in development may come about through certain kinds of experiences. The experiences include encountering conflict between different predictions, becoming more familiar with the task materials, trying out a strategy that works, and solving a series of similar problems. These experiences lead to new rules or strategies, which in turn lead to better (or at least different) memory, representation, and problem solving. For example, teaching children what information to encode (both distance and number of weights) enables them to learn from feedback regarding their predictions on the balance scale and subsequently to adopt new rules for problem solving (Siegler, 1978).

A much smaller group of psychologists has used self-modifying computer simulations to look at mechanisms of development (Klahr, 1999; Simon & Klahr, 1995). In production systems, change occurs when the system creates new productions or modifies existing productions, as described earlier. Such change can occur when children analyze their stored record of previous behavior and its results. They look for regularities and try to eliminate redundancy, thus producing sleeker productions. They often organize subsystems according to their similarity and relatedness. In these ways, children develop new rules for solving the problem, strengthen certain old rules, generalize old rules, and restrict the situations in which an old rule is used. A child can, for example, add or delete conditions to the condition side of the "If *X*, then *Y*" rule. If the conditions become more general, then generalization has occurred. If the conditions become less general, then more specific thinking is possible.

A very simple example of some of these activities is that on many occasions a child might count objects, move them, count them again, and compare the results of the two countings. The type of objects and the type of transformation would vary, but the constancy of the number before and after the transformation would be common to the situation. This rule gradually becomes more general to include, for example, larger numbers. Finally, redundancy is eliminated, for example, by removing the second counting because it is not needed if the objects are only moved.

When no production works in the current situation, a mechanism called *analogy* comes into play (Anderson, 1993). The system searches for a similar situation by finding an example of a production that worked with a similar goal and using the same steps that worked for achieving that goal. Or a desperate system can even randomly "mutate" some conditions in existing rules, and the fittest (most successful) survive. For more complex examples and a fuller account of these and other principles of change, including those of connectionist systems, the reader is referred to Klahr and McWhinney (1998). In connectionist systems, as a result of input the system changes the relative strengths of various connections in the system, as described earlier. The essence of these changes in both production and connectionist systems is that they reflect the operations of a self-modifying system. The system works on itself to produce change. Although these principles involve change during a short period of time, the experimental session, developmental changes over longer periods of time could involve similar principles (Klahr, 1982).

Klahr argues that it is crucial to develop specific, explicit, formal accounts of mechanisms of transition, in contrast to vague verbal statements: "For 40 years now, we have had *assimilation* and *accommodation,* the mysterious and shadowy forces of equilibration, the 'Batman and Robin' of the developmental processes. . . . Why is it that after all this time, we know no more about them than when they first sprang upon the scene?" (1982, p. 80). The information-processing approach probably has better theoretical equipment for achieving this goal of *specific* accounts of cognitive change than do most other theories.

POSITION ON DEVELOPMENTAL ISSUES

Human Nature

In an update of Newton's view that humans are machines, humans are now computers. (Presumably, children are microcomputers, especially laptop computers!) In this mechanistic view, we have input followed by a series of events and finally output. Although the information-processing approach is mechanistic in that it posits input–output machinelike devices, it is organismic in its emphasis on cognitive organization and on an active organism. The ultimate goal of the information-processing models is to characterize the organization of cognitive processing into a system, not just an aggregate of parts. Information-processing theorists believe this holism is achieved by control processes that organize and direct the varied cognitive components. Most adherents to the information-processing point of view do not, however, posit the tightly knit, organized set of underlying logical mental operations proposed by Piaget.

Like social learning theory, the information-processing approach has been criticized for positing a passive organism (Shaw & Bransford, 1977), perhaps because the models and metaphors seem to suggest passivity. Flowcharts seem to portray static structures nudged into activity by intruding arrows. Also, a computer must wait for environmental input. And, robots aside, computers and flowcharts typically do not move themselves and never ask questions of adults, call a friend, or select a good book to read. However, there certainly is nothing inherent in the information-processing approach that would call for a passive organism. It is true that people react to input in what has been called "bottom-up processing"—from the stimulus "up" to the higher levels of the cognitive system. And when processing is automatic, the organism can be characterized as passive. However, there is also "top-down processing" as long-term memory interprets the input, applies rules and strategies, searches for further information in the environment, or even "constructs" information as it makes inferences based on the input and on previous knowledge.

Humans are also active in that they are self-modifying cognitive systems, as reflected in certain computer simulations. People bring about their own learning and development, with boosts from nature and nurture, of course. In addition, children become more active cognitively with increasing age as they develop metamemory to enhance their memory by rehearsing, making written reminders, and relating new information to old.

Finally, the theories rarely are contextual, except for their careful attention to the nature of the task situation in which the child is operating. Little research examines the social content of information processing or social influences on thinking.

Qualitative Versus Quantitative Development

Information-processing theories allow for both qualitative and quantitative development. Most do not have the emphasis on the strongly qualitative, stagelike development found in Piagetian and psychoanalytic theory, but they do identify more qualitative change than does social learning theory. Examples of qualitative development are the emergence of new strategies for storage or retrieval, rules for problem solving, or modes of representation (for example, verbal representation after language is developed). Quantitative development appears in increases in the number of items remembered, in the amount of information in semantic memory, in the number of strategies in one's repertoire, and in the increasingly efficient application of strategies. There is often interplay between quantitative development and qualitative development, as when experience with weights leads to a new rule about balance scales, which then becomes more efficiently and consistently applied to a variety of situations. Or, in connectionist systems, a quantitative strengthening of connections can lead to crossing over a threshold, which produces a new behavior that looks qualitatively different from previous behaviors (Elman et al., 1996).

Nature Versus Nurture

The two influences of nature and nurture interact to produce change. The impact of the environment is obvious as it continually brings input to the cognitive system. On the nature side, examples of important influences are that neurological development increases the efficiency of the transmission of neuronal impulses and that the visual system limits how long information can stay in the visual sensory register. Also, the tendency toward economical, nonredundant, efficient processing may be innate (Klahr & Wallace, 1976), and the processing system may be pretuned to process certain types of stimuli, such as linguistic input (see modularity nativism theories in Chapter 8).

Promising recent work on neuropsychological parallels to connectionist models is beginning to influence developmental views of information processing. For example, connectionist models suggest how learning might occur within the constraints of the developing brain (Elman et al., 1996; Mareschal et al., 1999). They also show that "new structures can emerge at the interface between 'nature' (the initial architecture of the system) and 'nurture' (the input to which that system is exposed)" (Bates & Elman, 1992, p. 15).

What Develops

Stated most generally, cognitive processing develops. It becomes more efficient and organized in its operation and acquires more and more content as the child explores the world. More specifically, children acquire strategies, rules, scripts, patterns of connections, or a broader knowledge base, depending on the particular approach. Another way to describe what develops comes from Brown (1975): "knowing" (development of knowledge about the world), "knowing about knowing" (metacognition), and "knowing how to know" (development of strategies). A major goal of current research is to map out the developmental relationships among these three areas.

APPLICATIONS

Researchers and educators have applied information-processing theory to education in three ways. First, classroom instruction on "learning how to learn" has incorporated information about metacognition and the acquisition of strategies (e.g., Hacker, Dunlosky, & Graesser, 1998). Teachers emphasize, for example, choosing a good strategy, self-testing, and planning. Second, task analyses of reading and mathematics break these tasks into their component parts and identify the cognitive skills in each phase of processing needed to complete each part successfully. For example, one poor reader might have problems in the initial phase—encoding—whereas another poor reader might have trouble integrating the meaning of consecutive sentences.

A third implication for classroom instruction concerns individual differences in children's knowledge. If material that a child must memorize is not represented in a way that fits into that child's knowledge base, then his considerable knowledge about the material may not be utilized. For example, for the child dinosaur expert, presenting categories of "large plant eaters" and "armored dinosaurs," which are congruent with his own categories, would lead to greater recall than would categories formed on some other basis, such as dinosaurs' aggressiveness or time of emergence during evolution.

Sternberg has applied his theory of intelligence to instruction by constructing, for example, a social studies curriculum for third-graders and an introductory psychology curriculum for eighth-graders. Students who had instructions based on his triarchic model—componential, experiential, and contextual—performed better on a variety of measures than did children who received either a traditional curriculum or a critical-thinking curriculum (Sternberg, Torff, & Grigorenko, 1998). He also developed a curriculum based on his theory for teaching creative-thinking skills (Sternberg & Williams, 1996, p. 926).

An important recent application of memory research is to children's eyewitness testimony. At least 100,000 children testify in court cases in the United States each year (Ceci & Bruck, 1995), among criminal trials most frequently for sexual abuse (13,000 children). Researchers typically study eyewitness testimony in two ways. One is to create experimental settings that reproduce some elements of the abuse situation in an ethical way, for example, to study children's memory for events during a Simon Says game in which the child and the experimenter touch parts of each other's bodies (Ceci, Leichtman, & White, in press). The other is to study naturally occurring mildly traumatic, but nonabusive, experiences, such as going to the dentist or receiving a shot in a doctor's office. Although younger children usually do not recall as well as older ones, their errors usually are errors of omission rather than of providing false information. Of particular interest now is the issue of how suggestible very young children are and whether they are more suggestible than older ones. For a discussion of these and other issues, such as how best to elicit accurate testimony from children, see Bjorklund (2000b), Goodman and Quas (1997), and Ceci and Bruck (1998).

EVALUATION OF THE THEORY

The information-processing approach has greatly influenced not only work on cognitive development but also other areas. For example, in social development, information-processing notions appear in Bandura's social learning theory, in research on social interaction (Dodge, 1986; Lemerise & Arsenio, 2000), and in social scripts (Nelson, 1986,

1996). Despite the theory's considerable influence on developmentalists, it is not often scrutinized with respect to its strengths and weaknesses as a *developmental* theory. The theory's strengths lie in its ability to express the complexity of thought, its precise analysis of performance and change, and its rigorous methodology. Its weaknesses include the shortcomings of computer models and metaphors, problems with addressing certain developmental issues, and a neglect of the context of behavior.

Strengths

Ability to Express the Complexity of Thought ■ In Chapter 3, social learning theory was criticized for its overly simple account of thinking and learning. In contrast, the information-processing approach, like Piagetian theory, addresses complex thinking. It tries to specify a variety of cognitive processes, ranging from the simple detection of a stimulus to the development of complex rules, strategies, and concepts. Furthermore, it attempts to characterize how perception, attention, memory, language, and abstract mental operations might be interrelated. The approach posits an intricate organization of thought in which control processes direct and supervise. For example, children learn to handle large amounts of information by "chunking" it or by relating it to what they already know.

Because both connectionist systems and rules used to solve problems are often written to describe individual children, they can highlight subtle differences in how people of the same age process information. Thus, it is possible to study individual differences in problem solving and tailor instructional materials to fit the individual needs of students.

Connectionist models have described how complex new behaviors sometimes emerge unexpectedly during learning: "In trying to achieve stability across a large number of superimposed, distributed patterns, the network may hit on a solution that was 'hidden' in bits and pieces of the data" (Bates & Elman, 1992, p. 15). For example, a child might have the insight that adding and multiplying, which actually is repeated adding, use the same input to produce the same output and thus are the same process.

Precise Analysis of Performance and Change ■ Perhaps the greatest strength of information-processing theories is that they make specific predictions about a child's behavior from moment to moment, on the basis of a fine-grained analysis of the task and the current state of the child's cognitive system. This statement is especially true for computer-simulation programs, which attempt to specify all assumptions and relevant variables. Psychologists are forced to clear up any muddled theoretical thinking. Regarding learning, microgenetic methods carefully document moment-to-moment changes from one problem to the next.

The Piagetian and information-processing approaches have much in common. Both attempt to explain how more advanced concepts grow out of earlier, simpler ones—specifically, how a child's current cognitive system both constrains and permits the emergence of new knowledge. However, information-processing investigators attempt to be more explicit about *how* children use their cognitive skills in a given situation. This is a theory of performance, which, as mentioned in Chapter 1, is weakly developed in Piaget's theory. Information-processing theories describe how attention, memory, strategies, representational processes, and logical operations "connect" with tasks. For example, if the task requires that a child decide whether objects on a balance scale will balance, the information-processing approach would specify how the child selects certain information about the objects (for example, number, distance from the fulcrum), encodes it, and applies rules from long-term memory. Piaget's décalages (asynchronies in applying a concept to different but related tasks or content areas) become less mysterious when investigators analyze the information-processing demands of each task. It is not surprising that tasks with different information-processing requirements elicit different behaviors. More generally, the information-processing approach emphasizes, more than does Piaget, processing limitations, strategies for overcoming these limitations, domain-specific knowledge about the task at hand, and specific behaviors involved in the process of change on a particular task (Siegler, 1998).

Rigorous Methodology ▪ One outcome of the theory's specificity is that hypotheses generated by the theory are testable—a trait shared with social learning theory, less so with Piaget's theory, and much less so with psychoanalytic theory. Information-processing researchers use stringent and precise experimental methods. As one psychologist comments, "Many of us have become methodological behaviorists in order to become good cognitive psychologists" (Mandler, 1979, p. 281). Laboratory research on basic processing often makes precise measurements of processing time. Computer simulation requires that all relevant information about the task or child be stated in the programs. Gaps, contradictions, and vague statements are not permitted. These strict requirements demanded by computers are not easy to meet.

For developmental research, error analysis and microgenetic designs have proved to be particularly powerful assessment procedures. By cleverly designing different types of problems, researchers have discovered two kinds of limitations in young children. One, illustrated by Siegler's balance-scale experiments, is that young children are using simpler, less-complete rules, procedures, or strategies than are older children. The other limitation is different. Children basically are using the correct rule, but they have various "bugs" in the application of the rules, which lead to errors. For instance, after Brown and Burton (1978) used error analysis to detect bugs in students' application of the subtraction procedure, they wrote a computer program appropriately dubbed "Buggy," which taught prospective teachers to detect various bugs in their students' math work. One subtraction bug, for example, involves knowing how to borrow but not borrowing when the top number is zero.

■ *Weaknesses*

The preceding short section on strengths is followed by a longer section on weaknesses. This imbalance does not necessarily reflect an abundance of weaknesses in the theory. Rather, most of the strengths were mentioned earlier in the chapter, whereas weaknesses have not been discussed and must now draw our attention.

Shortcomings of Computational Models and Metaphors ▪ A basic problem with flowcharts or computer-program simulations is that these models may adequately describe human output (behavior), given knowledge of the input, but still differ in important respects from the way people think. For example, a computer program might process the information sequentially, while a child might process all the information simultaneously, but both could arrive at the same decision (output) in the task. Similarly, it is possible for different programs to predict performance equally well. This is one limitation to the generally good testability mentioned earlier. To help avoid the problem, Simon (1972) proposed that models meet certain criteria. They should be consistent with what we know about the brain and about behavior in tasks other than the one examined. They should also be sufficient to produce the behavior of interest and should be definite and concrete. Still, it can be difficult to judge the psychological validity of a model that meets these requirements.

One problem specific to computer-simulation models is that writing simulations is a time-consuming, often tedious task. Part of the problem is that in order to be complete and to run successfully, the program must contain much that is psychologically trivial, such as which block is picked up first. Perhaps because of the sheer demands of constructing self-modifying production or connectionist systems, psychologists have produced relatively few. Moreover, the obvious must be included in the program. An example (cited by Kendler, 1987) is a college campus computer dating program that contained much information about the students' interests and attitudes. The results were not considered successful by a brother and sister who were paired together! No one thought to instruct the computer that siblings should not be paired.

Another problem with computer models is that they tend to be highly specific, precise models of very limited, specific behaviors. Because they must consider all relevant variables, it is difficult to develop more general models that can run successfully. Still, there now are several large production systems that begin with a few hundred productions and learn over 100,000 productions (Klahr, 1999). Finally, self-modifying production systems have been more useful for explaining previous findings than for generating new ones (Siegler, 1998).

The metaphors of information processing, like all metaphors, can introduce problems. Metaphors are useful in that they explain abstract cognitive structures and processes in terms of concrete objects already familiar to people. Furthermore, they have helped psychologists view cognition from a new perspective and have suggested new research. However, we should use them with caution because they are a potentially dangerous tool. As George Eliot cautioned: "We all of us, grave or light, get our thoughts entangled in metaphors, and act fatally on the strength of them." One example is that metaphors, and even the more formal models, usually have excess meaning that was not intended. For instance, flowcharts may make us erroneously think of memory as passive, spatially organized, unaffected by emotion, and unrelated to other cognitive processes. In addition, adopting a particular model may seriously limit our thinking. Once psychologists began to express memory as a series of discrete steps (boxes in a flowchart), it took several years before a less discrete, more gradual levels-of-processing approach could be seriously proposed. Thus, it must be kept in mind that a model is similar only *in certain ways* to the phenomenon to which it is applied.

One example of how metaphors can constrain our thinking is that they may overly encourage us to think about cognition in terms of spatial representations. Roediger (1979) points out that memory metaphors usually are spatial metaphors, implying that we "search" our mental space for objects stored in physical space. There almost seems to be a "homunculus" (little man) who rifles through the files of memory until he finds that necessary paper. In these files or in semantic networks, concepts are stored at different "distances" from each other. Examples of cognitive metaphors in Roediger's list include a workbench, a pushdown stack (of clean plates in a restaurant), an acid bath, a dictionary, and a subway map. In a spoof of memory models, Hintzman (1974) likened memory to a "cow's belly." Information (like food) is transferred from the "short-term stomach" to the "long-term stomach." In this way, we "ruminate" over ideas and "digest" information.

The technology of the times suggests certain metaphors, beginning with Plato's notion that memory is like the impression of a seal on a wax tablet, which in his time was a method of storing information. Much later we find the gramophone, switchboard, tape recorder, computer, and holograph used as metaphors. It has even been suggested (Langlois, Cooper, & Woodson, 1985) that a bank automatic teller machine (ATM) might be an appropriate metaphor for a child. It processes information, is somewhat interactive, and usually follows instructions but sometimes has a mind of its own! Today's computer metaphor may eventually seem as naive as Plato's wax tablet. What metaphors will future technology bring? For example, the Internet may become an apt metaphor for thinking.

Problems with Addressing Certain Developmental Issues ▪ The information-processing approach has advanced our understanding of adult cognitive systems. How successfully has it contributed to a description and explanation of behavior? With respect to description, the information-processing approach rates high marks for its careful, refined descriptions of the memory system at various cognitive levels. An exception is that there is relatively little work on information processing in adolescents or infants and toddlers. Recent methodological advances in studying infants are beginning to show unexpected representational competence early in life. This neglect of infancy is unfortunate because, to be a viable developmental theory, the information-processing approach must describe preverbal, cognitively immature humans. It is important, for example, to know what kinds of nonverbal representations infants are capable of and how these nonverbal representational systems are related to the later verbal representational systems. Connectionist approaches are beginning to address these issues.

Although the information-processing approach has greatly contributed to our knowledge about mechanisms of development, the specifics are often still unclear. For example, although the development of control processes and improved encoding appears to be important for memory and problem solving, the information-processing approach has not yet explained how this development comes about. Why are some dimensions, such as number of weights, easier for young children to encode than other dimensions, such as distance of the weights from the fulcrum? In natural settings, what causes children to eventually encode previously ignored dimensions?

Connectionist models of learning, though successful, have been criticized (Siegler, 1998). In particular, they often overstate their similarity to brain mechanisms, which are much more complex. Moreover, the models learn more slowly than do humans and often do not show sudden insight as humans would (Raijmakers, Koten, & Molenaar, 1996). Finally, they have not yet been able to successfully model certain kinds of thinking. They may be better for accounting for some kinds of cognitive activities, such as detecting regularities in language, than others, such as metacognition. In general, computer simulations have more successfully spelled out how children use the skills that they already have, such as selecting among currently available strategies, than described how children discover new skills and rules, such as new strategies.

One important developmental change to be explained is whether developmental change is the same as the novice-to-expert shift in adults. That is, is change in adults as they become more knowledgeable about an area equivalent to cognitive development during childhood? The theory's view of development is very closely tied to its view of change in adults. A child, in a sense, is a "universal novice" (Brown & DeLoache,

1978), lacking knowledge in more areas than adults do. One important difference is that when adults "learn" in an experimental session, they are simply learning to make efficient use of what they already know. For example, when learning to play chess, adults may grasp the rules by generalizing from other games they know and rearranging this previous knowledge to fit chess. Also, adults have more sophisticated strategies of learning that allow them to move from the novice to the expert stage more quickly and to generalize new knowledge to other situations. In contrast, much change in children is due to the acquisition of *new* rules, concepts, or cognitive skills, rather than the rearrangement of old ones. Before children can learn chess, they must develop the ability to mentally move the pieces according to certain rules, to form a cognitive map of the location of pieces on the board, and so on. It is not clear that studying change in adults would elucidate these kinds of changes in children.

A related problem is that it is difficult to relate the short-term, microgenetic changes examined by information-processing psychologists to the long-term, stagelike qualitative changes postulated by Piaget. It may be that the seemingly revolutionary changes from stage to stage can be reduced to short-term quantitative changes if the level of analysis is refined enough. Or it may be that the information-processing approach will need to add more principles of functioning that explain major qualitative changes in cognitive organization.

Neglect of the Context of Behavior ▪ Critics (e.g, Neisser, 1985) have attacked information-processing psychologists' insensitivity to the natural context of behavior. As one critic noted, what a reader would conclude about the mind after reading a 904-page book surveying cognitive science is "Minds talk a lot . . . they move a little, they see a little, but they don't feel much else" (Anderson, 1991, p. 287). The image of the child is of a "rational, decontextualized isolated mind with limited knowledge, without interests, without feelings, attitudes, or views of the world" (Sigel, 1986, p. 99). Information processing entered developmental psychology after the field had already gone through its natural-history descriptive phase. The approach has focused on the processing mechanisms the person brings to a task or setting and on the task parameters, more than on the interplay between the demands or possibilities of the larger setting and the needs, goals, and abilities of the person. We might ask, for example, how cognition is related to larger motor behaviors such as approaching or retreating from particular activities or surfaces. Gibson's ecological perceptual theory, described in Chapter 6, is more successful in this regard.

How children feel about the particular setting and about other people in that setting are important as well. Central questions about the relation between cognitive and socioemotional variables include the following: How do children's emotional states affect their learning at various ages? Are encoding and retrieval strategies applied to social as well as physical objects and events? Does acquiring social experience and developing social scripts provide a framework for attending to, encoding, interpreting, and storing social events? Recent work on memory of traumatic events and on distortions in memory due to scripts and gender or racial stereotypes is promising in this respect.

The contextualists' attitude toward knowledge can be expressed as follows: "Ask not what's inside your head, but what your head is inside of" (Mace, 1977). Only recently have information-processing researchers begun looking at social influences, as seen in the work described earlier in areas such as peer collaboration. Still, certain areas are neglected; for example, information-processing-oriented cross-cultural work is rare. These socially oriented research programs are important because, as we saw in the earlier section on the sociocultural context of strategic behavior, the results give a new slant on the learning process.

SUMMARY

The information-processing approach studies how human symbol-manipulation systems work. Investigators take the computer program as a model—either as a metaphoric heuristic device or as a way of simulating and testing their views concerning the nature of human thought. Children change developmentally in how they attend to, represent, store, weight, and combine information. These changes occur at various points in the system, for example, the sensory store, short-term memory, and long-term memory in some models. Much of development occurs via self-modification, as children formulate rules of decision making and modify them as a result of feedback. Investigators often begin by performing a task analysis. They then either formulate a computer program simulating how the child learns, solves a problem, or stores information or test the efficiency of the child's processing by conducting experiments.

Humans are limited in how much information they can process at a given time and in how fast they can process this information. Much of development involves learning how to overcome these limitations by acquiring efficient control processes. Research on memory, the most studied area of development in information processing, shows that much of memory development is caused by the acquisition of strategies, the growing store of domain-specific knowledge, increased metamemory, and greater functional capacity.

The discovery and selection of various strategies and changes in the rules for problem solving also alter the processing of information. There is turning out to be more variability, and less consistency, in children's strategies and performance than we once thought. Social influences appear to be quite important. Children acquire a series of rules for problem solving and acquire new information that can be expressed in both production and connectionist simulations. Intelligence can be seen as the efficient, insightful, and adaptive application of information-processing components.

Mechanisms of development such as encoding, generalization, strategy construction, and automatic processing cause more efficient processing (Siegler, 1998). Information-processing theorists view humans as active, organized, self-modifying systems. Development involves both quantitative and qualitative change and both genetic and environmental influences. The essence of development is an increasingly efficient system for controlling the flow of information.

The theory has been applied mainly to educational settings and to issues concerning the reliability of young children's eyewitness testimony. The strengths of the theory are its ability to express the complexity of thought, its precise analysis of performance and change, and its rigorous methodology. Weaknesses involve certain shortcomings of computational models and metaphors, problems with addressing certain developmental issues, and a neglect of the context of behavior.

SUGGESTED READINGS

The following books describe current research on specific topics in memory, attention, and problem solving:

Bjorklund, D. F. (2000). *Children's thinking: Developmental function and individual differences* (3rd ed.). Belmont, CA: Wadsworth.

Flavell, J. H., Miller, P. H., & Miller, S. A. (2001). *Cognitive development* (4th ed.). Upper Saddle River, NJ: Prentice-Hall.

Siegler, R. S. (1998). *Children's thinking* (3rd ed.). Upper Saddle River, NJ: Prentice-Hall.

Schneider, S., & Pressley, M. (1997). *Memory development between two and twenty* (2nd ed.). Mahwah, NJ: Erlbaum.

For a look at programs of research directed toward the computer simulation of children's thinking, the reader is referred to the following source:

Klahr, D. (1999). The conceptual habitat: In what kind of system can concepts develop? In E. K. Scholnick, K. Nelson, S. A. Gelman, & P. H. Miller (Eds.), *Conceptual development: Piaget's legacy*. Mahwah, NJ: Erlbaum.

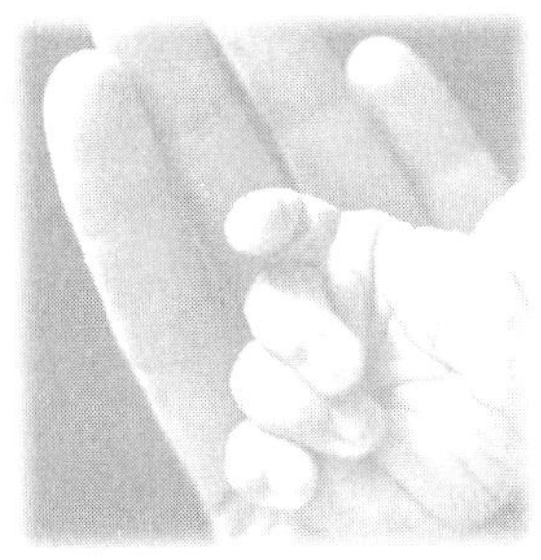

CHAPTER 5

Ethology and Other Evolutionary Theories

At the beginning of these experiments, I had sat myself down in the grass amongst the ducklings and, in order to make them follow me, had dragged myself, sitting, away from them. . . . The ducklings, in contrast to the greylag goslings, were most demanding and tiring charges, for, imagine a two-hour walk with such children — all the time squatting low and quacking without interruption! In the interests of science I submitted myself literally for hours on end to this ordeal

— *LORENZ, 1952, p. 42*

The initial phase, that of protest, may begin immediately or may be delayed; it lasts from a few hours to a week or more. During it the young child appears acutely distressed at having lost his mother and seeks to recapture her by the full exercise of his limited resources. He will often cry loudly, shake his cot, throw himself about, and look eagerly towards any sight or sound which might prove to be his missing mother. . . . During the phase of despair, which succeeds protest, the child's preoccupation with his missing mother is still evident, though his behavior suggests increasing hopelessness. The active physical movements diminish or come to an end, and he may cry monotonously or intermittently. He is withdrawn and inactive, makes no demands on people in the environment, and appears to be in a state of deep mourning.

— *BOWLBY, 1969, p. 27*

Developmental psychologists have not taken Shakespeare's advice, "Neither a borrower, nor a lender be." Some of the most fruitful ideas about development have been borrowed from other areas of psychology and even other sciences. The evolutionary approach, particularly ethology, sociobiology, and evolutionary psychology, is a good example of this. *Ethology* is the study of the evolutionarily significant behaviors of a species in its natural surroundings. As a subdiscipline of zoology, it looks at the biological and evolutionary blueprints for animal behavior. *Sociobiology*, which developed later, focuses on the evolutionary–genetic basis of human social behavior. The most recently developed theory, *evolutionary psychology*, examines the origins of human psychology, especially cognition, in our ancestors' adaptation to their environment. Related contemporary approaches, such as modern behavioral genetics and biological constraints approaches, also are part of the contemporary biological–evolutionary landscape. The chapter focuses on ethology, because it has provided the main theoretical foundation for the evolutionary perspective on development, particularly through John Bowlby and Mary Ainsworth's studies of infant attachment.

Evolutionary approaches place humans into a broad context, the animal world. It is humbling to contemplate the fact that there are more species of insects in a square kilometer of Brazilian forest than there are species of primates in the world (Wilson, 1975). The English geneticist Haldane, when asked about the nature of God, is said to have remarked that he displays "an inordinate fondness for beetles." The human species is just one small part of the huge, evolving animal kingdom. We are one of an estimated 3 million to 10 million species.

The chapter begins with a history followed by a general orientation. Then comes a section on the main contributions of ethology to human developmental psychology, followed by sections on mechanisms of development, the theory's position on developmental issues, applications, and evaluation.

HISTORY OF THE THEORY

Whoever achieves understanding of the baboon will do more for metaphysics than Locke did, which is to say he will do more for philosophy in general, including the problem of knowledge.

— CHARLES DARWIN

Ethology is linked to the German zoologists of the 1700s and 1800s who studied innate behaviors scientifically. The concept of evolution grew stronger after Darwin's painstaking observations of fossils and variations in plant and animal life. He, along with Alfred Wallace, concluded that nature ruthlessly selects certain characteristics because they lead to survival: "What a book a devil's chaplain might write on the clumsy, wasteful, blundering, low, and horribly cruel works of nature" (Darwin, quoted in Shapley, Rapput, & Wright, 1965, p. 446). As a result of this selective force, species changed and sometimes differentiated into subspecies. Thus, many animals, including humans, are related through common ancestors. Darwin proposed that intelligence and other behaviors, as well as physical structures, were products of evolution. If they increased the chances of survival, they were retained; if they did not, they disappeared. Darwin's claim of a common ancestry of humans and other primates was not received well in Victorian England: Montagu (1973) related an anecdote about a shocked wife of an English bishop. She said that she certainly hoped that the theory was false, but if it were true, that not many people would find out about it!

Darwin's careful observing and cataloging of plants and animals were imitated by ethologists years later. Just as he carefully described animal and plant life, Darwin also described his own infants' behavior, as in the following excerpt on fears:

> Before the present one was $4\frac{1}{2}$ months old I had been accustomed to make close to him many strange and loud noises, which were all taken as excellent jokes, but at this period I one day made a loud snoring noise which I had never done before; he instantly looked grave and then burst out crying. . . . May we not suspect that the vague but very real fears of children, which are quite independent of experience, are the inherited effects of real dangers and abject superstitions during ancient savage times?
>
> (1877, p. 289)

Ethology as a distinct discipline began in the 1930s with the European zoologists Konrad Lorenz and Niko Tinbergen. They developed, often in collaboration, many of the key concepts discussed in the next section. Tinbergen describes this new approach as having "started as a revolt by young zoologists against the dead animal" (Cohen, 1977, p. 316). Ethologists saw animals as active organisms living within a particular ecological niche, not as passive organisms prodded by stimuli, as in the tradition of learning theory. Their studies of species as diverse as ducklings, butterflies, and stickleback fish gave scientific meaning to the sometimes mystical term "instinct." Many of Lorenz's observations were of wild animals that wandered freely in and around his home. Lorenz and Tinbergen's work was honored with the Nobel Prize in medicine or physiology in 1973, which they shared with another ethologist, Karl von Frisch. For psychologists, Eibl-Eibesfeldt's work (1975, 1989), beginning in the 1950s and continuing in the present, is especially important, for he was one of the first to make a formal connection between psychology and ethology. This link with psychology fueled an interest in ethological accounts of human behavior.

Developmental psychology was receptive to ethology because developmentalists have a tradition of naturalistic observations of children and consideration of the biological basis of development. Many developmentalists continued to observe children even through psychology's behaviorist years. The most important figure to bring ethology to the attention of developmental psychologists was John Bowlby. His turning from a Freudian to an ethological account of infant–caretaker social attachment in the 1950s in England laid the groundwork for subsequent research in this area in both Europe and North America. (His work is described later.) Ethologically oriented psychologists also extended the approach to other areas of infant behavior, for instance, facial expressions and biases toward looking at certain objects, such as faces. With older children, the work focused on peer interaction. It is interesting that one of the founding fathers of ethology, Tinbergen, studied autistic children and interpreted their behavior as an extreme fear response to being looked at by other people (Tinbergen & Tinbergen, 1972). Developmental psychology welcomed ethology as a way to correct the extreme environmentalism of learning theory.

Ethology has continued to influence biologically oriented research on behavior in Europe and North America. Today, however, biologically oriented work on behavior includes many disciplines, for example, comparative psychology, psychobiology, neuropsychology, behavioral genetics, physiological psychology, behavioral ecology, and evolutionary biology. The word "developmental" could be placed in front of each label. In general, this work is more empirical and experimental and less speculative and theoretical than the earlier European "classical" ethological studies. The focus now typically is on the immediate causes of the behavior—for example, scent or temperature—rather than on the evolutionary origins of the behavior. The majority of the approaches favor a reductionist approach and study cells, neural impulses, and hormones rather than the behaviors of the whole organism in its ecological niche. This emphasis on laboratory research on various animal species contrasts with the ethological emphasis on observational research. However, ethology did bring a powerful methodology to biological approaches: "To have made 'inspired observation' respectable again in the behavioral sciences is, I believe, a positive achievement of ethology" (Tinbergen, quoted in Cohen, 1977, pp. 323–324).

Ethology was soon joined by sociobiology, defined by its main spokesman, E. O. Wilson, as the "study of the biological basis of all social behavior" (1975, p. 4). Although ethology and sociobiology overlap a great deal, the latter focuses on the species level and on social structures, such as customs, rituals, schools, and the legal system, rather than on the individual. People can pass on their genes either by reproducing or by furthering the survival of the genes of kin through altruistic behavior. Thus, a mother might risk her life for her young, which would not be adaptive for her as an individual but might further the survival of those with similar genes. The field is a hybrid of ethology, ecology (the study of how organisms are related to their environment), genetics, and population biology. Sociobiologists' work on such topics as reproductive patterns, altruism, parenting, and social hierarchies has had some influence on thinking about the behavior of parents and children. Still, the rise of sociobiology has minimally influenced developmentalists.

Evolutionary psychology, which arose after some of the criticisms of sociobiology as deterministic, reductionistic, and socially conservative, promises to have more impact on developmental psychology (Geary & Bjorklund, 2000). Evolutionary psychologists trace current psychological functioning to adaptations of our ancestors. This relatively new field was made possible "by the simultaneous maturation of evolutionary biology, paleoanthropology, and cognitive psychology" (Cosmides & Tooby, 1987, p. 302). Evolutionary psychologists use primatology, archaeological data, cultural anthropology, and data on contemporary human universals to relate current human cognition and behavior to adaptive ancestral behaviors. Most believe that there is little current evolutionary selection because of modern medicine, technological advances, and social services.

Developmental and biological approaches are very important to each other: "The developmental point of view is basic to an understanding of how evolutionary and ecological parameters are achieved in individuals and groups. The gap between molecular biology and natural selection will be filled by developmental analysis of the nervous system, behavior, and psychology" (Gottlieb, 1979, p. 169). The study of the development of behavior is "the backbone of comparative psychology. Shortcomings in its study inevitably handicap other lines of investigation, from behavioral evolution and psychogenetics to the study of individual and group behavior" (Schneirla, 1966, p. 283). Currently, developmental psychologists are quite interested in biological influences more generally, particularly in the areas of neuropsychology and domain-specific innate abilities for language, infant cognition, and early social development (see Chapter 8).

GENERAL ORIENTATION TO THE THEORY

Ethology is characterized by four basic concepts: (1) species-specific innate behavior, (2) the evolutionary perspective, (3) learning predispositions, and (4) ethological methodology. The theoretical notions described in this section are based primarily on "classical" ethology, that is, on the contributions of European ethologists, particularly Lorenz, Tinbergen, and Eibl-Eibesfeldt. These contributions have influenced ethological accounts of human development more thus far than have recent related approaches such as sociobiology or evolutionary psychology.

Species-Specific Innate Behavior

Innate behaviors, like organs of the body, are essentially the same in all members of a species, are inherited, and are adaptive (Lorenz, 1937). Just as physical structures are primarily under genetic control, so are certain behaviors. Although no physical structures or behaviors are completely innate, because they are always expressed in a particular prenatal and postnatal environment, ethology emphasizes the biological contributions to behavior.

Ethologists generally agree that a behavior is innate if it has these four characteristics (Cairns, 1979):

1. It is stereotyped in its form (that is, has an unvarying sequence of actions) across individuals in a species.
2. It is present without relevant previous experience that could have allowed it to be learned.
3. It is universal for the species (that is, found in all members).
4. It is relatively unchanged as a result of experience and learning after it is established.

For example, in certain songbirds, the same song appears in all members of the species at sexual maturity, even if they have never heard the song sung by other members of the species. As this example illustrates, some innate behaviors are not present at birth but appear later as a result of physical maturation. In contrast to primarily innate behaviors, learned behaviors, such as chimpanzees' use of sticks as "tools," vary in form from individual to individual, require relevant previous experience, usually vary in their occurrence among members of the species, and change as a result of subsequent experience.

Innate behaviors are termed *species-specific*, which means they occur among all members of the species or at least a particular subgroup, such as all the males or all the young. If another species also has the behavior, two inferences are possible. One is that the two species are related, perhaps having split into separate lines at some point in their evolution. That is, they have common ancestors. The other possible inference is that the behavior has evolved independently in the two species, perhaps because they had similar physical environments and needs. For example, in many species the young cling to the mother's fur—a necessity for survival if the infant must travel with its mother as she moves throughout an area in search of food or flees from predators. Ethologists must draw conclusions about similar behaviors in different species very cautiously, not only because the behaviors may have evolved independently but also because they may have different meanings or functions in the two species. An example is tail wagging in dogs and cats.

Two types of innate behaviors, reflexes and fixed action patterns, have particular relevance for humans. *Reflexes*, simple responses to stimuli, have long been familiar to psychologists. Examples from the human infant are grasping a finger placed in the hand, spreading the toes when the bottom of the foot is stroked, and turning toward a nipple when it brushes the cheek. Any long-haired parent would agree with ethologists' interesting observation that infants are particularly likely to grasp hair, especially during feeding. Ethologists speculate that this reflex originally served to facilitate clinging to the mother's fur. Many such reflexes are quite strong. A premature baby can grasp a clothesline and support its own weight, for instance. This ability is later lost. More complex reflexes are coordinated swimming, crawling, and walking movements when the body's weight is supported, in newborns or young infants.

Classical ethology (Lorenz and Tinbergen) emphasized fixed action patterns. A *fixed action pattern* is a complex innate behavior that promotes the survival of the individual, and thus the species. It is a "genetically programmed sequence of coordinated motor actions" (Hess, 1970, p. 7) that arises from specific inherited mechanisms in the central nervous system. For example, squirrels bury nuts, birds perform courtship "dances," spiders spin webs, and stickleback fish fight to protect their territory. A hand-fed starling with no experience in hunting prey attacks invisible insects, makes killing movements, and appears to swallow the insects (Lorenz, 1937). Fixed action patterns can become very elaborate, as when the male bowerbird spends hours building a love nest decorated with flowers, fruit, shells, and colorful beetles to attract a mate. He adjusts a twig here, adds a flower there, and seemingly stops to admire his work from time to time. The adaptive value of fixed action patterns lies in the fact that they often end in eating, mating, or protecting the species from harm.

A fixed action pattern is elicted by a *sign stimulus*—a particular stimulus whose presence automatically releases a particular fixed action pattern. Lorenz (1966) likens this process to a key opening a lock. For example, the red belly of a male stickleback fish venturing into another stickleback's territory is a sign stimulus that triggers fighting behavior. A decoy that only vaguely resembles the stickleback in shape but is red on its lower half elicits this fixed action pattern, whereas an accurately shaped decoy without the red area usually does not (Tinbergen, 1951). Thus, the sign stimulus is specific, and sometimes it must be in a particular orientation or position. Tinbergen (1958) discovered this particular sign stimulus when he noticed that his sticklebacks in an aquarium near a window facing a street would become agitated at a certain time of the day. He eventually realized that a red mail truck passed by at that time, a stimulus that approximated the natural sign stimulus. A further example of the specificity of the sign stimulus is that a hen will not rescue a distressed, flailing chick she can see under a glass bell but cannot hear. However, she will rescue the chick immediately if she can hear the distress cries even if she cannot see it (Bruckner, 1933).

When the sign stimulus is an appropriate exaggeration of the normal sign stimulus, it enhances the fixed action pattern. Fishermen take advantage of this fact by using lures that exaggerate the natural prey (the sign stimuli) of larger fish. At the other extreme, under certain conditions animals need very little from the environment to elicit a fixed action pattern, as when a female rat may try to retrieve her young shortly after birth even if no young are present; she will repeatedly grasp her own tail or one of her hind legs and carry it back to the nest (Eibl-Eibesfeldt, 1975). A human example is that infants who do not get enough opportunity to suck during feeding because the hole in the nipple is too large may make sucking movements even when no object is in the mouth (Spitz, 1957).

A fixed action pattern can arise from ambivalent behaviors due to conflict between two need systems. For instance, the male stickleback fish's zigzag courtship dance is a result of a "zig" toward the female that stems from aggression and a "zag" away from her that stems from the desire to lead her to the nest in order to mate. According to Lorenz (1966), this behavior has become ritualized into the innate courtship behavior of the species.

Ethologists have modified the concept of fixed action pattern in several ways (Beer, 1973; Dewsbury, 1978). For instance, research has found that many fixed action patterns are more variable than originally thought. They are now sometimes called "modal action patterns." Furthermore, most ethologists have rejected the classical ethological notion that the buildup and release of drives such as hunger, reproduction, aggression, and flight set the stage for fixed action patterns. They argue that the concept is not a useful one because it is not easily tested, is confusing, and leads to oversimplistic explanations of behavior.

Innate reflexes and fixed action patterns have developmental significance. These behaviors permit young infants' survival, either by allowing them to seek food and hide from predators on their own or by binding them to an adult caretaker through behaviors such as crying, grasping, sucking, or smiling. For example, the infant greylag gosling calls "wi-wi," especially when alone, and elicits a reassuring reply from its mother. Furthermore, with physical maturation come new behaviors such as nest building that allow even further adaptation to the environment. This fit between the organism's needs and the innate behaviors it possesses is not accidental but is the product of the long evolutionary history of its species.

The emphasis on innate behavior should not leave the impression that ethologists think learning is unimportant. Rather, most ethologists simply argue that it is necessary to describe and understand innate behavior before studying how it is modified by the environment. Most behavior is viewed as an interweaving of innate and learned components. A raven innately knows how to build a nest, but through trial and error learns that broken glass and pieces of ice are less suitable than twigs for this purpose (Eibl-Eibesfeldt, 1975). An innate skill can easily be adapted to new situations, as when English titmice quickly learned how to use innate gnawing behaviors to open milk bottles. The survival value of this interweaving of innate and learned behaviors is clear.

Waddington (1957) proposed a now-classic model of how biological regulating mechanisms constrain the course of development while allowing for the modification of development by the environment. He presented development as a ball rolling down an "epigenetic landscape." As the ball descends, this landscape becomes increasingly furrowed by valleys that greatly restrict the sideways movement of the ball. Slight perturbations from the developmental pathway can be corrected later through a "self-righting tendency," and the ball returns to its earlier groove. Thus, the general course of development is set, but some variation is possible because of particular environmental events. For a more complex description of contemporary systems models, see Gottlieb, Wahlsten, and Lickliter (1998).

Even a primarily learned behavior can contribute to survival. An example comes from Lorenz's description of how a learned act, "shaking hands," becomes an appeasement gesture:

> Who does not know the dog who has done some mischief and now approaches his master on its belly, sits up in front of him, ears back, and with a most convincing "don't-hit-me" face attempts to shake hands? I once saw a poodle perform this movement before another dog of whom he was afraid.
>
> (1950, p. 178)

Evolutionary Perspective

A chicken is just the egg's way of making another egg.

—ANONYMOUS

Evolution involves *phylogenetic* change, or change in a species over generations, in contrast to *ontogenetic* change, or developmental change in a single lifetime. From an evolutionary perspective, humans are an experiment in nature. A person is viewed "as though seen through the front end of a telescope, at a greater than usual distance and temporarily diminished in size, in order to view him simultaneously with an array of other social experiments" (Wilson, 1978, p. 17). Each species, including humans, is a solution to a problem posed by the environment. The problems include how to avoid predators, how to obtain food, and how to reproduce.

The course of development within an individual follows a pattern that was acquired by the species because it facilitated survival. The young must adapt to their environment in order to reach the age at which they can reproduce and transmit their genes into the next generation. Just as certain physical characteristics, such as the upright stance and the hand with opposable fingers and thumb, facilitated making and using tools, so did certain behaviors—reflexes and fixed action patterns—facilitate survival through mating, food gathering, caretaking, and so forth. Social behaviors, such as interindividual communication and cooperation, encouraged group cohesion and thereby increased the chances of survival. New behaviors arose through natural genetic variations or mutations and, if they allowed the organism to survive long enough to reproduce, were genetically transmitted to the next generation. These successful behaviors gradually became more common in the whole population over many generations.

Evolutionary theory has changed somewhat over the years, particularly in light of modern molecular genetics. Modern evolutionary theory combines Darwinian natural selection theory with population genetics. The latter views evolution as a "numbers game" (Surbey, 1998, p. 373) involving changes over generations in the relative frequencies of various genes. One current notion, for example, is that sudden changes during evolution may have been more common than Darwin thought.

Inferring the course of evolution is not as simple as it seems, however. It is not always obvious what the survival value of an innate behavior is. For example, a behavior may lead to the death of individuals but increase the survival of relatives or other members of the species. When an individual bird spots a predator, it gives a warning call to the flock, thus attracting the predator's attention and endangering its own life. The flock, however, survives. A further complication is that many existing behaviors, such as many of the reflexes in the human infant, are no longer necessary for survival; they appear to be relics. Many of the early arguments about evolution illustrate the dangers of armchair speculation about function. It was once claimed that flamingos are pink because that makes it difficult for predators to see them against the sunset (Thayer, 1909).

Learning Predispositions

Ethologists see the biological control of behavior not only in innate behaviors acquired during evolution but also in predispositions toward certain kinds of learning. Biology both enables and constrains learning. To a great extent the brain is "like an exposed negative, waiting to be dipped into developer fluid" (Wilson, 1975, p. 156). Species differ in which aspects of their behavior are modifiable, in what kinds of learning occur most easily, and in the mechanisms of learning. Learning predispositions include sensitive periods and general or specific learning abilities. *Sensitive*, or *critical, periods* are specific periods in which the animal is biologically ready to acquire a new behavior. During those times, the animal is especially responsive to particular stimuli and has certain behaviors that are particularly susceptible to modification.

The most popular ethological example of a sensitive period comes from Lorenz. Shortly after birth, usually in the first day or two, certain birds (for example, geese) are most able to learn the distinctive characteristics of their mother and therefore their species. During this sensitive period, the young learn to follow a stimulus and come to prefer that stimulus—a phenomenon called *imprinting*. Imprinting increases the survival of the young because it ensures that they stay close to the parent and, therefore, near food and shelter and far from predators and other dangerous situations. The stimulus to be followed must meet certain criteria; for example, it makes a particular call note or type of movement. The criteria vary from species to species, but the mother always meets these criteria. In the wild, a row of ducklings scurrying after their mother is a common sight. However, as Lorenz discovered, certain "unnatural" objects also meet the criteria. Young birds have become imprinted on flashing lights, electric trains, moving milk bottles, and a squatting, quacking Konrad Lorenz (see the excerpt at the beginning of this chapter). Horses and sheep have also become imprinted on humans. Lorenz considered imprinting critical because he thought it was irreversible; a duckling imprinted on a flashing light does not become imprinted on its real mother if she appears for the first time after the end of the sensitive period. More recently, however, ethologists have questioned this irreversibility. Still, ethologists agree that how experience affects the organism depends on the stage of development at which the experience occurs.

In many species, imprinting has a long-term effect on sexual behavior. Lorenz (1931) discovered that jackdaws raised by humans will join a flock of jackdaws but return to their first love, a human, during the reproductive season. They try to attract the human with their species' courting patterns.

Ethologists have also identified sensitive periods for behaviors such as learning bird songs, learning to distinguish males and females of the species, acquiring language, and forming a bond between the newborn and the mother. In the last case, for example, mother goats form a bond with their young in the first 5 minutes after birth. If the young are removed right after birth for 2 hours, the mother attacks them upon their return. Waiting 5 minutes after birth before removal, however, leads to their acceptance later (Klopfer, 1971).

Sensitive periods involve learning predispositions. In the case of imprinting, a young bird is biologically pretuned to notice certain types of objects, sounds, or movements, yet it links up a response to this stimulus as a result of experience, that is, of seeing the object and then following it. Thus, biology prepares the bird to learn from experience. The learning involved in imprinting or other behavior acquired during sensitive periods should not be confused with operant conditioning (discussed in the chapter on learning). Imprinting is acquired with no reinforcement; it even increases when punishment in the form of an electric shock occurs, and it resists extinction.

Developmental psychologists have drawn heavily on the concept of a sensitive period, and many have argued that early experience is particularly important for adult behavior, as suggested by Freud and others. Furthermore, all stage theories claim that at each stage the child is particularly sensitive to certain experiences, such as motor exploration in the sensorimotor period (Piaget), the meeting of one's needs by other people in the stage of trust versus mistrust (Erikson), and the satisfaction or deprivation of anal drives during the anal stage (Freud). Most nonstage theories also use the concept of readiness—the idea that the child is most likely to learn from an experience if it comes at the optimal time. The child may not profit from being shown how to put objects to be remembered into categories when she is 3 years old but may have increased recall as a result of this experience at age 6. Finally, it should be noted that sensitive periods are a central notion in embryological development. A particular drug taken by a pregnant woman will have no effect or a devastating effect on the fetus, depending on its stage of development.

In addition to sensitive periods, a second way in which biology indirectly controls behavior is found in *general and specific learning skills*. Particularly in humans, the genetic endowment includes a tremendous general ability to learn from experience. As Lorenz (1959) noted, humans are "specialists in nonspecialization." We have evolved a central nervous system that is capable of flexible thinking: humans can construct novel solutions to problems in various types of environments. Humans also have hands that can perform many different actions and a language system that permits symbolic thought and verbal communication. The advantage of this flexibility is that the organism can adjust to a changing environment. Humans rely less on fixed action patterns for survival, especially during adulthood. Another way in which a general learning ability is tied to innate factors is the ability to learn via reinforcement and punishment. The ability to be affected by the consequences of one's behavior must be built into the nervous system.

As a result of humans' biologically based general ability to learn, we have developed cultures to help us adapt. The culture is passed on to the next generation by imitation, instruction, and other forms of learning. Thus, even cultural adaptation has its biological origins.

General learning abilities are complemented by specific learning skills, each applied to a particular domain such as the representation of spatial locations. Specific learning skills reflect the fact that an organism does not learn everything equally easily. Each species has its own bias toward certain kinds of learning. The digger wasp, during its morning inspection of up to 15 nests, decides how much food is needed by each nest. He retains this information for the entire day. A well-known example of an amazing specific memory skill is the ability of salmon to return to their spawning ground by remembering the odor of the water in which they were born. Rats, which normally live in burrows, will learn to make their way through a psychologist's maze faster than herons and frogs (Eibl-Eibesfeldt, 1975). Wild rats quickly learn, after an unfortunate experience, to avoid poisonous bait (Barnett, 1963). When new bait is presented, rats will eat very small quantities and, if they fall ill, will subsequently avoid the bait.

Humans also have specialized learning skills. Chomsky (1965) and others have claimed that human infants are pretuned to process and acquire language. The rapid acquisition of language early in life, the culturally universal forms of early utterances, and the occurrence of babbling in infants born deaf all point to this conclusion. All infants are born with the ability to discriminate all human language sounds, but the particular subset of these phonemes that they still can discriminate by late infancy depends on the language or languages to which they were exposed during early infancy.

An interesting footnote to animal learning comes from Lorenz (1963), who suggests that once a behavior is learned, deviating from it often causes great fear. He offers the following anecdote to illustrate this point: A greylag goose that lived in Lorenz's room had developed a routine for entering the house every evening. At first she had always walked past the staircase to a window before climbing the stairs to her room. This detour was shortened until she merely turned toward the window at the foot of the stairs instead of going over to it. One evening Lorenz forgot to let the goose into the house. When he finally remembered as darkness approached, the goose ran in and immediately ascended the stairs:

> Upon this something shattering happened: Arrived at the fifth step, she suddenly stopped, made a long neck, in geese a sign of fear, and spread her wings as for flight. Then she uttered a warning cry and very nearly took off. Now she hesitated a moment, turned around, ran hurriedly down the five steps and set forth resolutely, like someone on a very important mission, on her original path to the window and back. This time she mounted the steps according to her former custom from the left side. On the fifth step she stopped again, looked around, shook herself, and performed a greeting display behavior regularly seen in greylags when anxious tension has given place to relief. I hardly believed my eyes. To me there is no doubt about the interpretation of this occurrence: The habit had become a custom which the goose could not break without being stricken by fear.
>
> (Lorenz, 1963, p. 112)

■ *Methodology*

Ethologists rely on two general methods for studying behavior: naturalistic observation and laboratory experimentation. Both are necessary to the theory. The insistence on observing organisms in their natural environments most clearly differentiates ethology from related disciplines such as evolutionary psychology and sociobiology. Ethologists' particular version of naturalistic observation ranks as one of their main contributions to psychology.

Naturalistic Observation ■ Although theories lead to particular methods, methods also influence theories. Rather than observe animal learning in the wild, learning theorists observed bar pressing in rats and table tennis in pigeons in the lab. These could hardly be considered typical species-specific behaviors. It is unlikely that interesting natural behaviors, such as defending a territory or building a nest, would occur often in barren laboratory cages. In contrast, ethologists emphasize naturalistic observation.

Naturalistic observation is closely tied to the three characteristics of the theory mentioned earlier. If one wants to describe species-specific innate behaviors or learning predispositions that evolved because they led to survival in a species' natural habitat, there is no substitute for observing animals in their typical environments. In particular, one can understand the function of a behavior only by seeing how it fits into the species' natural environment in order to satisfy the animals' needs. Giraffes' long necks make sense when we see them eating leaves from tall trees; we understand young gulls' innate "freezing" rather than fleeing in the face of danger by noting that their nests are built on narrow ledges or steep cliffs (Eibl-Eibesfeldt, 1975).

Observations of animals in captivity are inadequate because their behavior may be abnormal due to their atypical environment. One cause of abnormal behavior in this setting is the absence of sign stimuli that would release fixed action patterns. Thus, behavior is often redirected. Animals may restlessly pace back and forth, constantly rock, and kill their young. A simple change in the environment can often eliminate these abnormal behaviors. For example, an armadillo in the Amsterdam zoo made various abnormal, stereotyped movements until a layer of dirt was placed on the floor of its bare cage. The animal could then bury itself at night when it slept (Eibl-Eibesfeldt, 1975). Ironically, giving too much care to the captive animal may cause problems. Titmice in a zoo threw their young out of the nest soon after birth. The problem was that food was too readily available. The young quickly became full, stopped gaping, and consequently were taken for dead by the parents. Young titmice in the wild never stop gaping unless they are sick or dead, because the parents must hunt for food and the infants are never full (Koenig, 1951). In humans, abnormal behavior—for example, rocking—has been observed in children in unnatural environments such as orphanages and hospitals.

Ideally, ethologists follow a particular sequence of steps when studying an organism.

1 They develop an *ethogram,* an extensive, detailed description of the behavior of a species in its natural environment. An ethogram is like an inventory or a catalog. It includes the animal's behaviors, the characteristics of the environment, and the events immediately preceding and following each behavior. Of interest are not only the types of behaviors—for example, nesting and food gathering—but also their frequency, stimulus context, function, and ontogenetic development. Psychologists have been particularly oblivious to the frequency of a behavior in natural settings. The problem of not having scientific data

about frequency was noted long ago by Thorndike: "Dogs get lost hundreds of times and no one notices it or sends a scientific account of it to a magazine. But let one find its way from Brooklyn to Yonkers and the fact immediately becomes a circulating anecdote" (1898, p. 4).

It is as important to describe the environment as it is to describe the organism's behavior. In fact, a complete description of the setting essentially defines the animal that inhabits it: "If we specify in detail the niche of a fish (its medium, its predators and prey, its nest, etc.), we have in a way described the fish" (Michaels & Carello, 1981, p. 14).

The descriptive labels must be refined until two or more observers can agree, in nearly every case, regarding what behavior occurred and when it began and ended. Did a child smile or grimace, and for how long? When describing a behavior, ethologists examine the structure of that behavior: what elicits it, what the components are, in what order these components appear, and what ends the behavior. Note that these "raw data" in the ethogram focus on certain types of behaviors, namely, those that have evolved as an aid to survival. Furthermore, ethologists historically have been particularly interested in observing fixed action patterns that involve social behavior. Ethologists sometimes study human behavior by examining contemporary hunters and gatherers in order to understand the environment in which current human behaviors evolved.

2 Ethologists classify behaviors according to their function, that is, how they encourage survival. The categories—such as caretaking, mating, and defending territory—serve as working hypotheses that they modify after more observations. Ethologists often can identify function after determining which species do or do not exhibit the behavior and then finding out what differentiates these species. For example, they may find mother–child bonding only in species in which the young are helpless.

3 Ethologists compare how a given behavior, such as a fixed action pattern, functions in various species and how different behaviors meet the same need in different species. They are especially interested in similar fixed action patterns in closely related species. If several closely related species of birds have a similar courtship dance, they may have a common ancestor. Such species comparisons, along with changes in behavior inferred from fossils (for example, an increase in brain size), provide evidence about the evolutionary course of a behavior.

4 As described in the next section, ethologists use laboratory experiments to determine the immediate causes of the behavior described in the first three steps. From the viewpoint of ethologists, psychology has worked backward historically by performing laboratory research before obtaining a sufficient database of naturalistic observations.

Ethologists increase the power of the observational method by filming or videotaping their observations. They thus can return to an earlier observation to check a hypothesis formed after observations of many individuals. After observing many human babies, an investigator may notice that they seem to be less fearful of strangers when strangers kneel down than when they stand. By viewing all of the observations again, she can check this hypothesis.

Another advantage of videotaped observations is that the action can be sped up or slowed down. When this is done, previously unnoticed patterns of behavior sometimes emerge. For example, a flirting look often involves raising the eyebrows for only one-sixth of a second—a movement that becomes a noticeable invariant part of the flirting sequence only when the film is slowed down (Eibl-Eibesfeldt, 1975). By speeding up videotapes, investigators have noted that people who eat alone look up and around after every few bites, as if scanning the horizon for enemies, as baboons and chimps do (Eibl-Eibesfeldt, 1975). This is much less obvious at a normal camera speed.

Filming humans poses special problems because their awareness that they are being filmed is likely to change their behavior. The one-way mirror, which makes unobtrusive filming possible in the laboratory, is obviously of little use in field settings. Eibl-Eibesfeldt has made use of one clever solution to this problem. A mirror prism inserted in his camera allows camera operators to point the camera at a right angle to the target. Subjects know the camera is present but do not think they are being filmed.

Laboratory Studies ■ For an ethologist, a behavior has both a phylogenetic cause and an immediate cause. A spider spins a web "because" that innate food-gathering behavior has allowed the species to survive. In addition to this phylogenetic cause, various types of immediate causes can be identified. Spinning a web may be caused by specific physiological events, particular inborn neurological pathways, the presence of a sign stimulus, certain aspects of motor experience, and so on. Ethologists clarify these various causes of behavior suggested by the observational studies with controlled experiments.

The classical ethological experiment is the *deprivation study*, which determines whether a behavior is innate or learned. In this method, ethologists deprive the animal of specific experiences that could be relevant to the behavior of interest. Obviously, they do not deprive the organism of broad aspects of experience—a procedure that would cause widespread disruption of behavior or even physical deterioration. As an illustration of the deprivation study, an ethologist interested in the origin of nut-burying behavior raised squirrels in isolation in a cage with a bare floor and provided a diet of only liquid food. The squirrels had no exposure to other squirrels (who could serve as models), nuts, or earth (which could provide digging practice). Under these conditions, squirrels demonstrated a stereotyped sequence of nut-burying behaviors at the same age as do squirrels in the wild. When presented with a nut at this time, they ate until satiated, then dug an imaginary hole in the concrete floor, pushed the nut into the "hole" with their snouts, covered it with invisible soil, and carefully patted down the "soil" to finish the job (Eibl-Eibesfeldt, 1975). Thus, since they had no opportunity to learn this behavior, it must be an innate fixed action pattern of the species.

Other ethological laboratory experiments do not differ in method from those of comparative psychology or physiological psychology. They clarify which variables influence behavior and what the underlying physiological mechanisms are. For example, by systematically varying stimuli, researchers can determine which attributes of a stimulus are critical for eliciting the response. The experiments examine a variety of responses, ranging from pupil dilation (which indicates interest or attraction) to the amount of time spent near the stimulus. Although the laboratory experimental method is shared with the mainstream of experimental psychology, ethology maintains its distinctiveness by the content it chooses to study: behaviors tailored to the survival of the species.

CONTRIBUTIONS TO HUMAN DEVELOPMENTAL PSYCHOLOGY

Ethologists are interested in the same categories of adaptive behaviors in humans as in other animals, for example, feeding, communication, parent–child interaction, and reproduction. However, there is no unified ethological view of development. Instead, ethologically oriented psychologists have selected particular topics. The study of children has focused primarily on infant attachment but also has examined topics such as the organization of peer interaction and problem solving. Recent evolutionary accounts of development have focused on cognitive evolutionary psychology; cultural transmission, social cognition, and theory of mind; and the advantages of immaturity. A look at representative research in each of these areas will show ethology's imprint on both the content and the methodology of developmental research (see also Bjorklund & Pellegrini, 2000; MacDonald, 1998).

■ *Infant–Caretaker Attachment*

Bowlby's Theory ■ John Bowlby, a London psychoanalyst, is credited with bringing ethology to the attention of developmental psychologists. Because World War II had left many children as orphans, there were concerns about the effects of maternal deprivation. Bowlby's observations of infants separated for a long time from their mothers led him to conclude that an early social "attachment" between infant and caretaker is crucial for normal development. A disrupted relationship between mother and infant often leads to the infant's protest; then despair, characterized by grief and mourning; then detachment; and finally, in some cases, psychopathology (see the excerpt at the beginning of this chapter). Evidence for the attachment bond in normal situations includes protest when the parent leaves and greeting behaviors, such as smiling and babbling, when the parent returns. Children also seek their attachment figure when under stress.

Drawing on observations of mother–infant bonding in nonhuman primates, Bowlby [1969(1982)] proposed that attachment to a caretaker has evolved because it promotes the survival of helpless infants by protecting them from predators or exposure to the elements. Separation of the infant from its mother can be a fatal error in many animals. At birth and throughout early development, infants have a biological predisposition to maintain proximity to adults of the species. In animals other than humans, the young often use the mother's odor or the warmth of the nest to keep in contact with her (Moltz & Leon, 1983; Rosenblatt, 1976). Many of the human newborn's reflexes served this function during human evolution. One of these reflexes is grasping an object such as a finger or the hair when it contacts the infant's palm, just as many mammalian infants stay with the mother by clinging to her hair. Another reflex is an embracing movement in response to a sudden loud sound or a loss of support. This reflex may have prevented many ancestral infants from falling when the mother suddenly ran upon seeing a predator.

Of course, these reflexes have little value for attachment in human infants, who need not physically attach themselves to the parent in order to survive. Of more importance to human babies are signaling mechanisms such as crying, babbling, and smiling. These behaviors communicate infants' needs and encourage adults to come to infants, since young babies cannot go to adults. Just as following the imprinted object in ducklings maintains proximity, so do signaling behaviors serve this purpose in humans. The result is the same: the infant is protected and nurtured. These signaling behaviors are more complex than the simple reflexes and are considered by some to be fixed action patterns. Another ability found in young infants that may facilitate their relationship with their parents is imitation of facial gestures (Meltzoff & Moore, 1989). As the infant matures, other behaviors, such as crawling, walking, and talking, facilitate contact between parent and child.

Research supports Bowlby's notion that signaling behaviors are innate. Even infants born blind or blind and deaf acquire a social smile at approximately 6 weeks, as do normal infants. In fact, children blind and deaf since birth reveal a wide range of normal behaviors, including laughing, crying, babbling, and pouting, and typical facial expressions of fear, anger, and sadness (Eibl-Eibesfeldt, 1975, 1989). For example, they throw back their heads when laughing and stomp their feet when angry. Thus, these naturally occurring "deprivation experiments" show that visual and auditory experiences that would allow imitative learning are not necessary for these signaling or expressive behaviors to develop. Further evidence for the universality of the human smile and other expressions comes from observations of these behaviors in infants in many cultures (Eibl-Eibesfeldt, 1975). Darwin long ago observed smiling in infants of every culture with which he had contact.

It is highly unlikely that adults teach these expressive behaviors to normal infants or blind and deaf children. Smiling and laughing involve a complex sequence of coordinated movements or sounds. Eibl-Eibesfeldt (1975) describes a deaf and blind 12-year-old with severe brain damage who was unable to learn simple actions such as bringing a spoon to her mouth, in spite of an intense training program. Yet she was able to smile, laugh, and cry. Even the possibility that blind and deaf children might learn facial expressions by touching the mother's face and imitating her facial movements was ruled out by a child deaf and blind since birth who was born with no arms. Despite these handicaps, he showed normal facial expressions.

Bowlby proposed that these early reflexes and signaling behaviors, along with a bias toward looking at faces, leads to an attachment to adults in general and then, usually around 6 to 9 months of age, to one or a few specific adults. This specific attachment can be seen in the infant's protest when separated from a particular adult, as opposed to all adults. This separation is an innate "cue to danger" that elicits signaling behavior intended to restore proximity.

The infant and adult behaviors eventually become synchronized into an "attachment behavioral system," according to Bowlby. The appearance and behavior of each member serve as sign stimuli for the fixed action pattern in the other. Each member of the system comes to expect that the other will respond to its own behavior in certain ways. Children's expectations are part of their "internal working models" discussed in Chapter 2—mental representations of the attachment figures, the self, and the relationship. These models help children interpret and evaluate new situations and then choose a behavior such as playing or seeking the attachment figure for comfort. Between the ages of about 9 and 18 months, an infant's various individual behaviors, especially sucking, clinging, crying, smiling, and following, become incorporated into more complex, self-correcting "control systems."

Bowlby used control-systems theory from engineering as a model of how attachment forms an organizational system. Control systems are goal-directed and use feedback to regulate the system in order to achieve the goal. A simple control system is a thermostat, which maintains a particular room temperature (the goal) by comparing the actual temperature (the feedback) with the desired temperature. With respect to behavioral systems, Bowlby proposed that genetic action causes the behavioral system to develop but that the developed system is flexible enough to adjust to changes in the environment, within prescribed limits. Just as the human respiratory system works within a particular range of oxygen, a behavioral system operates efficiently within a certain range of variation in relevant features of the environment. The particular acceptable range of social and physical stimuli relevant for attachment varies from species to species. In human attachment, infants have a goal: an acceptable degree of proximity to the adult. When infants detect that the adult is too far away (feedback), they correct this state by crying or crawling, which reestablishes contact and reachieves equilibrium in the system. The limits of acceptable distance vary, depending on internal factors, such as hunger or illness, and external factors, such as the presence of an adult stranger or other cues of danger. The development of a secure attachment expands the distance acceptable by establishing the caretaker as a secure base from which the child can explore.

Bowlby's theory of attachment includes many of the characteristics of the general theory of ethology. Species-specific reflexes and fixed action patterns, which are the products of evolution, ensure the proximity of the mother to the child. Sensitive periods and general and specific learning abilities biologically predispose infants and caretakers to develop a system of synchronized interactions. In keeping with ethological theory, Bowlby relies heavily on observations of children. However, much of the more recent research on attachment stimulated by his theory was conducted in laboratory settings. Mary Ainsworth (Ainsworth, Blehar, Waters, & Wall, 1978) developed methods for assessing attachment and provided much of the empirical evidence for attachment theory in her research.

The ethological account of attachment, with its focus on innate behaviors, obviously contrasts with learning theory's focus on the reinforcement value of food (or, in later versions, other stimuli, such as warmth and physical contact), which establishes the mother as a secondary reinforcer. Although it seems likely that pleasant interactions have a positive effect on the bond between child and adult, ethologists point out that attachment occurs even when the attachment object physically abuses the infant. Ethological accounts also differ from Freudian theory's focus on the oral drive. Finally, ethology differs from both traditional learning and Freudian theory in stressing the infant's effect on the parent as much as the parent's effect on the child.

Bowlby later (1980) incorporated into his theory some of the notions of information-processing theory. He explained unsatisfactory early social relationships, abnormally strong repression, and thinking disorders in part by general principles of selective attention and selective forgetting. For example, if young children's attachment behavior is continually aroused but not responded to, they eventually exclude from awareness the sights, thoughts, or feelings that normally would activate attachment behavior.

Bowlby continually applied his ideas about attachment to his clinical work. Interestingly, his final book (1991), a biography of Darwin, traces Darwin's chronically poor health back to his failure to fully mourn his mother's death when he was 8 years old.

Adults' Responsiveness to Infants ▪ One important contribution of the ethological account of attachment is that adults, as well as infants, are biologically predisposed to develop attachment. Species in which infants depend on parents for survival should retain, over the course of evolution, innate caretaking responses in adults. Babies elicit adult attachment behavior by signaling behaviors or by their babyish appearance. Many infants emit calls to which the mother responds. For example, ultrasonic sounds from a young mouse elicit nest-building behavior in the adult female mouse (Noirot, 1974). Human signaling behaviors, such as smiling, visually fixating the face, and babbling, elicit the parent's attention and interest.

The infant's babyish appearance may elicit caretaking. Lorenz (1943) noted that the infants of many species, especially mammals, share certain physical characteristics, which are depicted in Figure 5.1. These characteristics include a head that is large in relation to the body, a fore-

Figure 5.1

Characteristics of babyishness or cuteness common to several species.

SOURCE: From "Die angeborenen Formen möglicher Erfahrung," by Konrad Lorenz, in *Zeitschrift für Tierpsychologie*, 1943, 5, 235–409. Reproduced by permission of Verlag Paul Parey.

head that is large in relation to the rest of the face, limbs that are relatively short and heavy, large eyes at or below the midline of the head, and round, prominent cheeks. This description is simply an objective description of what is better known as cuteness. This babyishness is exaggerated in baby dolls for children and in young animals in the Disney cartoon films. Interestingly, Gould (1980) observed that as Mickey Mouse became more lovable and well behaved over the years, his physical appearance became more babyish—a larger head with softer, more rounded features and larger eyes.

Infants' smiles also may be powerful elicitors of adults' attention. It has been suggested that the adaptive significance of an infant's smile is to make the tired, busy mother of the young infant feel that those difficult first months are worthwhile (Robson, 1967). Studies of adults' and children's responses to pictures of infants or to live infants have included physiological measures (pupil enlargement or changes in heart rate), behavioral measures (amount of interaction with the infant), or self-reports (rating the attractiveness of faces). This research shows that people respond positively to infant faces but that various factors affect the degree of their response. For example, 12- and 13-year-old girls who had begun menstruation rated pictures of infants more positively than did boys of the same age or girls of the same age who had not begun menstruation (Goldberg, Blumberg, & Kriger, 1982). However, responsiveness to infants is not always greatest among females or during the child-bearing years. The pattern of results depends on the type of response measure used, the physical and social nature of the testing situation, the person's experience with young children, and the person's cultural background (Berman, 1980). Thus, social factors, such as cultural expectations, appear to play at least some role in responsiveness to infants. Interpretation is also clouded by the fact that even infants prefer looking at babies to looking at children or adults (McCall & Kennedy, 1980).

The caretaker typically forms an emotional bond to the child in the first few hours or days of life. This *bonding* encourages caretaking and thus enhances survival. One of the most exciting discoveries from attachment research is a possible sensitive period for bonding during the first few hours after birth. It is tempting to draw an analogy with the sensitive period for imprinting in birds. Klaus and Kennell (1976) compared two groups of mothers and newborns. The control group followed usual hospital procedures, that is, a look at their babies at birth, brief contact at 6 to 8 hours, and 20 to 30 minutes of contact every 4 hours when they fed their infants. The "extra-contact group" received their nude babies for 1 hour of contact in the first 2 hours after birth and for 5 extra hours, compared with the control group, on each of the following 3 days. At the babies' examination 1 month later, the mothers from the extra-contact group held and soothed the infants more, showed more eye contact and fondling when they fed the infants, and reported they were less likely to leave the infants with another caretaker, in comparison to the control group. The differences were still present at 1 year. By 5 years of age, children in the extra-contact group had higher IQ and language-test scores. Although there is disagreement about the replicability of this research, its methodological adequacy, and its proper interpretation (Myers, 1984), the research does point to the importance of events that occur shortly after birth.

Contemporary Perspectives on Attachment ▪ Contemporary attachment research has focused on predispositions toward attachment in very young infants and on patterns of attachment identified by Mary Ainsworth. Young infants are biased toward attending to people. Newborns prefer to look at human faces rather than inanimate objects. Interestingly, infants prefer female faces that have been rated as attractive, rather than unattractive, by adults, even infants who are too young to have been taught this preference (Langlois et al., 1987). Even young infants gurgle and make various "pleasure sounds" in response to the sound of the human voice.

Infants also appear to be predisposed to learn to discriminate their mother's odor from that of others. Two-week-old breast-fed infants turned toward a pad that had been worn in their mother's underarm area rather than a pad worn by another lactating female (Cernoch & Porter, 1985). Just as infants can recognize their mother's odor, so do mothers quickly recognize their infant's distinctive smell. Six hours after giving birth, and after only a single exposure to their babies, blindfolded mothers could pick out, by smell alone, their own baby from a set of three babies (Russell, Mendelson, & Peeke, 1983).

One of Bowlby's colleagues, Mary Ainsworth, focused on the role of the attached parent as a "secure base" for exploration. The parent is a secure home base from which children venture to explore the next room or the next block and to which they return from time to time for "emotional refueling" (Mahler, 1968). If, however, the responses to children's signaling behaviors are inappropriate (unpredictable, slow, abusive, or not matched to the child's needs), children feel insecure and are less likely to use the mother as a base for exploring a strange environment (Ainsworth et al., 1978). Because the appropriateness of the adult's responses is more important than the total amount of interaction, infants become attached to fathers who respond appropriately to the child's signals, even if the total amount of time spent with the father is small.

Ainsworth (e.g., Ainsworth et al.,1978) devised the "Strange Situation" procedure, which lasts about 22 minutes, to assess babies' patterns of attachment to their mothers. The child, a parent, and a stranger in a laboratory setting proceed through a sequence of episodes, gradually moving from low stress (child with parent) to high stress (child with stranger in parent's absence). On the basis of their reactions to these events, children are classified as *securely attached* (approximately 65 percent of typical middle-class samples), *insecure–avoidant* (20 percent), or *insecure–resistant* (15 percent). However, it appears that some children do not fit easily into any of these categories and may form a fourth category—*disorganized or disoriented* (Main & Solomon, 1990). They have no consistent way of dealing with stress; they show contradictory behaviors such as calmness and anger. This disorganization is not surprising because they sometimes have parents who abuse them. The dyad's type of attachment depends on many factors, including parents' sensitivity to the child's needs, stresses on the family, parental psychopathology, and child characteristics such as Down syndrome or temperament (e.g., Thompson, 1998). Secure attachment predicts later child behaviors, particularly effective social functioning during childhood and adolescence (for reviews, see Cassidy & Shaver, 1999; Thompson, 1998).

A recent interpretation of these findings is that this variability in types of human attachment prepares the young of the species to adapt to their parents' pattern of investment in offspring, a notion from evolutionary approaches (Chisholm, 1996). Infants increase their chances of survival if they can adapt to their particular caregiving condition. If parents are heavily invested in their children and thus are sensitive and responsive, then environmental risk decreases and children can explore more freely from their safe base. If, because of environmental pressures such as scarce food, parents are unable or unwilling to invest heavily in caring for their children, then resistant or avoidant attachment may be more adaptive. In resistant attachment, clinging to the caregiver could elicit whatever meager resources are available. In avoidant attachment, a more independent infant can try to obtain resources from other adults. As Thompson concludes, "Attachment patterns that are adaptive for certain rearing conditions may be maladaptive for others, and patterns that are initially adaptive may not remain so if conditions change appreciably" (1998, p. 43).

Contemporary issues about attachment include the following, some of which challenge the original Bowlby–Ainsworth attachment theory (Cassidy & Shaver, 1999; Thompson, 1998): How stable over time is an infant's attachment classification? How broad is the effect of early attachment on later social relationships and cognitive abilities? Are aspects of the parent–child relationship other than attachment of equal importance? How are specific aspects of the attachment relationship related to specific later relationships? What is the child's active contribution (for example, temperament) to the attachment relationship? How, if at all, do child-care arrangements affect attachment and development? What accounts for the variability in a child's attachment behavior across situations? What effect does parental physical abuse of the infant have on the attachment bond?

One particularly interesting area of research concerns the possible link between insecure attachment and various sorts of later psychopathology. The early attachment pattern has an indirect effect in that it plays an ongoing role during development in the child's selection of environments, degree and type of engagement in activities in the environment, and interpretation of her experiences (Sroufe, Carlson, Levy, & Egeland, 1999). Also, work on young children at developmental risk, such as children with Down syndrome, cerebral palsy, or autism, promises to broaden our understanding of the variety of social attachments and the complex interweaving of genetic and environmental forces (Vondra & Barnett, 1999).

Today, researchers have added several perspectives to ethology to address broader questions about early social relations (Thompson, 1998). One is young children's theory of mind, such as their inferences of parents' feelings and intentions. This knowledge both affects and is affected by interaction with parents. Children's representation of events and their autobiographical memory also are important. Another perspective is cultural studies of attachment that clarify what cultural–ecological factors influence the security or insecurity of attachment. In general, Ainsworth's attachment patterns have emerged in studies in various countries, but the percentage in each category shows some variability from country to country and even within a country. For example, in one study (Van Ijzendoorn & Sagi, 1999), U.S. and Western European groups showed more avoidant infants than did groups from other regions. Still another perspective is related to the internal working models perspective described in Chapter 2. Young children's representations of the self and another person and their relationship could underlie the formation of later social relationships. As mentioned in Chapter 2, adults' memories of their own attachment as young children to their mothers fall into these same three categories and are related to how they treat their own infants. The initial attachment pattern sets in motion particular styles of thinking, feeling, and interacting that continue to influence the way children negotiate their environments throughout development. Attachment now is viewed as a lifelong process of forming affectionate bonds with various people (Ainsworth, 1989; Parkes, Stevenson-Hinde, & Marris, 1991).

■ *Peer Interaction*

Ethologists argue that children are innately predisposed toward interacting with other people in adaptive ways (Eibl-Eibesfeldt, 1989). Children's social interactions involve not only the family, especially the parents, but also the peer group. Ethological studies of animals' dominance hierarchies, aggression, play, altruistic behavior, and nonverbal communication led naturally to observations of these behaviors in groups of children in natural settings (Blurton-Jones, 1972; McGrew, 1972).

A basic feature of the organization of nonhuman primate groups is the *dominance hierarchy,* a pattern of social relationships related to the resolution of social conflict. It involves the distribution of power, especially access to resources such as food or mates, among group members by setting implicit "rules" as to who can control whom (Hinde, 1974). These dominance hierarchies also construct the social environment into which an infant is born. For example, in rhesus monkeys, which form large and complex social groups (troops), the matrilineal (mother's) dominance hierarchies affect the rank of the infant. All members of the highest-ranking matriline, even infants, outrank lower matrilines. Thus, a newborn "inherits" the status of the mother and outranks even adults of lower-ranking matrilines. Dominance hierarchies even affect how mothers treat their infants. High-ranking mothers are more "laissez-faire" in their supervision of their young than are low-ranking mothers. The latter are more limited in the social situations from which they can rescue their infants, so they are reluctant to let them explore much. Also, within each matriline, there is a clear hierarchy among females. Younger sisters outrank older sisters, even though the latter are much larger and stronger. Thus, mothers and the rest of the matriline give preference during sibling conflicts to younger sisters. This sibling hierarchy usually continues even after the sisters are fully grown. (See Sameroff & Suomi, 1996, for a review of this research.)

To illustrate ethologically oriented research on children's dominance hierarchies (see also Archer, 1992), we turn to a study by Strayer and Strayer (1976). They videotaped the free play of a group of preschool children toward the end of the school year, when the group had stabilized. The dominance relations could be inferred from the outcomes of three categories of naturally occurring social conflict between two children. These conflicts included physical attacks, threat gestures, and object or position struggles (physical or nonphysical struggles over a toy, standing at the front of the line, and the like). In response to these conflicts, a child could submit, seek help, counterattack, give up the object or position, or make no response. The child who wins in these encounters is considered to be the more dominant. These categories of initiated conflict and response to the conflict are quite similar to those used to study dominance in nonhuman primate groups. The analysis of the videotapes revealed a relatively rigid and stable dominance hierarchy in the group. Although boys initiated more conflict than did girls, boys were not higher in the hierarchy than girls overall. The fact that there were few counterattacks suggests that the stable dominance hierarchy minimizes group aggression, just as in nonhuman primate groups. Other research, in agreement with this argument, shows that conflicts are high among humans when groups first form, but then they drop drastically (Savin-Williams, 1976). Finally, research has suggested that boys' rough-and-tumble play may permit them to assess each other's relative strengths—one basis for dominance hierarchies—and to gain experience in dominant and subordinate roles (Biben, 1998; Pellegrini & Smith, 1998).

The Strayer and Strayer study reflects the ethological approach in its content (dominance hierarchies observed in animals), method (observation of behavior in its natural context and subsequent categorization of this behavior), and theory (emphasis on behaviors adaptive for the species). Ethologists have also studied peer interaction in play (Smith & Connolly, 1972) and children's appeasement behaviors, such as slumping the shoulders and bowing the head, which cause aggression to cease (Ginsburg, Pollman, & Wauson, 1977). The ethological approach clearly contrasts with social learning theory's focus on how a behavior (for example, aggression) in individual children is affected by reinforcement, punishment, and imitation. And, unlike Freud, ethologists focus on interpersonal processes more than individual psychological processes.

It may seem strange that researchers have shown more interest in negative, aggressive, power-oriented social relationships than positive, cohesive ones. Indeed, Strayer (1980), during a period of observation at a nursery school, saw fewer than 200 competitive or aggressive episodes in contrast to more than 1000 affiliative episodes. Sociobiologists have been interested in developing genetic models to outline a biological basis of altruistic behavior, in particular to show how self-sacrifice can be adaptive to the species. Moreover, some ethologists have argued that prosocial behaviors actually can be a form of competition for resources. In particular, when children enter grade school, they start rejecting dominant aggressive peers; most children learn that they must express dominance in more subtle ways in order to obtain resources—what Hawley (1999) calls "competing with finesse." Prosocial strategies such as persuasion, cooperation, and helping enable children to access resources such as toys or friends in ways that foster acceptance and maintain group harmony (see Hawley, 1999, for a review of developmental changes in strategies for obtaining resources). We now turn to recent evidence for this position.

At any phase in the life span it is adaptive to obtain resources from the environment. As Charlesworth expresses it:

> Whether it is an infant crying for attention, a preschooler struggling with a sibling over a toy, an adolescent trying to impress a peer, a graduate seeking a job, a scientist writing a grant proposal, or an octogenarian looking for someone to shovel snow, the possibility is always present of failing to acquire what one needs because of the competing needs of someone else. While all needs obviously do not have to be satisfied, a certain proportion of them must be if the individual is to carry out normal life functions.
>
> (1988, p. 24)

The task of obtaining resources changes developmentally. In most families infants need only signal their needs through crying or fussing in order to obtain resources. Later, during socialization, children acquire a variety of skills for obtaining resources—aggressing, lying, threatening, frightening, flattering, helping, sharing, and working together. Through experience, children learn which strategy is most effective in various situations. The types of resources that are most important also change developmentally. Charlesworth suggests that Erikson's eight developmental crises, or tasks, can be seen as changes in which resources are needed most critically—such as access to food and attention in infancy, materials and tools during grade school, and a mate during late adolescence.

Charlesworth (1988, 1996) studied the roles of cooperation and competition in establishing dominance and thereby obtaining resources in children age 4 to 8. He devised a situation in which four children attempted to obtain a resource—viewing a cartoon movie. One child could view the cartoon only if a second child turned on the movie light and a third turned a crank to start the movie. Thus, cooperation was necessary for anyone to see the cartoon. A fourth child had to simply be a bystander. From an analysis of the videotapes of the children's interaction, Charlesworth developed an observational scheme that categorized various types of resources, resource-acquisition behaviors, reactions to such behaviors, and outcomes of the interaction. Resource-acquisition behaviors included several types of verbal behaviors, such as requests, appeals to take turns, and threats, and several types of physical behaviors, such as touches, blocks, and attacks.

Using this ethological methodology, Charlesworth found that cooperative behavior led to inequitable outcomes for the children in the groups. By the end of 30 minutes, a few children saw some of the cartoons, but most did not. Some children were more skilled at obtaining resources than others. Successful children produced a mixture of assertive, selfish, deceptive, and cooperative behaviors. They somehow managed to get into the viewing position and then get others to turn on the light and crank the switch. That is, by engineering cooperation, they competed more successfully. For example, child A got child B to crank the switch but then looked at the cartoon longer. Child A also sometimes cleverly entertained the others, who could not see the cartoons, by narrating or acting out the cartoon events! The losers either did not detect the deception or inequity or were unwilling or unable to rectify it. Charlesworth has observed this pattern in all cultures studied thus far—American, Indian, Malaysian, and black South African—and thus argues for universality.

Dominance rank in the classroom, gender, age, and friendship predicted which children were most effective at obtaining resources. For example, high rank in the peer group enhanced a child's ability to get others to cooperate in ways that benefited the self. In addition, boys obtained more resources than did girls; boys used more physical behaviors than did girls, who used more verbal behaviors.

Ethology offers the intriguing notion that resources include not only materials and objects but also other people (MacDonald, 1998). From an evolutionary perspective, a child evaluates the resources to be gained from a peer—friendship, a play partner, cognitive stimulation. Popular children provide resources such as social status and the characteristics associated with it, such as friendliness, generosity, cheating, and helpfulness. As all the above programs of research show, ethology provides a powerful framework for understanding peer relations.

A final aspect of peer interaction is the maintenance of a preferred distance between the self and another person, just as birds on a wire keep a certain distance from one another. The desire to prevent another person from coming too close has been observed in many cultures, but the preferred distance may vary from culture to culture. One experiment (Barash, 1973) examined the response to violation of one's territory. A person sat down close to another person in a library with many empty seats. The latter person frequently turned away and sometimes built a barrier of books or other objects between the intruder and himself. The preferred distance may be related to the establishment of group territories. These territories are common in many animal species and serve to spread out the population to avoid starvation and overcrowding.

Problem Solving

I gather firewood
As if I had been at it
For a million years

—*Charlesworth,* One Year of Haiku, *1978*

Intelligence increases adaptation to the environment and therefore survival. As a result of evolution, the human brain is prepared for what is called an "evolutionarily expected environment." A species' cognitive system is designed to deal with a certain general type of environment, the type in which the species has evolved. What kinds of problems do children encounter in their daily lives and how do they solve them? In one ethologically oriented study, Charlesworth (1983) observed toddlers' responses to barriers (or "blocks") encountered in their everyday lives at home. Examples of these problems include being unable to reach a glass of juice (a physical block), being told by their mother to stop an activity (a social block), and being asked by someone to identify something (an informational block). In each case, the problem involves a relationship between the children and their environment. A block can come from outside of individuals or from individuals themselves—their need or desire for something unavailable. Charlesworth recorded all blocks to children's behavior and their response to each block, for example, compliance, ignoring, or hitting. The $3\frac{1}{2}$- to $4\frac{1}{2}$-year-olds, for example, encountered approximately 18 problems per hour and solved the problems 33 percent of the time. Many of the problem-solving episodes lasted several minutes. Social blocks occurred much more frequently than physical or informational blocks in these situations. It is therefore striking that solving social problems is not assessed to any extent on standard intelligence tests or on Piagetian cognitive tasks.

Charlesworth (1988) also has examined problem solving in a girl with Down syndrome and among preschoolers at nursery school in free play or instructional settings. In addition, he has documented the greater frequency of blocks, particularly informational and physical ones, among children with physical disabilities. These children interacted with the teachers more than did other children, who were involved in significantly more peer interaction. Finally, his ethological analysis included undergraduate honor students who faced blocks such as deciding what to wear in cold weather, running out of eggs for breakfast, having difficulty in finding library materials, being asked for advice by a friend, and forgetting how to make garlic bread.

The Charlesworth research illustrates the kind of information about cognition that we do not have from other current approaches to studying this topic. The intelligence-testing approach views intelligence as a trait or disposition that is revealed by certain tests administered by an adult, usually in a setting unfamiliar to the child. Laboratory studies of problem solving examine thinking out of context, usually about physical, nonsocial events. In contrast, Charlesworth's ethological research studies the function and ecological significance of the children's spontaneous use of their intelligence. This research tells us which features of everyday life pose problems, how children usually handle them, and how the children's reactions change developmentally. Such applications of intelligence in action help children adapt to the physical and social problems created by parents, peers, their own body, furniture, and toys in their environment.

Although Piaget's account of the sensorimotor period came from his observations of his own children, most of his information about children past infancy came from semistructured interviews. He had little concern with the frequency of occurrence of various categories of behavior because his focus was on the underlying knowledge structures. He also did not ask which kinds of everyday environmental circumstances require the use of such knowledge as conservation or transitive reasoning and whether these circumstances are more frequent at some developmental levels than at others. On the other hand, both Piagetian and ethological approaches are concerned with how an organism adapts to its environment. Both identify biological predispositions toward learning, for example, the assimilation–accommodation process (Piaget) and specialized learning abilities (ethology).

Recent Evolutionary Accounts of Development

One recent trend across developmental psychology is toward incorporating biological–evolutionary perspectives into accounts of development. In Chapter 4 we discussed Siegler's (1996) argument that strategy variability is adaptive for problem solving and that, after a process of competition, the most viable strategies prevail. Chapter 8 will present the *modularity nativist* and *biological constraints* arguments that infants are pretuned to process certain information in certain ways in certain areas. This view was stimulated in part by the recent findings of infant precocity in areas such as language, multimodal perception, and the perception of objects, causality, and animacy referred to in earlier chapters. These competencies appear so early and so easily that it is difficult to argue that they are acquired primarily through experience. They are the sorts of competencies that humans would be expected to have acquired during evolution.

Within neuroscience a sort of "neural Darwinism" (Edelman, 1987) proposes that during development competition among groups of neurons leads to the pruning away of certain neurons and the survival and enhancement of others. More generally, the current considerable interest in developmental neuroscience (Johnson, 1998), particularly brain development, is promoting a biological perspective on development (see Chapter 8).

Recent advances in developmental behavioral genetics and developmental psychobiology, along with the growing influence of person-in-context theories (Chapter 8), have stimulated developmentalists to construct more complex models of gene–environment interaction. These new models tend to emphasize bidirectionality—children actively select and change environments while environments are affecting them. The models give equal weight to contextual and genetic influences and include complex interactions among many levels from the level of protein production to the influence of the social environment. They tend to think in terms of holistic systems rather than take a reductionist stance A description of these models is beyond the scope of this book, but the reader is referred to the following sources: Gottlieb et al. (1998), Lerner (1991), Plomin (1998), and Scarr (1992, 1993). A main current issue in this area is to integrate the focus of developmental behavioral genetics on individual differences in the population with the focus of developmental psychobiology on development. Another main challenge is to integrate the mechanistic neuroscience approaches with the evolutionary and ecological study of primate behavior.

Other current evolutionary perspectives on development speculate about various aspects of social behavior. One is differences between males and females in their social behaviors, especially mating strategies and parenting behaviors, such as investment in their offspring (Bjorklund & Shackelford, 1999). Other behaviors for which evolutionary arguments have been made are male competition and violence; sex differences in play, risk taking, and the ability to inhibit behaviors; and parental investment in their children and child abuse (Bjorklund & Pellegrini, 2000).

Discussed below are three evolutionary perspectives currently influencing developmental psychology—cognitive evolutionary psychology, cultural transmission through social cognition, and cognitive immaturity. For additional research programs with evolutionary and biological frameworks, see various chapters in a volume edited by Langer and Killen (1998).

Cognitive Evolutionary Psychology ▪ The evolutionary perspective on cognition has had its impact mainly in recent years, though even Darwin (1890) studied the "mental power" of earthworms. Cognitive mechanisms may be the missing link between evolution and human behavior; that is, evolution may have led to changes in the brain, which changed thinking, which in turn changed behavior. Complex cognitive skills must have evolved to ensure finding a mate, hunting for food, recognizing group members, communicating with others, raising offspring, and cooperating for resources. The organism must attend to, encode, process, store, and access relevant information in order to survive and reproduce. In this way evolution would shape the neural mechanisms underlying cognition. That is, evolution selects for the psychological mechanisms that underlie adaptive social and cognitive behaviors. Cognition, then, serves to increase the chances of survival and reproduction. Thus, an evolutionary perspective is essential for understanding human cognition: "Understanding the process that designed the human mind will advance the discovery of its architecture" (Barkow, Cosmides, & Tooby, 1992, p. 3).

A subtle example of how cognition is critical for adaptation is that animals must cooperate with other members of their species in order to survive. It is important to be able to distinguish between individuals who share their genes (relatives) and those who do not. This requires complex cognitive skills such as remembering specific individuals and figuring out the costs and benefits of interacting with them, especially whether to risk one's life to help them. Cognitive skills also are necessary for group cooperative action, which is critical for gathering food, hunting, and warding off enemies.

Cosmides and Tooby (1987, 1992) are two of the main voices in this area. They have identified *Darwinian algorithms*—evolved cognitive mechanisms specific to particular domains. Each algorithm is "an expert in one area of interaction with the world" (Pinker, 1997, p. 21). The mind is like a Swiss army knife, with different tools for performing tasks well in different domains (Cosmides, 1994). Examples of these "core domains" are face recognition, language acquisition, certain characteristics of objects, and certain types of processing of social information. Infants are constrained (or, more positively, enabled) from acquiring and storing certain sorts of information needed for solving certain sorts of problems. Such behaviors bear some relation to fixed action patterns but are less tightly wired to particular stimuli; Darwinian algorithms are more flexible.

It is important to note that these cognitive skills enhanced adaptation for our ancestral hunters and gatherers: "Our psyche is not built for the present. It resonates to the vibrations of 200,000 generations ago" (Thiessen, 1996, p. 159). We do not do much hunting and gathering these days. Thus, the cognitive skills underlying these activities may not lead to survival and reproductive fitness in present-day humans, many of whom live in urban areas (for example, approximately three-fourths of the U.S. population). Still, we do have these ancestral ways of thinking that continue to influence our development and behavior in a world of shopping malls and computers, and the task of an evolutionary psychologist is to reveal how they are expressed in modern environments. One interesting hypothesis concerning the "modernization" of an ancestral cognitive module is that a module acquired to process information in one domain, such as the acoustical properties of the human voice, may be applied today to another domain, such as music. Music itself may not be essential for survival, but it may come from a module that is (Sperber, 1994).

Cultural Transmission, Social Cognition, and Theory of Mind ▪ Evolution often works in subtle ways. By giving humans the ability to acquire certain concepts, it can set the stage for the cultural transmission of knowledge needed for adaptation. In this sense, culturally based adaptation has a biological basis. Cultural change and transmission are particularly important because they can happen much more quickly than standard biological evolution. One recent version of this argument (Tomasello, 1999) focuses on *cultural transmission*, an evolved biological mechanism that enables an individual organism to take advantage of the knowledge and skills acquired over generations by the species. That is, adaptive cultural advances can accumulate over generations. For example, human children acquire the language and tools of their social group. Although young chimpanzees can communicate and learn how to use tools from the adults around them, Tomasello argues that only humans can engage in a cumulative process in which cultural products such as language and tool use develop over many generations. Later humans build on the knowledge of early humans. In this "ratchet effect" (Tomasello, Kruger, & Ratner 1993), social transmission of this knowledge through social learning serves as a ratchet that prevents slipping backward and losing the cultural knowledge. Thus, humans "are able to pool their cognitive resources in ways that other animal species are not" (Tomasello, 1999, p. 5). A simple example, based on evidence from artifacts, is that during human evolution hammers changed from simple stones to stones tied to sticks to modern metal hammers and mechanical hammers (Basalla, 1988).

Tomasello argues that humans have evolved one very special form of social cognition—the knowledge that other humans are like themselves, with intentional and mental properties. Inanimate objects do not have these properties. Once this social cognitive skill evolved, humans could "imagine themselves 'in the mental shoes' of some other person, so that they can learn not just *from* the other but *through* the other" (Tomasello 1999, p. 6). It is critical for children to understand this intentional aspect of others because it permits them to understand *why* others are using a tool or symbol—what the person intends to do with it. They can understand events from others' point of view. With this understanding, children can engage in a human-specific form of cultural learning. Consequently, humans can work together to create new knowledge about objects, quantities, tools, and social relations that cannot be created by a single individual. In the hammer example, humans were able to improve the tool because they understood what the purpose of the tool was (that is, what people *intended to do* with the hammer); they could go beyond simple imitation of someone using a particular type of hammer. Thus, Tomasello argues that a single evolved social cognitive ability permitted cumulative cultural transmission, which caused an explosion of rapid change in the human species that continues today. Indirectly, through this chain of events, a single unique product of evolution has led to modern humans, with all their wondrous positive and destructive knowledge and skills.

Newborns emerge into this situation. In a sense they encounter "ever-new artifacts and social practices which, at any one time, represent something resembling the entire collective wisdom of the entire social group throughout its entire cultural history" (Tomasello, 1999, p. 7). An infant can take advantage of the collective wisdom of the species and "participate in the collectivity known as human cognition, and so say (following Isaac Newton) that she sees as far as she does because she 'stands on the shoulders of giants'" (p. 8). In other words, children grow up surrounded by the very best tools and symbols that the species has developed. Much of development involves the internalization of these tools and symbols. Moreover, humans improve on these cognitive shoulders, and so the intergenerational cycle continues.

Young infants have come to experience themselves as intentional agents—they are trying to achieve some end, such as grasping a rattle just out of reach. Tomasello refers to the "9-month revolution" in which infants begin to understand others as intentional beings. They see others as similarly motivated by goals and thus begin to share attention, with other people, toward objects and events. They are sharing intentions as they are sharing attention. Consequently, they can begin to engage in cultural learning by imitating others. Later, this understanding of intentionality develops into the notion of the self as a mental agent with thoughts and beliefs that can differ from those of other people and from reality. This is, of course, the core notion in a theory of mind. This concept obviously sets in motion all sorts of useful further social and cognitive development, such as metacognition, self-regulation, and the construction of social relationships. Because of these species-specific social cognitive skills, throughout their development children engage in several types of cultural learning, including imitative learning, instructed learning, and collaborative learning (Tomasello et al., 1993).

In this process, language is particularly important. It transmits to young humans the ways of carving up the world into categories that have proved useful to the species. Another value of a language is that it assigns different words to a situation, thereby teaching children to represent a thing in multiple ways. Tomasello gives the example that a place can be labeled a "coast," "shore," "beach," or "sand," depending on the needs of a person and what he wishes to communicate. In addition to imparting this cognitive flexibility, language ensures that children engage in complex interactions with others that demand negotiation. These interchanges may lead to many useful social and cognitive developments, such as a more advanced theory of mind and the internalization of dialoguelike ways of thinking, described by Vygotsky (see Chapter 7).

Currently, a very active area of research among developmental comparative and evolutionary theorists concerns the similarities and differences between the social cognition of humans and that of other primates. There is considerable genetic similarity: chimpanzees and modern humans, for example, share approximately 99 percent of their genetic material, a proportion similar to that of species pairs such as lions and tigers or rats and mice (King & Wilson, 1975). Nonhuman primates clearly have certain humanlike cognitive and social skills. They can count, communicate, recognize themselves in a mirror, and understand object permanence. They also can deceive conspecifics (members of the same species), engage in pretense, and predict others' behavior on the basis of their emotional states and direction of locomotion. One example of deception is that chimpanzees learned to direct humans to a box without food so that the chimpanzees could obtain the one with food, although learning this took many trials with feedback (Woodruff & Premack, 1979). Also, chimpanzees have been observed pretending to pull an imaginary pull toy and even carefully disentangling the imaginary string (Hayes, 1951). Chimpanzees understand kinship and dominance relations, and they will select an appropriate ally, such as someone dominant over their opponent. Moreover, chimpanzees can be acculturated. Those raised by humans often show more humanlike linguistic and cognitive abilities than do mother-reared chimpanzees (Bjorklund, Bering, & Ragan, 1999; Call & Tomasello, 1996). Finally, monkeys can acquire new behaviors by imitating others. After receiving sweet potatoes, which were often sandy, one young monkey learned to wash them in sea water before eating them. Troop members imitated this and subsequently taught it to infants (Kawai, 1965).

As the above examples show, nonhuman primates clearly have some social understanding and engage in some sort of social learning. The issue is how how to interpret such examples. Tomasello concludes, after surveying the evidence (Tomasello & Call, 1997), that "nonhuman primates are themselves intentional and causal beings, they just do not understand the world in intentional and causal terms" (Tomasello, 1999, p. 19). They do not understand that there are underlying, unobservable physical and mental "forces" that mediate between an antecedent event and a consequent event. Only humans understand that the sharpness of a knife causes food to split in half or that another person reaches for an object because she desires it. Thus, only humans can engage in *cultural* learning. However, some investigators attribute a more advanced social cognition to nonhuman primates because of certain behaviors, such as deceiving conspecifics in order to obtain resources, and other sorts of creative intelligence that seem to reflect this understanding (Byrne, 1995).

A main forum for debates concerning the biological basis of social cognition is children's theory of mind—their understanding of the nature of mental states and activities such as desiring, representing, and believing. Research on biological contributions focuses on normal children versus autistic children and nonhuman primates (e.g., Baron-Cohen, 1995; Povinelli & Eddy, 1996; Whiten, 1998). This "mind-reading" skill clearly is fully developed only in normal humans and has obvious adaptive functions. The ability to interpret other people's behaviors by inferring the appropriate mental state is essential for predicting how someone else will treat oneself, for teaching the young, for engaging in cooperative activities with others, and so on. As discussed above, there is less agreement on whether chimpanzees engage in behaviors that reflect any understanding that people have beliefs (representations), especially ones that are false. Regarding people with autism, these children and adults have trouble interacting with other people. Consistent with this, they perform poorly on theory-of-mind tasks that most 4- and 5-year-olds have no trouble with, although they perform well on other, nonsocial tasks (Baron-Cohen, 1995). Children with mental retardation, such as from Down syndrome, do perform well on the theory-of-mind tasks. Thus, low general intelligence does not underlie the poor performance of autistic children on these tasks. The deficit is specific to the social–mental realm. This evidence taken together may point toward a specific biologically based ability to understand minds.

Advantages of Immaturity ▪ From an adult-centric view, children should show behaviors that are adaptive in that they prepare children for adulthood. Yet this may not be true. Some characteristics of infants and children may have evolved because they serve an adaptive function at a particular time in childhood. A case in point is certain reflexes, such as the grasping reflex, that are present in newborns but then disappear several months later after they have served their purpose of aiding survival during that particular period. Another example is the immaturity of young humans. As mentioned earlier, a general ability to learn is more useful to infants at that point in their development than a rigid set of fixed action patterns in response to sign stimuli. It is a risky strategy for the human species, because infants cannot obtain food or flee from enemies. Still, an extended childhood may be essential for learning all that is needed to survive to the age of reproduction in their particular complex and rapidly changing physical and social environment. For example, immaturity during childhood allows time for play. Although play probably has many functions, one may be to provide a sense of mastery and self-efficacy that encourages children to try out new activities and roles. These activities and roles provide opportunities for learning new skills.

This immaturity may play a more subtle role, however (Bjorklund, 1997; Bjorklund & Pellegrini, 2000). For example, young children have poor metacognition. As we saw in Chapter 4, they vastly overestimate how well they perform, even after feedback that they have performed poorly. More generally, until approximately age 7 children unrealistically think of themselves as "one of the smartest kids in my class" (Stipek, 1984). This seemingly nonadaptive characteristic may in fact be quite adaptive. This Pollyanna attitude may encourage them to keep trying to do activities that are beyond their current ability level. In this way they obtain valuable experiences that strengthen their skills. Because they do not expect to fail, they may not be afraid to try out a variety of new activities. Continuing to use strategies that do not yet help them—the utilization deficiency described in Chapter 4—may also reflect children's tendencies to not notice or to disregard negative feedback about their performance.

A particularly striking example of how an apparent deficit in young children actually may be an asset for adaptation in that particular developmental period is the notion of egocentrism, Piaget's concept discussed in Chapter 1. Children's bias toward perceiving and conceptualizing in terms of their own perspective obviously limits social understanding and interaction, but it may help them in other ways

(Bjorklund, 1997). Given that people tend to remember better when they relate the information to themselves (e.g., Pratkanis & Greenwald, 1985), egocentrism actually may help young children's recall.

Even toddlers' limited working-memory capacity can be seen as adaptive rather than as a liability (Bjorklund & Schwartz, 1996; Elman, 1994; Newport, 1991). Restricting how much language information can be processed simplifies the language corpus that is analyzed, and this in turn simplifies the process of acquiring language. Children first may acquire single syllables and then gradually deal with more information and increasingly complex information. If children could initially process more linguistic information, they might be overwhelmed by the amount of information and not be able to extract anything useful. In this case, less is more (Newport, 1991).

It is interesting that a connectionist simulation (see Chapter 4) appears to follow the same principle—"the importance of starting small" (Elman, 1994). Elman found that the connectionist network did not acquire a grammatical rule (subject–verb agreement for number) when the initial set of examples was a large corpus of sentences. Only after simplifying the corpus and then gradually introducing complexity did the network learn. Similarly, beginning with a small working memory and then gradually increasing it permitted the network to learn from a corpus of simple and complex sentences. In both cases, initial limitations (in the corpus or working memory) made language learning possible.

Thus, Bjorklund's evolutionary approach leads us to ask certain questions that other approaches do not. Specifically, although certain attributes of young children are nonadaptive in some ways, an evolutionary psychologist would ask whether these attributes might in fact also be adaptive in some way. We tend to see young children's apparent limitations as evidence that they are less advanced than older children and adults. Yet they may be quite well adapted to the demands of the particular developmental period. Bjorklund's argument reminds us that how we view development affects how we see children develop: Do we accentuate the positive or the negative?

MECHANISMS OF DEVELOPMENT

Because ethologists have chosen to focus on behaviors with a strong biological component, they stress biological processes as mechanisms of development. Physical maturation, including hormonal changes, locomotor development, and increased efficiency of the nervous system, underlies the emergence of sensitive periods or of fixed action patterns at appropriate times. For example, nest-building behavior surfaces when a bird matures to the point where reproduction is possible. All of the biological mechanisms of behavior interact with experience, of course. In addition, innate general and specific learning abilities built into the nervous system allow the organism to profit from its experience.

Although ethologists emphasize biological mechanisms, they also study learned behaviors that lead to adaptation. For example, even if it turns out that dominance hierarchies and altruism in children are entirely learned, such behavior patterns are still of interest because they lead to a socially cohesive group, which is considered an adaptive system.

POSITION ON DEVELOPMENTAL ISSUES

Human Nature

Human nature is just one hodgepodge out of many conceivable.

—WILSON, 1978, p. 23

Humans are social animals with certain species-specific characteristics. They are biological organisms that have evolved within a particular environmental niche. Human intelligence, language, social attachment, and perhaps even aggression and altruism are part of human nature because they serve or once served a purpose in the struggle of the species to survive. Children's developmental level, therefore, is defined mainly in terms of the biologically based behaviors they possess.

Identifying the theory's world view highlights the differences among ethological theorists. Lorenz stressed the mechanistic, automatic, elicited nature of behavior, such as sign stimuli that elicit fixed action patterns. He drew loosely on the reflex model and the hydraulic or "flush toilet" model (Dewsbury, 1978). Sign stimuli, fixed action patterns, and reflexes were hallmarks of the reflex, mechanistic, stimulus–response model, based on early views of how the nervous system operates. In contrast, Bowlby and many modern ethological theorists are more organismic. Humans spontaneously act to meet the demands of their environment. They actively search for the parent, food, or a mate. Children explore, play, solve problems, and seek out playmates. In Bowlby's control-systems approach, an infant seeks to maintain a certain state, for example, an acceptable degree of proximity to the caretaker. Finally, the theory is contextual in its focus on the links between the species' distant evolutionary history and the present and on the nature of the organism's immediate physical and social setting, to which it must adapt.

Qualitative Versus Quantitative Development

Ethology allows for both qualitative and quantitative change. It is not a stage theory and therefore does not posit large-scale qualitative changes in development. In a sense, there is qualitative change when biological maturation proceeds to the point where a sign stimulus triggers a fixed action pattern that has never appeared before. In this way, a new behavior appears in a more or less discontinuous fashion. Qualitative change also occurs when a system is expressed in different behaviors as the child develops. One such instance is attachment, the desire for which is expressed at first by crying or smiling and later by crawling toward the mother or talking to her. The underlying attachment, however, is changing quantitatively, usually toward increased organization, security, and efficiency.

Nature Versus Nurture

Although ethologists focus on the biological basis of behavior, like most of the theorists in this volume they are interactionists with respect to the effects of heredity and environment. The genotype and the environment operate together to produce changes in children over their lifetime. One implication of this interaction is that a particular experience has more impact if it occurs during a relevant sensitive period rather than at another time. Moreover, a given genotype is expressed differently in different environments. Also, one way to think about the importance of the environment is to note that it selects for or against genetic mutations that occur.

To complicate matters even more, genotypes influence what sorts of environments people select; children seek environments that are compatible with their genotype. These selected environments in turn affect the expression of the genotype and also define the nature of the settings to which people must adapt. Still, many behaviors are similar within a species because its members tend to have similar environments. In a sense, children inherit not only genes but also the "expectable" environment within which the species evolved that particular set of genes. It is the fit between the genes and a particular environment that is adaptive, not just the genes themselves. For example, ducklings still in the egg who are prevented from hearing both their mother's vocalizations and their own cannot recognize the call of their own species after birth (Gottlieb, 1976, 1991, cited by Bjorklund, 2000a). Ducklings with normal rearing can recognize the species' call because they inherit not only a genetic predisposition to do so but also the environment typical for their species, which provides the relevant experiences for expressing this predisposition.

Evolutionary theories' emphasis on the biological adaptiveness of human traits does not mean that the current human situation is "natural" and thus should be retained. Evolved human traits are not necessarily *ideal* adaptations. They are simply the best that the species could do, given what it had to work with.

■ *What Develops*

The most important behaviors to develop are species-specific behaviors that are essential for survival. These include such behaviors as social attachment, dominance–submission, eating, mating, social cognition, and infant care. Both general abilities to learn or process information and specific behaviors such as fixed action patterns or domain-specific cognitive algorithms are applied to the environment at hand. The theory seeks to explain similarities in what behaviors are acquired and how they develop in all humans and in both humans and other animals. The focus has been on what is universal for a particular species. Although interspecies differences in development are of interest, little attention is given to individual differences within a species. Phylogenetic outcomes constrain the range of possible differences between cultures or within a culture.

APPLICATIONS

Ethological work on attachment has had the most impact on real-life topics such as orphanages, adoption, day care, prolonged separation from the mother, and early contact between mother and child. Bowlby found pathological behaviors in children when they did not receive adequate attention from a caretaker early in life. Contemporary attachment research has identified lifelong relationship problems stemming from disordered early relations between mother and child. A main implication for parents is to respond promptly and appropriately when infants signal their needs. For a securely attached child, a parent serves as a safe base from which to explore the environment and establish independence. Parents should be sensitive to their children's emotional needs during separation caused by hospitalization or other events.

Charlesworth's work on children's strategies for obtaining resources provides a new perspective for thinking about children who have mental or physical limitations or who come from physically or psychologically impoverished environments. Such children may be at a disadvantage in obtaining the resources necessary for satisfactory development.

EVALUATION OF THE THEORY

Strengths

Both realized and potential contributions of ethology to developmental psychology are explored in three areas: theory, method, and content.

Theoretical Contributions ■ Ethology broadens our perspective on what constitutes an explanation of development. We can fully understand the child's behavior only if we expand our vision to include a larger space (the larger social context) and a larger time span (the history of the species). Tinbergen (1973) has identified four types of questions about the causes of behavior that developmentalists should try to answer about their topic of study. The questions are based in part on the time span involved, which varies from seconds to centuries. These "four whys" pertain to causes that are immediate, ontogenetic, functional, and phylogenetic.

1 *Immediate* causes are the antecedent external or internal events that come directly before the behavior. An infant smiles after viewing a human face or cries as a result of hunger pangs. Physiologically based motivation states are common immediate causes.

2 *Ontogenetic* causes encompass a longer time span—the genotype and the environment interact to produce changes in behavior over the child's lifetime. In this process, earlier events contribute to

later events, as when a secure attachment may later on allow the child to explore new environments confidently and even later encourage various independent behaviors.

3 *Functional* causes involve the immediate adaptive value of a behavior. An ethologist asks, "What is this behavior trying to achieve?" Children behave in certain ways in order to obtain food, protection, desired resources, and so on.

4 In *phylogenetic* causation, the cause of a behavior lies in the earlier forms of the behavior as it was shaped over generations as a result of the food supply, types of predators, mating patterns, and so on. Thus, a developmental psychologist seeking a phylogenetic cause of sex differences in behavior would consider environmental pressures in the early history of the human species.

Most developmental research has examined immediate causes or ontogenetic causes rather than phylogenetic causes or the behavior's functions (immediate function or survival value). Development cannot be completely understood, however, until researchers identify all these functions and causes. With the exception of Gibson, socioculturalists, and person-in-context approaches (see Chapter 8), most theories either have ignored the larger context of behavior or have simply acknowledged its influence but have not studied it. Piaget was concerned with adaptation to the environment but did not link it to evolutionary processes.

Related to the notion that there are various valid types of causes is the belief that there must be various levels of analysis of behavior. The organism, with its genetic, physiological, psychological, and behavioral aspects, is part of a system that includes the environment, with its physical, interpersonal, and cultural aspects (Hinde, 1992). Therefore, ethologists study each of these levels and their interaction, with the ultimate aim of understanding the entire organism–environment system. Each level of analysis contributes to our understanding of behavior and has its own set of principles. Behavior can never be reduced to any single level, such as the physiological. Only a theory with multiple levels of analysis is likely to disentangle the complex interweaving of innate and environmental forces during development. Although human developmental research currently proceeds at all these levels, progress at relating the various levels has been very slow. Ethological principles, because they concern many levels and their interrelationships, are potentially a unifying force in developmental psychology.

Ethology's focus on the function of behavior helps the investigator relate a child's behavior to its natural context. The way that investigators think about children's aggressive behavior changes if they discover that one of its functions is to increase the overall stability and cohesiveness of the group. The focus changes from a problem in the child to a feature of human groups. Thus, looking at function gives a broader context in which to embed a particular behavior.

Questions about function usually lead to questions about adaptation. Eibl-Eibesfeldt (1975) argues that ethology can fruitfully study cultural adaptation as well as the biologically based phylogenetic adaptation that is the theoretical core of ethology. Most human behaviors are not a matter of life and death. Few behaviors of the human child literally and directly avoid predators or avert starvation or exposure. Moreover, today infants with mental disabilities, poor health, or physical disabilities may survive and reproduce. In short, many of the evolutionary forces that operate on other species are less influential for human survival. Thus, the notion of adaptation in humans may be most fruitfully applied to the question of how behaviors taught by a society produce *optimal adaptation* (rather than biological survival). Optimal adaptation might include happiness, a feeling of competence at play, success at school, efficient use of tools (for example, eating utensils, scissors, and pencils), and so on. When Charlesworth studied how children solve problems, he did not see mistakes and inefficient problem solving leading to death and success leading to survival. He did, however, see how infants, by applying their intelligence, increase their control over their physical and social environment. If ritualistic behaviors, such as greeting, giving gifts, and communicating dominance or submission to others, lead to a more stable group, they are of interest to ethologists even if they turn out to be culturally based rather than biologically controlled adaptations. As these examples illustrate, looking at phylogenetic adaptation in other species can suggest hypotheses about cultural adaptation in humans.

Methodological Contributions ■ What can we learn from scientists who spend hours staring at crabs and birds? The most timely contribution of ethology is its method of observing behavior in its natural context. As Charlesworth commented, "the lab coat and microscope used to isolate biological variables to generate universal principles are no more important to acquiring understanding of the biological nature of human development than walking shoes and a clipboard used to discover organism–environment connections to identify significant individual differences in adaptation" (1992, p. 13). The field of developmental psychology has slighted its natural-history phase, which would have established a database. It has been suggested that the field moved too quickly into its experimental phase. Bronfenbrenner characterized much of developmental psychology as the "science of the strange behavior of children in strange situations with strange adults for the briefest possible periods of time" (1977, p. 513). Ethology can play a heuristic role in the field's relatively new interest in ecology. Although it certainly is not new for developmental psychologists to observe children at school or at home (for example, Barker & Wright, 1955), ethology provides *theoretically based* observational methods that supplement the more common empirical, atheoretical descriptions of ongoing behavior. Ethology suggests which behaviors are most important, stresses the need to note what environmental events precede and follow the behavior, and provides a detailed analysis of how the organism and environment interact. Such an analysis can show exactly how infants and their parents control and modify each other's behavior. It also describes the structure of the behavior and suggests how behaviors can be classified and compared with other species, cultures, or ages. In addition, federal social policy relevant to children badly needs a description of the present environments of children and an understanding of how these environments enhance or disrupt development.

Ethological observations of, for example, everyday problem solving can fruitfully be combined with traditional developmental laboratory methods and intelligence tests. Developmental psychologists, particularly those studying cognition during childhood, have relied too heavily on the questioning of children. As Charlesworth comments, "As soon as a research subject has the appropriate Piagetian operations and can talk, researchers stop observing and start asking. It's less strenuous that way" (1988, p. 298). Ethological observation could reveal how children vary in the form of a behavior, its time of acquisition, and its frequency. Another possibility, largely untapped, is ethologically based longitudinal research, in which the same children are observed over a period of months or years. This method could identify continuities and discontinuities not only in the child's behavior—the usual focus of longitudinal studies—but also in the child's environment and the interaction between the child and the environment. Ethology includes a changing physical and social world as well as a changing child in its account of development. The social environment changes its demands on the child during development, and the frequency of certain child behaviors changes.

The criticism in Chapter 4 that information processing is decontextualized points to the need for observational studies of cognitive and perceptual development. As an illustration, consider what ethologically oriented observational studies might contribute to the understanding of the development of attention. Developmental psychologists nearly always examine attention in the laboratory. They typically examine infants' preferences for attending to one of two stimuli placed in front of them or older children's attention to physical attributes, such as shape, color, or size. The child looks preferentially at one object rather than another, sorts the objects, or tries to remember them. An ethologist, in contrast, would ask the following questions: What types of objects or events does the child look at or listen to at home and at school? What events elicit attention, maintain it, and end it? What events distract the child? How often do distractions occur? Does efficient attention lead to efficient problem solving or other adaptive behaviors? How does attentional behavior differ from setting to setting? Does playful, exploratory attention resemble that observed in other primates, humans of other ages, and other cultures? We know, for example, that ethologists sometimes can infer the dominance hierarchy from who looks at whom and for how long.

Such questions are seldom, if ever, raised in studies of attention. The questions about how attention actually operates cause a shift in focus that makes previous research appear narrow and stripped of context. Paralleling Charlesworth's ethological studies of intelligence, it is likely that many distractions and other events controlling attention are social and dynamic, rather than nonsocial and static, as is assumed by laboratory researchers. Laboratory studies tell us what *can* happen during the attentional process. Ethological studies tell us what in fact usually *does* happen and what function the behavior has. Such studies suggest new variables to be examined in depth in the laboratory. In a similar way, ethological methods could be applied fruitfully to the other theories examined in this volume. We know little about the natural context of the spontaneous occurrence of defense mechanisms, mathematical reasoning, memory strategies, visual search for objects, and operant conditioning. A final example is the recent work on children's theory of mind. Although we now know a great deal about children's developing understanding of the mind, we are only beginning to study how they actually use this knowledge in their daily lives to function effectively in their social environment.

Content Contributions ▪ Ethology has influenced developmental psychology by bringing certain content areas to the attention of investigators. Bowlby's ethological account of attachment challenged learning theory and stimulated hundreds of studies not only of attachment but also of such related topics as sensitive periods and later social competencies, self-concept, and theory of mind. Also, ethology brought new life to research on peer interaction (for example, dominance hierarchies). In addition, ethology pointed out overlooked behavior such as averting one's gaze, hunching one's shoulders, sticking out one's tongue, and regulating the distance between the self and the mother. More distant causes that developmentalists have begun to examine include the evolution of self-knowledge and deception and the development of reproductive strategies (Bjorklund & Pellegrini, 2000). Finally, evolutionary approaches are aware of the importance of kinship relations, while experimental developmental psychology gives little attention to this social structure other than parent–child and, occasionally, sibling relations.

▪ *Weaknesses*

The following are critical shortcomings in theoretical, methodological, and substantive areas that must be addressed by ethological theory if it is to fulfill its promise as a theory of development. Some of these shortcomings merely reflect a lack of developmental research in certain areas; others are more serious because they reflect the incompleteness of the theory itself.

Theoretical Limitations ▪ As is true of other theories, ethology describes more than it explains. Many of the ethological notions that are most useful to developmental psychology require further elaboration if they are to serve as specific explanations of development. For example, concluding that children acquire a behavior "because" they are in a sensitive period is similar to concluding that they acquire conservation because they are in the stage of concrete operations. These general descriptive notions are only a first step. Invoking a sensitive period does not explain why the organism is pretuned to certain experiences at one time rather than another. A sensitive period must be understood not as a particular period of time but as a particular developmental level. A developmental level is a specific organization of capabilities that allows the child to interact with the environment in certain ways but not other ways. We need to be able to specify in a detailed way the exact process by which sensitive periods operate. What causes them to begin, have their effect, and end? More generally, what moves development along? Are the effects of extra contact between mother and infant in the first few hours after birth due to biological, perceptual, or cognitive variables or all these variables in interaction?

The lack of detailed explanation also can be seen in an example drawn from a typical topic of ethological research: the dominance structure of peer groups. By what process do children detect and understand the existence of this hierarchy and their own place in it? How do they use feedback from their interactions with other children in order to adjust their subsequent behavior? For example, the development of transitive reasoning ($A > B > C$ . . .) may be related to the perception of the dominance hierarchy in groups (Edelman & Omark, 1973). Since most human behavior is cognitively mediated, we need an account of the cognitive processes involved when social cues in the environment are interpreted and influence subsequent social behavior. In other words, how is information about the environment assimilated and linked up with behavior?

Similarly, in the area of attachment, there are no clear theoretical predictions as to what specific aspects of a secure or insecure attachment should predict what specific future social competencies. For example, "It is as important to determine what a secure attachment does *not* predict to, and why, as it is to understand its network of predictable consequences" (Thompson, 1998, p. 48). If it is true that different attachment patterns are adaptive for different environmental situations, then the expected long-term outcomes of each attachment type are less than obvious. Moreover, the specific mechanisms by which a child's early attachment leads to a particular set of outcomes need to be specified in more detail.

Another problem concerns identifying the function of a behavior. The phylogeny of anatomical structures can be gleaned from fossils, but we have no fossils of human behavior. At best we can examine other primates, contemporary hunter-gatherers, skulls, and archeological data such as diseases, housing, social structure, age distributions, and tools. We can speculate about how an upright stance, enlarged brain area, and increasingly sophisticated tools reflect changes in human behavior in our history. We can hypothesize what sorts of cognitive demands were made on early hunters and gatherers and the extent to which these demands are similar to or differ from those in modern human environments. What was adaptive generations ago may not be adaptive today, however.

To add a further complication, since the selection pressures differ at different ages, it is necessary to infer the adaptation for a particular developmental period. That is, one must make comparisons between human ancestral infancy and current infancy, between ancestral childhood and current childhood, and so on. It has been argued (Bjorklund & Pellegrini, 2000; Geary, 1995) that differences in ancestral and current environments may explain why some children have trouble adjusting to certain aspects of formal schooling that are not "natural," such as reading and higher mathematics. Some (Jensen et al., 1997) have even proposed that attention-deficit / hyperactivity disorder (ADHD) may consist of tendencies that were adaptive in early humans. Rapid scanning, quick responses, and high motor activity work better for monitoring threats and escaping from enemies than for reading and concentrating on homework.

Another problem with identifying a behavior's function is that the behavior may have a delayed function that cannot be validated until much later. For example, one function of attachment is to establish the mother as a secure base for the child's exploration later on. Moreover, the function of a behavior may be far from obvious. "Morning sickness" and the food aversions associated with it during early pregnancy may protect the fetus from toxic foods at a time when it is most vulnerable (Profet, 1992). Food aversions are most common for foods high in toxins. Moreover, women who have morning sickness have fewer spontaneous abortions than do pregnant women who do not (Weigel & Weigel, 1989).

It is important to note that not all behaviors are the result of evolution, and thus not all behaviors aid survival. A behavior may be an expression of some adapted cognitive mechanism that in fact did evolve, as in the example of music from a linguistic–acoustic processing module mentioned earlier. Or the behavior may have co-occurred with another behavior that was adaptive. As long as it did not hinder survival, it would continue to be transmitted across generations. Moreover, some characteristics that humans have retained during evolution because they held benefits also have certain costs. A cognitively flexible infant is also an at-risk organism because of reliance on adults. It is believed that benefits must outweigh costs in order for such characteristics to be retained.

Methodological Limitations ▪ One obvious limitation to applying ethological methods to humans is that the most critical experiments are unethical. We cannot perform deprivation experiments such as preventing an infant from seeing a human smile for the first few weeks of life in order to see if the social smile is innate. In an early misguided experiment, Frederick II (1194–1250) raised babies in silence and near isolation to find out if there is a "natural" human language. The babies, not surprisingly, died before the outcome was clear (Wallbank & Taylor, 1960). Instead of deprivation experiments, we must rely on naturally occurring deprivation, such as infants born blind or deaf, or maternal absence during early infancy. Bowlby's hypothesis concerning the effects of disrupting the early bond between mother and infant cannot be evaluated adequately because this event is confounded with changes in the organization of the entire family, economic changes within the family, changes in the father's behavior, the mother's detachment from the infant when she returns because she has changed during her long illness, and so on. For ethical reasons the necessary experimental manipulations cannot be performed.

Another limitation to applying the methods of ethology lies in three basic problems inherent in observational research. First, it is difficult, often tedious, research to do. One must invest large amounts of time and effort in videotaping, making detailed descriptions of the behavior, classifying the behavior, and establishing adequate interobserver reliability as to when the behavior begins and ends and how it should be classified (for example, as fear). Furthermore, it may be necessary to observe children in many different settings to obtain a description of typical behavior because it is not clear what constitutes a "natural environment" for children in a highly technological society. Should we study children running through a meadow, sitting in a classroom, or playing electronic games? Finally, so many events may be occurring simultaneously that not all the behaviors can be attended to and recorded. Even taping may miss certain important behaviors, such as facial expressions. In short, a comprehensive, detailed ethogram of a species is a large undertaking. As Charlesworth notes, "Unlike most tests, which throw out a small net with a small mesh, the present method throws out a big net with a small mesh and thereby catches many small fish. Herein, of course, lies a big problem of effort and cost. The net gets awfully heavy very quickly" (1979, p. 522).

A second problem with applying the observational method is that with humans there is a danger that the very presence of the observer changes the child's behavior. This is less of a problem when children are involved in group activities of interest to them and have become used to the observer's presence.

Third, there are conceptual problems in dividing the stream of behavior into units. It is not always clear what behaviors are relevant. An observer unfamiliar with Bowlby's work might well record that the infant crawled to the door of the adjoining room but would probably not record the distance between the mother and the infant. If one is interested in dependency behaviors, does one include touching others, looking at others, or asking for help? A related problem is that many behaviors have multiple meanings. When one child hits another child, this behavior may function as a sign of aggression or affection or playfulness.

Content Limitations ■ Certain psychological phenomena that are not consistently reflected in spontaneous behavior may not be easily studied from the ethological perspective. Charlesworth found it necessary to limit his investigation of problem solving to overt behaviors, such as removing a physical barrier blocking a desired object. Since behavior becomes more mediated and motivation becomes more complex with increasing age, observation of overt behavior may in general be more informative in infants and toddlers than in older children.

SUMMARY

Ethology, along with other evolutionary perspectives, is one of zoology's main contributions to developmental psychology. Thousands of hours spent observing animals have revealed important concepts concerning behavior. Each species, including humans, has a set of innate behaviors, specific to that species. These behaviors have evolved phylogenetically because they have increased that species' chances of survival in its particular environment. Some of the most important behaviors are social, such as mating dances, imprinting, dominance behaviors, and some forms of communication. Of particular interest are fixed action patterns elicited by sign stimuli. Even learned behaviors have a strong genetic component because each species has particular learning predispositions in the form of sensitive periods or general and specific learning abilities. Ethologists study behaviors by conducting both observations in natural settings and experimental studies in laboratories.

The ethological point of view has most influenced developmental psychology by stimulating work on attachment. There is some evidence that the very young infant and the adult are pretuned to respond to each other. This work has expanded to include the long-term effects of each pattern of attachment, individual differences, the role of fathers, bonding in newborns, and other social and social cognitive behaviors. Observation of dominance hierarchies in mammals and other animals has led to studies of the human peer group, especially in preschool groups. Investigators also have asked what kinds of problems children attempt to solve and how they try to solve them in natural settings. Main examples of contemporary developmental approaches are cognitive evolutionary psychology, the adaptive advantages of immaturity, and the biological basis of cultural transmission, especially regarding social cognition and theory of mind.

With respect to developmental issues, ethologists see humans as a species that has evolved in order to survive within a particular environmental niche. Theorists vary in whether this adaptation is primarily passive, in response to drives or sign stimuli, or active and self-regulating. Behavior changes both quantitatively and qualitatively as innate and environmental factors interact during development. The result is an organism that can operate efficiently within its environment.

Ethology has several strengths to offer the current field of developmental psychology. With respect to theory, it provides a broad evolutionary perspective on behavior that has encouraged investigators to look at the function of children's behaviors. Ethologists advocate more observational studies of children in natural settings in order to determine the function of particular behaviors. A final contribution is the identification of several content areas as particularly important in development, such as dominance hierarchies, attachment, and cognition.

Ethology has certain weaknesses, however, that limit its usefulness for developmental psychology. Its theoretical notions, such as sensitive periods, have not yet reached an explanatory level. With respect to methodology, the observational method poses difficulties, and deprivation experiments are not possible with humans. Finally, ethologists find it difficult to study certain aspects of development, such as language and abstract thought in older children.

In conclusion, ethology is a fruitful source of working hypotheses about what behaviors are important and why they are acquired. An ethological attitude opens the investigator's eyes to a broad context that spans space and time and various levels of analysis. In particular, ethologically based observations in the early phases of a research project can give the "big picture" of the behavior that will later be studied in a controlled laboratory setting.

SUGGESTED READINGS

The following readings survey evolutionary, including ethological, research on humans and animals:

Eibl-Eibesfeldt, I. (1989). *Human ethology*. New York: Aldine de Gruyter. This 848-page book provides a comprehensive journey, with many photographs, through work on human ethology. Much research on children is included.

Bjorklund, D. F., & Pelligrini, A. D. (2000). Child development and evolutionary psychology. *Child Development, 71,* 1687–1708.

Smith, P. K. (1990). Ethology, sociobiology and developmental psychology: In memory of Niko Tinbergen and Konrad Lorenz. *British Journal of Developmental Psychology*, *8*, 187–200. Smith presents an interesting historical account of the main leaders and ideas in ethology.

The following works focus on attachment:

Ainsworth, M. D. S., & Bowlby, J. (1991). An ethological approach to personality development. *American Psychologist*, *46*, 333–341. In this interesting article the authors provide a historical account of their research and theorizing on attachment.

Bowlby, J. (1982). *Attachment and loss: Vol. 1. Attachment* (2nd ed.). New York: Basic Books. This classic work is Bowlby's influential statement about attachment.

Cassidy, J., & Shaver, P. R. (Eds.). (1999). *Handbook of attachment*. New York: Guilford Press.

The chapter cited below describes contemporary models of genetic and environmental interactions during development:

Gottlieb, G., Wahlsten, D., & Lickliter, R. (1998). The significance of biology for human development: A developmental psychobiological systems view. In W. Damon (Series Ed.) & R. M. Lerner (Vol. Ed.), *Handbook of child psychology: Vol. 1. Theoretical models of human development* (5th ed., pp. 233–273). New York: Wiley.

Lorenz delights us with this account of his life with animals:

Lorenz, K. Z. (1952). *King Solomon's ring*. New York: Crowell.

CHAPTER 6

Gibson's Ecological Theory of Perceptual Development

We tested 36 infants ranging in age from 6 months to 14 months on the visual cliff. Each child was placed upon the center board, and his mother called him to her from the cliff side and the shallow side successively. All of the 27 infants who moved off the board crawled out on the shallow side at least once; only three of them crept off the brink onto the glass suspended above the pattern on the floor. Many of the infants crawled away from the mother when she called to them from the cliff side; others cried when she stood there, because they could not come to her without crossing an apparent chasm. The experiment thus demonstrated that most human infants can discriminate depth as soon as they can crawl.

— *Gibson & Walk, 1960, p. 64*

On uphill trials [on slopes in a laboratory] infants often attempted hills where they were likely to fall, despite falling on previous trials and in previous sessions. Crawlers usually struggled at the base of impossibly steep slopes for the entire duration of the trial, sometimes getting partway up, then sliding back down. After lengthy frustrated attempts, they tried equally hard moments later at the next impossibly steep slope. Walkers usually adopted a similar strategy, getting a running headstart on two feet and flinging themselves at impossibly steep inclines. Sometimes persistence paid off and infants eventually reached the summit.

— *Adolph & Eppler, 1999, p. 40*

Childhood is a time of perceptual discovery. Children look at and explore the wondrous objects, events, and surfaces in the environment occupied by the human species and thus learn what they can do in the world. They perceive faces to smile at, hills to climb, approaching objects to avoid, words to respond to, seashells to play with, and flowers to sniff. Although such discovery is exciting in itself, it also permits adaptation to this environment. Children are information "hunters and gatherers" trying to survive in an information-heavy world. Eleanor Gibson's focus on the importance of perception for adaptation makes this chapter a natural sequel to the previous one, on ethology. Gibson has taken on a question largely ignored by other theorists we have met: How do we learn to perceive our world? Surely this is a basic task of development. Gibson's answer to this question is that children learn to detect information that specifies objects, events, and layouts in the world that they can use for their daily activities.

The organization of this chapter is as follows: First is a biographical sketch, followed by a general orientation to the theory, and then a description of main developmental trends. A section on contemporary research on topics in infants' perceptual learning is followed by sections on mechanisms of development, the theory's position on developmental issues, applications, and an evaluation.

BIOGRAPHICAL SKETCH

Eleanor J. Gibson's studies in psychology began at Smith College, from which she graduated in 1931. She then stayed on as a teaching assistant and married a young faculty member, James Gibson, who also was to become an eminent psychologist. She earned her master's degree with a thesis on learning in 1933. Subsequently, she became an instructor at Smith and attended the Gestaltist Kurt Koffka's lectures regularly. Gibson moved on to Yale, hoping to study animal behavior, but instead studied people. In 1938, she obtained a Ph.D. under Clark Hull, the great learning theorist, at Yale. Gibson, however, did not feel intellectually comfortable in the stimulus–response learning climate of Yale. Her husband's relocation for military service during World War II temporarily interrupted her career. After the war, the Gibsons returned to Smith and later went to Cornell, where she became a research associate. They then spent their careers developing an ecological approach to perception.

Gibson's work in the 1950s and 1960s developed the new fields of perceptual learning and perceptual development. At Cornell she studied goats and sheep at the "Behavior Farm," babies on "visual cliffs," and children in reading-related situations in the laboratory. She became a professor at Cornell in 1966. Her book *Principles of Perceptual Learning and Development* (1969),which won the Century psychology prize, was hailed as one of the most influential books on development at that time (Hartup & Yonas, 1971). Her theory provided an alternative to learning theory and Piagetian approaches. In the next decade, she continued her wide-ranging research but turned her attention more and more to how children learn to read. Some of this work is summarized in *The Psychology of Reading* (1975), coauthored with Harry Levin. She then returned to infancy, to study early perceptual development. Cornell honored her with an appointment as the Susan Linn Sage Professor Emeritus of Psychology. Years after her "retirement," she continues her research and writing, and recently published *An Ecological Approach to Perceptual Learning and Development* (2000) with Anne Pick.

Her profession has awarded Gibson many honors, including the Gold Medal Award and the Distinguished Scientific Contribution Award from the American Psychological Association, the Howard Crosby Warren Medal from the Society of Experimental Psychologists, and the National Medal of Science. In addition, she was elected to the National Academy of Sciences, the American Academy of Arts and Sciences, and the National Academy of Education.

GENERAL ORIENTATION TO THE THEORY

Gibson's theory concerns perception, broadly defined. She asks four questions (Gibson & Pick, 2000): What do children perceive? How do they pick up this information? What actions or interactions take place? What are the consequences for knowledge? The following three sections examine characteristics of the theory that show how Gibson addresses these questions: the ecological approach, the notion that information for perception is specified in stimulation, and the active nature of human perceivers. The final section in this orientation examines her use of experimental methods that simulate natural environments.

■ *Ecological Approach: Affordances*

Only a theorist with an ecological perspective would ask Gibson's four questions because the questions address the function of perception in real settings. People need to perceive objects, spatial layouts such as floors or the ground, and temporal events in order to adapt to the world: to walk around in it, find things in it, play in it, and even survive in it. These stimuli are complex relational units, such as objects and events, not simple sensations of light or sound. Thus, unlike most theories of perception, Gibson's theory stresses the natural behavior of the perceiver in a particular environment.

Gibson's research and theorizing centers on *affordances*, a concept introduced by James Gibson (e.g., 1979b). Affordances are what an environment offers or provides for an organism; they are opportunities for action. Humans' environments "afford" surfaces of support for walking or crawling, objects for grasping, passageways allowing movement, and barriers preventing movement. Even the social environment offers affordances, for example, a smiling or angry face affords positive or negative interactions. Thus, the person and the environment have a reciprocal relationship. They fit together to form a whole, with a meshing of the person's activities and the environment's affordances. The utility of a property of the environment depends on the capacities of the organism. If an infant cannot yet walk, a solid surface does not afford "walking on." Affordances thus involve a relationship between the organism and its surroundings. Gibson claims that these affordances are perceived directly: "We do not perceive stimuli or retinal images or sensations or even just things; what we perceive are things that we can eat, or write with, or sit down on, or talk to" (1982, p. 60).

As children acquire new motor skills during development, they discover new affordances. When children start to walk, they learn to perceive whether a surface affords solid support for walking. This affordance is irrelevant for, and unknown to, a younger infant. In one experiment (Gibson et al., 1987), infants were placed on a walkway raised 4 feet from the floor. Their smiling mothers stood 6 feet away at the other end of the walkway. The walkway for one condition was a rigid surface (strong plywood covered with a patterned fabric), which affords locomotion for both crawling and walking. In the other condition, the walkway was a patterned fabric on a water bed, which affords crawling but not walking. The infants who could walk looked at and felt the water bed more than the rigid surface before they either walked on the rigid surface or crawled onto the water bed. The infants who could only crawl showed little, if any, differentiation of the two surfaces; they readily moved onto both of them. Thus, there is a fit between what the environment provides and the child's actions, goals, and abilities.

Like ethologists (see Chapter 5), Gibson emphasizes that the human species has evolved adaptive ways of perceiving the world. Each species is specialized for perceiving complex relations among stimuli specifying critical information in its environment. For example, bats are pretuned to use acoustic information (interpreting feedback from sounds) to help them navigate in dark caves. Birds and primates rely heavily on their visual perception of the spatial layout, prey, and predators, and hands permit humans and other primates to detect whether an object can be grasped and manipulated. Thus, what information an organism extracts from the environment depends on the species. The organism directly perceives affordances because the species has evolved a perceptual system that detects, or can learn to detect, the affordances that increase the likelihood of survival. The environment affords food, mates, and places to hide from predators.

Experience creates new affordances. Thus, within a species, individuals vary in their ability to use potential affordances: "A three-inch-wide beam affords performing backflips for a gymnast, but the affordance is not realizable by others; rock climbers learn to use certain terrains for support that do not appear to others to provide a surface of support" (Gibson & Pick, 2000, p. 17). Children's evolutionary heritage provides the perceptual equipment and motivation to perceive—or learn to perceive—the particular objects, events, and spatial layouts that the child needs in that setting. By exploring and playing, children learn the affordances of objects, events, and surfaces.

Information Is Specified in Stimulation

To begin to understand Gibson's answer to her first question, about what is perceived, we must understand her conception of the role of stimulation in perception. Her description of the active, self-motivated child exploring the stimulus world at first seems quite similar to Piaget's view of children. The theorists part, however, in their conceptions of how children "know" the world through activity. Piagetian children "construct" their knowledge by forming schemes based on their motor behaviors with objects. Because perception produces static images, it must be corrected by operational knowledge. Similarly, other cognitive and perceptual approaches see perception as an act of enriching a sparse, ambiguous, uninformative retinal image. For instance, information-processing approaches describe processes that add meaning to the stimulus by relating it to memories and knowledge in the long-term store.

They refer to going beyond the information given by making inferences based on knowledge of the world.

In contrast, Gibson believes that stimulation is a rich source of information that specifies objects, events, and surfaces. The developmental issue, then, is how children learn to extract more and more information from that stimulation. As children perceive, they differentiate information, rather than add to it. The assumption that complex information is inherent in stimulation is the most controversial claim in the theory. It is important, therefore, that we consider this claim carefully.

Information extends over time and space as people and objects move. That is, stimulation is not static and frozen in space and time. As Gibson comments, "There is no shutter on the retina, no such thing as a static image" (1988, p. 5). Stimulation specifies events, places, and objects. Thus, if children can extract this information, they perceive events, places, and objects and understand how the affordances fit with their abilities. They do not perceive a single, discrete "stimulus," such as an object. Rather, from the entire spatiotemporal array, they perceive the information that specifies particular objects. In other words, stimulation is a field of available information about affordances to be differentiated.

Stimulation carries many levels of information. At the simplest and most concrete level, a child discriminates objects by one or several *distinctive features*, or attributes, that differentiate them. Suppose a boy moves near an ocean and for the first time in his life encounters hundreds of shells. He begins a collection and attempts to identify the shells with the help of a guidebook with photographs. Although he is perceptually capable of telling all of the shells apart if he places them side by side, he actually notices only a few distinctive features at first, perhaps only salient differences in color, shape, and size. Only after much playing with the shells and comparing them with each other and with the pictures in the book does he realize that the stimulus class "shells" has a particular set of distinctive features that allows him to determine the appropriate label for each shell. Although size is a salient feature, it is seldom important for differentiating types of shells. In contrast, slight differences in the shape of the "crown" at the top of the shell or subtle differences in the colored pattern on the shell are quite important. Although this information was in the light stimulating the boy's eyes from the start, he did not really notice it or abstract it as a defining feature until he had more perceptual experience with the shells.

At a more abstract level of analysis, we can perceive a higher-order structure to light or sound. A good example is the musical pattern we call a melody. We abstract a melody from a succession of notes played on the piano. We recognize this melody as the same melody even if it is transposed to a different key or played at a different tempo or on a saxophone instead of a piano. The pattern is there in stimulation, but we may not have perceived it at first. Thus, perceptual learning is a process of learning to perceive what has always been there. Gibson has noted that her theory might be called a "seek and ye shall find" theory (1977, p. 157). Young children, having limited experience with objects and events in the world, often do not perceive subtle differences in the appearance of objects or patterns (organized light). They must search out these differences.

It is instructive to carry the musical example to perceptual learning. When we hear a new orchestral work, we have a relatively undifferentiated perception of the work after the first hearing. Only after listening to the work several times are we able to extract melodies and their transformations, grasp the overall structure of the piece, and perhaps even differentiate the various instruments of the orchestra. For most Americans, this task is more difficult with Eastern music or modern compositions using the 12-tone scale, which are less familiar, than with the first hearing of yet another Haydn symphony. In this musical example, stimulation has remained the same throughout the repeated playing of the record. What has changed is what information we have extracted. In the beginning we listened yet did not hear. We gradually perceived more and more of what had always been there. Our perception became both more specific, as we became aware of subtle musical qualities, and more abstract, as we perceived musical patterns. Thus, the information is in the stimulation, but sometimes we must learn to perceive it. Our perception improves not by filling in the raw auditory stimulus by adding words or applying schemes, not by cognitively gluing together the notes, but by listening to the music and directing our attention. We attend to relational information—distinctive features and patterns concerning relationships among the parts—not to bits and pieces of information. In Gibson's words:

> There is structure in the array, relational information that does not have to be pieced together because, like truth, it is already there. This is the assumption I want to proceed with. I do not want a construction theory, with processors at every stage like an assembly line.
>
> (1977, p. 157)

Information about the self also is important. Children must extract proprioceptive stimulation from their body in movement and detect information about their own effectiveness at making their way around their world. In this way they can perceive the relation between the environment and the self that together specify an affordance. Toddlers must be able to judge whether they can walk down a slope of a particular angle in order to detect whether the perceptual information about the slope specifies the affordance "walkability."

Humans as Active Perceivers

No parent would be surprised by the claim that children seem to be constantly in motion. Parents might, however, be surprised by the claim that this motion is essential to perceptual development, even in infancy. Gibson often refers to "the perceiver as performer" (Gibson & Rader, 1979). In her view, perception is an event. Children and adults discover, explore, attend, extract information, and differentiate objects, events, and arrays. These are the behaviors of an active organism that does something in order to learn about the world. Gibson holds an interactionist view of perception and action. Children act to discover the information, and by discovering information they can act. They actively extract affordances and by using them discover new affordances. For example, a child may perceive the affordances of various types of balls by kicking them, rolling them, and trying to bounce them. By then using them in a game for which they are suited, she discovers new affordances, such as passing the ball to teammates. This is Gibson's answer to her second question, about how information is picked up. Children actively perceive while dong things in their world.

Humans, as a species, are inherently motivated to explore and learn about their world. There are, however, goals and needs specific to each task or situation. A girl putting together a puzzle attends to shape and color because these attributes are information she needs to achieve her goal of completing the puzzle. A baby learning to walk must be very attentive to the position of his body in space and the distance between furniture. Young soccer players seek a different sort of information. They continually search for and track the ball, perceive the spatial relationship between other players and the ball, and use feedback concerning their attempts to kick the ball (falling down, kicking erratically, and so on). Adults also have different goals relevant to perception in different situations. Mountain climbers are more attentive to where they place each step than are people taking a leisurely walk (Gibson & Rader, 1979). In these examples, there is a relationship—ideally, a match—between the person's goals and the information extracted from the environment.

Methodology

Although Gibson's research, as well as other research stimulated by her theory, follows the experimental procedures of other areas of developmental psychology, it is unusual in one way. It tries to retain ecological validity in the experimental setting. This does not mean that Gibsonians necessarily observe perceptual activities in their natural settings. It does mean that they attempt to simulate (mimic important features), in the experimental setting, the stimulation, tasks, and goals of the child's natural environment. We can see the close connection between theory and methods in the materials and procedures Gibsonians select for their experiments. Multimodal stimulation (for example, faces that move and make sounds and objects that can be touched), various kinds of environmental supports for locomotion (for example, solid or nonsolid surfaces), and opportunities for obtaining feedback from exploratory activities (and thus detecting contingencies) are found in both the child's daily life and Gibson's laboratory.

In an early experiment on depth, for instance, Gibson, along with Walk (1960), constructed a "visual cliff," which simulates a cliff or drop-off in the real world. Gibson was inspired to create this miniature Grand Canyon after visiting the real Grand Canyon with her young child and pondering, with some concern, the child's ability to perceive it as a drop-off. The visual cliff is a table with a glass top that gives the impression of a solid surface on one-half of the table; on the other half of the table, the floor is visible through the glass. Thus, the apparatus displays information specifying a drop-off. Some of the results were described at the beginning of this chapter. Infants will crawl on the "cliff" half, but refuse to crawl onto the half of the glass that hangs over the apparent "thin air." The visual-cliff experiments demonstrated that children perceive depth at an edge at least as early as 6 or 7 months, when they begin to crawl. Research using heart rate indicates that even younger infants differentiate the cliff and noncliff sides (Campos, Langer, & Krowitz, 1970). The visual cliff has been used widely to study depth perception in many species.

DEVELOPMENTAL TRENDS

In Gibson's earlier work (1969) she focused on changes from infancy through childhood in how children detect the properties and structure of objects and symbols. Due to a growing range of experiences, children's perception of affordances becomes increasingly specific and economical. This is due in part to children's attention becoming more optimal. After the present section describing these trends, the following section examines how they play out in recent research on infancy, the age on which Gibson has focused more recently. In her infant work, the development of posture and its control, along with babies' use of information about objects, events, and layouts to exploit their affordances, takes center stage.

Increasing Specificity and Economy in the Perception of Affordances

During development, perception becomes more efficient. Children learn to select the right information, in the most economical way. They select the right information if they select information that provides a fit between the environment and themselves, for example, if infants check an adult's facial expression before deciding whether to approach a strange new object. They select economically if they select the minimal information that specifies the affordance for them.

There is a growing correspondence between what the child perceives and what information is in stimulation. In other words, perception becomes more exact. The toddler may be relatively insensitive to perceptual differences among members of the class "fish." The older child may discriminate among guppies, goldfish, and trout. Thus, perception has become more differentiated. As children explore objects and layouts in different environments, they learn about the important properties of objects and the affordances of these properties. Although the mechanisms for extracting information are the same throughout the life span, they become more efficient, or economical. Children achieve this economy by detecting distinctive features in stimulation, extracting invariants over time, and processing larger units of structure.

1 *Distinctive features* were introduced earlier in this chapter. They are critical features that can be used to discriminate between objects. Imagine, for example, that a practical joker mixed up the container

labels on the entire stock of ice cream in a 48-flavor ice-cream store. An efficient way to tell the flavors apart and group together identical flavors would be to pick out the minimal set of distinctive features that distinguish the types of ice cream. The set might include the following: color, nuts versus no nuts, sherbet versus nonsherbet, flavor (fruit-based, chocolate-based, or other), and smooth versus textured.

Faces are another group of objects that can be differentiated by distinctive features. Cartoonists take advantage of striking facial characteristics by exaggerating them in caricatures. Distinctive features of faces—a toothy grin or large nose—can bring instant recognition.

A classic Gibsonian experiment demonstrates the increasing specificity of perceiving distinctive features. Gibson, Gibson, Pick, and Osser (1962) presented letterlike forms—forms constructed on the same principles as printed capital letters in the English alphabet. On each trial the child's task was to select from a set of forms the two or three forms identical to the standard form. The nonidentical forms differed from the standard in several ways, for example, in orientation (reversed or rotated to an upside-down position, analogous to *M* versus *W*) or shape (a straight line changed to a curve or vice versa, analogous to *D* versus *O*). With increasing age, from 4 to 8, children were increasingly likely to differentiate the forms. That is, many of the forms that the younger children considered to be the same as the standard were, in fact, not the same. For example, the child might pick a reversal of the standard as a form that is the same as the standard, analogous to confusing *M* and *W* in our alphabet. The older children's perception corresponded more closely to the forms. That is, they usually picked forms that were exactly the same as the standard. Their superior performance presumably reflected their greater experience with letters of the alphabet.

2 A second aid to economy of information pickup, the extraction of *invariants*, is the search for relations that remain constant over change. Children extract what is permanent about objects despite changes in their appearance as the objects move toward or away from them. It is clearly more economical to perceive a single, constant mother of a particular size and shape than a succession of different mothers that expand and shrink.

One invariant examined experimentally by Gibson, Owsley, and Johnston (1978) is the perception of the rigidity, or lack of malleability, of a moving object. They asked whether the property of rigidity could be extracted when an apparently rigid object underwent various kinds of movement. Infants 5 months of age saw a round, disklike piece of foam rubber move in three ways, for example, rotation in the frontal plane, rotation around the vertical axis, and movement toward or away from them. The infants watched these rigid movements in succession until they habituated, that is, stopped looking at the object. Then they saw, in succession, a fourth rigid motion, perhaps rotation around the horizontal axis, and then a nonrigid, elastic motion. The latter was accomplished by having an experimenter continually squeeze and release the spongy disk. The infants showed little interest in the new rigid motion but much interest in the nonrigid motion. Thus, the infants discriminated rigid motions from nonrigid motions. The invariant property, rigidity, was extracted from the stimulus flux during the three types of movement. The authors concluded that the nonrigid movement "was perceived as different, presumably because it offered information about a new property of the object, that object being otherwise unchanged" (p. 414).

3 A third route to economical perception is the extraction of large units of perceptual *structure*. A basic tenet of Gibson's theory is that the world is structured and that we gradually become more aware of this structure. We do not impose structure on an unstructured world; our perceptual systems extract the structure. As mentioned earlier, music has a melodic structure that we may or may not detect immediately. Furthermore, much of learning to read is a process of detecting the structure in written discourse. Words and sentences have structure, or rule systems. The structure of words is apparent when we break words into letter clusters *(-ed, -ing, -ight)*. In addition, there are regularities in the spelling-to-sound correspondences, as in the unit *-ing* and the sound associated with that unit.

Children perceive economically if they pick the most useful level of analysis for the particular task: distinctive features, invariant relations, or higher-order structure. All are useful for discovering the affordances of objects.

■ *Optimization of Attention*

For Gibson, perceptual development is nearly synonymous with the development of exploratory activities, including active attention. The term *attention* refers to activities that gather information, especially information about the affordances of objects. Attentional activities include peripheral exploratory activities, such as looking back and forth between two faces, turning the head to facilitate locating a sound, and sniffing a rose. In addition, there are central, nonobservable attentional activities, for example, attending to an object's color rather than its shape. As a result of all these activities, the child extracts certain information and ignores other information. How efficiently children carry out attentional activities depends to a great extent on their developmental level. Although to some extent children perceive selectively from the beginning, during development they learn to tailor their perception to the requirements of each situation.

During development, attention becomes less captive and more under the child's control: Infants learn to actively scan an object rather than only passively react to a bright light or sudden movement that "catches" their attention. They gain control over their bodies and expand their exploratory potential. They work hard to use each new postural achievement to attend in new ways. Young infants struggle to hold their head and shoulders upright when carried so that they can look about. Later, trying to sit without support and attend to and slap at a toy require constant work to maintain balance. Still later, an infant just learning to stand suddenly falls to a sitting position when she lets go of a chair to attend to and pick up a block on the seat.

During childhood, attention also becomes more systematic and less random, more selective in the information picked up, and more exclusive, in that irrelevant information is ignored. For instance, if children are asked to decide if two drawings of houses are the same or different, older children, more than younger children, use efficient attentional strategies (Vurpillot & Ball, 1979). They actively and systematically look back and forth between corresponding parts of the two houses, attending to relevant features such as the windows, until a decision can be reached. Younger children settle for a few random glances before making their decision. Similarly, if children are asked to remember the locations of several pictures of objects but distracting pictures are also present, young children attend to both the pictures they are to remember and the distractors. In contrast, older children ignore the distractors (Miller, 1990). As these examples suggest, older children extract a more useful set of information because they more efficiently select information.

As children learn more about themselves and the world, they learn what kind of attention each setting requires. For instance, they attend differently when crossing a street, looking for a particular brand of cereal in a store, playing basketball, and reading a book. Much of the improvement in fitting attention to the setting comes from feedback in the form of successes and failures, such as avoiding bumping into furniture.

WHAT INFANTS LEARN ABOUT

In recent years, Gibson has emphasized infant development. Thus, this section describes the important developments during that time, including the trends described above. It is beyond the scope of this book to present adequately the many ingenious and compelling recent experiments that reveal an active infant fully engaged in discovering the world of people, objects, and events (see Gibson & Pick, 2000, for the full picture). This section tries to convey the important accomplishments in communication, interaction with objects, and locomotion in the spatial layout and presents a sampling of the methods for revealing these accomplishments.

Communication

The ecology of the human infant includes other people. Even before babies utter their first word or manipulate objects, they begin learning to participate in the social world. Newborns are familiar with their mother's voice, prefer it to an unfamiliar female's voice, recognize the overall pattern of speech, and discriminate between a foreign language and their own. Young babies learn the affordances of other people's facial expressions, gestures, vocalizations, and actions and learn to respond to them. For example, they can detect the emotional states of other people—an angry facial expression affords bad events, a happy one affords positive events. Babies thus come to anticipate the behaviors of others and to respond to them. Primitive nonlinguistic "conversations" are possible, for infants learn about turn taking and see themselves as able to control their interactions with others. Babies learn that they are agents with particular physical abilities and intentions. Eventually, babies and their parents engage in joint visual attention as they look at and talk about an object or event together. All of this is a perfect context for learning about language and social relationships. The following studies give a flavor of how perception relates to communication.

Two-day-old infants, born to either English-speaking or Spanish-speaking mothers, listened to a recording of a woman speaking one of these languages. The infants continued to suck, in order to keep the sound going, longer for their native language than the other language (Moon, Cooper, & Fifer, 1993). In another experiment, using a videotape of a face in the dark with small lights attached, Soken and Pick (1992) showed 7-month-olds patterns of moving lights specifying happy or angry faces. When infants heard a sound track of a happy or angry woman, they looked at the appropriate face, even though they could see no details of the face. As a final example, infants use information from their mother's face to avoid dangerous situations. A modified visual cliff displayed ambiguous information as to whether the "deep" side was safe to venture onto, because the apparent drop-off was not large. Infants whose mothers displayed a (coached) frightened face refused to venture onto the deep side, whereas infants whose mothers displayed a happy face would do so (Sorce, Emde, Campos, & Klinnert, 1985).

Interaction with Objects

Infants make use of whatever motor abilities they possess at any point to explore their environment. Even very young infants, by moving their head and eyes, can scan the visual layout and discover rudimentary properties of objects and layouts. As babies develop motorically and gain control of their head and of reaching for, and manipulating, objects, they learn more and more about the properties of objects. These properties will be important for specifying new affordances of the world. Because of recent research, much of it inspired by the Gibsonian approach, we now know that, as both babies and objects move, babies are surprisingly able to discover these properties. Consider, for example, a baby lying in her crib and gazing at her stuffed bear on a nearby shelf. She sees a single, solid, three-dimensional object separate from the shelf and from the other toys on the shelf. When her mother bends over the crib and occludes some of the bear, the baby does not think that her mother has bisected the bear. If the bear falls off the shelf, she expects that all parts will fall together but that the shelf and wall will not also fall. If the bear falls toward her, she does not think that it is becoming larger or that it is changing shape as its angle changes. And, finally, she knows that the falling bear may make contact with her face and most certainly will afford cuddling and chewing.

Infants' early perception of the separateness of objects was demonstrated in the following study (Needham & Baillargeon, 1998): Babies at $4\frac{1}{2}$ months of age saw either a cylinder or a tall blue box for several seconds. Then they saw both objects next to each other and watched as a hand appeared and pulled the cylinder. In one case the hand pulled the cylinder away from the box, and in the other case the cylinder drew the box with it. Babies looked longer when the objects moved together, an outcome that in infant research is taken to mean that the babies were surprised at this improbable event. The inference is that they had perceived the objects as separate. Remarkably, the results were the same when a 24-hour delay separated the presentation of one object and both objects. This outcome indicates that a very brief visual experience with a single object served to segregate it from an adjacent object, even at a later time. This experiment also serves as an example of the clever methods that have been constructed to assess early competencies. Similar experiments document infants' perception of number, solidity, size and shape constancy, substance, and texture.

One startling perceptual skill concerns babies' detection of the unity of objects and events. For example, 4-month-old infants perceive a long stick protruding on either side of a rectangular object as a single unbroken stick, rather than two short sticks separated by an object, which is literally what they see. However, they perceive this unity only if they see the stick move back and forth or in depth rather than remain stationary (Kellman & Spelke, 1983). Thus, action—of the object, the infant, or both—is essential for accurate perception. One of the most striking demonstrations of perceived object unity is the perception of a living object in motion. Fox and McDaniel (1982) presented a biological-motion light pattern—a videotape of 10 lights mounted on the joints of the arms, legs, and hips of a figure running in the dark. Another display included the same number of lights, but their movement was random. Infants age 4 and 6 months tended to look at the running pattern, which indicates both their ability to differentiate an object in biological motion from a random array and their preference for viewing a pattern of moving lights organized into a unitary object.

Babies learn about the various properties of objects as they develop optimal ways of exploring them, particularly as they gain control over their head and limb movements so that they can actively look at, listen to, and mouth objects, such as the fist, that they can get into their mouth. This exploration becomes increasingly multimodal, as eye, hand, ear, and mouth work together to capture the properties of a new toy. Babies learn that objects can be not only seen and heard but also squeezed, hit, banged, and thrown. And babies can detect the properties of various modalities that go together. For example, regarding touch–sight correspondences, infants can tactually recognize an object that they had previously only seen (Streri & Pecheux, 1986).

Let us consider in some detail the relations between sights and sounds. In a classic series of experiments that began in the late 1970s, Spelke and colleagues (Spelke, 1976, 1991) showed that young infants know something about this synchrony between modalities. The basic paradigm was to show two objects or events side by side, present a sound track in a neutral location (for example, the middle), and observe whether infants looked longer at the object or event whose sound track they were hearing. For example, 4-month-olds looked at a film of a hand hitting a wooden block and a tambourine rather than at a person playing peekaboo when the sound track for the former was played. They also looked more at a male face when they heard a male voice and more at a female face when they heard a female voice (Walker-Andrews, Bahrick, Raglioni, & Diaz, 1991) and at a child face rather than an adult face when a child sound track was played (Bahrick, Netto, & Hernandez-Reif, 1998). In fact, a recent study seems to show that even newborns look at the speaker whose mouth movements match the specific sounds they hear rather than the speaker making other sounds (Aldridge, Braga, Walton, & Bower, 1999).

Finally, by 7 to 9 months infants are even sensitive to the sight–sound correspondences of musical events (Pick, Gross, Heinrichs, Love, & Palmer, 1994). Infants heard a sound track in synchrony with two displays but specific to only one of the instruments. They appropriately looked at, for example, the musician playing a cello rather than a clarinet and the one playing a trumpet rather than a flute. Thus, experience with various instruments apparently is not necessary for detecting sound–sight correspondences and for differentiating instruments from different families.

Babies have a new awareness of the self as one object among many and can link proprioceptive information from their own body to a visual image of their body. Remarkably, Bahrick and Watson (1985) found that 5-month-olds could discriminate between a live video display of their own moving legs and that of another identically dressed infant or their own legs taped at another time. In the latter two displays proprioceptive and visual information were not synchronized. Moreover, infants even detect when the video display has reversed their right and left legs (Morgan & Rochat, 1995; Rochat & Morgan, 1998).

Locomotion in the Spatial Layout

When babies are too young to move about, they have only a "near" system—a hand–arm system for reaching, holding, and manipulating objects and near surfaces. After they can crawl or walk, they acquire a "far" system for exploring the outer space of their environments. As infants learn to roll, creep, crawl, and walk their way around their environments, their attention expands to larger arrays. As J. J. Gibson commented, "The surface is where most of the action is" (1979a, p. 127). Babies explore behind obstacles and themselves, around corners, on top of furniture, and inside of cabinets. Their perception of the layout guides their locomotion around obstacles, through openings, and onto safe, solid surfaces. A toddler crossing a room needs a great deal of affordance information in order to crawl under a table, over rather than around a blanket on the floor, and around rather than over the dog. Objects' affordance of being carried seems to fascinate toddlers, who often carry objects from one place to another, just for the sheer joy of doing so. Gibson (1988) notes that this affordance may take a while to be learned completely, for there are reports that toddlers sometimes try to carry a toy or piece of furniture almost as large as themselves.

Early locomotion requires constant decisions. A young child's toddling across the room may seem like a very simple action, but, as Adolph and Eppler explain, it is far from simple:

> Figuring out where to go and how to get there requires coordination of skills across a number of psychological domains and time scales: coping with the sheer biomechanics of moving the limbs in a gravitational field, contending with different ground surfaces and their effects on balance control, gathering perceptual information about the ground ahead and about infants' own propensities, searching out alternative means to traverse a surface or reach a location, and so on.
>
> (1999, p. 31)

Children must constantly tailor their locomotion both to the properties of the terrain and to their own developing abilities. In order to crawl or walk, infants need to find surfaces that afford crawling or

Figure 6.1

Adolph's walkway with adjustable slope used to test infants' judgments of whether to descend slopes that vary in steepness. The experimenter followed alongside to ensure the infants' safety.
SOURCE: "Learning in the Development of Infant Locomotion," by Karen Adolph, in *Monographs of the Society for Research in Child Development,* 1997, *62*(3, Serial No. 251). Adapted by permission of the Society for Research in Child Development.

walking. Two examples were presented earlier: the visual-cliff experiments revealed babies' refusal to enter an apparent drop-off, and the Gibson et al. (1987) study showed toddlers' perception of the solidity of walkways.

A more recent research example is Adolph's (1997) longitudinal study of infants encountering upward and downward slopes of various steepness—angles ranging from 0 to 36 degrees (see Figure 6.1). Infants had to decide whether they had the capability to climb or descend in this potentially (though not really) dangerous situation to reach a parent at the receiving end offering a Cheerio. Crawlers showed little caution and often just plunged ahead, even on the steepest slopes, and had to be rescued again and again (see the excerpt at the beginning of this chapter). Over weeks, as the infants' crawling expertise increased, their judgments improved. The infants tried out a variety of strategies. They sometimes tried various means of traversal down the slope by testing different sliding positions while still on the starting platform. They sat and hung their legs over the slope or changed into a backing position and looked over their shoulders down the slope. The babies eventually crawled on the safe slopes and refused to crawl on the riskier ones. Interestingly, later when they began to walk, they again judged poorly, but they again improved with experience. Thus, with each new postural advance, the infants had to relearn information about affordances tailored to their new ability. The better perceivers more effectively explored the slopes by looking, feeling, and trying out various positions, such as backing down or sliding. The fact that a control group without repeated experience with the slopes in the experiment exhibited the same pattern shows that specific learning on those particular slopes was not important. Rather, practice in maintaining posture and noticing consequences during daily activities transferred to the laboratory situation.

A more recent experiment (Adolph, 2000) also showed that experience with an earlier-developing skill does not transfer automatically to a later-developing one. Adolph examined 9-month-olds' willingness to reach over a risky gap to obtain an object. At this age infants are experienced at sitting but new at crawling. When in a sitting posture, they avoided reaching over the risky gap, apparently realizing that they would lose control of their body and fall. However, when in a crawling posture, they did not transfer this competency and consequently fell into the risky gap. Thus, this perceptual learning is surprisingly specific to a particular postural control system.

MECHANISMS OF DEVELOPMENT

The sections thus far have described a number of processes for bringing about development. Efficient exploratory activities lead to the economical extraction of information specifying affordances. For a 7-month-old, "fingering explores texture, hand-to-hand transfer and rotation explore shape, and squeezing and banging explore substance" (Gibson & Pick, 2000, p. 150). Children move their eyes to the television, turn their head toward the sound of a distant call, move their hands over sap dripping down a tree, sniff when they hear dinner being prepared, and cautiously roll a brussels sprout over the tongue. Consequently, children detect features, relations, and higher-order structure that specify objects, events, and layouts. Children also filter out irrelevant information, as in the "cocktail-party phenomenon" (or "birthday-party phenomenon" in children), in which all background noise is filtered out in order to hear a single voice. Maturational change permits new postures and motor skills that lead to new affordances.

POSITION ON DEVELOPMENTAL ISSUES

Human Nature

Gibson's view of human nature is much like Piaget's. In their organismic views, people are inherently motivated creatures who actively explore and try to extract sense from their world. Ideally, this is an organized and efficient process in which the child's needs and goals mesh with the nature of the environment. In Gibson's and Piaget's views, the child has a tremendous capacity to learn from experience and adapt to the environment. Both theorists describe complex organisms that are sensitive to the complex structure of the environment. The theorists differ, however, in the source of this structure. Gibson believes that in stimulation there is structure, which specifies the information available to be perceived. The child learns to detect this structure. In contrast, Piaget believes that to a great extent the nature of the interaction between the child and the world constructs the structure.

Qualitative Versus Quantitative Development

Just as perception in adults can gradually improve with practice, so does perception in children gradually improve as a result of experience. Perceptual development is not stagelike. There may, however, be specific qualitative changes in the exploratory strategies children use. For example, children's systematic visual comparison of two objects may replace their earlier random looking at the two objects.

Nature Versus Nurture

Gibson has been primarily interested in describing and explaining how children learn from experience and what they learn, especially affordances. Nurture and nature are inseparable, however. They do not just interact; they fit together. What information children extract from the environment depends on their evolved species-specific genetic endowment, in addition to their maturational level, immediate goals, and unique set of learning experiences. Babies are innately equipped to find out what the world is like and what it lets them do. Their growing control over their bodies and their awareness of their bodies in space is a big part of the story of perceptual learning and development.

What Develops

Gibson recently has identified four hallmarks of human behavior: agency, prospectivity, the search for order in the world, and flexibility (Gibson & Pick, 2000). *Agency* is "the self in control, the quality of intentionality in behavior" (p. 160). Even infants know that their actions have effects on the environment and that they can control their own behavior. They see themselves as distinct from, and capable of acting on, other objects. *Prospectivity* pertains to intentional, anticipatory, planful, future-oriented behaviors. Children reach, anticipate outcomes, and perceive where they are going in the array. The *search for order* involves children's tendencies to see order, regularity, and pattern and thus make sense of the world. Earlier sections described invariants, higher-order structure in stimulation, and economy of selecting information. Finally, regarding *flexibility*, "perception adjusts to new situations and to changing bodily conditions such as growth, improved motor skill, or a sprained ankle" (Gibson & Pick, 2000, p. 169). And as children move from one setting to another, they change their activities to seek whatever affordances they need in that situation.

APPLICATIONS

Gibson's book on reading, mentioned earlier, showed that perceptual learning about letters, correspondences between letters and sounds, and the structure of sentences is essential for learning to read. In addition, her theory suggests that to a great extent children can educate themselves about the world. A preschool teacher can provide interesting and varied objects and surfaces and let young children learn by moving around in that world and exploring objects. Finally, it is informative for parents that their young infants know much more about objects and events and are more ready to communicate with them than they might have thought.

EVALUATION OF THE THEORY

Gibson's theory is the most well known theory of perceptual development. It has inspired a great deal of creative research, especially regarding infants' early perceptual competencies. The evaluation will focus on the potential of Gibson's theory to guide not only perceptual research but also developmental research more generally and to tie perception to other areas of development. The strengths of the theory are its focus on the ecological context of perception and its putting the body back into developmental psychology. The main weakness is the unclear account of cognition.

■ *Strengths*

Focus on the Ecological Context of Perception ■ As Gibson comments, "Only a few hardy perception psychologists still study perception of the real world rather than small displays on computer screens" (1991, p. 607). For years, Gibson has been concerned with how perception serves us in our daily lives. She studies the perception of meaningful stimulation—patterns, objects, and events—rather than points of light or brief, static stimuli. In James Gibson's words, she works on "perception outdoors under the sky instead of perception of points in a darkroom" (1979a, p. xii). The perception of the affordances of natural units is essential for adapting to the environment. This ecological orientation has relevance for the current state of cognitive developmental research. Like ethological theory, Gibson's theory could enrich the information-processing approach by directing it toward (1) larger, more complex properties of the environment to be processed and (2) events rather than static stimuli.

First, Gibson criticizes the tendency of information-processing researchers to break down the world into objects and properties of objects. In Gibson's words, "Such a conception requires them to invent 'processing mechanisms' to put the world together" (1977, p. 156). In contrast, Gibson has shown that even young infants can detect complex and meaningful properties of the world such as pliability and traversability.

Second, information-processing approaches should take seriously her concern with the processing of events that occur over time: a rapidly approaching object, a ball rolling across the floor, one object striking another, liquid being poured out of a glass. This change in focus would broaden our understanding of processing based on the typically studied static stimuli, such as pictures, letters, objects, and written words. Most real-life events involve the movement of one or several objects or people—a complex set of information. Moreover, Gibson suggests that affordances provide a natural organization for knowledge, for example, a category of "things you can walk on."

Putting the Body Back into Developmental Psychology ■ Recall that in a previous chapter the information-processing approach was criticized for focusing on the child's cognitive skills and giving little attention to how these skills "fit" with the child's goals in a particular environment. Gibson certainly would agree with this criticism.

Current developmental research usually ignores the implications of thinking for children's actions. In contrast, Gibson's work does not leave the child wrapped in thought (Pick, 1992). Children do things. Thinking and perceiving are used to help us make our way around our world. The important categories are functional ones—what one can do with the objects. When we seek information about affordances, we do so because of our physical and psychological needs for moving toward resources, expressing ourselves, interacting with others, obtaining objects to work on, and so on. We explore to obtain information that will help us adapt. Thus, information-processing psychologists should ask questions such as: Why does a child try to memorize information or solve a problem? Why does an infant look carefully at a room before starting across it? How do these activities help them adapt to their environment?

Not only do perception and cognition help children locomote in adaptive ways, but the latter helps the former. Moving one's body across surfaces and around objects in turn helps cognitive development in that the detection of surfaces, events, and objects—and their affordances—is the foundation of knowledge about the world. Through exploratory behavior and perceptual learning we discover categories of events or objects (for example, "things you can walk on"), abstract properties such as number, and causal relations among objects or events. And we develop cognitive maps of the extended environment. As we learn to control our bodies, we also learn to control our cognitive activities such as the metacognitive activities of monitoring and checking.

The difference between the focus of most developmental theories on what children know and Gibson's focus on what children do can be subtle but telling. For example, developmentalists speak of a "self-concept," which connotes a static something that the child has, whereas Gibson speaks of self in terms of "agency," which connotes doing and action. This subtle difference has not-so-subtle implications for how we would assess the self and what questions we would ask about it.

Weaknesses

Unclear Account of Cognition ■ Contemporary psychologists tend to make a distinction between perception and cognition and then address how they interact. Gibson probably is correct that this distinction is misguided; it is artificial to try to separate the two. Still, her placement of many abilities that most psychologists would label as cognitive under the rubric of perception is puzzling to many in the field. The basic problem is that Gibson proposes a theory of the *direct* perception of the environment but then includes some behaviors that seem to many psychologists to involve indirect, interpretive cognition. For instance, Gibson's examples of perceptual learning include inferring emotions from a parent's face, reading maps, interpreting X-ray and aerial photographs, and identifying material under a microscope. Others include detecting means–end relations, perceiving causality, learning that events in the world can be contingent on one's own actions, and perceiving conservation as an invariance over time and over an event sequence (Gibson, 1969, pp. 8–9, 388). Furthermore, children are said to perceive affordances such as swinging (on swings), warmth and light for reading (from a fire), and hiding (behind a screen). Many psychologists seem uncomfortable designating these psychological activities as "perceptual." For example, Horowitz (1983) argues that instead of proposing that a chair affords sitting, one could propose more parsimoniously that the perceiver, because of previous experience, associates a chair with sitting. Although perceptual processes certainly are heavily involved in these cases, much of the learning concerns the interpretation and categorization of information. Stated differently, if one adopts Gibson's theory, it is not clear what is *not* perception. What are the limits to direct perception?

Even if one accepts Gibson's inclusion of perception and cognition within the same process—the detection of affordances and their meaning for the child—it still would be useful to address what seem to be some important differences along the continuum from discriminating two shapes to interpreting a shadow on an X-ray as tuberculosis

(Gibson, 1969, p. 9). And are there really no important differences between perceiving the size constancy of an object and perceiving the conservation of number?

SUMMARY

Gibson asks four questions: What is learned? How is this information picked up? What actions (or interactions) take place? What are the consequences for knowledge? Her answers are the following: Children learn to perceive affordances, namely, what it is that the events, objects, and layout in the environment offer that relates to the infant and can be controlled by the infant. An object's affordance is its meaning for what can be perceived. This relation is a fit between children and their environments. Children extract, from stimulation, information that specifies these places, objects, and events and their affordances for our actions. They learn to perceive invariants of events, objects, and layouts—what is unchangeable despite continual change as child and object move and as the setting changes. As they learn what is invariant in objects and events, children learn about themselves as objects that move about this world of variants and invariants. Because they know about events, they often can predict what people and nonhuman objects will do next. Infants also learn to participate in a communicative event. Importantly, children learn the consequences of their attempts to use affordances—successful exploration and play versus falling or not reaching a toy.

Perceptual development is largely a process of increasing the efficiency of perception as a result of experience. This is perceptual learning. The ecological context of this learning is important because children learn to perceive information that helps them adapt to this environment. In each setting, children's goals—whether playing or reading or climbing over a fence—guide their pickup of information. In general, the fit between the goal and perception improves during development.

Children show two main developmental trends. First, perception becomes more specific and economical as children learn to extract affordances efficiently. Children learn to extract information at the most useful level of analysis: distinctive features, invariant relations, or higher-order structure. Second, attention becomes more optimal as it becomes more active and selective. These and other developmental changes can be seen in recent work on children's learning about communication, interaction with objects, and locomotion and spatial layouts.

Regarding developmental issues, Gibson views humans as active, self-motivated creatures who develop primarily quantitatively but who also develop qualitatively. Nature and nurture together produce an efficient, adaptive perceptual system. The strengths of the theory are its focus on the ecological context of perception and its inclusion of the body in motion during cognition. An area of the theory needing further development concerns the nature of cognitive aspects of perceptual learning.

SUGGESTED READINGS

The best sources for Gibson's theory are her own publications:

Gibson, E. J., & Pick, A. D. (2000). *An ecological approach to perceptual learning and development*. New York: Oxford University Press. This is the most up-to-date comprehensive account of her theory.

Gibson, E. J. (1969). *Principles of perceptual learning and development*. New York: Appleton-Century-Crofts. This book presents Gibson's earlier work.

Gibson, E. J. (1992). How to think about perceptual learning: Twenty-five years later. In H. L. Pick, Jr., P. Van den Broek, & D. C. Knill (Eds.), *Cognitive psychology: Conceptual and methodological issues*. Washington, DC: American Psychological Association. In this chapter Gibson presents a short version of her theory.

Gibson, E. J. (1991). *An odyssey in learning and perception*. Cambridge, MA: Bradford/MIT Press. This collection of Gibson's major papers over her career also includes new material by her in introductions to each section and an epilogue.

The following article puts Gibson's career into a historical perspective and identifies her main contributions:

Pick, H. L., Jr. (1992). Eleanor J. Gisbson: Learning to perceive and perceiving to learn. *Developmental Psychology, 28*, 787–794.

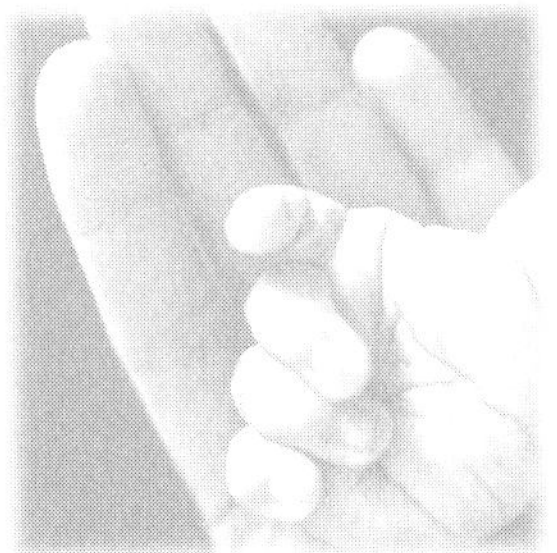

CHAPTER 

Vygotsky and the Sociocultural Approach

The experimenter has removed a crayon of a needed color before the child begins to draw. The child talks to himself:
Where's the pencil? I need a blue pencil. Never mind, I'll draw with the red one and wet it with water; it will become dark and look like blue.

—VYGOTSKY, *1962, p. 16*

Mothers and their children construct a jigsaw puzzle together. A $2\frac{1}{2}$-year-old:

C: *Oh. (glances at model, then looks at pieces pile) Oh, now where's this one go? (picks up black cargo square, looks at copy, then at pieces pile)*

M: *Where does it go on this other one? (child puts black cargo square back down in pieces pile, looks at pieces pile)*

M: *Look at the other truck and then you can tell. (child looks at model, then glances at pieces pile, then looks at model, then glances at pieces pile)*

C: *Well . . . (looks at copy, then at model) . . . I look at it. . . . Um, this other puzzle has a black one over there. (child points to black cargo square in model)*

M: *Um-hm.*

C: *A black one . . . (looks at pieces pile)*

M: *So where do you want to put the black one on this puzzle? (child picks up black cargo square from pieces pile, looks at copy)*

C: *Well, where do you put it there? Over there? (inserts black cargo square correctly in copy)*

M: *That looks good.*

—WERTSCH, *1979, p. 13*

A 4-year-old:

C: *I'll tell you when I need help, Mom.*

—WERTSCH & HICKMANN, *1987, p. 261*

Most of the theories that have influenced developmental research in the Western world have viewed individuals as separate from their social and physical environments. These theories, such as Piaget's, depict development primarily as an individual activity and the environment as simply an "influence on" an individual's development. In North America in particular, a democratic political philosophy, a focus on the rights of individuals, and, historically, the romantic ideal of a lone explorer separated from family in search of new land have directed developmental psychologists to an isolated autonomous individual. The environment simply facilitates or restricts development. A number of other social belief systems and their corresponding psychological theories, many of them Eastern, challenge this view (e.g., Markus & Kitayama, 1991). Of this group, the most influential for present-day developmental psychologists are the approach developed by the Soviet psychologist Lev Vygotsky and, more generally, the sociocultural approach. In the Vygotskian–sociocultural view, humans are embedded in a sociocultural matrix and human behavior cannot be understood independently of this ever-present matrix. As Bhaskar said, "To think of contexts as existing in addition to or apart from practices is like imagining smiles alongside or beside faces" (1983, p. 87)—like a Cheshire cat. Although the sociocultural approach has existed for some time, it appears late in this book because its main influence is recent.

Several influences and events have made developmentalists quite receptive to sociocultural approaches. Ethological and Gibsonian theorists directed our attention to the purposes of behaviors for daily life and the fit between human abilities and our ecological niche. However, they do not focus on the social–cultural aspects of this niche as much as do the socioculturalists. In addition, the neo-Piagetian findings of domain-specific (context-specific) developments, as discussed in the chapter on Piaget, also increased our interest in the contexts of development. However, the neo-Piagetians were more concerned with the nature of particular tasks or domains of knowledge than with the socially embedded nature of all types of knowledge. Trends in a discipline tend to "correct" the direction of previous trends. Thus, the sociocultural approach balances, or corrects, the Piagetian and information-processing focus on the individual. Socioculturalists point out that a culture defines what knowledge and skills children need to acquire and gives them tools such as language, technology, and strategies for functioning in that culture.

The organization of this chapter is as follows: First, in true Vygotskian style, a biographical sketch gives a historical perspective on Vygotsky. Much of the material for this sketch came from Luria (1979), Cole and Scribner (1978), and Wertsch (1985b). Next is a general orientation to sociocultural theory, followed by examples of typical research from this orientation. Then come sections on mechanisms of development, the theory's position on developmental issues, applications, and strengths and weaknesses.

BIOGRAPHICAL SKETCH

Lev Semyonovich Vygotsky was born in 1896, the same year as Piaget, into an intellectual Russian Jewish family. His large family valued stimulating conversations around the samovar. By age 15 Vygotsky was called the "little professor" because of his reputation as a leader of student discussions (Wertsch, 1985b). He often organized debates and mock trials in which his friends took the roles of historical figures such as Aristotle and Napoleon (Wertsch, 1985b). He was well educated. He received a degree in law from Moscow University, but he also read widely in literature, linguistics, psychology, the arts, social science, and philosophy. He later wrote his dissertation on Shakespeare's *Hamlet*. He expressed this interest in language and literature in his later work on cognitive development. Vygotsky taught psychology at a teacher's college in a provincial town in western Russia. In his work he encountered children with congenital defects such as blindness, deafness, and mental retardation. His search for ways to help these children fulfill their potential brought him face to face with issues in cognitive development.

Vygotsky's systematic work in psychology began in 1924 when the Russian psychologist Alexander Luria, impressed by the brilliance of one of Vygotsky's lectures, obtained a position for him at the Institute of Psychology in Moscow. Luria described this event starring an unknown young teacher from the provinces:

> When Vygotsky got up to deliver his speech, he had no printed text from which to read, not even notes. Yet he spoke fluently, never seeming to stop and search his memory for the next idea. . . . Instead of choosing a minor theme, as might befit a young man of twenty-eight speaking for the first time to a gathering of the graybeards of his profession, Vygotsky chose the difficult theme of the relation between conditioned reflexes and man's conscious behavior. . . . It was clear that

> this man from a small provincial town in western Russia was an intellectual force who would have to be listened to.
>
> (1979, pp. 38–39)

Vygotsky's speeches continued to inspire his listeners in the following years. Students sometimes even listened to his lectures through open windows when the auditorium was overflowing.

Vygotsky, Luria, and Leontiev, the "troika" of the Vygotskian school (Luria, 1979), enthusiastically constructed a new psychology based on Marxism as part of the construction of a new socialist state following the Russian Revolution. As Luria described it, "Our aim, overambitious in the manner characteristic of the times, was to create a new, comprehensive approach to human psychological processes" (1979, p. 40). Vygotsky's lack of formal training was not a problem to such a radical group! Wertsch (1985b) argues that it was largely because of the great social upheaval that Vygotsky was able to develop his theory and influence the psychology and education of the times.

Vygotsky and his colleagues wanted to change citizens' thinking from a feudal (landlords and serfs) mentality of helplessness and alienation to a socialistic mentality of self-directed activity and commitment to a larger social unit based on sharing, cooperation, and support. In the new Soviet view, each person was responsible for the progress of the whole society. A main goal was to eliminate the massive illiteracy of Soviet society. In reaction to previous Russian psychologists, Vygotsky and his colleagues constructed a cultural–historical view of developmental psychology and emphasized higher mental activities such as thinking, memory, and reasoning. Vygotsky drew on Pavlov's work on "higher nervous activity" and was aware of European psychologists such as Piaget, Binet, and Freud. In fact, several of his publications critiqued Piaget (e.g., Vygotsky, 1962).

Vygotsky extended Marx and Engels's ideas about economics and politics to psychology in three main ways, all of which will be described more fully later. First, he extended to human development their argument that humans transform themselves, as well as nature, through labor and tool use. The hand creates the mind. The mode of economic production—for example, socialist, capitalist, or feudal—determines people's working conditions and social interactions. These experiences in turn influence their cognition—cognitive styles, attitudes, perception of reality, and beliefs. As Vygotsky translated this to developmental psychology, children's interactions with others in social settings and the "psychological tools" such as language used in these interactions shape children's thinking. In an analogy with labor, children's actions with these tools create thought. Thus, both Piaget and Vygotsky thought that interaction with objects and materials direct cognitive development, but Vygotsky placed more emphasis on social interaction. Also, Vygotsky pointed out the cultural origins of physical objects such as machines and toys.

Second, Vygotsky argued that the economic collectivist principle of shared goods is parallel to socially shared cognition. The adult collective is responsible for sharing its knowledge with children and other less advanced members of society in order to advance their cognitive development. Third, Vygotsky advanced the Marxist principle (from Hegel) of *dialectical* change—that all phenomena constantly undergo change and move toward a synthesis of conflicting, contradictory elements. For Vygotsky, this process constitutes "development." Human thought, like other phenomena, can be understood only by examining its history. Conflict can occur between developing psychological structures, between a currently held concept and a new one, between the child and her environment, between nature and nurture, and so on. Cognitive development through resolving conflicts is similar to Piaget's notion of equilibration. Further discussion of dialectics appears later in the section on mechanisms of development.

Vygotsky remained interested in education, especially mental and physical disabilities and medical problems such as blindness, aphasia, and severe mental retardation. In fact, he undertook medical training for several years. He established several research laboratories, some of them dedicated to the study of children with physical or mental problems. Vygotsky lectured widely, conducted research continually, and published approximately 180 works.

In the early 1930s Vygotsky fell victim to the political strife surrounding Stalin's rule. The government accused him of being a "bourgeois psychologist" of the ilk of Piaget and other suspect Western psychologists. In fact, he was viewed suspiciously for often referring to these writers. The government also criticized him for suggesting that nonliterate minority people in the remote, nonindustrialized parts of Russia had not yet developed the intellectual prowess of those in more modern sections. Particularly suspect was his interest in intellectual testing—a "pedogogical perversion" denounced by the Communist party. The party blacklisted him during the Stalinist purges, as it did many psychologists. From 1936 to 1956 the government banned his work, though his writings continued to circulate underground. Vygotsky's influential book *Thought and Language* was published in

Russia in 1934, the year of his death. He died of tuberculosis at age 37 after only 10 years of professional work in psychology—though they were 10 quite remarkable years. Vygotsky's early brilliance and premature death led him to be called the "Mozart of psychology" (Toulmin, 1978). His theory "was sketchily proposed by a young genius in a mortal race with tuberculosis, during an intellectual revolution on foreign soil, over a half-century ago" (Rogoff & Goncu, 1987, p. 23).

Vygotsky's ideas continued through the work of Luria and others, particularly those in the Soviet Union who were building a "theory of activity." His influence continues there today. Only a few short articles by Vygotsky were available in English until a translation of *Thought and Language* was published in 1962. The efforts of several scholars, including Michael Cole, Barbara Rogoff, James Wertsch, Jean Valsiner, and Ann Brown in the United States, made Vygotsky's ideas more accessible to the English-speaking world. An important recent event was the publication of Vygotsky's collected works, with the sixth volume published in 1999 (Rieber, 1999). This increased accessibility should inspire even more research on his theory.

The last two decades have brought a renewed interest in Vygotsky's work and, more generally, in approaches that emphasize the social-cultural context of human development. Both the growing racial and cultural diversity of children within the United States and the globalization of contemporary life make it imperative that we understand cultural contributions to development.

GENERAL ORIENTATION TO THE THEORY

Vygotsky and present-day sociocultural psychologists share certain assumptions, which will be described below. However, they have certain differences, mainly in emphases, which will be pointed out. The main characteristics are the child-in-activity-in-cultural-context as the unit of study, the zone of proximal development, the sociocultural origins of mental functioning, the mediation of intellectual functioning by tools provided by culture, and sociocultural methodology.

Child-in-Activity-in-Cultural-Context Is the Unit of Study

Rather than focus on the Piagetian individual child, sociocultural psychologists view a child-in-context participating in some event as the smallest meaningful unit of study. "Context" refers to both the larger culture in which children live and its expression in the immediate setting. For example, U.S. culture creates settings such as malls, suburbs, schools, movies, and computers. In addition, of course, any culture has many subcultures, which create diversity in the contexts within the U.S. culture.

A child is not a constant, universal organism operating in a vacuum. Rather, the mind is inherently social: "The path from object to child and from child to object passes through another person" (Vygotsky, 1978, p. 30). The child, the other person, and the social context are fused in some activity. The sociocultural–historical context defines and shapes children and their experiences. At the same time children affect their cultures. Because of this interrelatedness, looking at children while ignoring their cultural contexts distorts our conceptions of them. Focusing on a child alone tends to encourage us to look for causes of behavior within the child rather than in the culture. However, the same developmental process can lead to different outcomes, depending on the cultural context.

This fusion of children and their contexts may not seem like a new concept, because several theories already discussed emphasize the interaction between children and their environments. The difference is that these previous accounts (except Gibson and some ethologists) consider the person and the environment to be separate entities that enter into interactions. In contrast, in the sociocultural view this perceived separation is artificial and distorting. Instead, a single unit exists: certain forms of social practice relate the child and her needs and goals to the environment and define what that environment means to the child. Children behave in certain ways because they have needs and goals that involve the environment. Goals are as diverse as planning a birthday party, trying to convince your parents to buy you a bicycle, attempting to remember which friend borrowed your baseball glove, and figuring out whether you have enough money to buy a candy bar. Social problem solving and communicating one's feelings and desires to others are not just "special cases" of predominantly "cold" cognition unrelated to personal needs; they are the fabric of everyday life and the essence of cognition.

Socioculturalists focus on children's participation in activities in the culture. The smallest reasonable unit of analysis is an individual participating in some cultural practice—an event that occurs routinely in everyday life in the culture—such as games, weaving, selling products on the street, and classroom practices in schools. Enculturation is not something that happens to children; it is something that children do.

And cognition is a dynamic process of trying to understand rather than a set of static stored knowledge. Much as Gibson emphasizes how perception of affordances happens during active exploration, sociocultural psychologists emphasize how children exploit opportunities offered by the culture during active participation in culturally organized activities such as rituals, narratives, and family structures. Much of development has to do with changes in how children participate in the activities offered by a culture; for example, they gradually take on more responsibility within the activity with others. These developmental changes in participation are linked with changes in cognition.

The mind is "socially distributed" (Hutchins, 1991). Consider the following exchange between a mother and her 24-month-old:

> M: Did you like the apartment at the beach?
> C: Yeah. And I have fun in the, in the, in the water.
> M: You had fun in the water?
> C: Yeah. I come to the ocean.
> M: You went to the ocean?
> C: Yeah.
> M: Did you play in the ocean?
> C: And my sandals off.
> M: You took your sandals off?
> C: And my jamas off.
> M: And your jamas off. And what did you wear to the beach?
> C: I wear hot cocoa shirt.
> M: Oh, your cocoa shirt, yeah. And your bathing suit?
> C: Yeah. And my cocoa shirt.
> M: Yeah. Did we walk to the beach?
> C: Yeah.
>
> (Hudson, 1990, pp. 181–182)

The dyad is carrying out the process of remembering. This child's mind extends beyond her skin. Her remembering flows into her mother's as her mother's remembering flows into the child's. It is hard to say where the child's mind ends and the external world begins.

What is culture? *Culture* consists of shared beliefs, values, knowledge, skills, structured relationships, ways of doing things (customs), socialization practices, and symbol systems (such as spoken and written language). Culture also includes social settings (such as schools) and physical settings (such as buildings and highways) and objects (such as tools, computers, television, and art). Culture is expressed through family routines and societal routines. For example, a going-to-a-restaurant script (such as the scripts described in Chapter 4) is a culturally organized pattern of behavior. Cultures use shared symbols, such as images, concepts, and narratives, to make sense of their experience. Within the overall culture, ethnic subcultures or pervasive different lifestyles present different contexts. For example, processes of child rearing differ among different races, social classes, dual-career versus one-career families, rural versus urban communities, single- versus two-parent families, and so on. Throughout this chapter are examples of how these aspects of culture influence (1) what children think about and acquire skills in (for example, academics, sports, weaving), (2) how they acquire information and skills (for example, from other children or from adults, verbally or nonverbally), (3) when in development children are allowed to participate in certain activities (for example, adult work, sex, care of younger siblings), and (4) who is allowed to participate in certain activities (for example, only one gender, certain social classes).

It is important to understand that culture also incorporates physical and historical influences. The climate, type of terrain, urban or rural setting, population density, health care, and physical risks are intertwined with social contexts. Culture is, to a great extent, a group's response to its physical ecology, which biases toward certain forms of economic activity, such as farming or hunting. These activities in turn dictate a particular social organization and division of labor, which in turn influence child-rearing practices, which influence children's concepts. Vygotsky also emphasized that the history of a culture powerfully shapes all levels of contexts. Wars, natural disasters, revolutions, economic depressions, and civil rights movements reverberate at all contextual levels. At any one point in history a culture is both a product of its own history and a provider of settings that shape children's development and, consequently, the future of the culture.

The various levels of cultural settings form a system in which changes at one level affect the other levels. A recession may cause a father to lose his job. This may lead to tension at home, which in turn may cause the child to have problems at school. Such rippling effects can move in the opposite direction as well (from developing child to culture) and bring about social change.

Vygotsky and his colleagues provide a striking illustration of how socioeconomic–cultural change brings psychological change in a naturally occurring experiment involving illiterate peasants working on small farms under a feudal lord in a remote area of the Soviet Union

(Luria, 1976). As part of the movement toward a modern socialist state, the peasants became involved in collective farming practices that required meetings to plan production and make other decisions. They also learned to read and write. Among the illiterate peasants without these new experiences, classification, concept formation, reasoning, and problem-solving skills were concrete and practical. For example, when told that all bears in the far north are white, the peasants would not predict what color a particular bear there would be. A typical reply was, "I don't know what color the bears there are; I never saw them" (p. 108). After even minimal schooling the farmworkers, in contrast, could consider this logical problem in the abstract and give an answer based on logic. It should be noted that Vygotsky may have overestimated the concreteness of the peasants' thinking (Cole, 1988). More recent research in traditional societies shows that these people do think in a logical abstract manner in certain contexts. The schooling and training may simply have taught the peasants to use their abstract thinking in contexts in which they previously did not use it.

A main current discipline associated with the Vygotskian approach is *cultural psychology*. Since the 1980s, the view within this discipline has become more compatible with Vygotsky's. Earlier, cultural psychologists studied culture by comparing cultures and emphasizing differences in behavior between cultures. In fact, the field often was called "cross-cultural psychology." This approach considered culture to be yet another independent variable that "affects" individual psychology, the dependent variable. However, this view is problematic. Culture cannot be separated out and treated as an external factor; culture is everywhere, and it serves to organize all experience. Mind and culture cannot be separated. As Cole (1999) points out, this older *culture-as-difference* approach ignores the fact that the ability to construct, and operate in, a culturally organized environment is a *universal*, species-specific characteristic of humans. We need to understand universal cultural mechanisms as well as the diversity of content they produce. Culture operates in all settings; particular cultures are only particular cases of culture. In this *culture-as-medium* approach, culture organizes the child's everyday experiences and, like good soil for plants, nurtures development. An example is the above conversation between mother and child, which incorporates the culture's world view that guides the child's cognitive structuring of her experiences. Culture-as-difference studies, typically laboratory studies, tend to take a task or procedure that has been studied in one culture to another culture in order to compare the outcomes. Culture-as-medium studies tend to select a task or procedure that makes sense within whatever culture is being studied. The latter approach stresses understanding a culture on its own terms.

As noted earlier, the more "distant" levels of culture, such as cultural beliefs about what kinds of skills children should acquire, often reach a child through the immediate social situation in which a child engages in activities with a parent, sibling, or peer who encourages these skills. Vygotsky expressed this process in his most well known concept—the *zone of proximal development*, our next topic.

Zone of Proximal Development

Vygotsky defined the zone of proximal (nearby) development as the distance between a child's "actual developmental level as determined by independent problem solving" and the higher level of "potential development as determined through problem solving under adult guidance or in collaboration with more capable peers" (1978, p. 86). A more competent person collaborates with a child to help him move from where he is now to where he can be with help. This person accomplishes this feat by means of prompts, clues, modeling, explanation, leading questions, discussion, joint participation, encouragement, and control of the child's attention. As Vygotsky explained, "learning awakens a variety of internal developmental processes that are able to operate only when the child is interacting with people in his environment and in cooperation with his peers" (1978, p. 90). The more skilled adult or peer builds on the competencies the child already has and presents activities supporting a level of competence slightly beyond where he is now.

The dyadic memory episode described earlier provides one example of the zone of proximal development. The mother's prompts and hints scaffold the child's attempts to recall and help her organize her memories. Because the mother and child have a shared understanding of the earlier event, they are able to talk about it together. Another example is the protocol at the start of this chapter in which a mother, helping her child construct a puzzle identical to a completed model, directs his attention to particular puzzle pieces in the model, points to corresponding pieces in his puzzle, and says the names of parts of the puzzle. The mother engages in "building bridges" (Rogoff, 1990, p. 8) between the child's present abilities and new skills. She does this by arranging and structuring his behavior in the task. An example from infancy is that parents draw their infant's attention to important aspects of the environment by carrying her close to, or pointing to, certain objects and events.

Each culture has its own "cultural curriculum" (Rogoff, 1990, p. 190). Children in various cultures learn skills valued by the culture—weaving, hunting, sorcery, healing, reading, taking a bus, or operating computers—by observing others and responding to their informal instruction. For example, a nomadic tribe of magicians and other entertainers in Pakistan highly values the skills of careful observation, refined visual discrimination, sensitivity to the characteristics of other people, and selective attention to the important aspects of a task (Berland, 1982). When adults were tested on a conservation task, if even a single grain of rice spilled out during the pouring or a few drops of water remained in the transfer container, they judged that there now was less. As one adult explained, "When there is little food and many stomachs, our eyes, ears, and noses are more sensitive than goldsmiths' scales" (p. 174). The adults engage in everyday activities with children that encourage these perceptual skills, which are relevant to their nomadic life (for example, acute awareness of surroundings) and magic performances (for example, control of the audience's attention). Thus, adults provide "user-friendly" contexts that help children perfect skills that are needed to survive or succeed in the culture.

Vygotsky described the relation between the actual and the potential levels as follows:

> The zone of proximal development defines those functions that have not yet matured but are in the process of maturation, functions that will mature tomorrow but are currently in an embryonic state. These functions could be termed the "buds" or "flowers" of development rather than the "fruits" of development. The actual developmental level characterizes mental development retrospectively, while the zone of proximal development characterizes mental development prospectively.
>
> (1978, pp. 86–87)

Vygotsky and other socioculturalists believe that development can be understood only by looking directly at the process of change, not at a static child frozen in one developmental moment. Process is more important than product (for example, correct or incorrect answers). They look directly at a child's series of actions and thoughts as she tries to solve a problem and, in the process, advance her own thinking. Rather than focus on what concepts a child "has," they examine what a child actually does over time when involved in an activity, typically with other people and objects. Vygotsky stated that to study a child's development means

> to study it in the process of change. . . . To encompass in research the process of a given thing's development in all its phases and changes—from birth to death—fundamentally means to discover its nature, its essence, for "it is only in movement that a body shows what it is."
>
> (1978, p. 65)

In Rogoff's (1990) extension of the notion of the zone, adults need not explicitly instruct children through face-to-face interaction; children can learn from skilled adults at a distance, by observing everyday activities in which there is no intention to teach the child. That is, instruction can be implicit as well as explicit. Learning is a natural by-product of involvement in tasks with adults or more competent peers. Any verbal explanation occurs naturally while they are working together rather than as part of intentional instruction. Interactions in the zone do not have to be verbal, especially those involving infants and young children. Their behaviors resemble "those appropriate for anyone learning in an unfamiliar culture: stay near a trusted guide, watch the guide's activities and get involved in the activities when possible, and attend to any instruction the guide provides" (Rogoff, 1990, p. 17).

Rogoff (1990, p. 191) expresses these ideas in her notion of *guided participation*, in which a child and an adult collaborate in everyday problem-solving activities. Adults guide children's participation in these activities, helping them adapt their knowledge to a new situation and encouraging them to try out their emerging new skills. Children share in the views and values of the more expert partner, offer their own views, and engage "in the process of stretching their concepts to find a common ground" (p. 196). Rogoff uses the metaphor of apprenticeship. These cultural apprenticeships "provide the beginner with access to both the overt aspects of the skill and the more hidden inner processes of thought" (p. 40).

We can see gradual learning within a cultural apprenticeship in the way Mayan girls learn how to weave—an important skill in that culture (Rogoff, 1990). Very young girls watch their mothers and other adult women weave on a loom. By age 5 they are plaiting long leaves on a play loom fashioned from pieces of thread they find. By age 7 they weave, with help, on real looms, and by 9 they weave simple items alone.

Learning within the zone is possible in part because of *intersubjectivity*—shared understanding, based on a common focus of attention and a common goal, between a child and a more competent person. For infants and young children, this person is most likely to be a parent because their frequent experience together builds these shared understandings. For example, in a laboratory classification task, a mother related the task to the kitchen in the child's home: "We're going to organize things by categories. You know, just like we don't put the spoons in the pan drawer and all that stuff" (Rogoff & Gardner, 1984). It is important to note that intersubjectivity not only contributes to learning from social interactions but also results from these interactions. Each builds on, and contributes to, the other throughout development.

Sociocultural psychologists sometimes use the metaphor of "scaffolding." Much as a temporary framework supports workers and materials involved in work on a building, more skilled people temporarily support a child's emerging skills. They adjust their degree of support according to how much help the child needs. It must be emphasized, however, that the child's behavior affects the adult's behavior as much as the adult's behavior affects the child. The child actively constructs new knowledge and skills with the help of more skilled others. Children actively contribute in that, motivated to learn, they "invite" the adult to participate and gradually take on more responsibility for carrying out the activity. And adults adjust their guidance according to the child's response. Thus, they "collaborate."

Although the zone usually refers to child–adult or child–skilled-peer interactions, Vygotsky actually had a broader definition in mind. The zone can refer to any situation in which some activity is leading children beyond their current level of functioning. Thus the zone can operate during play, work, school studies, and other leading activities (Griffin & Cole, 1984). Play supports young children's emerging ability to use objects in a symbolic way—to substitute one object for another and thereby separate the object's meaning from the object itself. When children "ride" a stick, they separate the stick from its usual meaning. They can think of a stick as both a stick and a horse. Play creates a zone of proximal development for a child because he can operate at a higher level than is possible in nonplay activities: "In play it is as though he were a head taller than himself" (Vygotsky, 1978, p. 102).

■ *The Sociocultural Origins of Individual Mental Functioning: The Intermental Constructs the Intramental*

What happens to children cognitively when they interact with adults? Vygotsky's answer is that interaction between a child and an adult or older child on the intermental (between-minds) plane becomes internalized into the child's mind, the intramental (within-mind) plane. External interaction becomes internal interaction. In this sense, thinking is always social and reflects the dyad's culture. Thinking, remembering, and attending are activities not only of an individual; they first were carried out between individuals. A mental activity "appears twice, or on two planes. . . . It appears first between people as an intermental category, and then within the child as an intramental category" (Vygotsky, 1960, pp. 197–198).

This movement from the intermental to the intramental is related to the first two characteristics described in this section. First, it explains why a child-in-activity-in-context is the smallest possible unit to study. Intramental activity cannot be divorced from intermental activity between children and people in their social context. Second, the internalization of social processes occurs during a child's movement through the zone of proximal development. Children eventually internalize the mode of problem solving that was first supported socially. As Vygotsky expressed it, "children grow into the intellectual life of those around them" (1978, p. 88). They internalize both social nonverbal interaction and the language involved. In a sense, children mentally interact with themselves as they did earlier with other people. Learning to have a conversation with someone else leads to the ability to mentally talk to oneself when thinking through a problem; an external dialogue becomes an internal dialogue. In this way, children gradually take on more and more responsibility for problem solving and become self-regulated rather than other-regulated.

The notions that social activity shapes the mind and that a collectivist society shares its knowledge and experience with less advanced members of society come from Marxist philosophy. The view that intermental (between-people) activity is primary and intramental (within-a-person) activity is secondary—derived from the former—is opposite to the view of much of contemporary Western psychology, which locates cognition "inside" an autonomous individual.

Different types of settings offer different types of interpsychological activities. Teacher–student cognitive activities may be more formal, verbal, and objective than parent–child or older-peer–younger-peer activities. Scientific thinking may emerge from the first, whereas intuitive, concrete thought may be more prevalent in the latter two. Because children encounter a variety of settings, they incorporate a variety of mental processes (Tulviste, 1991).

Both Vygotsky and Piaget emphasized the internalization of interaction between a child and the world. However, Vygotsky stressed the internalization of social interaction, whereas Piaget was more interested in the internalization of motor actions on physical objects. For Piaget, for example, physical reversibility, such as crawling from A to B and back to A or pouring liquid from container A to B and back to A, later becomes the important concrete operation of mental reversibility. The process, but not the content, is similar for Vygotsky. For Vygotsky, the structure of conversations becomes the structure of thought. Collaboration and dialogue between two people lead to these sorts of mental activity during individual private thought. Although Piaget also recognized the influence of other people on a developing child, he emphasized internalization of regularities in the child's motoric interactions with physical objects. Also, he did not address the changing nature of society itself during the life of an individual or over generations.

Intramental processes and structures do not copy intermental ones perfectly. Rather, intermental processes are transformed during the internalization process. The process is active, not passive. For example, inner speech, to be described later, is an abbreviated, personal version of external speech. Rogoff emphasizes that children actively constrain what they retain from social exchanges, a process that she calls *appropriation*. During a shared activity a child assimilates (much as Piaget uses the term) certain meaning but not other possible meanings. Rogoff (1990) uses an analogy of the constant exchange of water and air between the body and the environment. Just as bodies filter and transform air and water to meet biological needs, so do our minds selectively assimilate the social activities in our "social sea" to our current needs and abilities. The child learns something and can now better handle another, similar situation.

A child's selective appropriation of a new idea from a social exchange can be seen in the following conversation between a mother (P. Miller) and her (then) 4-year-old daughter:

M: What do you think you'd like to be when you grow up?

C: A mommy!

M: That's nice . . . but if you want, you can be a mommy and something else.

C: I just want to be a mommy.

M: You know, I'm a mommy and a teacher—two things. You could do that too.

C: I just want to be a mommy.
(This continues for a while until the child concedes—sort of.)
C: Okay . . . I'll be a mommy and a bird!

The child appropriated certain meanings from this conversation and ignored other aspects of the mother's meaning.

Rogoff (1990, 1998) favors the notion of appropriation over internalization because the latter connotes a boundary or barrier between the individual and interpersonal aspects of functioning—a barrier that does not in fact exist. She argues that because "internal" and "external" blend naturally in the shared meaning of social exchanges, no barriers exist between self and other; internal and external are intermixed. As Rogoff states, "It is impossible to say 'whose' an object of joint focus is, or 'whose' a collaborative idea is" (1990, p. 195). In Rogoff's view, children's changed understanding is a natural by-product of their active participation in joint thinking, not an external idea gone underground.

■ *Tools Provided by a Culture Mediate Intellectual Functioning*

As mentioned earlier, Vygotsky and other Soviet social theorists claimed that humans create themselves (that is, their intellectual functioning) through activity: "Humans master themselves from the outside—through psychological tools" (Vygotsky, 1981, p. 141). Peers and adults assist in this self-shaping process by helping children learn how to use their culture's psychological and technical tools. Psychological tools include language systems, counting systems, writing, diagrams, maps, conventional signs, and works of art. Other examples are various strategies for learning, attending, or memorizing, like those described by information-processing psychologists. Some tools that influence thinking are physical devices such as computers, calculators, and electronic games. Tools have ideas and skills built into them. For example, research shows that playing computer games improves spatial skills (Greenfield, Brannon, & Lohr, 1994). People use psychological tools to control thought or behavior, just as they use technical tools such as axes and plows to control nature. Both kinds of tools mediate between the child and the environment. However, technical tools are externally oriented—toward changing objects—whereas psychological tools are internally oriented—toward changing ways of thinking and toward controlling and organizing behavior.

Psychological tools transform the *elementary mental functions*—mental abilities we have in common with other animals—into *higher mental functions* such as voluntary attention and logical and abstract thinking. Elementary mental functions are controlled by external stimuli, as when perception and attention are elicited by a physical object. Higher mental functions use language and other symbol systems for voluntarily thinking about such objects and using them to solve problems.

Each tool involves a different cognitive skill or style. For example, the invention of paper influenced cognition by making the rote memorization of oral texts less important. Today, people's style of thinking may be transformed when they "write" with a computer rather than with a pen or typewriter. A computer lets people reorganize their thoughts and move around sentences and paragraphs. Will children who use computers to write and to seek information over the Internet during their cognitive formative years develop thinking that differs from that of previous generations?

These examples show that a culture's tools connect children, through their activities, with the physical and social world. A culture creates these tools to help people master the environment, the favored tools are passed on to children during social interchanges, and in turn the tools shape children's minds. Children use tools to help themselves think; the tools actually transform thought. For example, once children learn to use language to help them remember, the nature of remembering may change to a more verbal form.

For Vygotsky, language is the most important psychological tool. It frees us from our immediate perceptual experience and allows us to represent the unseen, the past, and the future. Thinking and language are dynamically related; comprehending and producing language are processes that transform, not merely influence, the process of thinking. In Vygotsky's words, "Just as a mold gives shape to a substance, words can shape an activity into a structure" (1978, p. 28). Although language is primarily a device for social communicating with others, this social tool also goes into the mental underground. There, language directs thinking, controls the child's behavior, organizes categories of reality, represents the past, and plans for the future. Again, the intermental becomes intramental. When children use language, they are using a system of meanings constructed by their culture that shapes their attempts to make sense of their world. They are learning to participate in a system of meaning provided by the culture.

Language also transforms the way children use technical tools. It reorganizes and controls their behavior with these objects, thus permitting new forms of problem solving. For example, Vygotsky (1978) describes Levina's observations of children trying to obtain a piece of candy out of reach in a cupboard. Preschoolers typically first try to get the candy silently and then begin to talk aloud to themselves about the problem. Eventually the speech becomes more planful and addresses, for example, the possible usefulness of a stool and a stick. Vygotsky concluded: "Children not only speak about what they are doing; their speech and action are part of one and the same complex psychological function, directed toward the solution of the problem at hand. . . . Children solve practical tasks with the help of their speech, as well as their eyes and hands" (pp. 25–26). There is a unity of perception, speech, and action. Language is a tool and works in conjunction with other tools.

Although language was a product of history, it then changed the course of history. Language changed the way that adults interacted with each other and raised their children. Moreover, cultures vary in how much parents use language in their interactions with children. For example, the Navajo tend to teach quietly by demonstration (Cazden & John, 1971). The direction of gaze and facial expression can be effective nonverbal teaching cues. Verbal communication may be more necessary in cultures in which children are separated from adults and have little opportunity to observe and participate in adult occupational and recreational activities (Rogoff, 1990). When infants are carried on cradleboards on the mother's back all day and children are in the setting where their parents work, and thus can observe work activities, explicit verbalizations about how to do things may be less important.

Contemporary socioculturalists also point out that using language to solve problems is more prevalent in the Western industrialized world. For example, Kearins (1981, 1986) compared Australian aboriginal children of desert origin and European-Australian children on visual spatial memory tasks. She showed children age 6 to 17 an array of items and asked them to re-create the array after she piled the items together. The aboriginal children performed better than the European-Australian children. The latter tried to use verbal mediational strategies, such as rehearsing the names of the items, which were inefficient for this type of task. In contrast, the aboriginal children were more successful because they used relevant visual strategies developed to help them find their way around the desert.

Different cultures emphasize different kinds of tools (for example, verbal or nonverbal), skills (reading, mathematics, or spatial memory), and social interaction (formal schooling or informal or formal apprenticeships) because of different cultural needs and values. Many cultures use schooling to transmit important tools to children. A culture that emphasizes the memorization of religious texts instills different cognitive skills than a culture with schools stressing conceptual understanding and scientific reasoning. The latter are intellectual skills needed in a highly technological society relying heavily on communication through books and other symbolic media. We should not assume that these values are shared by all cultures or even that they would be adaptive in other cultures. Rogoff (1990) notes that in 1744 a group of North American Indians politely declined an invitation from commissioners from Virginia to send boys to William and Mary College. The Indian leaders explained that several of their youths who had been instructed in such institutions returned "ignorant of every means of living in the woods; unable to bear either cold or hunger; knew neither how to build a cabin, take a deer, or kill an enemy . . . neither fit for hunters, warriors, or counselors; they were totally good for nothing" (Drake, 1834, p. 25). More generally, the definition of intelligence differs from one culture to another. For instance, adults in a Ugandan village describe an intelligent person as slow and careful, whereas westernized groups emphasize speed of thinking (Wober, 1972). Kenyans include the responsible participation in family and social life in their definition of intelligence (Super & Harkness, 1983).

■ *Methodology*

For Vygotsky, methods must capture the dynamic nature of development and social interaction. He favored a *dynamic assessment* of children's potential developmental levels rather than only a static assessment of their actual levels. He felt that what children can do with the assistance of others (the zone of proximal development) is a better reflection of their intellectual ability than what they can do alone. A child "is" what he "can be." A dynamic assessment directly measures children's readiness or potential for learning, rather than the products of previous learning. Standardized intelligence tests assess the latter.

One can assess the zone of proximal development in several ways (see Grigorenko & Sternberg, 1998, for a recent review of various sorts of contemporary dynamic testing). For example, an adult might provide a single clue and observe how much the child improves. Ferrara, Brown, and Campione (1986) favored providing an increasingly specific series of clues and determining how many are needed for a child to solve the problem. Children were to pretend they were a spy who wanted to send a message in a secret code. To figure out the code, they had to find the pattern in a series of letters and add the next four letters, for example, "NGOHPIQJ _ _ _ _." The first clue was "Is this problem like any other you've seen before?" A later clue was "Point to the *N* and *O* in the alphabet . . . and to the *G* and *H* . . . . Does that help at all?"

Vygotsky's studies of the zone illustrate his more general method of studying development by looking at change during one or several experimental sessions. This has been called the *microgenetic method*, which was later adopted by information-processing psychologists, as we saw in Chapter 4. The researcher studies the *process* of problem solving and tries to capture a "developmental moment." For example, Vygotsky set up obstacles that disrupted routine procedures of problem solving and observed the child's attempts to cope with this change (see the observation at the beginning of this chapter). In another example, researchers provide various materials or tools that can be used for problem solving and then observe how children of different ages select from, and use, these objects. Because the task typically exceeds a child's cognitive level, she must construct a new skill. Some of these methods will be illustrated in the next section by "double-stimulation" studies.

Contemporary sociocultural research often uses conventional observational methods to study dyads or larger social groups, rather than a child alone, in everyday settings. For example, some studies find that young children often reveal greater social cognition in family contexts than they do when tested individually in the laboratory. At home they effectively use their social intelligence on what matters most to them emotionally—their own rights, needs, and interests. For example, Dunn (1988) describes a 24-month-old with an older sister who had three imaginary friends—Lilly, Allelujah, and Peepee. The younger child taunted her sibling by announcing that she was Allelujah! This rather advanced understanding of what would upset her sister and the ability to pretend to have a different identity are skills that are more advanced than those usually seen in the laboratory in children this young. Finally, other sociocultural methods include ethnographies (interpretive descriptions of a culture) and other interpretive methods, often taken from cultural anthropology.

Researchers must be very careful when choosing the methods for assessing abilities in cultures other than their own. Consider how one might assess whether a person can classify objects in an abstract way, characteristic of adults in literate societies. Cole, Gay, Glick, and Sharp (1971) reported that African Kpelle farmers, when asked to put together the items that go together, sorted 20 objects into functional groups (for example, knife with orange, potato with hoe) rather than into abstract categorical groups (for example, foods, tools). Knife and orange go together, for example, because you cut an orange with a knife. (Such functional groupings are also typical of young children in literate societies.) At one point the experimenter happened to ask how a fool would do it. The farmers immediately put the foods together, the tools together, and so on, as adults in literate societies would! It should not be concluded that people do not possess a particular cognitive skill when they do not demonstrate it. They may be capable of abstract thinking but simply consider other ways of thinking to be more useful for certain everyday activities. This is an example of Wertsch's "toolkit" metaphor for both cultural differences and age differences (1991, p. 93). Cultural groups differ in cognitive functioning not so much in what processes they possess as in which settings they use them in—which psychological tool they select from their toolkit in a particular setting.

For doing research in other cultures, Shweder et al. (1998) suggest two general methods. One is to start with what people do, such as common ways of solving a problem, and then "explore the consequences or the correlates of particular modes of participation" (p. 912). The other method is to "start from some aspect of cognitive functioning (e.g., from a particular understanding of number, biology, or ownership) and ask—again in ethnographic or experimental fashion—what might establish or maintain such forms of mentality" (p. 912).

EXAMPLES OF VYGOTSKIAN AND OTHER SOCIOCULTURAL RESEARCH

The following examples of Vygotskian and related research illustrate the above characteristics of the theory. Vygotsky also studied mental retardation, adolescence, deafness, play, emotions, personality, multilingualism, memory, mathematics, perception, and attention. His work also included schizophrenia, negativity in adolescents, the psychology of art, and even creativity in actors.

The topics in the first two sections below—private and inner speech, and the development of concepts—flow directly from Vygotsky's research. Those sections describe both his research and contemporary research on these topics. The other three topics—collaborative problem solving, research across cultures, and socialization through narratives—are areas that in contemporary research are often associated with sociocultural approaches, though Vygotsky conducted little such research himself.

Private Speech and Inner Speech

Vygotsky saw a powerful interplay between mind and language. He proposed that speech and thought at first are independent. Babbling and other such sounds are speech without thought. Infants' sensorimotor thinking, from Piaget's work, is thought without speech. Vygotsky felt that speech and thought begin to merge at around age 2. At that time "the knot is tied for the problem of thought and language" (Vygotsky, 1962, p. 43). Children learn that objects have names, and thus they use words as symbols. Next, at about age 3, after children learn to talk, speech between people splits into communicative speech to others and *private speech* (sometimes called "egocentric speech" or "speech for self"), which is audible speech for oneself. In private speech, children talk aloud to themselves in a running dialogue but use this speech to guide their thinking, to think through a problem and plan their actions. An example mentioned earlier is children talking to themselves while trying to obtain out-of-reach candy. By approximately age 7, private speech becomes *inner speech*. Children now can silently "think in words," though inner speech is more abbreviated, idiosyncratic, and fragmented than spoken language. Just as children earlier used language only to influence others, they later use it in private and inner speech to influence themselves. In this way, internalized language reflects its social origins: "When children find that they are unable to solve a problem . . . instead of appealing to the adult, children appeal to themselves" (Vygotsky, 1978, p. 27). The intermental becomes the intramental; interpersonal communication becomes intrapersonal communication.

Note that in form (auditory spoken), private speech is like speech between people. However, in function it is like inner speech because both serve to direct thinking and behavior. Private speech is spoken because children do not yet fully differentiate speech for others (communicative speech) and speech for self. As evidence, Vygotsky observed that children produced less private speech in situations in which communication with others was impossible or difficult (a noisy room, a deaf or foreign-speaking peer, no one present) or undesirable (a stranger present). When children differentiate speech for others and speech for self, private speech becomes inner speech.

Vygotsky found that private speech increased when he made the task more difficult so that children could not solve it directly with other tools at their disposal. Some of Vygotsky's manipulations were to remove paper or a pencil of a needed color before a child began to draw, as seen in the protocol at the beginning of this chapter. With these impediments, private speech nearly doubled among 5- to 7-year-olds (Luria, 1961). In a more recent study (Duncan & Pratt, 1997), preschoolers used more private speech on difficult and novel tasks than on easy and familiar tasks. Moreover, private speech declined across sessions as the children became more expert in the activity. It should be noted, however, that private speech never disappears entirely. Adults occasionally use such speech to direct their activities for difficult tasks, as when they mutter to themselves while filling out income tax forms or assembling a bookshelf.

Although Piaget also studied private speech, he thought it simply reflected the child's egocentric inability to take another person's perspective. It has no use to children. In contrast, Vygotsky thought that such speech helps children direct their problem-solving activities. Another difference is that Piaget thought that private speech just fades away, whereas Vygotsky thought it becomes inner speech. More generally, Piaget and Vygotsky have very different views of the relationship between language and thought. Piaget thought that cognition is prior to, and broader than, language. Children develop through the sensorimotor period before acquiring language, and language is but one expression of the emerging symbolic ability around 18 to 24 months. Vygotsky felt that language and thought begin independently and then partially merge. As a result, language gives a tremendous boost to cognition, permitting forms of thinking that are not possible without the help of language.

Speech and thought never completely overlap, even in adults. There is always some nonverbal thought, such as that involved in tying one's shoes or playing the piano, and some nonconceptual speech—rote verbalizations such as saying a familiar address. Even when thoughts are expressed in words, they are never the same thing, according to Vygotsky. There is always a hidden subtext in our speech. For example, Vygotsky (1962) described a passage by Dostoevsky in which six drunken workmen conduct a brief, but complex, conversation, though the only word they speak is a single profane word. Depending on the way it was spoken, it indicated contempt, doubt, anger, delight, and so on. The developmental implication is that language acquisition is more than learning language structure and word meanings; it also requires that the child understand intonations of speech and the dynamics of social contexts and detect the thoughts and feelings of the speaker. Vygotsky was years ahead of his time in this very contemporary-sounding view of language pragmatics and theory of mind.

■ *Development of Concepts*

This section describes Vygotsky's idea that even higher mental functions are social in origin. One of Vygotsky's applications of the microgenetic method described earlier is the *double-stimulation method*. He gave a child a task in which she could select certain materials to serve as a new means to solve a problem. The term "double stimulation" refers to the presence of two stimulus sources—typically, a stimulus with symbolic qualities, such as a word, and a nonsymbolic stimulus, often with perceptual qualities, such as a colored block. An older child is more likely than a younger child to use symbolic as well as nonsymbolic stimulus sources to solve a problem. By observing the child's choice of objects, actions on those objects, and remarks while thinking about the problem, the experimenter can infer the small cognitive advances emerging during the session.

To examine the development of concepts using this method, Vygotsky designed a set of 22 wooden blocks of different colors, shapes, heights, and sizes (horizontal area), now cleverly called "Vygotsky blocks." No two blocks are identical. On the bottom of each block is one of four nonsense words: "bik," "cev," "mur," or "lag." "Bik" appears on all short, large blocks, regardless of color or shape; "cev" on all short, small ones; "mur" on all tall, small ones; and "lag" on all tall, large ones. The experimenter first spreads the blocks randomly in front of the child and then turns over one block to expose its name. The child is asked to select all the blocks she thinks are the same kind. After the child does this, the experimenter turns over one of the selected blocks that he knows is wrong (was not in the same verbal category) and shows the child that it does not have the correct word. He asks the child to try again. This sequence is repeated until the child discovers which characteristics define the word. For example, a child's first collection for "bik" might consist of all short blocks, thus including some "cev" blocks as well. Eventually she would eliminate the latter blocks. Not only the child's initial collection but also her response to correction and efficiency in finding a solution indicate her cognitive level. Thus, in this double-stimulation method, Vygotsky looked at children's use of verbal versus nonverbal concepts. The physical characteristics of the objects are one source of stimulation, and the nonsense words—the symbolic means to solving the problem—are another source. Notice that this study also illustrates movement through the zone of proximal development.

From various studies with these blocks, Vygotsky inferred three stages of conceptual development: (1) unorganized categories (for example, a random heap), (2) complexes (for example, a chain in which a large red block is next to a large blue block because of their identical size, the large blue block is next to a small blue block because of their identical color, and so on, so that each block is similar in some concrete way to the block next to it but no single abstract characteristic unites all the blocks), and (3) concepts (correct sorting on the basis of height and size, possible because the child can use the nonsense word to abstract out dimensions and detect similarities along these dimensions among the blocks). Note the Vygotskian emphasis on how language helps direct the child's problem-solving activities.

Vygotsky was particularly interested in logical concepts, which he called *scientific concepts* (even though they need not have science content). Children can use these concepts consciously and deliberately because they are "distanced" from them. In contrast, *spontaneous concepts* are intuitive, concrete concepts based on everyday experience. For example "grandmother," as a spontaneous concept, is defined as "She has a soft lap" (Vygotsky, 1978, p. 50). As a scientific concept, "grandmother" is understood as an abstract familial relationship that is expressed by many different specific people, some of whom may not have soft laps.

Vygotsky thought that scientific concepts formed one of the most powerful psychological tools developed by modern society. Children enter into this type of thinking with their teachers at school and subsequently internalize it. However, "development in children never follows school learning the way a shadow follows the object that casts it" (Vygotsky, 1978, p. 91). Rather, children's minds are "ready" to accept this overlay; abstract thinking simply formalizes their preexisting intuitive concepts based on everyday experience. Scientific concepts handed down from above by teachers meet children's intuitive concepts halfway and become intertwined with them. Scientific concepts become more concrete, and spontaneous concepts become more logical and abstract. Vygotsky gave the example that when teachers introduce the abstract concept of class conflict, children use their concrete personal knowledge ("spontaneous concept") of poor and rich people to assimilate the new concept. As intuitive concepts are transformed into scientific concepts, they are decontextualized—taken from the child's concrete experience into a context-free formal system. Children become conscious of these concepts and skills and consequently can voluntarily make use of them in a variety of contexts. This "meeting of the minds" that characterizes the interaction between teachers and students during the process of acquiring scientific concepts is yet another example of both the social nature of learning and movement through the zone of proximal development.

Vygotsky argued that instruction in school requires children to form concepts by thinking about speech in a new way: children no longer can simply think about words as ways of communicating meaning; the words themselves become the objects of communication. Teachers direct children's attention explicitly toward the meanings of words and the relationships among these words—a system of knowledge. For example, they teach children to examine the logical consistency of written statements isolated from their referents. Moreover, children become conscious of their own thought processes—a harbinger of what today is called "metacognition."

■ *Collaborative Problem Solving*

Present-day sociocultural psychologists have devoted only moderate research efforts to Vygotskian views on language and concept formation. In contrast, they have shown a great deal of interest in three research areas: the one presented in this section, collaborative problem solving, and the ones presented in the next two sections, research across cultures, and use of language for narratives.

A central idea in Vygotskian and other cultural approaches is that when two or more people interact, they coconstruct a conversation, event, or activity. Developmentalists have been particularly interested in collaborative problem solving between parent and child or between two peers (see Rogoff, 1998). An example of the former, which also illustrates the basic principles of the zone of proximal development, is a study by Freund (1990). Children ages 3 and 5 helped a puppet move his furniture into his new house—basically a sorting task in which doll-house furniture was sorted into a living room, kitchen, and so on. The experimenter told the children to put the objects into the rooms in which they belonged. A child could, for example, place a sofa, chair, small table, and lamp into one room and label it a living room. In the same way children formed other rooms as well. This procedure assessed how well they could perform on their own—their current level of functioning. Next, half of the children interacted with their mothers on easy and difficult versions of the task. The latter had more rooms and more objects. The experimenter instructed the mothers to help their children but not explicitly teach them. The other half of the children spent this time working on the tasks by themselves rather than with their mothers; the experimenter did, however, give them the correct solution at the end. In a posttest, the children once again performed a similar task on their own.

The children who had worked on the problem with their mothers performed at a more advanced level on the posttest than the children who had practiced on their own, even though the latter had been given the correct solution by the experimenter. Mothers acted in the way advocated by Vygotsky for optimal movement through the zone of proximal development. In particular, they adjusted their behavior to the child's cognitive level. For example, they gave more specific content (such as "That stove goes in a kitchen") to the 3-year-olds than to the 5-year-olds. Mothers gave the older children more general help such as planning and keeping the goal in mind (e.g., "Let's make the bedroom and then the kitchen"). Mothers' sensitivity to the 3-year-olds' greater potential on the easy task than the hard one led them to give these general prompts to some extent on the easy task. Mothers tended to talk more in the difficult version. Thus, the mothers were giving their children as much responsibility as they thought they could handle, given their age and the difficulty of the particular task. They tried to structure their children's activities so that the children could move through the zone and gradually take on more responsibility for placing the objects. The dyads also showed intersubjectivity and use of their shared past experience in statements such as "Where do we keep our refrigerator at home?" Finally, the children also contributed to the exchange by ac- attempting to solve the problems and adjusting their behavior in se to feedback.

The above collaborative problem solving with much verbal interaction and direct instruction is typical of a Euro-American dyad. The interaction may differ in cultures in which most of the child's guided participation takes place while the child watches the mother and other adults doing important daily activities. One study (Rogoff, Mistry, Goncu, & Mosier, 1993) examined mothers with their toddlers in four cultures—Salt Lake City, Kecioren in Turkey, Dhol-Ki-Patti in India, and the Guatemalan Mayan town of San Pedro. In the latter two cultures, mothers transmit culturally important information in, rather than out of, context. Thus, in the study they used more nonverbal communication, such as putting the child's hands in the correct position for a jumping-jack toy, and rarely instructed their children directly. These children had developed powerful skills for learning by observing others that are less necessary in the United States and Turkey.

Peer collaborations differ from parent–child ones because peers' competencies are more equal. Also, conflict may be more frequent than with a typically more patient parent. Experiences within a more equal relationship may provide opportunities to learn how to take the perspective of others and how to resolve conflicts. As in parent–child collaborations, the critical process is shared understanding of what the activity is all about. Simply having two children work together does not ensure improved performance or cognitive growth. As we saw in the peer-collaboration research on problem solving in Chapter 4, the positive or negative reactions of one peer to the other one's ideas is a critical shaper of the outcome of the collaboration. The goals of collaborations may differ across cultures, thus leading to differences in the nature of the collaboration. For example, in one study (Ellis & Siegler, 1997), when children collaborated to solve a maze, the Navajo children were more planful than the Euro-American children. This was attributed to Navajos' lesser concern with fast performance. In addition, cultures vary in whom children choose to collaborate with at various developmental levels; this may lead to differences in the relative influence of parents and peers. For example, U.S. adolescents of Chinese, Vietnamese, Filipino, and Mexican descent value discussions with their parents and other relatives when making important decisions more than do adolescents of European descent (Cooper, 1999). This was true even for their degree of comfort with discussing sensitive topics such as sexuality and school performance.

Some of the issues in this area are the following: Do adult–child and peer collaborations differ in their effectiveness and, if so, under what circumstances of age, gender, setting, expertise, and so forth? Are the patterns of thinking and talking together and the mechanisms of change different for adult–child, sibling, and peer collaborations? Can collaboration lead to regression as well as progression? Which specific aspects of collaboration affect which specific aspects of cognitive progress? Do cultures vary in their use of collaborations for enculturation or cognitive progress?

Research Across Cultures

Cross-cultural research is one method within cultural psychology. Such research on cultures other than one's own or on several cultures contributes to our understanding of development by identifying what is universal about development and the mechanisms by which culture affects development and what is culture-specific. In this way, we can see what is "invisible" in our own culture, such as the effects of schooling, because we are so accustomed to its presence. Thus, cross-cultural research prevents us from overgeneralizing our findings.

One good example of how cross-cultural research can identify specific cultural practices that lead to particular child behaviors is infant sleeping arrangements. Nearly all American babies sleep in their own beds and, by the end of infancy if not sooner, in a different room from the parents. This practice seems wrong and bizarre to adults in many parts of Asia, Africa, and Central America, where children sleep with their parents even when there is plenty of sleeping space for separate sleeping arrangements (Shweder, Balle-Jensen, & Goldstein, 1995). Mayan mothers, for example, expressed pity for U.S. babies when told that they sleep in their own rooms (Morelli, Rogoff, Oppenheim, & Goldsmith, 1992). They consider this harmful for the babies. Japanese parents believe that babies are born separate beings who must be taught feelings of interdependence with other people, and sleeping with parents is thought to encourage feelings of closeness and solidarity with others in the family (Caudill & Weinstein, 1969). In contrast, U.S. parents (and most Western social developmental theorists) believe that babies are born dependent and must develop independence; a separate bed is thought to facilitate this. It is interesting to think about this cultural difference in light of the discussion of bonding and attachment in Chapter 5.

Related to these sleeping arrangements, American parents encourage their babies to sleep through the night. In contrast, parents need not push babies toward sleeping through the night in cultures such as rural

Kenya, where parents and infants share a bed so that nursing on demand is possible, where parents need not live by the clock, and where babies are strapped to their mothers' backs while they work during the day (Super & Harkness, 1983). As this research on infant sleep shows, even very early experiences are organized by the culture.

Another cultural difference in adult–child interaction patterns is that North American middle-class mothers usually hold their infants facing toward them, whereas in many cultures, such as in the Marquesas Islands in the South Pacific, mothers hold their infants facing away from them (Martini & Kirkpatrick, 1981). Facing babies outward may reflect both a de-emphasis on parent–child verbal interaction and an attempt to encourage children to observe and interact with older siblings and other members of the community. This orientation of children away from the parent and to the larger community may indicate the sense of community typically found in these villages. Community members may share in the socialization of the young, reprimanding misbehavior in other people's children.

These cultural differences may affect not only social interaction but also even basic cognitive tendencies. In one study (Chavajay & Rogoff, 1999), toddlers and their caregivers from a Guatemalan Mayan community were more likely than those in U.S. families of European descent to attend simultaneously to two or more competing events in the environment. The U.S. dyads tended to alternate their attention between the events. Thus, even attention management is culturally formed; when it is important that children attend to multiple events in the community around them, cultural practices guide children in that direction.

Bornstein and his colleagues (Bornstein, Tal, & Tamis-LeMonda, 1991; Bornstein, Toda, Azuma, Tamis-LeMonda, & Ogino, 1990) have observed American and Japanese (Tokyo) mothers interacting with their 5-month-old infants. At this point infants in both cultures show equal amounts and types of orientation to their mothers and to physical objects in the environment. However, mothers respond differently in the two cultures. American mothers are more responsive when babies orient to physical objects; Japanese mothers are more responsive when their babies orient to them. When the babies' preferences for what to look at did not fit the mothers', the mothers tried to change their babies' attention to fit their preferences—toward themselves for the Japanese and toward objects for Americans. Japanese mothers in general continue to encourage their young children's dependence on them. These specific behaviors are a concrete expression of a very general cultural belief system. The Japanese culture values social ties and dependency; American culture values autonomy and independence. Culture clearly is directing development.

When Japanese children enter preschool, this setting continues to instill the value placed on group harmony (Cole, 1992). For example, American educators viewing a videotape of a Japanese preschool were shocked that there were 30 preschoolers and only one teacher. In contrast, Japanese educators viewing the American classroom with only a few students per teacher expressed concern for the children: "A class that size seems kind of sad and underpopulated," and "I wonder how you teach a child to become a member of a group in a class that small" (Tobin, Wu, & Davidson, 1989). In the Japanese mind, "A child's humanity is realized most fully not so much in his ability to be independent from the group as [in] his ability to cooperate and feel part of the group" (p. 39). As Markus and Kitayama (1991) observe, in America "the squeaky wheel gets the grease" and in Japan "the nail that stands out gets pounded down."

Culture touches concepts even as universal-sounding as mathematics. First, numerical symbol systems differ. Certain cultures in New Guinea, for example, use the names of parts of the body for their counting system. Counting begins with the thumb of one hand and progresses through 27 separate locations (each finger, wrist, elbow, shoulder, right ear, right eye, nose, left eye, and so on) to the far side of the other hand (Saxe, 1981). Second, the form of mental calculation varies as a function of the culture's symbol system. In many Asian countries, people often use abacuses to solve math problems. At least among older children who achieve expertise, these devices encourage people to solve calculation problems in their head by forming a mental image of the abacus (Stigler, 1984). As evidence, when they make an error, it is of the type that would be expected if they were reading off of such a mental image rather than the type of error made by people in cultures where the abacus is not used.

Third, cultures vary in the contexts in which children develop mathematical skills. One example comes from Saxe's (1999) research on child candy vendors on the streets of Brazil. These 6- to 15-year-old boys are poor, and many have little or no schooling. Many need the money to help their families survive and may work as much as 14 hours per day and 60 to 70 hours per week. When selling their products, they must very quickly perform various numerical activities—purchase candy in bulk, decide on a sale price per unit that ensures enough markup, negotiate the price (for example, a discount for larger quantities), make change, and so on. Despite their generally disadvantageous childhood environment, they develop impressive mental calculation abilities. They often perform mathematical calculations in their heads, adjust for inflation, and use a complex system to figure out markups. For example, 10-year-old Luciano paid 7000 cruzeiros at a wholesale store for his 30-unit box of candy bars and must calculate how much to sell the candy for so that he sells it quickly and makes a good profit. This competency is especially remarkable given that, because of inflation, the child vendors have to deal with very large numbers, often in the thousands. They have constructed their own mathematical system and strategies that bear little resemblance to those taught in schools. For example, a child might use a strategy of many-to-one correspondences: setting three bars to one 1000 cruzeiros bill and then adding together many of these sets. In Vygotskian fashion, older children, storekeepers, or parents serve as social supports for the young vendors by helping them set the markup. Developmental changes in participation in the social practice, such as figuring out markup by oneself, lead to cognitive changes, such as an increasingly abstract and hypothetical selling plan. Interestingly, when researchers ask child street vendors to solve similar math problems, but without the vending context, they perform much more poorly; nonvendors show the opposite pattern (Carraher, Carraher, & Schliemann, 1985).

An example of cultural support for participation in mathematical activities is that Asian children surpass American children in their mathematical prowess (though not in overall intelligence). One cause may be that Asian mothers generally attribute mathematical performance to trying hard and not giving up, and they instill these behaviors in their children. This attitude is consistent with their cultural belief in improving oneself through hard work. In contrast, American mothers tend to emphasize inherent ability, an attribution that does not encourage studying hard or trying harder next time if one does poorly on a test (Stevenson, Lee, & Stigler, 1986). Surprisingly, American mothers tend to overestimate their children's abilities and are more satisfied with their children's performance than are Chinese or Japanese mothers! Another cultural influence may be that the Japanese language system encourages attention to the quantitative aspect of reality. Japanese has separate words for counting people, birds, four-legged animals, broad thin objects such as sheets of paper, and long thin objects such as sticks. And Japanese mothers encourage even very young children to play counting games, such as "Let's count birds" (Hatano, cited in Siegler, 1998).

Socialization Through Narratives

Probably all cultures use narratives, or stories, for organizing experience over time and for interpreting human action. As a device for socialization, they maintain the moral system of the culture. These myths and moral tales communicate "lessons" about cultural beliefs and practices. Cultural themes are expressed not only in narratives shared by the entire culture but also in personal narratives within families. A study comparing middle-class Chinese families in Taipei, Taiwan, and middle-class European-American families in Chicago (Miller, Fung, & Mintz, 1996) provides an example. Chinese families were more likely than the ones in Chicago to tell stories about the child's past misbehaviors and to weave into the stories moral and social rules about these transgressions. When the European-American families did construct stories about the child's misdeeds, they tended to downplay this aspect of the story. The Chinese parents may have been operating within a Confucian emphasis on teaching, strict discipline, social obligations, and the value of feeling shame, whereas the American parents may have been more concerned with the child's self-esteem. Thus, cultures select differently from the past when constructing personal narratives and, consequently, children learn what experiences are important and how they should assess them.

Conversations between parents and their children also communicate cultural expectations about gender roles. For example, middle-class European-American parents subtly incorporate these beliefs into their conversations with their preschoolers (Fivush, 1990). Parents coconstructed more elaborate stories about sadness and discouraged feelings of anger more with their daughters than with their sons.

Finally, narratives not only transmit cultural values and meaning but also contribute to children's cognitive skills, memory systems, representations of time, and ability to communicate (Nelson, 1996). Nelson refers to the "emergence of the storied mind" and to the "emergence of the historical self," as when narratives help children develop a sense of self through, for example, autobiographical remembering with adults. Narratives also may contribute to the understanding of others' mental states (Nelson, 1996). Language, along with culturally specific social experiences, allows children to compare their thoughts and beliefs with those of others and thus develop a theory of mind. This perspective contrasts with most accounts of theory of mind that emphasize innate modules or the construction of abstract theories for various domains.

MECHANISMS OF DEVELOPMENT

Vygotsky focused on change and its mechanisms, rather than on the outcome, or performance, of the child. For Vygotsky, development follows a *dialectical process* of thesis (one idea or phenomenon), antithesis (an opposing idea or phenomenon), and synthesis (resolution), which produces a higher-level concept or more advanced functioning. Examples of these two opposing ideas, phenomena, forces, or events are spontaneous, intuitive concepts versus scientific concepts (see earlier), children's level of cognitive functioning with and without an adult's help, the child versus the problem to be solved, and nature versus nurture. These opposing elements confront each other, intertwine, and become transformed into a new and higher level.

Klaus Riegel (1976) identified four sources of developmental change in a dialectical process: (1) inner biological, (2) individual psychological, (3) cultural sociological, and (4) outer physical. Conflict can occur within each dimension, for example, parent–child conflict in the individual–psychological dimension or conflict between racial groups in the cultural–sociological dimension. In addition, as each of these four factors undergoes change, it affects and is affected by changes in the other three factors. These various causes are not simply added together; they interact. A serious illness (inner-biological change) may thwart one's career and cause family tensions (individual–psychological dimension). Changing a child's schooling from a traditional classroom to an "open" classroom (cultural–sociological change) may cause confusion and insecurity (individual–psychological dimension).

Riegel emphasized that life is a sequence of *concrete* interacting events and episodes as the individual grows within a sociohistorical context. At any point in time, the four factors may be in or out of synchrony, but a lack of synchrony is much more common. Development is a lifelong process of trying to resolve the inevitable conflicts among these factors and within each factor. An active individual tries to cope with an active world and learns to live with a certain amount of contradiction. In fact, conflict plays a major role in bringing about successful development.

The idea that there is continual conflict punctuated by momentary stable structures is similar to Piaget's notion of equilibration. Both Vygotsky and Piaget saw a dialectical process at work. However, Piaget did not include a changing society or changing physical environment as possible sources of disequilibrium. That is, he saw an active organism but a somewhat passive environment. Vygotsky, of course, assigned a greater role to social forces, such as parental guidance, teacher instruction, and language, in this process than did Piaget. Another difference is that Vygotsky emphasized the collaboration of people or ideas in this process, whereas Piaget emphasized conflict between one's own concepts and those of a peer or adult.

The dialectical process proceeds through various means. Verbal and nonverbal interaction with adults or more advanced peers, play, and using technological and psychological tools are all important. Engaging in progressively more complex activities and tasks and internalizing social interaction and psychological tools bring about much of the change during development. Modern socioculturalists emphasize that children are exposed to increasingly diverse settings during development that permit them to acquire many kinds of skills.

The specific processes of change during the dialectical process of adult–child and child–child interaction were described earlier in this chapter. During the internalization (or appropriation) process the intermental becomes intramental. Through guided participation, children respond to support and instruction from others and actively contribute to the instructional process. A child and an adult collaborate, and the child gradually takes on more responsibility for problem solving or other activities. Language (or other cultural tools) and observation of other people's activities contribute to the process of change. Once inner speech and various skilled activities are acquired, they in turn stimulate more advanced thinking.

Vygotsky emphasized change resulting from interaction between a child and a more skilled person, usually an adult, perhaps because he was interested in formal instruction and other settings in which children are taught how to use psychological tools to develop the higher mental functions. More recently, socioculturalists have also been interested in cognitive progress resulting from interaction between peers with comparable knowledge and skill levels. Such dyads permit a more equal contribution and avoid the imbalance inherent in adult–child dyads. Peers often *coconstruct* new (to them) knowledge that is a product of their collaboration. The novel outcome does not clearly belong to one child or the other.

Finally, developmental processes may vary from one culture to another. For example, parents from different cultures or subcultures vary in how they attempt to instill values in their children. Cultures may vary in the use of verbal instruction, modeling, and punishment. One particularly compelling example concerns Baumrind's (e.g., 1973) often-cited research demonstrating the superiority of the authoritative pattern of child rearing (a combination of firmness and support) over highly controlling or permissive patterns for increasing achievement and independence in children. This conclusion is questioned by more recent findings (Dornbusch, Ritter, Leiderman, Roberts, & Fraleigh, 1987) that this result appears mainly among Euro-Americans, not African-Americans, Asians, or Hispanics. For example, the Asian parents were high on control, but their children generally received high grades in school. And controlling parents were associated with low grades among Hispanic girls but not boys. Thus, the same parent–child behaviors may have different meaning in different cultures and for different social categories of children. Parental control may be interpreted as caring in one culture and as a negative attitude in another.

POSITION ON DEVELOPMENTAL ISSUES

Human Nature

Sociocultural theories obviously fall within the contextualist world view. Human nature is created in the medium of culture and thus can be understood only in cultural context. Humans are not independent entities that engage their environment; they are part of it—a person-in-context. A child is an active, inherently social, organism in a broad system of interacting forces in the past, present, and future. A child's actions occur in the context of others' actions. Children actively seek out, and respond to, a variety of social and physical contexts. These activities in turn change children cognitively, and this subsequently changes the nature of their future activities. Children cognitively transform their social experiences rather than passively internalize them. They contribute to, and select from, their participation in cultural practices and thus transform the interpersonal plane into the intrapersonal plane.

Qualitative Versus Quantitative Development

In Vygotsky's view, development is both quantitative and qualitative, with periods of calm alternating with periods of crisis or "turning points . . . spasmodic and revolutionary changes" (1978, p. 73). In a dialectical process two elements may develop in a quantitative way, but then as a result of the process of synthesis a qualitatively new form emerges. Important examples of qualitative change are the acquisition of inner speech, moving from an intuitive, spontaneous concept to a scientific (logically defined) concept, and progressing from elementary mental functions to higher mental functions. During such qualitative changes the psychological system reorganizes itself.

Although socioculturalists typically do not posit stages of development, they are not opposed to them. One stage account is Cole and Cole's (2000) proposed series of universal bio-social-behavioral shifts—at birth (transition to life) and then at ages $2\frac{1}{2}$ months (formation of cortical–subcortical brain connections, social smiling, caretaker's new sense of connectedness with the baby), 7 to 9 months (wariness of novelty, fear of strangers, attachment), and 24 to 30 months (grammar-based language). Later shifts occur at 5 to 7 years (independent work responsibilities, formal instruction), 11 to 12 years (sexual maturation), 19 to 21 years (responsibility for self, raising the next generation), and during adulthood and aging (changes in social categories and involvement). During each shift, a convergence of biological, social, and behavioral changes reorganizes the way children interact with their environment. For example, the shift at age $2\frac{1}{2}$ months involves brain maturation and increased wakefulness (the "bio"), caretakers' growing emotional contact with their babies and a sense that they can communicate with them (the "social"), and increased visual acuity, social smiling, decreased fussiness, and improved learning and memory (the "behavioral"). Vygotsky had little interest in describing a set of specific stages, but he and his colleagues did sketch out some possible themes for stages: affiliation (infancy), play (early childhood), learning (middle childhood), peer activity (adolescence), work (adulthood), and theorizing (old age).

Nature Versus Nurture

Socioculturalists see nature and nurture as intertwined. Vygotsky stated that biological and cultural forces "coincide and mingle with one another. . . . The two lines of change interpenetrate one another and essentially form a single line of sociobiological formation of the child's personality" (1960, p. 47). Thus, for socioculturalists, the question is not "how much" culture affects development; rather, the question is, "By what process do biology and culture coconstruct development?"

Even biological influences are mediated by culture, as when the impact of a newborn's sex depends on the culture's social construction of the meaning of this biological fact. For example, the birth of a girl often elicits comments from adults such as "It can't play rugby" and "I shall be worried to death when she's eighteen" (Macfarlane, 1977). Such cultural attitudes about the girl's future constrain and organize her present experiences and thus create a self-fulfilling prophecy. Another example of how cultural beliefs influence parents' reactions to biologically based differences in their children concerns reactions to temperament. In many cultures, parents prefer an "easy" baby who is calm, attentive, and easy to care for. However, a study of Brazilians who live a hard life in the harsh environment of the slums found a preference for "fighters":

> I prefer a more active baby, because when they are quick and lively they will never be at a loss of life. The worst temperament in a baby is one that is dull and *morto de esprito* [lifeless], a baby so calm it just sits there without any energy. When they grow up they're good for nothing.
> (Scheper-Hughes, 1987, p. 194)

Although socioculturalists acknowledge the importance of biology, they choose to concentrate on environmental forces—particularly cultural ones. The activities of others, such as communication, formal and informal instruction, and the use of technical and psychological tools, engage children in collaborative activities. Vygotsky, of course, also emphasized the sociohistorical forces expressed in the environment, although today little attention is given to these forces. Finally, Vygotsky pointed out that people change their environments to some extent through the use of technical and psychological tools.

What Develops

The Vygotskian view of what develops is very broad—a culture (sociocultural history), a species (phylogenesis), a child (ontogenesis), and a cognitive skill (microgenesis). Ontogenetically, an active-child-in-cultural-context is the unit that develops. This unit constructs a variety of cognitive skills, most importantly a system of meaning and its psychological tools—a culturally constructed system of knowledge. Goals, values, and motivation are inseparable from cognitive activity, and thus follow a parallel developmental course. Development has no universal ideal end point; what constitutes an ideal end point depends on the goals of a particular culture. However, Vygotsky, like Piaget, clearly favored higher mental functions, particularly scientific concepts.

APPLICATIONS

Vygotsky's theory and other sociocultural theories have emphasized the importance of schooling for human development. Vygotsky saw school as a way that a culture turns children's intuitive concepts into formal ("scientific") abstract ones. Also, he wrote often about the education of children with low intelligence or learning disabilities.

Contemporary Western schooling tends to teach cognitive skills removed from the practical contexts in which children will use them (Cole, 1996; Rogoff, 1998). These decontextualized activities include memorizing unrelated pieces of information, learning procedures for mathematical calculation, and mastering a written language system. Teachers usually transmit information verbally—through spoken or written language—an approach that encourages abstract, reflective thought and general rules. An important message for teachers is that in many cultures children are taught behaviors that, in a school or testing setting, would make it seem that they do not know something. Examples are not to talk back to a person of higher status, not to act in a way that would draw attention to themselves, not to initiate a conversation, not to appear to be a fool by giving an obvious answer, and not to produce information that the questioner might not have. Navajo children, for example, tend to pause when they answer a question, which gives a non-Navajo teacher the impression that they have finished their answers. Thus, they often are interrupted before they have finished their answers (White & Tharp, 1988).

Cultures in which some children attend school and some do not provide a clearer way to look at effects of schooling. Schooling seems to have more effect on some cognitive skills, such as using memory strategies, forming abstract categories of objects, and engaging in metacognition, than on other skills such as Piagetian concepts (at least through concrete operations). However, it is difficult to determine whether schooling has significant effects on general cognitive development, because unschooled children, who appear to perform poorly, may simply be unfamiliar with the language and procedures of testing—the "rules of the game" of testing.

Vygotsky's notion of the zone of proximal development has important implications for how one assesses a child's ability. A test for assessing intelligence, for example, should assess not what the child knows and understands right now, the typical approach of such tests, but what she can know and understand with help. Similarly, instruction, whether formal schooling or informal apprenticeships, should be based on children's potential level (their "readiness") more than on their actual level.

Dynamic assessments often reveal performance gains that are undetected by standard assessments. This is especially true of "underachievers," who do not typically work up to their ability level.

To illustrate how dynamic and traditional assessments can lead to different conclusions, Vygotsky presented the following example:

> Imagine that we have examined two children and have determined that the mental age of both is seven years. This means that both children solve tasks accessible to seven-year-olds. However, when we attempt to push these children further in carrying out the tests, there turns out to be an essential difference between them. With the help of leading questions, examples, and demonstrations, one of them easily solves test items taken from two years above the child's level of (actual) development. The other solves test items that are only a half-year above his or her level of (actual) development.
>
> (1956, pp. 446–448)

These two children with the same score obviously are not the same cognitively. One can proceed far with help, and thus is said to have a "wide" zone; the other cannot and thus has a "narrow" zone.

Palincsar and Brown (1988) have incorporated the notion that children learn through social interaction in their "reciprocal-teaching" intervention program. In this instruction, a child alternates between the roles of questioner and respondent during reading lessons. A main goal is a shift from teacher-regulated activity to child self-regulation. Another Vygotskian-based school instruction emphasizes apprenticeships with experts in a content area of interest (for example, sculpting) for students with specific learning disabilities (McPhail, Pierson, Freeman, & Goodman, in press). Still another provides unconventional learning tools, such as graphic representations, to students who do not respond to conventional school tools such as reading and writing (Palincsar, Collins, Marano, & Magnusson, 1998). Finally, some schools are incorporating so-called cooperative learning techniques in which a more advanced peer tutors a less advanced one or two peers at roughly the same level collaborate during the learning process.

EVALUATION OF THE THEORY

The strengths of the sociocultural approach are widely acknowledged today and can be described rather quickly. Thus, this section focuses on its weaknesses, particularly its limitations, with an eye toward needed future research. The strengths are the theory's attention to the social-cultural context, integration of learning and development, and sensitivity to the diversity of development. Weaknesses include the vagueness of the notion of the zone of proximal development, insufficient attention to issues of development in the zone, difficulties of studying cultural–historical contexts, and failure to provide a legacy of prototypic tasks revealing interesting developmental phenomena.

■ *Strengths*

Attention to Social-Cultural Context ■ Ethologists and Gibsonians emphasize the evolutionary history of the species and adaptation to the immediate physical–social context, but neither they nor other developmental theorists seriously address the broader sociohistorical context of development. Vygotsky's theory is unique in developmental psychology in weaving together insights from history, sociology, economics, political science, linguistics, biology, art, and literature into psychology. This broader context is not simply another "influence" on children. Rather, it defines children and their activities. Thus, the Vygotskian–contextualist approach "corrects" other approaches.

Vygotsky's theory gives us a different perspective on major topics in development. For example, the significance of attachment is that it serves not only to initiate a strong social relationship with other people and to develop a sense of trust in others but also to involve infants in shared activities with adults and the cultural practices of society. In this way children acquire language and other cultural tools.

Particularly useful for contemporary developmental psychology is Vygotsky's focus on the fluid boundary between self and others. Society and a child make cognitive exchanges at this boundary; society shares its cognitive goals with the child, and the child shapes the environment. The zone of proximal development, intersubjectivity, and internalization all refer to phenomena at this border.

The task for developmentalists is to focus on the specific *processes* involved in this interface between child and setting—the joint operation of forces in the child and in the environment. That is, what do a child and other people actually do together moment to moment in a particular setting, and how does this interaction affect the child's development? Why are certain ecological niches favorable for the development of particular types of children?

In a sense, development occurs at the child–society border rather than in the individual child. This notion is very difficult for the Western mind to assimilate. We tend to dichotomize the individual and the external world, including society, and to situate development within the individual. Vygotsky's view challenges our basic assumption about the nature of reality and, consequently, of psychological development and how to study it.

Integration of Learning and Development ▪ A main theoretical contribution is the account of the relation between development and learning—one of the most important issues of cognitive development. Vygotsky argued that learning drives development. As children learn (proceed through the zone of proximal development), they achieve a higher level of development. In turn, children's level of development affects their readiness to learn a new concept. This theoretical focus on change, along with the method of dynamic assessment, makes this a truly developmental theory (but see the section on weaknesses below).

Children learn how to use materials and people in their specific circumstances to obtain goals: "Cognitive development consists of coming to find, understand, and handle particular problems, building on the intellectual tools inherited from previous generations and the social resources provided by other people" (Rogoff, 1990, p. 190).

Sensitivity to Diversity of Development ▪ Most developmental theories focus on universal aspects of development. In contrast, sociocultural psychologists acknowledge both individual differences within a culture, such as wide versus narrow zones, and differences among cultures. This sensitivity to diversity is quite important, because much of the knowledge base of contemporary developmental psychology comes from research on white, middle-class Western (mostly North American) children. What is true of this group may not be universally true. Shweder et al. (1998) use the phrase "one mind, many mentalities" to express the idea that the mind is both universal and specific to its cultural milieu. Cultural psychology raises the question of whether there is a universal end point of development. Ideal thinking and behavior may differ for different cultures with their particular social and physical circumstances and types of tools available. And different historical and cultural circumstances may encourage different developmental routes to any given developmental end point.

▪ *Weaknesses*

Vagueness of the Notion of the Zone of Proximal Development ▪ Paris and Cross (1988) have noted two main ambiguities in or limitations to Vygotsky's concept of the zone. First, knowing only the width of children's zones does not provide an accurate picture of their learning ability, style of learning, current level of development compared to other children of the same age, and degree of motivation. For example, children who have narrow zones may have so little inherent learning ability that they are unable to profit from assistance. These children may be functioning at a very low level. Or children with narrow zones may be successful independent learners who nearly have achieved their potential. Consequently, social assistance helps them only slightly. Similarly, low-achieving children who have wide zones may be unable to solve problems independently and so rely on help from adults. Or high-achieving children may have wide zones because they have high learning ability but, due to low motivation or lack of appropriate learning strategies, rely on adults for help. Thus, having a wide zone (or a narrow zone) can be desirable or undesirable, depending on its causes. Moreover, children may appear to have a narrow zone simply because adults have failed to provide appropriate instruction. In short, simply assessing children's zones provides a very incomplete developmental picture.

Second, the zone has problems of measurement. Although the metaphor of a spatial zone implies a metric of distance, there currently is no metric for determining this "distance" (Paris & Cross, 1988). For example, one child needs help sounding out words during reading, a second child needs help connecting ideas across sentences, while a third only needs encouragement. Even if these children need an equal number of prompts, do they actually have equally wide zones? No common scale exists for answering this question. Vygotsky sometimes measured the zone in terms of age, such as when a child with an actual level of functioning of age 6 and a potential level of functioning of age 9 has a zone of 3 years. Yet this is a very global metric, and it cannot be assumed that the difference of 3 years between ages 2 and 5 is equal to that between ages 6 and 9.

There are still other problems with the zone notion. One is that the exact psychological processes involved in internalization of the intermental to the intramental (Vygotsky) or appropriation of a shared activity (Rogoff) remain unclear. For example, what sorts of mental representations of social interaction are formed? Also, we know little about the generality and stability of an individual child's zone. Does a child tend to have a wide zone (or a narrow zone) across most domains? Is the size of the zone a stable individual characteristic that is constant over the years? Moreover, we need more information about the developmental implications of the zone. Is guided participation from adults necessary or only helpful for development? Is improvement resulting from the zone long-lasting? Can it generalize to other similar situations?

Another limitation is that most of our knowledge about the zone concerns mother–child and, to a lesser extent, peer dyads. Do father–child, adult–infant, sibling, and multiperson units operate in the zone in different ways? Also, not all parents are eager and competent guides, and many children in hostile environments may learn not to seek contexts with adults. Finally, we know little about the role of affect in the zone. Children seek out contexts that satisfy their needs for affection, food, stimulation, and so on. They enter contexts with their own emotion-laden agenda. Moreover, they often have a preexisting emotional (positive or negative) relationship with the people in these contexts that colors the nature of their social interaction. A child asks her mother to show her how to ride a bicycle because she wants to be able to engage in this activity with her friends. Another child is asked by a disliked relative to listen to instructions on using a vacuum cleaner so that she can help clean the house. The nature of learning in the zone will differ in these two cases. The general point is that our knowledge about zones must be broadened.

Insufficient Attention to Developmental Issues ▪ Although Vygotskian theory is a quintessential developmental theory, in some ways the approach does not really seem very developmental, especially in work on the zone of proximal development and other studies of the social context of problem solving. As Bronfenbrenner put it, "In place of too much research on development 'out of context,' we now have a surfeit of studies on 'context without development'"(1986, p. 288).

We need a more developmental account of both contexts and children. Regarding contexts, we have little description of contexts of children of various ages or developmental levels. The culture has different expectations for children of different ages and thus places them in different settings. As children grow older, the culture puts new pressures on children and grants them new social freedoms. Society introduces older children to schooling, work responsibilities, clubs, and organized athletic and social activities. It allows or encourages different activities at different ages.

Regarding a developmental account about children, children's abilities, needs, and interests at each age influence the nature of the settings they seek out and the effect that a particular setting has on them. We have little idea how the child's cognitive level both permits and constrains processes in the zone of proximal development. Sociocultural research rarely addresses the nature of the cognitive skills that are required for responding to prompts, joint attention, learning from observation, and collaborative dialogue. Developmental changes in these skills affect both the breadth of the zone and how quickly a child can move through it. Specifically, the most helpful hints, modeling, direct instruction, explanations, and motivators surely differ for children of different cognitive or social developmental levels. All of these require certain developing cognitive skills such as attention, memory for action sequences, mental imagery for comparing the actions of the self and others, verbal encoding, and inference of intentions.

For instance, at any age children's developmental level constrains what they can acquire in the zone of proximal development. We know, for example, that 3-year-olds benefit less than 4-year-olds from nondirective prompts (Plumert & Nichols-Whitehead, 1996). Moreover, among children who cannot count by themselves, 4-year-olds are more likely to shift to counting with their mothers' help than are 2-year-olds (Saxe, Guberman, & Gearhart, 1987). As still another example, preschoolers may profit less in the cognitive realm from peer-collaborative activities than do older children, and even when collaborating with skilled partners they may have difficulty engaging in certain cognitively sophisticated activities, such as abstract planning (Rogoff, 1998). Without an account of how cognitive development affects the processes and outcomes of collaboration, we have no clear idea of how the processes of learning and development operate in, for example, a 2-year-old's zone compared to an 8-year-old's:

> It seems reasonable that naivete and lack of experience may underlie zones at some ages or in some domains and that poorly structured knowledge, lack of strategies, inappropriate expectations, and so forth may determine the widths of zones at other ages or in other domains.
>
> (Paris & Cross, 1988, p. 35)

Vygotsky began to address this issue and suggested, for example, that the emerging speech and mobility after the first few months of life dramatically change children's potential for social interaction and the kinds of settings they can enter. One example is Luria's (1961) description of developmental changes in young children's ability to use language to regulate their behavior.

Tomasello, Kruger, and Ratner (1991) have proposed a promising account of developmental changes in the capacity for acquiring culture through interacting with other people. As children's social cognition, particularly their ability to take the perspective of other people, matures, they are capable of increasingly advanced forms of cultural learning. Nine-month-olds can acquire new behaviors through *imitation* because they understand that people are intentional agents. They know what goal the other person is trying to achieve through his behavior. Around age 4 children see others not only as intentional agents but also as mental ones. Their emerging understanding of representation allows them to represent someone else's representation of the situation and to try to reconcile it with their own. As a result, they can benefit from *instruction* from others and can internalize the instructions, which is similar to Vygotsky's notion of internalizing dialogue. By age 6 they can engage in *collaboration* with a peer at their level of competence because they can integrate the mental perspectives of two people who can think about each other's thinking. With a peer they coconstruct knowledge and internalize the coconstruction. In this model, intersubjectivity, because it permits social perspective taking, is central to cultural learning.

Another important developmental difference affecting behavior in the zone may be a child's level of expertise or phase of stagelike development. For instance, children who are acquiring new skills or just entering a new stage may have a wider zone than children who are experts or are solidly in that stage. The former may have a tenuous grasp of their new skills and concepts and need scaffolding from adults in order to perform at the level of the new stage. In contrast, the latter children have a solid, stable understanding that allows them to function on their own, creating a narrow zone because they already have proceeded nearly as far as they can. Similarly, modeling may be a more effective clue than verbal explanation for 4-year-olds because the latter may be beyond their comprehension ability. They would appear to have a wide zone in the former case and a narrow one in the latter.

Finally, the effects of major sociohistorical events depend on developmental characteristics of the child and other individual characteristics. For example, the Great Depression had its most negative effects on boys of preschool age (Caspi, Elder, & Herbener, 1989); both age and gender mediated this sociohistorical variable.

Vygotsky also gave little attention to the role of physical maturation. Specifically, the neurological, sensory, cognitive, and motoric abilities of a 1-year-old and a 3-year-old surely affect which contexts are available to them and how people treat them in these contexts. Also, human infants are biologically predisposed toward acquiring some concepts more easily than others, as a result of phylogenesis (see Chapters 5 and 6). This puts constraints on the degree to which social experiences can influence various skills during infancy. Contemporary sociocultural theorists are addressing this issue. For example, Cole and Cole's (2000) notion of bio-social-behavioral shifts is a promising attempt to add a developmental dimension to contextualism.

The overall point here is that a child's cognitive and physical developmental level influences (1) what contexts a child enters, (2) the nature of the social–cognitive processes involved in the dyadic interaction, and (3) the effect of sociohistorical events on the child. "Developmental level" includes children's knowledge, motives, reasoning skills, attentional biases, metacognition, social skills, language ability, self-concept, and so on. Children of different developmental levels bring different things to a setting.

Difficulties of Studying Cultural–Historical Contexts ▪ Nearly all developmental psychologists would agree that it is important to examine the social, cultural, and historical contexts of development. Yet few studies examine, or even vary, the social and cultural context. And many fewer study the historical context. Why this discrepancy between attitudes and behavior? A main reason is the practical difficulty of conducting this type of research. Observing parent–child or older-peer–younger-peer dyads in action is difficult and time-consuming. Investigators must develop a sensible classification system for coding the behaviors, use this system to code the videotaped interactions, establish interrater reliability, and then code all of the tapes. Cross-cultural research often requires expensive travel, extensive learning about the other culture, careful translation of materials, and identification of appropriate testers. And it is difficult to interpret cultural differences in the results because they could be caused by many differences between the cultures. It is even more difficult to study historical influences because the relevant events no longer are occurring. One historical moment can never be directly compared with another, and it is difficult to detect which of the many differing aspects of a different historical moment, for example, an economic depression, is responsible for the behavior. Even Vygotsky conducted little research on larger historical–cultural forces such as class struggles, racial unrest, and alienation of certain groups. The links between broad social–historical contexts and specific parent–child interactions, in particular, need to be worked out better (see also Paris & Cross, 1988).

No Legacy of Prototypic Tasks Revealing Interesting Developmental Phenomena ▪ One reason that Piaget's theory stimulated much productive research by others is that he provided several tasks that revealed interesting, even surprising, developmental phenomena.

The conservation, object permanence, spatial perspective-taking, class-inclusion, and transitivity tasks come to mind. These served as arenas for fruitful empirical skirmishes for many years. Similarly, information-processing-oriented investigators had these Piagetian tasks plus problem solving, attention, and memory tasks; ethology had imprinting, attachment, and peer dominance hierarchies; social learning had imitation paradigms; and Gibson had the visual cliff, reading, and traversability tasks. No such prototypic tasks from sociocultural approaches have caught the imagination of current developmentalists and stimulated an outpouring of research. Although Vygotsky developed several tasks to use with children, as described earlier, researchers have rarely adopted these tasks in recent years. Even when Vygotsky did conduct experiments, he typically described his procedures in a very sketchy way and presented little or no data, relying instead on general summaries. His studies were more like pilot studies, or demonstrations used to illustrate what he saw as the basic principles of cognition and development. Given the urgency of his mission and his chronically poor health, he directed his energy toward opening up new lines of research rather than fully examining any one area.

Sociocultural psychologists today use many different types of tasks. In a way this diversity is advantageous. We can test the theory more generally, and research does not become the mindless, pedestrian varying of one factor after another on the same task. However, the lack of prototypic tasks and sets of interesting developmental findings connected with these tasks makes an explosion of sociocultural research unlikely. Moreover, a systematic, coherent, well-documented account of development in a single domain may never emerge. The body of contextual research may always seem scattered and unfocused, and it may be difficult to compare findings from studies using different tasks.

CONCLUDING COMMENTS

Given this account of Vygotskian sociocultural research, how much of the recent "Vygotskian" research is actually Vygotskian? The assimilation of Vygotsky into contemporary work on developmental psychology provides an interesting case study of sociocultural influences on science. When researchers take a theory from a different culture and historical time, they necessarily distort the theory in some way—much like the distortion that occurs when people assimilate, in the Piagetian sense, something into their current mental structure. In the case of Vygotsky, something is lost in the translation, so to speak. What contemporary developmental psychology needed from Vygotsky was a sensitivity to the social and cultural context of development. And that is what we took. In this sense there now have been quite a few Vygotskian studies. The prototypic current sociocultural study focuses on peer or mother–child collaboration during problem solving or looks at behaviors in another country. However, three main aspects of Vygotsky's theory do not fare as well in our individual-oriented world view and so have been relatively ignored. First, much current sociocultural research looks at how social settings influence behavior or how a child's performance shifts from setting to setting. It does not start with the child-in-context as its basic unit. The social context is grafted on to individual development, rather than considered an inherent part of it.

Second, the notion of the zone of proximal development has been plucked out of its social–political context. Vygotsky saw interactive learning processes in the zone as an expression of collectivism; society shares its mental skills during "shared consciousness" much as it shares its material goods. In contrast, current Vygotskian research still conveys the impression that an individual child's cognitive development is guided by an individual adult rather than by society in general.

Third, many recent studies of the zone that are presented as Vygotskian-inspired are little more than traditional studies of mother–child interaction and do not incorporate the principles that distinguish Vygotskian studies from any study of adult–child interaction. Researchers still view cognition as something that happens inside a child's head—an adult simply helps put it there. Truly Vygotskian studies must (1) look at both adult and child behavior and at how each adjusts to the previous response of the other, (2) assess what a child can do both alone and with an adult's help, and (3) look at the gradual shift in responsibility from adult to child over the course of the session. Such studies must also (4) assess how the adult structures the learning process, tries to pull the child to a slightly higher cognitive level, relates the problem to the child's previous experience, and adjusts the amount of help to the difficulty of the task and (5) examine how the culture and its history shape the nature of the parent–child interaction. Some studies incorporate only certain aspects of this approach, such as looking at how adults "scaffold" (provide physical, social, or intellectual support for) children's emerging abilities (Griffin & Cole, 1984). Very few studies include all five aspects.

It is not necessarily wrong to selectively assimilate a theory. Scientific progress often comes from taking only what is most useful from a theory. But it should be recognized that Vygotsky's theory is often misunderstood.

SUMMARY

Developmental sociocultural approaches have many roots, but Vygotsky was the main historical force. Vygotsky's theory currently has considerable influence on developmental psychologists, especially in the area of cognitive development. Unlike most theories, this approach focuses on the child-in-activity-in-cultural-context, rather than on the child alone. The higher mental functions are social; children use cultural tools, such as symbol systems, to solve problems in their everyday attempts to meet their goals within a social reality. Culture constructs settings and shapes the interactions of people in them. A child's participation in various cultural routines nurtures particular ways of thinking. Cultural beliefs, knowledge, values, artifacts, and physical settings influence what settings children are encouraged to enter and when they can enter them, what they learn in these settings, how they acquire skills, and who can enter particular settings. Thus, sociocultural approaches force researchers to reexamine dichotomies such as culture versus mind, thought versus action, and person versus context.

Besides a child-in-activity-in-cultural-context as the unit of study, several other characteristics define settings. Children develop in a zone of proximal development—the distance between what a child can do without help and what he can do with help. A more skilled person uses prompts, discussion, modeling, explanation, and so on to guide and collaborate with children to move them through the zone. Because the child and a familiar adult share a past and have a common goal in the task, they have a shared understanding of the problem. Children actively contribute to their movement through the zone by seeking out particular settings, influencing the course of the activity, and bringing personal qualities and developmental skills to the interaction. Vygotsky argued that only by looking directly at moment-to-moment change over time can we understand development; intelligence is not what you know but what you can learn with help.

As children engage in activities with others, intermental activities, particularly dialogue, become intramental. In this way individual mental functioning has sociocultural origins. Language between people eventually becomes spoken speech for self (private speech) and then silent, mental, speechlike inner speech. Children internalize (Vygotsky) or appropriate (Rogoff) information and ways of thinking from their activities with parents, teachers, other adults, and more skilled peers.

Technical and psychological tools provided by the culture mediate intellectual functioning. Language, in particular, helps children direct their own thinking efficiently; they plan, think logically, and form abstract concepts. However, nonverbal interaction with others encourages cognitive skills as well. If culture constructs the mind and if culture changes, then it follows that we must study the mind by looking at how it changes.

The above theoretical considerations mandate a dynamic assessment of children's potential levels of development rather than a static assessment of current levels. The microgenetic method involves an analysis of moment-to-moment changes as a child moves through the zone of proximal development. In this approach, Vygotsky sometimes used the method of double stimulation to see if children could use materials as symbolic tools to solve a problem beyond their current ability. Vygotsky thought that psychologists should study development over four time frames: microgenetic, ontogenetic (development), phylogenetic (history of the species), and sociohistorical (for example, the emergence of new technologies).

Prototypic Vygotskian research includes topics such as private speech and the development of concepts (particularly "scientific" ones taught in school). Today, sociocultural research is more likely to examine collaborative problem solving, multiple cultures, and socialization through narratives. For Vygotsky, the most general mechanism of development is the dialectical process in which two contradictory ideas or phenomena are synthesized into a new idea or phenomenon. Several types of forces enter into this dialectical process: inner-biological, individual–psychological, cultural–sociological, and outer-physical change. The dialectical process operates mainly during interaction with adults, more skilled peers, or peers of equal ability and during play. Movement through the zone is a dialectical process as the child collaborates with another person and they coconstruct the meaning of the task, a goal, and a solution.

Regarding the theory's position on developmental issues, it holds a contextualist view of human nature; human nature develops in a social context. The temporal dimension (past, present, and future) is cross-woven with the spatial dimension (social settings). Development is both quantitative and, when synthesis results during the dialectical process, qualitative. Nature and nurture also enter into a dialectical process, but socioculturalists focus on the social strands of this process. Finally, what develops is an active-child-in-context.

Regarding applications, Vygotsky wrote about learning in the classroom and about children with special needs. More recent applications focus on collaborative peer learning, interactive learning, and the zone of proximal development. The strengths of the sociocultural approach are its attention to the social–cultural context of development, integration of learning and development, and attention to the diversity of development. Weaknesses are the vagueness (or limitations) of the notion of the zone of proximal development, insufficient attention to setting and child-developmental aspects of the zone of proximal development, the difficulties of studying cultural–historical contexts, and the failure to provide prototypic tasks revealing interesting developmental phenomena. Although sociocultural theory has stimulated research on social influences, few studies have incorporated the aspects of the theory that do not fit easily into the contemporary Western cultural belief system.

SUGGESTED READINGS

The following two books by Vygotsky provide a good introduction to his theory:

Vygotsky, L. S. (1978). *Mind in society: The development of higher psychological processes*. Cambridge, MA: Harvard University Press.

Vygotsky, L. S. (1986). *Thought and language*. Cambridge, MA: MIT Press.

Vygotsky's works are being collected into a series:

Rieber, R. W. (Ed.). (1987–1999). *The collected works of L. S. Vygotsky* (Vols. 1–6). New York: Plenum Press.

For a recent overview of developmental sociocultural psychology, the following sources are useful:

Cole, M. (1999). Culture in development. In M. Bornstein & M. Lamb (Eds.), *Developmental psychology: An advanced textbook* (4th ed.). Mahwah, NJ: Erlbaum.

Shweder, R. A., Goodnow, J., Hatano, G., LeVine, R. A., Markus, H., & Miller, P. (1999). The cultural psychology of development: One mind, many mentalities. In W. Damon (Series Ed.) & R. M. Lerner (Vol. Ed.), *Handbook of child psychology: Vol. 1. Theoretical models of human development* (5th ed., pp. 865–937). New York: Wiley.

Rogoff, B. (1998). Cognition as a collaborative process. In W. Damon (Series Ed.) & D. Kuhn & R. S. Siegler (Vol. Eds.), *Handbook of child psychology: Vol. 2. Cognition, perception, and language* (5th ed., pp. 679–744). New York: Wiley.

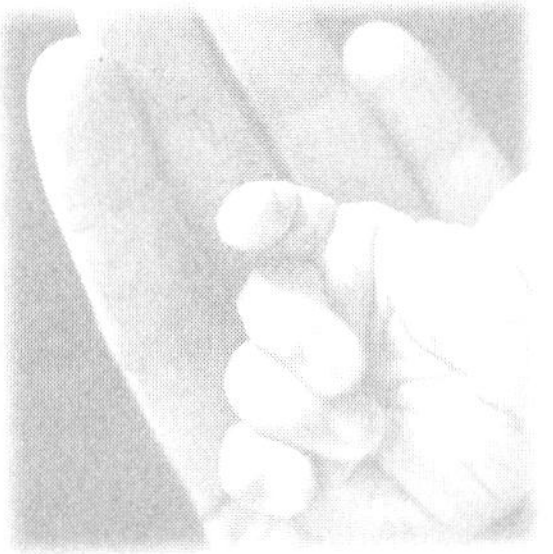

CHAPTER 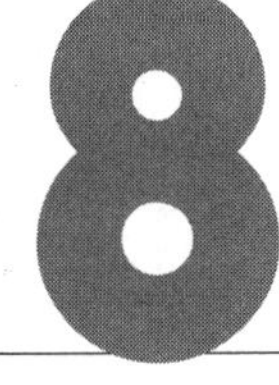

Contemporary Minitheories and Emerging Approaches

An experimenter shows a 5-year-old a candy box with pictures of candy on it and asks her what she thinks is in it. "Candy," she replies. She then gets to look inside and discovers to her surprise that it actually contains pencils. What would another child who had not yet looked inside think was in it, the experimenter next asks. "Candy," says the child, amused at the deception. The experimenter then tries the same procedure with a 3-year-old. The response to the first question is the expected "candy," but the response to the second is an astonishing and unamused "pencils." More surprising yet, the younger child also claims, in response to further questioning, that he himself had initially thought that pencils would be in the box—and had even said there were.

—FLAVELL & MILLER, 1998, p. 851

The preferred states of infants' motor systems in nonreaching movements—their individual instrinsic dynamics—profoundly influenced the nature of the transition to reaching. . . . Two infants, Gabriel and Nathan, had large and vigorous movements; the other two were quieter and generated fewer and slower, less forceful movements. The task for all the babies was the same: to get their hands in the vicinities of the desired objects. But they had different problems to solve to do this: Gabriel and Nathan had to damp down their forceful movements to gain control; Hannah and Justin had to produce more muscle force to extend their arms forward in space and hold them stiffly against gravity.

—THELEN & SMITH, 1998, p. 608

Developmental theories, like the children they describe, are always in motion, always changing. Each chapter in this book on the "big" approaches also described some of their contemporary relatives currently stimulating research and tried to convey a sense of the sort of research associated with each. Examples of these current perspectives are neo-Piagetian approaches, connectionism, modern attachment theories, and evolutionary psychology. To complete the picture of contemporary theories, this chapter provides a slice of theoretical life in developmental psychology today. The currently influential theoretical approaches described here either do not emerge obviously from the theories covered earlier or are distinct enough from their theoretical relatives to deserve our undivided attention. Each approach is placed within the current context of developmental research and theorizing. A main goal is to convey the current issues these approaches address. References for each theory provide direction for further reading for more details. The approaches included are the theory theory, modularity nativism, developmental neuroscience, dynamic systems, developing person-in-context, and critical psychology.

THE THEORY THEORY

Children are told the following story, which the experimenter acts out with dolls (Wimmer & Perner, 1983). A boy puts some chocolate in a blue cupboard and goes out to play. In his absence, his mother moves the chocolate into a green cupboard. After the boy returns for his chocolate, the children are asked where the boy will look for it. Three-year-olds immediately say "the green cupboard," where the chocolate actually is, even though the boy in the story could not possibly know that the chocolate was moved. In contrast, the 4- and 5-year-olds usually say "the blue cupboard," because, unlike the 3-year-olds, they have an understanding of mind in which people act on the basis of their beliefs, even when the beliefs are false. This surprising and compelling demonstration of 3-year-olds' belief system, and its relatively rapid change over the next year or two, became the basic paradigm for *theory-of-mind* (see below) research. One could say that the 3-year-old and the older child have different theories of mind—different underlying principles about mental states and their connections to behavior and the physical world.

Theory of mind is a main topic within the *theory theory*, an influential current theory of cognitive development (Gopnik & Meltzoff, 1997; Wellman & Gelman, 1998). This theory proposes that children, and perhaps even infants, have the capacity to construct intuitive, folk, everyday, naïve "theories" that attempt to explain a particular domain. For example, children have theories of biology, physics, and mind. This approach arose in part because of dissatisfaction with Piaget's claim of domain-general concepts and ways of thinking. Recall from Chapter 1 that children often do not seem to have concepts characteristic of a particular stage that they apply consistently across tasks. Also persuasive was the discovery of specific cognitive or linguistic deficits in children with disorders believed to be biologically based, for example, a lack of understanding of certain aspects of mind in children with autism. Such evidence of domain-specific concepts led to the theory-theory view. Also, young infants' apparently advanced concepts of the physical world, described in earlier chapters, suggested that even young children might have a belief system or intuitive "theory" that is more abstract than the thinking that Piaget attributed to them.

According to the theory theory, children's thinking progresses much as does scientific discovery. Children are little scientists (and perhaps scientists are grown-up children). Children are born with a tendency to form naïve, or folk, theories. Such a theory is an organized representation about a particular domain in the world, such as a theory of mind. Typically theories infer unobservable causal relationships that underlie observable phenomena. A simple example is the knowledge that desires lead to intentions; a child might understand that another child *wants* to find her new game and thus *intends* to look for it. Or, in the cupboard example, 4- and 5-year-olds think that beliefs lead to behavior, even when the belief is false. The claim is that young children's theories, and perhaps even those of infants, are somewhat abstract, coherent, and internally consistent. Children use these causal-explanatory theories to interpret the world, predict future events, and explain previous events, just as do scientists.

Children test their theories and may be in a temporary state of cognitive disorganization if a theory does not hold up. However, their theories are resistant to change. Children initially tend to try to ignore disconfirming evidence or perhaps patch up the theory. An implication for education is that children (and even adults) resist giving up their theories, for example, their belief that the world is flat, based on their everyday experience, even when teachers provide evidence that the world is round. Getting children to give up an old theory is as important as providing them with a new theory.

As counterevidence continues to build, infants and children may construct a new and improved theory. Consider a 9-month-old baby who has a simple theory of action (Gopnik & Meltzoff, 1997). He believes that he can influence people's actions by communication but objects' actions only by making physical contact with them. This theory about the role of force on physical objects works fairly well much of the time for a 9-month-old. However, counterevidence arises when he tries to put a block into a bottle with a narrow neck. He repeatedly but unsuccessfully tries to force it into the bottle but eventually must reconsider his theory, and by 18 months he has a new and better theory that acknowledges that brute force does not always work with physical objects. The new theory in turn has a new set of interpretations, predictions, and explanations that he will test.

The new theory may be a revision of the old theory, as in the above example of physical force. Or the new theory may be quite different from, and incompatible with, the old theory (Carey, 1991). An example is the change from a flat-world to a round-world theory. This radical theory change constitutes a cognitive revolution, similar to the scientific revolution in changing from a Newtonian to an Einsteinian physics in the history of science.

According to the theory theory, children have the innate ability to abstract information from events and this helps them construct their theories. Within this broad predisposition, experience (evidence and counterevidence) contributes to the specific theory they construct. Consequently, the type of theory a child has would differ from one domain to another and would evolve at different rates in different domains. Not only would 6-year-old's theory of biology be very different from her theory of mind, but also one theory could be more advanced than the other.

Many sorts of evidence support the claim that children have theories of physics, biology, and mind. Regarding a theory of physics, many examples of recent demonstrations of young infants' considerable knowledge about properties of objects, such as their permanence and continuity, and correlations between their sights and sounds appeared in the chapters on Piaget's and Gibson's theories. Also, the information-processing chapter reported adults' and children's adherence to their theory that objects fall straight down even though they saw evidence to the contrary when watching an object dropped from a moving toy train. An example of young children's changing theory of biology is their awareness of some, but not all, properties that distinguish living from nonliving entities. They are puzzled by plants, for example, because plants grow, like animals, but do not have self-initiated movement, unlike animals. Other evidence is that young children seem to have some notion of the "essence" of an animal, because they can ignore physical similarity or dissimilarity and detect underlying essences. For example, they consider a realistic-looking mechanical monkey to be more like a hammer than a real monkey (Carey, 1985). However, some essences are harder for young children to maintain. This was demonstrated when children were told a story about a scientist who operated on a horse to make it look like a zebra (Keil, 1989). The scientist added stripes to the horse, cut off its mane, taught it to live in Africa, and so on. Is it still a horse? Young children had trouble continuing to think of it as a horse, but older children did not.

Theory of mind currently is the most active area of theory-theory research and perhaps of the entire field of cognitive development (see Flavell & Miller, 1998, and Wellman & Gelman, 1998, for reviews). Older children and adults seem to have a *desire–belief theory of mind*. They predict and explain others' behavior in terms of what people *want* to do and what they *believe* about reality—true or false. John looked around the neighborhood for his puppy because he thought it had gotten lost and he wanted to find it, even though it actually was asleep under the bed. The candy-box experiment presented at the beginning of this chapter is another example of theory of mind in young children.

Let us now look more carefully at the claims that children have naïve *theories* of the world as opposed to just any sort of knowledge about the world (Wellman & Gelman, 1998). First, the theory theory proposes that children divide the world into fundamentally different sorts of "things"—for example, thoughts versus solid physical objects. Second, children understand that each domain involves fundamentally different sorts of causes—for example, in the physical domain one object collides with another object, causing it to move, but desires and intentions cause human behavior. Third, children refer to distinctive underlying constructs in their understandings—for example, the mind consists of mental representations, but solid objects are composed of physical substances. Fourth, concepts form a larger system. Desires are connected to intentions to perform certain actions, as when a desire for candy leads to the intention of obtaining some, which leads to a trip to the store.

In other words, children should honor distinctions among these domains as to the sort of entities they are and use distinctive causal principles when reasoning about various domains. They also should construct theories such that each domain is represented by a distinct set of unobservable and interconnected causal notions.

It is important to emphasize that children's theories are everyday, commonsense, folk theories, not scientific theories. The theories organize and structure children's everyday understanding of phenomena. Theories are called "foundational" in that they address particularly important aspects of daily life, such as the properties of physical objects, and are influential for shaping and constraining other concepts during development.

It is clear that the theory theory still looks somewhat Piagetian in its claims that knowledge is organized, children construct new knowledge, current knowledge constrains what sort of change can occur, and a period of instability accompanies change. However, the approach differs from Piaget's in that it tends to consider each theory to be domain-specific and relatively separate from the others. Also, the capacity to construct theories is considered to be innate, and theories appear much earlier than Piaget thought. Some versions of the theory theory make even a stronger claim about the extent to which a theory is innate.

What is the current status of theory theories? They have produced a rich body of knowledge about children's understanding of mind and behavior. Moreover, developmentalists are impressed by infants' seemingly precocious knowledge, by the domain-specific deficits in special populations, and by demonstrations of the fairly rapid qualitative shift to an understanding of false belief. However, many developmentalists question whether infants and young children have anything abstract, coherent, and consistent enough to be called a "theory." Preschoolers' understanding of mind may involve a more concrete and limited body of knowledge acquired from interaction with family and peers and from their knowledge of their own desires and intentions. Also, as Lillard asks: "When a 42-minute-old infant imitates an adult's tongue protrusion, is it really right to say the infant is guided by an abstract theory?" (1998, p. 664). Another caution is that the need for coherence and internal consistency in a theory may not have a high priority in all cultures (Lillard, 1998).

Finally, it is not clear what can count as a domain. When we describe how people carve the world at its joints, how do we identify the joints and decide how large or small a domain can be? For example, do we have a theory of paper clips or of the kitchen sink? How can we tell if a theory refers to a foundational, or core, domain? And, of course, what is the process of change from one theory to the next?

MODULARITY NATIVISM

Somewhat related to the theory theory is what might be called *modularity nativism*. Modularity nativism provides an alternative to Piaget's theory and information-processing theory that is even more radical than most theory theories because it takes an even stronger position about what is innate. The claim is that the mind consists of a loosely connected set of innate modules, structures, or constraints (Fodor, 1983). Each module is specialized for perception and/or cognition in a particular domain, such as language (Chomsky, 1988) or mind. That is, the brain is wired in such a way that it makes certain assumptions about these entities. Modules are preprogrammed to respond to specific sorts of information. A module requires little experience in order to be triggered, much like fixed action patterns in ethological theory or the Darwinian algorithms of evolutionary psychology described in Chapter 5. For example, simply being exposed to language may be sufficient for normal language development. Evidence has little effect other than to serve as content that fits into the innate structure; counterevidence cannot overturn the modules. Any developmental changes in thinking are caused by factors external to the module, such as maturation that brings a later module or more efficient processing of information. A module specifies a limited number of end points in each domain and cannot be tested and changed. Thus, infant minds in many ways are not that different from adult minds.

In contrast, in theory theories infants and children engage in testing their theories and thus, if they have different experiences, can end up at a variety of end points. And because theories are constructed rather than simply elicited early on, children's theories typically look rather different from adults' theories. The theory-theory approach's nativism is only a "starting-state" nativism (Gopnik & Meltzoff, 1997): infants have an innate ability to construct a set of representations of input and rules for operating on those representations, but these initial "theories" will be revised later and continually in light of evidence as infants explore the world. For example, infants are pretuned to infer rules about objects' behavior, such as "one solid object cannot pass through another solid object." In other words, there is a human tendency to theorize.

Modularity nativists argue that humans have evolved specific perceptual and cognitive abilities essential for adaptation. Because of their innate modules, infants' brains have certain assumptions about the nature of physical and social entities and language. That is, there are mandatory links between input and output. Thus, children can acquire a complex system such as language very early and quickly (Pinker, 1997). Humans can develop only a limited set of possible grammars because of brain-based constraints. Theory of mind and physics also may develop in this way (Gelman & Williams, 1998; Spelke & Newport, 1998). The concepts that children acquire look very much like the theories of the theory-theory approach in that they are somewhat abstract and allow children to make predictions that go beyond the perceptual input and infer minds, other essences of objects, and rules of grammar.

Modularity nativism draws on many of the same sorts of research evidence as described above for theory theories, such as young infants' precocious knowledge and evidence for a biological basis for cognitive deficits in autistic children. Other evidence includes the selective impairment of grammatical abilities after brain damage, the rapid acquisition of complex language despite meager environmental data, critical periods for language development, and correlations between physical maturation and the emergence of new concepts. Some researchers (Pinker, 1997) argue for an evolutionary–neurological basis for modules, which makes research on animals other than humans and cognitive neuroscience research (see below) useful as well.

Not all developmentalists who think that children's knowledge is domain-specific are modularity nativists. For example, many of the neo-Piagetians described in Chapter 1, especially Kurt Fischer, also emphasize the context-specific nature of cognitive performance. In addition, Howard Gardner (1993) proposes domain-specific intelligences in several domains: linguistic, spatial, logical-mathematical, musical, bodily-kinesthetic, intrapersonal (understanding the self), and interpersonal (understanding others). Although some of these forms of intelligence are assessed on IQ tests, some, particularly musical and kinesthetic intelligence, are not. In Gardner's view, professional musicians and dancers, first-rate quarterbacks, plumbers, and car mechanics display high intelligence of nontraditional sorts.

Regardless of whether developmentalists ultimately will adopt the strong biological stance of modularity nativism or the weaker biological stance of certain theory theories, or neither, these approaches have placed a central issue on the table: What constrains learning and development? What, how, and how fast a 1-year-old or a 4-year-old can learn in a particular domain may be constrained by her modular brain or her current conceptions of reality or a variety of other subtle constraints (or, more positively, "enabling constraints"). Also, how can we account for the recently demonstrated apparent precocious knowledge in infants? For an account of theoretical and empirical developments concerning constraints, see Gelman and Williams (1998).

How might we reconcile nativism and the constructivism of the theory theory and Piagetian approaches? One example of theorizing about this issue is Karmiloff-Smith's (1992) account of how representations might change through a constructive process. In her *representational redescription* theory, she proposes that children develop from innately programmed, highly specific and modular processors of information to more flexible processors with an awareness of their own thinking. At first children simply have problem-solving behaviors. Later they have representations of the world but are not conscious of them or able to generalize them. The representations may emerge from the innate, domain-specific modules. Later, children gradually come to form representations of these representations; they think about and talk about their representations. That is, by reflecting on their own mental representations, children acquire new knowledge. What once was an encapsulated module of implicit knowledge can become a more generally available skill or explicit concept about a particular domain.

DEVELOPMENTAL NEUROSCIENCE

Strictly speaking, the developmental neuroscience approach should not be called a theory. However, because it does include an identifiable set of concepts, methods, and assumptions, and because it currently is a main rising "star" in developmental psychology, and in fact throughout psychology, we must consider it at least briefly here. It obviously is not possible to cover the many fascinating facts revealed about the developing brain. (For good recent descriptions, see Johnson, 1998, 2000.) Instead, this account outlines the developmental issues that the neuroscience approach addresses and identifies the questions it asks, thereby suggesting the sorts of findings that are likely to modify our theories of development. Neuroscience is most obviously related to the ethological, evolutionary psychology, connectionist, neo-Piagetian, and modularity-nativist approaches. However, findings potentially have relevance for any developmental theory.

Recent technological advances, particularly brain-imaging techniques, partly account for the current boom in neuroscience. Neuroscientists generate maps of brain activity based on changes in blood flow, metabolic activity in the cerebrum, or electrical activity. For example, they place sensitive electrodes on the scalp, which measure the electrical activity generated by the firing of groups of neurons. In this way they identify the pattern of the activity when, for example, a stimulus is presented. Or cerebral blood flow generates images indicating brain activity. Thus, one could compare the spatial patterns of brain activity in children of different ages or ability levels working on the same task or those of children of the same age working on different sorts of tasks. Such comparisons provide clues about developmental changes in cognitive processing and about the relations among different cognitive processes. For instance, changes in brain activity are correlated with the change from nonconservation to conservation (Stader, Molenaar, & van der Molen,1993). Other knowledge of brain development comes from work with animals and with humans with brain damage or other brain disorders.

The approach obviously addresses the nature–nurture issue. Brain development used to be considered a static unfolding of the genetic blueprint. Modern neuroscience, however, views brain development as a complex interaction of nature and nurture. Behavior affects brain development, just as brain development affects behavior. For instance, some evidence suggests that there are slight initial brain constraints or biases in that, for a particular task and situation, some neural pathways are more easily activated or more easily connect to certain outputs. Examples are infants' biases toward looking at faces or analyzing language sounds. However, infants in turn seek out these appropriate stimuli, which further strengthen and specialize these pathways (Johnson, 2000). Thus, infants may be slightly biased to look at particular types of stimuli, but the small biases become further amplified through specialized activity. The developmental end result of this "activity-dependent development" is specialization of brain pathways, because the infant does not use the other pathways that initially could have been used.

Another example of the complex relations between biology and experience is that there is a biologically driven overproduction of synapses early in development but certain ones are pruned because they are not stimulated by experience. Most children, because they are physically normal and are raised in an environment typical for the species, have more or less the same sorts of experiences at about the usual time. Thus, the pruning proceeds along similar lines for most children. However, what about atypical situations, such as children who are deaf or blind and thus do not receive auditory or visual stimulation? In deaf children, certain areas of the brain that normally would be devoted to auditory processing if the brain received both auditory and visual stimulation instead gradually become devoted to visual processing (Neville, 1995). Conversely, in blind children, areas normally devoted to visual processing when receiving both auditory and visual stimulation instead are devoted over time to auditory processing. Thus, when an area of the brain does not receive its normally expected input, it can be used for other purposes. The nature of experience, and consequently the nature of brain activity, determines which synapses are pruned and which survive. The brain is preset to rapidly guide children along certain developmental paths, but it is also flexible enough to deal with adverse circumstances.

Researchers are addressing the molecular, cellular, and behavioral levels for a complete account of how brains develop from their initial plasticity to their final specialization as a result of experience. Research has examined the brain basis of behaviors such as face recognition, visually guided action, memory, language acquisition, speech recognition, object permanence, planning, and emotional development.

Some of the questions that neuroscientists ask that are most relevant to theories of development are the following: Are changes in the brain during development correlated with changes in cognition? Do areas of the brain become more specialized during development? How does experience contribute to this specialization? Does the spatial pattern of activity in the brain while the child is performing a particular task change during development? Are there different developmental timetables of specialization for different domains, different sorts of cognition, and different areas of the cortex? How early does the primary visual cortex process visual input, and how does it come to be involved in visually guided motor behavior such as reaching? Is there evidence for domain-specific modules? Neuroscience also has important practical applications. Increasingly accurate assessments of brain damage or of abnormal brain activity in psychologically abnormal or developmentally delayed populations broaden our understanding of disorders and suggest effective interventions.

Neural findings may play two roles regarding theories of development. One is that they may constrain them. Certain theoretical claims may appear implausible in light of new findings about the brain. For instance, the competition among brain pathways during infancy suggests cognitive models that posit multiple competing representations stimulated by particular stimuli or tasks, rather than a single representation (Johnson, 2000). Second, neural findings may raise new questions and suggest new hypotheses that enrich our current theories or suggest new ones. For example, we need psychological theories that explain apparent regressions, as when synapses increase in density during infancy but then decrease to an adult level several years later (Johnson, 1998).

A cautionary note is that there is a danger that findings from neuroscience are being considered more important—more basic and explanatory—than purely behavioral findings. In fact, each level of analysis from the molecular to the behavioral to the ecological is an integral part of the story of development. No one level is privileged, and all are intertwined. Moreover, although neuroscientists know that showing the brain basis of behavior reflects how experience affects the brain as well as how the brain affects behavior, other people sometimes neglect this point when interpreting findings.

DYNAMIC-SYSTEMS THEORY

The dynamic-systems theoretical approach would be on anyone's list of influential and promising current theories. Thelen and Smith (1998) and Lewis (2000) provide a comprehensive account. Key phrases are "order in complexity," "patterns that live and change in time and space," and "the whole is more than the sum of its parts." *Dynamic-systems theory* comes from work on complex, nonlinear systems in physics and mathematics, but it fits into models of biology and the organismic tradition in developmental psychology. The theory addresses changes over time in complex holistic systems, especially self-organizing ones. (One self-organizing system from an earlier chapter is Piaget's cognitive structures that reorganize themselves in order to maintain equilibrium.) In dynamic systems' "big-picture" view, one can understand development only by considering "the multiple, mutual, and continuous interaction of all the levels of the developing system, from the molecular to the cultural" and "nested processes that unfold over many time scales, from milliseconds to years" (Thelen & Smith, 1998, p. 563). This inclusiveness distinguishes it from the other theories in this book.

A mountain stream serves as a good metaphor for a dynamic system (Thelen & Smith, 1998). At various points down the mountain the stream is expressed as a fast stream, a small trickle, a waterfall, or a still pool, depending on many factors, such as the rate of flow of the water downstream, the terrain, and weather conditions. Most of the time this pattern is about the same. After a heavy rain or a drought, however, the configuration of the water changes, though in predictable ways. To understand the current dynamic state of the stream and how it self-organizes, we must consider many time frames, from the ancient geological history of the mountain to the recent rainstorm. We also must consider many levels of "cause," from the terrain of the mountain and gravity to water molecules. The same is true of changes in human dynamic systems. Developing children show patterns, self-organization, and interconnected changes on many levels, ranging from culture to molecules.

Dynamic-systems theory asks, "Where do new behaviors come from?" New complex forms or skills emerge from interactions of the parts of a complex system—from the relations among the parts and the self-organizing nature of living organisms. They can be said to "fall out" of the current status of the system in its present context, just as a new stream falls out of an existing stream after a heavy rain. Given the overall state of the system in its current setting, a certain outcome is inevitable. The development of an embryo from one cell through various more complex organizations is a good metaphor of how a new organ or limb emerges during prenatal development through a predictable set of configurations.

One example of the emergence of a new ability is that when babies do not have the motor skill to perform some desired action, such as obtaining an attractive toy, they have to create a behavior that works. In trying to assemble a new motor behavior on the spot, such as trying to obtain a toy out of reach or walking on a water bed for the first time, infants draw on the motor skills they already have. First they randomly try out many different behaviors in an attempt to find one that works. Then, after seeing which behaviors work, or appear promising, they put together and fine-tune a new behavior, such as pulling on the cloth on which the desired toy rests. Thus, both the nature of the task and the child's current motor skills and motivations determine what develops in a particular situation at a particular time. "Individual speed 'personalities'" (Thelen & Smith, 1998, p. 609) also play a role, as seen in the second quotation at the start of this chapter. A more cognitive example, in an older child, is the emergence of a new strategy in response to information specifying the task in its physical environment. That is, given the child's current strategies and skills, the nature of the task materials, and the child's goal, he assembles a new strategy.

Consider a classic dynamic-systems experiment: Newborns have a stepping reflex. They appear to walk, much like a toddler does, when supported in an upright position with their feet touching the floor. The fact that this reflex disappears around 2 months of age traditionally has been interpreted as showing that higher brain functions begin to inhibit lower-level reflex behaviors. However, the dynamic-systems approach suggests another explanation (Thelen, Fisher, & Ridley-Johnson, 1984). The fact that babies older than 2 months continue to show this "walking" pattern when lying on their backs argues against the traditional explanation. Thelen and her colleagues proposed instead that as babies gain weight over their first few months, their legs become too heavy to lift when babies are upright. Their evidence was that these older babies, who apparently had lost the walking reflex on the usual measures, suddenly began showing it again when held in a waist-high tank of water that made their legs less heavy. Thus, an infant's behavior depends on the particular configuration of infant skills and intentions and the affordances of the immediate setting. If you change one element, you change the interaction of the parts. The irreducible unit is the organism-in-context. In this way, the approach resembles sociocultural approaches or the developing-person-in-context approaches discussed later in this chapter.

An important notion in the theory is that of a *preferred state*—a state in which the system tends to reside. Although behaviors can vary, the organism tends toward a preferred form. A 4-year-old tends to walk in a particular way, at a particular speed, but this changes somewhat when walking very fast or when walking on a water bed or a boat. An 8-year-old tends to use a particular addition strategy but uses others if the numbers get so large or so small that other strategies work better or a less effortful strategy can be used. In large time frames, even stages such as Piaget's can be considered preferred states with periods of instability between them.

Several subtle principles of change make intriguing predictions about development. One is that a small initial difference or effect can have reverberations that culminate in large, dramatic differences or effects later. This would tell a strategy researcher to look for causes of new strategies not only on the trials immediately preceding the one on which a new strategy emerges but also on trials, or perhaps even sessions, much earlier (Miller & Coyle, 1999). The child may early on try out a small variation that, after many trials, grows strong enough to stand on its own. A related prediction is that a small change causes changes throughout the system. Thus, dynamic-systems researchers might look for effects of instruction on tasks other than the ones on which they trained the child. Moreover, quantitative change can lead to qualitative change as a skill gradually changes until it passes a critical threshold and then seems to emerge as a qualitatively different skill. For example, an infant's muscles gradually become stronger to the point that he can—apparently suddenly—sit without support.

Given the above principles, it is obvious that the theories' methods must examine moment-to-moment changes over time. This characteristic is shared with information-processing approaches. Microgenetic methods (Chapters 4 and 7) and longitudinal designs are the best methods for looking at change. By looking at behavior over a period of time, researchers can identify the preferred state. They also can identify the point of most rapid and significant change when the system is self-organizing to a new developmental level. At this unstable point a system reveals itself, especially its processes of change. One technique for measuring the dynamic pattern of locomotion and its change is to dress babies in black bodysuits with reflective markers (like baby bikers) at their joints. As the babies learn to move across a surface by creeping, crawling, or scooting, a computer reads the reflections to determine the speed, direction, and pattern of the movements over time (Freedland & Bertenthal, 1994). By looking at how each behavior flows from previous behaviors and from the current environment, such as the surface on which the baby crawls, it is possible to hypothesize what variables (for example, body weight, body proportion, perceptual ability) are controlling behavior. Finally, the experimenter tests this hypothesis experimentally; an example is the earlier experiment in which babies walked in water.

A main attraction of the dynamic-systems approach is its inclusion of many aspects of development and many levels of analysis. In principle, one could study any sort of content from a dynamic-systems perspective, a characteristic that distinguishes it from the other theories in this book. The approach shares with Piagetian theory a desire to describe the overall organization of behavior and dynamic equilibration. Most of the theories in this book tend to break complex systems into simpler, more easily studied parts, thereby limiting their scope. However, the inclusiveness of dynamic-systems theory makes it difficult to conduct research from this perspective. It is difficult to examine all potential causes of a behavior and their complex interactions.

Dynamic-systems theory provides a general approach that can be applied to many areas of developmental psychology. Most of the developmental research thus far has examined infants' motor behaviors, such as walking, reaching, and searching for hidden objects, and the relevant research is most easily applied to such motor behaviors. However, the approach also has been applied to more cognitive skills, such as word learning and the concept of object permanence (Thelen & Smith, 1998), and to social development (Lewis, Lamey, & Douglas, 1999). And more applications appear regularly.

DEVELOPING-PERSON-IN-CONTEXT

Approaches emphasizing the settings in which people develop (see Lerner, 1998) arose in reaction to the decontextualized, reductionist laboratory studies of children that dominated the 1960s and 1970s. Context-sensitive theories are closely related to the sociocultural perspectives in the previous chapter but differ enough to warrant separate coverage in this chapter. Both approaches insist on the situated nature of all behavior and thinking and often study behaviors in everyday contexts. Both question any claims of universal characteristics of humans. However, cultural psychology tends to focus on how children's participation in the customs, practices, and shared meanings of a culture is intertwined with the development of the mind in various cultures. For example, tools such as language mediate reality. In contrast, much of the person-in-context research examines populations in the United States and describes how the social and physical environments form layers of influence on the child. Also, these models vary in whether the context influences the child, whether they influence each other, or whether they form a complex system of influences between contexts and between contexts and children. The most recent models tend to be of the latter sort and often are labeled a "systems approach," in some ways similar to the dynamic-systems approach. Systems theories focus on the integration of various levels of organization, ranging from biology to culture to history.

Person-in-context approaches typically describe multiple levels of contexts in which developing children are embedded. Contexts change over time, as a result of sociohistorical changes. The Great Depression and World War II obviously changed the contexts of childhood in major ways. As a contemporary example, a person-in-context theorist might hypothesize that deteriorating social conditions in the home, including the availability of guns, increase children's violent behavior in the schools; this increased violence in schools in turn affects other parents' beliefs about how to raise their children and increases parents' contact with the schools. Moreover, the particular pattern would depend on the child's age. Contextualists also examine whether one context supports another. For example, do parents ensure that children do the homework assigned at school? Another important notion in person-in-context approaches is the goodness of fit between a person and her context. A particular school may work well for one child but not another. A poor but talented musician is more likely to obtain the needed musical training in a culture that values and supports its musical culture.

Although developing-person-in-context approaches have been around for a number of years, they have become more salient in recent years as part of the more general renewed interest in situated accounts of development, along with Vygotskian and other sociocultural approaches. Also, many models of interactions of biology and ecology within a system have drawn on contextual models. Finally, the extension of person-in-context models to historical contexts in life-span psychology (Elder, 1998) has enriched, and created interest in, the approach. Discussions of developing-person-in-context approaches can be found in Magnusson and Stattin (1998) and Moen, Elder, and Luscher (1995). We will focus our discussion on one of the most influential models—Bronfenbrenner's (1989a; Bronfenbrenner & Morris, 1998) *ecological-systems approach*.

Bronfenbrenner (1989a, pp. 226–229) sees the context as a set of nested structures, like nested Russian wooden dolls. These structures range from the immediate face-to-face interaction with another person to very general cultural belief systems:

1. A *microsystem* is a "pattern of activities, roles, and interpersonal relations experienced by the developing person in a given face-to-face setting." The setting includes (a) particular physical and material features and (b) other people with particular temperaments, personalities, and systems of belief. A child's home, school, and peer group are important microsystems.

2. The *mesosystem* includes "the linkages and processes taking place between two or more settings containing the developing person." For example, we might ask if the peer group and school system support or contradict the parents' value system. Thus, a mesosystem is a system of microsystems.

3. The *exosystem* "encompasses the linkage and processes taking place between two or more settings, at least one of which does not ordinarily contain the developing person." Events in this system "influence processes within the immediate setting that does contain that person." An example is the relation between the home and the parent's workplace. A stressful work environment may increase a parent's irritability at home, and this could lead to child abuse. This level includes the major institutions of society, such as the economic system, the transportation system, local government, and the mass media. As an example of the latter, watching television may interfere with family interaction.

4. The *macrosystem* "consists of the overarching pattern of micro-, meso- and exosystems characteristic of a given culture, subculture, or other broader social context." Of particular importance are the "belief systems, resources, hazards, life styles, opportunity structures, life course options, and patterns of social interchange that are embedded in each of these systems." The macrosystem is a general cultural "blueprint" that helps design the social structures and activities occurring at lower, more concrete levels. This blueprint influences how parents, teachers, and significant others in the child's life "consciously or unconsciously define the goals, risks, and ways of raising the next generation." There tends to be consistency among the important settings of a particular culture. Bronfenbrenner points out that within a given society, one elementary school classroom looks and operates

much like every other. The nature of the prototypic classroom reflects unstated beliefs of the society.

These four levels interact. What happens in one level impacts the other levels, as when the Depression affected family dynamics and thus the children of that time (Elder, 1998). Bronfenbrenner (1989a, 1989b) also emphasizes that children actively shape the nature of their social contexts. For example, personal attributes encourage or discourage reactions from other people that facilitate or damage psychological development (see also Bandura's "triadic reciprocal determinism" in Chapter 3). A fussy baby, a physically unattractive preschooler, or a hyperactive school-age child may repel adults. A happy, smiling baby, a beautiful preschooler, or a good-natured, calm 8-year-old has the opposite effect and thus creates a different environment for herself. She is likely to respond in kind to warm social attention, setting in motion a chain of reciprocal exchanges that chart a course of development for her that is rather different from that of the other child.

Another way in which children shape their contexts is that they display individual differences in their tendency to approach or avoid particular aspects of the social and physical world. Temperamental differences are expressed in social extroversion, shyness (avoiding social stimulation), resistance to changes in the environment, a high activity level, and so on. Consequently, different children seek out different types of contexts and thus engage in somewhat different developmentally relevant activities. One child may prefer to be a "child-in-structured-quiet-, two-person-context" whereas another may tend to be a "child-in-unpredictable-, loud-, multiperson-context." In this way, different skills and learning styles may develop. Differences in creativity and the need for change also affect children's choice of settings.

Bronfenbrenner's most recent accounts (e.g., Bronfenbrenner & Morris, 1998) have an even more developmental and interactive flavor. In his "bioecological model," as he sometimes refers to it, Bronfenbrenner emphasizes the *processes* by which child and context directly (proximally) affect each other during frequently occurring interactions, for example, comforting a baby, peer play, problem solving, and athletic activities. The particular nature of these processes depends on characteristics of the developing person, as described above, and of the environment in which the processes are taking place.

Ceci's (1996) bioecological theory of intelligence provides an example. He emphasizes how domain-specific knowledge and basic cognitive processes intertwine to generate intelligent behavior. The human species has evolved basic information-processing skills, such as encoding, storage, and retrieval, that contribute to adaptation. However, these processes may work better in some contexts (the "ecological" part of the theory) than in others. Thus, a particular child appears more intelligent in some contexts than others. Although schooling encourages the sort of intelligence assessed on IQ tests, it may not contribute as much to other sorts of intelligence that are important for other contexts. Ceci's research often examines context-specific expertise—advanced cognitive skills, for example, as seen in the child experts described in the discussion of information processing in Chapter 4 and the Brazilian street vendors in Chapter 7. In addition, contexts differ in whether they frame a task in a meaningful way, which affects how intelligently a child functions. Ceci (1996) found, for example, that 10-year-olds had great difficulty learning to predict the movement of a geometric shape across a computer screen until the context for the same rule was changed to that of a video game of catching butterflies in a net. Thus, Ceci argues for intelligence-in-context, rather than the more traditional "general-intelligence" view.

CRITICAL PSYCHOLOGY: ARE THEORIES OF DEVELOPMENT GENDERED?

Recent critiques of theories of psychology have identified biases that reflect the belief system of the larger culture in which psychologists work (e.g., Fox & Prilleltensky, 1997). One aspect of culture, for example, is its conception of masculine and feminine gender roles. In recent years, feminist theories have critiqued, and provided an influential alternative perspective for, a wide range of disciplines across the sciences and humanities (Alcoff & Potter, 1993; Tong, 1998). For example, in the field of history, adding the activities of women to what is studied changes models of history from a focus on wars, generals, and rulers to the inclusion of everyday life and social reforms.

Developmentalists recently have applied feminist perspectives across several areas of cognitive and social development (Miller & Scholnick, 2000). This work builds on earlier work by Gilligan (1982) on caring-based moral judgments, by Belenky, Clinchy, Goldberger, and Tarule (1986) on "women's ways of knowing," and by Burman (1994) on theoretical critiques of models of development.

Parallel to the change from cross-cultural psychology to cultural psychology described in Chapter 7, work on gender is changing somewhat from the gender-differences approach that has characterized the field of psychology to a gender-psychology, or feminist-psychology, approach. In the latter view, gender is not just another individual difference—an independent variable that causes differences in thinking and behavior. Rather, like culture (and in fact a main aspect of culture), gender pervades all human situations and is an inextricable part of any event. Also, like cultural beliefs, beliefs about gender are so pervasive and deeply ingrained that they are often invisible to people within a culture. Finally, models of behavior and development arising from one culture or gender may not be universal or appropriate for understanding all behaviors.

Developmentalists and feminist scholars ask some of the same questions—about the process of acquiring knowledge, the effects of social institutions on people, the effects of experience on one's perspective, and the construction of social categories. There are a number of feminist theories, such as liberal (positivist), socialist, African-American/ethnic, essentialist, existentialist, psychoanalytic, radical, postmodern, and postcolonial theories (Rosser & Miller, 2000). Each offers a framework through which to explore various central issues in developmental psychology. However, despite their differences, these theories have certain commonalities. In particular, they focus on the notion of connections rather than separation, distance, and dichotomy (see examples below). That is, development is as much a process of developing relationships with others and developing an understanding of the complex connections in the social and physical world as it is a process of establishing autonomy and supposed objectivity and of analyzing reality into objects and properties. Moreover, feminist approaches focus on the cultural, institutionalized organization of social relations according to gender, race, class, and ethnicity (and therefore differences in power).

The following are several examples of attempts, inspired by feminist theories, to provide a broader conception of development (Miller & Scholnick, 2000). Metaphors can depict development as a process of argument, survival of the fittest, an arrow, and building or, in contrast, from a feminist perspective, a process of friendship, conversation, apprenticeship, and narrative (Scholnick, 2000). Aggression can be physical or relational, such as gossip (Crick & Rose, 2000). Thinking can be linear, distanced from the object of study, and reductionist, or it can be contextual–relational, situated, reciprocal, dialogical, connected, co-constructed, experientially based, and diverse (Miller, 2000). Developmentalists have raised other issues, such as these: Who has the authority to author an autobiographical memory; whose voice and memory counts (Fivush, 2000)? Does the world as viewed from the margins look different from the world as viewed from the center (of power)? How do sociocultural macrosystems support the maintenance of gender divisions in daily interactions at the microsystem level (Leaper, 2000)? How do children's essentialist concepts of gender and developmentalists' essentialist concepts of children impact development and its study (Gelman & Taylor, 2000)? Feminist approaches clearly have close ties to the sociocultural and person-in-context theories within developmental psychology. The inclusion of feminist theories in developmental psychology is part of a larger movement toward a broader, more diverse, multicultural vision of people and their development.

POSITION ON DEVELOPMENTAL ISSUES

Regarding world views, the dynamic-systems and theory-theory approaches are the most organismic because they emphasize that a child constructs a concept, skill, or behavior during experience. The person-in-context and critical-psychology approaches are the most contextual in their emphasis on people in settings created by social systems. Developmental neuroscience work tends to be mechanistic or organismic, rather than contextual. All the approaches include both quantitative and qualitative change, but none are stage theories. Modularity nativism and developmental neuroscience emphasize nature; person-in-context and critical-psychology approaches emphasize nurture; and the theory-theory and dynamic-systems approaches are the most interactionist. Finally, the "what" of development includes new theories, encapsulated knowledge, neural pathways, and skills in contexts within a cultural system of beliefs.

CONCLUDING THOUGHTS

Where are we now in our theorizing about development? There is no one dominant theory of development. In terms of research publications, the most active theories currently probably are information-processing, sociocultural, person-in-context, neo-Piagetian broadly defined, and domain-specific conceptual development (for example, theory-theory) theories. Neuroscience and connectionism, which are as much methods as they are theories, are attracting much attention. Dynamic-systems and biological theories (for example, evolutionary psychology, behavioral genetics, and various biopsychology approaches) also are salient. Others are influential for specific topics, such as Bowlby's "internal working models" for attachment and Gibson's theory for infant perception. Developmentalists seem to be constructing both small, focused theories that are energizing research in specific areas and general models that incorporate various levels of biology and environment in complex interaction. The latter are satisfying in their all-encompassing nature but unsatisfying in their generation of research because of the complexity of the models. Both types of theories are useful. And all address what is perhaps the most important and difficult question about development: How does change come about? That is, by what processes do new concepts, skills, and behaviors emerge?

How are developmental theories likely to change? We have seen that both technological innovations and changing social structures have an impact on children and on theorizing about children. The automatic washing machine and disposable diapers made early toilet training less important to busy parents and less of an issue for theories of socialization. Television (for example, *Sesame Street*) and child-care centers brought instruction and a wider set of social models to children. Computers and the Internet have made new forms of instruction and recreation possible. Will we continue to extend the computer metaphor? A look at the keyboard shows "delete," "control," "insert," and "break" but also, thankfully, "pause," "end," and "home." The menu on the screen has "file," "edit," "tools," "cut," "paste," and "merge" but also, thankfully, "help." Does this common system reflect the cognitive processes that seem natural to us, given our cognitive system, or will the system become more than a metaphor and actually cause some changes in the way children think, just as earlier cultural tools, such as a system of writing, may have. Similar questions can be asked about the Internet. We use outdated conceptions of cognition when we study concepts of objects, classes, and events. That is, we know very little about children's concepts and skills that are most relevant to navigating on the Internet—connections among categories, interconnected networks of knowledge, skills for conducting efficient searches, communication with other people, and evaluation of the sources of information. Our theories have not kept up with children's rapidly changing lives.

Social changes will change theories as well. The United States is becoming increasingly culturally and ethnically diverse. The employment of both parents outside the home, increased diversity in what constitutes a family, later first marriages, and the trend toward smaller families create a different environment for most children today than that for a child 30 years ago. Today few children in the United States live in a middle-class Euro-American household with two parents, in which the father works outside the home and the mother does not. Will attachment, identification, independence training, and other aspects of socialization proceed in the same way as they have before? It seems unlikely.

SUMMARY

Developmental theories develop. Several approaches in addition to the "big" theories of previous chapters currently are influencing developmentalists. The theory theory examines children's coherent, causal-explanatory "theories" about particular domains, for example, "theory of mind." They test their theories, but resist changing them, though they eventually construct better theories. According to modularity nativism, such domain-specific knowledge is largely innate. A module for language, for example, predisposes infants to process linguistic information and thereby acquire language quickly. The developmental neuroscience approach is rapidly gaining influence in developmental psychology. It promises to reveal links between brain activity and behavior that can both evaluate current beliefs about human development and also suggest new hypotheses. The approach addresses the nature–nurture issue, in particular, because it shows how each enables and constrains the other.

Dynamic-systems theory is a broad theory that tries to encompass all relevant factors operating at a particular developmental moment. The theory focuses on change at multiple levels and on the child's construction of a new skill on the spot. The developing person-in-context approach embeds development within a social ecology consisting of various levels from near to far. Sociohistorical events, such as the Great Depression, provide contexts that shape development, but children are active participants in these contexts as well. Finally, critical psychology reminds us that theorists are products of their own culture. We should become aware of the biases that influence the sorts of theories they construct.

SUGGESTED READINGS

The section for each theory refers to good sources for further reading. In addition, the following four-volume set includes chapters on most of the approaches.

Damon, W. (Series Ed.). (1998). *Handbook of child psychology* (5th ed.). New York: Wiley.

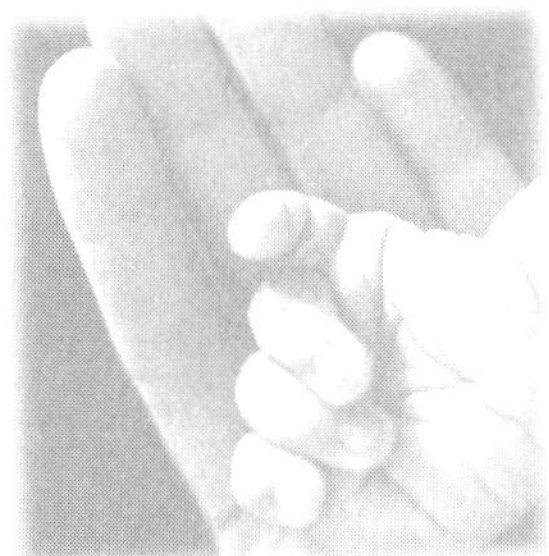

CHAPTER 9

Reflections

The beginnings and endings of all human undertakings are untidy, the building of a house, the writing of a novel, the demolition of a bridge, and, eminently, the finish of a voyage.

—JOHN GALSWORTHY

Although it is tempting to tidy up the assortment of theories presented here by offering an orderly set of conclusions, that aim is not realistic. Developmental psychology is a huge, multifaceted discipline that has produced a diverse group of theories. Some theories are bold and speculative, while others are cautious and precise; some are large-scale and rambling, while others are modest and systematic. Furthermore, they ask different questions about development. Consequently, they address different levels of reality, ranging from a simple motor response to a complex personality structure to a child-in-context. Any attempt to integrate all the theories would be foolish at best and misleading at worst.

This chapter, then, offers several "untidy" thoughts that linger after we have delved into the theories of this book. The first section summarizes the theories' positions on the four developmental issues that were raised in each chapter. In the second section we revisit the issue of mechanisms of development—the most serious limitation of developmental theories. In the third section, we view the history of developmental theory from two points of view. In the traditional view of scientific progress, research and theories build on previous work and thereby increase our knowledge base in a linear fashion. An opposing view, proposed by Thomas Kuhn, sees successive theories as supplanting previous theories rather than building on them and improving them.

DEVELOPMENTAL ISSUES REVISITED

Human Nature

The distinction among organismic, mechanistic, and contextualist world views served as a useful heuristic for understanding developmental theories, even though some theories do not fall neatly into one category. Most contemporary versions of the theories portray children as active agents in their own development, to varying degrees. Children assimilate, accommodate, and equilibrate (Piaget); strengthen ego processes (Freud); construct a sense of identity (Erikson); and develop self-regulatory mechanisms (social learning). In addition, they develop a set of strategies and procedures for problem solving (information processing), search their environment and elicit reactions from others (ethology), explore environments for their affordances (Gibson), and acquire cultural tools that help them coconstruct knowledge and skills with other people (sociocultural). Children also construct and test naïve theories (theory theory), self-organize (dynamic systems), and select environments (developing-person-in-context approaches). Active self-regulation, in particular, is important for social learning theory, Vygotsky, Piaget, Bowlby, information processing (control processes), and dynamic systems. Some of the theories include passive biological- or environmental-based processes as well. Examples include the push from biological drives (Freud, Erikson, ethology), the expression of innate cognitive modules (modularity nativism), the registering of co-occurring events (connectionism, neuroscience, reinforcement contingencies in learning theory), and the response to sign stimuli (ethology).

Another dimension separating mechanistic and organismic approaches ranges from antecedent causes of isolated behaviors to inherent causes within a whole structure. The former causes include S–R associations (learning theory), fixed action patterns (ethology), and input–output procedures (information processing). The latter are illustrated by cognitive structures (Piaget) or theories (theory theory), the organization of the id, ego, and superego (Freud), the knowledge base or system of processing information (information processing), intrinsic motivation (Gibson), control systems of behavior (Bowlby's ethological theory), dialectical systems (sociocultural), and the self-organizing tendencies of a system (dynamic systems).

Overall, Piagetian and dynamic-systems theories are the most clearly organismic theories, whereas traditional learning theory is the most clearly mechanistic. Later, learning theory added some organismic, self-regulatory features, especially as a result of Bandura's theoretical work.

In addition to differences in the theories' world views, there are striking differences in the theories' overall views of human nature: whether humans develop into rational, efficient "scientists" or into social cognitive beings that develop more intuitive concepts and "hot" cognition (emotions). Piaget and information-processing theorists emphasize the rational; Freud and Erikson emphasize how motives and needs affect thinking. The other theories are more neutral on this issue. For example, in social learning theory the models that children imitate may demonstrate either logical or irrational thinking. Ethologists, evolutionary psychologists, Gibsonians, socioculturalists, modularity nativists, and person-in-context theorists emphasize the adaptation required for survival or optimal functioning in the particular environment. Rational, scientific thought is most adaptive for some settings, whereas sensitivity to interpersonal relationships and emotions may be more adaptive in other settings.

Our theorists' view of human nature is not a trivial matter, because it influences their theorizing. As the critical-psychology theorists point out, developmentalists are influenced by their culture and need to be aware that both the field of developmental psychology and the definition of development are sociological phenomena to some extent. For example, feminist approaches note that society's emphasis on science and technology and on interindividual competition encourages developmentalists to study the development of the child as a solitary, distanced, scientific thinker who develops concepts of isolated objects in the world and competes with others for resources. In contrast, some societies are more concerned with interpersonal connections (Markus & Kitayama, 1991).

■ *Qualitative Versus Quantitative Development*

All the theorists see a number of ways in which development increases quantitatively—in amount, frequency, or degree. With increasing age, children strengthen and generalize their cognitive skills (Piaget), increase their ego strength (Freud and Erikson), imitate more accurately (social learning theory), and process information more efficiently (information processing). They also refine the interweaving of innate and learned components (ethology), detect more affordances (Gibson), and develop their skills gradually as they move through the zone of proximal development (Vygotsky). In addition, children refine their theories (theory theory) and strengthen certain neural pathways at the expense of others (neuroscience and connectionism). Although all the theories posit at least minor qualitative change, only Piaget, Freud, and Erikson—the stage theorists—make qualitative change a central part of their theories. In the other theories, the most common qualitative change is a new strategy of learning or problem solving. Dynamic-systems approaches address how quantitative change, once it crosses a certain threshold, can lead to a qualitative reorganization of a whole system. A major current question regarding the issue of qualitative, stage-like change concerns the apparent unevenness in a child's cognitive performance across tasks or content areas. Domain specificity, which is addressed mainly by neo-Piagetian, information-processing, theory-theory, and modularity-nativist theorists, has been a major challenge for developmental theorizing during the past decade.

■ *Nature Versus Nurture*

All the theorists agree that development springs from a complex interweaving of innate and experiential influences. However, they vary in their degree of concern with this issue and in which influences they choose to study. Piagetian, neo-Piagetian, theory-theory, and dynamic-systems theories most clearly are interactionist theories. Piaget, for example, sees development as an interaction of two innate factors (physical maturation and equilibration) and two types of experience (social and physical). Erikson also stresses both biological and social changes, showing that as drives change, they mesh (or conflict) with social institutions. Moving from the middle of the spectrum toward one end, we see that social learning theory, sociocultural theories, and person-in-context approaches focus on the effects of experience. Toward the other end of the spectrum, ethologists, neuroscientists, modularity nativists, and to a lesser extent Freud emphasize the effects of innate factors. The other theories do not focus on this issue but imply interactionism. In information processing, for example, neurological development obviously increases the potential efficiency of the information-processing system, and problem-solving experience leads children to adopt new strategies when they receive feedback during attempts at problem solving. And Gibson's theory posits the evolution of perceptual learning abilities that permit adaptation to the environment.

What Develops

The diverse answers to "What develops?" illustrate why an integration of theories is so difficult. The theorists attend to very different levels of behavior and select different content areas. The stage and dynamic-systems theorists look at stage-defining characteristics and therefore operate at a general level. In their view, the most important developments are cognitive structures (Piaget), personality structures (Freud and Erikson), or self-organizing systems (dynamic systems). Other theorists focus on more specific acquisitions, often limited to certain situations or types of stimulation: rules (information processing and social learning theory), the perception of affordances (Gibson), adaptive behaviors (ethology), naïve theories (theory theory), and culturally constructed systems of knowledge (sociocultural). With respect to content, the theories range from stressing social behaviors and personality (Freud, Erikson, social learning theory) to thinking (Piaget, information processing, Vygotsky, theory theory, modularity nativism) to perception (Gibson) but have an overall bias toward cognitive aspects of development. The sociocultural, person-in-context, dynamic-systems, ethological, and neuroscience approaches study a variety of skills. It is clear that development proceeds on several levels and in many content areas simultaneously. No one theory has unraveled this complex process. Finally, feminist and other critical-psychology theorists point to diversity between cultures and within a culture in what develops and direct attention to the contributions of race, culture, gender, and social class. There also may be various end points to development and various routes for reaching any end point.

A NEED FOR BETTER THEORETICAL ACCOUNTS OF MECHANISMS OF DEVELOPMENT

A common weakness of developmental theories is that they lack an adequate account of mechanisms of development. It was stated in the Introduction that a developmental theory must *describe* development within one domain and the relationship among simultaneously developing domains and that it must *explain* the course of development that has been described. For example, Piaget, Freud, and Erikson have given us a rich description of development, but their mechanisms of development—equilibration and the invariant functions for Piaget, drives for the psychoanalysts—are vague. We cannot easily observe and study these mechanisms. In contrast, social learning theory, information processing, ethology, Gibsonian theory, Vygotsky–sociocultural theories, and dynamic-systems approaches emphasize processes of change but are weaker at describing what develops. Even these process theories, however, do not provide satisfactory mechanisms of development. Social learning theory posits observational learning, which includes verbal instruction and imitation of models, and cognitive processes. However, it is not clear how these processes actually operate. The processes have been given labels but do not really serve as explanations of development. Observational learning involves symbolically representing the sequence of behaviors to be imitated, constructing an image of a new behavior from printed words, integrating new information into previous knowledge, and translating new information into a course of action. One must still explain how these processes operate to cause change. In other words, it is not enough to identify the conditions facilitating observational learning and list the components involved (attention, retention, motor reproduction, and motivation). The identification step merely pushes the explanation back to another level.

The same problem arises with information-processing, ethological, Gibsonian, and sociocultural theories. Exactly how do we acquire new strategies, encode new information, develop control processes, overcome production deficiencies, integrate individual innate behaviors into a system, detect affordances, and learn new skills in social contexts? The precise cognitive, neurophysiological, or perceptual processes are still unspecified. Moreover, a key question, as yet unanswered, is how mechanisms of development change over the life span. More generally, we need to tie together the theories of childhood, adolescence, adulthood, and aging to create a true life-span theory of development.

Future theories need to examine two roles of developmental mechanisms: (1) to facilitate the acquisition of new skills and (2) to make these skills readily accessible. Any given mechanism may play one or both roles. Examples of mechanisms proposed by theorists to explain acquisition are the equilibration process, dialectical process changes in biologically based drives, identification, ego development, observational learning, acquisition of strategies of information processing, automatization, perceptual learning, and self-organization. Theorists have given much less attention to how these new acquisitions become readily accessible and expressed in performance. This is a critical issue, particularly in the area of cognitive development, because recent research suggests that much of development involves children's learning to *use* the skills they have already acquired. Children can verbally mediate long before they spontaneously verbally rehearse a list of items to be remembered. Young children have a rudimentary understanding of number but are easily diverted from using this understanding by distracting stimuli or a large amount of information to process. Adolescents use formal operations in some content areas but not others. Social learning, person-in-context, neo-Piagetian, information-processing, and sociocultural theorists have identified a number of situational variables that facilitate or discourage the application of knowledge, but they have not satisfactorily explained why or how these variables have an effect on performance.

In looking for mechanisms, we should keep in mind one of the main messages of the more ecologically oriented theories, such as sociocultural, person-in-context, and Gibsonian theories: that we should take an event as our unit of analysis. Children do something, in some setting, with some goal in mind. They move about, explore their world, and interact with other people. Developmentalists are becoming aware that we have looked at cognition, personality, and perception as decontextualized for too long.

On a more optimistic note, recent theoretical and empirical advances in the study of mechanisms of development may preview exciting breakthroughs in the next few years. Connectionists' focus on learning, neuroscientists' account of changes in neural pathways, and dynamic-systems theorists' research on mechanisms of self-regulation are particularly promising. In addition, sociocultural and person-in-context approaches are identifying the processes involved in development in cultural context.

HISTORICAL PROGRESS OF DEVELOPMENTAL THEORIES

A succession of developmental theories has waxed and waned in influence. Are we left with a sense of scientific progress? Has each successive theory been better than the one before it? The traditional view of scientific progress, also the commonsense view, sees the history of a discipline as a cumulative enterprise. Each new discovery or theory builds on previous work and is a refinement of it in the search for ultimate truth. Each theory stands until empirical observations cast doubt on its validity. People believe that the evaluation of facts is totally objective: "There is only one established dogma in science—that scientists do not blindly accept established dogma" (Brush, 1976, p. 68).

Clearly, there is continuity and a sense of theory development between Freud and Erikson within the psychoanalytic tradition or between classical learning theory and social learning theory within learning theory. Over a longer period of time, however, the historical progression of theories in this volume does not seem to follow this pattern. One is struck more with discontinuity than with continuity in moving from Freud to learning theory to Piaget to information processing to the theory theory. Each theory challenged a previous one and proposed an attractive alternative conception of development more than it refined the earlier theory. Often a new theory is accepted because it corrects the excesses of an established theory, as when developmentalists are attracted to sociocultural and person-in-context approaches because they address the social context of thinking, which is relatively ignored by information-processing approaches. Similarly, the theory-theory and modularity-nativism approaches offer a plausible account for the counterevidence regarding Piaget's theory. This switch of allegiance occurs despite the fact that newer theories are less well worked out than the abandoned theories. The history of developmental psychology suggests that when a theory cannot be modified satisfactorily, the stage is set for change. A discipline seems to have a particular need at some point in history and embraces a new theory that offers a more satisfactory view of that discipline.

Such discontinuities from one theory to another become understandable if one looks at Thomas Kuhn's (1970) account of the growth of scientific knowledge. Kuhn provides an alternative to the traditional account (see also Lakatos, 1978). He posits the following historical sequence within any scientific discipline: First is a "preparadigmatic phase," in which no one theory or generally agreed-upon way of studying the discipline's subject matter has emerged. There is debate over fundamental issues within the discipline. Next comes a period of "normal science," in which one paradigm dominates the field or at least an important subarea of the field. A *paradigm* is a generally accepted set of assumptions as to what should be studied, what questions should be asked, how these questions can be studied, and how the results should be conceptualized. For example, the information-processing approach emerged from a general agreement among developmental psychologists to study the flow of information through a processing system that resembles the operations of a computer and, furthermore, to ask how that information is stored, not how it is repressed as a result of anxiety. An investigator using this paradigm therefore is likely to measure reaction time, types of errors, or number of items correct but probably will not ask about dreams or fantasies. Thus, a paradigm serves as a working model of how to do science.

A paradigm is larger than a theory. It is both an intellectual framework and a sociological phenomenon. Examples of this intellectual framework are the organismic, mechanistic, and contextualist world views. One holding a mechanistic world view, for instance, would be more likely to develop a theory that posits external mechanical rather than internal cognitive causes of behavior. With respect to the sociological aspect of paradigms, Kuhn points to a "community" of scholars who share certain assumptions or ground rules. The scholars can make rapid progress during the period of normal science because, instead of questioning the assumptions of the approach, they can concentrate their efforts on gathering data and solving problems identified by the paradigm. It is a time for "mopping-up operations" (Kuhn, 1970) to tidy up the paradigm. Scientists maintain the paradigm by training students to carry on the tradition. The students absorb the conventions for solving problems in the field and thereby "step into the circle" of that paradigm. An old paradigm never dies immediately; it just fades away, as students trained in the new paradigm enter the field and believers in the old paradigm are ignored and left behind.

The change from one paradigm to another follows a typical pattern. At some point a crisis arises. Phenomena may be discovered that cannot be explained by the current paradigm and consequently cause a crisis of confidence in the paradigm. If a more promising alternative paradigm appears on the scene, it may win the allegiance of the field and begin its own phase of normal science. Thus, after a first paradigm emerges in a discipline, there is a continual back-and-forth movement between normal science (a time of stability) and scientific revolution (a time of change). The history of a science is cyclic more than continuous, according to Kuhn.

Obvious examples of scientific revolutions are Darwinian theory, Einstein's theory of relativity, and the Copernican revolution, which brought the view that the sun rather than earth is the center of the universe. Each of these paradigms brought a gestaltlike shift in the way scientists looked at facts.

It is interesting that whether a new theory, set of findings, or method influences the field and eventually becomes a paradigm depends on many factors that have nothing to do with the work itself. A good case in point is the fact that Binet, the IQ pioneer, conducted experiments on conservation and other concepts of number before Piaget was even born. In fact, he published over 200 books and papers on topics such as children's memory and cognitive styles that had nothing to do with IQ testing. Yet this work was, and still is, ignored for various historical and sociological reasons (Siegler, 1992; Wesley, 1989).

Psychologists disagree about the value of Kuhn's model for the social sciences and about where to locate psychology in this history-of-science model. Is psychology in a preparadigmatic phase, or has it entered the cycle of paradigms and scientific revolutions? There has never been a paradigm that was accepted by the entire field of psychology or even developmental psychology. Today, psychologists still question basic assumptions about development, such as whether newborns have any innate knowledge. However, a paradigm can be restricted to a subarea within the field. From this perspective, there are several candidates for paradigms in developmental psychology. In fact, each of the theories described in this book has won over a group of scholars who have accepted the assumptions and gone about the business of solving problems defined by these assumptions. The general-orientation section of each chapter in this book roughly defines the paradigmatic characteristics of the theory. Each theory has had its community of productive investigators. One example is the Piagetian group in Geneva. A group of investigators accepted Piaget's intellectual framework and proceeded as though they were working out the details of this framework. Piaget's theory never quite reached this status among American researchers in cognitive development. Other paradigmatic communities can be identified for computer-simulation, particularly connectionist, approaches at several U.S. universities, for ethology in Germany, learning in the early 1960s, and the theory theory in parts of the United States and Europe.

Regardless of whether future generations will look back on today as a time of preparadigmatic or paradigmatic science, Kuhn's view of science as both continuous and discontinuous seems to have some validity in the history of theories of developmental psychology. Both continuity and discontinuity are apparent in information processing, for example. It built on the precision and analytic posture of learning theory but won followers in part because of dissatisfaction within the ranks of learning researchers, rather than simply because it produced a better version of learning theory.

CONCLUSIONS

As Beilin comments, "History makes every theory look deficient in some way" (1985, p. 9). Because no one theory satisfactorily explains development, it is critical that developmentalists be able to draw on the content, methods, and theoretical concepts of many theories. The various theories supply multiple levels of analysis, from the neurological to the sociological level. A knowledge of the developmental theories in this volume can serve as a heuristic for developmental researchers and professionals working with children. Shifting from theory to theory provides a flexible perspective on children's behavior.

Suggesting the value of using theories flexibly does not mean, however, that there is no place for developmentalists who operate within a single theory. There is value to pushing a single theory to its limits. As Kuhn noted in his discussion of paradigms, sometimes rapid progress is most likely when investigators do not question the assumptions of their field. Finding out where a theory breaks down can be very informative. As the English logician Augustus De Morgan commented, "Wrong hypotheses rightly worked from have produced more useful results than unguided observation." Given the current level of knowledge in developmental psychology, we need both eclectics and true believers.

> "Where shall I begin?" asked the White Rabbit.
> "Begin at the beginning," the King said gravely, "and go on till you come to the end, then stop."
>
> —Lewis Carroll

REFERENCES

Adolph, K. E. (1997). Learning in the development of infant locomotion. *Monographs of the Society for Research in Child Development, 62*(3, Serial No. 251).

Adolph, K. E. (2000). Specificity of learning: Why infants fall over a veritable cliff. *Psychological Science, 11*, 290–295.

Adolph, K. E., & Eppler, M. (1999). Obstacles to understanding: An ecological approach to infant problem solving. In E. Winograd, R. Fivush, and W. Hirst (Eds.), *Ecological approaches to cognition: Essays in honor of Ulric Neisser.* Mahwah, NJ: Erlbaum.

Ainsworth, M. D. (1989). Attachments beyond infancy. *American Psychologist, 44*, 709–716.

Ainsworth, M. D., Blehar, M. C., Waters, E., & Wall, S. (1978). *Patterns of attachment*. Hillsdale, NJ: Erlbaum.

Alcoff, L., & Potter, E. (Eds.). (1993). *Feminist epistemologies*. New York: Routledge.

Aldridge, M. A., Braga, E. S., Walton, G. E., & Bower, T. G. R. (1999). The intermodel representation of speech in newborns. *Developmental Science, 2*, 42–46.

Alexander, J. M., & Schwanenflugel, P. J. (1994). Strategy regulation: The role of intelligence, metacognitive attributes, and knowledge base. *Developmental Psychology, 30*, 709–723.

American Psychologist. (1981). *36*, 27–34.

American Psychologist. (1982). *37*, 74–85.

Anastasi, A. (1958). Heredity, environment, and the question "How?" *Psychological Review, 65*, 197–208.

Anderson, J. (1991). Comments on *Foundations of cognitive science*. *Psychological Science, 5*, 283–287.

Anderson, J. (1993). *Rules of the mind.* Hillsdale, NJ: Erlbaum.

Archer, J. (1992). *Ethology and human development*. Hemel Hempstead, UK: Harvester-Wheatsheaf.

Averill, J. R. (1976). Patterns of psychological thought: A general introduction. In J. R. Averill (Ed.), *Patterns of psychological thought.* Washington, DC: Hemisphere.

Bahrick, L. E., Netto, D., & Hernandez-Reif, M. (1998). Intermodal perception of adult and child faces and voices by infants. *Child Development, 69*, 1263–1275.

Bahrick, L. E., & Watson, J. S. (1985). Detection of intermodal proprioceptive-visual contingency as a potential basis of self-perception in infancy. *Developmental Psychology, 21*, 963–973.

Baillargeon, R. (1987). Object permanence in 3.5- and 4.5-month-old infants. *Developmental Psychology, 23*, 655–664.

Baltes, M. M., & Barton, E. M. (1979). Behavior analysis of aging: A review of the operant model and research. *International Journal of Behavioral Development, 2*, 291–320.

Bandura, A. (1965). Influence of model's reinforcement contingencies on the acquisition of imitative responses. *Journal of Personality and Social Psychology, 1*, 589–595.

Bandura, A. (1967). Behavioral psychotherapy. *Scientific American, 216,* 78–86.

Bandura, A. (1971). Vicarious and self-reinforcement processes. In R. Glaser (Ed.), *The nature of reinforcement.* New York: Academic Press.

Bandura, A. (1977). *Social learning theory.* Englewood Cliffs, NJ: Prentice-Hall.

Bandura, A. (1986). *Social foundations of thought and action.* Englewood Cliffs, NJ.: Prentice-Hall.

Bandura, A. (1989). Social cognitive theory. In R. Vasta (Ed.), *Annals of child development* (Vol. 6). Greenwich, CT: JAI Press.

Bandura, A. (1997). *Self-efficacy: The exercise of control.* New York: Freeman.

Bandura, A., Grusec, J. E., & Menlove, F. L. (1966). Observational learning as a function of symbolization and incentive set. *Child Development, 37,* 499–506.

Bandura, A., & McDonald, F. J. (1963). The influence of social reinforcement and the behavior of models in shaping children's moral judgments. *Journal of Abnormal and Social Psychology, 67,* 274–281.

Bandura, A., Ross, D., & Ross, S. A. (1961). Transmission of aggression through imitation of aggressive models. *Journal of Abnormal and Social Psychology, 63,* 575–582.

Bandura, A., & Walters, R. H. (1959). *Adolescent aggression.* New York: Ronald Press.

Bandura, A., & Walters, R. H. (1963). *Social learning and personality development.* New York: Holt.

Barash, D. P. (1973). Personal space reiterated. *Environment and Behavior, 5,* 67–72.

Barkow, J. H., Cosmides, L., & Tooby, J. (1992). *The adapted mind: Evolutionary psychology and the generation of culture.* New York: Oxford University Press.

Barnes, M. A., Dennis, M., & Haefele-Kalvaitis, J. (1996). The effects of knowledge availability and knowledge accessibility on coherence and elaborative inferencing in children six to fifteen years of age. *Journal of Experimental Child Psychology, 61,* 216–241.

Barnett, S. A. (1963). *A study in behavior.* London: Methuen.

Baron-Cohen, S. (1995). *Mindblindness: An essay on autism and theory of mind.* Cambridge, MA: MIT Press.

Basalla, G. (1988). *The evolution of technology.* Cambridge: Cambridge University Press.

Bates, E. A., & Elman, J. L. (1992). *Connectionism and the study of change.* (Tech. Rep. No. 9202). La Jolla: University of California, San Diego.

Bauer, P. J., & Mandler, J. M. (1992). Putting the horse before the cart: The use of temporal order in recall of events by one-year-old children. *Developmental Psychology, 28,* 441–452.

Baumrind, D. (1973). The development of instrumental competence through socialization. In A. D. Pick (Ed.), *Minnesota symposia on child psychology* (Vol. 7). Minnapolis: University of Minnesota Press.

Beer, C. G. (1973). Species-typical behavior and ethology. In D. A. Dewsbury & D. A. Rethlingshafer (Eds.), *Comparative psychology: A modern survey.* New York: McGraw-Hill.

Beilin, H. (1971). The training and acquisition of logical operations. In M. F. Rosskopf, L. P. Steffe, and S. Taback (Eds.), *Piagetian cognitive-developmental research and mathematical education.* Washington, DC: National Council of Teachers of Mathematics.

Beilin, H. (1985). Dispensable and core elements in Piaget's research program. *The Genetic Epistemologist, 13*, 1–16.

Beilin, H. (1992). Piaget's new theory. In H. Beilin & P. B. Pufall (Eds.), *Piaget's theory: Prospects and possibilities*. Hillsdale, NJ: Erlbaum.

Beilin, H., & Fireman, G. (2000). The foundation of Piaget's theories: Mental and physical action. In H. Reese (Ed.), *Advances in child development and behavior* (Vol. 27). New York: Academic Press.

Belenky, M. F., Clinchy, B. M., Goldberger, N. R., & Tarule, J. M. (1986). *Women's ways of knowing: The development of self, voice, and mind*. New York: Basic Books.

Berland, J. C. (1982). *No five fingers are alike: Cognitive amplifiers in social context*. Cambridge, MA: Harvard University Press.

Berlyne, D. E. (1965). *Structure and direction in thinking*. New York: Wiley.

Berman, P. (1980). Are women more responsive than men to the young? A review of developmental and situational variables. *Psychological Bulletin, 88*, 668–695.

Bhaskar, R. (1983). Beef, structure and place: Notes from a critical naturalist perspective. *Journal for the Theory of Social Behaviour, 13*, 81–97.

Biben, M. (1998). Squirrel monkey play fighting: Making a case for a cognitive training function for play. In M. Bekoff and J. A. Byers (Eds.), *Animal play*. New York: Cambridge University Press.

Bigler, R. S., & Liben, L. S. (1993). A cognitive-developmental approach to social stereotyping and reconstructive memory in Euro-American children. *Child Development, 64*, 1507–1518.

Bijou, S. W., & Baer, D. M. (1961). *Child development* (Vol. 1). New York: Appleton-Century-Crofts.

Bjorklund, D. F. (1987). How age changes in knowledge base contribute to the development of children's memory. *Developmental Review, 7*, 93–130.

Bjorklund, D. F. (1997). The role of immaturity in human development. *Psychological Bulletin, 122*, 153–169.

Bjorklund, D. F. (2000a). *Children's thinking: Developmental function and individual differences* (3rd ed). Belmont, CA: Wadsworth.

Bjorklund, D. F. (Ed.) (2000b). *False memory creation in children and adults: Theory, research, and implications*. Mahwah, NJ: Erlbaum.

Bjorklund, D. F., Bering, J., & Ragan, P. (1999, October). *A two-year longitudinal study of deferred imitation of object manipulation in an enculturated juvenile chimpanzee (Pantro glodytes) and orangutan (Pongo pygmaeus)*. Poster presented at the meeting of the Cognitive Development Society, Chapel Hill, NC.

Bjorklund, D. F., Miller, P. H., Coyle, T. R., & Slawinski, J. L. (1997). Instructing children to use memory strategies: Evidence of utilization deficiencies in memory training studies. *Developmental Review, 17*, 411–442.

Bjorklund, D. F., & Pellegrini, A. D. (2000). Child development and evolutionary psychology. *Child Development*, 71, 1687–1708.

Bjorklund, D. F., & Schwartz, R. (1996). The adaptive nature of developmental immaturity: Implications for language acquisition and language disabilities. In M. Smith and J. Damico (Eds.), *Childhood language disorders*. New York: Thieme Medical Publishers.

Bjorklund, D. F., & Shackelford, T. K. (1999). Differences in parental investment contribute to important differences between men and women. *Current Directions in Psychological Science, 8*, 86–89.

Bjorklund, D. F., & Zeman, B. R. (1982). Children's organization and metamemory awareness in their recall of familiar information. *Child Development, 53,* 799–810.

Blurton-Jones, N. (1972). *Ethological studies of child behavior.* Cambridge, England: Cambridge University Press.

Bornstein, M. H., Tal, J., & Tamis-LeMonda, C. S. (1991). Parenting in cross-cultural perspective: The United States, France, and Japan. In M. H. Bornstein (Ed.), *Cultural approaches to parenting*. Hillsdale, NJ: Erlbaum.

Bornstein, M. H., Toda, S., Azuma, H., Tamis-LeMonda, C. S., & Ogino, M. (1990). Mother and infant activity and interaction in Japan and in the United States: II. A comparative microanalysis of naturalistic exchanges focused on the organization of infant attention. *International Journal of Behavioral Development, 13*, 289–308.

Bower, T. G. R. (1974). *Development in infancy.* San Francisco: Freeman.

Bowers, K. S. (1973). Situationism in psychology. *Psychological Review, 80,* 307–336.

Bowlby, J. (1958). The nature of the child's tie to his mother. *International Journal of Psychoanalysis, 39,* 350–373.

Bowlby, J. (1969). *Attachment and loss: Vol 1. Attachment*. New York: Basic Books.

Bowlby, J. (1980). *Attachment and loss: Vol. 3. Loss.* New York: Basic Books.

Bowlby, J. (1982). *Attachment and loss: Vol. 1. Attachment.* (2nd ed.), New York: Basic Books. Original work published 1969.

Bowlby, J. (1991). *Charles Darwin: A new biography*. London: Hutchinson.

Bradley, B. S. (1989). *Visions of infancy*. Oxford: Polity/Blackwell.

Brainerd, C. J. (Ed.). (1996). *Psychological Science* celebrates the centennial of Jean Piaget. [Special section of journal]. *Psychological Science, 7,* 191–225.

Brainerd, C. J., & Reyna, V. F. (1998). Fuzzy-trace theory and children's false memories. *Journal of Experimental Child Psychology, 71*, 81–129.

Breland, K., & Breland, M. (1961). The misbehavior of organisms. *American Psychologist, 16,* 681–684.

Bretherton, I., & Munholland, K. A. (1999). Internal working models in attachment relationships: A construct revisited. In J. Cassidy and P. R. Shaver (Eds.), *Handbook of attachment*. New York: Guilford Press.

Bringuier, J. (1980). *Conversations with Jean Piaget.* Chicago: University of Chicago Press.

Bronfenbrenner, U. (1977). Toward an experimental ecology of human development. *American Psychologist, 32*, 513–531.

Bronfenbrenner, U. (1986). Recent advances in research on human development. In R. K. Silbereisen, K. Eyferth, and G. Rudinger (Eds.), *Development as action in context: Problem behavior and normal youth development.* New York: Springer-Verlag.

Bronfenbrenner, U. (1989a). Ecological systems theory. In R. Vasta (Ed.), *Annals of child development: Vol. 6. Six theories of child development.* Greenwich, CT: JAI Press.

Bronfenbrenner, U. (1989b, April). The developing ecology of human development: Paradigm lost or paradigm regained. Symposium conducted at the meeting of the Society for Research in Child Development, Kansas City, MO.

Bronfenbrenner, U., & Morris, P. A. (1998). The ecology of developmental processes. In W. Damon (Series Ed.) & L. M. Lerner (Vol. Ed.), *Handbook of child psychology: Vol. 1. Theoretical models of human development* (5th ed.). New York: Wiley.

Brown, A. L. (1975). The development of memory: Knowing, knowing about knowing, and knowing how to know. In H. W. Reese (Ed.), *Advances in child development and behavior* (Vol. 10). New York: Academic Press.

Brown, A. L. (1978). Knowing when, where, and how to remember: A problem of metacognition. In R. Glaser (Ed.), *Advances in instructional psychology* (Vol. 1). Hillsdale, NJ: Erlbaum.

Brown, A. L., & DeLoache, J. S. (1978). Skills, plans, and self-regulation. In R. S. Siegler, (Ed.), *Children's thinking: What develops?* Hillsdale, NJ: Erlbaum.

Brown, A. L., & Smiley, S. S. (1978). The development of strategies for studying texts. *Child Development, 49,* 1076–1088.

Brown, J. S., & Burton, R. B. (1978). Diagnostic models for procedural bugs in basic mathematical skills. *Cognitive Science, 2,* 155–192.

Brückner, G. H. (1933). Untersuchungen zur Tiersoziologie, insbesondere der Auflösung der Familie. *Zeitschrift für Psychologie, 128,* 1–120.

Bruner, J. S. (1987, December). The artist as analyst. A review of *A way of looking at things: Selected papers from 1930 to 1980,* by E. Erikson. *The New York Review, 3,* 8–13.

Brunk, M. A., & Henggeler, S. W. (1984). Child influences on adult controls: An experimental investigation. *Developmental Psychology, 6,* 1074–1081.

Brush, S. G. (1976). Fact and fantasy in the history of science. In M. H. Marx & F. E. Goodson (Eds.), *Theories in contemporary psychology* (2nd ed.). New York: Macmillan.

Bryant, P. E. (1986). Theories about the causes of cognitive development. In P. L. C. Van Geert (Ed.), *Theory building in developmental psychology.* Amsterdam: North Holland.

Burman, E. (1994). *Deconstructing developmental psychology*. London: Routledge.

Bussey, K., & Bandura, A. (1992). Self-regulatory mechanisms governing gender development. *Child Development, 63,* 1236–1250.

Bussey, K., & Bandura, A. (1999). Social cognitive theory of gender development and differentiation. *Psychological Review, 106,* 676–713.

Byrne, R. W. (1995). *The thinking ape*. Oxford: Oxford University Press.

Cairns, R. B. (1979). *Social development: The origins and plasticity of interchanges*. San Francisco: W. H. Freeman.

Call, J., & Tomasello, M. (1999). A nonverbal false belief task: The performance of children and great apes. *Child Development, 70,* 381–395.

Campos, J. J., Langer, A., & Krowitz, A. (1970). Cardiac responses on the visual cliff in prelocomotor human infants. *Science, 170,* 196–197.

Carey, S. (1985). *Conceptual change in childhood*. Cambridge, MA: MIT Press.

Carey, S. (1991). Knowledge acquisition: Enrichment or conceptual change? In S. Carey & R. Gelman (Eds.), *The epigenesis of mind: Essays on biology and cognition*. Hillsdale, NJ: Erlbaum.

Carraher, T. N., Carraher, D. W., & Schliemann, A. D. (1985). Mathematics in the streets and in schools. *British Journal of Developmental Psychology, 3,* 21–29.

Case, R. (1992). *The mind's staircase: Exploring the conceptual underpinnings of children's thought and knowledge.* Hillsdale, NJ: Erlbaum.

Case, R. (1998). The development of conceptual structures. In W. Damon (Series Ed.) & D. Kuhn & R. S. Siegler (Vol. Eds.), *Handbook of child psychology: Vol. 2, Cognition, perception, and language* (5th ed.). New York: Wiley.

Case, R., & Okamoto, Y. (1996). The role of central conceptual structures in the development of children's thought. *Monographs of the Society for Research in Child Development, 61* (1–2, Serial No. 246).

Caspi, A., Elder, G. H., & Herbener, E. S. (1989). Turning points in the life course. In A. Caspi (Chair), *Surmounting childhood disadvantage: Pathways to change.* Symposium conducted at the meeting of the Society for Research in Child Development, Kansas City, MO.

Cassidy, J., & Shaver, P. R. (Eds.), (1999). *Handbook of attachment: Theory, research, and clinical applications.* New York: Guilford Press.

Cassirer, E. (1951). *The philosophy of the enlightenment.* Boston: Beacon Press.

Caudill, W., & Weinstein, H. (1969). Maternal care and infant behavior in Japan and America. *Psychiatry, 32,* 12–43.

Cazden, C. B., & John, V. P. (1971). Learning in American Indian children. In M. L. Wax, S. Diamond, & F. O. Gearing (Eds.), *Anthropological perspectives in education.* New York: Basic Books.

Ceci, S. J. (1996). *On intelligence: A bioecological treatise on intellectual development* (expanded ed.). Cambridge, MA: Harvard University Press.

Ceci, S. J., & Bruck, M. (1995). *Jeopardy in the courtroom: A scientific analysis of children's testimony.* Washington, DC: American Psychological Association.

Ceci, S. J., & Bruck, M. (1998). Children's testimony. In W. Damon (Series Ed.) & I. E. Sigel & K. A. Renninger (Vol. Eds.), *Handbook of child psychology: Vol. 4. Child psychology in practice* (5th ed.). New York: Wiley.

Ceci, S. J., Caves, R. D., & Howe, M. J. A. (1981). Children's long-term memory for information that is incongruous with their prior knowledge. *British Journal of Psychology, 72,* 443–450.

Ceci, S. J., Leichtman, M., & White, T. (in press). Interviewing preschoolers: Remembrance of things planted. In D. P. Peters (Ed.), *The child witness in context: Cognitive, social, and legal perspectives.* Dordrecht, The Netherlands: Kluwer.

Cernoch, J. M., & Potter, R. H. (1985). Recognition of maternal axillary odors by infants. *Child Development, 56,* 1593–1598.

Chapman, M. (1988). *Constructive evolution: Origins and development of Piaget's thought.* Cambridge, England: Cambridge University Press.

Charlesworth, W. R. (1978). *One year of haiku.* Minneapolis, MN: Nodin Press.

Charlesworth, W. R. (1979). Ethology: Understanding the other half of intelligence. In M. von Cranach, K. Foppa, W. Lepenies, & D. Ploog (Eds.), *Human ethology: Claims and limits of a new discipline.* Cambridge, England: Cambridge University Press.

Charlesworth, W. R. (1983). An ethological approach to cognitive development. In C. Brainerd (Ed.), *Recent advances in cognitive developmental theory.* New York: Springer-Verlag.

Charlesworth, W. R. (1988). Resources and resource acquisition during ontogeny. In K. B. MacDonald (Ed.), *Sociobiological perspectives on human development.* New York: Springer-Verlag.

Charlesworth, W. R. (1992). Darwin and developmental psychology: Past and present. *Developmental Psychology, 28*, 5–16.

Charlesworth, W. R. (1996). Cooperation and competition: Contributions to an evolutionary and developmental model. *International Journal of Behavioral Development, 19*, 25–38.

Chavajay, P., & Rogoff, B. (1999). Cultural variation in management of attention by children and their caregivers. *Developmental Psychology, 35*, 1079–1090.

Chen, Z., & Siegler, R. S. (2000). Across the great divide: Bridging the gap between understanding of toddlers' and older children's thinking. *Monographs of the Society for Research in Child Development, 65*(2, Whole No. 261).

Chi, M. T. H. (1978). Knowledge structures and memory development. In R. S. Siegler (Ed.), *Children's thinking. What develops?* Hillsdale, NJ: Erlbaum.

Chi, M. T. H., & Koeske, R. D. (1983). Network representation of a child's dinosaur knowledge. *Developmental Psychology, 19,* 29–39.

Chisholm, J. S. (1996). The evolutionary ecology of attachment organization. *Human Nature, 1*, 1–37.

Chodorow, N. (1978). *The reproduction of mothering: Psychoanalysis and the socialization of gender.* Berkeley: University of California Press.

Chomsky, N. (1959). A review of *Verbal behavior,* by B. F. Skinner. *Language, 35,* 26–58.

Chomsky, N. (1965). *Aspects of the theory of syntax.* Cambridge, MA: MIT Press.

Chomsky, N. (1988). *Language and problems of knowledge.* Cambridge, MA: MIT Press.

Cohen, D. (1977). *Psychologists on psychology.* New York: Taplinger.

Cole, M. (1988). Cross-cultural research in the sociohistorical tradition. *Human Development, 31*, 137–157.

Cole, M. (1992). Culture in development. In M. Bornstein & M. Lamb (Eds.), *Developmental psychology: An advanced textbook* (3rd ed.). Hillsdale, NJ: Erlbaum.

Cole, M. (1996). *Cultural psychology: A once and future discipline.* Cambridge, MA: Harvard University Press.

Cole, M. (1999). Culture in development. In M. Bornstein & M. Lamb (Eds.), *Developmental psychology: An advanced textbook* (4th ed.). Mahwah. NJ: Erlbaum.

Cole, M., & Cole, S. R. (2000). *The development of children* (4th ed.). New York: Worth.

Cole, M., Gay, J., Glick, J. A., & Sharp, D. W. (1971). *The cultural context of learning and thinking.* New York: Basic Books.

Cole, M., & Scribner, S. (1978). Introduction. In L. S. Vygotsky, (Ed.), *Mind in society: The development of higher psychological processes.* Cambridge, MA: Harvard University Press.

Coleman, P. K., & Karraker, K. H. (1997). Self-efficacy and parenting quality: Findings and future applications. *Developmental Review, 18*, 47–85.

Collins, J. L. (1982, March). *Self-efficacy and ability in achievement behavior.* Paper presented at the meeting of the American Educational Research Association, New York.

Commons, M. L. (1994). A summary of the general stage model (GSM). *Behavioral Development, 4*, 6–7.

Cooper, C. R. (1999). Multiple selves, multiple worlds: Cultural perspectives on individuality and connectedness in adolescent development. In A. S. Masten (Ed.), *Cultural processes in child development*. Mahwah, NJ: Erlbaum.

Cosmides, L. (1994, August). *Emergence of evolutionary psychology.* Paper presented at the meeting of the American Psychological Association, Los Angeles.

Cosmides, L., & Tooby, J. (1987). From evolution to behavior: Evolutionary psychology as the missing link. In J. Dupré (Ed.), *The latest on the best: Essays on evolution and optimality*. Cambridge, MA: MIT Press.

Cosmides, L., & Tooby, J. (1992). Cognitive adaptations for social exchange. In J. H. Barkow, L. Cosmides, & J. Tooby (Eds.), *The adapted mind: Evolutionary psychology and the generation of culture*. New York: Oxford University Press.

Coyle, T. R., & Bjorklund, D. F. (1997). Age differences in, and consequences of, multiple- and variable strategy use on a multitrial sort-recall task. *Developmental Psychology, 33*, 372–380.

Crick, N. R., & Grotpeter, J. K. (1995). Relational aggression, gender, and social-psychological adjustment. *Child Development, 66*, 710–722.

Crick, N. R., & Rose, A. J. (2000). Toward a gender-balanced approach to the study of social-emotional development: A look at relational aggression. In P. H. Miller & E. K. Scholnick (Eds.), *Toward a feminist developmental psychology*. New York: Routledge.

Darwin, C. (1877). A biographical sketch of an infant. *Mind, 2*, 285–294.

Darwin, C. (1890). *The formation of vegetable mould, through the action of worms, with observations on their habits.* New York: Appleton.

Davidson, P. (1988). Piaget's category-theoretic interpretation of cognitive development: A neglected contribution. *Human Development, 31*, 225–244.

Decarie, T. (1965). *Intelligence and affectivity in early childhood.* New York: International Universities Press.

Dekker, E., & Groen, J. (1956). Reproducible psychogenic attacks of asthma: A laboratory study. *Journal of Psychosomatic Research, 1,* 58–67.

DeLoache, J. S., Cassidy, D. J., & Brown, A. L. (1985). Precursors of mnemonic strategies in very young children's memory. *Child Development, 56*, 125–137.

DeMarie-Dreblow, D. (1991). Relation between knowledge and memory: A reminder that correlation does not imply causality. *Child Development, 62,* 484–498.

Demetriou, A., Efklides, A., & Platsidou, M. (1993). The architecture and dynamics of developing mind: Experiential structuralism as a frame for unifying cognitive developmental theories. *Monographs of the Society for Research in Child Development, 58*(5–6, Serial No. 234).

Demetriou, A., & Raftopoulos, A. (1999). Modeling the developing mind: From structure to change. *Developmental Review, 19*, 319–368.

Dewsbury, D. A. (1978). *Comparative animal behavior.* New York: McGraw-Hill.

Dodge, K. A. (1986). A social information processing model of social competence in children. In M. Perlmutter (Ed.), *Cognitive perspectives on children's social and behavioral development.* Hillsdale, NJ: Erlbaum.

Dollard, J., Doob, L., Miller, W. N. E., Mowrer, O. H., & Sears, R. R. (1939). *Frustration and aggression.* New Haven, CT: Yale University Press.

Dollard, J., & Miller, N. E. (1950). *Personality and psychotherapy.* New York: McGraw-Hill.

Dornbusch, S. M., Ritter, P. L, Leiderman, P. H., Roberts, D. F., & Fraleigh, M. J. (1987). The relation of parenting style to adolescent school performance. *Child Development, 58,* 1244–1257.

Dorr, D., & Fey, S. (1974). Relative power of symbolic adult and peer models in the modification of children's moral choice behavior. *Journal of Personality and Social Psychology, 29,* 335–341.

Drake, S. G. (1834). *Biography and history of the Indians of North America.* Boston: Perkins and Hilliard, Gray.

Duncan, R. M., & Pratt, M. W. (1997). Microgenetic change in the quantity and quality of prechoolers' private speech. *International Journal of Behavioral Development, 20,* 267–383.

Dunn, J. (1988). *The beginnings of social understanding.* Oxford: Basil Blackwell.

Edelman, G. M. (1987). *Neural Darwinism: The theory of neuronal group selection.* New York: Basic Books.

Edelman, M. S., & Omark, D. R. (1973, March). *The development of logical operations: An ethological approach.* Paper presented at the meetings of the Society for Research in Child Development, Philadelphia.

Eibl-Eibesfeldt, I. (1975). *Ethology: The biology of behavior* (2nd ed.). New York: Holt, Rinehart & Winston.

Eibl-Eibesfeldt, I. (1989). *Human ethology,* New York: de Gruyter.

Elder, G. H. (1998). The life course and human development. In W. Damon (Series Ed.) & R. M. Lerner (Vol. Ed.), *Handbook of child psychology: Vol. 1. Theoretical models of human development,* (5th ed.). New York: Wiley.

Elkind, D. (1968, May 26). Giant in the nursery—Jean Piaget. *New York Times Magazine.*

Ellis, S., & Johns, M. (1999, April) *Children's understanding of wrong reasoning as a function of domain knowledge.* Paper presented at the meeting of the Society for Research in Child Development, Albuquerque, NM.

Ellis, S., Klahr, D., & Siegler, R. S. (1993, March). *Effects of feedback and collaboration on changes in children's use of mathematical rules.* Paper presented at the meeting of the Society for Research in Child Development, New Orleans, LA.

Ellis, S., & Siegler, R. S. (1997). Planning as a strategy choice or why don't children plan when they should? In S. Friedman & E. Scholnick (Eds.), *Why, how, and when do we plan: The developmental psychology of planning.* Mahwah, NJ: Erlbaum.

Elman, J. L. (1994). Implicit learning in neural networks: The importance of starting small. In C. Umilta and M. Moscovitch (Eds.), *Attention and performance: XV. Conscious and nonconscious information processing.* Cambridge, MA: MIT Press.

Elman, J. L., Bates, E. A., Johnson, M. H., Karmiloff-Smith, A., Parisi, D., & Plunkett, K. (1996). *Rethinking innateness: A connectionist perspective on development.* Cambridge, MA: MIT Press.

Erikson, E. H. (1950). In M. J. E. Senn (Ed.), *Symposium on the healthy personality.* New York: Josiah Macy, Jr. Foundation.

Erikson, E. H. (1951). The California loyalty oath: An editorial. *Psychiatry, 14,* 244–245.

Erikson, E. H. (1958). *Young man Luther.* New York: Norton.

Erikson, E. H. (1959). Identity and the life cycle. *Psychological issues* (Monograph No. 1). New York: International Universities Press.

Erikson, E. H. (1963). *Childhood and society* (2nd ed.). New York: Norton.

Erikson, E. H. (1968). *Identity: Youth and crisis.* New York: Norton.

Erikson, E. H. (1969). *Gandhi's truth.* New York: Norton.

Erikson, E. H. (1973). The wider identity. In K. Erikson (Ed.), *In search of common ground: Conversations with Erik H. Erikson and Huey P. Newton.* New York: Norton.

Erikson, E. H. (1977). *Toys and reasons.* New York: Norton.

Erikson, E. H., Erikson, J. M., & Kivnick, H. Q. (1986). *Vital involvement in old age.* New York: Norton.

Eron, L. D. (1987). The development of aggressive behavior from the perspective of a developing behaviorism. *American Psychologist, 42,* 435–442.

Evans, R. I. (1967). *Dialogue with Erik Erikson.* New York: Harper & Row.

Evans, R. I. (1973). *Jean Piaget: The man and his ideas.* New York: Dutton.

Evans, R. I. (1989). *Albert Bandura: The man and his ideas—A dialogue.* New York: Praeger.

Fabricius, W. V., & Hagen, J. W. (1984). Use of causal attributions about recall performance to assess metamemory and predict strategic memory behavior in young children. *Developmental Psychology, 20,* 975–987.

Ferrara, R. A., Brown, A. L., & Campione, J. C. (1986). Children's learning and transfer of inductive reasoning rules: Studies of proximal development. *Child Development, 57,* 1087–1099.

Ferrari, M., & Sternberg, R. J. (1998). The development of mental abilities and styles. In W. Damon (Series Ed.) & D. Kuhn & R. S. Siegler (Vol. Eds.), *Handbook of child psychology: Vol. 2. Cognition, perception, and language* (5th ed.). New York: Wiley.

Fischer, K. W., & Bidell, T. R. (1998). Dynamic development of psychological structures in action and thought. In W. Damon (Series Ed.) & R. M. Lerner (Vol. Ed.), *Handbook of child psychology: Vol. 1. Theoretical models of human development* (5th ed.). New York: Wiley.

Fisher, S., & Greenberg, R. P. (1996). *Freud scientifically reappraised: Testing the theories and therapy.* New York: Wiley.

Fivush, R. (1990, August). *Self, gender, and emotion in parent-child conversations about the past.* Paper presented at the meeting of the American Psychological Association, Boston.

Fivush, R. (1997). Event memory in early childhood. In N. Cowan (Ed.), *Development of memory in childhood.* Hove East Sussex, UK: Psychology Press.

Fivush, R. (2000). Accuracy, authority, and voice: Feminist perspectives on autobiographical memory. In P. H. Miller & E. K. Scholnick (Eds.), *Toward a feminist developmental psychology.* New York: Routledge.

Flavell, J. H. (1963). *The developmental psychology of Jean Piaget.* Princeton, NJ: Van Nostrand.

Flavell, J. H. (1971a). First discussant's comments: What is memory development the development of? *Human Development, 14,* 272–278.

Flavell, J. H. (1971b). Stage-related properties of cognitive development. *Cognitive Psychology, 2,* 421–453.

Flavell, J. H. (1982). On cognitive development. *Child Development, 53,* 1–10.

Flavell, J. H. (1992). Cognitive development. *Developmental Psychology, 28*, 998–1005.

Flavell, J. H. (1996). Piaget's legacy. *Psychological Science, 7*, 200–203.

Flavell, J. H., Beach, D. R., & Chinsky, J. M. (1966). Spontaneous verbal rehearsal in a memory task as a function of age. *Child Development, 37,* 283–299.

Flavell, J. H., Friedrichs, A. G., & Hoyt, J. D. (1970). Developmental changes in memorization processes. *Cognitive Psychology, 1*, 324–340.

Flavell, J. H., & Hill, J. (1969). Developmental psychology. In P. H. Mussen & M. R. Rosenzweig (Eds.), *Annual review of psychology* (Vol. 20). Palo Alto, CA: Annual Reviews.

Flavell, J. H., & Miller, P. H. (1998). Social cognition. In W. Damon (Series Ed.) & D. Kuhn & R. S. Siegler (Vol. Eds.), *Handbook of child psychology: Vol. 2. Cognition, perception, and language* (5th ed.). New York: Wiley.

Flavell, J. H., Miller, P. H., & Miller, S. A. (2001). *Cognitive development* (4th ed.). Englewood Cliffs, NJ: Prentice-Hall.

Flavell, J. H., & Wellman, H. M. (1977). Metamemory. In R. V. Kail & J. W. Hagen (Eds.), *Perspectives on the development of memory and cognition.* Hillsdale, NJ: Erlbaum.

Flavell, J. H., & Wohlwill, J.F. (1969). Formal and functional aspects of cognitive development. In D. Elkind & J. H. Flavell (Eds.), *Studies in cognitive growth: Essays in honor of Jean Piaget.* New York: Oxford University Press.

Fodor, J. A. (1983). *The modularity of mind.* Cambridge, MA: MIT/Bradford Books.

Fox, D., & Prilleltensky, I. (Eds.). (1997). *Critical psychology: An introduction.* London & Thousand Oaks, CA: Sage.

Fox, R., & McDaniel, C. (1982). Perception of biological motion by human infants. *Science, 218,* 486–487.

Freedland, R. L., & Bertenthal, B. I. (1994). Developmental stages in interlimb coordination: Transition to hands-and-knees crawling. *Psychological Science, 5*, 26–32.

Freud, S. (1953a). The interpretation of dreams. In J. Strachey (Ed. & Trans.), *The standard edition of the complete psychological works of Sigmund Freud* (Vols. 4 and 5). London: Hogarth Press. (Original work published 1900).

Freud, S. (1953b). Fragment of an analysis of a case of hysteria. In J. Strachey, (Ed. & Trans.), *The standard edition of the complete psychological works of Sigmund Freud* (Vol. 7). London: Hogarth Press. (Original work published 1905).

Freud, S. (1953c). Three essays on the theory of sexuality. In J. Strachey (Ed. & Trans.), *The standard edition of the complete psychological works of Sigmund Freud* (Vol. 7). London: Hogarth Press. (Original work published 1905).

Freud, S. (1955a). Analysis of a phobia in a five-year-old boy. In J. Strachey (Ed. & Trans.), *The standard edition of the complete psychological works of Sigmund Freud* (Vol. 10). London: Hogarth Press. (Original work published 1909.)

Freud, S. (1955b). Notes upon a case of obsessional neurosis. In J. Strachey (Ed. & Trans.), *The standard edition of the complete psychological works of Sigmund Freud* (Vol. 10). London: Hogarth Press. (Original work published 1909).

Freud, S. (1955c). Totem and taboo. In J. Strachey (Ed. & Trans.), *The standard edition of the complete psychological works of Sigmund Freud* (Vol. 13.). London: Hogarth Press. (Original work published 1913).

Freud, S. (1955d). The Moses of Michelangelo. In J. Strachey (Ed. & Trans.), *The standard edition of the complete psychological works of Sigmund Freud* (Vol. 13.). London: Hogarth Press. (Original work published 1914).

Freud, S. (1955e). From the history of an infantile neurosis. In J. Strachey (Ed. & Trans.), *The standard edition of the complete psychological works of Sigmund Freud* (Vol.17). London: Hogarth Press. (Original work published 1918).

Freud, S. (1955f). Beyond the pleasure principle. In J. Strachey (Ed. & Trans.), *The standard edition of the complete psychological works of Sigmund Freud* (Vol. 18). London: Hogarth Press. (Original work published 1920).

Freud, S. (1957). Instincts and their vicissitudes. In J. Strachey (Ed. & Trans.), *The standard edition of the complete psychological works of Sigmund Freud* (Vol. 14). London: Hogarth Press. (Original work published 1915).

Freud, S. (1959a). An autobiographical study. In J. Strachey (Ed. & Trans.), *The standard edition of the complete psychological works of Sigmund Freud* (Vol. 20). London: Hogarth Press. (Original work published 1925).

Freud, S. (1960). The psychopathology of everyday life. In J. Strachey (Ed. & Trans.), *The standard edition of the complete psychological works of Sigmund Freud* (Vol. 6). London: Hogarth Press. (Original work published 1901).

Freud, S. (1961a). The ego and the id. In J. Strachey (Ed. & Trans.), *The standard edition of the complete psychological works of Sigmund Freud* (Vol. 19). London: Hogarth Press. (Original work published 1923).

Freud, S. (1961b). Some psychical consequences of the anatomical distinction between the sexes. In J. Strachey (Ed. & Trans.), *The standard edition of the complete psychological works of Sigmund Freud* (Vol. 19). London: Hogarth Press. (Original work published 1925).

Freud, S. (1961c). The future of an illusion. In J. Strachey (Ed. & Trans.), *The standard edition of the complete psychological works of Sigmund Freud* (Vol. 21). London: Hogarth Press. (Original work published 1927).

Freud, S. (1961d). Dostoevsky and parricide. In J. Strachey (Ed. & Trans.), *The standard edition of the complete psychological works of Sigmund Freud* (Vol. 21). London: Hogarth Press. (Original work published 1928).

Freud, S. (1961e). Civilization and its discontents. In J. Strachey (Ed. & Trans.), *The standard edition of the complete psychological works of Sigmund Freud* (Vol. 21). London: Hogarth Press. (Original work published 1930).

Freud, S. (1963a). Introductory lectures on psycho-analysis. In J. Strachey (Ed. & Trans.), *The standard edition of the complete psychological works of Sigmund Freud* (Vol. 15). London: Hogarth Press. (Original work published 1916).

Freud, S. (1963b). Introductory lectures on psycho-analysis. In J. Strachey (Ed. & Trans.), *The standard edition of the complete psychological works of Sigmund Freud* (Vol. 16). London: Hogarth Press. (Original work published 1917).

Freud, S. (1964a). New introductory lectures on Psycho-analysis. In J. Strachey (Ed. & Trans.), *The standard edition of the complete psychological works of Sigmund Freud* (Vol. 22). London: Hogarth Press. (Original work published 1933).

Freud, S. (1964b). Why war? In J. Strachey (Ed. & Trans.), *The standard edition of the complete psychological works of Sigmund Freud* (Vol. 22). London: Hogarth Press. (Original work published 1933).

Freud, S. (1964c). An outline of psycho-analysis. In J. Strachey (Ed. & Trans.), *The standard edition of the complete psychological works of Sigmund Freud* (Vol. 23). London: Hogarth Press. (Original work published 1940).

Freund, L. S. (1990). Maternal regulation of children's problem-solving behavior and its impact on children's performance. *Child Development, 61,* 113–126.

Furth, H. G. (1987). *Knowledge as desire.* New York: Columbia University Press.

Garcia, J., & Koelling, R. A. (1966). Relation of cue to consequences in avoidance learning. *Psychonomic Science, 4,* 123–124.

Gardner, H. (1993). *Multiple intelligences.* New York: Basic Books.

Gardner, R., & Heider, K. G. (1969). *Gardens of war: Life and death in the New Guinea stone age.* New York: Random House.

Garmezy, N., & Tellegen, A. (1984). Studies of stress-resistant children: Methods, variables and preliminary findings. In F. Morrison, C. Lord, & D. Keating (Eds.), *Applied developmental psychology* (Vol. 1). New York: Academic Press.

Geary, D. C. (1995). Reflections of evolution and culture in children's cognition: Implications for mathematical development and instruction. *American Psychologist, 50,* 24–37.

Geary, D. C., & Bjorklund, D. F. (2000). Evolutionary developmental psychology. *Child Development, 71,* 57–65.

Gedo, J. E. (1999). *The evolution of psychoanalysis: Contemporary theory and practice.* New York: Other Press.

Gelman, R. (1969). Conservation acquisition: A problem of learning to attend to relevant attributes. *Journal of Experimental Child Psychology, 7,* 167–187.

Gelman, R. (1972). Logical capacity of very young children: Number invariance rules. *Child Development, 43,* 75–90.

Gelman R., & Gallistel, C. R. (1978). *The child's understanding of number.* Cambridge, MA: Harvard University Press.

Gelman, R., & Williams, E. M. (1998). Enabling constraints for cognition development and learning: Domain specificity and epigenesis. In W. Damon (Series Ed.) & D. Kuhn & R. S. Siegler (Vol. Eds.), *Handbook of child psychology:Vol. 2. Cognition, perception, and language* (5th ed.). New York: Wiley.

Gelman, S. A., & Taylor, M. G. (2000). Gender essentialism in cognitive development. In P. H. Miller & E. K. Scholnick (Eds.), *Toward a feminist developmental psychology*. New York: Routledge.

Gibson, E. J. (1969). *Principles of perceptual learning and development.* New York: Appleton-Century-Crofts.

Gibson, E. J. (1977). How perception really develops: A view from outside the network. In D. LaBerge & S. J. Samuels (Eds.), *Basic processes in reading: Perception and comprehension.* Hillsdale, NJ: Erlbaum.

Gibson, E. J. (1982). The concept of affordances in development: The renascence of functionalism. In W. A. Collins (Ed.), *The concept of development.* Hillsdale, NJ: Erlbaum.

Gibson, E. J. (1988). Exploratory behavior in the development of perceiving, acting, and the acquiring of knowledge. In M. R. Rosenzweig & L. W. Porter (Eds.), *Annual review of psychology* (Vol. 39). Palo Alto, CA: Annual Reviews.

Gibson, E. J. (1991). *An odyssey in learning and perception.* Cambridge, MA: Bradford/MIT Press.

Gibson, E. J., Gibson, J. J., Pick, A. D., & Osser, H. (1962). A developmental study of the discrimination of letter-like forms. *Journal of Comparative and Physiological Psychology, 55,* 897–906.

Gibson, E. J., & Levin, H. (1975). *The psychology of reading.* Cambridge, MA: MIT Press.

Gibson, E. J., Owsley, C. J., & Johnston, J. (1978). Perception of invariants by five-month-old infants: Differentiation of two types of motion. *Developmental Psychology, 14,* 407–415.

Gibson, E. J., & Pick, A. D. (2000). *An ecological approach to perceptual learning & development.* New York: Oxford University Press.

Gibson, E. J., & Rader, N. (1979). The perceiver as performer. In G. Hale & M. Lewis (Eds.), *Attention and cognitive development.* New York: Plenum Press.

Gibson, E. J., Riccio, A., Schmuckler, M., Stoffregen, T., Rosenberg, D., & Taormina, J. (1987). Detection of the traversability of surfaces by crawling and walking infants. *Journal of Experimental Psychology: Human Perception and Performance, 13,* 533–544.

Gibson, E. J., & Walk, R. D. (1960). The "visual cliff." *Scientific American, 202,* 64–71.

Gibson, J. J. (1979a). Foreward: A note on E. J. G. by J. J. G. In A. D. Pick (Ed.), *Perception and its development: A tribute to Eleanor J. Gibson.* Hillsdale, NJ: Erlbaum.

Gibson, J. J. (1979b). *The ecological approach to visual perception.* Boston: Houghton-Mifflin.

Gigerenzer, G. (1991). From tools to theories: A heuristic of discovery in cognitive psychology. *Psychological Review, 98,* 254–267.

Gill, M. M. (1959). The present state of psychoanalytic theory. *Journal of Abnormal and Social Psychology, 58,* 1–8.

Gilligan, C. (1982). *In a different voice: Psychological theory and women's development.* Cambridge, MA: Harvard University Press.

Ginsburg, H. J., & Opper, S. (1979). *Piaget's theory of intellectual development* (2nd ed.). Englewood Cliffs, NJ: Prentice-Hall.

Ginsburg, H. J., Pollman, V. A., & Wauson, M. S. (1977). An ethological analysis of nonverbal inhibitors of aggressive behavior in male elementary school children. *Developmental Psychology, 13,* 417–418.

Goldberg, S., Blumberg, S. L., & Kriger, A. (1982). Menarche and interest in infants: Biological and social influences. *Child Development, 53,* 1544–1550.

Goodman, G. S., & Quas, J. A. (1997). Trauma and memory: Individual differences in children's recounting of a stressful experience. In N. L. Stein, P. A. Ornstein, B. Tversky, & C. Brainerd (Eds.), *Memory for everyday and emotional events.* Mahwah, NJ: Erlbaum.

Gopnik, A., & Meltzoff, A. N. (1997). *Words, thoughts, and theories.* Cambridge, MA: MIT Press.

Gottlieb, G. (1976). The roles of experience in the development of behavior and the nervous system. In G. Gottlieb (Ed.), *Neural and behavioral plasticity*. New York: Academic Press.

Gottlieb, G. (1979). Comparative psychology and ethology. In E. Hearst (Ed.), *The first century of experimental psychology.* Hillsdale, NJ: Erlbaum.

Gottlieb, G. (1991). Experiential canalization of behavioral development: Results. *Developmental Psychology, 27*, 35–39.

Gottlieb, G., Wahlsten, D., & Lickliter, R. (1998). The significance of biology for human development: A developmental psychobiological systems view. In W. Damon (Series Ed.) & R. M. Lerner (Vol. Ed.), *Handbook of child psychology: Vol 1. Theoretical models of human development* (5th ed.). New York: Wiley.

Gould, S. J. (1980). *The panda's thumb.* New York: Norton.

Graham, T., & Perry, M. (1993). Indexing transitional knowledge. *Developmental Psychology, 29,* 779–788.

Greenfield, P. M., Brannon, C., & Lohr, D. (1994). Two-dimensional representation of movement through three-dimensional space: The role of video game expertise. *Journal of Applied Developmental Psychology, 15*, 87–103.

Griffin, P., & Cole, M. (1984). Current activity for the future: The Zoped. In B. Rogoff & J. V. Wertsch (Eds.), *Children's learning in the "zone of proximal development."* San Francisco: Jossey-Bass.

Grigorenko, E. L., & Sternberg, R. J. (1998). Dynamic testing. *Psychological Bulletin, 124*, 75–111.

Grotevant, H. D. (1998). Adolescent development in family contexts. In W. Damon (Series Ed.) & N. Eisenberg (Vol. Ed.), *Handbook of child psychology. Vol. 3: Social, emotional, and personality development* (5th ed.). New York: Wiley.

Guttentag, R. E. (1995). Mental effort and motivation: Influences on children's memory strategy use. In F. E. Weinert & W. Schneider (Eds.), *Memory performance and competencies: Issues in growth and development*. Hillsdale, NJ: Erlbaum.

Hacker, D.J., Dunlosky, J., & Graesser, A. C. (Eds.). *Metacognition in educational theory and practice*. Mahwah, NJ: Erlbaum.

Haith, M. M., & Benson, J. B. (1998). Infant cognition. In W. Damon (Series Ed.) & D. Kuhn & R. S. Siegler (Vol. Eds.), *Handbook of child psychology: Vol 2. Cognition, perception, and language* (5th ed.). New York: Wiley.

Halford, G. S. (1993). *Children's understanding: The development of mental models*. Hillsdale, NJ: Erlbaum.

Halford, G. S. (1999). The properties of representations used in higher cognitive processes: Developmental implications. In I. E. Sigel (Ed.), *Development of mental representations: Theories and applications*. Mahwah, NJ: Erlbaum.

Hall, C. S. (1954). *A primer of Freudian psychology.* New York: World.

Hall, C. S., & Lindzey, G. (1957). *Theories of personality.* New York: Wiley.

Harris, F. R., Wolf, M. M., & Baer, D. M. (1967). Effects of adult social reinforcement on child behavior. In W. W. Hartup & N. L. Smothergill (Eds.), *The young child: Reviews of research.* Washington, DC: National Association for the Education of Young Children.

Hartmann, H. (1958). *Ego psychology and the problem of adaptation.* New York: International Universities Press.

Hartup, W. W., & Yonas, A. (1971). Developmental psychology. In P. H. Mussen & M. R. Rosenzweig (Eds.), *Annual review of psychology* (Vol. 22). Palo Alto, CA: Annual Reviews.

Hawley, P. H. (1999). The ontogenesis of social dominance: A strategy-based evolutionary perspective. *Developmental Review, 19*, 97–132.

Hayes, C. (1951). *The ape in our house.* New York: Harper.

Hebb, D. O. (1949). *The organization of behavior.* New York: Wiley.

Hebb, D. O. (1960). The American revolution. *American Psychologist, 15,* 735–745.

Hebb, D. O. (1980). *Essay on mind.* Hillsdale, NJ: Erlbaum.

Hess, E. H. (1970). Ethology and developmental psychology. In P. H. Mussen (Ed.), *Carmichael's manual of child psychology* (Vol. 1, 3rd ed.). New York: Wiley.

Hicks, V. C., & Carr, H. A. (1912). Human reactions in a maze. *Journal of Animal Psychology, 2,* 98–125.

Hilgard, E. R. (1965). *Hypnotic susceptibility.* New York: Harcourt.

Hinde, R. A. (1974). *Biological bases of human social behavior.* New York: McGraw-Hill.

Hinde, R. A. (1992). Developmental psychology in the context of other behavioural sciences. *Developmental Psychology, 28*, 1018–1029.

Hintzman, D. L. (1974). Psychology and the cow's belly. *Worm Runner's Digest, 16,* 84–85.

Hitch, G. J., & Towse, J. (1995). Working memory: What develops? In F. E. Weinert & S. Schneider (Eds.), *Memory performance and competencies: Issues in growth and development*. Hillsdale, NJ: Erlbaum.

Hopkins, J. R. (1995). Erik Homburger Erikson (1902–1994). *American Psychologist, 50*, 796–797.

Horney, K. (1967). *Feminine psychology.* New York: Norton.

Horowitz, F. D. (1983). A behavioral alternative to an ecological approach to understanding the development of knowing in infancy: A commentary. *Developmental Review*, *3,* 405–409.

Hudson, J. A. (1990). The emergence of autobiographical memory in mother-child conversation. In R. Fivush & J. A. Hudson (Eds.), *Knowing and remembering in young children.* Cambridge, England: Cambridge University Press.

Hutchins, E. (1991). The social organization of distributed cognition. In L. A. Resnick, R. Levine, & A. Behrend (Eds.), *Perspectives on socially shared cognition.* Washington, DC: American Psychological Association.

Iaccino, W. J., & Hogan, J. D. (1994, March). *Plotting the impact of Piaget*. Paper presented at the meeting of the Society for Research in Child Development, Boston.

Inhelder, B., & Piaget, J. (1980). Procedures and structures. In D. R. Olson (Ed.), *The social foundations of language and thought: Essays in honor of Jerome S. Bruner.* New York: Norton.

Inhelder, B., Sinclair, H., & Bovet, M. (1974). *Learning and the development of cognition.* Cambridge, MA: Harvard University Press.

Jensen, P. S., Mrazek, D., Knapp, P. K., Steinberg, L., Pfeffer, C., Schwalter, J., & Shapiro, T. (1997). Evolution and revolution in child psychiatry: ADHD as a disorder of adaptation. *Journal of the American Academy of Child and Adolescent Psychiatry, 36,* 1672–1681.

Johnson, M. H. (1998). The neural basis of cognitive development. In

W. Damon (Series Ed.) & D. Kuhn & R. S. Siegler (Vol. Eds.), *Handbook of child psychology: Vol. 2. Cognition, perception, and language* (5th ed.). New York: Wiley.

Johnson, M. H. (2000). Functional brain development in infants: Elements of an interactive specialization framework. *Child Development, 71,* 75–81.

Johnston, M. K., Sloane, H. N., & Bijou, S. W. (1966). A note on the measurement of drooling in free-ranging young children. *Journal of Experimental Child Psychology, 4,* 292–295.

Jones, E. (1953). *The life and work of Sigmund Freud* (Ed. and abridged by L. Trilling & S. Marcus) (Vol. 1). New York: Basic Books.

Jones, E. (1955). *The life and work of Sigmund Freud* (Ed. and abridged by L. Trilling & S. Marcus) (Vol. 2). New York: Basic Books.

Jones, E. (1957). *The life and work of Sigmund Freud* (Ed. and abridged by L. Trilling & S. Marcus) (Vol. 3). New York: Basic Books.

Jones, E. (1961). *The life and work of Sigmund Freud* (Ed. and abridged by L. Trilling & S. Marcus). New York: Basic Books.

Jones, M. C. (1924). A laboratory study of fear: The case of Peter. *Pedagogical Seminary, 31,* 308–315.

Justice, E. M. (1989). Preschoolers' knowledge and use of behaviors varying in strategic effectiveness. *Merrill-Palmer Quarterly, 35*, 363–377.

Kail, R. V. (1997). Processing time, imagery, and spatial memory. *Journal of Experimental Child Psychology, 64,* 67–78.

Kail, R. V., & Salthouse, T. A. (1994). Processing speed as a mental capacity. *Acta Psychologica, 86*, 199–225.

Kaiser, M. K., McCloskey, M., & Proffitt, D. R. (1986). Development of intuitive theories of motion: Curvilinear motion in the absence of external forces. *Developmental Psychology, 22*, 67–71.

Karmiloff-Smith, A. (1992). *Beyond modularity: A developmental perspective on cognitive science.* Cambridge, MA: MIT Press.

Kawai, M. (1965). Newly acquired precultural behavior of natural troop of Japanese monkeys. *Primates, 6*, 1–30.

Kearins, J. M. (1981). Visual spatial memory in Australian Aboriginal children of desert regions. *Cognitive Psychology, 13*, 434–460.

Kearins, J. M. (1986). Visual spatial memory in Aboriginal and white Australian children. *Australian Journal of Psychology, 38*, 203–214.

Keeney, T. J., Cannizzo, S. R., & Flavell, J. H. (1967). Spontaneous and induced verbal rehearsal in a recall task. *Child Development, 38,* 953–966.

Keil, F. C. (1989). *Concepts, kinds, and cognitive development.* Cambridge, MA: MIT Press.

Kellman, P. J., & Spelke, E. (1983). Perception of partly occluded objects in infancy. *Cognitive Psychology, 15*, 483–524.

Kendler, H. H. (1987). *Historical foundations of modern psychology*. Chicago: Dorsey Press.

Kimble, G. A. (1961). *Hilgard and Marquis' conditioning and learning* (2nd ed.). New York: Appleton-Century-Crofts.

King, M., & Wilson, A. (1975). Evolution at two levels in humans and chimpanzees. *Science, 188*, 107–116.

Klahr, D. (1982). Nonmonotone assessment of monotone development: An information processing analysis. In

S. Strauss (Ed.), *U-shaped behavioral growth.* New York: Academic Press.

Klahr, D. (1984). Transition processes in quantitative development. In R. J. Sternberg (Ed.), *Mechanisms of cognitive development.* New York: Freeman.

Klahr, D. (1985). Solving problems with ambiguous subgoal ordering: Preschoolers' performance. *Child Development, 56,* 940–952.

Klahr, D. (1989). Information processing approaches to cognitive development. In R. Vasta (Ed.), *Annals of child development.* Vol. 6. Greenwich, CT: JAI Press.

Klahr, D. (1999). The conceptual habitat: In what kind of system can concepts develop? In E. K. Scholnick, K. Nelson, S. A. Gelman, & P. H. Miller (Eds.), *Conceptual development: Piaget's legacy* (pp.131–161). Mahwah, NJ: Erlbaum.

Klahr, D., & McWhinney, B. (1998). Information processing. In W. Damon (Series Ed.) & D. Kuhn & R. S. Siegler (Vol. Eds.), *Handbook of child psychology: Vol. 2. Cognition, perception, and language* (5th ed.). New York: Wiley.

Klahr, D., & Siegler, R. S. (1978). The representation of children's knowledge. In H. W. Reese & L. P. Lipsitt (Eds.), *Advances in child development and behavior* (Vol. 12). New York: Academic Press.

Klahr, D., & Wallace, J. G. (1976). *Cognitive development: An information-processing view.* Hillsdale, NJ: Erlbaum.

Klaus, M. H., & Kennell, J. H. (1976). *Maternal-infant bonding.* St. Louis, MO: Mosby.

Klein, G. S. (1970). *Perception, motives, and personality.* New York: Knopf.

Klopfer, P. H. (1971). Mother love: What turns it on? *American Scientist, 59,* 404–407.

Knight, C. C., & Fischer, K. W. (1992). Learning to read words: Individual differences in developmental sequences. *Journal of Applied Developmental Psychology, 13,* 377–404.

Koenig, O. (1951). Das Aktionsystem der Bartmeise *(Panurus biarmicus* L.*). Oesterreichische Zoologische Zeitschrift, 1,* 1–82.

Kohlberg, L. (1969). Stage and sequence: The cognitive-developmental approach to socialization. In D. A. Goslin (Ed.), *Handbook of socialization theory and research.* Chicago: Rand McNally.

Kreutzer, M. A., Leonard, C., & Flavell, J. H. (1975). An interview study of children's knowledge about memory. *Monographs of the Society for Research in Child Development, 40* (1, Serial No. 159).

Kuhn, D. (1989). Children and adults as intuitive scientists. *Psychological Review, 96,* 674–689.

Kuhn, D. (1999). Metacognitive development. In C. Tamis Le-Monda (Ed.), *Child psychology: A handbook of contemporary issues.* New York: Garland.

Kuhn, D., & Pearsall, S. (1998). Relations between metastrategic knowledge and strategic performance. *Cognitive Development, 13,* 227–247.

Kuhn, T. (1970). *The structure of scientific revolutions* (2nd ed.). Chicago: University of Chicago Press.

Lachman, R., Lachman, J. L., & Butterfield, E. C. (1979). *Cognitive psychology and information processing: An introduction.* Hillsdale, NJ: Erlbaum.

Lakatos, I. (1978). *The methodology of scientific research programs.* Cambridge, England: Cambridge University Press.

Lamb, M. E. (Ed.). (1997). *The role of the father in child development* (3rd ed.). New York: Wiley.

Langer, J. (1969). *Theories of development.* New York: Holt, Rinehart & Winston.

Langer, J., & Killen, M. (Eds.). (1998). *Piaget, evolution, and development.* Mahwah, NJ: Erlbaum.

Langlois, J. H., Cooper, R. G., & Woodson, R. H. (1985). The child: Many views, many fields [Review of the book *Handbook of child psychology]. Contemporary Psychology, 30,* 357–369.

Langlois, J. H., Roggman, L. A., Casey, R. J., Ritter, J. M., Rieser-Danner, L. A., & Jenkins, V. Y. (1987). Infant preferences for attractive faces: Rudiments of a stereotype? *Developmental Psychology, 23,* 363–369.

Leaper, C. (2000). The social construction and socialization of gender during development. In P. H. Miller & E. K. Scholnick (Eds.), *Toward a feminist developmental psychology*. New York: Routledge.

Lemerise, E. A., & Arsenio, W. F. (2000). An integrated model of emotion processes and cognition in social information processing. *Child Development, 71*, 107–118.

Leon, M. (1984). Rules mothers and sons use to integrate intent and damage information in their moral judgments. *Child Development, 55,* 2106–2113.

Lerner, R. M. (1991). Changing organism-context relations as the basic process of development: A developmental contextual perspective. *Developmental Psychology, 27,* 27–32.

Lerner, R. M. (1998). Theories of human development: Contemporary perspectives. In W. Damon (Series Ed.) & R. M. Lerner (Vol. Ed.), *Handbook of child psychology: Vol. 1. Theoretical models of human development* (5th ed.). New York: Wiley.

Levy, R. I. (1969). On getting angry in the Society Islands. In W. Caudill and T. Y. Lin (Eds.), *Mental health research in Asia and the Pacific.* Honolulu: East-West Center Press.

Lewis, M. D. (2000). The promise of dynamic systems approaches for an integrated account of human development. *Child Development, 71*, 36–43.

Lewis, M. D., Lamey, A. V., & Douglas, L. (1999). A new dynamic systems method for the analysis of early socioemotional development. *Developmental Science, 2*, 457–475.

Liben, L. S. (1977). Memory from a cognitive-developmental perspective: A theoretical and empirical review. In W. F. Overton & J. M. Gallagher (Eds.), *Knowledge and development* (Vol. 1). New York: Plenum Press.

Lillard, A. (1998). Casting the theory net wide [Review of the book *Words, thoughts, and theories]. Contemporary Psychology, 43*, 663–665.

Lindsay, R. K. (1991). Symbol-processing theories and the SOAR architecture [Review of the book *Unified theories of cognition*]. *Psychological Science, 5*, 294–302.

Loevinger, J. (1976). *Ego development.* San Francisco: Jossey-Bass.

Looft, W. R., & Svoboda, C. P. (1971). *Structuralism in cognitive developmental psychology: Past, contemporary, and futuristic perspectives.* Unpublished manuscript, Pennsylvania State University, University Park.

Lorenz, K. Z. (1931). Beiträge zur Ethologie sozialer Corviden. *Journal für Ornithologie, 79,* 67–127.

Lorenz, K. Z. (1937). Über die Bildung des Instinktbegriffes. *Naturwissenschaften, 25,* 289–300, 307–318, 325–331.

Lorenz, K. Z. (1943). Die angeborenen Formen möglicher Erfahrung.

Zeitschrift für Tierpsychologie, 5, 235–409.

Lorenz, K. Z. (1950). *So kam der Mensch auf den Hund.* Wien: Verlag Borotha-Schoeler.

Lorenz, K. Z. (1952). *King Solomon's ring*. New York: Crowell.

Lorenz, K. Z. (1959). Psychologie und Stammesgeschichte. In G. Herberer (Ed.), *Evolution der Organismen*. Stuttgart: Fischer.

Lorenz, K. Z. (1963). *Das sogenannte Böse.* Wein: Verlag Borotha-Schoeler.

Lorenz, K. Z. (1966). *On aggression.* New York: Harcourt, Brace and World.

Lourenco, O., & Machado, A. (1996). In defense of Piaget's theory: A reply to 10 common criticisms. *Psychological Review, 103*, 143–164.

Luria, A. R. (1961). *The role of speech in the regulation of normal and abnormal behavior*. New York: Liveright.

Luria, A. R. (1976). *Cognitive development: Its cultural and social foundations*. Cambridge, MA: Harvard University Press.

Luria, A. R. (1979). *The making of mind: A personal account of Soviet psychology* (M. Cole & S. Cole, Eds.). Cambridge, MA: Harvard University Press.

MacDonald, K. B. (Ed.) (1988). *Sociobiological perspectives on human development*. New York: Springer-Verlag.

MacDonald, K. B. (1998). Evolution and development. In A. Campbell and S. Muncer (Eds.), *The social child*. East Sussex, UK: Psychology Press.

Mace, W. M. (1977). James J. Gibson's strategy for perceiving: Ask not what's inside your head, but what your head's inside of. In R. Shaw & J. Bransford (Eds.), *Perceiving, acting, and knowing.* Hillsdale, NJ: Erlbaum.

Macfarlane, A. (1977). *The psychology of childbirth.* Cambridge, MA: Harvard University Press.

MacWhinney, B. (1996). Lexical connectionism. In P. Broeder & J. M. J. Murre (Eds.), *Models of language acquisition: Inductive and deductive approaches.* Cambridge, MA: MIT Press.

MacWhinney, B. J., Leinbach, J., Taraban, R., & McDonald, J. L. (1989). Language learning: Cues or rules? *Journal of Memory and Language, 28*, 255–277.

Maddux, J. E. (1998) Why the little blue engine could: Self-efficacy and the real power of positive thinking. [Review of the book *Self-efficacy: The exercise of control*]. *Contemporary Psychology, 43*, 601–602.

Magnusson, D., & Stattin, H. (1998). Person-context interaction theories. In W. Damon (Series Ed.) & R. M. Lerner (Vol. Ed.), *Handbook of child psychology: Vol. 1. Theoretical models of human development* (5th ed.). New York: Wiley.

Mahler, M. S. (1968). *On human symbiosis and the vicissitudes of individuation: Vol. 1. Infantile psychosis.* New York: International Universities Press.

Mahler, M. S., Pine, F., & Bergman, A. (1975). *The psychological birth of the human infant.* New York: Basic Books.

Main, M., & Goldwyn, R. (1998). Adult attachment rating and classification systems. In M. Main (Ed.), *Assessing attachment thought discourse, drawings, and reunion situations*. New York: Cambridge University Press.

Main, M., & Solomon, J. (1990). Procedures for identifying infants as disorganized/disoriented during the Ainsworth Strange Situation. In M. T. Greenberg, D. Cicchetti, & E. M. Cummings (Eds.), *Attachment in the preschool years*. Chicago: University of Chicago Press.

Mandler, G. (1979). Emotion. In E. Hearst (Ed.), *The first century of experimental psychology*. Hillsdale, NJ: Erlbaum.

Mandler, J. M. (1998). Representation. In W. Damon (Series Ed.) & D. Kuhn and R. S. Siegler (Vol. Eds.), *Handbook of child psychology: Vol. 2. Cognition, perception, and language* (5th ed.). New York: Wiley.

Marcia, J. E. (1967). Ego identity status: Relationship to change in self-esteem, "general maladjustment," and authoritarianism. *Journal of Personality, 35*, 118–133.

Marcia, J. E. (1999). Representational thought in ego identity, psychotherapy, and psychosocial developmental theory. In I. E. Sigel (Ed.), *Development of mental representation: Theories and applications*. Mahwah, NJ: Erlbaum.

Mareschal, D., Plunkett, K., & Harris, P. (1999). A computational and neuropsychological account of object-oriented behaviours in infancy. *Developmental Science, 2*, 306–317.

Markus, H. R., & Kitayama, S. (1991). Culture and the self: Implications for cognition, emotion, and motivation. *Psychological Review, 98*, 224–253.

Martini, M., & Kirkpatrick, J. (1981). Early interactions in the Marquesas Islands. In T. M. Field, A. M. Sostek, P. Vietze, & P. H. Leiderman (Eds.), *Culture and early interventions*. Hillsdale, NJ: Erlbaum.

Matthews, A., Ellis, A. E., & Nelson, C. A. (1996). Development of pre-term and full-term infant ability of AB, recall memory, transparent barrier detour, and means-ends tasks. *Child Development, 67*, 2658–2676.

McAdams, D. P., & de St. Aubin, E. (Eds.). (1998). *Generativity and adult development: How and why we care for the next generation*. Washington, DC: American Psychological Association.

McCain, G., & Segal, E. M. (1969). *The game of science*. Belmont, CA: Brooks/Cole.

McCall, R. B., & Kennedy, C. B. (1980). Attention to babyishness in babies. *Journal of Experimental Child Psychology, 29,* 189–201.

McGrew, W. C. (1972). *An ethological study of children's behavior*. New York: Academic Press.

McPhail, J. C., Pierson, J. M., Freeman, J., & Goodman, J. (in press). The role of interest in fostering sixth grade students' identities as competent learners. *Curriculum Inquiry*.

Meacham, J. A., & Santilli, N. R. (1982). Interstage relationships in Erikson's theory: Identity and intimacy. *Child Development, 53,* 1461–1467.

Meltzoff, A. N., & Moore, M. K. (1989). Imitation in newborn infants: Exploring the range of gestures imitated and the underlying mechanisms. *Developmental Psychology, 25*, 954–962.

Meltzoff, A. N., & Moore, M. K. (1998). Object representation, identity, and the paradox of early permanence: Steps toward a new framework. *Infant Behavior and Development, 21*, 201–235.

Michaels, C. F., & Carello, C. (1981). *Direct perception*. Englewood Cliffs, NJ: Prentice-Hall.

Miller, N. E., & Dollard, J. (1941). *Social learning and imitation*. New Haven, CT: Yale University Press.

Miller, P. H. (1978). Stimulus variables in conservation: An alternative approach to assessment. *Merrill-Palmer Quarterly, 24,* 141–160.

Miller, P. H. (1990). The development of strategies of selective attention. In D. F. Bjorklund (Ed.), *Children's strategies: Contemporary views of cognitive development*. Hillsdale, NJ: Erlbaum.

Miller, P. H. (2000). The development of interconnected thinking. In P. H. Miller & E. K. Scholnick (Eds.), *Toward a feminist developmental psychology*. New York: Routledge.

Miller, P. H., & Coyle, T. R. (1999). Developmental change: Lessons from microgenesis. In E. K. Scholnick, K. Nelson, S. A. Gelman, & P. H. Miller (Eds.), *Conceptual development: Piaget's legacy*. Mahwah, NJ: Erlbaum.

Miller, P. H., & Scholnick, E. K. (Eds.). (2000). *Toward a feminist developmental psychology*. New York: Routledge.

Miller, P. H., & Seier, W. L. (1994). Strategy utilization deficiencies in children: When, where, and why. In H. W. Reese (Ed.), *Advances in child development and behavior* (Vol. 25). New York: Academic Press.

Miller, P. J., Fung, H., & Mintz, J. (1996). Self-construction through narrative practices: A Chinese and American comparison of early socialization. *Ethos, 24*, 237–279.

Miller, S. A. (1976). Nonverbal assessment of Piagetian concepts. *Psychological Bulletin, 83,* 405–430.

Moen, P., Elder, G. H., & Luscher, K. (1995). *Examining lives in context*. Washington, DC: American Psychological Association.

Moltz, H., & Leon, T. M. (1983). The coordinate roles of mother and young in establishing and maintaining pheromonal symbiosis in the rat. In L. A. Rosenblum and H. Moltz (Eds.), *Symbiosis in parent-offspring interactions.* New York: Plenum Press.

Montagu, A. (1973). The new litany of "innate depravity," or original sin revisited. In A. Montagu (Ed.), *Man and aggression*. New York: Oxford University Press.

Montangero, J., & Maurice-Naville, D. (1997). *Piaget or the advance of knowledge*. Mahwah, NJ: Erlbaum.

Moon, C., Cooper, R., & Fifer, W. (1993). Two-day-olds prefer their native language. *Infant Behavior and Development, 16*, 495–500.

Morelli, G. A., Rogoff, B., Oppenheim, D., & Goldsmith, D. (1992). Cultural variation in infants' sleeping arrangements: Questions of independence. *Developmental Psychology*, 28, 604–613.

Morgan, R., & Rochat, P. (1995). The perception of self-produced leg movement in self- versus object-oriented contexts by 3.5-month-old infants. In B. G. Bardy, R. J. Bootsma, & Y. Guiard (Eds.), *Studies in perception and action III*. Hillsdale, NJ: Erlbaum.

Munakata, Y., McClelland, J. L., Johnson, M. J., & Siegler, R. S. (1997). Rethinking infant knowledge: Toward an adaptive process account of successes and failures in object permanence tasks. *Psychological Review, 104*, 686–713.

Munn, N. L. (1954). Learning in children. In L. Carmichael (Ed.), *Manual of child psychology* (2nd ed.). New York: Wiley.

Murray, F. B. (1983). Learning and development through social interaction and conflict: A challenge to social learning theory. In L. Liben (Ed.), *Piaget and the foundations of knowledge*. Hillsdale, NJ: Erlbaum.

Needham, A., & Baillargeon, R. (1998). Effects of prior experience on 4.5-month-old infants' object segregation. *Infant Behavior and Development, 21*, 1–24.

Neisser, U. (1985). Toward an ecologically oriented cognitive science. In T. M. Shlechter & M. P. Toglia (Eds.), *New directions in cognitive science.* Norwood, NJ: Ablex.

Nelson, K. (1978). How children represent knowledge of their world in and out of language: A preliminary report. In R. S. Siegler (Ed.), *Children's thinking: What develops?* Hillsdale, NJ: Erlbaum.

Nelson, K. (Ed.). (1986). *Event knowledge.* Hillsdale, NJ: Erlbaum.

Nelson, K. (1996). *Language in cognitive development: The emergence of the mediated mind.* New York: Cambridge University Press.

Neville, H. J. (1995). *Brain plasticity and the acquisition of skill.* Paper presented at the Cognitive Neuroscience and Education Conference, Eugene, OR.

Newcomb, A. F., & Collins, W. A. (1979). Children's comprehension of family role portrayals in televised dramas: Effects of socioeconomic status, ethnicity, and age. *Developmental Psychology, 15,* 417–423.

Newell, A., & Simon, H. A. (1961). Computer simulation of human thinking. *Science, 134,* 2011–2017.

Newport, E. L. (1991). Constraining concepts of the critical period for language. In S. Carey & R. Gelman (Eds.), *The epigenesis of mind: Essays on biology and cognition.* Hillsdale, NJ: Erlbaum.

Noam, G. G. (1996). Reconceptualizing maturity: The search for deeper meaning. In G. G. Noam & K. W. Fischer (Eds.), *Development and vulnerability in close relationships.* Mahwah, NJ: Erlbaum.

Noelting, G. (1980). The development of proportional reasoning and the ratio concept. *Educational Studies in Mathematics, 11,* 217–253, 331–363.

Noirot, E. (1974). Nest-building by the virgin female mouse exposed to ultrasound from inaccessible pups. *Animal Behaviour, 22,* 410–420.

Ormiston, L. H. (1972). *Factors determining response to modeled hypocrisy.* Unpublished doctoral dissertation, Stanford University, Stanford, CA.

Ornstein, P. A., & Naus, M. J. (1985). Effects of the knowledge base on children's memory strategies. In H. W. Reese (Ed.), *Advances in child development and behavior* (Vol. 19). Orlando, FL: Academic Press.

Ornstein, P. A., Naus, M. J., & Liberty, C. (1975). Rehearsal and organizational processes in children's memory. *Child Development, 46,* 818–830.

Overton, W. F. (1984). World views and their influence on psychological theory and research: Kuhn-Lakatos-Laudan. In H. W. Reese (Ed.), *Advances in child development and behavior* (Vol. 18). Orlando, FL: Academic Press.

Palincsar, A. S., & Brown, A. L. (1988). Teaching and practicing thinking skills to promote comprehension in the context of group problem solving. *Remedial & Special Education, 9(1),* 53–59.

Palincsar, A. S., Collins, K. M., Marano, N., & Magnusson, S. M. (1998, November). *Methodological considerations in constructing cases of "included" students in guided inquiry science.* Paper presented at the meeting of the National Reading Conference, San Antonio, TX.

Paris, S. G., & Carter, A. Y. (1973). Semantic and constructive aspects of sentence memory in children. *Developmental Psychology, 9,* 109–113.

Paris, S. G., & Cross, D. R. (1988). The zone of proximal development: Virtues and pitfalls of a metaphorical representation of children's learning.

The Genetic Epistemologist, 16(1), 27–37.

Parkes, C. M., Stevenson-Hinde, & Marris, P. (Eds.). (1991). *Attachment across the life cycle.* London: Tavistock/ Routledge and Kegan Paul.

Pascual-Leone, J. (1970). A mathematical model for the transition rule in Piaget's developmental stages. *Acta Psychologica, 32,* 301–345.

Pascual-Leone, J., & Johnson, J. (1999). A dialectical constructivist view of representation: Role of mental attention, executives, and symbols. In I. E. Sigel (Ed.), *Development of mental representation: Theories and applications.* Mahwah, NJ: Erlbaum.

Patterson, G. R. (1980). Mothers: The unacknowledged victims. *Monographs of the Society for Research in Child Development, 45*(5, Serial No. 186).

Patterson, G. R., & Bank, C. L. (1989). Some amplifying mechanisms for pathologic processes in families. In M. R. Gunner & E. Thelen (Eds.), *Minnesota symposia on child psychology: Vol. 22. Systems and development.* Hillsdale, NJ: Erlbaum.

Patterson, G. R., & Reid, J. B. (1984). Social interactional processes within the family: The study of the moment-by-moment family transactions in which human social development is imbedded. *Journal of Applied Developmental Psychology, 5,* 237–262.

Pellegrini, A. D., & Smith, P. K. (1998). Physical activity play: The nature and function of a neglected aspect of play. *Child Development, 69,* 577–598.

Pepper, S. C. (1934). A contextualistic theory of possibility. *University of California Publications in Philosophy, 17,* 177–197.

Pepper, S. C. (1942). *World hypotheses: A study in evidence.* Berkeley: University of California Press.

Perry, D. G. (1989, April). Social learning theory. In R. Vasta (Chair), *Theories of child development.* Symposium conducted at the meeting of the Society for Research in Child Development, Kansas City, MO.

Piaget, J. (1918). *Recherche* [Research]. Lausanne, Switzerland: La Concorde.

Piaget, J. (1926). *The language and thought of the child.* New York: Harcourt, Brace. (Original work published 1923)

Piaget, J. (1928). *Judgement and reasoning in the child.* New York: Harcourt, Brace. (Original work published 1924)

Piaget, J. (1929). *The child's conception of the world.* New York: Harcourt, Brace. (Original work published 1926)

Piaget, J. (1930). *The child's conception of physical causality.* London: Kegan Paul. (Original work published 1927)

Piaget, J. (1932). *The moral judgment of the child.* London: Kegan Paul.

Piaget, J. (1950). *The psychology of intelligence.* New York: Harcourt, Brace. (Original work published 1947)

Piaget, J. (1951). *Play, dreams and imitation in childhood.* New York: Norton. (Original work published 1945)

Piaget, J. (1952a). Autobiography. In E. G. Boring, H. S. Langfeld, H. Werner, & R. M. Yerkes (Eds.), *A history of psychology in autobiography* (Vol. 4). Worcester, MA: Clark University Press.

Piaget, J. (1952b). *The origins of intelligence in children.* New York: International Universities Press. (Original work published 1936)

Piaget, J. (1954). *The construction of reality in the child.* New York: Basic Books. (Original work published 1937)

Piaget, J. (1964a). Development and learning. In R. E. Ripple & V. N.

Rockcastle (Eds.), *Piaget rediscovered.* Ithaca, NY: Cornell University Press.

Piaget, J. (1964b). *The early growth of logic in the child.*

Piaget, J. (1969). *The child's conception of time.* London: Routledge & Kegan Paul. (Original work published 1946)

Piaget, J. (1970). *The child's conception of movement and speed.* London: Routledge & Kegan Paul. (Original work published 1946)

Piaget, J. (1971). The theory of stages in cognitive development. In D. R. Green, M. P. Ford, & G. B. Flamer (Eds.), *Measurement and Piaget.* New York: McGraw-Hill.

Piaget, J. (1972a). Intellectual evolution from adolescence to adulthood. *Human Development, 15,* 1–12.

Piaget, J. (1972b). *Psychology and epistemology: Towards a theory of knowledge.* Harmondsworth, England: Penguin. (Original work published 1970)

Piaget, J. (1979). Correspondences and transformations. In F. B. Murray (Ed.), *The impact of Piagetian theory: On education, philosophy, psychiatry, and psychology.* Baltimore, MD: University Park Press.

Piaget, J. (1980). *Experiments in contradiction.* Chicago: University of Chicago Press. (Original work published 1974)

Piaget, J. (1981). *Intelligence and affectivity: Their relationship during child development.* Palo Alto, CA: Annual Review Monographs. (Original work published 1954)

Piaget, J. (1983). Piaget's theory. In P. H. Mussen (Series Ed.) & W. Kessen (Vol. Ed.), *Handbook of child psychology: Vol. 1. History, theory, and methods,* (4th ed.), New York: Wiley.

Piaget, J. (1985). *The equilibration of cognitive structures.* Chicago: University of Chicago Press. (Original work published 1975)

Piaget, J. (1987). *Possibility and necessity: Vol. 1. The role of possibility in cognitive development: Vol 2. The role of necessity in cognitive development.* Minneapolis, MN: University of Minnesota Press. (Original work published 1981)

Piaget, J. (1995). *Sociological studies.* London & New York: Routledge. (Original work published 1965)

Piaget, J., & Garcia, R. (1991). *Towards a logic of meanings.* Hillsdale, NJ: Erlbaum.

Piaget, J., & Inhelder, B. (1969). *The psychology of the child.* New York: Basic Books. (Original work published 1968)

Piaget, J., & Inhelder, B. (1973). *Memory and intelligence.* New York: Basic Books. (Original work published 1968)

Pick, A. D., Gross, D., Heinrichs, M., Love, M., & Palmer, C. (1994). Development of perception of the unity of musical events. *Cognitive Development, 9,* 355–375.

Pick, H. L. (1992). Eleanor J. Gibson: Learning to perceive and perceiving to learn. *Developmental Psychology, 28,* 787–794.

Pinker, S. (1997). *How the mind works.* New York: Norton.

Plaut, D. C., McClelland, J. L., Seidenberg, M. S., & Patterson, K. (1995). Understanding normal and impaired word reading: Computational principles in quasi-regular domains. *Psychological Review, 103,* 56–115.

Plomin, R. (1998). Behavioral genetics. In M. Bennett (Ed.), *Developmental psychology: Achievements and prospects.* Philadelphia: Psychology Press.

Plumert, J. M., & Nichols-Whitehead, P. (1996). Parental scaffolding of young children's spatial communication. *Developmental Psychology, 32*, 523–532.

Poincaré, J. H. (1908). *Science and hypothesis.* New York: Dover. (1952)

Povinelli, D. J., & Eddy, T. J. (1996). What young chimpanzees know about seeing. *Monographs of the Society for Research in Child Development, 61*(3, Serial No. 247).

Pratkanis, A. R., & Greenwald, A. B. (1985). How shall the self be conceived? *Journal for the Theory of Social Behavior, 15*, 311–328.

Pressley, M. (1982). Elaboration and memory development. *Child Development, 53*, 296–309.

Pressley, M., Borkowski, J. G., & Schneider, W. (1987). Cognitive strategies: Good strategy users coordinate metacognition and knowledge. In R. Vasta & G. Whitehurst (Eds.), *Annals of child development* (Vol. 5). Greenwich, CT: JAI Press.

Price-Williams, D. R., Gordon, W., & Ramirez, M., III. (1969). Skill and conservation: A study of pottery-making children. *Developmental Psychology, 1*, 769.

Profet, M. (1992). Pregnancy sickness as adaptation: A deterrent to maternal ingestion of teratogens. In J. H. Barkow, L. Cosmides, & J. Tooby (Eds.). *The adaptive mind: Evolutionary psychology and the generation of culture*. New York: Oxford University Press.

Quillian, M. R., Wortman, P. M., & Baylor, G. W. (1964). *The programmable Piaget: Behavior from the standpoint of a radical computerist*. Unpublished manuscript, Carnegie Institute of Technology, Pittsburgh.

Raijmakers, M. E. J., Koten, S. V., & Molenaar, P. C. M. (1996). On the validity of simulating stagewise development by means of PDP networks: Application of catastrophe analysis and an experimental test of rule-like network performance. *Cognitive Science, 20*, 101–139.

Rapaport, D. (1960). The structure of psychoanalytic theory: A systemization attempt. *Psychological Issues*, (Monograph No. 6). New York: International Universities Press.

Recht, D. R., & Leslie, L. (1988). Effect of prior knowledge on good and poor reader's memory for text. *Journal of Educational Psychology, 80*, 16–20.

Reddy, V. (1991). Playing with others' expectations: Teasing and mucking about in the first year. In A. Whiten (Ed.), *Natural theories of mind: Evolution, development and simulation of everyday mindreading*. Oxford: Basil Blackwell.

Reese, H. W. (1991). Contextualism and developmental psychology. In H. W. Reese (Ed.), *Advances in child development and behavior* (Vol. 23). San Diego, CA: Academic Press.

Reyher, J. (1967). Hypnosis in research on psychopathology. In J. E. Gordon (Ed.), *Handbook of clinical and experimental hypnosis.* New York: Macmillan.

Rieber, R. (1999). *The collected works of L. S. Vygotsky: Vol. 6. Scientific legacy*. New York: Plenum.

Riegel, K. (1972). Influence of economic and political ideologies on the development of developmental psychology. *Psychological Bulletin, 78*, 129–141.

Riegel, K. (1976). The dialectics of human development. *American Psychologist, 31*, 689–700.

Robson, K. S. (1967). The role of eye-to-eye contact in maternal-infant attachment. *Journal of Child Psychology and Psychiatry, 8*, 13–25.

Rochat, P., & Morgan, R. (1998). Two functional orientations of self-exploration in infancy. *British Journal of Developmental Psychology, 16*, 139–154.

Roediger, H. L. (1979). Implicit and explicit memory models. *Bulletin of the Psychonomic Society, 13,* 339–342.

Rogoff, B. (1990). *Apprenticeship in thinking: Cognitive development in social context*. New York: Oxford University Press.

Rogoff, B. (1998). Cognition as a collaborative process. In W. Damon (Series Ed.) & D. Kuhn & R. S. Siegler (Vol. Eds.), *Handbook of child psychology: Vol. 2. Cognition, perception, and language* (5th ed.). New York: Wiley.

Rogoff, B., & Gardner, W. P. (1984). Guidance in cognitive development: An examination of mother-child instruction. In B. Rogoff & J. Lave (Eds.), *Everyday cognition: Its development in social context*. Cambridge, MA: Harvard University Press.

Rogoff, B., & Göncu, A. (1987). Vygotsky and beyond [Review of the book *Vygotsky and the social formation of mind*]. *Contemporary Psychology*, *32*, 22–23.

Rogoff, B., Mistry, J., Goncu, A., & Mosier, C. (1993). Guided participation in cultural activity by toddlers and caregivers. *Monographs of the Society for Research in Child Development, 58*, (Serial No. 236).

Rose, S. A., & Blank, M. (1974). The potency of context in children's cognition: An illustration through conservation. *Child Development, 45,* 499–502.

Rosenblatt, J. S. (1976). Stages in the early behavioral development of altricial young of selected species of nonprimate mammals. In P. P. G. Bateson & R. A. Hinde (Eds.), *Growing points in ethology.* Cambridge, England: Cambridge University Press.

Rosenthal, T. L., & Zimmerman, B. J. (1978). *Social learning and cognition*. New York: Academic Press.

Rosser, S. V., & Miller, P. H. (2000). Feminist theories: Implications for developmental psychology. In P. H. Miller & E. K. Scholnick (Eds.), *Toward a feminist developmental psychology*. New York: Routledge.

Rovee-Collier, C. K. (1999). The development of infant memory. *Current Directions in Psychological Science, 8*, 80–85.

Rovee-Collier, C. K., & Gerhardstein, P. (1997). The development of infant memory. In N. Cowan (Ed.), *The development of memory in childhood*. Hove, East Sussex UK: Psychology Press.

Ruffman, T. (1999). Children's understanding of logical inconsistency. *Child Development, 70*, 872–886.

Russell, J. (1982). Cognitive conflict, transmission, and justification: Conservation attainment through dyadic interaction. *Journal of Genetic Psychology, 140*, 283–297.

Russell, M. J., Mendelson, T., & Peeke, H. V. S. (1983). Mothers' identification of their infants' odors. *Ethology and Sociobiology, 4,* 29–31.

Sameroff, A. J., & Suomi, S. J. (1996). Primates and persons: A comparative developmental understanding of social organization. In R. B. Cairns, G. H. Elder, & E. J. Costello (Eds.), *Developmental science*. Cambridge, England: Cambridge University Press.

Savin-Williams, R. C. (1976). An ethological study of dominance formation and maintenance in a group of human adolescents. *Child Development, 47,* 972–979.

Saxe, G. B. (1981). Body parts as numerals: A developmental analysis of numeration among the Oksapmin in

Papua New Guinea. *Child Development, 52*, 306–316.

Saxe, G. B. (1999). Source of concepts: A cultural-developmental perspective. In E. K. Scholnick, K. Nelson, S. A. Gelman, & P. H. Miller (Eds.), *Conceptual development: Piaget's legacy.* Mahwah, NJ: Erlbaum.

Saxe, G. B., Guberman, S. R., & Gearhart, M. (1987). Social processes in early number development. *Monographs of the Society for Research in Child Development, 52*(2, Serial No. 216).

Scarr, S. (1985). Cultural lenses on mothers and children. In L. Friedrich-Cofer (Ed.), *Human nature and public policy.* New York: Praeger.

Scarr, S. (1992). Developmental theories for the 1990s: Development and individual differences. *Child Development, 63,* 1–19.

Scarr, S. (1993). Biological and cultural diversity: The legacy of Darwin for development. *Child Development, 64*, 1333–1353.

Schank, R. C., & Abelson, R. (1977). *Scripts, plans, goals and understanding.* Hillsdale, NJ: Erlbaum.

Schauble, L. (1996). The development of scientific reasoning in knowledge-rich contexts. *Developmental Psychology, 32*, 102–119.

Scheper-Hughes, N. (1987). Culture, scarcity, and maternal thinking: Mother love and child death in Northeast Brazil. In N. Scheper-Hughes (Ed.), *Child survival.* Boston: D. Reidel.

Schlein, S. (Ed.). (1987). *A way of looking at things: Selected papers from 1930 to 1980. Erik H. Erikson.* New York: Norton.

Schneider, W., & Bjorklund, D. F. (1998). Memory. In W. Damon (Series Ed.) & D. Kuhn & R. S. Siegler (Vol. Eds.), *Handbook of Child Psychology: Vol. 2. Cognition, perception, and language* (5th ed.). New York: Wiley.

Schneider, W., Körkel, J., & Weinert, F. E. (1989). Domain-specific knowledge and memory performance: A comparison of high- and low-aptitude children. *Journal of Educational Psychology, 81*, 306–312.

Schneider, W., & Pressley, M. (1997). *Memory development: Between two and twenty* (2nd ed.). Mahwah, NJ: Erlbaum.

Schneider, W., & Weinert, F. E. (1989). Memory development: Universal changes and individual differences. In A. de Ribaupierre (Ed.), *Transitional mechanisms in child development: The longitudinal perspective*. Cambridge, England: Cambridge University Press.

Schneider, W., & Weinert, F. E. (1995). Memory development during early and middle childhood: Findings from the Munich longitudinal study (LOGIC). In F. E. Weinert & W. Schneider (Eds.), *Memory performance and competencies: Issues in growth and development*. Hillsdale, NJ: Erlbaum.

Schneider, W., & Weinert, F. E. (Eds.) (1999). *Individual development from 3 to 12: Findings from the Munich Longitudinal Study*. Cambridge, England: Cambridge University Press.

Schneirla, T. C. (1966). Behavioral development and comparative psychology. *Quarterly Review of Biology, 41*, 283–302.

Scholnick, E. K. (2000). Engendering development: Metaphors of change. In P. H. Miller & E. K. Scholnick (Eds.), *Toward a feminist developmental psychology*. New York: Routledge.

Sears, R. R., Rau, L., & Alpert, R. (1965). *Identification and child rearing*. Stanford: Stanford University Press.

Shapley, H., Rapput, S., & Wright, H. (Eds.) *The new treasury of science*. New York: Harper & Row.

Shaver, P. R., & Hazan, C. (1993). Adult romantic attachment: Theory and evidence. In D. Perlman & W. H. Jones (Eds.), *Advances in personal relationships*. London: Jessica Kingsley.

Shaw, R., & Bransford, J. (1977). Introduction: Psychological approaches to the problems of knowledge. In R. Shaw & J. Bransford (Eds.), *Perceiving, acting, knowing: Toward an ecological psychology.* Hillsdale, NJ: Erlbaum.

Shiffrin, R. M., & Atkinson, R. C. (1969). Storage and retrieval processes in long-term memory. *Psychological Review, 76,* 179–193.

Shultz, T. R. (1997). *A computational analysis of conservation*. Unpublished manuscript, McGill University, Department of Psychology, Montreal, Canada.

Shultz, T. R., Schmidt, W. C., Buckingham, D., & Mareschal, D. (1995). Modeling cognitive development with a generative connectionist algorithm. In T. Simon & G. Halford (Eds.), *Developing cognitive competence: New approaches to process modeling*. Hillsdale, NJ: Erlbaum.

Shweder, R. A., Balle-Jensen, L., & Goldstein, W. (1995). Who sleeps by whom revisited: A method for extracting the moral goods implicit in praxis. In J. J. Goodnow, P. J. Miller, & F. Kessell (Eds.), *Cultural practices as contexts for development: New directions for child development*. San Francisco: Jossey-Bass.

Shweder, R. A., Goodnow, J., Hatano, G., LeVine, R. A., Markus, H., & Miller, P. (1998). The cultural psychology of development: One mind, many mentalities. In W. Damon (Series Ed.) & R. M. Lerner (Vol. Ed.), *Handbook of child psychology: Vol. 1. Theoretical models of human development* (5th ed.,). New York: Wiley.

Siegal, M. (1991). *Knowing children: Experiments in conversation and cognition*. Hillsdale, NJ: Erlbaum.

Siegler, R. S. (1978). The origins of scientific reasoning. In R. S. Siegler (Ed.), *Children's thinking: What develops?* Hillsdale, NJ: Erlbaum.

Siegler, R. S. (1992). The other Alfred Binet. *Developmental Psychology, 28,* 179–190.

Siegler, R. S. (1995). How does change occur: A microgenetic study of number conservation. *Cognitive Psychology, 28*, 225–273.

Siegler, R. S. (1996). *Emerging minds: The process of change in children's thinking*. New York: Oxford University Press.

Siegler, R. S. (1998). *Children's thinking.* (3rd ed.). Upper Saddle River, NJ: Prentice Hall.

Siegler, R. S. (2000). The rebirth of children's learning. *Child Development, 71*, 26–35.

Siegler, R. S., & Chen, Z. (1998). Developmental differences in rule learning: A microgenetic analysis. *Cognitive Psychology, 36*, 273–310.

Siegler, R. S., & Crowley, K. (1991). The microgenetic method: A direct means for studying cognitive development. *American Psychologist, 46,* 606–620.

Siegler, R. S., & Ellis, S. (1996). Piaget on childhood. *Psychological Science, 7,* 211–215.

Siegler, R. S., & Jenkins, E. (1989). *How children discover new strategies*. Hillsdale, NJ: Erlbaum.

Siegler, R. S., & Stern, E. (1998). Conscious and unconscious strategy discoveries: A microgenetic analysis. *Journal of Experimental Psychology: General, 127*, 377–397.

Sigel, I. E. (1986). Mechanism: A metaphor for cognitive development? A review of Sternberg's *Mechanisms of cognitive development. Merrill-Palmer Quarterly, 32,* 93–101.

Signorella, M. L., & Liben, L. S. (1984). Recall and reconstruction of gender-related pictures: Effects of attitude, task difficulty, and age. *Child Development, 55,* 393–405.

Simon, H. A. (1972). On the development of the processor. In S. Farnham-Diggory (Ed.), *Information processing in children.* New York: Academic Press.

Simon, T. J., & Klahr, D. (1995). A theory of children's learning about number conservation. In T. J. Simon & G. Halford (Eds.), *Developing cognitive competence: New approaches to process modeling*. Hillsdale, NJ: Erlbaum.

Skinner, B. F. (1948). *Walden two*. New York: Macmillan.

Skinner, B. F. (1967). Autobiography. In E. G. Boring & G. Lindzey (Eds.), *A history of psychology in autobiography* (Vol. 5). Englewood Cliffs, NJ: Prentice-Hall.

Skinner, B. F. (1971). *Beyond freedom and dignity.* New York: Knopf.

Skinner, B. F. (1980). The experimental analysis of operant behavior: A history. In R. W. Rieber & K. Salzinger (Eds.), *Psychology: Theoretical-historical perspectives.* New York: Academic Press.

Smith, P. K., & Connolly, K. (1972). Patterns of play and social interaction in preschool children. In N. G. Blurton-Jones (Ed.), *Ethological studies of child behavior.* Cambridge, England: Cambridge University Press.

Soken, N., & Pick, A. (1992). Intermodal perception of happy and angry expressive behaviors by seven-month-old infants. *Child Development, 63,* 787–795.

Sorce, J., Emde, R., Campos, J., & Klinnert, M. (1985). Maternal emotional-signaling: Its effect on the visual cliff behavior of 1-year-olds. *Developmental Psychology, 21,* 195–200.

Spelke, E. S. (1976). Infants' intermodal perception of events. *Cognitive Psychology, 8,* 553–560.

Spelke, E. S. (1991). Physical knowledge in infancy: Reflections on Piaget's theory. In S. Carey & R. Gelman, (Eds.), *The epigenesis of mind: Essays in biology and cognition*. Hillsdale, NJ: Erlbaum.

Spelke, E. S., & Newport, E. L. (1998). Nativism, empiricism, and the development of knowledge. In W. Damon (Series Ed.) and R. M. Lerner (Vol. Ed.), *Handbook of child psychology: Vol. 1. Theoretical models of human development* (5th ed.). New York: Wiley.

Sperber, D. (1994). The organization of lexical knowledge in the brain: Evidence from category- and modality-specific deficits. In L. A. Hirschfeld, & S. Gelman (Eds.), *Mapping the mind: Domain specificity in cognition and culture*. Cambridge and New York: Cambridge University Press.

Spiker, C. C. (1966). The concept of development: Relevant and irrelevant issues. In H. W. Stevenson (Ed.), Concept of development. *Monographs of the Society for Research in Child Development, 31*(5, Serial No. 107).

Spitz, R. A. (1945). Hospitalism: An inquiry into the genesis of psychiatry conditions in early childhood. *Psychoanalytic Study of the Child, 1,* 53–74.

Spitz, R. A. (1957). *Die Entstehung der ersten Objektbeziehungen*. Stuttgart: Klett.

Sroufe, L. A., Carlson, E. A., Levy, A., & Egeland, B. (1999). Implications of attachment theory for developmental psychopathology. *Development and Psychopathology 11*, 1–13.

Stauder, J. E. A., Molenaar, P. C. M., & van der Molen, M. W. (1993). Scalp topography of event-related brain potentials and cognitive transition during childhood. *Child Development, 64*, 768–788.

Steele, H., Steele, M., & Fonagy, P. (1996). Associations among attachment classifications of mothers, fathers, and their infants. *Child Development, 67*, 541–555.

Stern, D. N. (1974). Mother and infant at play: The dyadic interaction involving facial, vocal, and gaze behaviors. In M. Lewis & Rosenblum (Eds.), *The effect of the infant on its caretaker*. New York: John Wiley.

Stern, D. N. (1985). *The interpersonal world of the infant*. New York: Basic Books.

Stern, D. N. (1995). *The motherhood constellation*. New York: Basic Books.

Sternberg, R. J. (1979). The nature of mental abilities. *American Psychologist, 34,* 214–230.

Sternberg, R. J. (1985). *Beyond IQ: A triarchic theory of human intelligence.* New York: Cambridge University Press.

Sternberg, R. J. (1986). *Intelligence applied.* San Diego, CA: Harcourt Brace Jovanovich.

Sternberg, R. J. (1999). Looking back and looking forward on intelligence: Toward a theory of successful intelligence. In M. Bennett (Ed.), *Developmental psychology: Achievements and prospects.* Philadelphia: Psychology Press.

Sternberg, R. J., & Lubart, T. I. (1995). *Defying the crowd: Cultivating creativity in a culture of conformity*. New York: Free Press.

Sternberg, R. J., & Rifkin, B. (1979). The development of analogical reasoning processes. *Journal of Experimental Child Psychology, 27,* 195–232.

Sternberg, R. J., Torff, B., & Grigorenko, E. L. (1998). Teaching triarchically improves school achievement. *Journal of Educational Psychology, 90*, 374–384.

Sternberg, R. J., & Williams, W. M. (1996). *How to develop student creativity.* Alexandria, VA: Association for Supervision and Curriculum Development.

Stevenson, H. W., Lee, S., & Stigler, J. W. (1986). Achievement in mathematics. In H. Stevenson, H. Azuma, & K. Hakuta (Eds.), *Child development and education in Japan*. New York: Freeman.

Stigler, J. W. (1984). "Mental abacus": The effect of abacus training on Chinese children's mental calculation. *Cognitive Psychology, 16*, 145–176.

Stipek, D. (1984). Young children's performance expectations: Logical analysis or wishful thinking? In J. G. Nicholls (Ed.), *Advances in motivation and achievement: Vol 3. The development of achievement motivation*. Greenwich, CT: JAI Press.

Strauss, S., & Levin, I. (1981). Commentary. *Monographs of the Society for Research in Child Development, 46* (2, Serial No. 189).

Strayer, F. F. (1980). Social ecology of the preschool peer group. In W. A. Collins (Ed.), *Development of cognition, affect, and social relations.* Hillsdale, NJ: Erlbaum.

Strayer, F. F., & Strayer, J. (1976). An ethological analysis of social agonism and dominance relations among preschool children. *Child Development, 47,* 980–999.

Streri, A., & Pecheux, M. (1986). Vision-to-touch and touch-to-vision transfer of form in 5-month-old infants. *British Journal of Developmental Psychology, 4,* 161–167.

Super, C. M., & Harkness, S. (1983). *Looking across at growing up: The cultural expression of cognitive development in middle childhood.* Unpublished manuscript, Harvard University, Cambridge, MA.

Surbey, M. K. (1998). Developmental psychology and modern Darwinism. In C. Crawford & D. L. Krebs (Eds.), *Handbook of evolutionary psychology: Ideas, issues, and applications.* Mahwah, NJ: Erlbaum.

Thayer, G. H. (1909). *Concealing coloration in the animal kingdom.* New York: Macmillan.

Thelen, E., Fisher, D. M., & Ridley-Johnson, R. (1984). The relationship between physical growth and a newborn reflex. *Infant Behavior and Development,* 7, 479–493.

Thelen, E., & Smith, L. B. (1998). Dynamic systems theory. In W. Damon (Series Ed.) & R. M. Lerner (Vol. Ed.), *Handbook of child psychology: Vol. 1. Theoretical models of human development* (5th ed.). New York: Wiley.

Thiessen, D. (1996). *Bittersweet destiny: The stormy evolution of human behavior.* New Brunswick, NJ: Transaction.

Thompson, R. A. (1998). Early sociopersonality development. In W. Damon (Series Ed.) & N. Eisenberg (Vol. Ed.), *Handbook of child psychology: Vol. 3. Social, emotional, and personality development* (5th ed.). New York: Wiley.

Thorndike, E. L. (1898). Animal intelligence: An experimental study of the associative processes in animals. *Psychological Review: Series of Monograph Supplements, 2*(4, Whole No. 8).

Tinbergen, E. A., & Tinbergen, N. (1972). *Early childhood autism: An ethological approach.* Berlin: Parey.

Tinbergen, N. (1951). *The study of instinct.* London: Oxford University Press.

Tinbergen, N. (1958). *Curious naturalists.* New York: Basic Books.

Tinbergen, N. (1973). *The animal in its world. Explorations of an ethologist 1932–1972* (Vols. 1 & 2). Cambridge, MA: Harvard University Press.

Tobin, J. J., Wu, D. Y. H., & Davidson, D. H. (1989). *Preschool in three cultures.* New Haven, CT: Yale University Press.

Tolman, E. C. (1959). Principles of purposive behavior. In S. Koch (Ed.), *Psychology: A study of a science.* New York: McGraw-Hill

Tomasello, M. (1999). *The cultural origins of human cognition.* Cambridge, MA: Harvard University Press.

Tomasello, M., & Call, J. (1997). *Primate cognition.* New York: Oxford University Press.

Tomasello, M., Kruger, A. C., & Ratner, H. H. (1991). *Cultural learning* (Tech. Rep. No. 21). Atlanta, GA: Emory University, Emory Cognition Project.

Tomasello, M., Kruger, A. C., & Ratner, H. H. (1993). Cultural learning. *Behavior and Brain Sciences, 16,* 495–552.

Tong, R. (1998). *Feminist thought* (2nd ed.). Boulder, CO: Westview Press.

Toulmin, S. (1978, September). The Mozart of psychology. *New York Review of Books.*

Tuddenham, R. D. (1966). Jean Piaget and the world of the child. *American Psychologist, 21,* 207–217.

Tulviste, P. (1991). *Cultural-historical development of verbal thinking: A psychological study*. Commack, NY: Nova Science Publishers.

Van den Daele, L. (1969). Qualitative models in developmental analysis, *Developmental Psychology, 1,* 303–310.

Van Ijzendoorn, M. H., & Sagi, A. (1999). Cross-cultural patterns of attachment: Universal and contextual dimensions. In J. Cassidy & P. R. Shaver (Eds.), *Handbook of attachment theory and research: Theory, research, and clinical application*. New York: Guilford Press.

Vondra, J. I., & Barnett, D. (Eds.). (1999). Atypical attachment in infancy and early childhood among children at developmental risk. *Monographs of the Society for Research in Child Development, 64*(3, Serial No. 258).

Vurpillot, E., & Ball, W. A. (1979). The concept of identity and children's selective attention. In G. Hale & M. Lewis (Eds.), *Attention and cognitive development.* New York: Plenum Press.

Vuyk, R. (1981). *Overview and critique of Piaget's genetic epistemology, 1965–1980* (Vol. 1). London & New York: Academic Press.

Vygotsky, L. S. (1956). *Selected psychological investigations*. Moscow: IAPN-SSSR.

Vygotsky, L. S. (1960). *Development of the higher psychical functions*. Moscow: APN.

Vygotsky, L. S. (1962). *Thought and language*. Cambridge, MA: MIT Press.

Vygotsky, L. S. (1978). *Mind in society: The development of higher psychological processes.* Cambridge, MA: Harvard University Press.

Vygotsky, L. S. (1981). The instrumental method in psychology. In J. V. Wertsch (Ed.), *The concept of activity in Soviet psychology*. Armonk, NY: M. E. Sharpe.

Waddington, C. H. (1957). *The strategy of the genes.* London: Allen & Unwin.

Walker-Andrews, A., Bahrick, L., Raglioni, S., & Diaz, I. (1991). Infants' bimodal perception of gender. *Ecological Psychology, 3*, 55–75.

Wallbank, T. W., & Taylor, A. M. (1960). *Civilization past and present.* Chicago: Scott, Foresman.

Wason, P. C., & Johnson-Laird, P. N. (1972). *Psychology of reasoning.* Cambridge, MA: Harvard University Press.

Watson, J. B. (1924). *Behaviorism.* New York: Norton.

Watson, J. B. (1928). *Psychological care of infant and child.* New York: Norton.

Watson, J. B., & Rayner, R. (1920). Conditioned emotional reactions. *Journal of Experimental Psychology, 3,* 1–14.

Wegman, C. (1985). *Psychoanalysis and cognitive psychology: A formalization of Freud's earliest theory.* Orlando, FL: Academic Press.

Weigel, R. M., & Weigel, M. M. (1989). Nausea and vomiting of early pregnancy and pregnancy outcome: A meta-analytic review. *British Journal of Obstetrics and Gynecology, 96*, 1304–1318.

Welch-Ross, M., & Miller, P. H. (2000). Relations between children's theory of mind and a selective attention strategy. *Cognition and Development, 1*, 281–293.

Wellman, H. M., & Gelman, S. A. (1998). Knowledge acquisition in foundational domains. In W. Damon (Series Ed.) & D. Kuhn & R. S. Siegler (Vol. Eds.), *Handbook of child psychology: Vol. 2. Cognition, perception, and language* (5th ed.). New York: Wiley.

Wertsch, J. V. (1985). *Vygotsky and the social formation of mind.* Cambridge, MA: Harvard University Press.

Wertsch, J. V. (1991). *Voices of the mind: A sociocultural approach to mediated action*. Cambridge, MA: Harvard University Press.

Wertsch, J. V., & Hickmann, M. (1987). Problem solving in social interactions: A microgenetic analysis. In M. Hickmann (Ed.), *Social and functional approaches to language and thought*. Orlando, FL: Academic Press.

Wesley, F. (1989). Developmental cognition before Piaget: Alfred Binet's pioneering experiments. *Developmental Review, 9*, 58–63.

White, B. L. (1969). Child development research: An edifice without a foundation. *Merrill-Palmer Quarterly, 15*, 47–78.

White, R. W. (1963). Ego and reality in psychoanalytic theory: A proposal regarding independent ego energies. *Psychological Review* (Monograph No. 11). New York: International Universities Press.

White, S. H. (1970). The learning theory approach. In P. H. Mussen (Ed.), *Carmichael's manual of child psychology* (Vol. 1, 3rd ed.). New York: Wiley.

White, S. H. (1976). The active organism in theoretical behaviorism. *Human Development, 19*, 99–107.

White, S., & Tharp, R. G. (1988, April). *Questioning and wait-time: A cross-cultural analysis*. Paper presented at the meeting of the American Educational Research Association, New Orleans.

Whiten, A. (1998). Evolutionary and developmental origins of the mind-reading system. In J. Langer & M. Killen (Eds.). *Piaget, evolution, and development*. Mahwah, NJ: Erlbaum.

Wilson, E. O. (1975). *Sociobiology. The new synthesis.* Cambridge, MA: Belknap Press of Harvard University Press.

Wilson, E. O. (1978). *On human nature.* Cambridge, MA: Harvard University Press.

Wimmer, H., & Perner, J. (1983). Beliefs about beliefs: Representation and constraining function of wrong beliefs in young children's understanding of deception. *Cognition, 13*, 103–128.

Winnicott, D. W. (1953). Transitional objects and transitional phenomena. *International Journal of Psychoanalysis, 34*, 89–97.

Winnicott, D. W. (1971). *Playing and reality.* New York: Basic Books.

Wober, M. (1972). Culture and the concept of intelligence: A case in Uganda. *Journal of Cross-Cultural Psychology, 3*, 327–328.

Woodruff, G., & Premack, D. (1979). Intentional communication in the chimpanzee: The development of deception. *Cognition, 7*, 333–362.

Zajonc, R. B. (1980). Feeling and thinking: Preferences need no inferences. *American Psychologist, 35*, 151–175.

Zimmerman, B. J. (1974). Modification of young children's grouping strategies: The effects of modeling, verbalization, incentives, and praise. *Child Development, 45*, 1032–1041.

NAME INDEX

SUBJECT INDEX

Note: locators in *italics* indicate display material